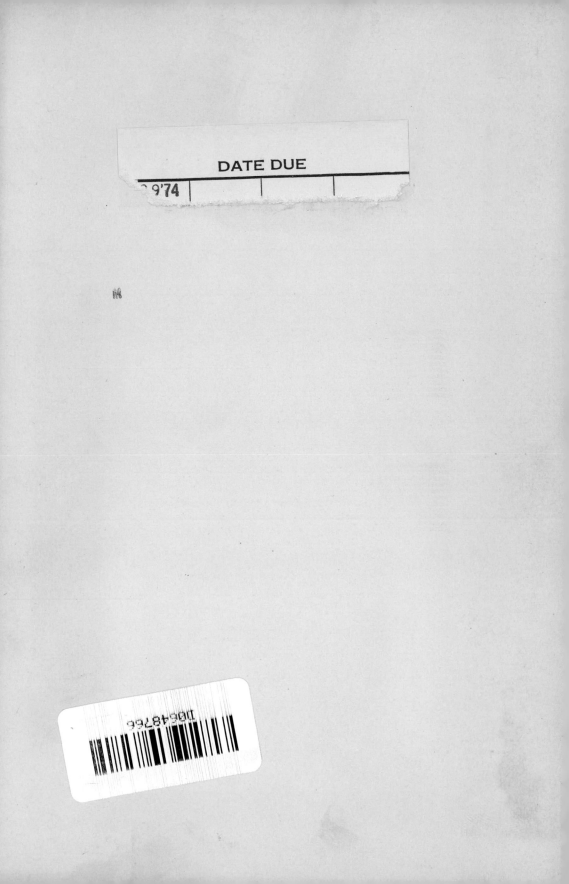

Frances Koltun's
complete book
for
THE INTELLIGENT
WOMAN TRAVELER

SIMON AND SCHUSTER • NEW YORK

To
My Mother and Father

Acknowledgments

I owe a great debt of gratitude to Katharine Davis Fishman, whose wisdom and friendship are a very real part of this book. She has counseled me throughout its preparation, and her encouragement, suggestions and generous advice are warmly acknowledged, appreciated—and woven into this text.

I should also like to express my deep appreciation to Eve Auchincloss, who read the entire manuscript and made many valuable suggestions for its improvement. She was of inestimable help.

Thanks are due, too, to the good men and women of the foreign tourist offices, the airlines, the ship lines and the travel industry at large, who helped to assemble and verify much of the information here. They are William J. Walker and Donald C. Beresford, Australian National Travel Association; Rudolph F. Mattesich, Austrian State Tourist Department; Joseph A. Murphy, Hill and Knowlton, Inc.; Brenda D. Gilkes, Barbados Tourist Board; Peter A. De Maerel, Official Belgian Tourist Bureau; James Forbes, Bermuda Trade Development Board; James Turbayne, Edmund

Antrobus, Dorothy L. Harmshaw, and William Houlton, British Travel Association; Roland de Grosbois, Canadian Government Travel Bureau; Susan Baumgartner, Spanish National Tourist Office; Axel Dessau, Danish National Travel Office; Eva and Herman Ramo, Finnish National Travel Office; Myron Clement, French Government Tourist Office; Hans J. Baumann and Ruth Aldendorff, German Tourist Information Office; John Fanelli, Stephen Goerl Associates, Inc.; Alex Alexandrakis, Greek National Tourist Organization; Richard F. MacMillan and Anne Holt, Hawaii Visitors Bureau; S. D. Khanna, Leela S. Nadhan, and Bina Krishnamurti, Government of India Tourist Office; Kevin Durnin, J. P. Murray, Gordon Clark and Maurice Dunne, Irish Tourist Board; Laurence J. Pett, Israel Government Tourist Office; Dr. Renato Guerrieri, Josephine Inzerillo and Laura Falbo, Italian Government Travel Office; De Witt S. Davidson, Wesley Advertising; Peter J. Celliers, Mexican National Tourist Council; Onno Leebaert, Netherlands National Tourist Office; Jan Aaron, Edward Gottlieb and Associates Ltd.; Per Prag and Kaare Brekke, Norwegian National Travel Office; Evelyn J. Heyward, Heyward Associates, Inc.; José López-García and Joseph Petrocik, Commonwealth of Puerto Rico Department of Tourism; M. Louis Pare, Province of Quebec Department of Tourism; Warren F. West, South African Tourist Corporation; Enrique Garcia-Herraiz, Spanish National Tourist Office; Ake Gille and Uno W. Grönkvist, Swedish National Travel Office; Hans Baertschi, Bruno Baroni and Max Lehmann, Swiss National Tourist Office; Stojan Pudar, Yugoslav State Tourist Office; Joseph Le Tourneau and David Walley, Alitalia; Patricia Montgomery, American Airlines; Eugene Du Bois, Eastern Air Lines; Jane Kilbourne, Pan American Airways; Christian Castenskiold, Scandinavian Airlines System; R. H. Braun, Alcoa Steamship Company; Sam N. Mercer, American President Lines; George O'Reilly and James C. Murray, Cunard Steamship Company; J. Robert Bielskas, Farrell Lines; Oscar F. Kolb, Holland-America Line; Howard S. Kennedy, Moore-McCormack Lines; Carl W. Hallengren, Swedish American Line; Jacques Meinnier, French National Railroads; May P. Jackson, Trans-Atlantic Passenger Steamship Conference; Wayne Kennedy, J. Walter Thompson Company; Sheridan H. Garth, Thomas Cook and Son; Michael Fooner, Fred Rosen Associates; Warren Kraemer, Warren E. Kraemer Associates; A. Slavnov, Intourist; George Burns, Pan American Airways.

I would also like to express thanks to Simone Swan, A. Michael Finn, Beverley Lehman, Josefina Feliu, Maud McDougall, Manolita T. Doelger, Richard Eisley, Harold Underhill, Virginia Radcliffe, Aly Kamel, M. Fouad Shadi, Adela Lindeman, Helen Kahn, the Ambassador from Brazil to Canada, Dora A. de Vasconcellos, and Tandy Van Doren, who helped in preliminary research.

I am indebted to David Gollan of Travel Agent Magazine *for his assistance with information on fares, stopovers and charters, and his generous editorial comments.*

I asked a number of specialists to read various sections of the book in order to check the authority and accuracy of its information. Among those who kindly cast their practiced eyes on the manuscript were Arthur Settel, Bureau of Customs; Dr. Ben Kean; Nicholas L. Deak, Deak & Company; S. Ralph Cohen, Scandinavian Airlines System; Herbert Buhrman, American Society of Travel Agents; Jack Jonas, American Automobile Association; John L. Young, World Touring and Automobile Organization; Harold Wolfe, Information Officer, National Institute of Health; Gustav A. Pfuhlman; T. Anthony, Sr., T. Anthony Luggage; Frances G. Knight, Director of the United States Passport Office; Edward J. Hickey, United States Passport Office; Barbara H. Mayer, Hammacher Schlemmer; Ben Thirkield, Department of State; Robert Brown, Kimberly Knitwear Inc.; Jacques Kaplan, Georges Kaplan; Anita Brielke, Bonwit Teller; Nancy Sirkis; Maeve S. Fitzgibbon, Shannon Free Airport; Don Weiss, U.S. Golf Association; William Pahlmann, William Pahlmann Associates; David Nash, Sotheby's of London Ltd.; Dr. Lewis Bronstein; Dr. Louis Bush; Dr. Philip Weissman; Dr. Jules Klein; David A. Brice, Milbanke Travel Ltd.; The Right Reverend Monsignor Joseph L. Zryd, Superior, North American College, Rome; The Very Reverend Monsignor Thomas McGovern, Archdiocese of New York; John A. C. Cannon, Fourways Travel Ltd.; Robert Burstein, Civil Aeronautics Board; William Wallace; H. J. Wellman; Joseph Gould; Mary Connolly Sargenti; and Harvey Katz, Pan American Airways.

Gratitude is due, too, to Dr. Jack Tabor, whose encouragement helped along the way; to Somerset R. Waters of Child & Waters, Inc., who, as Street and Smith's travel consultant introduced me to the travel business; and to Helen Valentine, the first editor-in-chief for whom I worked as travel editor, who gave me the world to roam and lent me her support in a thousand ways.

It also goes most warmly to the readers of my newspaper column. Their letters and search for information led me to these pieces and prompted this book.

Part of the book was written in the serenity of the Newfane Inn in Newfane, Vermont, where Mr. and Mrs. René Chardain looked after me.

Sandra Reimer Lucas cheerfully helped with typing and correspondence at one period.

Janet Bush and Sheila Barry are two wonderful girls who brightened my life considerably—and a very special note of affection is due them.

I am grateful, too, to Charlotte Seitlin of Simon and Schuster, a sympa-

thetic, congenial editor who accepted, with infinite patience, the delays of a peripatetic writer.

And finally, I should like to say thank you to Betsy Talbot Blackwell, editor-in-chief of Mademoiselle *magazine. Mrs. Blackwell has been a pioneer in travel coverage as in many other fields. Her enthusiasm for presenting fresh travel news and her lively interest in all that goes on in the field have made our association constantly stimulating.*

Contents

Preface

I STARTED to travel when I was quite a young woman in 1948, during the first postwar spurt of tourism, when a visiting American woman was still a fresh and curious sight on the boulevards of Paris. I have been traveling, as a writer and editor, ever since (sometimes as much as 95,000 miles a year). Looking back over these years, I cannot imagine what my life would have been like without that first trip, which brought on the traveler's happy, permanent addiction. I would certainly have missed the pleasant company of many warm friends, and the new cadence of language spoken by Irish, Indians, Greeks, French, Italians—the singing lilt, the spilling melody, the outpouring of rich, almost palpable sound. I would have missed the first moving view of the Acropolis in the clear light of a Greek morning, the radiance of the Taj Mahal, the shimmering temples of Bangkok, the picture of the last surfers coming to shore in Hawaii when the sea, sand and horizon turn amethyst in the twilight. I would have known less about French furniture and English drawings and I would not have the lovely antiques that are now part of my home and give me constant pleasure. Then there are the private experiences that live forever in the senses: swimming in the soft, clear sea off Eleuthera, in the Bahamas, watching the dawn come up (the only time I was free of business); snorkeling for the first time off Virgin Gorda, when I wanted to call to everybody in sight and say, "Hey, come see what's out there"; all the tastes of food, from the first croissants in Paris and the hot coffee which was half milk to the thick cream the English pour over dessert, the chicken tarragon at a lake resort in France, sukiyaki in Kyoto, all the meals I have had in gardens, the crabs and lobsters and crayfish; the light taste of ouzo as I sat in the trance of early evening on a Greek island; the taste of sangría on the sunlit terrace of a pension in Majorca; and the sounds—all those bells and fountains; the swell of music at Royal Festival Hall in London, the roar of a jet, the clear voices rising in the theater at Epidaurus; the excitement of seeing my first Balenciaga collection, my first row of poplars lining a French country road, my first all-French conversation, throwing open the shuttered windows on my first morning in St.-Paul-de-Vence, to see the lemon, lime and orange trees and all the white doves flying about; and the children, with shining eyes and tinkling voices—all different around the world, and the differences sharpening themselves against one another, so that everything is the better for it.

This outpouring—or one like it, but ever so personal—can be yours, too. In the span of a single generation, *the* world has become *our* world—and because of travel we have gained the freedom to know it well. My hearth and my country are richer and clearer to me because I have seen what lies beyond them—and it will be the same for you.

I know that many women with the means to travel (and more women than ever have the means, if they make the effort) are held back by reticence, self-consciousness and fear. I have written this book in the hope that it will dissolve much of the difficulty, and therefore the fear of travel; I want to tell the timid that the world is mostly a pleasant and congenial place, that the unknown does not remain that way for long. And I hope to be helpful, too, to veteran travelers, who love to trade tricks and systems.

The subjects covered here are those which have come up most often in letters from my readers; the material is meant to give the traveler rules of thumb for nearly all the situations she is likely to encounter. As well as explaining how matters should be handled, I've also tried, where possible, to supply some background about manners and customs—how rules or situations have evolved through history or circumstance—a framework which has often helped me. Finally, I hope you will enjoy reading the book, that you will want to carry it and jot things down in the margins.

Today, I fly to London for a day and to the West Indies for the weekend. And each time I do, I wish I could say to every woman in the country, "Come, do it too." Don't put it off! Scrimp. Save. Sacrifice. Open up your life—and make travel part of it.

Go unafraid of the foreign or of foreigners. Remember as you ask directions in the Paris Métro, however halting your French, that people have been lost in your home town, and didn't meet hostility. The least important thing you share with a Frenchman is temporary ignorance of each other's ways.

Go with zest, to see how other people work out their lives, and show admiration and understanding of all they are proud of. Enjoy what lies before you without "missing the smile of the absent cat." Go with common sense, curiosity and a clear knowledge of your own interests.

Go, because it has never been more important to you and to the world: Knowing more of life, you will enjoy and cherish it more; and to cherish the world with its peoples and treasures is to help it stay peacefully together.

—FRANCES LANG KOLTUN

New York City, September 1966

Travel information, especially that concerning fares and charters, is highly volatile because it is subject to constant review. You should therefore always check carefully at the time of your trip on what fares the current agreements permit. Although this book was being updated right up to the last possible moment, it is inevitable, since fare agreements are always in such a state of flux, that certain changes may have occurred.

After all, life, for all its agonies of despair and loss and guilt, is exciting and beautiful, amusing and artful and endearing, full of liking and of love, at times a poem and a high adventure, at times noble and at times very gay; and whatever (if anything) is to come after it, we shall not have this life again.

ROSE MACAULAY, *The Towers of Trebizond*

I am much pleased that you are going on a very long journey, which may by proper conduct restore your health and prolong your life. Observe these rules:

1. *Turn all care out of your head as soon as you mount the chaise.*
2. *Do not think about frugality; your health is worth more than it can cost.*
3. *Do not continue any day's journey to fatigue.*
4. *Take now and then a day's rest.*
5. *Get a smart sea-sickness, if you can.*
6. *Cast away all anxiety, and keep your mind easy.*

—SAMUEL JOHNSON, Letter to Henry Perkins, July 28, 1782

Airports

BACK IN the early 'twenties when commercial aviation was just getting started, an airfield was any flat grassy stretch—a cow pasture, a prairie, even a military parade ground—and the terminal little more than a barrackslike shed. The plane taxied up to its door, the passengers stepped gingerly onto the lower linen-covered wing, were bundled into the tiny cabin, and the plane took slowly, quiveringly to the air, carefully clearing the barbed-wire fences as it gained altitude.

Today, an airfield sprawls for miles. When a jet roars smoothly, strongly into the sky, it leaves behind a complex of buildings and services the near equal of a small city. Paris's peerless Orly, for example, which started life as a grassy strip in World War I, is almost one-fifth the size of the city of Paris, and it is equipped with enough services to keep you coiffed, well fed and entertained for weeks.

Therefore, whether you are grounded for hours while in transit or the victim of a delayed departure or are just passing through, remember that a big-city airport is much like an iceberg: Few of its

1

comforts or amusements, except for shops, show on the surface. Airport space is parceled out among concessionaires, many of whom are tucked away in out-of-the-way corners where rents are lower. At a first-rate airport you can find a movie theater, a beauty salon, or a place for a quiet nap as a substitute for hours of wilting boredom. This just calls for a little previous knowledge or on-the-spot investigation.

To use "in transit" or waiting time profitably, find out *exactly* how long you will be on the ground. Then ask the airport's information desk or the airline's ground personnel what services the airport offers.

However, airports reflect a nation's purse—as well as its pride—and facilities vary greatly from place to place. Where the economy is sluggish, the airports will naturally have little to beguile you and may even be rather shabby. Where tourism and a strong flow of business and cargo are essential to local well-being, the airports are likely to represent the best architecture and interior design the country can muster and may offer the attractions of a pavilion at a minor World's Fair.

To give you an idea of what to expect, here is a sampling of the facilities provided by some of the top airports around the world.

You will find some or all of these bounties at places like London's Heathrow, Brussels' National, Paris's Orly, Copenhagen's Kastrup, Amsterdam's Schiphol, Tokyo's International, Ireland's Shannon, and Honolulu's International.

FACILITY	EXAMPLES
One or more hotels. Some have rates for fractions of days; others charge daily or overnight rates; all have special facilities for passengers—from soundproof rooms to free transportation to and from the airport.	At London's Heathrow Airport the new Fortes Airport Hotel is linked to the main concourse by an underpass. At Tokyo's Airwait Hotel you can take a room for 3 hours for $2.78, need only pay 50 cents for each additional hour. At Copenhagen you can rent a cabin which contains a bed, lamp and telephone for $1.55. Book it at the information desk; you'll be awakened 45 minutes before your plane leaves. This airport also has cots with blankets and cushions, free of charge.
Showers. For a small sum, you can rent a towel, bathrobe and other toilet articles to freshen up between flights.	Zurich, Manchester, Schiphol, Orly

Movie theater	Orly. (At New York's Kennedy Airport there is even a theatrical group which performs at scheduled intervals.)
Chapel (usually nondenominational)	Orly, Kennedy and others
Medical and dental facilities	Schiphol, Kennedy, Orly
Beauty salon and barbershop	At most major airports, e.g., Zurich, Kennedy, Schiphol. In the Relaxation Center of Paris's Orly, you can get a beautifying and reviving massage or oxygenation treatment.
Pressing service, shoe repair	Most new major airports
Local tourist information desks	Most major airports
. Nursery and play areas for children	At Brussels National Airport there's a nursery with a playroom, six-bed dormitory, kitchen and nursing staff which functions from 7 A.M. to 10 P.M. 7 days a week, free. At Copenhagen there are play pens, baby-sitters, free diapers, baby powder and safety pins. At London's Heathrow there's a boating pond; at Honolulu's International Airport a playground with a spiral slide and a "hill of bars" for children beyond the toddler age. For infants there is a nursery where mothers can prepare or warm baby's bottle and lay him down for a nap.
Restaurants and bars	At every new major airport

You will also find such ubiquitous conveniences as photographers, banks, currency exchange counters, cars for hire, flight insurance, post offices, duty-free shops (see Duty-Free Shopping, page 117), transportation into town (sometimes free), cable desks, telephones.

Besides these major comforts, you will run into local refinements: At Amsterdam's Schiphol Airport you can buy flowers from vending machines; and in Honolulu's airport a coin-fed machine will sell you a handful of dried silkworms, so you can feed the beautiful Japanese carp in the swimming pools.

In recent years one more embellishment has been added to keep you from pacing restlessly between planes: quick sightseeing tours. In Amsterdam, for example, you can have one called a Minitour, or 200 minutes of touring in or around the capital every morning or afternoon in a tiny Austin driven by a pretty hostess who works for the Amsterdam Tourist Association. (If there are 7 or more, she will arrange for a bus.) You can see the city, the flower auctions at Aalsmeer or the gardens at Keukenhof, for $4 a head, with tea included. At Orly, Air France has organized tours of Paris and its environs which last from 3 to 7 hours and cost from $6 to $12. If you have a 24-hour stopover at Shannon Airport, you can take a one-day tour, culminating in a rich medieval banquet at Bunratty Castle, 6 miles from the airport. For $23 you get, in addition to the banquet, a large helping of "Instant Ireland" including a drive through the countryside, tea at a thatched cottage, a visit to a typical village, a room with bath at Shannon's International Hotel, breakfast and lunch, dinner in an Irish home, a tour of Limerick, and plenty of time for the airport's duty-free shops. Passengers may join the tour whenever they arrive; they are met at their plane and escorted throughout the tour. It is available from April 1 until October 31. You can also take quick air tours at airports. Paris's Orly, for example, offers two via Air Paris: A 50-minute flight over the city's rooftops is $7; a two-hour one over the chateaux of the Loire is $30.

At any airport where there is a tour desk—or even a local taxi driver who "has some English"—you can arrange your own sightseeing on the spot.

Finally, while some airports provide special facilities for unexpected sports (Buenos Aires's Ezeiza has a swimming pool), even the shabbiest offers plenty of one wholesome activity: walking. Airport sprawl is a chronic condition around the world. As terminals developed, they began to sprout "fingers"—long covered walkways to loading gates that could be extended when additional parking space was needed for aircraft. Today some of these "fingers" are like endless hallways. The average walking distance at larger terminals is estimated at about 950 feet, or a little under one fifth of a mile. If you are staggering under a load of hand luggage or packages, ask for carts to wheel them along—or throw yourself on the mercy of the airline's personnel. Until moving sidewalks or mobile lounges become standard equipment, airport sprawl is one of several good reasons for wearing your most comfortable shoes (see Shoes, page 325) on a flight. The long walk from airplane to airport will give you your first sights and sounds and smells of a new country. You will enjoy them more if your attention is not half absorbed by aching feet.

Antique Shops

AT LEAST half the fun of antiques is the process of acquiring them. The search goes on in shops, auction rooms and markets, and the rules in each are quite different. To keep your foraging successful, here are some general guidelines for making your way about the antique shops. (For more about antiquing, see Auctions, page 9, and Markets, page 226.)

1. Generally antique shops are clustered in a single neighborhood or even on one street. Ask your concierge where to find them. In Vienna, for example, the antique district is the Kohlmarkt; in Dublin most of the shops are on Lower Ormond Quay and Lower Liffey Street; in Amsterdam on Nieuwe Spiegelstraat; in Athens on Pandrossou Street; in Lisbon on the Rua Dom Pedro V; in Stockholm in the Old Town; in Copenhagen they run parallel to the main shopping district of Strøget.

Sometimes a large city like Paris or London will have more than one quarter for antiques, and prices vary according to local rents. You may want to do your browsing in the posh district and buy in the low-rent one. In Paris, for example, the area around the Rue du Faubourg St.-Honoré or the Rue Royale near Place Vendôme is chic and expensive; your money will probably go a little further on the Rue du Bac or the Rue Jacob.

Many tourist offices publish a list of reliable antique shops. If you don't have a notebook of gleanings from friends, get the tourist office list of recommended shops or the list published by the local antique dealers' trade association. (Only a certified antique dealer can supply guarantees of authenticity. Secondhand dealers, junk shops, and flea-market stalls, while often sources of bargains, cannot.) In London, the British Antique Dealers' Association, 20 Rutland Gate, London S.W.7, compiles an annual list of its members. This can be your guide wherever you go in the country. (Each dealer also has an identifying sign in his window.) This Antique Dealers' Association booklet includes not only its members, their addresses and the merchandise in which they specialize, but it also lists the names of carriers and shipping agents who are expert in packing and transporting antiques and works of art all over the world.

Always go to well-established and reputable sources. Be wary of places recommended by taxi drivers or guides you don't know well. They are bound to get a "cut" for producing your business, which you pay for. Furthermore, a business that indulges in this disreputable practice probably won't be squeamish about misrepresenting the value and authenticity of its wares.

2. The antique fairs held throughout Europe are still the world's biggest source of antiques, and you should include some in your itinerary. Typical are the Swiss Antiques Exhibition in Bern in October or the Antique Dealers Fair in Delft the last week in August or the beginning of September. Britain's fairs are marvelous for antique buffs—and extremely well organized. The oldest and most famous is the Antique Dealers' Fair and Exhibition held annually at Grosvenor House, Park Lane, London, in June. This is one of the leading events of its kind in the world and so charged with excitement that it has become an outstanding social occasion. The best, most comprehensive collection of antiques for sale in the world is gathered under one roof and prices are quite fair.

Other fairs in London are held in the Town Halls at Chelsea in May and October, and at Kensington in August and September. Outside London, there are antique fairs at Harrogate, in the Brontë country of Yorkshire; at the seaside resort of Brighton; and at Chesford Grange, Kenilworth, in Warwickshire in the Midlands.

At all British Antiques Fairs, every piece on the stands is for sale, and has been declared authentic by a committee of experts. If more than slight restoration work has been done on a piece, the committee will not accept it. As an item is sold it is replaced by another, so the exhibits are always stocked with an enormous variety of merchandise.

3. The lighter the traffic in a shop or an area, the lower the prices are likely to be. Antique shops in small towns and villages, or in countries which, like Ireland, are not yet flooded with tourists, are relatively untouched and may offer bargains. The price tag on an antique reflects the number of people who have owned it. Each time a piece goes from one dealer to another, one more person makes a profit. Therefore it is usually a sound rule to catch local antiques as early as possible in the season before they have had much chance to change hands.

4. In areas once colonized by Europeans, watch local newspapers for the sale of great houses or look in the shops for the furniture and bric-a-brac of the original settlers, or the often beautiful but oddly accented furniture made to European designs by native craftsmen. Caribbean plantation houses, for example, harbor furniture which came out with the early colonists; Australia, too, is a good source of Georgian and Victorian oddments.

5. Bargaining or haggling over price is acceptable, even mandatory, in an open-air market, but is in bad taste in an established antique shop. On the other hand, if an antique dealer himself opens the way for some polite "negotiating," follow his lead. This is more likely to happen in out-of-the-way shops. Like open market stalls, shops in the country are sensitive to weather. If rain has kept people off the roads, prices may come down. During your stay in a large city, go off antiquing in the countryside after a heavy siege of rainy weather; if you have had three rainy weekends in a row, get on the prowl as soon as the sun comes up on the fourth.

6. Be sure to add the cost of mailing or shipping to that of your "bargain" to determine how much of a bargain it really is. Leave the details to the shop. An established one will have a long-standing relationship with a reliable shipper. If this can't be done, ask your concierge for help. He will either put you into the hands of a good shipper or wrap and send the package himself. If the package is reasonably manageable, take it along with you. This forestalls waiting, frustration, and expense.

Any piece dated earlier than 1830 (except rugs and carpets, which must have been made before 1701, and violins, violas, and cellos which must predate 1801) is classified by United States Customs as an antique, and is therefore duty-free. This includes furniture, marble, bronze, brass, porcelain, chinaware, and any object of artistic value. However, whether a painting was finished 24 hours or 240 years before your return to the States, it may be brought in without duty. Be sure to ask the antique or art dealer for a bill that identifies the piece, gives its date and guarantees its authenticity. (See Customs, page 95.)

While most countries are happy to have you buy anything you like, they do have rules about art, antiques, and archaeological finds. This is to stop the drain on national treasures, and the regulations vary in strictness from one type of antique to another, as well as from one country to another. The average shopper, however, seldom runs into the regulations. Reputable antique dealers know the rules and will help you with the proper forms whenever they're necessary.

In India, for example, no article over one hundred years old may be taken away from Madras, Delhi, or Calcutta without the permission of the head of the Archaeological Survey; or from Bombay without the permission of the director of the Prince of Wales Museum. (Local tourist offices will put you in touch with the proper person in each city.) In Egypt, only replicas of antiques are allowed out of the country. In Greece, Greco-Roman and Byzantine articles won't be released by local customs officials without written permission from the Greek Ministry of Education. In Mexico, you must get a special permit from the National Institute of Anthropology and History to take out an archaeological find. In Mexico, too, you may no longer remove from the country any painting by a nationally recognized Mexican artist who has died, e.g., Diego Rivera. Moreover, countries may impose a limit on how much you can take out in cash value without special permission. In Austria, for example, if you want to carry off goods worth more than $400, you need an export permit which costs 20 cents. In Britain, on the other hand, with its plenitude of antiques, you can buy up to $2,800 worth of art and antiques without a license.

You'll find nearly all governments sympathetic to your antique hunting. Unless you want to take away one of their exceptionally valuable national treasures, obtaining permits is relatively simple.

7. Don't overlook the antique shops in department stores. I have had good luck with the collection at the Central Cottage Industries Emporium in New Delhi and the corner basement shop at Takashimaya in Tokyo.

8. If you really want something desperately—and can afford it— buy it. Heaven knows when you will get back to Bangkok or Jaipur, and the thought of the carved chest you pass up may gnaw at you the rest of your life. Your only regret will be for the things you were strong-minded about—and didn't buy. On the other hand, don't buy something just because it's a bargain. $4 is little enough to pay for a 5-foot-square heavy baroque frame; but if you live in a small apartment and have no particular need for it, you haven't bought a frame but a white elephant.

Finally, here are some basic rules recommended by decorators for collecting antiques: If you want first-rate pieces but can't afford perfect specimens, buy examples that are broken, faded or otherwise in need of repair. The price will be a tiny fraction of what the unflawed piece can command. Buy what is out of fashion or handicrafts that are rapidly being replaced by machine-made goods. (In Belgium, for example, as machines take over lacemaking, handmade lace becomes rare and antique lace even rarer.) Study the antiques at museums; go to auctions to familiarize yourself with current values. If you are prepared to spend a lot of money, get the advice and assistance of an expert. Unless you are a serious collector, buy a piece for the pleasure it gives you, never for the investment value. Don't be afraid of being "taken"—it's most unlikely in a reliable shop.

William Pahlmann, the distinguished interior designer, says, "Never buy anything that doesn't mean something personal to you. It must reflect a sense of place or country, but most especially it must give *you* a sense of joy!"

Auctions

WHILE THE auctioneer's gavel can certainly be heard on other continents, it is in Europe's great salesrooms that most of the world's treasures change hands from one owner to another, just as they have done for hundreds of years. Whether you are a serious collector, an enlightened amateur, or simply one who finds auctions exciting, you will want to pay some attention to the public sales of paintings, furniture, porcelain, antiquities, books, silver and jewelry in the course of your travels.

Though Europe has many auction houses, authorities list these as outstanding: Sotheby's and Christie's (known formally as Christie, Manson and Woods, Ltd.) in London; Hôtel Drouot in Paris; Klipstein and Kornfeld in Bern; Galerie Fischer in Lucerne; Kunsthaus Lempertz in Cologne; and the Dorotheum in Vienna. In addition, you will find other auctioneers in the telephone directories and newspapers or by asking the local tourist association.

In France, keep your eye out for the names of distinguished *commissaires-priseurs*, known in English as auctioneer-appraisers. These gentlemen, among whom Maurice Rheims is probably the best-known, are retained to handle a sale and then pick the salesroom in which to conduct it. Where they go, you should follow.

Don't be intimidated by stories about Renoirs that sell for $200,-000, Rubenses at $400,000 or Rembrandts for over $1,000,000. Millionaires and dealers don't buy everything, and most sale prices are not astronomical. In fact, you may be astonished to learn that Sotheby's, the grandest of all auction rooms, sells about three quarters of its lots for less than $280, and more than one third for less than $56! So, even if your budget for *objets d'art* is no bigger than your weekly paycheck, you still have status as a bidder.

Buying at auctions abroad has the same sorts of advantages and drawbacks it has at home, compounded by the difficulties of negotiating in a foreign language and dealing with foreign currency and measurements. The big advantage is, of course, the chance to save money—you are avoiding the dealer's markup by buying directly from the owner. The difficulty is that no auction house will guarantee the authenticity of any object, although no reputable house will sell anything it does not *believe* to be genuine. There is always the possibility that you may find yourself bidding against a dealer or collector who has his heart set on the item, and the price may be pushed up to shop levels. Again a piece may have flaws that are not apparent from where you sit (though the auctioneer usually points out those he is aware of).

Since all bidders face these disadvantages, auction houses have done what they can to ease them. If you behave like an experienced dealer, you can generally circumvent these problems. Here is what to do:

First, all merchandise is exhibited for several days before it is sold. Be sure to inspect carefully any lot in which you are interested before you bid on it.

Next, each house publishes a catalog describing the items on sale, in considerable detail. Buy one and use it as a guide. The descriptions often provide clues to an item's authenticity. Sotheby's, for example, uses the full name of the artist when convinced the work is authentic, only the initials if there is the least doubt.

Finally, although few buyers are aware of this service, all reputable houses will give you their estimate of the price a lot should bring. If you consult them before a sale, they will tell you the range of prices in which any given lot should fall. This can keep you from overbidding. For example, you may be willing to bid $150 for a Georgian mustard pot, but if the auction house tells you it should go for between $40 and $50, you can be fairly sure that a good antique shop would sell it for $100.

Since you will be bidding in a foreign language, you will need someone to sort out the francs, pounds and schillings. You can ask your concierge to suggest a guide who, for a small fee, will act as a translator. He will keep up a steady stream of translations and computations, tell you how big a table is in inches, not in centimeters, and generally guide you through the maze. If you expect to make sizable purchases, enlist the services of a dealer, who will charge you a small percentage as a fee. He will do the actual bidding, which often calls for a cool head and unflurried judgment.

If you do your own bidding, handle it just as you would in this country—by raising your hand or waving your program—and do it clearly and decisively. Auctioneers are driven absolutely wild by women whose motions are so unclear that they don't know whethe. they are greeting a friend or making a bid.

In France, don't be surprised when you are nicked for roughly 10 to 16 per cent on top of your successful bid. It's a purchase tax levied by the government.

Auctions are held not only in established salesrooms, but also in private houses, and if you are an experienced auction buff, these present an opportunity to pick up enormous bargains. Even though the custom of bringing home castles stone by stone went out with Mr. Hearst, you might find carved paneling, doors or mantels that would cost the earth in a shop. Your best guide to these auctions is again the local newspaper.

Remember that while an auction house will arrange to pack and ship your purchase, you pay extra for this service. If you buy something at a private sale, your concierge, an exporter or a shipper will have to take care of this chore for you.

Some houses hold auctions regularly, others sporadically, but the big season everywhere is between October and July. If you mean to try your hand at an auction or two, ask your concierge to check the days and hours as soon as you arrive. Some countries have specific regulations concerning the export of objects of artistic, cultural or historical value, and you may need some sort of official permission to take home what you buy. (See Antique Shops, page 5.)

A final word: The *International Art Market,* an American publication which carries the details of major auction sales here and abroad, quotes the advice of André Fage, a French authority, on bidding for paintings at auctions:

"Never bid for a painting you have not subjected to personal examination at close range."

"Never tell the person next to you that you are interested in a particular lot; he may be bidding against you."

"Never make the first bid; let someone else establish the pace for you."

Background Reading

SINCE Karl Baedeker first published his thorough guides nearly a hundred years ago (". . . to enable the traveler so to employ his time, his money, and his energy, that he may derive the greatest possible amount of pleasure and instruction from his visit . . ."), travelers have depended on books to light their way. Today, there is a vast body of literature which will, among other things, explain a country's form of government, list its charming pensions, grade its restaurants, describe its weather, and speak poetically of its buildings, feelingly of its people, and statistically of its natural resources.

You are, presumably, a believer in background reading of one sort or another; you wouldn't be looking at this book if you weren't. You know it is folly to travel uninformed, for to arrive anywhere in a state of total ignorance can be bad manners (you run the risk of committing terrible *faux pas*) and wasteful (why miss the great sights, notable restaurants, and shopping bargains the books describe?). In travel, as in most other things, what we understand best we enjoy the most. When you visit a country, you should know at the least those facts about its religion, history, arts, and politics that are dearest to its people.

There are two general categories of travel books. Try to do some reading in each. First, there are the books that give specific, immediately useful information, and they, in turn, fall into two groups: general books about a country's history, architecture, art, music, etc.; and guidebooks which deal with the practical matters in a traveler's life. Many of these how-to books incorporate some "background" information, but their chief role is to serve as reliable advisers on hotels, restaurants, sightseeing, excursions, and the like. At their best, they give ample facts, prices, and opinions. Look at several guidebooks until you find one whose author's taste seems to be sympathetic to yours. Three useful books that I like especially are Naomi Barry's *Paris Personal*, the best guidebook to come out on that city; Kate Simon's *Mexico: Places and Pleasures*, a literate and informative view of that country; and Leila Hadley's *How to Travel with Children to Europe*, filled with sensible, thoughtful information.

Some guidebooks are much like encyclopedias—lots of facts, no opinions. A good example is Pan American's *New Horizons World Guide*, which gives basic information in capsule form for 112 countries.

Some books of personal reminiscences incorporate excellent travel information. Ilka Chase's books, *The Carthaginian Rose* about a trip through Europe and Southeast Asia and *Elephants Arrive at Half-Past Five* about a photo-safari through East Africa, are bright, amusing reading, liberally sprinkled with useful tips. H. V. Morton's series of books called "In Search of . . ." (e.g., *In Search of England, In Search of Scotland, In Search of London*) are not meant to be ordinary guidebooks but accounts of the author's wanderings. In the course of these, he absorbs a country's spirit and transmits it to his readers.

There is, too, the venerable *Guide Michelin*, which first appeared about sixty years ago and remains in a class by itself. It rates restaurants and hotels from information gathered by a team of professional inspectors, and is so dependable that travelers of all degrees of sophistication use it. If the *Guide* gives a restaurant three stars, you can be sure the food will be superb and the restaurant will be worth a special journey. Only 12 restaurants received this accolade in 1965. While *Guide Michelin* started in France and was for many years devoted solely to that country, today there are *Guides* for Italy, Switzerland, Austria, Germany, Spain, and the Benelux countries.

There are maps, dictionaries, picture books, books about a single aspect of travel (such as restaurants, museums, walking tours, shops, etc.), and finally there are excellent brochures published by tourist offices and transportation companies which are available, free.

The second category of travel books lies half buried all through literature; any book that throws light on a place obliquely rather than directly belongs to it. It may have been written five, fifty, or five hundred years ago, but the truth of its observations makes it as pertinent and revealing today as when it was published.

Novels, adventure stories, thrillers, poetry, drama, essays, even cookbooks all add flesh to the skeleton of facts and give you the "feeling" of a place. Read books like Giuseppe di Lampedusa's *The Leopard* on Sicily; Ernest Hemingway's *Death in the Afternoon* on bullfighting in Spain; or Lawrence Durrell's *Prospero's Cell* and *Reflections on a Marine Venus* about the life and temperament of Greek islanders; or any of Elizabeth David's cookbooks for a sense of the rhythm and the texture of the Mediterranean world as well as its smells and colors. These books say little about monuments and museums and much about the way human beings behave and feel.

The body of distinguished travel writing grows. It would seem that as differences diminish, fine writers have grown keener to seek and celebrate them—read V. S. Pritchett, Mary McCarthy, Elizabeth Bowen, Eleanor Clark, Sybille Bedford, William Sansom, Laurie Lee, Anthony Carson, D. H. Lawrence, Rose Macaulay, James Morris, Patrick Leigh Fermor and perhaps the greatest writing traveler of our time, Freya Stark.

Bathrooms

WHILE IT IS true that the United States has 90 per cent of the world's bathtubs and Americans have a fondness for bathing unequaled by any people since the ancient Romans, you needn't fear that, having crossed an ocean, the facilities will be medieval. It just isn't so. The bathrooms in the Hotel Ritz in Lisbon are more luxurious and beautiful than any found in these fifty states; those in the Rambagh Palace in Jaipur, India, are bigger and loftier than our hotel rooms.

There are, however, some less enviable differences between bathrooms here and those abroad that must be pointed out. Since the rest of the world shares the remaining 10 per cent, you won't find bathrooms everywhere. Except for those in private houses, the others show up strategically in the best, most modern hotels or wherever Americans are likely to turn up. Also, when you do find them in vintage hotels, they may not contain *all* the usual articles of plumbing. Europeans—and those countries that follow European hotel standards—take the word "bathroom" literally. To them it means what it says—a room to take a bath in. It may be the size of a ballroom, but it doesn't necessarily house more than a bathtub and washbowl. The toilet, known as the "W.C."—for water closet—will often be found in a small room of its own at the end of the corridor. If you'd rather not put up with all this shuttling about, be sure to specify a room with a bathroom *and* toilet when you make your hotel reservations.

This inconvenience apart, the average European bathroom—and those in good hotels around the world—is both efficient and immaculate. In Europe, especially, the bathtubs are so big that while the water is steaming into one end, it is cooling off at the other. While stall showers don't exist, you will often find a needle spray hanging from the wall beside the bathtub, and it's wonderful for rinsing your hair or spraying your back. You will also find a bidet, that neat porcelain apparatus that seems to shock so many Americans on first acquaintance. (Because it comes as such a surprise to the American traveler, and because it's such a useful item, the bidet is treated separately on page 36.) You're also likely to see, folded on a chair or hanging behind the door, a tent of terry cloth in which to wrap yourself after a bath. This is such a practical garment that it has been copied by American department stores. Towels dry on pipes that carry hot water (and are often hot to the touch, so be careful).

As for hot water, you'll find it's plentiful except at times in places like the Virgin Islands and Hong Kong, which suffer from chronic shortages of fresh water. Apropos of hot water, stamp into your memory the fact that when you get to Spain, France, Italy, Latin and South America, the letter "C" on the tub and washbowl taps stands for steaming hot, not as in the U.S.A. or Britain for "cold." *Calda* (Italian), *chaude* (French) and *caliente* (Spanish) spell scalding in their native languages. In those countries, if you want cold water, turn the tap marked "F" for *friggia* (Italian), *froide* (French), or *frio* (Spanish). The German language is not so confusing. In Germany and Austria, you'll find "H" for *heiss* (hot) and "K" for *kalt* (cold).

There's another oddity about Continental bathrooms. If when you've melted into your bath, you notice a worn, dingy cord or a button on the side, don't pull or press unless you mean to sound a note of alarm that may ring clear down to the cellar. Both sound summonses for help, which may arrive in the form of the valet with a bristling mustache and a stack of towels. If you've locked your room from the inside, you'll have to get out of the bathtub, lather and all, or the staff will be sure you've fainted and tear the door down to keep you from drowning.

In Japan, all reports to the contrary, men and women do not ordinarily bathe together in communal baths unless they live in a remote country village or go to a spa for the hot mineral waters. (While mixed nude bathing is still practiced, it's confined mostly to simple, strictly Japanese inns outside the tourist orbit; or to hotels famous for their mineral waters such as the Dai-ichi Takimoto Inn in Noboribetsu, Hokkaido, with its huge indoor bath hall.) If you stay at a Western hotel, your bathroom will look pretty much the same as it might in a hotel in Dallas except that the bathtub will be traditionally Japanese—square and so deep you can soak up to your chin. If you go to a good *ryokan*, the traditional Japanese inn, you'll find a good-sized bathroom containing a washbowl and large wooden or tile tub. (As in Europe, the W.C. is usually separate.) The tub is filled with hot—indeed *very* hot—water, but you never get into it until you have first soaped yourself and rinsed off the lather with a small pan of clear water. The Japanese believe one should enter one's bath clean and consider it the worst possible manners to soap oneself in the tub. The tub is strictly for a long, hot soak.

There are small hotels abroad where you will have to pay extra to use the common bath; there are vintage hotels with splendid lofty rooms and bathtubs to go with only a few of them; there are glossy international hotels in which a bathroom comes with a room as inevitably as sheets on the bed; and there are a few truly luxurious hotels like the Ritz in Lisbon whose bathrooms are a sybarite's daydream. Naturally, you pay for what you get.

Beaches and Swimming Pools

IF THE alchemy of sun, sea and sand works wonders for you, plan to allow time for it, even on a city-hopping vacation. An interlude on a beach—whether an afternoon or long weekend—will give you not only a suntan but a rewarding sense of physical well-being. The museum treasures of The Hague in the Netherlands seem even more lustrous after a few hours of lazy sunning at Scheveningen, a few minutes away from the city; and the Parthenon in moonlight will look more mysterious and moving after a day in the sun at Vouliagméni, the smooth beach 30 minutes out of Athens. Besides providing a physical tonic, a foreign beach will give you a chance to meet the locals (who are much more approachable without their formal city manners—and clothes) as well as *other* visiting foreigners. The seaside resorts of Normandy, for example, are as close to London as to Paris, and for many years the British have streamed across the Channel to share the beaches with the French. The beaches at Rhodes are as international as the U.N. delegates' lounge.

You will find beaches nearly everywhere you go, often in unexpected places, like Salvador, Brazil's old capital; Mahabalipuram, a lovely stretch of sand and sea 37 miles away from Madras in India; and Hammamet outside Tunis, on the Mediterranean's southern shore. Europe and Australia, with their thousands of miles of seacoast, are belted with them, in enormous number and variety. But it doesn't take a seacoast—there are wonderful beaches along the landlocked lakes of Switzerland, for example, especially at Geneva, Maggiore and Lugano.

You have two decisions to make: The first is which beach style appeals to you; the second is how best to fit some beach life into your itinerary.

Though Europeans were fairly late to discover the virtues of sea air (the mountains, especially the Alps, came into vogue two or three generations earlier), as the seaside resorts sprang up, an elaborate social life evolved in many. Today, for example, the French resort of

Deauville glitters with diamonds and ball gowns in August; unless you are equipped appropriately, stay away from the big hotels in this area. At Belgium's Knokke, also a *luxe* resort, the after-five diversions include the opera or a concert. On the other side of the scale are the simple fishing villages like those in Brittany, whose chief concern is not tourism but the coming and going of the fleet and the richness of the catch. Here you are strictly on your own—to search out a private cove, to take the sun in solitude, or dine at a small quayside restaurant when the sun goes down in the Atlantic.

If you haven't time to travel far for beach life, investigate local possibilities. There are, for example, three major beaches close to Rome; if you get an early start, especially on Sunday, you should be able to reach any of them in about an hour by car, bus, or subway. The Lido of the ancient Roman town of Ostia is popular and the center of beaches which stretch up and down the coast for miles; Fregene, edged with pines, is quieter and attracts the Roman *bel mondo;* Santa Marinella, 37 miles north of Rome, is also fashionable and pretty. Athenians bolt out of their offices at the stroke of two and head for an afternoon of sunning at Glyfada, Vouliagméni, or Lagonissi, all about a half to three quarters of an hour's drive from the city. Estoril and Cascais are even closer to Lisbon, and the beach of Bygdøy is only 15 minutes by bus from Oslo's extraordinary City Hall. You can find relief from Tangier's intense summer heat on a fine beach 10 miles west of the city. But remember that beaches near the big cities, particularly those in the south, will be crowded, especially on weekends. On Fridays in August, half of Rome's population escapes the city for seashore or mountains.

You may be surprised to discover that beach manners are generally more relaxed abroad than at home. (For "do's" and "don'ts" about bikinis, see page 41.) Europeans everywhere are infinitely more casual about changing clothes than we are. If tents or lockers are not available—at many public beaches, facilities for changing are sparse to nonexistent—they shrug and twist their way into their bathing suits under a large beach towel in full view of the crowd. It's perfectly acceptable to wear your bathing suit to the beach under a loose sheath dress and to simply step out of the dress on the sand. Large beaches have restaurants and snack bars; or you can take a picnic lunch. Many resorts have sports events and facilities unknown in the U.S.A. At Deauville, for example, it's fashionable to take an early morning canter along the hard-packed sands before the tide comes in. Naturally, the more secluded the beach, the fewer the safety facilities, so step gingerly where a beach is uncrowded, and always check with the concierge or manager of your hotel about local conditions before leaving on a day's outing. (And in Denmark, where people are jovial, easygoing and devoted to beach life, three rules are laid down: Don't build castles and moats in the sand, don't fly a foreign flag, and if you like to swim in the nude, do so only if you can find a place where no one can see you even through binoculars from far, far away.)

If a taste of beach life is impossible, consider the local swimming pools. Young Parisians pick up their suntans along the Seine at, among others, the Bain Royal or—more chic—the Piscine Deligny. During the long lunch period and over weekends, the pools are alive with bikinied young men and women. Entrance fees are from 50 to 70 cents and pools stay open from early morning to mid-evening, sometimes even later. The pools, built on barges moored in the Seine, are in business from May until mid-September, when they are dismantled for the winter.

Many of London's parks have open-air swimming pools, too, notably Hyde Park (the Serpentine), Roehampton, Finchley, Chiswick and Parliament Hill—and they fill up whenever the weather is hot. Entrance fees are only 14 cents for adults, 7 cents for children. Rome has one indoor and two outdoor swimming pools in the Piscina del Fore Italico, which are jammed over weekends.

The Cavalieri Hilton has an Olympic-size pool that's popular with young Romans; the Hotel Caesar Augustus a rooftop pool with a panoramic view of the city; and the new Americana two pools—one for adults and one for children. The famous Moscow swimming pool is large, outdoors, heated and open every day of the year. It draws Muscovites even when the temperature is below zero. There are also splendid pools in Milan, Oslo, Helsinki and many other cities on the Continent.

In warm-weather cities, such as Tehran, you can always count on an elaborate swimming pool in the local Hilton or Intercontinental hotel. If there are no beaches nearby, the locals as well as visitors flock to it to cool off over weekends.

Big-city swimming pools around the world seem to be the natural habitat of the young. If you find yourself in a large city during a midsummer heat wave, head for its nicest public swimming pool. It's bound to be the coolest, gayest place in town.

Beauty en voyage
and Hairdressers

IT'S A rare woman who can enjoy beautiful surroundings when she's conscious of looking rather unattractive herself. Bangkok won't seem particularly enchanting when the humidity has made your hair frizz like Brillo; and you'll be miserable stretched out on the beach at Acapulco when you know you are in sore need of a leg waxing. By the same token, Paris will look lovelier than it already does when you feel that you are a well-groomed, lovely little part of it.

Far from the *terra cognita* of your own dressing table, familiar brand names, and an infallible hairdresser just a telephone call away, your beauty morale may go into a swift decline; therefore it's worth a bit of extra effort and planning to keep yourself looking well while traveling. Here, then, are a few suggestions on preparation, maintenance, and some current products that can make you and the world look rosier.

BEFORE YOU GO: Two or three weeks before you leave, tell your hairdresser you're planning a trip abroad. If you need a new permanent wave, have it then. By the time you take off, your hair will be soft and well-behaved. If you are heading for hot, humid places and your problem is curly hair, this may be the time to have it straightened. About ten days before departure, review the products you use daily, weekly and monthly and do the necessary replenishing. Give some thought to the climate of your destination, which may require some adjusting of your usual beauty habits and products. You need tropical-weight cosmetics, for example, for tropical climates; the after-bath lotion that's smooth and creamy up north can feel too sticky in the heat. If your hair needs coloring, have it done a week before you leave. At your last session with the hairdresser, ask for a diagram and instructions for setting and combing. They will be useful whether you intend to manage on your own or as a guide to the foreign coiffeur, to whom you will then only have to say, for example, "Four big rollers straight back." Some experienced travelers go to their home salons three or four days before departure, then splurge on a fresh coiffure as soon as they arrive at their destinations; altitude and sleeping aloft, they say, makes even freshly done hair go limp. Others prefer to be coiffed at the last minute so they can then go a week without losing precious travel time under the hair dryer. Whichever plan you follow, include manicure, pedicure, and perhaps leg waxing. If you have foot problems, be sure to see a chiropodist.

HAIR AND SALONS: It's reassuring to know that wherever you may go, you will find a reasonably good hairdresser close at hand. In every first-class hotel or department store there is usually a highly trustworthy hairdresser on the premises, and the hotel's concierge or manager usually has a list on hand. The best hotel in town often has one of the best hairdressing salons. Also see page 28 for a list of good hairdressers in major cities around the world. In foreign parts, you do run the slight peril of being made to look a little more native than you'd like. Expect your hair to be teased à la Farah Diba in Tehran, or set like a Dutch matron's in Amsterdam. But, with slight local variations, you will find that foreign coiffeurs keep up with current fashion trends. Most of the operators in big-city salons speak English, but some knowledge of local beauty terms will help avert catastrophe. When the hairdresser in Madrid hovers over you with scissors poised for the kill, "*no demasiado corto*" will save you sooner than just "Help!" It means "not too short." Helene Curtis has put out a booklet called "How to Talk Beauty in Five Languages," which covers the major contingencies in French, Italian, German, Spanish and Japanese. It is divided into sections dealing with the shampoo, haircut, set, permanent, manicure and pedicure, and hair coloring, and is available for 25 cents in coin from Helene Curtis, Suite 1300, 75 East Wacker Drive, Chicago, Illinois 60601.

Aside from your regular trips to the hairdresser, you might enjoy a session at one of the great European salons—and a chance to experiment with new products and looks. The Romans have a fascinating flair for avant-garde makeup and are clever innovators. French coiffeurs start the trends that American salons follow; the Swiss and the Danes achieve the greatest advances with chemistry in beauty products. A visit to a big salon in one of these countries can be exciting and reward you with a bagful of new tricks. The Finnish sauna has become an indispensable part of the major cosmopolitan beauty salons and the Finns believe that a woman looks most beautiful three hours after a sauna. Who could resist finding out just how beautiful that is?

Always make an appointment ahead of time (your concierge can do this for you). Prices, except in such famous salons as Alexandre in Paris, are usually lower than those in the U.S.A. The better coiffeurs in Europe, the Middle East and the Pacific have been trained in Paris or elsewhere on the Continent. In Italy and France, even village hairdressers are good. Don't expect the lightning speed and efficiency you get at home unless you're patronizing one of the top salons that are accustomed to the pace of American tourists. If you go to the local branch of an American salon such as Elizabeth Arden or Helena Rubinstein, you can be reasonably sure that home standards are maintained and home products used whenever possible. The chic places such as the Côte d'Azur, Biarritz, Deauville, Chamonix, Vichy, et al., have branches of big salons or top-caliber hairdressers. At most resorts, hairdressers are open until 8 or 9 P.M. Salons in late-dining countries (Greece, Spain) are also still buzzing at 8 P.M. Tipping is pretty much the same the world over (see pages 359 to 366). In sum, don't expect the foreign beauty shop to do things just as they're done at home—but do expect to come away looking clean and well-coiffed.

While you will see many familiar American products abroad, it's safer to take your own shampoo (check first to be sure it will lather in hard water) and hair spray (foreign brands are often tough lacquer). If you are going on a long trip and normally have your hair tinted, ask your hairdresser for your hair-coloring formula; it can then be reassembled from the same or similar ingredients anywhere. If your trip will be too short to have coloring done but long enough for the sun to bleach your hair, ask your hairdresser to give you a small bottle of rinse to go over it when it's washed. It tones down the harsh brassy color the sun produces. If your hair-coloring method is no more than a particular brand of shampoo, rinse or brightener, take it with you.

Little hairpieces—wiglets or *postiches*—are the best answer for hair that's gone limp from humidity or salt water. They are lifesavers in places where sun, sea, and humidity play mischief with your hair: the coastal cities of South America—Santiago, Rio, Buenos Aires; the West Indies; along the Mediterranean; India, Hong Kong, Singapore, Hawaii. They should be packed in silk scarves rather than plastic, which locks in the dampness and ruins a hairpiece. Foreign salons, incidentally, are no strangers to wiglets; their customers have been wearing them for years.

Even if you're supplied with hairpieces, take precautions with your hair from day to day. Keep it covered in the sun; if it gets soaked while swimming, rinse it with fresh water and dry it in the shade. Be careful where you have tinting done on a trip; changes of climate and water can cause alterations in color, turning a sunny blond into a light brunette. In the Orient and Pacific hair is teased heavily and larded down with spray; indeed, heavy teasing and spraying are things you'll have to be hawk-eyed about in all but the first-class salons wherever you go.

SKIN: If you use a moisturizer at home, it will be doubly useful in foreign climates, where sun can parch the skin and hard water dry it out. In the tropics you may want to use a lighter cream than usual; also, cleansing lotion is better than cream in hot climates. A good hand and body lotion, a water softener, bath oil or special soap are potent ammunition against the hard water you'll find in many places. (In spite of the talk of English rose-petal skins, London will have yours feeling like leather in three days. Hard water also is the rule in balmy islands like the West Indies.) Sometimes you may have to wait for a hot bath, especially in exotic places; a refreshing substitute might be a rubdown with a cologne-dampened washcloth. Cologne has alcohol to cleanse the skin, fragrance to brighten the spirits. Pack a slew of ten-cent washcloths that can be left behind without a pang if they are too wet to pack. Cologne also works as a substitute shampoo, once you've brushed all the dust from your hair. Transfer all your usual skin preparations from their big glass jars into smaller unbreakable plastic ones. The thin paper squares called Face Savers absorb grease without disturbing the matte finish of your makeup; they're handy to tuck in your purse, and to use before re-powdering.

During flights, wear as little makeup as possible, preferably only lipstick and eye makeup so your skin can breathe while you catnap. (If you insist on powder and want to feel pretty aloft, a pinkish shade is most flattering under plane lights.) You will feel thoroughly refreshed, no matter how much sleep you have missed, if you clean your face and put on fresh makeup at your destination. While the baggage is being unloaded and everyone else has lined up for passport inspection, you head for the ladies' room armed with your cosmetics. Whenever you're traveling, even if complete repairs are impossible, take two minutes to clean off the old lipstick (tired lipstick can make your face look drab) and whisk on the new.

Sunning and skiing require special procedures. A suitcase tagged for beach resorts should carry a strong suntan preparation—those with moisturizers are especially efficient. In places where the sun is particularly strong—such as Greece and Israel—you will need a powerful, no-nonsense lotion that prevents the burning which can make a stay on the brilliant Greek islands more pain than pleasure. Allow a maximum of ten minutes' tanning time the first day, increasing your exposure gradually as your skin gets accustomed to the sun. Avoid the lethal twelve-to-two-o'clock sun shift. If your suntan preparation isn't waterproof, be sure to reapply it after swimming. Skiers also suffer from parched skin and lips, sun and windburn; a vacationer at St. Moritz should be as careful as the traveler to St. Tropez. Baby oil is a good lubricant for winter parching; it also helps a tan along.

EYES: Traveling can be irritating to the eyes. Long flights may cost you a night's sleep, and in places dust and grit may be heavy. In the tropics the glare from the sun and the salty sea can cause your eyes to smart. Take eye drops (Italian women use them automatically before applying their makeup). If you use cake mascara or eye liner that needs dampening, apply eye-drop lotion rather than water. Also carry eye pads that can be dampened just before use. Carry two pairs of sunglasses and two pairs of your regular glasses, plus their prescriptions.

LEGS AND FEET: Before you leave, be sure to clear up any potential foot problems; bumps or irritations can be aggravated by days of sightseeing and museum-hopping. If you're headed for beaches or expect to go without shoes in public (in Japanese shrines, for example), take care that your pedicure is flawless. Don't overlook the advantages of local pedicures. In London, for example, pedicurists are also chiropodists; after a half hour in their hands, you walk out on air. They are also very good in Hong Kong, Manila, and Rome. The best remedy for feet swollen from tramping is elevation and soaking in cool water. There are a number of excellent foot sprays on the market. Tuvache puts out a spray talcum powder that cools as it goes on. Since feet and legs work overtime on any trip, they deserve pampering. Imperfections are more glaring when stockingless legs and sandal-shod feet are exposed in the harsh light of the noonday sun.

NAILS: Take your usual manicuring equipment. There is, also, a new product called Glamour Girl Pink Pads which could be a welcome auxiliary to your supplies. They are neat, compact, premoistened cotton pads, individually wrapped in aluminum, each saturated with enough nail-polish remover to clean all ten nails; one less bottle to pack, and a handy way to eliminate bulky cotton. They cost

29 cents for a six weeks' supply, and sell at drug and five-and-dime stores.

Scent: Perfume, cologne and toilet water are, of course, a favorite buy in many countries. Start out with a supply sufficient to tide you over till you hit the shops. Don't wear heavy perfume in the close quarters of a plane. And if you are going to hot climates, take a light floral scent in toilet water. Splashed generously on your skin, it can be more refreshing than perfume.

Cosmetics to take: Unless you use a special brand, you can be sure that at least one reliable line of American drugs and toiletries has found its way into the local drugstore, even if it has a thatched roof. Chances are you'll find Coty in Calcutta and Revlon in Reykjavik. Max Factor products are sold all over Japan. You'll never be completely out of luck—but American brands will be more expensive abroad and you'll never be sure of finding the special shade of lipstick or the night cream you can't be happy living without. When you do need a new lipstick or night cream, search out the local "American" or English pharmacy; nearly all capitals have one or both.

Take all your usual cosmetics, but in small sizes. Even hair spray and eye drops come as small as handbag size. Transfer them as far as possible into plastic jars, for glass is heavy. These days you can get almost any of your pet cosmetics in plastic containers; if not, they are available at every drugstore.

Pack the favorite, familiar things you know work for you. To keep your cosmetic weight down, wherever possible take one beauty aid that can do the work of two: a single moisturizing cream or lotion, for example, that can serve as an all-in-one night cream, foundation, sun protection and hand lotion. Don't fill plastic containers any more than ¾ of the way with liquid, and squeeze them lightly as you put on the cap. For extra protection, seal the caps with Scotch tape.

Here is a checklist of all the beauty aids that might be needed on a trip. But naturally take only those you use at home or those that would be especially useful on the trip you are making.

Deodorant—spillproof, roll-on

Bath oil or water softener

Kleenex (You'll find it abroad, but it may cost 75 cents a box; take small packets and tuck them into corners.)

Soap (see page 335)

A magnifying mirror (If poorly placed, poorly lighted hotel mirrors irritate you.)

Cleansing cream or lotion

Toilet water, stick cologne, perfume

Talcum powder (preferably spray-on, spillproof)
Cotton pads
Toothbrush and toothpaste
Depilatory or razor, tweezers
All-purpose moisture cream
Suntan cream, spray or oil (perhaps with built-in bug repellent)
Eye drops
Hand and body lotion
Wash 'n Dri packets
Face Savers
Toilet paper (For trips abroad. Take half-used rolls, remove center cylinder, press into packable size.)
Scotch tape for sealing plastic bottles

Usual makeup, powder, lipstick, eye makeup
Expendable washcloths
Comb and brush
Hair spray or cream
Shampoo—for hard water
Shower cap
Rollers, clips, hairpins as needed
Pocket comb and/or hairbrush
Hair net or nylon nightcap to cover rollers
Chiffon scarves—as protection from wind, sun, dust, etc.
Portable hair dryer (If you are going to the beach, won't be moving around from place to place, and your luggage doesn't weigh too much already.)

DON'T TAKE: a massive leather cosmetic case. Work out your own lightweight arrangement.

Following is a list of good hairdressers in the major cities of the world. If you're sailing—especially on a tropical cruise that includes swimming—be sure to set up your hairdressing appointment at the ship's beauty salon immediately after embarkation, for the salons are small and the demand for their attentions heavy. If you don't have your hair done aboard ship, you will either have to sacrifice precious shore time or go unkempt for the duration. For more about beauty, see Light and Lipstick, page 207.

AMSTERDAM, NETHERLANDS

Beauty Salon, *Amsterdam Hilton*
Duller, *P.C. Hooftstraat 115*
Failé, *Apollolaan 83*
Heidstra, *American Hotel*
Michel, *Kalverstraat 175*
Piet Akkermans, *Vondelstraat 2–4*
Vand der Laaken, *Leidseplein 35*

ANKARA, TURKEY

Figaro, *Tuna Caddesi*
Zeki's, *Ataturk Boulevard 70*

ATHENS, GREECE

Angelos, *28th October Street 50*

Costi and Taki, *Athens Hilton*
Haute Coiffure Angelos, *Omirou Street 17*
George and Rena, *Kanari Street 4*
Haute Coiffure Georges, Branch A, *Grande Bretagne Hotel*
Haute Coiffure Georges, Branch B, *King's Palace Hotel*
Salon de Coiffure Kammer, *Venezelos 11*

AUCKLAND, NEW ZEALAND

Alex Vogel, *Dilworth Building, Customs Street East*
Bruce London Hair Salon, *10 Vulcan Lane*

French Salon, *145 Karangahape Road*

Kay's Continental Salon, *Victoria Arcade*

Salon Rubinstein, *246 Queen Street*

BANGKOK, THAILAND

Anna's, *Gaysorn Road (near Erawan Hotel)*

Dawrung, *Rajtavi Road*

Nancy, *Patumwan Road (near Erawan Hotel)*

Beauty Salon, *Erawan Hotel*

Beauty Salon, *Hotel Rama*

BARCELONA, SPAIN

Izquierdo, *Paseo de Gracia 100*

Rafael Pages, *Muntaner 361*

Vda. de Abdon, *Muntaner 193*

BEIRUT, LEBANON

Jean D'Estrées, *Phoenicia Intercontinental Hotel*

Milady Beauty Salon (Joseph Najjar), *Moukarzel Building, Lyon Street*

BELGRADE, YUGOSLAVIA

Frizerski Salon-Krasic Nedeljkovic, *Hotel Majestic*

Frizerski Salon-Krasic Nedeljkovic, *Nusiceva 8*

BERLIN, GERMANY

Beauty Salon, *Berlin Hilton*

Willy Lefevre, *71 Fasanenstrasse (Berlin 15)*

Salon Vicky, *Knesebeckstrasse 68 (Berlin 12)*

Zumsteg, *Kurfürstendamm 187 (Berlin 15)*

BRIDGETOWN, BARBADOS

Coiffure de Paris, *Hastings, Christ Church*

Lillian's Hair Studio, *Hastings House, Hastings, Christ Church*

Toni's Hair Styling, *Hastings, Christ Church*

BOGOTÁ, COLOMBIA

Rodríguez y Talero, *Carrera 10, No. 24–76*

Rueda Hernández & Cia. Ltda., *Calle 54, No. 13–09*

Beauty Salon, *Tequendama Hotel*

BRUSSELS, BELGIUM

Charles of the Ritz, *50 Boulevard de Waterloo*

Elizabeth Arden Salon, *65 Boulevard de Waterloo*

La Maison Delbove, *11 Boulevard de Waterloo*

La Maison Delbove, *37 Marché aux Herbes*

Roger, *88 Avenue Louise*

BUENOS AIRES, ARGENTINA

Harrod's, *Florida No. 877*

Helena Rubinstein, *Santa Fé No. 865*

CAIRO, U.A.R.

Costi and Taki Salon, *Nile Hilton*

Socrate, *Kasr El-Nil Street*

CANNES, FRANCE

Alexandre de Paris, *30 Boulevard de la République*

Antoine, *Rue Jean-Baptiste Dumas*

Elizabeth Arden Salon, *Résidence Médicis, Rue Frédéric-Amouretti*

Jean-Pierre Virgile, *1 Square Mérimée*

CAPRI, ITALY

Eve, *Camerelle 19*

Tonino d'Emilio, *Camerelle 6*

CARACAS, VENEZUELA

Beauty Parlor Capri, *Capri Building, Altamira*
Beauty Salon, *Hotel Tamanaco, Las Mercedes*

CHARLOTTE AMALIE, ST. THOMAS, VIRGIN ISLANDS

Casa Vanitas, *Palm Passage*
Beauty Salon, *Virgin Isle Hotel*
Tany's, *Creque's Alley*

CHRISTIANSTED, ST. CROIX, VIRGIN ISLANDS

Elysée Coiffure, *King's Wharf*

COLÓN, PANAMA

Mavis Beauty Shop, *Avenida del Frente, 8030*

COPENHAGEN, DENMARK

Du Barry Salon, *23 Bredgade*
Helmersen, *47 Vimmelskaftet*
Karl Vinholt, *46 Vesterbrogade*
Ole Tage Hansen, *3 Østergade*
Beauty Salon, *Palace Hotel, 57 Raadhuspladsen*
Viggo Grantzau, *1 Nyhavn*

DUBLIN, IRELAND

Beauty Salon, *Brown Thomas, Grafton Street*
Leon's, *King Street*
Michael of London, *Creation Arcade*
Peter Mark, *Grafton Street*
Beauty Salon, *Switzer's, Grafton Street*
Thullier's, *Duke Street*
Thullier's, *Nicholas Street*

DÜSSELDORF, GERMANY

Karl Degenhardt, *98 Königsallee*
Salon von der Gathen, *Breitestrasse 2*

Beauty Salon, *Breidenbacher Hof*

EDINBURGH, SCOTLAND

Greens, *4 Castle Street*
Beauty Salon, *Jenners Ltd., Princes Street*
J. Stewart, *122 Princes Street*
Struans Hairdressing Ltd., *1 Atholl Place*

FLORENCE, ITALY

Dante, *Lugarno Corsini 36*
Eve, *Piazza del Pesce 1*
Renato Bianchi, *Piazza Strozzi 4 R*
Valentino, *Via Tornabuoni 105 R*

GENEVA, SWITZERLAND

Ernst Zaech, Haute Coiffure, *1 Vieux Collège*
Geiser & Neuhaus, Haute Coiffure, *4 Rue Bonivard*
Jean Kaufmann, Haute Coiffure, *16 Rue de Rive*
Noel Schenk, Haute Coiffure, *4 Rue du Mont-Blanc*

GLASGOW, SCOTLAND

Elizabeth Arden Salon, Pettigrew and Stephens Ltd., *Sauchiehall Street*
Leon Ltd., *89 St. Vincent Street*
Robert Hely Hair Artists, *Clifton Place C3*
Rodolfo Pediani Ltd., *111 Union Street*

GUATEMALA CITY, GUATEMALA

French Beauty Parlor, *Palace Hotel*
La Casa Musica, *6 Avenida at 12 Calle*

THE HAGUE, NETHERLANDS

Elizabeth Arden Salon, *Plaats 24*

Henry van der Poel, *Hoge Nieuw-straat 32*

Jacques de Moor, *25-A Hoogstraat*

Robert, *92 Lange Voorhout*

HAMILTON, BERMUDA

Betty's Hairdressing Salon, *Front Street West*

Ideal Beauty Salon, *South Shore, Paget West*

Jane Hairdressers, *The Hayward Building, Bermudiana Road*

Marie's Bermudiana Salon, *Hotel Bermudiana*

The Princess Salon, *Princess Hotel*

HELSINKI, FINLAND

Beauty Salon, *Aleksanterinkatu 17*

Monsieur Heikki, *P. Roobertinkatu 10 C*

Monsieur Robert, Salon New York, *Kluuvikatu 8*

HONG KONG

Antonio Beauty Parlor, *39A Carnarvon Road, (Kowloon)*

Beten's Salon, *Gloucester Hotel Building*

Beten's Salon, *Mandarin Hotel*

Beten's Salon, *Peninsula Hotel (Kowloon)*

Beauty Salon, *Hongkong Hilton*

Michel's, *Hotel Peninsula Court*

Simone's Beauty Parlor, *207 Central Building, Pedder Street*

HONOLULU, HAWAII

Elizabeth Arden Salon, *115 Kaiulani Avenue*

Beauty Salon, *Royal Hawaiian Hotel Arcade*

Beauty Salon, *Kahala Hilton*

ISTANBUL, TURKEY

Beauty Salon, *Divan Hotel*

Beauty Salon, *Istanbul Hilton*

KINGSTON, JAMAICA

Elizabeth of Sweden, *42 Constant Spring Road*

Elizabeth of Sweden, *Sheraton Kingston Hotel*

Je Reviens, *13A Ripon Road*

Myrtle Bank Beauty Salon, *Harbour Street*

Valerie of New York, *119 Old Hope Road*

KYOTO, JAPAN

Beauty Salon, *Miyako Hotel*

LIMA, PERU

Elizabeth Arden Salon, *Ocona 154*

Elizabeth Arden Salon, *San Isidro*

LISBON, PORTUGAL

Beauty Salon, *Hotel Ritz*

Bruna & Renzo, *Largo de São Carlos 8*

Danova e Margarida, *Praça Luis de Camões, Rua das Flores 113*

Malheiros, *Arcadas do Parque (Estoril)*

LONDON, ENGLAND

Alan Spiers, *27 Berkeley Square (London W.1)*

Aldo-Bruno, *22 Motcomb Street (London S.W.1)*

André Bernard, *10A Old Bond Street (London W.1)*

André Bernard, *16 Berkeley Street (London W.1)*

Charles of the Ritz, *Brook House, Park Lane (London W.1)*

Elizabeth Arden Salon, *25 Old Bond Street (London W.1)*

French, *6 Cork Street (London W.1)*

Helena Rubinstein, *3 Grafton Street (London W.1)*

Martin Douglas, *72 Southhampton Row (London W.C.1)*

Raymond, *18 Grafton Street (London W.1)*

Raymond, *39 Brompton Road (London S.W.3)*

Réné of Mayfair, *66 South Audley Street (London W.1)*

Riché of Hay Hill, *Berkeley Square (London W.1)*

Steiner, *66 Grosvenor Street (London W.1)*

Vidal Sassoon, *Grosvenor House Hotel (London W.1)*

Vidal Sassoon, *171 New Bond Street (London W.1)*

MADRID, SPAIN

Carita, *Serrano 26*

Beauty Salon, *Castellana Hilton, Paseo de la Castellana 55*

Elizabeth Arden Salon, *Plaza de la Independencia 4*

Edouard, *Avenida du José Antonio 58*

Molina, *Infantas 40*

Peluquería Sras. Prieto, *Marqués do Urquijo 20*

MANILA, PHILIPPINES

Army and Navy Beauty Shop, *Luneta*

Ben Farreles, *Quezon Boulevard Extension, Quezon City*

Gloria's Beauty Salon, *Manila Hotel, Katigbak Drive*

Pierre French Beauty Shop, *536 United Nations Avenue*

MARRAKESH, MOROCCO

Beauty Salon, *Hotel Mamounia*

Salon Christine, *19 Avenue Mohammet V*

MELBOURNE, AUSTRALIA

Antoine de Paris, *The Myer Emporium, Bourke Street*

Elizabeth Arden Salon, *Buckley & Nunn Ltd., 310 Bourke Street*

Lillian and Antonio, *8th floor, Howey Court, 234 Collins Street*

William Grau House of Coiffure, *Southern Cross Hotel, Exhibition Street*

MEXICO CITY, MEXICO

Coiffure Romans, *Génova 34*

Elena, *Londres 205*

Beauty Salon, *Maria Isabel Hotel, Tiber y Reforma*

Pierre Jacy, *Continental Hilton Hotel, Paseo de la Reforma 166*

MILAN, ITALY

Attilio Trevisan, *Via Cartesio 2*

Elizabeth Arden Salon, *Via Montenapoleone 2*

Ghisletti, *Via Montenapoleone 3*

Nino Laurora, *Via Montenapoleone 27*

Livio Fanelli, *Via Manzoni 23*

MONTEGO BAY, JAMAICA

Beauty Salon, *Casa Blanca Hotel*

Beauty Salon, *Montego Beach Hotel*

Beauty Salon, *Sunset Lodge Hotel*

MONTREAL, CANADA

Antoine Salon, Henry Morgan & Co. Ltd.

Elizabeth Arden Salon, Robert Simpson Montreal Ltd.

Gibson Beauty Salon, *The Queen Elizabeth Hotel*

Salon Alaine, *8397 St. Denis Street*

Bernard, *1185 Ste. Catherine Street*

Salon Laurentian Hair Stylists, *Laurentian Hotel*

Maxine et Michel, *Place Ville Marie*

MUNICH, GERMANY

Edward Bachmaier, *Schützenstrasse 9/11, (part of Excelsior Hotel)*
W. Herrmann, *43/1 Maximilianstrasse*

NASSAU, BAHAMAS

Barbara Beauty Salon, *Boyle Building Arcade, Bank Lane*
Barbara Beauty Salon, *British Colonial Hotel*
Barbara Beauty Salon, *Montagu Beach Hotel*
Barbara Beauty Salon, *Nassau Beach Hotel*
Barbara Beauty Salon, *Nassau Harbour Club*
Beauty Salon, *Emerald Beach Hotel*
Hibiscus Beauty Salon, *Bay Street*
Rosemary's Salon of Beauty, *Bay Street*

NEW DELHI, INDIA

Beauty Salon, *Oberoi Intercontinental Hotel*
Beauty Salon, *Ashoka Hotel*
Beauty Salon, *Imperial Hotel*
Cosmetic Stores, *Janpath*
Roy & James, *N. Block, Connaught Circus*

NICE, FRANCE

Albert de Paris, *1 Avenue Gustave-V*
Antoine de Paris, *11 Rue Croix-de-Marbre*
Coiffure Lafayette, *55 Rue Gioffredo*
Michel de Paris, *20 Rue de la Liberté*
Salon Mariano, *9 Rue Masséna*

Salon Pascal, *20 Rue de la Buffa*

OCHO RIOS, JAMAICA

John's Playmate Parlour, *Jamaica Playboy Club-Hotel*

ORANJESTAD, ARUBA, N.A.

Beauty Salon, *Arcade, Aruba Caribbean Hotel-Casino, Palm Beach*
Madame Alice, *Nassaustraat 83A*

OSLO, NORWAY

Broadway Frisersalong, *Pilestredet 8*
Leif G. Johansen, *Karl Johansgate 20*
Lilla Frisersalong, *Universitetsgaten 7*
Liv. E. Nielsen, *N. Slottsgate 8*
Marlen Damefrisor, *Kronprinsesse Marthas Pl. 1*
Trygve Salberg, *Karl Johansgate 27*

PALMA DE MAJORCA

Carita, *Avenida Jaime III, 86*

PANAMA CANAL ZONE, PANAMA

Brenda's Tivoli Beauty Shop, *Hotel Tivoli*

PANAMA CITY, PANAMA

Salon de Belleza Charl's, *Calle 55, 7–60*
Salon de Belleza Tony, *Avenida I. y. Calle 31*
Beauty Salon, *El Panama Hilton, Avenida 7, Espana III*

PARIS, FRANCE

Alexandre, *120 Rue du Faubourg St.-Honoré (Paris 8e)*
Antoine, *5 Rue Cambon (Paris 1er)*
Carita, *11 Rue du Faubourg St.-Honoré (Paris 1er)*

Charles of the Ritz, *51 Avenue Montaigne (Paris 8ᵉ)*

Desfossé, *19 Avenue Matignon (Paris 8ᵉ)*

Elizabeth Arden Salon, *7 Place Vendôme (Paris 1ᵉʳ)*

Fernand Aubry, *5 Rue du Cirque (Paris 8ᵉ)*

Guillaume, *5 Avenue Matignon (Paris 5ᵉ)*

Henri Prévost, *400 Rue Saint-Honoré (Paris 1ᵉʳ)*

Michel Kazan, *3 Place du Théâtre-Français (Paris 1ᵉʳ)*

Pierre Jacy, *45 Avenue Franklin-Roosevelt (Paris 8ᵉ)*

PORT OF SPAIN, TRINIDAD

Kim's Beauty Salon, *58 Pembroke Street*

QUEBEC, CANADA

Salon du Chateau, *Chateau Frontenac Hotel*

Beauty Salon, *Holt Renfrew Ltd., 35 Buade Street*

RIO DE JANEIRO, BRAZIL

Beauty Salon, *Copacabana Palace Hotel*

Emilio Cabeleireiro, *Avenida Copacabana 1017*

ROME, ITALY

Attilio, *Hotel Excelsior*

Attilio, *Piazza di Spagna 68*

Elizabeth Arden Salon, *Piazza di Spagna 19*

Eve, *Piazza di Spagna 51*

Femme Sistina, *Via Sistina 74–75*

Filippo, *Via Condotti 91*

Giulio, *Via Fontanella di Borghese 25*

Leonardo, *Via Prisciano 66*

Liliana Santini, *Via Emilia 47*

Pino, *Hotel de la Ville, Via Sistina*

Nino e Carlo, *Via Bonconpagni 14 D*

Riccardo, *Via Veneto 92*

ST. MORITZ, SWITZERLAND

Parfumerie Albert Ryf, *Hotel Caspar-Badrutt*

SAN JUAN, PUERTO RICO

Beauty Salon, *Caribe Hilton*

Beauty Salon, *La Concha Hotel*

Elizabeth of Sweden, *Puerto Rico Sheraton Hotel*

Lolita Reilova Beauty Salon, *Ashford Medical Center (Condado)*

Naida Varela, *1468 Wilson (Santurce)*

Oshier's Salon of Beauty, *Condado Beach Hotel*

SANTIAGO, CHILE

Instituto Franca, *Hotel Carrera*

SINGAPORE, SINGAPORE

Beauty Salon, *Cathay Hotel*

Duchesse Beauty Salon, *Raffles Hotel Building*

Little's Beauty Salon, *Raffles Place*

Maison Moderne, *126 Orchard Road*

STOCKHOLM, SWEDEN

Beauty Salon, NK, *Hamngatan 18–20*

Beauty Salon, *Hotel Foresta*

Björn Axén Coiffeur de Dames, *51 Sibyllegatan*

Ingvar Carell AB, *2 Styrmansgatan*

Salon Åke, *5 Östermalmstorg*

Salon Belleza, *153 Valhallavägen*

Salon Robert, *15 Stureplan*

SYDNEY, AUSTRALIA

Elizabeth Arden Salon, *109 Elizabeth Street*

Helena Rubinstein, *82 Castlereagh Street*

Peter Hanlon, *207 Darlinghurst Road, King's Cross*

Philippe and Maurice of Paris, *155 King Street*

TAIPEI, TAIWAN

Beauty Salon, *Friends of China Club*

Beauty Salon, *Grand Hotel*

TEHRAN, IRAN

Costi and Taki, *Royal Tehran Hilton Hotel*

TEL AVIV, ISRAEL

Annetta, *Mapoo Street 18*

Beauty Salon, *Hotel Dan*

Ninabella, *Ben-Yehuda Street 7A*

TOKYO, JAPAN

Arden Yamanaka Beauty Salon, *Nikkatsu Arcade*

Maya Kataoka, *6–2 Ginza, Chuo-Ku*

Oba Beauty Salon, *Imperial Hotel Arcade*

Aiko Yamano, *3–4 Ginza, Chuo-Ku*

TORONTO, CANADA

Beauty Salon, Henry Morgan and Company Ltd., *56 Bloor Street West*

Elizabeth Arden Salon, Robert Simpson Co., Ltd.

Paula Hair Stylist, *1263 St. Clair Street West*

Peter Edelmayer Hair Design Salon, *836 Yonge Street*

TUNIS, TUNISIA

Beauty Salon, *Tunis Hilton Hotel*

Mimi, *Rue St. Vincent de Paul*

VANCOUVER, CANADA

House of Beauty, *619 Seymour Street*

Hudson Bay Salon, *Georgia and Granville Streets*

Maison Antoine, Eaton's of Canada, *515 West Hastings Street*

Raymond Salons, *Woodward Stores, Abbott and Hastings Streets*

VENICE, ITALY

Anna and Silvestro, *Via XXII Marzo 2090 pt. S. Moise*

Beauty Salon, *Hotel Danieli*

Carol, *opposite Hotel Gritti Palace*

Cervieri, *Hotel Excelsior, Lido*

Elizabeth Arden Salon, *Hotel Gritti Palace, St. Mark's Square*

VIENNA, AUSTRIA

Eckel, *2 Maysedergasse*

Kampits, *11 Weyburggasse*

VIÑA DEL MAR, CHILE

Elizabeth, *Galería Couve, Hotel O'Higgins*

WILLEMSTAD, CURAÇAO, N.A.

C. de Groot, *Helfrichplein*

WINNIPEG, CANADA

Beauty Salon, T. Eaton Co. Ltd., *Portage and Donald Streets*

Cecilia's Hair Design and Fashion Ltd., *302 Kennedy Street*

Hudson's Bay Store, *Memorial Boulevard and Portage Street*

La Femme Beauty Salon, *95 Osborne Street at River*

YOKOHAMA, JAPAN

Arden Yamanaka Beauty Salon, *No. 1, 1-Chome, Minami, Saiwai-cho, Nishi-ku*

Maxine Beauty Salon, *170,*
4-Chome, Motomachi, Naka-ku

ZURICH, SWITZERLAND

Parfumerie Albert Ryf, Haute Coif-
fure, *Pelikanstrasse 19*
Bachann, *12 Poststrasse*
De Neuville & Seilaz SA, Haute
Coiffure, *Paradeplatz 2*

Elizabeth Arden Salon, *Bahnhof-
strasse 1*
Elsasser, *Poststrasse 8*
Gebr. Bachmann, Haute Coiffure,
Poststrasse 12
Georges Meyer, Haute Coiffure,
Strehlgasse 8
W. Kaiser, Haute Coiffure, *Werd-
muehleplatz 3*
Georges Lenhard, *Bahnhofstrasse 39*

(*One brief note about the foregoing list of hairdressers: As every woman
knows, good hairdressers come and go almost as swiftly as the seasons. On
your arrival in these cities, you may find that others have set up shop, or
these closed down. At this writing, these can be vouched for as good and
reliable.*)

Bidets

ALONG WITH hot water pipes for drying towels and
bedside buttons for summoning waiter, maid and valet, there is one
other fixture you seldom find at home for which you should be prepared. It's called a bidet (pronounced bee-day), and it's a ceramic
basin with pipes and drains, found in bathrooms, which has per-
plexed American tourists since the middle of the eighteenth century,
when it came into use—though in those days it was often richly decorated and sometimes even concealed cleverly in desks, easy chairs,
or dressers. While it *can* be used for soaking tired feet, its classic purpose is personal hygiene, both masculine and feminine. Once you
have used it properly, you'll wonder why more bidets are not sold in
the United States. (We manufacture almost as many as France does,
but sell most of them to South America.) However, the fashion for
them is growing here as more Americans travel abroad—and the
bidet, along with fine French furniture and piped music, is rapidly
becoming a status symbol.

The bidet was invented in France and has been used for centuries
throughout Europe, South America and wherever the pattern of liv-

ing is European. Originally created for *chevaliers* who spent long hours on horseback and wanted a quick way to refresh their saddle-worn haunches, the bidet is still shaped like a saddle. (In fact, the word "bidet" originally referred to a small saddle horse.)

To use one, just turn on the hot and cold water, adjusting the temperature as you like, let the water run until it reaches just below the rim, straddle the fixture as you would a saddle, facing the faucets, wash as in any sitz bath, and rinse. As you will see, it's a splendid invention. Although Americans take more baths and use more soap than any other nation past or present, we haven't caught on to *all* the tricks for keeping clean.

Big-City Dressing

No MATTER how free and independent a spirit you may be, there is one rule you must follow relentlessly to be well dressed in cities everywhere around the world: Blend into the populace. Your clothes should be so natural to the surroundings that even the natives cannot spot you as a foreigner.

This is far easier to manage than most women realize. To help simplify the problem of what to wear and where to wear it, follow this formula: Climate + (a city's) Character + Clothes that please you = what-to-wear, anywhere. Here's how it works:

Take the first "C"—Climate. This must, of course, be the first consideration when you pack—and the major clue to climate is temperature. To compare the climate of your destinations with that you know at home, study the facts on pages 425 through 444.

While admittedly temperature is not synonymous with weather—altitude, ocean currents and humidity can cause places of identical latitudes to have entirely different weather—it *is* a reliable starting point. Notice in the Weather chapter, for example, that during July and August Europe's leading cities are far cooler and rainier than those in the U.S.A.

The second "C" is Character (not yours, but the cities'). This is a composite of elements that range from history to the social position of women. A city's character produces its mood—and its mood governs the colors that look right on its streets. For example, temperate cities that have (or once had) courts such as London, Tokyo, Copenhagen, Paris, Stockholm, Brussels and Amsterdam have an atmosphere of formality and sophistication, which calls for tailored city clothes in neutral or dark colors. In young, warm-weather nations such as Israel and India, life is less formal and restrictive; there's a freer attitude about fashion, and you will want to wear brighter colors. While you might confidently arrive in New Delhi in a bright pink suit, you would feel far more comfortable stepping into London's Heathrow Airport dressed in beige or gray. Cities with long Spanish traditions such as Mexico City tend toward conservatism, strong rules of decorum and plenty of black; South American cities are not resorts, as so many women believe, but highly sophisticated metropolises that demand all the fashion you can muster.

The final "C" is Clothes, and as always, the best bit of advice is the most realistic: There is no ironclad formula for being perfectly dressed at all times, in all places. There is no way of guaranteeing that you will pack the right clothes for every occasion—or that you will wear everything you pack. No one does. All you can hope to achieve is a high batting average. The following basic rules are designed to give you just that.

1. If you live in or near a city, you undoubtedly own, right now, nearly all the clothes you will need for a big-city itinerary. So start preparations for your trip in your own closet. This rule is not meant to deprive you of the delights of shopping, but simply to shift its scene. Unless you are a size 4 or 44 or have a chronic problem of finding clothes that fit, hold off your spending for the enchanting boutiques you will find abroad (see Boutiques, page 51). Besides being much more fun, buying fill-ins on the spot assures you of the right fashion look for the local scene.

2. Don't change your fashion habits for a trip. It will make you uncomfortable and self-conscious. If, for example, you don't like wearing a raincoat in Philadelphia, don't buy one for Copenhagen. Rely instead on your customary umbrella. If you don't bother with drip-dries at home, a pleasure trip is no time to get involved with them. If separates leave you feeling slightly confused, don't try making them do in Helsinki.

3. Take clothes whose flattery never fails you, and take *only* your favorites. Never pack anything that makes you feel drab, just because it's "safe." Then forget about what you are wearing—and concentrate on what you came to see.

4. Limit the colors of your accessories so that heavy objects like handbags and shoes can be kept to a minimum.

5. As a rule, sunny places call for a sunny clothes palette. Even in such places as Hong Kong, which is hot most of the year but cool enough during its brief winter to warrant wool, keep your woolens light and bright in color as well as light in weight.

With these basic principles firmly in mind, let's move on to the specifics:

1. The daytime city uniform for most of the year in Europe, South America, Australia, New Zealand, South Africa—in short, every-where—is a discreet lightweight woolen suit (in a flat worsted or a tightly woven tweed). It should have an easy skirt and be worn with a sweater or overblouse (silk sweaters are marvelous), and low-heeled walking shoes.

In the fall, winter and spring, supplement the suit with several woolen dresses. One might be simple and dark to do for sightseeing during the day, and a *bistro* at night. Another could be a knitted dress, perhaps with its own jacket. If you head for northern Europe in the summer, you will have to pack for a range of climate. Countries like Ireland, Britain and France are far cooler and damper than the U.S.A., and you are apt to find yourself yearning for wool in mid-August. When the sun shines, however, you will need silks and linens. Make it a rule never to leave for Europe without woolens in your suitcase even if you pack in a blazing heat and can't imagine wanting them. Lightweight worsted wool is one of a traveler's chief blessings: It's porous, crisp, holds its shape, and doesn't crease.

Southern Europe gets hot during the summer and you will need an ample supply of sleeveless dresses in pale, sunny colors plus a silk or cotton suit. In sizzling climates, avoid heavy linen; it tends to be too hot. Also, dry cleaning is unreliable. Instead pack some cotton and cotton-and-Dacron dresses that can be washed with soap and water.

2. Take one or two outfits for sightseeing that "walk well"—a dress or a suit with a skirt that is pleated, gored, flaring or split like a culotte. In general, concentrate on clothes that move well, are uncluttered, and give you a sense of freedom. Never take anything you haven't worn at least once before. When everything else is new and strange, it's comforting to wear easy, undemanding, familiar clothes.

3. Pack several dresses to wear after 5 o'clock. One should be a theater suit, i.e., a brocade dress and jacket; two should be "little black" dresses. The latter in rayon or silk crepe are right nearly everywhere in the world, but "nearly" is the key word here. In London in early summer (where women bloom in flowered silks), in big

cities on the palmy coastlines of the Rivieras, in brilliantly sunny cities like Bangkok, black looks too "heavy." On the other hand, it is utterly appropriate for twelve months of the year in such black-dress capitals as Rome, Madrid, Paris, Lisbon and the South American cities. Take one or two black dresses that are not cut low. In Europe, houses and theaters are heated to just one degree above freezing by American standards and if you are in décolletage, your teeth will be chattering so that you can't speak to your dinner partner.

4. Always take one soft crepe dress in a medium shade. It's utterly dependable for tea or a midweek dinner at someone's house or in the gentle haze of a London summer where soft colors are as much at home as flowers.

5. Along with worsted wool, the fabrics that seem at home everywhere and in nearly all climates are silk chiffon and silk knits. They can be packed in a small space and need little, if any, pressing.

6. Most American women overdo the use of fur stoles and coats abroad. If you plan on leading a gay, brilliant social life, pack your furs. Otherwise, remember that few countries in the world can afford the lavish furs we wear, and as it's rather tactless to dress more opulently than your hosts, you may feel unpleasantly conspicuous (see Furs, page 139).

7. In areas like northern Europe where you are bound to run into rain, take a collapsible umbrella, a collection of scarves, and a raincoat if you like one. Today many raincoats are cut with the flair of evening coats and often double for them.

8. Take at least one outfit that works in layers to meet the changes in the day's temperatures.

9. Never leave home without a coat: lightweight wool or linen for warm climates, a heavier wool for cooler places.

10. Even if you are heading for the tropics in August, take a cardigan sweater or two as armor against air conditioning. You will also need one for the cool morning hours in warm countries like Greece.

11. Don't bother with formal clothes unless you *know* you will use them—even then, keep them slim and simple (a crepe sheath, for instance, would be fine and take up little packing space). First nights at the opera always call for formal dress; likewise Friday night at Maxim's in Paris. In London, however, if your hostess says dinner will be "black tie," a pretty cocktail dress or the bare-ish dress of your theater suit will rise to the occasion.

12. If you are going around the world, concentrate on such transseasonal fabrics as silk. Instead of weighing yourself down with things you won't be wearing for long stretches of your trip, airfreight

ahead, to the places you'll need them, such things as beachwear and heavy woolens.

13. If you head for Europe in midwinter, pack warm lingerie such as a sheer wool robe, a flannel nightgown, or even a silk undershirt. Hotel rooms are often so underheated by our standards that you'll cherish these comforts.

14. Take a supply of stockings in two shades; one for day, the other for evening; two pairs of gloves; two scarves; two or three brightly colored small handbags (the most lightweight way of brightening your wardrobe); and a minimum amount of jewelry.

Two final notes: No matter what the character of a city, there are three things you must never wear: strapless sundresses, slacks or shorts, and glitter by day. They are always in inexcusably bad taste.

Since there is no way of forecasting the vagaries of weather or anticipating unexpected occasions, don't fret about whether you've brought everything you could conceivably need. Pack by the basic rules and if you find you'd like something special on the spot, such as a print dress for a London cocktail party in June, a silk suit for dinner in New Delhi, or a "little black" dress for dancing in Rome, buy it wherever you happen to be. It's the best excuse there is for treating yourself to the fun of shopping abroad.

Bikinis

THIS FASHION whirlwind, which has swept many beaches of the world bare, originated in Europe, was introduced to the United States about 1950, and is still battering at some rocks of conservatism—though a recently discovered mosaic shows that ancient Roman girls wore them too. If you're a devotee of bikinis, you will have to become sensitive to where they are and aren't acceptable.

As a guide to the world's beach manners (often fashionable areas not more than 50 miles apart have completely opposite rules), here are some rules of thumb.

If you are devoted to your bikini and headed for the Orient, draw a sigh and leave it home. Although a tiny number of "emancipated" local women wear them, most Orientals consider bikinis highly improper. If, on the other hand, you are planning to tour Hawaii, Europe, South America or the Caribbean, you can take it along, but be sure to pack a second, more conservative bathing suit.

Because one beach's rules may be completely different from its neighbor's, always check with the concierge of your hotel about the local customs before venturing out.

Don't make the mistake of thinking that a bikini is the only bathing suit you may blush to wear. Too much can be just as embarrassing as too little. If you step onto a beach like St. Tropez in the south of France wearing a one-piece bathing suit, you'll feel about as out of place as you would in Grandmother's bloomers. A recent survey of the beach at Cannes discovered not a single covered sunbather of either sex or any age. The Riviera calls, at the very most, for a bare-ish two-piece suit.

Regardless of how sheltered and socially protected the women of certain countries are, bikinis will be "in" if its beach resorts have attracted international café society. The women of the country will frown on them, but as a visiting foreigner you can get away with one. Some good examples are Spain and Puerto Rico. Portugal, which still wraps its black-dressed women in rigid tradition, is a unique case. While, for instance, you could wear a bikini at the famous beach at Estoril, where the Almanach de Gotha suns itself, you cannot wear one on other Portuguese beaches. Take a conservative one-piece bathing suit, for even two-piece ones are rarely seen. In Mexico, bikinis are appropriate only on the beaches of the American-patronized resorts such as Acapulco, Puerto Vallarta and Cozumel. Avoid them altogether in Argentina.

In Scandinavia and in the sunny countries that ring the Mediterranean—France, Italy, Greece, Israel—bikinis look as natural on all beaches as fur hats in Russia. (The French take credit for the bikini and describe it as *la mode qui fait boom*—its style having first appeared around the time of the atomic explosion at Bikini.) In Turkey they are worn in the cosmopolitan resorts, but you might feel better in a one-piece suit.

Bikinis are also accepted without fuss in Britain, although, curiously enough, in countries with strong British ties and tradition, such as Jamaica and Canada, conservatism dies harder. In Canada one would feel terribly out of place in a bikini, and in Jamaica one would tend to step gingerly, examining the local scene closely first before blazing forth semi-naked. Bermuda and the Bahamas, on the other hand, have been so Americanized by waves of tourists that their pattern follows that of most U.S.A. beaches—and bikinis are acceptable. In the Virgin Islands both visitors and islanders wear them.

As for Australia, that vigorous land, bikinis are more popular and briefer there than in the U.S.A. It was, after all, an Australian swimmer, Annette Kellerman, who made it acceptable for women to compete in swimming meets, and who introduced the shocking notion of a one-piece bathing suit in 1909. Australia was also among the first countries to allow desegregation of the sexes on public beaches.

In Ireland, where nobody will raise an eyebrow if you wriggle into your bathing suit on the beach hidden under a big towel, bikinis are never, nowhere, acceptable.

Boarding Planes
and Disembarking

THESE DAYS, airlines and governments are so busy trying to make our international comings and goings smoother that it's as easy to catch the 10 A.M. flight to Istanbul as the 5:01 commuter train to Islip.

Here are a few simple rules followed by all experienced air travelers, for boarding a flight with aplomb:

Check last-minute details before leaving home. Is your handbag carrying airline tickets, confirmation of your hotel reservations, passport, smallpox vaccination certificate, travelers checks and cash, international driver's license, address book and letters of introduction? If all are firmly in place, you are ready to lock the door behind you.

Check in at the airlines terminal building—and take the airline bus from there to the airport. Do this even if you have money to burn, for the anguished moments it may save you. If you insist on private transportation and get stuck in traffic, you may end up fuming on the freeway while your flight leaves. When you come by airline bus, the responsibility for making the flight is off your shoulders, since the airlines must wait for these connections. If you leave from mid-Manhattan for Kennedy Airport, you can take New York Airways' helicopter service from the top of the Pan Am building. It covers the distance in 7 minutes and costs $7 one way.

When you arrive at the terminal, have your ticket (plus passport and vaccination certificate if you're bound for a foreign country) at the very top of your handbag. A porter will take charge of your luggage and lead you to the check-in counter. The airline personnel will examine your ticket and passport, weigh in your luggage, staple your receipts to your ticket envelope, tag your hand luggage, assign your seat, and give you a boarding pass. (You can stick this like a bookmark into the paperback you're carrying, since you will turn it in a few minutes later.) For seating, see page 318. Once this bit of business is taken care of at the terminal, you can take a few minutes to buy flight insurance if you want to. You then enter the bus and are driven to the airport, where you board the plane with no more chores.

You can of course go directly to the airport, where you will go through the same procedure. If you do, arrive with plenty of time to spare—between 45 and 60 minutes before an overseas flight. The movie heroine who arrives breathlessly, surrounded by mounds of luggage, five minutes before takeoff would be instantly recognized offscreen as a novice. The knowing traveler comes to the airport calmly, early and neatly.

As soon as your flight is called, queue up at the gate. Some airlines board their passengers in groups or let them trickle onto the aircraft so that a vague semblance of order is maintained. Others less efficiently choose to board them all at once, causing instant bedlam as more than 100 people struggle out of their coats, find space for hand luggage and squeeze past other passengers in the tiny aisle. Whichever system your airline uses, do your best to settle in early.

For those who live outside of New York City and fly into Kennedy Airport to connect with a Pan American flight, the airline provides a quick transfer to its terminal via station wagon. Some domestic flights are met automatically; others will be if PAA is notified in advance. A similar service is provided at the Chicago and Los Angeles airports.

You're allowed to carry coats, umbrella, briefcase, camera, binoculars, books, magazines and a small cosmetic case. (This last item is supposed to be weighed in with the rest of your luggage, so watch those heavy jars and bottles; briefcases and overnight bags may also be weighed.) If you want to look like a woman who winters in Jamaica and summers in Cap d'Antibes, keep what you carry aboard to a spartan minimum. Knowing women travelers carry a handbag, or airplane case, a coat and a paperback book. That's all.

If you are traveling with friend, husband or children, your luggage can be weighed in together. (Children are given the same baggage allowance as adults.) Overweight will cost you dear and it's practically never worth it. If you must have extra luggage, you will pay about $2 a pound on a flight from New York to London. To cushion the blow, the airlines have devised other ways of shipping extra luggage. You can send it air freight as unaccompanied baggage if you arrive at the airport ahead of time, let's say 2 hours before flight. By this method, the overweight charges are far lower. Or you can send your luggage by sea while you fly; in this case, allow at least a month for your belongings to arrive at the rendezvous point. American Express can also be helpful on this score. If your excess baggage weighs 25 pounds or more, they will make arrangements to forward it as air freight. Call the nearest American Express office or the one at Kennedy International Airport in New York at least 72 hours before you leave. They will handle all the paper work, pick up your pieces, fill out customs declarations and arrange to have the luggage shipped on the first available flight to the airport of your destination.

If you have a foreign-made camera, and are headed out of the country, you *must* register it with the United States Customs Bureau at the airport—unless you have a bill of sale or insurance certificate —or you'll be asked to pay a high import duty when you bring it in again.

Airsickness is an anachronism nowadays. Jets fly so high they seldom encounter rough weather. Still, if your stomach is empty, you're likely to be sensitive to even the slightest bump. It's a good rule never to board a moving vehicle without eating something beforehand.

This doesn't mean bolting down rich food and drink—lots of champagne can be heavenly while you're on the ground but hellish once you're up in the air. While airlines usually serve meals, you can't always depend on their adequacy. Certainly, you are amply fed en route to Europe, South America, or Hawaii. Domestic or Caribbean flights are something else again. (I've been caught on a flight which left New York City for San Francisco at 8 P.M. I boarded the flight with a splendid appetite, only to discover that the airline felt the hour was "too late" for dinner. I had to mull over this philosophy for 5½ hours on an empty stomach.) Worse, if you run into bumpy weather, you may not get dinner for hours—and there's nothing you can do about it. Check with the airline, which will tell you if and when a meal is to be served and nibble beforehand accordingly.

When you arrive in a foreign airport, disembarking, going through immigration and customs, and collecting your luggage are simple to manage. Airline personnel will direct you to the arrival hall. You will have to queue up for health and passport inspection but you are usually waved through without delay. These days customs means a cursory examination of your bags; they are seldom opened. Porters stand by to help you with your luggage and into a taxi. If your tour includes being met by a guide, one of the airline staff who meets your plane will see that you are brought together. The guide usually wears an armband with the name of his travel agency.

Many airports are miles out of town. If there are three or more in your party, it's generally better to take a taxi to your hotel; you may even want to spend the substantial amount on your own, for sheer convenience. Or the airline bus will take you to the city's air terminal building, where you will have to gather your luggage again, find a porter, tip him, and take a taxi to your hotel.

However you go, you'll have to accept the fact of traffic tie-ups and bumper-to-bumper crawling. The drive from Leonardo da Vinci Airport to Rome, for example, ordinarily takes 45 minutes, but you can use up twice that time in summer when the roads are especially crowded.

Some forward-looking cities have solved the problem of airport-to-midtown drives. Tokyo International Airport has a monorail whose overhead trains speed from the airport to Tokyo in 15 minutes. Since it skirts the edge of Tokyo Bay, the monorail provides a sightseeing introduction as well. Brussels operates a train from the airport to its downtown air terminal.

When you are ready to leave a foreign country, you generally go through the same procedure as you did on leaving the U.S.A., with the single additional step of having to pay a head tax, or departure tax. Nearly all governments levy them, and they vary from place to place and time to time. As of this writing, they can range from 90 cents in Spain to $6.72 in Peru. Paris's Orly charges from $5 down, depending on your destination. The important point about a departure tax is to remember that when you leave a country, you should have enough small local currency on hand to pay for it.

Bon Voyage Gifts

TRAVELERS, like chess champions and bird watchers, move in the same circles, and you are likely to be giving *bon voyage* gifts as often as receiving them.

Decades ago, when people traveled with steamer trunks, a proper *bon voyage* gift was a lavish floral arrangement or an enormous basket of fruit. Today, when the air travelers with two canvas suitcases outnumber those who go by sea with no luggage limit (though even the smart sea voyager travels as light as possible), *bon voyage* gifts have been considerably pared down.

A successful *bon voyage* gift should pass muster on these counts: Is it light (is it, in fact, the *lightest* of its genre)? Is it easy to pack? Is it disposable en route? Does it give pleasure? Or is it truly practical? Is it small? Unless a gift qualifies on all or at least some of these counts, don't give it. Avoid, for example, bulky gifts of fruit or candy —they're a colossal nuisance. *Bon voyage* gifts of food were devised originally for the servants of wealthy travelers to supplement the thin rations aboard ship. Today, no one is in danger of malnutrition aboard ship or plane.

To these rules, add two more: A *bon voyage* gift should be given before packing time so it can be neatly tucked away. Please don't shove a great bundle into the hands of an air traveler just as she is about to step aboard her flight. She will smile her thanks wanly and wonder where in heaven's name she is going to put it. Also, consider the destination of the traveler, and don't send coals to Newcastle (gloves to someone destined for Paris or Rome, or a transistor radio to someone embarking on a Caribbean cruise with stops at duty-free ports).

With these considerations in mind, here is a list of likely *bon voyage* gifts:

A silver ballpoint pen. Travelers use pens constantly and fountain pens are apt to leak in the air due to changes in pressure. Consider, too, a ballpoint pen with its own light, described on page 124.

A set of foreign language dictionaries. The Macmillan Company has put out a tiny set that fits into the palm of your hand. They hardly make a bulge in pocket or purse; each book is $1.

A piece of luggage known as an "airline cheater," which can be used instead of a handbag and is normally not weighed in with the rest of one's luggage. (See Luggage, page 208.) It is roomy enough, however, to enclose a handbag and half a dozen other heavy necessities.

A folding laundry kit with a Flex-O-Line braided rubber clothes line that adheres to the wall of a bathroom without hooks or hangers.

A suitcase that folds flat and can be stored at the bottom of one's luggage until it's needed to carry home bargains, laundry, or whatever. There are many styles on the market and they keep multiplying.

A white cardigan sweater, the single most useful piece of clothing a traveler can pack. It acts as bed jacket and light wrap in air-conditioned planes and restaurants or chilly museums and churches and goes with anything.

A collection of paperback books, to be tossed or given away as you finish reading them so that their weight is not a burden throughout the trip.

An immersion heater for making coffee or bouillon. See Electrical Appliances, page 122.

An umbrella with a handle that folds over so as to fit into a suitcase.

A miniature game. It can be Scrabble, chess or backgammon. It helps to while away all the long boring hours spent at airports or in transit.

A set of scented pellets which, dropped into water, expand into washcloths in 30 seconds.

Soap, soap, soap. Small boxes of scented personal soap; liquid soap for laundry; a small plastic case for carrying a cake of soap in a handbag.

A selection of foreign magazines to give the traveler a quick preview of local life and events at her destination.

Money, i.e., small packets of prepacked foreign currency from $10 up to save untold amounts of nerve-racking confusion on arrival. It's wonderful for tips, or for taxi or bus fares into town. See Currency, page 92, for where-to-buy information.

The electrical appliances mentioned on pages 123-124.

Other possibilities:

A small jewel case
A lightweight travel robe
A set of lingerie cases
A passport wallet
A raincoat in its own case
A sewing kit
A transistor radio
Personalized luggage tags
Folding travel slippers
A currency converter
Pill bottles in a case
A traveling clock

Plastic inflatable clothes hangers
Beauty products that come in tubes, such as hand cream or water softener
A set of shoe mitts
A diary
Lightweight, folding drinking cups
Binoculars
A tiny flashlight
A cigarette lighter
A collapsible traveling lamp.

If you can't cope with finding a *bon voyage* gift yourself, there is a service called Manna Unlimited (550 Fifth Avenue, New York, New York 10036, PLaza 7-9577). It takes orders only by phone or through the mail and will make up a *bon voyage* basket of all sorts of fancifully wrapped, useful gifts. The donor fills out a questionnaire which gives the clues to the traveler's tastes, destination, etc., and the baskets are assembled accordingly. Even the basket itself is useful and handsome (it might be, for instance, a brightly colored woven carryall). Such a collection of small presents has all the fun of a Christmas stocking: guide and phrase books, inflatable pillows and hangers, sleeping masks, small sewing kits, pocket knives, playing cards, key chains, money converters, shoe and laundry bags, folding travel mirrors, marking pencils and maps, folding drinking cups, washcloths in their own plastic case, tiny bags of soap, etc. Baskets start at $12.50 and the assortment depends, of course, not only on your friend's interests but on what you want to spend.

Recently a style of *bon voyage* gift has developed which is given in your name but not in your presence. Meant to bring cheer while people are *en voyage*, these "absentee gifts" include the following:

A bottle of wine or champagne, or bar credits to be used at sailing time or during the voyage. Call or write the office of the steamship company or arrange this while you are seeing a friend off. Remember that bar credits go a long way on a ship; liquor is untaxed and drinks cost about half the shoreside price.

A bouquet of flowers. These can be delivered in several ways. You can go to a florist who is a member of FTD, the Florists' Transworld Delivery Association, and wire flowers anywhere in the world. For a friend who is in a dreary hotel in far-off Jakarta, this can be a particularly cheering gift. However, allow several days for the flowers to arrive. You might, on the other hand, give a Flora-Cheque, also available at FTD florists. This is a gift certificate that can be cashed at any of the 33,000 member florists around the world. It starts at $5 and is as good in Monaco or Malaya as in Montana. Finally, you can have flowers delivered to a friend's cabin after the ship sails if there is a florist aboard the liner. It's important to remember that if you decide to wire flowers abroad, you must do this at the very beginning of someone's stay in a city or your bouquet may arrive just as its recipient is checking out of her hotel.

A Rolls-Royce—a ride in one, that is. You can arrange to have friends met at London Airport and driven to their hotel in a Rolls-Royce with chauffeur. The cost is $10.80. There are less exalted automobiles available for a similar service at docks and airports in other countries. Get in touch with a travel agent or Auto-Europe, Inc., 25 West 58th Street, New York, New York 10019, or Auto-Europe offices in Chicago, Beverly Hills, Seattle or Toronto.

Tickets to European theaters and festivals. Arrangements for many of these can be made on this side of the Atlantic. Write to the tourist offices on page 479 for information.

Be My Guest gifts. This service, available to holders of American Express Company credit cards, provides a welcoming gift for the new arrival. Calling itself an "international host," it will arrange an evening's entertainment to be presented to the traveler at her destination in the form of a formal invitation, ranging from dinner at a small Spanish restaurant in the Philippines to a night on the town, including wine with dinner, in Paris. Dinner invitations are coded, so that only the restaurant need know how much you've spent. You can reach Be My Guest at American Express, Box 700, New York, New York 10003, or, for rush deliveries, by calling Western Union. Tell the telegraph company that you want to send a Be My Guest telegram. Like all services, Be My Guest charges a fee: in this case $1 per guest. It is nice to know that you can arrange an evening's entertainment by charging the works to your American Express Credit Card. For a directory listing member establishments, write to Be My Guest at the address given above.

It is relatively simple to send a gift to a ship. Address the package with the passenger's name, the class in which she is sailing, if possible the cabin number, name of the ship, sailing date, name of the steamship company, pier number and address. For example: Miss Jane Doe, First Class, Room A 128, *S.S. France,* sailing date, French Line, Pier 88 N.R., Foot of West 48th Street, New York, New York 10036. Having a gift delivered to a flight, on the other hand, is a difficult and uncertain business, and it's best to avoid it. There is one exception, however. Perera Company, whose main job is buying and selling foreign currency, will also sell you such duty-free items as French perfume, Swiss watches, transistor radios and electric shavers at New York's Kennedy Airport to be given departing travelers. Here's how it works: You call Perera's airport office, (656-8444) and order the item you desire—for about a 50 per cent saving on New York prices—and they will put it on board the recipient's plane. Your friend will be presented with the gift at her first landing in Europe.

Don't ever have flowers delivered to an air passenger. There's barely enough room to fold your legs comfortably aloft, let alone store a bouquet; and a corsage is not only useless—it's downright hickish.

Boutiques

IMAGINE a screeching red slicker, a bracelet with a tiger's-head clasp studded with obviously fake jewels, three bogus lemon trees, two lynx pillows, a white brocade pullover, a buttercup-yellow linen shift, a small army of carved wooden toy soldiers, a gilded unicorn once a sign for a seventeenth-century shop, a mauve crocheted at-home dress, several extravagant beach hats, a set of flowery egg cups, an ostrich boa, and an immense butter-soft suede carryall, all gathered under one roof—and you will have a good idea of the stock of a typical boutique. The French word *boutique*, which once signified a decidedly low-class shop, has become, in the past twenty years or so, synonymous with slightly giddy high fashion. Technically, the current meaning of boutique is a small shop filled with one-of-a-kind items, not necessarily related to each other. Their only common bond is individuality and uninhibited flair. A good boutique is a little show, filled with wit and glitter that give the shopper the feeling that clothes and household accessories are pure fun and adventure.

You will never find anything you *need* at a boutique. You won't see a good gray dress for job-hunting, a neat little black for meeting your husband's boss or a discreet printed lawn to wear to a garden party. What you will find is that wonderful splurge that buoys up the spirits—the slinky jump suit, the wildly flattering burgundy-colored hat, the sleek knitted pullover that makes you feel like a *contessa*. The boutique produces a you-and-you-alone look—and that is both the strength and the weakness of boutique shopping. Because items are one-of-a-kind, stocks are limited. If you covet a dress that's not in your size, you may have to wait weeks for a special order, or it may be run up in three days, or you may just be out of luck.

Boutique clothes always appeal more to the daring than to the classicist. The boutique owner knows her customers have a taste for the unique, even the bizarre, and generally the looks to carry it off; she knows, too, that she needn't touch all the bases, as the department store buyer whose clientele comes in all sizes, shapes and ages must do. Prices may go from microscopic to astronomical, because boutique customers simply don't care about money. They are rich enough to pay a small fortune, and secure enough to come home with a thrift-shop bargain. They are the women who own sable but prefer to wear guanaco for every day. For this reason, boutiques come in very handy when you need a dress for some chic gathering and haven't much money. "Kooky little nothings" cost far less than Scaasi ball gowns—and are often just as widely admired. By being on the *qui vive* for boutiques wherever you travel, you can assemble a handsome and original wardrobe. Even if your tastes are conventional, you can always find some elegant shoes and handbags.

Nearly every great fashion house in Europe has a boutique on its ground floor. Some of these carry only perfume and a few choice accessories. Others have added a small ready-to-wear collection with the house's label; some, like Galitzine and Pucci, design special collections for their boutiques. The couture boutiques are, as a rule, not so young and zany as their lesser-known counterparts. But they give you the heady feeling of owning a Cardin without having paid a skyscraper price for an original. At Dior, whose boutique is particularly elaborate, you will find not only women's things but a small collection for men and a limited selection of frivolities for the house such as embroidered linens and Limoges egg cups signed "Christian Dior." While you need a special appointment to see the regular collection at a *maison de haute couture*, you can stroll into its boutique on a whim. For a listing of Europe's great fashion houses, see page 86.

Besides these small couturier shops, there are innumerable attractive boutiques cropping up in all of Europe's large cities. Madrid's carry exquisite handwork, embroideries, leather goods and the like.

Italian boutiques have especially whimsical and flamboyant clothes. Recently over three dozen young boutiques have opened on the Rue de Sèvres in St.-Germain-des-Prés, in Paris, where every young girl and her mother goes shopping. Among the most notable are Marie-Martine and Dorothée Bis.

Look for boutiques, also, in the West Indies and in Hawaii, or at such developing beach resorts as Mexico's Puerto Vallarta. Resort boutiques, usually less expens've than those in the big cities, deal in splashy shifts and patio dresses washed by the brilliant colors of the tropics. In many resort areas, there's usually a small atelier in the back of a shop, which runs up the silk shirts and pants that local women wear as a uniform. In Hong Kong and the Bahamas, the boutiques have enticing collections of duty-free goods. A boutique's character depends on its neighborhood: On the Via Veneto, expect an expensive look and prices to match; in London's Chelsea, look for way-out clothes; and in artists' colonies, count on slightly artsy-craftsy handmades.

Since boutiques appear and disappear like the sun in Ireland, you will have to do your own sleuthing on the spot. Ask your concierge or the manager of your hotel—if it's a posh one—or walk over to the best hotel in town and ask there. Call the fashion or women's editor of the local English-language newspaper; boutiques are her beat and she should know the ones that are hot. On the theory that "like knows like," go to the best shop selling shoes, gloves or lingerie and ask for the names of good boutiques. Check with the leading hairdresser in town; sometimes, like Elizabeth Arden in Rome, it has a boutique of its own.

Because the word "boutique" has become automatically exciting, there are many shops that use it, although inexactly. You may find belt boutiques, glove boutiques and such. One big art gallery in Paris, the Galerie de France, has even opened a "bargain bas ment boutique" to sell low-cost original paintings and lithographs. But the true boutique, anywhere, remains a potpourri of delectable one-of-a-kind clothes and accessories for women.

Most knowledgeable women use boutiques to add spice to their basic wardrobes. If you've never shopped in one, you may feel a bit extravagant at first—but the odd-looking fisherman's sweater, the wildly striped patio dress, the vinyl trench coat, often turns out to be the thing you live in for years to come.

Budget

UNLESS you are the wife or daughter of an oil million-
aire, you have probably had some sort of experience with budgeting.
You learned at a fairly early age to give priority to some yearnings
over others. Travel budgeting is, first, deciding what denials will finance what treats, and, second, a rough guide to where your money
will go.

Painless budgeting on a trip is a matter of degree and common
sense. Once you have made a budget, you needn't be as slavish as an
ant in following it. A holiday is certainly no time to try to change
the habits of a lifetime. If, for example, you can't get through a morning at home without a hearty breakfast of cereal, bacon and eggs and
toast, don't try to cut corners by eating a roll-and-coffee Continental
breakfast on your trip. Shopping with that extra dollar or two will
be no fun on an empty stomach.

While restaurants and accommodations around the world generally cost less than in the U.S.A., you can live abroad at any level you
like. You might very well enjoy combining levels, staying at a pension in one city and at the best hotel in another.

The idea of doing a city on $5 or $10 a day has been widely touted,
but it is difficult and uncomfortable for almost everyone over twenty-
one. A more normal figure is $20 a day and even that doesn't buy
luxury. If, however, I had to choose between traveling on $10 a day
and not traveling at all, I would never hesitate to travel—and I
would use all the canny, penny-pinching devices I knew to obtain as
much pleasure and comfort as any few dollars ever bought.

Let's see how to make a travel budget.

Take the total amount of money set aside for your trip. Subtract
from it the total fare from your home town to your destination; this
should include the trip to New York or San Francisco or wherever
you catch the plane or ship to go abroad. You can even save money on
this first step through night flights, driving, traveling by bus, etc.

Now allocate a realistic sum of money for shopping and subtract *it.* (You are allowed to bring into the U.S.A. $100 worth of duty-free merchandise and to send home an unlimited number of $10-or-under gifts. See Customs, page 95.)

Divide the balance by the number of days you will be away. This will give you, roughly, the amount you have for each day's expenses: hotel, food, local transportation (don't forget transfers to and from the airport), sightseeing fees, amusement, tips, telephone calls, mail, laundry, sundries like film and developing charges, and a small daily splurge like a foreign magazine or a bottle of good wine.

Apportion the amount you will spend each day on each of the categories listed, and you will have a rough budget.

The table below, which was drawn up by the research department of the AAA, estimates the average American traveler's daily expenditure for Europe, the Far East and the Pacific, and South America.

Approximate daily cost for an American tourist traveling in:

	EUROPE	FAR EAST AND PACIFIC	SOUTH AMERICA
Lodging	$7.50–$8.50	$7.50–$8.50	$10–$11
Food	$6.20–$7.75	$6.00	$9
Other expenses: including transportation, admissions and miscellaneous	$7–$8.75	$7.50	$10
Totals:	$20.70–$25.00	$21–$22	$29–$30

Total expenditure by length of stay:

	EUROPE		FAR EAST, PACIFIC	SOUTH AMERICA
Average length	20 DAYS	30 DAYS	35 DAYS	20 DAYS
Lodging	$150–$170	$225–$255	$262–$297	$200–$220
Food	$124–$155	$186–$232	$210	$180
Other Expenses	$140–$175	$210–$262	$262	$200
Totals:	$414–$500	$621–$749	$734–$769	$580–$600

Now, let's refine that budget a bit. First, if your trip will take you touring in several countries, make a note of the country in which each day will be spent. The cost of living differs widely from area to area, even from country to country. Recently, the Center for Financial Statistics of Florence published an estimate of the daily expenditure of a tourist traveling first and second class in 43 countries. They divided the figures into two categories: high and medium. Each class's expenses included the cost of hotel plus meals taken either at the hotel or in restaurants of comparable grade, plus the costs of porters, theaters, tips, two daily trips in a local city bus, and small expenditures such as clothes pressing, newspapers, etc., which might crop up. Here's how the daily expenditures in several countries stack up as of this writing:

COUNTRY	HIGH CATEGORY	MEDIUM CATEGORY
Argentina	$22.55	$10.80
Austria	17.08	10.17
Belgium	20.16	12.96
Brazil	18.23	12.25
England	22.94	15.88
France	29.04	19.54
Greece	16.55	9.48
Italy	21.84	14.69
Netherlands	20.80	14.37
Spain	14.51	8.79
Sweden	23.51	15.73
Switzerland	21.57	13.82
West Germany	22.53	14.33
Yugoslavia	10.96	7.38

(In the U.S.A. by the same reckoning, the daily expenditure of a tourist in the high category was $34.48, medium $22.46.) Since, for example, Greece is a less expensive country than Italy, you should budget different amounts for each place.

Prices are also controlled by regional variations within a country. Cities are more expensive than rural areas unless the rural area also happens to be a posh resort. In Britain you can find dozens of charming country inns that charge $3 a night for a single room; in London such accommodations are scarce. Even in an inexpensive country like Portugal, the cost of a big-city first-class hotel room with private bath and three meals ranges from $6 to $8.50 a day; in the country inns or *pousadas* the price is about $4 a day, including the wine of the region.

Getting there and back is the biggest expenditure in your budget, and it offers the best chance to save. Investigate all the possibilities in charter flights, stop-over plans, seasonal, excursion and tour-basing fares. (These subjects are covered in the following sections: Charters and Group Fares, page 68; Fares, page 129; Stopovers, page 341.)

The next largest amount will probably go for hotels (see the section on Hotels, page 168). The third largest will be spent getting from one country to another and seeing the sights en route. You can reckon roughly that a tourist-class flight costs 10 cents a mile, a first-class flight 13 cents; second-class trains and buses average about 3 cents a mile; self-drive automobile about 3½ cents a mile. Half-day motor-coach sightseeing trips with English-speaking guides range from $2.50 to $3.50; full-day city sightseeing about $5. These are rough estimates, as costs vary from place to place. For example, a bus in Europe which drives along a mountainous route costs more per mile than one that covers flat country. See the sections on Buses, page 59; Motoring Abroad, page 255; and Trains, page 374.

All prices are subject to seasonal variations; sometimes even a difference of a few days can spell a large saving in money. Plan your trip clearly knowing when air and ship fares change, and when hotel rates rise, as the season advances. If you travel on a package tour— either as one of a group on a conducted tour or on an F.I.T. or Foreign Independent Trip, you will know most of your expenses before you start, an advantage for those who are weak-willed about budgeting. The disadvantage of spending money this way is that few, if any, operators will break down the costs item by item. If, however, your trip is booked country by country, hotel by hotel, you can probably save money by adjusting your choices according to the area.

Here are 14 rules of thumb for planning and stretching your budget (you'll find many more scattered throughout this book):

1. In estimating your hotel costs, be sure to include service charges. These can add up to as much as 26 per cent above the listed room rate in luxury hotels.

2. Figure out all money-saving arrangements such as Eurailpass, Eurotourpass and Eurotelpass *carefully*. Take a paper and pencil and see if the dazzling bargains they seem to offer at first glance will fit into the general plan of your trip. Most of these arrangements are very useful over a long period, but if yours is a short trip, you might find the bargain costing you more than you would have spent in the normal way. For example, a month's Eurailpass costs $130, but if your only train ride is a $41 run from Paris to Rome, you'll be out $89. Figure out the point of diminishing returns in terms of *your* itinerary.

3. Combine travels in expensive and inexpensive countries, expensive cities and the inexpensive countryside.

4. A trip must be costly in either time or money. The more time you have, the less money you need and vice versa. With time, you can take slower, cheaper transportation, search out more modest ho-

tels, take subways instead of taxis. You can also, for example, live in small hotels on the outskirts of town, always less expensive than those in the center.

5. Don't take lots of luggage. Tips to porters can add up. To avoid overweight charges, ship back old clothes as you accumulate new ones; and mail home books, pamphlets and the like as printed matter at low rates.

6. Don't always take a room with a private bath. The bath can add $2 to $3 to the single-room rate, more to the double. If you are willing to walk down the hall and ask the maid to run your bath, the extra charge will be only 50 to 75 cents.

7. Sharing a double room is cheaper than taking a single room; dividing the cost of taxis, car hire and tips also helps reduce expenses.

8. Use airline buses or limousines rather than taxis or hired cars between city and airport. These distances are usually long and the taxi fares mount.

9. Watch your mail costs; sending letters and postcards airmail more than doubles the cost. Use aerogrammes wherever possible. (See Mail, page 214.)

10. Don't eat two big meals a day; you probably never do at home. Take either lunch or dinner at an inexpensive pub or café.

11. Pay in travelers checks where you can save money. In France, for example, Americans get discounts of 20 per cent on many purchases. (See Travelers Checks, page 386.)

12. If you find yourself booking transportation in Europe, investigate night and excursion flights. They save substantial amounts of money. (See Fares, page 129.)

13. Stick to local wines, spirits, liqueurs, beer and the like. Imports will cost you dear.

14. Paper products are expensive abroad. Pack lots of small packets of Kleenex and toilet tissue.

15. Tip only in local currency. (See Tipping, page 359.)

Watch your economies, however; some you may regret. For example, taking a less expensive seat at a bullfight will mean hours of sitting in the hot, nearly unendurable, sun.

Buses

IF YOU LIVE a suburban, car-to-train life at home, you may not climb on a bus from one year's end to the next. Even if you live in a city, you may confine your bus travel to the daily haul between home and office. Abroad, especially in Europe, buses are not only the usual way to get about a city but a sightseeing and touring lifeline across the countryside. In some cities, sightseeing buses have introduced innovations that have made them tourist attractions themselves. The Cityrama buses of Paris, for example, are double-decked, glass-wrapped marvels with hostesses, bar service, and individual speakers that confide tape-recorded commentaries in nine languages. In Japan, passengers on buses between Tokyo and Kobe, or Tokyo and Hakone, can tune in on ten different languages. Cross-country buses have been made enormously comfortable, even luxurious. When you travel in Europe, possibly Japan, there's a strong chance that at some time during your trip you will ride a bus. It will be as different from the homely vehicle that lumbers down the street at home as a 1952 Studebaker is from a new Mercedes.

Buses designed for long-distance travel may have individual air conditioning, toilets and washbasins, cloakroom, refrigerator, bar service, radio. On many there are only 36 seats, reclining, and as comfortably upholstered as armchairs; yards of window that give superb visibility; individually adjustable window ventilators; footrests and individual lighting. They have pneumatic suspension, soundproofing, call signals and plenty of room to stretch. On the luxury bus lines, such as Europabus and CIAT, there are also English-speaking hostesses or couriers who look after you and your luggage. On some, you can have a drink and meet other passengers in a small parlor lounge that seats four.

You can take half-day and full-day sightseeing excursions by bus, short trips into the countryside, 2–3-week tours covering an area like the Adriatic Coast or the Costa Brava, and grand tours that travel from country to country for a period of six weeks. There are also "centered" and "stay-put" tours—those that go to a specified point which becomes your base for exploring the area. There are hundreds of de luxe and standard tours built around bus travel which provide hotel accommodations, some or all meals, sightseeing, all local tips, taxes, entrance and service fees and baggage handling. Often the bus picks you up at the airline terminal, the quay or your hotel, and while you are usually limited to two pieces of luggage, on some lines they may weigh as much as 110 pounds. (On others, the limit is the same as that for transatlantic economy air travel, 44 pounds.) The more stretch in your budget, naturally, the more luxury you can afford. The price of a bus tour, like that of any other tour, depends on the quality of the hotel and the meals, whether you have a private bath, and the leisureliness of the itinerary—as well as the number and quality of springs in the bus seats.

While Americans tend to look upon buses as the most modest means of travel, which they are, so far as expense is concerned, European buses are so comfortable, even luxurious, that many well-heeled travelers prefer them. Motorcoach touring is markedly on the upswing for reasons that have nothing to do with economy.

Among the big companies are Europabus, the motorcoach system of the European Railways, an international network of bus lines that cover the length and breadth of Europe; CIAT, an Italian bus company with excellent equipment; Linje-Tours, a company with tours throughout Europe, which allows stopovers on certain of its itineraries; ATESA and Melia Tours, the principal companies of Spain; Globus, a Swiss company, offering a wide choice of tours; Global of London, Britain's largest motorcoach operator, which has tours through Europe from $12 a day; and Fourways, which operates the Fourways and Val-U-Tour programs.

It's best to book your bus tour with a travel agent before you start. But if you haven't booked it here, look into the offerings of Fourways, Global, et al., when you are in London, generally the best city for booking economical bus travel. Incidentally, the British use the word "coach" to refer to a bus used for touring or long-distance travel; a "bus" is used only for local transport.

The prices of bus tours range from $10 to about $23 a day, everything included; there are even some as low as $8 a day. You might, for example, take a 2-day tour of the Castles of the Loire from Paris for $36; a 7-day Swiss Alpine tour from Zurich for $110; a 3-day tour of Holland from Amsterdam for $68; a 15-day tour of Italy and Yugoslavia from London for $212.

Besides tours, there are regular bus services which crisscross the landscape. Their fares are usually the equivalent of—or lower than—second-class rail fare. For example, the fare from London to Edinburgh by bus, one way, is $7; by first-class train it is $18.80, second-class $12.60, and via air, economy class, $22.90 in summer. Fares vary from country to country. In Europe, a journey of 500 kilometers on a flat road or *Autobahn* will cost less than the same distance on mountainous roads.

Like every other means of travel (and like most things in life), the bus has its pluses and minuses. There are probably more of the former. Here are some:

IT'S EASY: On group tours, and on some regular city-to-city bus runs, you and your luggage are picked up and set down directly at your hotel. A tour operator has made all the arrangements in advance. The itinerary is tried and true; you follow the smoothest roads, your meals are ready when you arrive, and so is your room. You need never pick up your suitcase. The courier handles all the operations—luggage, connections, preparations. A tour has knowledgeable commentary by the courier all along the route; even some city-to-city bus companies have instituted this.

IT CAN BE INEXPENSIVE: A low-priced inclusive bus tour is among the least costly ways to travel. If you are traveling with a group, you can hire your own bus, driver and guide, and your travel agent or the motorcoach company will design and book a complete itinerary to fit your group's interests. Because of their low prices, bus tours are becoming more and more popular with families, who are usually interested in budgeting.

IT PROVIDES COMPANY: A busload of people is a small community brought together by common interests. You are always sure of finding someone to talk to, and an atmosphere that is friendly and relaxed. If you travel on a regular city-to-city bus line, you will meet locals on *their* vacations or visiting friends and family, and tourists from other European countries; on a bus tour that you book in this country, you usually travel with other Americans. If you are at all timid or shy, this a comfortable, cozy way to go.

IT'S SCENIC: You see more through a bus window than from a plane or train. You travel more slowly, and are in the midst of the countryside. If you really want to see a country, you must do it by bus or car, and buses have the great advantage over cars of costing little and saving you wear and tear.

THE MINUSES: Bus travel is at its best on short hops; it is no pleasure to sit up, for example, without stopovers on a trip from Naples to Florence. You must have time to break it up. You cannot take long walks from car to car, as you would on a train. A group tour, of course, has its own minuses: The same daily organized routine, though you change seats every day, and the same faces can make you feel rather cut off from the country itself. There is seldom enough time to be adventurous on your own, to go off on tangents.

Be sure to book a bus tour only with a reliable firm. There are a number of fly-by-night operators in the field that may take your money and leave you stranded. A tour arranged by an airline or a reputable travel agent or bus company is unquestionably good.

As for the public transportation buses in a foreign city, if you are the least bit adventurous and can spare the extra few minutes they take, they can be great fun and a pleasant way of saving money. (At major bus stops in some cities—Paris is one—you must get a numbered ticket from a dispenser. It denotes your priority to board the bus.) In Venice the *vaporetti* operate like buses and move along the lengths of the canals.

Also consider taking public buses for excursions out of the city. They are more intimate than the typical tourist sightseeing ones.

Arm yourself with a phrase book, and you will find the locals courteous and eager to help; sometimes they will even get off and walk with you to your destination.

Castle Hotels
and Country Inns

ONCE UPON a time, a castle was a private preserve, the home of a noble family that might include a few golden-haired young princes and princesses and a coroneted ghost or two. It was a place of marvelous enchantment—and every little girl who read fairy tales knew all about them. The little girls grow up, the fairy tales get lost, and the noble families sometimes depart, but the castles remain, and in many of them you can actually stay today.

Wherever there has been wealth and nobility, castles have been built, and in recent years these castles and other great dwellings—manor houses, mansions, country estates, palaces, hunting lodges, medieval towers and monasteries—menaced by taxation and the servant problem, have opened their gates to guests. In Switzerland the Hotel Drachenburg, a bishop's castle built on Lake Constance in the thirteenth century, is now a lovely inn; in France the Château de Pray, once used by Charles VII as a hunting lodge, has become a fine small hotel; in Udaipur, India, the extraordinarily beautiful rooms of a Maharana's summer palace—a white jewel in the middle of a lake

—now house nonroyal travelers. The estate is called the Lake Palace Hotel. In Ireland turreted sixteenth-century Dromoland Castle, standing in a forest of oaks by a lakeside, offers every luxury, including tennis, golf and fishing. In England Le Talbooth in Dedham, Essex, a half-timbered Flemish weaver's house, is today a charming country hotel; and in Germany the medieval fortress of Waldeck, complete with dungeons and torture chambers, offers bed and board for about $2 a day.

And so it goes throughout most of Europe and occasionally on other continents as well. Often the property is still in the hands of the family whose forebears built it, and the traveler is welcomed like a personal guest by M. le Comte himself. Even when the historic building has been bought for the express purpose of conversion into a hotel, in spite of the loss of some intangible charm, the atmosphere is nevertheless unusually beguiling. Knowing travelers make it a point to search out castle hotels whenever they find themselves in the countryside. Here are some of their advantages:

First, romantic and luxurious as castle hotels may be, they are, paradoxically, among the least expensive places to stay. While they run the gamut in price and exclusiveness from the Duke of Bedford's Woburn Abbey—where bed, board and extras will cost you $100 a day—to the lovely Matzleinsdorf, a castle pension in Austria where room and board come to about $4 to day, they are, for the most part, not nearly so budget-breaking as the luxury they offer would seem to warrant. In Portugal, Germany and Austria, rates range from $4 to $10 a day for room and meals; in France and Britain prices are somewhat higher. In a number of places, castles are even inexpensive youth hostels.

Castle hotels sit in commanding parts of the countryside: in deep parks or on mountaintops where they were originally built for security against warring neighbors. Therefore the views are almost always glorious: from the Castle of Braemar, in Aberdeenshire, Scotland, there's a sweep of green hill, meadows flecked with flowers, a sparkling river and flocks of sheep; from the Château de Pray you have a view of the Loire, with Renaissance gardens and terraces.

Since most castle hotels have room for only a handful of guests— the average number is 25, although it can go as low as 4 or as high as 99—you are drawn cozily into its life and into conversation with other guests. In many castles, especially those run by the descendants of the original families such as the Schloss Sighardstein near Salzburg, Austria, life has the gaiety and friendliness of a particularly successful house party.

The food is far, far better, as a rule, than that served at commercial hotels in the same price range. For generations the castle has lived off its land, dining on the trout from its streams, the produce from its gardens, the meat from its herds, and the wines from its vineyards.

It usually does the same today, and you are often served matchless fish, fowl and fresh little wines.

You are surrounded by exceptionally beautiful things that are part of a family's and a nation's history—perhaps the guns used by Emperor Maximilian the Great, or the Persian rugs brought back from the East by an empire builder, or porcelains used by popes.

Finally, as if these were not inducement enough, many castles have added the pleasures of resort life: swimming pools, riding, shooting, tennis, skiing and of course fishing. Somehow, the best fishing in most countries is invariably near castles.

It is, no doubt, abundantly clear at this point that I am devoted to castle hotels and stay in them whenever I can. But it is only fair to point out their few disadvantages. The mechanical problem of boring through walls several feet thick that may date back to Charlemagne's time cuts down on the twentieth-century amenities. For example, there are many more bedrooms than bathrooms. If this disturbs you, make your reservation far ahead and ask for a private bathroom. Although in *some* places they come with every room, these are the exceptions. The same thick walls occasionally even make central heating impossible. Since Europeans tend to keep their room temperatures lower than ours anyway, the electric heaters usually provided may not be enough. (To solve this problem, just pack some cashmere cardigans.) Furthermore, sitting as they do in the midst of the countryside, castle hotels are best reached by car. Although the hotel will send a driver to meet your plane or train, without your own transportation you are a prisoner of the castle. It's best, therefore, to make castle-visiting part of a driving itinerary, unless you've come for the express purpose of rest and solitude. Because their capacity is small, many castles require the guarantee of a minimum stay in season, which can be anywhere from 2 to 4 days. And finally, if yours is a restless spirit, face up to the fact that, after nightfall, there's little in the way of entertainment except conversation, reading and occasional musical programs arranged by your hosts or the local village.

Austria is richest in castles but France, Germany, Spain, Switzerland, Belgium, Ireland, Portugal and Britain are generously supplied. If "castling" interests you, check the appendix for the address of each country's tourist office and write for a list of castle hotels. France has two castle chains. One is called the "Relais de Campagne" and includes about 70 places. The second group is known as "Châteaux-Hôtels de France" and numbers 36. Both are collections of castles, manors, country houses and old mansions converted into hotels. Also see Pensions and "P.G.'s," page 292, for information about a fairly new organization called ORSEC or *Organisation de Sejours en Châteaux*. This is a group of about 70 attractive medieval and Renaissance chateaux that take paying guests. Germany's Castle Hotel Association (Vereinigung der Burg und Schlosshotels) has 32 members. The state of Hesse alone has so many castle hotels that it issues its own brochure, obtainable by writing to Suite 1825, 250 West 57th Street, New York, New York 10019.

If you plan to motor through Europe, an organization called Open Road Tours, 407 North Eighth Street, St. Louis, Missouri 63101 (see Motoring Abroad, page 255), will "package" a string of manor houses and castles plus transatlantic transportation, car rental, breakfast, dinner, maps, and touring information. Their itineraries are quite good and their service is reliable. Study their brochures and ask your travel agent to do the booking.

Nearly everything written about castles applies to the country inns of Europe. The only big difference is that being small, inns are cozier, warmer, more intimately involved with the locals. They are also, for the most part, inexpensive: In Portugal, for example, a *pousada* will usually charge $4.03 a day per person—or $6.83 for two—for a room with full board, including free wine with lunch and dinner. What's more, the food is ample and good. (See Hotels, page 168.) France has a string of small country inns called Logis de France and Auberges Rurales where a single room often costs no more than $1 for the night. There's usually a bath at the end of the hall; average price for a hot tub is 50 cents. A French family, sometimes including a great-aunt or two, runs the establishment, doing the cleaning and cooking. About 2 thousand of these inns are scattered all over France.

Inns can be found on sites where the scenery is especially dramatic —the *parador* at Pajares, Spain, is at the summit of the majestic Pajares Pass—and you can often enjoy activities that are normally found only in a resort. Pajares, for instance, draws mountaineers and fishermen.

Because they are usually out of the way, inns are steeped in the lore and habits of a country. Denmark's country inns, or *kroer*, were the centers for village life, and you'll often find them opposite an old village church with, perhaps, a view of a serene blue lake and flower-flecked meadows. Many of the old inns are on secondary roads, which are in good condition and fine for driving; newer inns have been built along the main express roads. Denmark is known for its marvelous food, and you'll probably want to stop in the older inns for a home-cooked meal. But generally accommodations are simple (bath in the hall), so stay at the newer ones if you want a private bath. Rates at the old inns average $6–$9 a day for two, at the newer ones $12–$15 a day for two.

For centuries, the Japanese have been enthusiastic travelers—and their roadside inn has been the traditional *ryokan*. The pattern of this kind of hotel living still follows the ritual laid down hundreds of years ago. There is a room maid to cook and serve your food, prepare your bath, run your errands, do your laundry and otherwise wait on you in a dozen ways. Prices go from modest to quite high; a luxurious *ryokan* will charge as much as a good Western-style hotel. The Japan Ryokan Association publishes a free guide in English that tells all you need to know about staying in a *ryokan;* it is available from the Japan National Tourist Organization, whose address is on page 484. I have always found these Japanese inns a delight.

Probably no country in the world has woven the intimacy of the inn into the fabric of its national life as England has. You sense it best in late afternoon, when the tavern is filled with locals who have dropped by for a drink, or a game of dominoes or cribbage. In various stages of England's history, the inn has represented different things. At one time, many were posting inns, providing hasty travelers with a change of horses. When railroads came, with them came the big railroad hotels, and many inns dwindled to the status of pubs. Automobiles and new roads restored them to their traditional function as centers of hospitality. Today, with their oak-beamed ceilings, paneled rooms and open brick hearths untouched, the inns carry on that tradition, and inn-hopping by car can be one of the nicest ways to see England.

One English firm, Boswell and Johnson Travel Service, has motoring itineraries which can be followed by chauffeur-driven limousine, or by driving yourself. Their rates are low, and include accommodations, full English breakfast, gratuities, and use of a car, with unlimited mileage. (Boswell and Johnson are located at 119 Oxford Street, London, W.1.) Even if you decide to take your own car and do your own routing, you will find that prices in English inns are generally low. In summer, they average $3.50–$5 a day per person, and most of the inns have between 6 and 20 bedrooms. It's wise to write ahead of time for reservations.

Perhaps the chain best known for quality and variety is the Trust House group, which has more than 230 members throughout England

and includes the famous Shakespeare Inn in Stratford, where every bedroom is named for a play. (Imagine sleeping in *Othello* on your honeymoon.) Most of the Trust chain are small; the Dorset Arms Inn in Withyham, Sussex, with one room to rent, is an extreme example, and of course there are exceptions. Rates for room and breakfast average about $10 a day for two, about $5 a day for one, depending on location and season. A three-course dinner costs $1.50–$2 almost everywhere. An annual brochure giving rates, locations and facilities of all Trust House hotels is available, in limited number, from the British Travel Association in New York (see National Tourist Offices, page 483, for address). The address in London is Trust House Hotels Enquiry Office, 81 Piccadilly, London, W.1.

The development of government-operated inns in some countries has removed the disadvantage of the shared bathrooms and listless heating you will have to put up with elsewhere. Although rates are low, the facilities in many of Spain's *paradores* are on a par with those in de luxe hotels. Though some are located in new buildings, many of them are ancient dwellings with twentieth-century polish. In Granada, the Parador de San Francisco is within the actual walled fortress palace of the Alhambra. The Parador de Mérida is a baroque-styled monastery dating back to the early sixteen-hundreds.

There's a country inn wherever there's a countryside, and the designation "inn" insures reasonable prices. Even in Austria, where the construction of first-class hotels is booming, the new inns, or *Gasthöfe*, are almost always inexpensive. Like all other country inns, they have the charm of being close to the land because they are really inseparable from it.

Charters and Group Fares

CLUBS THAT used to celebrate July 4 with a picnic or a moonlit boat ride are now flying to Paris or Dublin, for travelers have discovered that plane fares, like eggs and oranges, come cheaper by the dozen. Today you can fly anywhere in the world as one of a company that charters a plane or half a plane and splits the cost among its members, saving everyone a substantial amount over the regular individual commercial fare. No wonder, then, that the charter business has been zooming since 1955.

However, travelers investigating charters are often like people investigating sin. It's done mostly in whispers—and lots of misinformation is the result.

Quite understandably, travel agents are afraid that they are losing clients and commissions through the charter boom. While charters were originally designed to fill up planes that would otherwise be empty, the airlines also fear that too much chartering will siphon off passengers from regular commercial flights. But for the traveler, a charter flight is superior only to not flying at all; there are enough disadvantages (I'll talk about these later) so that anyone who can possibly afford to will take a commercial flight. For many people who would not ordinarily be going abroad, the charter is a boon. Having traveled once, they get the bug—and become excellent future prospects for repeated commercial flights.

The Civil Aeronautics Board tries to make charter flights available to "a broad segment of the public" but not to "the general public." Under regulations of the CAB, charter flights are available to bona fide chartering organizations. Resolutions of the International Air Transport Association (IATA), which are similar to the CAB regulations, govern on route charter operations of IATA member carriers. There are, therefore, certain requirements which every group must meet in order to charter, and which travelers must satisfy in order to board a charter flight. To follow these rules is important both for your safety and as a matter of personal conscience, but their pursuance does allow some leeway.

The CAB states that a chartering group must have been in existence for some reason other than just the purpose of travel. Individuals are required to have been members of the organization for at least six months in order to be eligible to participate in the proposed charter. The group might be a garden club that wants to see the seventeenth-century gardens of France; a group of nursery school teachers interested in seeing how other schools work; or simply a bridge club splurging its winnings on a few weeks of fun. Lawyers' groups charter, doctors' groups charter, and so, presumably, do clubs for chicken breeders and lepidopterists; indeed, the members of corporations, companies, grange or 4-H clubs, professional, social, religious, trade, union, civic, veterans', charitable, ethnic, student and teachers' associations are all eligible. No group may advertise or promote a charter flight to the general public, nor may an airline or travel agent give out information on which groups are booked to charter or solicit individual members for participation in the charter flight.

To qualify as a charter passenger, you must have been a member of the *particular* group for six months prior to takeoff. You can't just ring up the airlines or breeze into your travel agent's office to ask which groups are booked to travel together. Members of your immediate family who live in your household (spouse, children and parents) can qualify as part of your group as long as they are traveling in your company. If you must cancel your reservation, the family can still take the trip but you may have to forfeit your fare if the organization can't find an eligible substitute passenger for your seat.

The CAB polices charter flights as carefully as it can. Groups must keep clear membership lists to verify that all their members fulfill the six-month requirement. If one ringer is discovered, even at the very last minute, the entire flight could be canceled, leaving perhaps 120 innocent passengers sitting on their suitcases in Kennedy Airport at midnight. The necessity of joining an absolutely bona fide group and the moral obligation to be on the level yourself are obvious.

The question is: how can you morally, legally, safely get on a charter flight? If you already belong to a group such as those described above, you are in the clear; if the group is planning a charter flight, it will announce the fact to its members, whether by newsletter or bulletin-board notice. But a non-joiner need not despair; there are honest ways of finding a charter.

There is bound to be some group whose non-charter activities interest you, and which you are eligible to join; ask all friends and acquaintances if they know of an organization planning a trip. There are several good criteria for discovering whether the group is legitimate and not an association set up for literally fly-by-night purposes. Have you heard or read of the group's regular activities in your community? Do they, for instance, do charity work, run tours of historic houses, agitate for better schools? Do they issue a newsletter? Have they offices or a meetinghouse? Observe the way they handle your membership application. First, of course, reject the offer of any group that offers to sell you a ticket when you haven't been a member for six months, or that agrees to backdate your membership. More positively, do they ask you to sign up for committee work, decorate the next party, address envelopes and make telephone calls? A club which demands nothing of its members may be suspect. By the same token, if requested to help out in club functions, you should agree to some minimum of work with good grace; if they are getting you to

Paris cheaply, it's the very least you can do. You may, actually, develop a hitherto dormant interest in gardens or bridge; some groups apparently institute charters as an incentive for membership.

Your contract should contain a clause that allows you to get a refund if the flight is canceled; sometimes an organization, in perfectly good faith, will schedule a charter, then discover it can't fill enough seats and must cancel. If you must take your vacation at a certain date, make sure the flight plans and cost will be verified within a reasonable time before takeoff, and find out how far ahead you can cancel and still receive a refund. Should you want to protect yourself in case of accident or illness (either before you take your trip or *en voyage*) that would force you to change or cancel your ticket, the American Casualty Company of Reading, Pennsylvania, offers a new kind of insurance plan for charter groups at rates ranging from $5 to $12.50 per person. (They will reimburse you in amounts from $200–$500.) You must apply for the insurance at least 21 days before leaving; otherwise you can buy it only for the return flight.

Since charter groups pay a flat rate for the plane and distribute the cost among their members, the price of your ticket depends on the size of the group: An organization of 80 people will charge more per person than another with 100 people. A round-trip charter to London can cost each member as little as $200, but generally the fare runs about $250–$260 for a transatlantic trip.

Chartered planes are generally the same as those used in regular service; whether your plane is an old DC-6B or a current-model jet, it has undergone the same rigid safety checks as any commercial aircraft. Food depends on what the chartering group chooses; it ranges from full first-class service with unlimited free drinks to soup and sandwiches only.

Flying charter is a splendid means of getting abroad when you can't afford to go any other way; if you can comfortably afford an economy-class commercial ticket, however, you'd be slightly mad not to buy one. Here are some of the flies in the charter ointment:

1. The dates and length of your stay are fixed by the group, not by your personal convenience. If your Aunt Millie gets sick or if a business emergency arises, you can't postpone the trip two days; and if Cousin Jim suddenly decides to get married, you can't come home a day earlier without forfeiting the price of your return charter ticket, *plus* paying for a commercial flight home. Nor can you decide to stay a week longer and see Rome with the handsome Italian you met the night before takeoff.

2. Your itinerary is, to some extent, controlled by that of the flight.

While the charter group can (and usually does) disperse during its stay abroad, reconvening for the trip home, all non-charter traveling is done at regular commercial rates. Therefore, when your charter plane lands in Amsterdam, you can't go to Athens without paying a very pretty extra penny indeed, and most charter passengers limit themselves to the general area of the arrival and departure cities.

3. The cost, being regulated by the conditions described above, is subject to change. If 20 people cancel out, the others must divide their shares of the bill.

4. Shady practices can result in last-minute cancellation—and however innocent you may be, you're stuck.

5. While charter planes themselves are both as safe and as comfortable as commercial flights, they seem to suffer a high percentage of delays in takeoff and landing. Any airport delays result in maximum waiting around for charter passengers—and even the most efficiently managed charter flight has often been known to leave 2, 3, 5, 7 hours late. If you are due back home at a definite hour, you can't depend on a charter to get you there on time.

Impressed by the success of charters, the airlines, steamships and railroads have instituted their own low fares, available to groups who board regular commercial trips together. (They are usually smaller than groups who charter.) On most scheduled airline group flights, you must number 25 or more, but this figure varies with your destination and can be as low as 10. There are group fares operating on flights all over the world. Under the scheduled airline group plan you must all stay together during every leg of the journey; if the itinerary calls for London–Paris–Rome–Madrid–New York, all of these segments must be traveled by the whole group simultaneously. If you separate from the group and return on a different flight, you forfeit the discount, paying the difference between regular and group fares. While they are available most of the year, group fares are not operative for certain short periods during the peak season when there is an exceptional demand for space. Since these dates tend to change from time to time, be sure to check them with the airline concerned. A group fare includes round-trip jet transportation, economy class, with its usual baggage allowance of 44 pounds. There is no limit to the time the group can be away.

How much money does group travel save you? From New York to Rome, for example, a regular round-trip economy-class ticket costs $629.90 in the high season; a 21-day excursion fare is $409; group fare is also $409 but you can stay away longer than the 21 days permitted under the excursion fare. Traveling with a group around the world, you save about $340. On some routes, there are several group fares, depending on the size of the group.

There is a special fare to Israel which is calculated simply on people traveling together, but the group need have no affinity. All that's needed is 25 people in winter or 40 in summer who travel to Tel Aviv on the same plane and spend at least 8 days in Israel. This move reduces the usual high-season economy round-trip fare from $883.50 to $535. Here's the way it works. A travel agent or the airline promotes a trip. Twenty-five or more people (they can all be strangers to each other) decide to go and are booked on the same aircraft. The group is allowed two predetermined stopovers in Europe on its return trip. Forty, for example, can fly from New York to Tel Aviv, go their separate ways in Israel, then board the same flight for Rome and after a few days there proceed to another city which might be Paris. If they leave from there and come back to the U.S.A. together, both stops are included in the $535 fare. Stopovers are *only* permitted on the homeward leg of the flight. If passengers make additional stops, they forfeit the group fare, and must pay for the separate segments.

Actually, this is a group fare in name only, for you make your booking as an individual and are only joined to 24 or 39 other passengers by the travel agent or airline as a technicality. You need never be with the group at your destinations and you needn't fear that 25 or 40 people are trouped through countries as a group. Dozens of departures are listed each season so you are sure to find a tour whose dates, duration and itinerary suit you. If you are interested, see your travel agent or an airline, or watch the newspapers, for these particular Israel group fares can be organized and publicized by a travel agent.

If you are enterprising enough to organize a group, even if it's too small to charter and has no affinity, the airline will provide your transportation as the tour conductor, depending on the size of the group. Generally, you get one free ticket for every 15 passengers and a 50 per cent reduction for every 10 to 14 passengers.

Ships also offer reductions of 25 per cent round trip for groups of 25 or more traveling during the off season. The rates are available in cabin and tourist classes or on one-class ships, and members of a party need not travel in the same class. Also, you may go by one line, return by another. For every 25 people, one free round-trip passage is given to the party leader. As with air fares, a written application containing the names of the passengers must be submitted to the ship line. On some lines, you may make an individual reservation and still benefit from the group rate on specific sailings. Ask about this when you book your passage.

Even trains now offer reductions to people traveling together. Eurailgroup entitles any group of at least 10 people to a reduction; for groups of 25 it is even more. For the first 15 to 50 passengers, one member is carried free; an additional free passage is given for every 50 paid fares thereafter. There are special group rates for young travelers under the age of 21. An adult escort who travels with the group also receives the youth rate for every group of 10 and one more for every 10 thereafter.

Church Deportment

A MOSLEM sightseeing in St. Peter's, a Protestant touring a shrine, or a Buddhist observing the services in a synagogue have one thing in common: diffidence. *Grande dame* or schoolgirl, we are all somewhat unsure of ourselves in a church, especially if it is in a foreign country and not of our own religion.

Churches are built to inspire reverence, but all too often reverence can become inhibition. Yet the service is, after all, only the formal expression of how we govern our lives—hopefully, with kindness, respect for each other, and mercy. It's perfectly natural to be afraid of showing, even unwittingly, the slightest shred of disrespect to any religion. But this can be carried too far. Remember first, that if you *feel* respectful toward other religions, you will not be misunderstood in a place which is devoted to tolerance and gentleness. You are there to look at beauty and to learn, and if you let yourself be frozen by self-consciousness, you are depriving not only yourself but the church as well.

Since you will be constantly going in and out of churches, here are a few rules to observe which should put you at ease. If you want any further help, ask the concierge of your hotel or your tour guide for a briefing on the decorum observed in local churches.

People who are not Moslems are welcomed warmly at any mosque. You must, however, remove your shoes (Mohammedans touch their foreheads to the floor during prayers). Should you enter during the service, do not walk among the worshipers.

In Japan's Buddhist temples a Western observer should sit as still as a flower on the tatami matting while watching the ritual. At Shinto shrines you can stand during the service or sit on the benches that are provided for visitors. In India's Moslem mosques, women—whether or not they are of the faith—are not permitted to participate in services, but if you would like to see the building itself, you may do so after the prayers are over. Non-Hindus may visit only the outer precincts of Hindu temples; only believers are allowed in the inner sanctum.

Israel's synagogues are orthodox, which means that women are separated from men; if you plan to stay through a service, you and your husband must be prepared to sit in different sections. In Greek Orthodox churches, women may not go behind the altar.

Should you come into a Catholic or Protestant church in northern Europe during services, you may either stand quietly in the back or slip into a seat or even participate, kneeling, rising, and singing hymns with the congregation. If you aren't of the faith, you need not follow the conventions of the church or take part in any of the ritual. Wherever you are, however, only one thing is required: Be as inconspicuous as possible and do not disturb the worshipers. It is bad manners, therefore, to use a camera in church while services are in progress without receiving permission to do so beforehand.

Catholic Latin countries are a curious mixture of strict observance and relaxation. While they have explicit, carefully maintained rules for dressing (see Church Dressing, page 76), they seem casual in matters of decorum. It usually comes as a surprise to Americans that people move around during Mass. There is a constant coming and going: Visitors can walk through church (though not in front of the altar while Mass is being celebrated); worshipers come in for a few minutes, then leave. Some people stand, some kneel, and often the words of the priest are lost in the general hum. Do not mistake this flurry for lack of piety; quite the opposite is true. People move in and out of their churches this way because religion is an immediate part of their daily lives, not relegated to Sunday.

Don't be surprised if you find a church closed during the siesta hours in Spain, Mexico or Italy. Check before you go; otherwise you may travel miles on a hot day only to find that even a cathedral is locked tight between 12 and 3:30 or 4 P.M. Many churches will be closed at other times as well, although you can always get into any one you want to see by making special arrangements. Also, should you want to pay a call on a convent, you must obtain permission in advance. Write ahead or check with the local tourist office and ask them to make the arrangements.

Many churches have an attendant to explain works of art and to take you into locked chapels. Be sure to show your appreciation of his courtesy by putting a donation into the collection box in his presence. About 25 cents a person will do.

In Italy where churches have enjoyed perhaps the most glorious marriage to art, mechanization is setting in. You may occasionally find a machine into which you deposit 100 lire (16 cents), dial a language and listen to a running commentary on the church via earphones.

Church holidays are the occasion of many of the world's most colorful celebrations; they are called variously festas, fiestas, feast days, festivals. Even though you are not particularly devout, you will be caught up in the spontaneous warmth of these lively festivals —which have nothing of the hush of a cathedral. In Israel, for example, during Simhath Torah and Purim, there are floats, brightly costumed marchers, dancing and singing. Japanese religious holidays are celebrated with splendid pageantry. In Portugal, from Easter until mid-October, there's scarcely a village or hamlet without a "festa" and the folk costumes, bullfights, fantastic fireworks displays, parades and folk dancing that go with it. For more on this subject, see Festivals, page 132.

Church Dressing

WHETHER YOU were last in church as a beribboned child or attend services every Sunday, once abroad, you'll find yourself constantly drifting in and out of churches. You will go not so much to worship, although you may be sure of finding a church of your faith in nearly every large city, but for the same reasons that would move you to a museum: to look and admire. To bypass churches is to miss Michelangelo's most glorious paintings, little-known Giottos hidden behind black altar cloths, the heavenly stained-glass windows of

Chartres, the gemmed mosaics of a mosque in Istanbul. In churches you will find not only much of the world's most exalted art and architecture, but a better understanding of the history and spiritual beliefs of its peoples.

But no matter why you visit churches, there are strict ground rules for dress and behavior. Both must be unexceptionably "inconspicuous." While most foreigners will be charming and forgiving about other informalities, they are deeply offended, and quite rightly, by a woman who shows up in a halter and shorts at their cathedral. (It happens!)

It goes without saying that if you attend a service, you dress just as you would at home: dress, hat, gloves and stockings. If you "do" the church as a sightseer, you may leave off the stockings in warm climates and substitute a scarf or mantilla for the hat. *Never* wear slacks or shorts or any sort of décolletage in a church. There's only one exception to this rule, and that, curiously, is in otherwise proper Bermuda. If you're sightseeing on a sunny day in St. George Parish and want to visit St. Peter's Church, the oldest Anglican church in continuous use in the Western Hemisphere, you *can* enter if you are wearing the Bermuda uniform, i.e., long shorts and a shirt; but you must be sure to have a scarf along to cover your head.

Just as in America, the rules for being covered are stricter in Catholic than in Protestant churches. In Finland's Lutheran churches, for instance, a visitor needn't wear a hat or scarf. In Mexico's Catholic churches, on the other hand, if your arms are bare, you'll probably be barred.

Assume, then, for safety and propriety's sake, that it's always a good idea to have something on your head (even when not required, it's considered more respectful). The only other variable then, is whether or not your arms can be exposed. Here the answer depends partly on the country but also on the rules of a given church, how strictly the locals or parishioners observe them and whether the church is in a big city like Paris or the provinces like Brittany.

As a general rule, however, in strongly Catholic countries like Portugal, Ireland, Belgium, Spain and Mexico, even if you wear a dress with a train, your arms should be covered. In Greece, Britain, Puerto Rico, Germany and most of France, as long as your head is shielded, your arms needn't be. The prettiest and easiest solution to handling the various rules would be to buy a long lace mantilla as soon as you arrive in a Latin country. It's a flatterer nonpareil, wraps becomingly around your head and arms, and when not in use lies neat and flat at the bottom of your handbag. Otherwise, you'll be forced to sightsee in dresses with sleeves or to carry a cardigan sweater. In other than Latin countries, carry a generous silk scarf; if you wear a simple sheath dress, the scarf can sit prettily around your shoulders when it's not in use in church.

Having muffled your head all over Europe, when you arrive in Japan you'll be expected to uncover it, for here it is considered respectful for women to bare their heads when they enter a Buddhist temple or a Shinto shrine. As for sleeves, the Japanese are indulgent with visitors and you may go without them, but some kind of sleeves are nevertheless preferred.

Religious etiquette involving shoes is also varied. They are always removed before entering temples and shrines in Japan, mosques in the Middle East and Hindu or Sikh temples in India. You'll be given a pair of slippers to wear over—or instead of—your shoes. The doorkeeper or porter who supplies these will expect you to tip him lightly. A pair of Peds or knitted socks tucked into your handbag—the kind of slipper socks the airlines give out to passengers—is just fine for this purpose. When you're sightseeing in countries where you have to slip in and out of shoes, avoid laced oxfords, ghillies and the like. Constantly tying and untying them can be a nuisance.

Remember that you are always, of course, welcome everywhere, regardless of whether you are of the faith or not (except for the Temples of Kartik Mundi in India or Mt. Athos in Greece) as long as you do your strolling about with the hush and lightness of a butterfly.

Cigarettes and Matches

Oscar Wilde said, "A cigarette is the perfect type of a perfect pleasure. It is exquisite and it leaves one unsatisfied. What more can one want?" If cigarettes give you pleasure, you can enjoy them to the fullest, throughout your travels, with a little planning.

Actually, the innovations that keep smokers smoking in the U.S.A. also exist abroad. Today there is no major country in which you cannot find king-sized and filter-tipped cigarettes. Only the mentholated varieties are elusive. They are not manufactured everywhere, and if you are wedded to them, you'll have to plan your cigarette rationing carefully.

As soon as a country can afford to, it manufactures its own cigarettes, so nearly everywhere you go, you will be within reach of the comforts of tobacco. But if you aren't willing to experiment with local varieties, plan on taking your quota of American cigarettes. In most countries, this is 400 or two cartons. In some, this amount drops to 200, so be sure to check the regulations of the *first* country on your itinerary which you'll be entering with your tobacco supplies at their fullest. In a few, the quota is higher: Ireland allows 1,000 cigarettes, Brazil 800; in others, lower—Turkey allows only 50.

Should you be rigidly devoted to a particular brand, your loyalty will cost you dear once you're abroad. You will have to pay a stiff duty on whatever you bring in above your quota. If you buy American brands abroad, you will find that they are expensive—anywhere from 40 cents, unless locally manufactured, to over $1.50 a package in glossy hotels. In London shops a package of Pall Malls costs about 80 cents. In Switzerland, however, if you are a Kent or Marlboro smoker, you are in luck: Both brands are manufactured in the country and cost only 28 cents a package.

On the other hand, if you will be tolerant of other countries' tobacco, you can happily smoke your way around the world. Simply tell the tobacconist the sort of cigarette you like, and he'll produce the local American-type version. In France, for example, Maryland and Fontenoy are the two brands which most resemble ours. At first the flavor of native cigarettes may seem strange, but once you acquire the taste, you'll probably become devoted to it. There's even a bit of snobbery involved in smoking foreign cigarettes. The bitter French cigarette, Gauloises, is now a status symbol in the U.S.A., and in Greece, while you are smoking Papastratos, the Greeks will be relishing Kents.

Generally, to name just a few countries, Spanish, French and Colombian cigarettes are usually stronger than ours; Austrian, South African, Canadian, and Italian brands are milder; and Norwegian are about the same. Each Greek cigarette manufacturer makes cigarettes of several strengths, both with and without filters. In Britain, tobacconists sell a far larger variety of cigarettes than we have here. There are several sizes: small, medium, thick, medium with cork tips, medium with filters, and king-sized. Abroad, a package of native cigarettes costs anywhere from 17 to 70 cents and holds either ten or twenty.

Don't be surprised when you are asked to pay for matches. Only in the U.S.A., and on nearby islands such as Bermuda, the Bahamas and the Caribbean Islands where American habits wield influence on the local scene, are matches supplied free. Everywhere else, you must pay for them. The cost is little enough, only 1 to 5 cents. It's a practical way of getting rid of your small coins, and in these tiny denominations they are unconvertible, anyway. The matches are attractively boxed, sturdy and much nicer than ours.

However, since matches are not always available a cigarette lighter becomes a handy item to carry with you. This may be the moment to invest in a butane lighter. (It's also a splendid *bon voyage* gift, should anyone ask.) The alternative is to pack a small box of matches. Without one or the other you could easily find yourself touring the countryside, miles from a small town—and a tobacconist—hungering vainly to light a cigarette.

A good place to save money on tobacco is the tax-free shop at an airport. It sells a wide variety of brands, and prices are considerably lower than any you'll find outside. If you fly from Kennedy Airport, leave yourself time to stock up on cigarettes from the duty-free shop where they cost about $2.00 a carton.

If you haven't time to do this, a last resort is the airplane, which carries a limited stock of cigarettes to sell during its flight across the Atlantic at prices a bit lower than those in U.S. stores. On most airlines, for example, a carton of Winstons costs $2.50 en route to London.

However, if you sail, buy nothing on shore and wait for the ship's stores to open; a package usually costs about 20 cents.

As for stories about how eager foreigners are to smoke American cigarettes, they are part of the lore of the war and immediate postwar years, and have little reality now. Expensive brands of American cigarettes can be a status symbol, but by and large, today, no one is particularly impressed by them. Since they are not greatly coveted, don't plan on taking them abroad as inspired gifts.

Clothes Care

BECAUSE YOU travel with only a few clothes, which constantly submit to being packed, unpacked, crumpled on long bus rides, worn on dusty sightseeing expeditions and generally given as rough wear as a soldier's fatigues, you will find yourself playing lady's maid with more zeal abroad than at home. At luxury and first-class hotels the housekeeping and valet staffs will help: The chambermaid will handle your personal laundry; the valet will take charge of pressing and cleaning outer garments. At smaller, simpler hotels the chambermaid functions as an all-in-one assistant. At third-class hotels *monsieur le patron* will help you get the necessary chores done.

First, there is the matter of laundry. If you can possibly afford to, send it out. Make a list for yourself and give the bundle to your chambermaid. Large hotels often have same-day service for a small surcharge; normal service takes no more than 24 to 48 hours. Like the price of eggs, laundry prices around the world vary. Where labor costs are high, you will pay as much to have a blouse or shirt done as in the U.S.A. Where they are low, your laundry bill will be modest. Foreign laundries seem to do better with cotton than synthetics, perhaps because so many of them believe in using actively boiling water to get clothes clean. (Watch out for such things as linen dresses in the Far East. In Bangkok, for example, they will come back with spirits broken, having been parboiled.) But you will always be enchanted with the pressing. Each tiny pleat will have a razor's edge, every ruffle will bounce and curl. The same painstaking care that still goes into making exquisitely intricate handicrafts turns slips, nightgowns and blouses into things of beauty.

If you are budgeted down to your last sou, use the public launderettes in large cities. Like our laundromats, they return your clothes spanking clean but unironed; you can have the chambermaid at your hotel iron the important pieces or ask your concierge or the local tourist association for the nearest laundry. For example, the British Travel Association will give you the names and addresses of laundries in London that can do a job in 24 hours, and the Institute of British Launderers Ltd., 16 Lancaster Gate, London W.2. (tel. PADington 2454), will supply the names of other laundries throughout the country. Paris has a new completely automatic self-service launderette that's open around the clock, every day of the week. It's called the Laverie Self-Service and is at 37 Rue Didot, Paris 14*e*.

For the bits and pieces you want to launder by hand, take a traveling laundry kit. (See Soap, page 335.) While not the most glamorous *bon voyage* gift in the world, it's one that gets used. It contains plastic clothespins, a few folding hangers and a braided latex line with looped ends to keep it stretched taut. Since many foreign bathrooms do not have overhead showers, there are no shower rods to hang things on. This line can be looped around a water faucet, towel rack, doorknob or any other handy projection.

In places where the humidity soars, blot the extra moisture out of your laundry with bath towels before hanging it up to dry—or you may find yourself sitting on a plane for hours in clammy underwear. If you go swimming, remember to rinse your bathing suit after each swim (swish it through some suds first) to remove the sea's salt, the pool's chlorine or the sharp bits of sand which often cut fabrics. Carry a couple of lightweight plastic bags. They are a blessing if your lingerie and/or bathing suits are still damp when you are ready to start off in the morning.

As for pressing—there are four ways to revive wrinkled clothes. First, as with laundry, you can have the hotel do it. Ring for the valet and let him take over. You won't get your clothes back for several hours, perhaps not until the next day, and the prices will be rather high. (At resort hotels, which are self-sufficient entities, pressing is done on the premises and the service is usually quite fast.) Second, ask the valet to sponge and brush them himself; often this is all the care that's needed. Third, try the old-fashioned steam-and-dry method. Moisture and heat can remove wrinkles as well as pressure, and hanging them in the bathroom with the hot water faucets turned on strongly in the bathtub so that steam rises (be sure the door is closed) can refresh them in 15 minutes. Be sure, however, to let them air and dry before wearing. This method is chiefly effective with wools and silks which are naturally springy. Fourth, just hang your clothes in the open rather than the closet, giving the fresh air a chance to get at them. Often the natural moisture in the air plus some brushing on your part will be enough to restore them.

Should you get caught in a heavy London fog or a spring shower in Paris, let your clothes dry at normal room temperature, away from direct heat or radiators, then brush them.

Most cruise ships have laundry and dry cleaning facilities. You can always ask your steward or stewardess to take care of pressing or use the ship's iron and pressing room to do the job yourself.

This is the moment to mention travel irons. They are splendid in theory but a nuisance in practice. If your clothes are packed well (see Packing, page 281) and made of even reasonably sensible fabrics (cotton and linens with crease-resistant finishes, lightweight silks and worsteds, synthetics such as Dacron or Orlon or either of these combined with silk, cotton or wool), you will never need a travel iron.

And finally, dry cleaning. Don't count on it. In many cities of the world the service equals ours. In others it's fairly chancy. Generally foreign cleaners are more expensive and slower than the ones at home; same-day service is almost nonexistent. Sometimes the results can be catastrophic. Unless someone sloshes a pot of coffee down the front of your dress, be prepared to function as your own "spotter," the trade term for the man who takes the stubborn spots out of clothes. So be sure to pack the essential tools for the job: a dry-cleaning fluid or a spot-removing stick, and a clean rag.

As a general rule, the more charmingly rustic the hotel, the fewer the chances of finding highly organized laundry, pressing and dry cleaning facilities. In such places call for the maid. She will wash some of your lingerie and press one or two dresses. If you go to a Japanese inn, a *ryokan*, the room maid takes care of such matters automatically.

There is one attention that first surprises, then delights, Americans. You'll find it wherever European customs prevail—in a small Alpine village chalet, an inn in the Scottish highlands, or a seafront pension in the Balearic Islands. If you place your shoes outside your door when you go to bed, you will find them polished to a gleam in the morning. Like a brownie, the valet or his substitute gathers them up in the night and magically refreshes them. When it comes to leathers, the Europeans have a persuasive touch. See Leather Goods, page 204. Even a tired handbag can be revived by the valet. Be sure to tip for these services when you check out. See Tipping, page 359.

Concierge

YOUR STAUNCHEST ally on the European Continent may well be a gentleman in a blue uniform with gold braid and a crossed-keys insignia on the lapels, who stands at the front desk of your hotel. In France* he's called a concierge, in Yugoslavia he's a *sef recepcije*, and in other countries his name is a slight variation of the word porter: *portiere*, *Portier*, *portero*, *porteiro*, or, quite simply, hall porter. He's a sterling breed found everywhere in Europe, occasionally in South America, never in the Orient or the Caribbean, and rarely in the U.S.A.

* In France the word "concierge" also means the janitor-guardian of an apartment building, but it is not this man who concerns us here.

Whenever you find the concierge, count yourself blessed. He performs a multitude of services that otherwise would keep a team of hardworking elves busy. Yet few American travelers realize his omnipotence or make good use of him, perhaps because his like is so little known in this country. Where the concierge doesn't exist, his functions are divided among a hotel's desk clerk, travel desk, bell captain, doorman, social hostess, and manager! In short, he is the person who understands the petty problems of life in a strange city and knows how to solve them.

He knows, for example, where to find an English-speaking dentist or the best *fraises des bois*. He can wangle tickets to the opera or the bullfight—and tell you where to sit. He will help locate a long-lost friend, make your telephone calls, wrap packages for mailing and arrange to ship your luggage. He's a fountainhead of all sorts of reservations: your next hotel, a rented car, a sightseeing tour. If you have work to do, he'll find you a typewriter, and a typist.

As you gather, he's a marvel—and a man of infinite discretion, so sophisticated that you needn't feel shy about asking him where to have your hair colored or where to buy underwear.

After all this devoted and indispensable service, you will, of course, want to tip a concierge. There is, however, a certain etiquette to be observed in tipping him. Since he is not a servant but a unique combination of secretary, majordomo, ticket booking agent, adviser and confidant, his post carries with it a measure of dignity. Some concierges are nearly as famous as their hotels and may make up to $2,000 a month. Therefore never tip a concierge at the moment he performs a service—though it's not a bad idea to give him a small tip at the beginning "to put him on your side." The main tip is given when you check out—an amount commensurate with the time he's spent on your requests. Usually, $1–$2 is enough for a stay of a few days, $2–$5 for a week, the scale depending on the class of your hotel. In some hotels, shifts of concierges work round the clock, and you may never get to meet the night man. In that case, leave your tip in an envelope marked "concierges" with the man on day duty and ask him to distribute it among his colleagues.

Consuls

THE NORMAL course of a tourist's life need never lead inside an American embassy, legation or consulate. If something abnormal occurs, however, get in touch immediately with a representative of our Foreign Service.

The United States maintains 111 embassies, 2 legations and about 150 consulates abroad. They range in size from the large, impressive Saarinen-designed building on Grosvenor Square in London, which has several hundred local and American employees, to a tiny consular office in Enugu, Nigeria, staffed only by a few Americans. In France, for example we have an embassy in Paris and consulates general, or consulates in Nice, Bordeaux, Lyon, Marseilles, and Strasbourg. Where we maintain an embassy (in capital cities), consular functions are included in the overall operation of the embassy; where we do not, they are handled by a Consulate General, or a Consulate.

A U.S. consular office functions as, among other things, a special sort of welfare and protective agency for American tourists. If you get into trouble, it will see that you receive emergency assistance. If, for example, you are injured or become seriously ill, it will guide you to good medical care. If you lose your money and must reach your family back home, it will act as an intermediary. If your passport expires or needs changing while abroad, it will issue, renew, amend or extend it. If someone in your party dies, it will handle the disposition of the person's possessions and other relevant business. (You will have to pay the costs of some of these services, but charges, as for cables or shipping, are minimal.) If you break the foreign country's laws, the consular office will see that you receive just treatment and have access to legal counsel. Remember, however, that if you violate a law such as exchanging money illegally, you are subject to the penalties of the host country—and the consulate cannot prevent punishment from being meted out to you.

In short, if your life and liberty are threatened, our consulates will come to your rescue. The pursuit of happiness, however, is strictly your own affair. Reservations at hotels and transportation are not a consulate's province.

Don't, for example, expect the consulate to arrange a car and guide, or to straighten out a snarled car-hire situation. If you have to be home the first week of September and find yourself stranded because you didn't book a return reservation early enough, the consul cannot get you a ticket. If you are fleeced by a local shopkeeper, he cannot intervene in your behalf. In crises such as these, count, respectively, on the concierge of your hotel, a travel agent or airline, and the local police as your allies.

There are, however, two circumstances in which you should register with the consulate: first, if you plan to stay in a foreign country for any considerable length of time; and second, if you travel in a truly remote area of the world. In the latter case, call the diplomatic or consular post in each city you visit and tell them where you plan to stay and when you will be leaving.

Couture Houses

IN FRANCE, to be chic is to be worthy of attention; and to be worthy of attention is the business of every Frenchwoman. Since Marie Antoinette decreed that special costumes be worn at her court for different daily occasions, France has had a highly organized interest in fashion unequaled by any other country. Today what its *haute couture* does to the cut of a shoulder, the length of a skirt, the shape of a collar, the set of a sleeve, the position of a waistline becomes hot news that is flashed by wire services around the world.

The affairs of the French fashion industry are governed by an organization known as the Chambre Syndicale de la Couture Parisienne. Its membership of several hundred firms is divided into groups, the most renowned being the small band that makes up the *haute couture*, or high-fashion, contingent.

Their genius governs the "looks" that you, I—and millions of women the world over—wear. For example, about a month to six weeks after Chanel shows her collection in an elegant mirrored mansion on the Rue Cambon, line-for-line copies appear on the streets of New York, Rome, and Montevideo.

The feverish excitement, secrecy, and technical jargon that accompany each collection's opening tend to frighten most women. It's a common misconception that the showings of the *haute couture* are closed to all but a privileged few. This is simply not true. Dior, Givenchy, Cardin, Yves St.-Laurent and their colleagues are as eager for business as the small shop on the corner. They couldn't exist without customers for their clothes. Of course, like the corner shop, they prefer paying customers to browsers, but they recognize that even spectators have an indirect value. Whether or not you can afford to buy from the *haute couture*, you can gain admittance to a showing by following certain steps. And who knows? If you really adore clothes and are willing to forgo a lot of embroidered sweaters, beaded evening bags and such, you might even be able to afford an original.

At the end of January and the first two weeks of February, and the end of July and the first two weeks of August (the exact dates vary from year to year), the showings are closed to all but buyers, accredited press representatives and a handful of distinguished clients whose patronage of a house has been long established. Once the flurry of the openings is over, the collections are shown to private clients. This is usually a month after the opening date when deliveries have been made to buyers.

To arrange a visit, do one of two things: Either write ahead to the house while you are still in the U.S.A., stating your preferred date; or when you arrive in Paris, ask the concierge of your hotel to telephone and make the arrangements. If you fly first class over the Atlantic, your airline can be of assistance, too, for nearly all the transatlantic lines know the *haute couture* and can lend a hand in opening doors. The important thing is that someone—you, the concierge, or the airline—must pave the way so that you are expected at the showing. When you arrive, you will be asked for your passport (this is to make sure that you are not a designer in disguise or a pirate of fashion ideas); you will then be shown to a small gilt chair, with your name on a card tacked to its back. (During the frenzied days of the openings, the spindly gold chairs are trucked from house to house to accommodate the crowds of press people and buyers. The vans stand outside, waiting for each showing to end.)

The clothes are shown every afternoon, Monday through Friday.

At 3 o'clock, the mannequins come gliding into the high-ceilinged showroom, and for the next hour and a half a *vendeuse*, or saleswoman, intones the number and name of each design. If you like one of them, you write the number on a pad that has been handed to you.

When the showing is over, you can ask the *vendeuse* who has been assigned to you to show you the favored dresses at close range. Should you place an order, your *vendeuse* will watch over you and your dress with the greatest solicitude; she will see it through the atelier, supervise the fittings, check the progress of the garment, make certain it's ready for delivery on time.

The price of an original in Paris ranges from $500 to $3,000. (Couture is less in other great European cities.) For this not inconsiderable sum, a daytime dress, coat, suit, or evening dress is made to your measurements after several fittings. It is sewn entirely by hand by women who are superb seamstresses. It is cut from exquisite fabric, which is seamed, stretched, shaped, very nearly molded to your figure. The fit must be perfection itself; the house will take more pains with this than you could ever imagine demanding. And when it is finished, it is a marvel of construction, made by a single worker who has been trained from the start of a collection in the intricacies of that particular garment. (For all the faithful care given to the copies you can get for a fraction of the Paris price in the U.S.A., this all-important matter of fit can never be duplicated.)

If these prices are clearly out of your reach, you should investigate two other parts of a *maison de haute couture:* One, the invariable "back room," which closets a small stock of slightly used originals at slashed prices. If you can fit into them—i.e., if you are as thin and flat as the mannequin—you can pick up a terrific bargain. Two, the boutiques. These range from small areas set aside for perfumes and accessories to separate shops with their own collections of semi-custom-fitted clothes and/or ready-to-wear. (See Boutiques, page 51.)

While the instructions given above refer to the French *haute couture*, they apply in basically the same manner in Spain, Ireland, England and Italy, each of which has a small number of excellent high-fashion houses.

If you buy *couturier* clothes, be sure to list each item on your customs declaration. You won't fool the inspectors by clipping out the labels. Customs men have learned to look at side seams, zippers and the like—they know a good thing when they see it.

Here is a list of the *haute couture* houses in England, Ireland, France, Spain and Italy. Since new names keep coming up, no list can stay up-to-date for long.

ENGLAND—LONDON

John Cavanagh Ltd., *26 Curzon Street, W.1*

Clive Ltd., *17 St. George's Street, W.1*

Hardy Amies Ltd., *14 Savile Row, W.1*

Norman Hartnell Ltd., *26 Bruton Street, W.1*

Lachasse Ltd., *4 Farm Street, W.1*

Mattli Ltd., *63a South Audley Street, S.W.1*

Michael Ltd., *2 Carlos Place, W.1*

Ronald Paterson Ltd., *25 Albemarle Street, W.1*

Worth Ltd., *50 Grosvenor Street, W.1*

IRELAND—DUBLIN

Sybil Connolly, *71 Merrion Square*

Irene Gilbert, *117 St. Stephen's Green*

FRANCE—PARIS

Balenciaga, *10 Ave. George-V*

Pierre Balmain, *44 Rue François-Ier*

Capucci, *4 Rue Cambon*

Pierre Cardin, *118 Rue du Faubourg St.-Honoré*

Castillo, *95 Rue du Faubourg St.-Honoré*

Chanel, *31 Rue Cambon*

Courrèges, *40 Rue Francois Ier*

Christian Dior, *30 Ave. Montaigne*

Louis Feraud, *88 Rue du Faubourg St.-Honoré*

Givenchy, *3 Ave. George-V.*

Grès, *1 Rue de la Paix*

Jacques Griffe, *5 Rue Royale*

Jacques Heim, *15 Ave. Matignon*

Lanvin, *22 Rue du Faubourg St.-Honoré*

Ted Lapidus, *29 Rue Marbeuf*

Guy Laroche, *29 Ave. Montaigne*

Molyneux, *5 Rue Royale*

Jean Patou, *7 Rue St.-Florentin*

Madeleine de Rauch, *37 Rue Jean-Goujon*

Nina Ricci, *20 Rue des Capucines*

Yves St.-Laurent, *30-bis Rue Spontini*

Philippe Venet, *62 Rue François-Ier*

SPAIN—MADRID

Asunción Bastida, *Hermosilla 18*

Elio Berhanyer, *Ayala 124*

EISA (Balenciaga's Spanish firm), *Avenida José Antonio 9*

Herrera y Ollero, *Almirante 9*

Marbel, Jr., *José Ortega y Gasset 25*

Vargas Ochagavia, *Avenida Calvo Sotelo 16*

Pertegaz, *Paseo de la Castellana 54*

Pedro Rodríguez, *Alcalá 54*

ITALY—ROME

Antonelli, *Via Lucullo 24*

Carosa, *Piazza di Spagna 93*

De Barentzen, *Via Gregoriana 5*

Fabiani, *Via Barberini 36*

Fontana Sorelle, *Via San Sebastianello 6*

Forquet, *Via Condotti 9*

Galitzine, *Via Veneto 155*

Gattinoni, *Via Toscana 1*

Schuberth, *Via XX Settembre 4*

Valentino, *Via Gregoriana 54*

ITALY—FLORENCE

Battistoni, *Via Vacchereccia 6R*

Palloni, *Lungarno Vespucci 2*

Pucci, *Palazzo Pucci, Via dei Pucci 64*

If you need further help on the spot, get in touch with these organizations: in London, the Incorporated Society of London Fashion

Designers, 315 Regent Street, W.1; in Paris, Chambre Syndicale de la Mode Parisienne, 102 Rue du Faubourg St.-Honoré; in Rome, Comitato Nazionale della Moda Italiana, Piazzi della Repubblica 59; and Centro Romano Alta Moda Italiana, Via Torino 107; in Florence, Centro di Firenze per la Moda Italiana, Via Tornabuoni 1.

Credit Plans

EVEN IF you are low in cash, you can take off for any part of the world by saying "Charge it, please" and deferring payment for your flight, hotels, meals, even sightseeing, in one of several ways. These days, it doesn't take ready money to travel. It just takes a good credit rating or a nationally recognized, general-purpose credit card.

One plan is lightheartedly known as "Fly Now, Pay Later," and here's how it works: You apply for a round-trip ticket or a package tour through your travel agent or carrier. Either one will process your application for credit, which usually clears in about 24 hours or less. You pay 10 per cent of the total cost and the rest in monthly installments for 3, 6, 12, 18, or 24 months. While the loan is made through the travel agent or carrier, the payments go back to a bank or finance company. (Of course, you can also take out a loan for travel *directly* from your bank as you might for an antique table, caps on your teeth, or a fur coat. Doing it through an agent or carrier simply saves you one step.) If, for example, you applied for a loan of $600 to cover a 3-week trip to five European countries, to be repaid in 12 months, each monthly payment would amount to $52.25. Interest on the entire amount would be about $27. Do shop around, however, for the best interest rates. They can vary from airline to airline; there are also differences between banks and airlines.

Other credit plans involve the use of credit cards. American Express cards, which can be used to rent a car, or charge meals, accommodations, clothing and sightseeing, now insure instant credit for air transportation at almost any travel agency or ticket counter in the country. This plan, sponsored by the American Express Company in connection with the major airlines, is called "Sign and Fly," and all you need is your Amex card and a fountain pen. There is no down payment; you simply put your name on the dotted line and travel. You pay for the ticket later in one of two ways. On the "current" basis, the total cost is billed on your next regular monthly Amex bill, and there is, of course, no service charge. On the "deferred" basis, you pay over a period of 3, 6, 9 or 12 months at low credit rates: 1 percent a month on the unpaid balance. On a $100 ticket, you would pay $2 over a period of 3 months; $3.50 over a period of 6 months; $5 over a period of 9 months; $6 over a period of 12 months. American Express also has a program called "Sign and Travel" which allows you to charge any of its escorted tours, through their offices or your travel agent.

Another credit card which is honored by many airlines and steamship lines is Bank Americard, issued by the Bank of America. On the bank's Travel Loan-Travel Goal program, you can apply for a direct, immediate loan (Travel Loan), or a loan which goes into operation several months before your trip (Travel Goal). On the latter, you deposit a certain amount into a savings account at the bank each month up until your departure; then you withdraw it and make a down payment on the trip. The balance of the cost is added to it in the form of a loan. Loans are made for any reasonable amount you will need, not just for transportation alone, and the interest rate, if you extend payments, is 1½ per cent on the outstanding balance each month (with a minimum of $10). If you repay the full amount within 25 days of billing, there is no service charge. Several airlines and railroads, among them Air Canada and the Canadian National Railways, have their own credit cards, for travel on their lines.

You can also use Diners' Club, Carte Blanche, Bank of Hawaii, Mellon Bank or Citizens and Southern National Bank of Atlanta cards for "quick cash." Whichever one you finally use puts upon you, naturally, the responsibility of regarding it as cash. Make sure you get your card back every time you use it.

Check each charge slip before you sign it, and see that the total is written plainly in the "total" space. Save your receipts and double-check your monthly statements; even machines make errors. Report a lost or stolen card immediately, in writing, to the issuing company, and if you receive an unsolicited credit card, and are not going to use it, tear it up immediately or send it back to the company.

Most plans provide approximately the same arrangements: credit for 30 days with no interest charged or a time payment plan up to 2 years, at nominal interest rates. It's interesting to know, too, that if your husband has a Universal Air Travel Plan card or any other good general purpose credit card that can be used as a credit reference, Pan American Airways will book your transportation—and bill you later. And Eastern Airlines has just announced "Charge-a-Trip," a credit plan which enables you to book your air ticket or tour by telephone, requires no down payment and allows you up to 24 months to pay for your trip.

Since a trip, unlike the aforementioned fur coat, is not a tangible possession, only you can decide whether you have the temperament to pay for it cheerfully after the pleasures have become memories. You might well be the sort of person who would prefer to save now and go later. It's good to know, however, that should the chance, temptation or mood strike, you can fly from these shores by depositing as little as $12, the down payment on a trip to Bermuda, by flashing your credit card, or merely by picking up the telephone and charging it to your account.

Currency

EVEN IF you were a dud in mathematics as a schoolgirl, you needn't be worried about handling the coin of other realms. The moment you find yourself paying for something in a foreign currency is no time to pretend to be anything other than what you are: a newcomer to the country. No matter how self-reliant you may be, reach for a currency-converter (it should be sitting in the top of your handbag) and sail through the transaction with precise knowledge of what you are spending. (The alternative is to carry around an abacus or an adding machine.)

If yours is a rather typical itinerary taking in four European countries in 3 weeks, you will be handling about 28 different coins and about 25 different bills. Don't expect to learn the exact value of each one instantly, or even by the end of your visit. If you are blessed with the sort of mind that works well with fractions and conversion tables, so much the better—but this talent is not essential. Either buy a converter at your local book or luggage store or ask the airline that will be whisking you across the Atlantic for one. Nearly all major airlines give them away, free.

Of course, if you plan to visit only one country or, perhaps, take a 2-week vacation in Jamaica or Mexico, you can memorize the currency down to the last shilling and peso—and you should.

To feel comfortable with foreign money quickly, memorize two items: the coin or bill that "works" like our quarter (you'll need it to tip as you go) and the coin or bill that equals our dollar, so that you have a clear idea of how much things cost. If on the plane or boat, you memorize the basic tipping unit for porters in the first country you'll hit—100 lire in Italy, for example—your entry can be smooth and untroubled. The rest can come later. (See Tipping, page 359.) This "quarter rule" does not mean that every country has a coin or bill that exactly equals 25 cents. It does mean that everywhere you go there is a denomination that will nearly always do the *work* of a quarter (such as a shilling in Britain, which is actually worth 14 cents, a franc in France, worth 20 cents, and a 5-drachma coin in Greece, worth 17 cents), and it should be used in comparable ways.

The price of currency fluctuates just like that of any other commodity; sometimes you can save some money by buying foreign currencies in the U.S.A. This is not true, however, in the case of European currencies, which are so stable that they fluctuate hardly at all. In the Far East and Africa, money markets are far less firm and you may well be able to get a rupee for a lot less in New York than in Pakistan. But before rushing out to buy fistfuls of strange colored money, find out how *much* currency each country will allow you to bring in. Only 80 of those rupees, or $12, can be legally taken into Pakistan, so what's the point? With Japan, the story is different; you can save by buying yen here—and there are no restrictions. In Europe, Austria, Belgium, Denmark, France, Great Britain, Italy, Portugal, Switzerland and West Germany impose no limits. The same is true of most Central and South American countries. On the other hand, you are not allowed to take a ruble into Russia or a rupee into India, and can bring only 100 pounds ($35) into Israel and 2,000 drachmai ($65) into Greece. Travelers to Israel, India and the United Arab Republic can buy currency at the American Embassy. You receive the official rate of exchange and because the Embassy draws on counterpart funds, your dollars remain in U.S.A. hands. The best source of advice in these matters is your bank or a foreign exchange company like Perera Company, Inc. in New York.

Regardless of the legal limits on the legal tender you can take across the borders, most of your money should be in travelers checks. (See Travelers Checks, page 386.) You may lose a tiny amount in the foreign exchange, but you will more than make it up in peace of mind.

The rest should be a nominal amount in $1 and $5 bills, which are a blessing when you are leaving a country and need just small bits of money for things like the last day's breakfast, a cup of coffee at the airport or airport departure taxes. Travelers checks save you from getting stuck with a big bundle of foreign currency and also provide the change you'll need when you land in the U.S.A. again. On a 3-week trip to Europe, you might take about $35 in $1 bills, $75 in $5 and $10 bills and the rest in travelers checks, to avoid ending up with too much change in another currency. Don't expect to use personal checks. They are generally extremely hard to cash abroad.

Wherever you travel, add one other item: an envelope filled with $10 worth of each foreign country's currency (if it's allowed).

These envelopes, prepacked by foreign currency firms, are available for about 15 countries. They come in $10, $20 and $50 amounts and can be bought at your bank or at a company like Perera Company which has two offices in New York City, two at John F. Kennedy International Airport, and another in Miami. If you write or go to their main office, at 29 Broadway, New York, New York 10006, or their affiliate at 636 Fifth Avenue, New York, New York 10020, they will assemble these packets to suit your itinerary. The average charge for this service is 75 cents on $10 envelopes; $1 on $20; and $1.50 on $50. The packets are enormously useful, giving you just enough small cash for the porters and bus at the airport and the porters at your hotel. While every major air terminal and seaport has a bank or currency exchange bureau, it's a relief to avoid the chore of changing money when you arrive tired in a strange country and still have immigration, customs and transportation to cope with. Once at your hotel, the concierge will exchange money, as will the local bank and Thomas Cook and American Express offices.

When you return, Perera Company's or the First National City Bank's counters at Kennedy Airport will convert most of your foreign change, except for the really small amounts like centimes and pennies. You can throw them into the collection box for a worthy charity which is stationed at the end of Kennedy's Custom Hall (or give them to your favorite small boy). By all means, avoid leaving any foreign country with a sizable chunk of its currency, for, with the exception of Swiss francs, you can't get back the same number of dollars you spend for them.

Three final words: Don't think it's cute or feminine to be helpless about money when you're in a foreign country. It's maddening to see a woman stick out a palmful of money when she wants to tip and say

"Help yourself." The money she is treating so cavalierly is not just so many pretty coins and colored pieces of paper—it means as much to another national as dollars mean to her. No one will admire you or the U.S.A. for seeming to handle francs, yen and pesos as though they had little value.

Don't get involved with black market transactions. Black markets flourish where currencies are weak, and they are a thoroughly risky business. Resist the temptation, because you invariably end up victimized; and since you've done something illegal, you'll get no protection from the police.

Finally, remember that if you run out of money, banks abroad will cable your own bank for funds—merely for the cost of the cable.

Customs

THE CUSTOMS inspector you meet today is a professional descendant of the Roman *portitor* who levied duties and tolls nearly two thousand years ago. In Britain he actually stood on the very site of the present London Custom House. In our own country, the second act of the First Congress on July 4, 1789, provided for levying duties on merchandise imported into the U.S.A.; the fifth act, passed four weeks later, laid the basis for the U.S. Customs Service.

At every border in the world you will find customs officials doing their ancient jobs: those of protecting their countries from floods of unwanted goods or from deprivation of rightful goods and duties. You will also find that they are decent, efficient, if sometimes harried, men, as little interested in having a fuss with you (unless you have done something wrong) as you with them. These days foreign customs officials are so lenient with American tourists that you can easily make a 6-week, 8-country tour of Europe without opening your luggage once. On the other hand, since you are legally accountable to customs officials for the goods you carry, you should know the rules to avoid unnecessary complications.

Let's start with the customs regulations of the U.S.A., the all-important ones you face on your return from a trip.

1. Once every 31 days, any resident of the U.S.A. may bring back articles valued up to $100 free of duty. Their value is determined by the fair retail price of each item in the country where it was obtained. The articles must have been acquired abroad for her personal or household use, and must be carried back by her as baggage on her return (except for the under-$10 gifts sent to others; see point 8). The word "acquired" is an important one here, for besides purchases it includes any gifts given to you by a friend or even by your husband *en route.* If you buy a suit in Paris at the beginning of your trip and wear it thin while you're doing the Continent, it nevertheless counts as an acquisition. If you take a watch abroad to have it repaired, the repairs are dutiable. In brief, anything added to the value of goods with which you started out must be declared.

There is one exception to the $100 limit. If you return from United States possessions—the American Virgin Islands, American Samoa, or Guam—and any of these islands is included in your itinerary, you are allowed to bring back an additional $100 in merchandise, duty free, or a total of $200. This total, however, cannot include more than $100 worth of goods acquired elsewhere than these islands. Thus, for example, if you travel to several Caribbean islands and end your trip in the American Virgin Islands, the value of the goods you have purchased before you reach St. Thomas cannot add up to more than $100 if they are to enter your home port within your duty-free exemption limits.

2. Every member of your family who lives at the same address and makes the trip with you is entitled to the $100 exemption, including your six-months-old baby. If you, your husband, mother-in-law, three-year-old son and infant daughter travel together, your family's total allowance is $500. Only one member of the family need make the declaration for the whole group.

3. To qualify for the exemption, you must have been out of the country for at least 48 hours, unless you traveled in Mexico or the U.S. Virgin Islands, where trips do not require a minimum absence. If you are the rare one who weekends in Europe and are out of the country less than 48 hours, you're limited to $10 in duty-free purchases.

4. To come in free of duty, an item must be purchased only incidentally—you must not have made the trip just to buy it. As a rule, if you order something before you go, pick it up while abroad, and bring it back with you, the customs inspector has the responsibility to ask for a duty payment.

5. Within your $100 exemption you can bring back, tax free and

duty free, a quart of liquor if you are twenty-one or over and 100 cigars. (There's no limit on cigarettes.) Again, if you are returning from the American Virgin Islands, American Samoa, or Guam, and any one of these islands is any one of your stops, you may bring back a gallon rather than a quart of liquor (not more than one quart of this quota may be acquired elsewhere than in these islands). Gallon or quart size, your liquor must accompany you. It is important to remember that if yours is not a "wet" state, the customs officer, co-operating with the state, will not release the liquor to you.

6. If you take along foreign-made valuables such as watch, camera, binoculars or professional books, register them with customs before you leave or carry a bill of sale or insurance papers. This is to prove that they were not bought on your journey and are therefore not subject to duty on your return.

7. Watch out for "swing back" trips (i.e., ones that take you back into U.S.A. territory in the midst of a trip), and consult the nearest customs officer about your rights. An example of a "swing back" trip would be one that took you from Mexico to Jamaica via San Juan. San Juan, sharing common customs formalities with the U.S.A., will require your going through the examination there. On your return to home port you may get exemptions only on the purchases you made in Mexico, not in Jamaica.

8. To ease your exemptions and luggage weight, mail gifts home. If they are valued at $10 retail or less, they are free of duty and need not be listed on your customs declaration, which can be kept for the things you buy for yourself. The packages should be sent via International Parcel Post and must be clearly marked "Gift Enclosed— Value under $10." You can send a stream of ties, scarves, gloves, etc., but you cannot send gifts of alcoholic beverages or tobacco. Perfume may be sent as a gift if the total value of the package is not more than $1. Also, you can mail gifts to as many people as you like, and over a period of time you can mail more than one gift to any one person. You must, however, be certain that no more than one gift is received by any one person on one day. If your addressee does receive more than one $10 gift in one day, he will have to pay customs duty. Each package must contain a card or note from the donor as evidence that it is a bona fide gift.

At this writing, the Bureau of Customs, irritated at the large number of abuses of the $10 evaluation rule, is cracking down on violations. If a gift is found to be valued at more than $10, penalties will be levied against the traveler, and falsely labeled or undervalued packages will be confiscated. Don't let a shopkeeper persuade you to split one $50 shipment meant for your use into five $10 ones which are then mailed to five innocent friends.

9. On your return to the U.S.A., you must go through customs inspection at your port of entry. (In Nassau, Bermuda, Winnipeg, Montreal, and Toronto you can go through customs inspection before you leave and have nothing more to do when you arrive in the U.S.A.) While still on the aircraft or ship, you will receive a form which asks for your name, nationality, passport or tourist card number, address, flight or voyage number, and place of embarkation. All other information such as the description of your purchases can in most instances be given orally to the inspector.

If you have acquired an automobile abroad, you may use all or part of your exemption toward its value if it accompanies you.

Since the customs inspector is interested chiefly in two things, articles purchased and prices, make his job—and your return—easy, by keeping them in one place. Pack all your parcels either in a single bag or in one spot in your suitcase. Clip all your receipts together or put them into one envelope, along with a list of purchases. Then the inspector need only look at your declaration sheet, check your items, and wave you through. Declare the price you paid for new merchandise or repairs. Give him a fair estimate of any gifts you have received—and tell him if you are bringing in something at someone else's request or if you have an article to be used in your business. Don't guess or fudge on what anything is worth. U.S. Customs inspectors know just what things cost all over the world. They can recognize the difference between a custom-made Dior suit and one bought at Dior's boutique. They know whether a porcelain plate is a piece of eighteenth-century Sèvres or a nineteenth-century imitation. They know the difference between an Hermès handbag and its cheap "knock-off." The process of trying to outwit our customs officials will cost you dearer than you may imagine—as it did 45,000 otherwise respectable citizens in a recent year. At the least, you will have to pay a fine equal to the price you would pay for the article in the U.S.A., plus its price once again if you want to keep it. A suit which costs you $150 in London, on which you might have to pay $31.50 in duty, can end up costing you $550. Also, just about anything you buy abroad and bring in with an intention to sell cannot be passed duty free under your personal exemption.

What articles are free of any duty? Typewriters, signed original paintings, drawings and sculptures regardless of date, are admitted free (copies are not), so are etchings, engravings and woodcuts, if they are the artist's proofs. Antiques dated before 1830 are also admitted duty free, except for rugs and carpets, which must predate 1701, and violins, violas and cellos, which must have been made before 1801. Books more than twenty years old are admitted free of duty. Antique furniture, however, if it is worth more than your exemption, must be examined at any of the major ports of entry. Be sure you have a certificate or a letter guaranteeing antiquity from your dealer.

There are some articles on which our government casts a jaundiced eye, and they are either completely forbidden in this country or so restricted that you will need special permission to bring them in. Here are some examples:

1) Any product suspected of being of Red Chinese, North Korean, North Vietnamese or Cuban origin may not be brought into the U.S.A. If you are tempted by a teakwood chest in Hong Kong, you don't stand a chance of getting it through customs unless you have a Certificate of Origin, issued by the Hong Kong government. This costs about 90 cents and covers purchases valued up to $250 made at the same store. Customs is very severe about enforcing this rule. You must have paper proof that a product was not made in those countries. A mere sales slip or the label of a shop is not enough. Without a Certificate of Origin, your purchase will be confiscated by customs.

2) Avoid bringing back fruits, vegetables, plants, cuttings, seeds and unprocessed plant products. Customs, acting for the U.S. Department of Agriculture, won't let them through, as a rule, since one bug on a small leaf can cause huge damage to our plant life. If you do want to bring in a plant, you can sometimes make arrangements in advance by writing to the Import and Permit Section, Plant Quarantine Division, 209 River Street, Hoboken, New Jersey 07030. Cured and cooked meats are also forbidden.

3) Bringing in a pet is subject to the regulations of the Public Health Service, Department of Health, Education and Welfare. Write to the Division of Foreign Quarantine, U.S. Public Health Service, Silver Springs, Maryland 20910, or to the nearest Public Health Service quarantine officer if you wish further information.

4) There is a limit on some registered trademarked items (watches, cameras, musical instruments, tape recorders, lenses, optical goods and the like) and on certain well-known brands of perfume. Legally, these items cannot be brought into the U.S.A. at all, or else in limited amounts, without the consent of the trademark owner. Check with the nearest Customs Office before leaving the U.S.A., so you

will know what's in store for you; there is a pamphlet available which lists these trademarks.

If you want to go on a buying spree while abroad, remember that there is no limit to the amount of merchandise a returning citizen may bring in. Duties range from 4 per cent to 55 per cent on popular tourist items. Even after the Bureau of Customs has collected its due, you may still have a bargain. A common misconception is that expensive items are always charged with high duty and inexpensive one's with low. This isn't always so. Customs regulations require inspectors to apply your exemption to your highest-duty articles and charge duty on the merchandise with the lowest rates. A camera priced at $260 in a free port would cost $39 in duty—figuring 15 per cent duty—and sell for about $485 in the U.S.A.

The International Department of the AAA has issued a list of U.S. Customs duties on articles of special interest to American tourists. Use the following AAA list only as a rough guide, since there are numerous exceptions and duty rates change frequently. The rates quoted are "ad valorem," or based on invoiced value.

ARTICLE	DUTY LEVIED, IN PER CENT OF ITS COST
Alcohol: spirits (whiskey, gin, etc.)	$.85 to $5.00 per gallon, plus $10.50 per gallon Internal Revenue tax
Alcohol: wines, champagnes	less than spirits—increases with higher alcoholic content
Automobiles, new or used	6½
Books, of foreign authorship	3 (free if printed in foreign language or more than 20 years old)
Cameras	15, unless the lens is the camera's chief value, in which case duty goes up to 25 per cent.
Chinaware, bone	35
Cigarette lighters	30 to 50
Dolls	35
Embroidered or appliquéd cloth or garments	42½ to 45
Furniture, chief value in wood:	
chairs	17
other	10½
Garments—cotton:	
coats (outerwear)	10
shirts	25
most others (plain)	20
Garments—silk: all wearing apparel	32½

Garments—wool:

coats	21
jackets, suits	21
dresses, skirts	21
sweaters (incl. cashmere)	20 (plus 37½ cents per lb. of net weight)

* Jewelry:

gold, platinum, silver	24
with gold, platinum or silver portion valued at over $1.50	24
pearls, if not strung or temporarily strung, i.e., no clasp, no knots between pearls	3 to 5
pearls, strung	55
most other—necklaces, brooches, rings, etc.	55

Lace—shawls, scarves	42½

Leather goods:

belts	17½
handbags of reptile leather	17½
handbags of other leathers	20
luggage	same as handbags
tobacco pouches	16
wallets, key cases, coin purses of reptile leather	14
wallets, key cases, coin purses of other leathers	16

Linen handkerchiefs (plain)	6½ to 24
Linen sheets, pillow cases (plain)	8½
Perfume—containing alcohol	16 cents per lb. plus 15 per cent

Toys:

metal	21
mechanical	44
other	35

Watches (depending on movement and case):

movement:	
less than 18 jewels	up to $3.85
18 jewels or over	$10.75
case:	
base metal	20
gold, platinum, ornamental, jeweled	30
Watches with special properties (e.g., self-winding)	subject to additional duty

* *Duty on unset stones ranges from 5 to 10 per cent, whereas duty on set stones runs as high as 55 per cent.*

So far, we have been talking about U.S. Customs. Abroad, you will find most customs men are lenient with American tourists. They will give your luggage a cursory examination—indeed, sometimes they only spot-check about one out of every ten pieces coming in. In Britain there is no written baggage declaration. I have never had a bag opened in the dozens of trips I have made there.

As a temporary visitor anywhere, you are allowed to bring in—and take out—the usual accouterments of a traveler: clothing, personal cosmetics and toiletries, cameras, film (in reasonable amounts), radio, typewriter, sports equipment, baby carriage, bicycle, musical instrument, binoculars and the like, plus several hundred dollars' worth of purchases in that country. (For the limitations on antiques and national treasures see Antique Shops, page 5.) There *are* limitations on the cigarettes, tobacco, alcoholic beverages and perfumes that you may take in. While these figures vary from country to country and should be checked in terms of your destination before you start, you are generally allowed 400 cigarettes, or 100 cigars, 1 bottle of perfume, 2 bottles of liquor or wine and a pound of tobacco. (See Cigarettes and Matches, page 78.)

Should you plan to take gifts to a country's nationals, see Gifts to Take Abroad, page 148, for the regulations and price limitations. If you are carrying heavily taxable items bought in one country but not to be used in another, ask the customs officers if you can leave them in bond at the airport or pier until you leave.

And finally, follow these hints for making all customs procedures easy:

1. Get a sales slip or receipt for everything you buy abroad.

2. Never accept a shopkeeper's offer of a false invoice. A fraudulent bill of sale is one of the most serious customs violations. Also, a shopkeeper who will offer a fraudulent bill will often turn informer and tell customs about your would-be smuggling for a 25 per cent reward.

3. Keep a running record of all the articles you acquire while you're abroad. Don't wait until the last minute to make your list.

4. If you leave a foreign country through a duty-free port, you will probably be tempted into last-minute purchases. Save some of your $100 exemption for them. (See Duty-Free Shopping, page 117.)

5. There are three ways to ship goods to the U.S.A.: mail, express (including air freight) and sea freight. The least expensive and troublesome of the three is by mail (including parcel post, provided your package meets the requirements of the exporting country as to weight, size and measurement). Be firm with the store about its sending your package via mail. If it is sent by freight or express, it must

be handled by a licensed customs broker and his fees and commissions can spiral. (Occasionally, an unscrupulous storekeeper will promise to send the goods by mail and ask you to pay for postage. Then, after you have left, he will pocket the postage money and send the package by freight, so that you have to pay charges when it arrives.) As much as possible, carry purchases yourself; or put the matter into the hands of a shipping agency like American Express or ask your concierge to help you.

6. Most customs officials believe you to be innocent of mischief unless you give them reason to believe otherwise. Don't be impatient or hasty, and have all your papers in order. Treat the inspector as the man he is—a government official anxious to do his job easily, pleasantly. If you do, things will be easy and pleasant for you too.

Department Stores

YOU MAY GO abroad armed with the names of dozens of "wonderful little shops," but it's unlikely that anyone will have drawn you aside to confide the name of a department store. Perhaps because it's hard to be cozy and confidential about a behemoth, or because department store shopping seems so "American," the names of the world's big department stores are not as likely to be breathlessly passed from friend to friend as are those of small boutiques. A building that covers a floor area of 60 acres (Myer in Melbourne), or is over 250 years old (Fortnum and Mason in London), or looks like a Victorian convention hall (Nordiska Kompaniet, or NK, in Stockholm), would seem to speak for itself.

So, with a very few exceptions, foreign department stores go largely unsung. Yet continuity—of the sort that makes it possible to buy tea from the grocer who shipped it over for the Boston Tea Party in 1773 —endows many of the stores around the world with the grandeur of tradition and a highly developed sense of service. The great foreign stores, with their vaulted ceilings and splendid wrought-iron stair-cases, have so entwined themselves around the life and needs of their cities and countries that their complex services are much more highly developed than those of some of their American counterparts.

Since many travelers tend to bypass these splendid giants, which elicit the same intense loyalty from local women as do our Macy's or Marshall Field, it's worth noting the shopping advantages they offer. Here are a few:

As in our own large stores, there are interpreters to guide you through the departments.

Stocks are ample; having them under one roof makes it easy for you to tick off your errands efficiently. Usually, they carry products from all the different regions of their country, making it unnecessary to buy a set of pottery dishes in Lyon, carry it to Nice and then Paris, as I once did. There's a good chance that I would have found the same set in a Paris department store.

Many stores, especially those in Scandinavia, have constant exhibitions of the best of their country's design, and are, to an extent, patrons of its art. NK in Stockholm is a case in point. Its giant initials stand out on the skyline. It is the merchandising hub of the city, indeed, the country, and its products are in every Swedish home. The store is so deeply involved in Swedish design that it owns its own furniture factory, maintains its own fabric studio, and sponsors competitions for young designers. It holds first-rate art shows and concerts. It is a home away from home for all Swedish women—and 9 out of 10 women visitors who are in Stockholm for more than a day come to shop here.

It is easy to ship goods home from a department store. Most stores will insure your package and assume responsibility for its arriving in good condition, and will replace it in case of loss or damage, a highly important and comforting fact if you are sending home dozens of glasses or a stock of china. The stores usually have an export department which will make all arrangements. If you buy something in a store in a small town or even in a tiny shop in the capital, they will wrap it up casually, perhaps in a sheet of newspaper, lightly tied with string; whereas a department store will pack goods securely, making them less of a nuisance to handle as you travel.

Many stores, besides being generally excellent, have particularly notable departments: The antiques departments of Takashimaya in Tokyo and Au Printemps in Paris are good places for finding bibelots at fair prices. In Helsinki, Stockmann's Academic Bookstore is one of the largest in the world and has hundreds of titles in English. In London, Fortnum and Mason—which started life as a grocery shop (it helped to feed Wellington's hungry officers, Florence Nightingale's soldiers in the Crimea and homesick troops in India)—still has a marvelous grocery department with food from all over the world and shop assistants who wear striped trousers and morning coats. Harrod's in London even has a zoo, and there is the apocryphal story which illustrates the vast range of its stocks and the imperturbability of its salespeople: A woman tourist approached a salesman and said, "I want to buy an elephant." Without twitching a muscle he asked, "African or Indian?"

Most of the stores will deliver purchases to your hotel the same day without charge; many will also accept credit cards from the Diners' Club and/or American Express. In the department stores in Yugoslavia and France, you receive a discount of 20 per cent if you pay in travelers checks. This is also true in France if your purchases are delivered to your airplane or ship as individual luggage. There is an additional discount of 20 per cent on certain brands of perfume in France, bringing the total to 40 per cent. The tourist desk on the main floor of every Paris department store will tell you the brand names of the perfumes it sells. Many stores will also accept your personal check if you have sufficient identification. In Oslo, Steen and Strøm will ship all your purchases home and, of course, give you a discount of 10 per cent, which the government allows only on articles shipped out of the country.

All the stores have good, comfortable restaurants for luncheon or tea, some of a certain distinction. Fortnum's Fountain in London, for example—which is open until 11 P.M. although the rest of the store closes at 5:30—is chic among Londoners for after-theater supper; at Switzer's in Dublin, morning coffee at 11 at the Downstairs Café is a popular ritual. Many stores have roof terraces where you can dine with a wonderful view of the city: From NK in Stockholm there's a sweeping vista of islands and waterways; from Galeries Lafayette in Paris you can see Sacré-Coeur; and from the roof garden of Ka-De-We in Berlin, the city spreads below. Many stores also have departments which will send you *hors d'oeuvre* for 6 or handle a sit-down dinner for 1,600. If you want to do any entertaining but feel unsure of how to go about it abroad, call on a local department store to take over the problem.

What sort of shopping, then, should you do at a department store?

In general, look for the best-known indigenous products of a country: cashmere sweaters in Britain, linens in Ireland, kitchen equipment in France. In Paris's Samaritaine, for example, browse among the household wares and pick up oyster and snail dishes, salad baskets, wine racks and hundreds of other efficient gadgets that usually enliven a French kitchen.

Be on the lookout for line-for-line copies of Paris fashions now carried in most large stores, often inexpensively. In Oslo's Steen and Strøm, for example, you can have a French original copied and custom-made to your measurements at prices far lower than in the U.S.A.

Watch for inexpensive chic ready-to-wear. Some countries, notably Britain, have made such strides in this area in the last six or seven years that American stores now import clothes with the "London look." In London itself, go to the specialty store, Woollands', whose "21" shop is where chic young English women spend their pounds. Also, look in on any one of the phenomenal Marks and Spencer stores, by strict definition *not* department stores, but a chain of nearly 250 shops throughout Britain where it has become absolutely *de rigueur* to buy some of one's clothes. The Duchess of Windsor shops there, as do Princess Grace of Monaco and Princess Alexandra, along with secretaries and housewives. The lowest price is 30 cents for children's underwear, the highest $22.50 for a wool suit. There are no fitting rooms, you search for what you want on counters, but the merchandise is absolutely the best of its kind at the price, for it's quality-controlled down to the number of stitches to the inch. About 10,000,000 customers, or roughly a fifth of Britain's population, go through the stores every week.

You will also find corners in department stores stocked with handsome imports. If your itinerary will not take you to Florence and you crave some of its leather goods, you can probably find them in a Paris store. Don't buy at a second-string department store. If a city doesn't have distinguished big department stores—Athens, for example, doesn't—then stick to specialty shops and boutiques.

How to use a department store:

Go first to the information desk and ask for a directory and an interpreter or special shopper, if you think language will be a problem. The majority of salespeople speak some English. The Magasin du Nord in Copenhagen, for example, gives special courses for its salespeople. Check your hat, coat and parcels; ask for the outstanding departments and head for them; ask also about current sales and exhibitions. Plan on having luncheon or tea in the store. Pay a visit to the children's department and to the grocery department. Think of a department store, especially one abroad, as a local fair. Much goes on in a busy store. Being where local women are gives you a chance to catch a glimpse of their lives—mothers outfitting their children for school, newlyweds picking furniture for their first apartment, young married working women on their lunch hour buying dinner groceries. Everywhere, women's lives are caught up inextricably with department stores, and there's no better place to see them in action.

Watch the local department store hours, which differ from country to country or district to district within a country. In Amsterdam and Paris, for example, they are closed Monday morning; in Copenhagen, Saturday afternoon.

And finally, learn what special services are available. You will find that stores have booking offices for theater tickets; banks; post offices; nurseries; travel agencies. There are information bureaus to tell you where to stay, to eat, to shop, and what sights to see. There are good beauty salons and machines where you can have photography and photoprinting done. If your heels need lifts, you can have them replaced in minutes; if something needs dry cleaning, the stores have facilities. In Finland, when your car breaks down, Stockmann, the largest department store in Helsinki, will repair it for you or sell you a new one. Myer's in Melbourne, Australia, will take care of your child if you want to park him while you have a permanent wave. It also offers a 24-hour laundry service for shirts and rents skis and boats.

As for Harrod's in London, no store in the world has departments and services that can compare in number and variety with those of this hushed, genteel institution. Its cable address is Everything, London, which puts the case succinctly. The store will arrange a lovely wedding, a child's christening, or even a funeral, always in the most discreet manner. It will auction your goods and chattels, and find a school for your child. Its telephone service works around the clock. If a craving for *fraises des bois* strikes you at two in the morning, it will send some round to your hotel, right away. Like Fortnum and Mason, it started out as a grocery store, and its grocery and meat department is one of the wonders of London. There are close to 250 varieties of cheese, 15 kinds of bread, and hundreds of cuts of meat. The pet shop has night monkeys, squirrels, bush babies, snakes and dingoes in stock and will special-order lions, rhinoceroses or any other animal except a protected creature such as a Kiwi. Like the duck that looks so calm and dignified above the water although it is paddling furiously all the time underneath, the atmosphere of Harrod's is calm, unruffled, carpeted and quiet. The salesclerks address everyone as Sir or Madame, to avoid difficulties in protocol in case they happen to be

serving a maharani or a member of European royalty. If you are
London, go to Harrod's to see what a velvety experience shoppin
can be.

Dieting

IF YOU don't want to come home from a trip looking like
a pigeon—pleasantly rounded—you must give a little thought to how
quickly calories can pile up *en voyage*. Don't be put off by the purists
who scoff, "A trip is no time to count calories!" They are usually
either thin to start with or have given up the struggle against weight.
Of course, it isn't the time for dieting to *lose* weight. But if your
weight rises and falls with your caloric intake as a normal person's
does, you must be cautious of fettucini, soufflés and baklava, if only
to come out even. (I am still haunted by the memory of the awful
swiftness with which I added 15 pounds on my first trip abroad, and
the painful slowness with which I took them off at home.)

The object of "dieting" while traveling is simply to preserve,
roughly, the same measurements as those with which you started.
You can, and will, sin a lot of the time—it is sheer folly to miss the
great dishes of the world—but you must also be sensible, if only to
avert shock when you weigh in at home.

You could, of course, diet like mad a few weeks before your departure and then set off happily with the knowledge that if you
gained 5 or 10 pounds, your clothes would still fit. If you can't manage this ploy, here are a few rules of thumb to make weight-watching
and high living mutually compatible.

1. Every national cuisine has great dishes of a low caloric content
as well as those that are fattening. Learn to strike a balance between
the two at each meal, or during each day. Allow yourself not more
than one rich dish a day, and fill out your meals with those that are
not calorie-loaded. In France, for example, if you order saddle of
veal Prince Orloff (veal, foie gras and truffles) and *vacherin* (ice
cream, meringue, crème Chantilly and fruit) at luncheon, have a
simple *entrecôte* or omelet for dinner. Alternate dishes made with

villainous cream sauces, like *gratin de homard neuburg* and *poularde normande*, with such nonlethal national specialties as *pot-au-feu*, *petite marmite*, *coq-au-vin*, *artichaut vinaigrette*, *asperges*, and the like. In Italy eat the baby lamb, mushrooms, cheese, and fruit, but pass up the fettucini and *zuppa inglese*.

In Britain feed up on the roast beef, avoid potatoes in all their variety, and go easy on the Yorkshire pudding as well as the thick cream that is poured over fruits. Britain, incidentally, can be harder on the waistline than France. French food is so rich and sauce-filled that it demands discretion; English cuisine is so undramatic, the tea table so innocently loaded with apple cakes and clotted cream, the country air so intoxicating, that you can arrive home pounds heavier with utter, unsuspecting ease. Japan, to skip over the Continent, presents few worries. Its cooking has a minimum of sauces, and its specialties such as sashimi (raw fish), sukiyaki, tempura and the like are high in protein, low in calories.

Wherever you go, try beefsteak (preferably grilled) and seafood—boiled, baked or grilled. Many countries eat much more fish than we and have created marvelous national delicacies out of the "fruits de mer." Remember that 15 to 20 good-sized Greek shrimps or 30 of the smaller pink Danish variety contain only 100 calories, as do 8 Dublin Bay oysters or 12 tiny, fresh Portuguese clams. In France try the *bouillabaisse* (fish and spices with only a bit of that wicked olive oil), trout, filet of sole poached or *bonne femme* (go easy on the accompanying sauce); in Portugal the fish stew, *caldeirada;* in Spain *zarzuela de mariscos;* in Barbados the flying fish; in England oysters, trout, and sole; in Newfoundland cod; in Australia rock oysters; in Belgium sole.

2. Save up for national cuisines most worth splurging on. Go light on pasta and pastries during part of your trip so that when you get to France, for example, you can eat what tempts you.

3. Adopt the Continental habit of having cheese and fruit for dessert. In Italy this might be a slice of Bel Paese or Gorgonzola, then a pear; in France a wedge of Camembert, Port-Salut or Pont l'Evêque, all lower in calories than our own cream cheese. Try the *framboises* (raspberries) or the *fraises des bois* (tiny wild strawberries). If you fall into the habit of tea or coffee in the afternoon, be strong-willed about the *patisserie*.

4. In countries where an afternoon siesta is part of the daily routine, avoid going to sleep *immediately* after a heavy meal. Walk it off a bit, first. Nothing adds weight so speedily as a two-hour siesta after a big luncheon.

5. In a part of the world that serves highly seasoned foods, take some occasionally that are plain. Highly seasoned dishes stimulate the appetite.

6. Try the vegetarian health-food restaurants in any big city. The yoghurt-wheat germ-vegetable juice fad is everywhere. You will find that there isn't a capital or major city without its share of special shops and restaurants. Many are favored by the smart local women and offer two bonuses: They are inexpensive and there won't be another tourist in sight. One that I like in Edinburgh, for example, is whitewashed and neatly scrubbed Henderson's on Hanover Street, where an ample lunch of a huge salad, crunchy brown bread and dessert costs 75 cents.

7. Don't combine your customary eating and drinking habits with those of the locals. Europeans have a simple breakfast (watch the croissants, however; they are light but have a soul of butter), and a substantial luncheon. Americans at home often reverse this order. Decide which pattern you are going to follow and stick to it. Combining a heavy breakfast with a heavy luncheon will, obviously fill you out in no time at all. Also, follow local drinking tastes. Instead of bourbon and Scotch at 80 or 90 calories a drink, or a martini at 160, take a glass of vermouth or white wine at 75. Sherry is a mere 60 calories a drink, and a leisurely lemonade (*citron pressé*) on a warm French afternoon will add only 75 calories.

8. In some countries, notably Switzerland, the portions are enormous. Instead of ordering a complete dinner, have only the main course.

9. Beware the coffee in many parts of the world such as Greece, Turkey, the Middle East, Japan and Brazil, where it is so heavily sweetened that you will be drinking dozens of calories with each cup.

10. Avoid olive oil as much as you can. It will be hard, it's true, in Italy and Spain, but merely a matter of watching each day's or meal's balance.

11. And finally, don't allow yourself to arrive at meals ravenously hungry or you will fill up on the rolls and butter while you are waiting to be served. Since people in most parts of the world dine later than Americans, break the long period between lunch and dinner with a cup of tea or bouillon and some dry crackers. Pack a fat-free snack kit made up of instant coffee, tea bags, bouillon cubes and the ever-useful immersion heater described on page 124. Take along some low-calorie candies, biscuits and cookies. The following dietetic supplies can also take the edge off your hunger: instant chicken broth (only 6 or 8 calories a cup), a box of Oysterettes (about 1

calorie each), some boxes of De Boles Arti-Nuggets-Stix (about 5 calories each), Arti-Rusks (about 6 calories each), Tiger Milk cookies (about 42 calories each), and some Weber's cookies (about 6 calories each). Biscuits and cookies fill the echoing cavity in your stomach without making you pay in calories. One Weber cookie can stave off your hunger for hours.

Since my travels often require nonstop activity for about 18 to 20 hours a day, my "survival" food is low-calorie honey drops, candies that taste like the real thing, but are only about 10½ calories each. Many times in hot, humid countries these honey drops have propped up my flagging spirits and heavy eyelids by giving me quick energy.

Dieting *en voyage* shouldn't be made a deadly serious pursuit, but a light challenge. You can still eat like a gourmet and have great pleasure on few calories, without gaining. It may also be cheering to remember, when you are wandering through famous buildings and museums, that walking burns up 216 calories an hour.

Dieting has been discussed here only as a staying action to keep you from gaining weight. If you are on a salt-free or other medical diet, you will find that airlines, steamships, and most major hotels and restaurants are prepared to serve your needs. When you make your reservations, tell the carrier of your special diet requirements (kosher, vegetarian, salt-free, etc.), and special food will be served to you while other passengers are dining on the standard menu. If you must follow religious dietary laws, there are restaurants catering to them in just about any major city you may visit.

Dining Solo

It is RARE that people willingly dine alone. A charming companion with whom to enjoy the surroundings, the food, the wine, is after all one of the greatest pleasures of a meal. But sometimes, if your husband is off on business, your traveling companion is out with a new beau (or insists on seeing every painting at the Tate Gallery), or simply if you are making the whole trip solo, you will have to dine alone. Let the prospect hold no terror for you, as it does for many women. There are few moments in life when we can be as blessedly anonymous and detached as when we are foreigners in another country. When you sit down to dinner alone, you are giving yourself a wonderful chance to watch the fascinating flow of life around you. Welcome the opportunity—don't bemoan it. (As a travel writer, I've often found myself alone in foreign countries and was glad of every meal I could have by myself.)

Here's the way to handle the situation smoothly:

Dine early. If you feel self-conscious about walking into a restaurant alone, slip in ahead of the full flood of diners. In a country like Spain where women rarely go out alone at night, and the height of the dinner hour is 10:30 or 11 in the evening, get to the restaurant about 9 or 9:30.

Carry a book. The proverb that "A good book is the best of friends" is never more true than when you and the book are together at the dinner table. There's something rather forbidding about a lone woman diner with a book. If you actually read it while waiting to be served, you will have made a loud, ringing declaration that you are neither a hopeful pickup nor a lost creature about to dissolve into tears.

There are certain restaurants which, like Noah's Ark, are confined to couples and off limits to a solitary woman: those with floor shows, those that tend to be "dives," however attractive, island restaurants that are largely native hangouts, and extremely expensive, posh restaurants that attract a black-tie crowd, like Maxim's in Paris on Friday night. Just resign yourself to missing these—where you wouldn't be happy alone anyway—and carry on. There are thousands of other small, chic, pleasant places where women are welcome: *bistros* in Paris, *tavernas* in Athens, restaurants in London's Chelsea—the list is endless. Make just one concession. When you dine alone, dress discreetly. Don't wear anything with a décolletage. This is one occasion that calls for the most understated simple "little nothing" dress or suit you own.

Hotel dining rooms are always safe and comfortable for women alone, and some—not all, certainly—have a distinguished cuisine. The Connaught Hotel in London, for example, has one of the best tables in the city; its dignified wood-paneled dining room is a haven not only for women alone but for writers, editors, actors, and polished City types. But, for heaven's sake, don't fall into the habit of dining only at your hotel as many timid women do. Hotel dining rooms tend to be rather alike the world over, and you will get much closer to the life of a city by dining occasionally farther afield.

As in the United States, tearooms, coffeeshops, student restaurants, and places that draw a "family crowd" are comfortable for a woman alone. If you have any doubts or questions about suitable restaurants, ask your concierge for advice, and, where possible, have him make the booking.

These are good general rules, but they vary slightly from place to place. In countries with strong Spanish traditions such as those in South America, the sight of a woman alone in the evening is so rare that it is easier to dine in hotels. Women simply don't appear in public without men. However, don't mind eating lunch alone in city restaurants. It isn't done commonly, but you need not feel uncomfortable. The same general rules apply in South Africa.

Japan is one place where a woman can feel completely at ease on her own. In sukiyaki restaurants the rooms are small and separate, and each diner or dining party is served apart. No one can tell whether you are alone or with ten. India has the classic double standard—one for natives, the other for tourists. An Indian woman dining alone would be an odd sight indeed, but no impropriety is felt if the woman is a foreigner. If you go to a good restaurant that normally attracts tourists, no one will raise an eyebrow.

In Scandinavia you can feel even freer than you would at home. Go anywhere within the limits of the general rules. Finns are especially zealous about the independence of women; Finnish women, back in 1906, were the first in Europe and the second in the world to receive the right to vote. If you ask a Dane to suggest a rule of thumb for the woman traveling alone, and who must, after all, have her dinner, he will probably say, "Don't look too dull."

In France, Ireland, Britain and the like, again if you follow the general rules, you can dine everywhere in comfort.

Except for having to pay her own bill, the woman dining alone has no real problem, once she stops feeling self-conscious, and this doesn't last long.

Dressing for Flights

THE CLOTHES you wear for flying reflect your experience as a traveler with all the subtlety of a billboard. If you board an airplane wearing anything that flutters or tinkles or swoops, you are marked immediately as a rank amateur. Dressing for a flight is a discipline demanded by sheer physical circumstances and a need to be comfortable for hours at a stretch. Quite simply you must pare down your clothes and carryalls to the core.

Consider your situation.

First, you will be sitting in one place for a long time. Flying time between New York and London, for example, is 6½ hours. Furthermore, that one place will be none too generous—economy-class seats in a jet measure a scant 18 inches across. (About 91 per cent of air travel today is done in economy class; and things are so little different in first class that the same advice holds for the other 9 per cent.) Still further, the "kingdom" you call your own—overhead rack, coat closet space, the area under your feet—is doll-size. Obviously if you're to be at all comfortable and attractive, you must get rid of absolutely all extraneous matter. That means almost literally *paring down to the core.*

These days, it is good fashion to wear a dress or a suit while traveling—and, of course, to carry a coat. Whichever you choose, the skirt should be neither so bulky with pleats, seams or gathers that you will sit for hours on yards of crumpled fabric nor so narrow that it hikes up or gets rump-sprung. If you wear a suit, your jacket should be cut and fitted very easily, one you can shrug around in. Under it wear a loose silk overblouse or a sweater—never anything that tucks in, because what tucks in slides out. Roughly speaking, dress as you would for a comfortable day's shopping in town.

Avoid all flaring fleecy travel coats. While they are touted as "going over everything," this usually means they are so bulky and clumsy that even before your plane is airborne you will be hating every monstrous inch. The ideal travel coat should be cut straight and fold into a small, flat square. You're sure to have to crush it into the overhead rack above your seat, which is also stuffed with pillows, blankets, your neighbor's four topcoats, a sport jacket, several hats, and heaven knows what else. Jersey or some other knitted wool, or spongy fabrics like camel hair or soft tweed are good travelers—warm as they are light—and if your coat is rainproof, so much the better. In fact, the most intelligently designed travel coats are likely to turn up in the raincoat department.

As for hats, if you don't wear them at home, you needn't cart them abroad. (See Hats, page 162.) You certainly don't need one for a flight. If you feel underdressed without one, wear the smallest, most crushable one you can find—a pillbox, a beret or a turban. A dear little hat with a veil is strictly for the mythical little old lady from Dubuque.

As for accessories, the fewer the better. Heavy bracelets and neck-laces become hateful burdens, sparkling earrings are as out of place as sneakers with a ball gown, and charm bracelets will only succeed in snagging your neighbor's sleeve; seats are *that* close. The white collar and cuffs that look so crisp in an office wilt visibly en route, so leave them behind. The same holds true for white gloves. Beige has far greater staying power.

Carry a small bag (see Luggage, page 208) to accommodate the following necessities:

1. your gloves (so they won't get lost)
2. a cardigan sweater (It's often drafty in aircraft.)
3. toothpaste and toothbrush (After sitting, sometimes dozing, for hours, your mouth feels like sandpaper.)
4. perfume (Assuming that you came aboard with reasonably fresh makeup, the only other beautifiers you'll need are lipstick and face powder which are already in your handbag.)
5. a chiffon scarf for your hair (Breezes on airfields generally seem like baby cyclones.)
6. a pair of travel slippers (the kind that fold into their own case)

It would be nice to say leave off everything that pulls or holds you together—brassieres, girdles, shoes and belts—but belts aside, that would be dreaming. All that can be realistically recommended is that you wear your loosest shoes, most comfortable brassiere, and oldest girdle (or, if your figure can take it, an unfettering garter belt or panty stockings). Shoes are covered in a separate chapter on page 325, but because they can take on such nightmarish importance in traveling, here are a few reminders: Don't wear brand-new shoes, avoid high heels that will trip you on the ramp, and bring along a pair of folding slippers for the flight. You know from movie- or thea-ter-going that when you sit in one place your body seems to expand. Well, a flight from New York to Europe is longer than an O'Neill play, and you can be sure that if your girdle and shoes are tight, you'll be brought to the screaming point of discomfort. In fact, Amer-ican Airlines says—and their longest nonstop flight is about 5½ hours from New York to San Francisco—that the item turned into the Lost and Found department most often is girdles! *Their* explana-tion is that women who can't bear another minute of torture remove their girdles in the washroom, and lose or forget them before the flight is over.

To step down the ramp as unrumpled as possible, wear a dress or suit in worsted—it's springier, more tightly spun and woven, flatter and sturdier than plain wool—or a knit blended of Dacron or Orlon with naturally resilient wool or silk. The more I travel, the more I see chic women slipping off to the washroom once the plane has leveled off, to change into another dress or a pair of slacks. The great American designer Norman Norell has recently created travel costumes with slacks, the latter meant to be worn during flight. The idea is fine if you like to wear them; otherwise choose an easy, fluid dress or suit.

Even if you're taking off on a bleak, gray day in January, take a pair of sunglasses, for up at around 35,000 feet the sun is brilliant—nay, blinding.

As for color, wear what makes you feel pretty provided it isn't black or white, since the one shows dust and lint, the other dirt. Choose it, however, with your destination in mind. If you're arriving in a big, gray, conservative city like London, a bright color will seem out of place. If, on the other hand, you're headed for Honolulu or Jamaica, look summery. Which brings us to the business of coping with temperature differences between departure and arrival points. The only solution is one used by our armed forces in the Arctic: layers. Even if you leave Chicago for the Caribbean on the rawest of March days, you can take your departure comfortably by wearing cashmere cardigan over blouse, suit jacket over cardigan, and lightweight coat over suit. And you simply peel off a few layers for your arrival in the sun. There's nothing that looks so wrong or so uncomfortable in the tropics as a heavy winter or fur coat. Besides, you'll have to cart your coat from place to place—a bore if you're island-hopping.

Practically everything that has been said about dressing for a flight is just as true for train, bus and automobile travel. If you go "clothed in reason's garb," you'll look like a worldly woman, even before you've seen the world.

Duty-Free Shopping

IN 1947, the Irish Parliament ruled that any goods brought directly into Shannon Airport from abroad would not be liable to duty or local taxes. It was an historic decision that paved the way for the phenomenal growth of duty-free shopping throughout the world. At Shannon itself, it transformed a small, plain kiosk into a handsome complex that does a multimillion-dollar business annually. In fifteen years of operation, it has never been closed. So that you can never say that your flight arrived at the wrong time, Shannon's airport shops are open 24 hours a day, 7 days a week.

Much of Shannon's successful pattern has become the model for other duty-free airports, everywhere. Today the drive to sell duty-free goods is so feverish, the shopping bug so virulent, that besides airports, you will find duty-free shops at resorts, in the hearts of cities and even as small mobile units that are wheeled down the aisles of aircraft. Any traveler knows that "duty-free goods" means goods sold at prices lower than their equivalent in the U.S.A. Here's why:

Every government, to protect its own industries, levies duties on certain imported goods. It can, therefore, lift those duties when and where it chooses. Usually goods that are duty free are also free of local taxes. Relieved of duties and taxes, their prices naturally plummet—and the consumer gets the benefit. This means that identical goods will often cost from 20 to 60 per cent less in duty-free shops than they do in the U.S.A.

You can, for example, buy French perfume at duty-free shops around the world, for less than you'd pay in France, and half the American price. You will find English china at prices minus the usual U.S.A. duty and taxes of 30 to 60 per cent; cashmere sweaters minus the usual 20 per cent duty; German cameras minus both the 15 to 25 per cent duty and our 10 per cent excise tax. A good duty-free shop is loaded with temptations: a compelling reason to save some of your shopping dollars for the airports you will hit on the way home. You will see china, crystal, silverware, watches and clocks, linens, brushes, rugs, stoles, blankets, cameras, projectors, binoculars, radios, fabrics, sweaters, leather goods, gloves, woolens, handbags, antiques, cigars, perfumes, gold and diamond jewelry—and liquor. At Shannon the usual $6.25 bottle of whisky costs only $2.50; a liqueur that is $8 or $9 in the States is only $3 or $4 there. The savings are a result not only of the absence of duty but of internal taxes, as well.

The goods are imported into each country in bond—and stored in bonded warehouses. This enables governments to exercise a tight control in order to isolate the merchandise from a country's mainstream of goods. At airport shops, only people in transit can buy duty-free items; you may be asked to show your ticket to prove you are just passing through. At some resorts, merchandise can be bought just by those who are leaving. Only if an entire area or a port has declared itself duty free can you shop for and use the goods on the spot. Otherwise, your purchases will be sent directly to your plane or ship.

You can buy as much as you want to take into the U.S.A. under your customs allowance, and you can pay in local or American currency. At an airport shop, you can use currency left over from other countries you have visited, and you take your purchases with you. (If you have bought them at an airport or quayside shop, you are not supposed to open or use your purchases until you are airborne or on the high seas.)

Duty-free airport shops are found in nearly every major country. Located chiefly in the large international terminals, they exist in Tokyo, Manila, Sydney, Suva, London, Paris, Rome, Amsterdam, Copenhagen, Geneva, Zurich, Düsseldorf, Munich, Tel Aviv, Vienna, Brussels, Frankfort, Nice, among other places. Some, naturally, display a more complete selection of goods than others. At Brussels National Airport's shop, for example, there's even a selection of cut diamonds.

At airports where there is no duty-free shop, there may be counters that sell a product or two, such as liquor, cigarettes or perfume.

Duty-free shopping is a beloved institution of most of the Caribbean islands; Jamaica, for example, has about 50 "in bond" or duty-free shops. There are two large centers along the Canadian border, one at Niagara Falls, the other at the Thousand Islands. Hong Kong, the Canary Islands, and the Virgin Islands have such low duties as to be virtually duty free. At Amsterdam's Schiphol Airport, the duty-free shopping center even sells automobiles. Whenever you step off your plane, any day of the week, the airport showroom will sell you a car on the spot and you can drive away within an hour, all documents and insurance papers completed. You can use the car to tour the Continent, take it home, and, having reduced taxes and duty, save a sizable amount in the process. Cars are of English, French, German, Swedish and Italian makes and are fitted with speedometers that tick off miles instead of kilometers, laminated windshields and reinforced bumpers. Since you are buying a car free of European duties and taxes, you are issued a special license plate which is valid for only one year and is available only to nonresidents. If you want to place your order for a special car in advance, get in touch with ShipSide Car Delivery, Inc., 609 Fifth Avenue, New York, New York 10017, or ShipSide, Schiphol Airport, Amsterdam.

If you are tempted by the goods at the duty-free shops or in their catalogs even if you've already filled your $100 exemption, you may buy these goods, provided you pay United States duty. Many times, even with U.S.A. duty added, they will still cost less than the identical item at home—because you have eliminated several middlemen who all make profits by importing. You need only send your order and check to the duty-free shop, which will immediately acknowledge its receipt and send the goods, at your instructions, by air or by surface mail. At a good and experienced duty-free shop such as the one at Shannon, the merchandise is packed securely; any damaged goods are cheerfully replaced. When it arrives, you pay the duty to the mailman. If, for example, you buy a Pringle cashmere cardigan in the States, it costs $28; if you order it from Shannon, you pay $18.75, plus 50 cents for mailing, $3.10 in duty, and 33 cents U.S. Post Office clearance fee, or a total of $22.68. The duty on a fisherman's knit sweater, the kind handmade by the Aran islanders, is $3.50, the sweater at Shannon is $18.50, the clearance fee again 33 cents, and there's postage of $1.15, bringing the total cost to $23.48; the same sweater or one like it is $30–35 in the States.

Japan has many licensed tax-free shops where you can save yourself taxes amounting to 20 to 25 per cent on such things as cameras, radios, and pearls. By showing your passport in the shop where you buy, you get a Record of Purchase form, which you later present at customs.

If you do any duty-free shopping, remember these points:

1. Airport counters get crowded, so move quickly during your transit time.

2. It might even be worthwhile to stop over at a good duty-free airport.

3. Many of the duty-free shops accept credit cards from American Express or Diners' Club.

4. In many places your purchases must remain in bond until you leave the area. You are given a receipt but not the item, which is put either into the "in bond" window at the airport (where you collect it), or directly aboard your aircraft or ship. Don't fret. These systems are tried and true; and you will get your package.

5. If you are buying gifts, remember that duty-free shops will mail any number of gifts priced at $10 retail or under, except liquor, tobacco or perfume valued at more than $1.00. You need not pay duty or include them on your customs declaration. Each person to whom you send a gift, however, can receive only one $10 gift in a single day. (See Customs, page 95).

6. Many airlines roll a trolley of merchandise up and down their aisles during a flight, from which you can select cigarettes, perfume,

scarves, neckties, liquor, lighters, even watches, at prices which reflect large savings.

7. As you leave the U.S.A. from John F. Kennedy International Airport, you can buy cigarettes, perfume, liquor and other duty-free gifts at substantial savings. Place your order about an hour before your flight leaves. It will be put aboard your outbound plane, and the steward will give you the package just before you land. Such items are sold by the International Shoppes and the Bon Voyage Liquor Corp. at the International Arrivals Building.

8. Many of the larger stores abroad—to compete with the savings offered by duty-free shops—will deliver purchases to your plane or ship, which enables them to eliminate local taxes. Check into this when you shop, for these levies, especially luxury taxes, can be high.

Electrical Appliances

IF YOURS is a sybaritic nature—and you are willing to pay the price in space and weight—you can travel with all the comforts of home. The American genius for gadgetry has produced a string of electrical appliances that travel; they work like a breeze, and are certain to keep you fed, warm and neat. (Incidentally, they make splendid *bon voyage* gifts.)

There are only two important considerations in determining what makes an electrical appliance usable abroad: current and socket. Our country and most places in the Western Hemisphere operate on 110 volts. Most of the rest of the world, however, runs on a variety of voltages, usually ranging from 220 to 240. For example, Buenos Aires operates on 220; Sydney, 240; Rio de Janeiro, 125; London, 240; Athens, 220; Mexico City, 125. And not only do the characteristics of each country's electric current differ—they often differ from city to city in the same country.

The safest rule to follow is to take only those appliances that work both on the U.S.A. current of 110 and the foreign current of 220. (Generally speaking, electrical equipment geared to 110 volts will work for 125, and 220 for 240.) Otherwise, you'll have to carry a transformer which can be a heavy and expensive nuisance.

As for sockets, ours take the familiar flat-pronged plug. Those abroad take round prongs. Therefore, you will need to adapt your American plug to foreign sockets by adding an adapter plug. Most appliances made for travel are packaged with adapter plugs. If you need extras, they can be bought at hardware and electrical appliance stores here and abroad for about 35 cents. Actually, you may need two different types for use abroad. Britain and Ireland take a round plug with short, stubby prongs; the Continent and much of the rest of the world needs a plug with long, slender prongs.

The electrical appliances (none weighs more than 4 pounds) that seem to give travelers the greatest amount of comfort, ease and pleasure are these:

Razor. If you are wedded to an electric one, take it. Try a Remington or Schick that works on both 110 and 220 volts. If you don't want to buy a new one, you can use your 110-volt razor simply by attaching a resistor cord, which costs about $1.50 and comes with adapter plug already attached. If you have forgotten yours, ask your concierge to lend you one.

Iron. I find this item highly overrated and have never traveled with one (see Clothes Care, page 80). On the other hand, if you have a large family and a small budget or feel more secure having an iron with you, take a General Electric or Westinghouse. The compact GE model can be used with steam or dry. To use it abroad, push down the small red lever to "220 volts"; at home, push up the lever to "110 volts." It sells for about $15.

Heating Pad. You *could* make do with a hot-water bottle as the British do. On the other hand, it does cool off toward morning, and those thick-walled, underheated castles are chilly. For people who hate cold feet and clammy beds, Kaz makes a small 10-inch-square heating pad which comes in handsome plaids, will work everywhere and sells for about $8.

Hair Dryer. There are two that work both here and abroad. One is the Oster model, a blower-and-hood type that costs about $30. The other is made by Schick and includes a power manicure attachment with fine and coarse emery wheels, nail buffer and brush, plus a built-in nail-polish dryer. It sells for about $35. Both are a blessing for women who like to set their hair frequently, or on any vacation that includes lots of water sports.

Tensor Light. This might seem to be carrying things too far, but if reading in bed at night is one of your cherished indulgences, you will be unhappy in many hotel rooms whose only light is often a wan overhead bulb. One style in these small lamps is geared to 220 volts, weighs 3 pounds, and sells for about $20.

Immersion Heater. This is simply a coiled electric rod. When it is put into a cup of water, it brings it to a boil. Most immersion heaters are sold in cases that also contain two cups, two spoons, two plastic jars—one for instant coffee, the other for powdered milk—and cost about $10 or less, depending on the equipment. Travelers who have used immersion heaters become fiercely devoted to them. With some packaged bouillon or chocolate, you can be free from the vagaries of room service any time, however unlikely, you want a hot drink.

In the battery and transistor classifications, there are two particularly useful items: one, a transistor radio. It may be so tiny that it fits into the palm of your hand, but it can bring you the full sounds of music, language and a feeling of companionship and life in a foreign country (it's especially nice when you're dressing). There are many styles and types in transistor radios; take one that fits your budget and is lightest in weight. Two, an item called a "night writer," a ballpoint pen with its own light. If you want to write letters while your husband is asleep this is the gadget for keeping you both happy in the limited space of a hotel room. It sells for $6.

Bear in mind these four rules about traveling with electrical appliances:

1. Whenever you see a round outlet in the wall, you know that it will take *only* appliances that run on 220 volts. Read the voltage on yours—it always appears on appliance or plug—and, if in doubt, don't plug it in, or all that you'll remember of that charming inn in the Cotswolds is that evening you blew out all the lights.

2. Adapter plugs don't change voltages. They only make it possible for you to plug your appliance into a foreign socket.

3. If you are in doubt about electrical requirements, get your concierge to spell out the local situation. Most big hotels keep a supply of adapter plugs, resistor cords and transformers on hand.

4. Be extremely careful about any electrical appliances you use on a plane. *Never* turn on a transistor radio. It may interfere with the aircraft's delicate communication and navigation instruments. On a ship, check voltage with the steward before you plug in a razor or iron. You could damage your appliance or even the ship's electrical system.

5. If you can't find any of the items listed above locally, all can be

ordered by mail from Hammacher Schlemmer, 145 East 57th Street, New York, New York 10022. This is a distinguished old store that has been selling household equipment and the like since 1848. It has the largest collection of products and gadgets for travel of any store in the country.

Evenings

FOR THE traveler—especially a woman alone—evenings often seem as long as days and much more of a problem. When dusk falls, lights brighten the foreign city, and its inhabitants withdraw behind their curtains, even the most dedicated wanderer, though she may have been striking up sunlit conversations in a bookshop or on a ferry, sometimes turns coward and longs for home. Often, however, the traveler's own attitude intensifies her loneliness. She expects every single hour of the twenty-four, for 2, 4 or 6 weeks running, to be filled with magic—an unreasonable kind of optimism even for a honeymoon. But a trip is memorable for the richness of the experience as a whole; and a certain amount of time should be spent digesting it. Get rid of the frantic, compulsive feeling that every minute must count, and relax about the evenings. Expect to spend some alone; others will be what you've dreamed about. Evenings are not just for dancing and casinos, but for theater, movies, concerts, ballet, even sightseeing, all of them pleasures to be enjoyed alone as well as with company. Even the fizzier nighttime diversions can be arranged for a lone woman these days, and I'll talk about this later on.

First, ask yourself what you would be doing at home, come nightfall. Some evenings you would probably stay home to write letters, wash your hair, read, watch television or just chat with your family. Except that your hotel room will give you less roaming space and there will be fewer people around, you can and should do the same thing while you travel. No one can be on the move 16 hours a day, absorbing new sights and stimuli for days at a time; the chance for a breather is salubrious.

Then, think of what diversions give you pleasure after dark at home. The movies? Every big city has large cinemas or small art houses. American films, often subtitled in the native language, are international favorites and often funny. (I once saw a western in Paris in which the hero's order, "Give me a shot of whiskey," was subtitled, *"Un apéritif, s'il vous plaît."*) The great artists of the world move around. You can probably catch up with Yehudi Menuhin in New Delhi, Van Cliburn in Vienna. To these add a particularly European delight that seems designed to make unaccompanied women happy: a long, leisurely dinner at a seaside café, a *taverna*, a small *bistro*. Most Europeans would rather linger late over a fine dinner than rush away to a nightclub; restaurateurs, understanding this, do not hover over you, and by the time you've finished the brandy and coffee it's close to midnight. (See Dining Solo, page 112.)

Some countries specialize in a particular form of entertainment, which invariably costs less than it would in America. Britain's superlative theater offers often-brilliant plays and always-brilliant acting; tickets are available (ususually for the same night) and cheap, with $4.20 the top price and about 70 cents the bottom. Theaters are small, so you can see and hear from any seat. A woman alone or two women together can feel perfectly at ease at an evening performance, even to the point of popping into the bar for a drink between acts. Some dedicated visitors to London go every night and twice on Saturday. London also has superb ballet at the Royal Opera House, Covent Garden, and great vaudeville entertainment at the Palladium. In Vienna, Rome, Munich, Milan, and Naples, go to the opera. Seats cost between $2 and $8, averaging $4 for a good one, and they go quickly. Make your reservations as soon as you arrive. In Paris, try the government-subsidized national theaters, all inexpensive: the Comédie Française; the Théatre de France (Odéon), run by Madeleine Renaud and Jean-Louis Barrault (it offers more variety than the Comédie Française); and the Opéra and Opéra-Comique. In Denmark, see the ballet; in Athens, plays again, some in English, some the ancient Greek tragedies and comedies (these are given at the foot of the Acropolis during August and September). Indeed, wherever you go, see a local play, perhaps a musical comedy, even if you don't understand the language. The staging, atmosphere and acting technique can still be interesting, and you are often given a synopsis in English.

Your concierge will get you tickets to all performances, putting the cost on your bill, so see him just as soon as you've decided what you want to do.

An evening spent at one of the charming small concerts or plays given in town squares, castles and museums is often among your warmest memories. Go, for example, to the museum at Sceaux, about 20 minutes from Paris, the eighteenth-century Drottningholm Court Theater outside Stockholm, and the Sunday evening concerts in the open-air courtyard of the Victoria and Albert Museum in South Kensington, London.

Gravitate to the places where young people go; the atmosphere will be more informal, less likely to depend on people in pairs.

Go sightseeing by night. Don't miss the *Son et Lumière* (Sound and Light) spectacles which are given at many historic buildings: a number of the great châteaux along the Loire Valley, Versailles, the Cathedral of Notre Dame in France; the Forum in Rome; the Acropolis in Athens; Hampton Court in Great Britain; the pyramids of Egypt; and the Belvedere Palace in Vienna, among other places. They go on only after dark, and present an interplay of sound (voices, music and sound effects) and powerful illumination which weaves a dramatic history of the building you are visiting with a stirring, often eerie flourish. It is easy to imagine the effect when you know that the idea was conceived by a French architect while watching a storm of thunder and lightning breaking over Chambord one night.

Try an amusement park, such as the famously wonderful Tivoli Gardens in Copenhagen—an endless potpourri of restaurants, theater, ballet, and carnival midway fun-and-games. No one will notice if you're without a man.

Take a carriage ride, a lovely way to see the city's boulevards and its strollers. Fix the price with the driver before you start and tip him at the end.

The leisurely evening boat ride is a classic summer amusement in any capital city built along or around a river. The *bateaux mouches* are a Paris signature and from them the city is more rosy and beautiful than ever; the 8:30 sailing includes dinner aboard, for a well-deserved sum of about $10. In London you can ride up the Thames from Westminster Pier to the Tower of London for about $1; the trip lasts from 7:50 to 9:30 P.M., and since London's summer light lasts until 10, you have a fine dusk view of the bridges and the Houses of Parliament. Or go up the river to Greenwich to see the *Son et Lumière* there, and come back by dark.

Become a sports fan. You may feel you wouldn't be caught dead at Candlestick Park or Shea Stadium, but the cheers of the crowd acquire a certain charm in a foreign language. The bullfights in Madrid start anywhere between 5 and 7 and *jai alai* is also a popular twilight entertainment. At Lisbon's new stadium, the hubbub of soccer fans is part of the music of a summer evening. Then there are the active sports which attract the young: *le bowling* in Paris, ice skating at the Palais de Glace on the Champs-Élysées, and in London at Queen's Club in Bayswater.

To find out what's available, turn to the local English-language newspapers or buy the weekly entertainment magazines—*What's On in London*, *Semaine de Paris*, et al.—available at newsstands, which give complete listings of theatrical productions, concerts, movies, art shows, sports events, etc., for their cities.

And if you don't feel like doing anything, just walk and watch. Window-shop. Stroll. Go into the shops that are open late. Leave your hotel room and look at life around you. In many countries (especially Latin ones), the evening stroll between 8 and 11, in the main square or along the main street, marks the pleasant, unhurried end to the day.

Stay away from preserves meant for pairs: cabarets, casinos, smart supper clubs, dimly lighted jazz clubs, big brassy dance halls, smoky cellars and discothèques. You will only depress yourself and those around you, and confirm the foreign contention that American women are too independent and aggressive. If you want a quick whirl through some sort of night life, you can do one of two things. Join an organized, guided nightclub tour, which includes a while at several different places with something to eat or drink at each (prices range from $10 to $20). In Paris, the tour that visits the Lido is fun, for its extravaganza of rising and sinking stages and disappearing scenery, decorated by the well-known semi-dressed girls. Your concierge or the local American Express office can arrange this sort of nightclub visit.

The foregoing is addressed to a woman traveling by herself or with another woman. If you are with your husband, no place is off limits unless it is disreputable and dangerous. Use your common sense. You probably wouldn't go down to the skid row or dock areas of your home town, so don't go there after dark in a foreign city.

What is known as the Action is to be found in the discothèque. Along with Bogner ski pants, op art and ostrich feathers, it is a chic international institution. Some discothèques are organized as private clubs, to circumvent national licensing laws; others are open to all. At any rate, the term "private club" as applied to places of evening entertainment is a euphemism, because any tourist who calls ahead can usually get in; a "temporary membership" is immediately arranged for a small fee. The spots swing in and out of favor every few months, so you'll have to check them on arrival with your concierge or the concierge of the best hotel in town.

Fares

MANY PEOPLE believe that the price of an airline or steamship ticket is as uniform as the postal rates. They are wrong. The only absolutely certain, unchanging fact is that all airlines that are members of the International Air Transport Association (IATA) must charge the same rates for a trip between any two given points— in other words, whatever airline you fly from New York to London, for example, the fare is the same.

Air and steamship lines, however, do provide a range of fares based on season, day of the week, class, length of stay abroad, type of tour, etc. The fares are designed to encourage travel when planes and ships are least likely to be filled—in short, to level out peaks and valleys in the flow of travelers abroad. It is the practice of both to experiment with special rates in the hope of spreading their business. Those who want to travel with the crowd at the season's peak must pay for the privilege; business travelers, a group that the travel industry feels can afford to pay higher fares, must pay more for a quick trip than a pleasure traveler does for a slower one. Thus, the man who flies to

Paris for a 48-hour business session pays a higher fare ($526.30) than the person who travels for 21 days, in peak season ($331.00). If you fly to London during the summer, economy class will cost you $484.50; the rest of the year it will be $399. When you shop for transportation, then, know what the differences are and plan accordingly.

If you travel by air to Europe you can choose from these basic fares:

TYPE	SAMPLE ROUND-TRIP FARES NEW YORK—PARIS	CONDITIONS AND RESTRICTIONS
First-Class Fare	$754.30	None—just lots of money. Used by business travelers and wealthy pleasure travelers who can afford it.
Regular Economy Fare	$440.80	Basic economy fare in effect most of the year. Not available on certain dates.
Peak-Season Economy Fare	$526.30	Economy fare for traveling during the peak summer months. In effect only on certain dates.
14–21 Day Excursion Fare	$331.00	Primarily meant for the two- to three-week vacationer, not the business traveler. This fare is the lowest IATA one across the Atlantic. You must stay in Europe no fewer than 14 days and no more than 21; you must fly across the North Atlantic between Monday and Thursday. Calculate the days of your trip carefully to avoid getting trapped into returning too late, which can cost you dear, e.g., $195.30 more on a round-trip ticket between New York and Paris. Applicable the entire year except for certain peak weeks in summer.
Inclusive Tour Basing Fare Package	starting at $371.00	Subject to the same seasonal and weekend restrictions as excursion fare. An ITF includes round-trip transportation, hotels and sightseeing which must be paid in full before you go. While the actual fare is $30 less than the excursion fare, you are obliged to buy the total tour which must cost at least $40 more.
Affinity-Group Fare	$331.00	Available for qualified groups of 25 or more. See Charters and Group Fares, page 68, for details.

(Note that all round-trip fares save you 5 per cent over the equivalent two one-way fares. This is also true on ships.)

As you can see, the range in fares is great. It's important, then, to discuss them carefully with your travel agent or the airline at the time you book your ticket.

Be on the lookout, too, for special excursion fares designed to boost travel to specific destinations. They sometimes spring up overnight. There is, for example, a special excursion rate to the Arab countries for a trip of no fewer than 11 days, no more than 21. There's a special group fare to Israel (see page 73). There are several fares for a flight between New York and San Juan, Puerto Rico, depending on the time of the day, the day of the week, and the weeks of the year. There are both a 16-28-day tour basing fare and a 16-28-day excursion fare to India, Pakistan, Ceylon or Nepal.

Also take a fresh look at round-the-world fares. Once you are far from home, it is considerably less expensive to return by circling the globe than you might imagine. For example, on a flight from New York to Athens in summer, you will have spent $776.40 for an economy-class round-trip ticket; for another $486.85, you can come back via Hong Kong. If you have gone as far as Tel Aviv in summer for $883.50, you can return to New York via Bangkok for $379.75 more. A passenger flying west from New York to Hong Kong can continue on around the world for just $125.25 more than it would cost her to return the way she came across the Pacific. If she goes westward from Chicago to New Delhi, she has gone halfway around the world; hence, she can circle back through Europe at no additional cost.

The steamship lines also offer a wide assortment of fares. They vary according to the season, location and size of your cabin (i.e., inside, outside, upper deck, lower deck), its amenities (i.e., bath or shower, beds or berths), etc.

Basically, transoceanic ship fares are divided into summer season (roughly May till the beginning of August) and thrift season. During the thrift, or low, season, fares are reduced as much as 8 to 20 per cent below the summer rate for a one-way trip, the exact amount varying with the difference in services, ships, and types of accommodations. In addition, there are reductions on round-trip tickets (5 per cent), excursions, and group fares.

Minimum rates will vary with the age, size and speed of the ship. For example, if you sail from New York to a port in Britain, they might range as follows:

TYPE	SUMMER SEASON	THRIFT SEASON
First Class	$343 to $473	$288.50 to $440
Cabin Class	$274 to $289	$244 to $271
Tourist Class	$230 to $265	$194.50 to $235

If you land in a French Channel port, a North Atlantic port, or one in the Mediterranean, the rates will be a little higher.

Should you want the best of both worlds, you can go one way by sea, the other by air. You will get a 5 per cent reduction in total fare, provided that the sea portion of your ticket falls in the thrift season and you have booked your passage in advance.

Like airlines, steamship lines also have an excursion rate for the short-term overseas traveler. If you sail both ways and spend up to 30 days ashore, you get a 15 per cent reduction in the price, provided you leave between early fall and the beginning of the peak season in the spring. This excursion fare is applicable on all ships and in all classes on the transatlantic lines and on any combination of lines, routes, ships or classes. There is also a group fare by ship which gives organized parties of 25 or more adults a reduction of 25 per cent in cabin and tourist classes and on one-class ships (see Charters and Group Fares, page 68).

This is the fare picture as this book goes to press. However, the fare situation is regularly reviewed by the International Air Transport Association and the Steamship Conferences, and changes are continually being made. Therefore, check your travel agent, the airline or ship line for the latest news. Ferreting out the facts may take the nose of a detective and the mathematical skill of an accountant—but it is labor that will save you money.

See also Charters and Group Fares, page 68.

Festivals

TRADITIONALLY festivals have been holidays of communal feasting and celebration in honor of some happy event—the return of the fishing fleet, the longest day of the year, the eve of a religious fast, the harvest of an important product. They have been celebrated by processions winding through streets, dancers in blazing color, music of all kinds; and they have taken the form, among others, of Mardi Gras carnivals, Holy Week pageants, and Easter celebrations.

In Thailand, banana-leaf boats kindled with tiny flames are set afloat on streams and canals one night each November as prayers to the Mother of the Waters. Halfway around the world, at the golden autumn harvest, the great vintage regions of France, Italy and Switzerland devote weeks of celebration—with bonfires, banquets, and tastings—to the glories of wine. Musicians serenade the workers as they pluck the grapes and carry them to the wine presses; mountain villages are gay with music, plays and costume parades. In Mexico there are almost as many fiestas as there are patron saints, providing a year-round explosion of fireworks and processions to mark each anniversary.

While the ancient feasts still go on in the picturesque backwaters of the world, a new festival concept has taken hold in many other places: programs of concerts, operas, dramas, films and the like which are slated, usually annually, for several days or weeks. They draw a drove of talented people who perform, one after the other, in a richly packed program. At the well-established festivals, both the performers and the works in which they appear are exceptional.

The cultural festivals take place in great metropolises like Berlin and Edinburgh, sometimes lovely old cities like Salzburg and Spoleto. They may honor an artist at his birthplace, or perform his work in the most appropriate surroundings: You can go to Salzburg for Mozart, to Bayreuth for Wagner, to Helsinki for Sibelius, to Bergen for Grieg and to Duszniki in Poland for Chopin. For less eclectic tastes, there are jazz festivals in Warsaw, folk-song and bagpipe festivals in Ireland, and operettas performed on barges moored in the Rhine.

There are other festivals built around a galaxy of talent which is brought together in one place—and in one short space of time. The famous Edinburgh International Festival draws great performers, exhibitions, ballet companies and films from all over the world. Because audiences, temporarily at leisure and relaxed, have traveled expressly to listen and hear, they are usually more receptive to the unfamiliar. Festivals, therefore, have even become experimental workshops and important as a creative force in the evolution of the arts.

They are often held in the midst of beautiful surroundings—ancient ruins, castles, cathedrals, squares, parks and gardens. Whatever the festival, you will enjoy a special occasion in that great intensity of atmosphere that goes with any holiday. You will be among people who share a common interest. The normal barriers fall faster and the camaraderie at festival time makes it a happy occasion for meeting people. Even at the traditional local festivals, some of which have survived unchanged for centuries, visitors are generally welcome guests.

Since it would be a pity to miss their richness of regional costume, special dishes, happy children, traditional toys, games and processions, be sure to find out from the national tourist offices (see page 479) whether any local native festivals will be held during your stay in any country you plan to visit. Mexico, Japan, Portugal, Spain and India are especially festival-rich. For a good Pacific calendar, write to the Pacific Area Travel Association, 442 Post Street, San Francisco, California 94102. *Mexico This Month*, a magazine with offices at Atenas 42, Mexico 6, D.F., publishes a fine annual calendar of its country's fiestas, available for about $1, and Pan American Airways, among other airlines, puts out a comprehensive and succinct calendar of special events all over the world.

If you hope to see the big festivals listed by the airline calendars, be sure to secure hotel reservations *well* in advance. Also, be warned that in many places hotel rates go up during festivals. The spring *feria* in Seville, for instance, has become so popular and fashionable that room costs soar higher in price for the duration. Another way of beating the price hitch in countries with efficient public transportation (Germany, Netherlands or Switzerland) is to get a room out of town; you can depend on the electric railways to carry you swiftly to the festivities.

When it comes to the traditional folk festival, it is safe to say that the smaller, lesser known—and less commercialized—are often the most rewarding. You may not even be able to find these provincial Passion Plays, lake festivals, costume and flower parades listed in the big calendars, but the national travel offices will be able to fill you in. For instance, spend Midsummer Eve (June 23) not in Copenhagen but in some Danish village where you will see real folk dancing, singing, bonfires leaping up on the beaches all through the faintly sunlit night. Try Walpurgis Night (April 30) in a Finnish village. Go to the lusty folk fair of Salat Kirmess at Ziegenhain in the West German state of Hesse from May 30 to June 1. Or the pre-Lenten candlelight festivals held at Patras and Nauplion in the Greek Peloponnesus. Or the festival of Perahera in Kandy, Ceylon, where Buddha's tooth is paraded through the streets in a golden casket on the back of an elephant. Or the Spring and Flower Festival in Istanbul with Karagoz shadow puppet plays in the Topkapi Palace Gardens. Or the festival of the whirling dervishes, which takes place in Konya, 4 hours from Ankara, in December.

At the great Gypsy Festival in Saintes-Maries-de-la-Mer in Provence, May 24–25, to which gypsies come from everywhere to honor their patron saint, statues of the three Marys are escorted to the sea by Camargue cowboys; girls in Arlesian costume dance in the streets; horse races, bullfights and religious ceremonies are performed by gypsies in white tunics who escort the statues back from the sea. One of the most moving and impressive religious festivals in the world takes place in Spain during Semana Santa, the week preceding Easter. Solemn candlelit processions, silent but for the sounds of trumpets and drums, and the soft tread of bare feet, move through towns and villages throughout the countryside; the largest is in Seville.

In Portugal, in Vila Franca de Xira, on two July weekends, there is the great Festival of the Red Waistcoat, with bull-catching in the streets, fireworks, folk dancing, and a great supper. A 300-year-old Christmas Fair takes place in Nuremberg from December 4 to 24, with many happy children, much music and singing, entrancing booths selling Christmas delights, and a large Nativity scene.

The most enthusiastic Bastille Day celebration outside of France takes place in Tahiti. During this festival, which goes on for days, dancers and singers from Tahiti and other islands come to the capital, Papeete, and compete for top honors. There are also javelin-throwing contests, outrigger canoe races, and fire-walking ceremonies. The Indian city of Jaipur also has a gay July fete—the "Teej" festival. Swings are hung from trees in all parts of the city, and the colorfully dressed women rock back and forth watching a procession of elephants, camels and folk dancers.

Other festivals have a note of exotic danger. On Corpus Christi Day in Mexico, the Volador dance is performed in Papantla near the Gulf Coast in the state of Veracruz, once an ancient religious center belonging to the Totonac Indians. Following Totonac ritual, five Indian dancers ascend a bare tree trunk which can be sixty to ninety feet high. One plays a reed flute and drum on a tiny platform at the top. The others wrap ropes around their ankles and at a given signal dive backward into space and revolve to earth head downward. When they reach ground they swing their bodies upward and nimbly land on their feet.

Whatever and wherever the festival, if it lasts several days it is likely to become most colorful toward the end. So if you haven't much time, try to come on the last day or so.

As for the great cultural festivals that have established themselves in recent times, they can provide worthwhile focus to part of your trip. There are few times or places where you can see and hear so much of the best the world has to offer. The Casals Festival, held in San Juan,

Puerto Rico, each June, is now a musical landmark; some conducting is done by the maestro, Pablo Casals, who makes his home on the island; in past years other musical treats have included performances by Leonard Bernstein and Yehudi Menuhin. The Glyndebourne Festival in England is a gem of a summer opera season; not only are the programs, performances, and staging of the highest order, but the setting (a superb English garden) and the atmosphere (Rolls-Royces, full evening dress, picnic hampers, champagne in the intervals) are uniquely civilized and charming—and very English. Some of the most magnificent Welsh singing can be heard at the annual Llangollen International Musical Eisteddfod in Wales in July.

Spoleto in Italy was a sleepy medieval city until Gian-Carlo Menotti brought in an annual avant-garde culture binge which runs every year from mid-June to mid-July. Everything—music, drama, ballet, opera—is contemporary but the setting; sculpture stands dramatically in the cobbled streets.

Mid-June brings the Festival of Epidaurus to Greece. Classic Greek drama is performed on weekends by stars of the Greek National Theater in the ancient amphitheater. The acoustics are so perfect that you can hear a stage whisper from the highest seat—which is so high up that the actors themselves look minuscule.

Every summer, usually from July to September, the great festival at Salzburg honors Mozart with superbly performed concerts and operas in a peerless mountain setting. During the same period, the Baalbek International Festival draws the world's greats to the silent grandeur of Baalbek, set amid Lebanon's Bekaa Plain. This ancient city, which has passed through Canaanite, Greek, Roman, Christian, Arab, Crusader, Mongol and Turkish hands, has now been restored by archaeologists. With its pagan temples, towering stone slabs, and immense columns, it forms a powerful backdrop for the festival, which in past years has featured Dame Margot Fonteyn and Rudolf Nureyev. For light opera, you might enjoy the festival of Bregenz in Austria, where the stage is a barge floating by the shore of Lake Constance.

There are other great music festivals—some with theatrical performances as well: at Aix-en-Provence (featuring Mozart), Athens (drama), Berlin, Dubrovnik (where the medieval setting is a joy in itself), Lucerne (whose festival was founded by Toscanini), Prague, Vienna—to mention only a few of those immensely worth traveling to attend.

Scandinavian countries get together for a festival series, which you can follow, as if it were a progressive dinner party, from capital to capital during the summer. You begin in Copenhagen with the Royal

Danish Ballet; proceed to Bergen for Grieg; on to Stockholm, which offers opera in the exquisite eighteenth-century Drottningholm Court Theater; and finally to Helsinki for Sibelius.

If you like films, then by all means visit Cannes for the annual Film Festival early in May, or try the International Film Festival in Venice, late in August. With all the mobs of bikinied starlets, oglers, photographers, and capital-P Personalities, they are ecstasy for the gregarious, a nightmare for quiet types. At either place reservations must be made ages ahead. A calmer event is the Dublin Theater Festival in late September and early October, where young writers have a chance to see their plays produced. It may not be always up to O'Casey and Abbey Theater standards, but there is a good deal that is well worth while.

If you dislike crowds and any disruption of routine, stay away from a city or village where a festival is going on. But they are wonderful events to seek out if you enjoy seeing things at a high pitch of excitement and, usually, of excellence. A whole summer of festivals would pall dreadfully, but let them punctuate your trip with bright exclamation marks.

Flowers

"THERE'S ROSEMARY, that's for remembrance; pray love, remember: and there is pansies, that's for thoughts."

Ophelia's lines sound elfishly pretty now, but in the seventeenth century the "language of flowers" was put to literal use. It was understood even in America a hundred years ago, and today it maintains its currency in Europe. When a dashing Italian sends you a bunch of jasmine, he could be saying: "Start now to love me."

Certainly Americans are fond of flowers. For us, however, they do not have the importance and subtle significance that they have for the people of European and Oriental countries. In these countries the actual cultivation of flowers is a passionate pursuit, deeply rooted in local mores. (If you are lucky enough to be in London in mid-May, go to the Chelsea Flower Show and observe the rapt expressions of normally impassive, well-tailored English gentlemen carrying furled umbrellas. It is a revelation.)

Europeans plant flowers everywhere. In London, crowded and traffic-jammed, window boxes brighten sober office buildings. In Switzerland, railroad stations are brilliant with masses of red geraniums. In Holland's Schiphol Airport, flowers for greeting and farewells are sold in vending machines like Coca-Cola or cigarettes.

While fresh flowers are often a luxury in this country, in Europe and elsewhere they are so inexpensive and readily available from street carts that they are used on the slightest pretext, as a sign of warmth, affection and appreciation. If you would like to be remembered as a courteous American, here are some of the rules to observe governing the use of flowers abroad:

1. If you are invited to dine at someone's house on the Continent, bring flowers with you unless it is a formal dinner, in which case you would send them the next day with a note of appreciation. In Britain, even for informal dinners, send them the following day. In Holland, where flowers are exchanged for any reason, the hostess who expects eight guests for dinner has eight vases lined up in the kitchen, ready for their bouquets.

2. If someone has given you a pleasant, hospitable treat—a sightseeing or shopping excursion, lunch, or a visit to their house—flowers are in order. If, for example, you and your husband are entertained by a business associate and his wife at a restaurant, it would be gracious to send flowers to the wife afterward. In neither case should you be showy or extravagant. Flowers bought from the corner cart and wrapped in newspaper still make a pretty gesture.

3. In Scandinavian countries if you send only one kind of flower, try to remember to send an odd number—3, 5, 7, 9, 11 or 13—rather than our standard dozen. This has become the convention, and the rule may exist because odd-numbered flowers seem easier to arrange. But if you forget these figures, don't fret; a dozen flowers will do beautifully anywhere.

4. Greater symbolism is attached to flowers abroad than at home. Watch out for chrysanthemums: In Belgium, Italy and France, among other places, they are associated with funerals. In Japan, on the other hand, where they are the national flower, they are great favorites, especially in white, but camelias, lotus blossoms and lilies are associated with death. Red roses stand for deep, undying love in most European countries. Lilies except in Bermuda, go to funerals. White, pink and purple flowers are also used for condolence. Whenever one says "goodbye" and there is a chance of not meeting again, the occa-

sion calls for a farewell bouquet of violets, forget-me-nots, asters, carnations or gladioli.

In India and Hawaii, garlands are draped over the heads of arriving or departing guests as signs of welcome and affection. Indeed, in Hawaii leis are presented often: A man will bring one to his date, or a guest may occasionally take one to her hostess. In southern India, flowers are sold by the yard, beautifully woven garlands of jasmine, champacs, and tuberoses; and in many homes these garlands are delivered as regularly as milk or groceries.

Where people feel this intensely about flowers, it's natural that flower shows should be impressive events, and flower markets places of joy and color. You might enjoy a visit to Aalsmeer, 30 minutes from Amsterdam, where flower auctions are as tense and exciting as the sale of silver at Sotheby's. The best days to go are Tuesday and Thursday, when cut flowers are auctioned from 7:30 in the morning till just before noon. Tables and wagons are loaded with flowers that were cut at dawn, are auctioned at 7:30 and may be selling anywhere in Europe by 3 in the afternoon. It's a serious pursuit. Only wholesalers can bid, but, as a visitor, you are welcome to watch for the fun of it.

Let yourself be caught up in this flower fever. Buy a bouquet of flowers from a street vendor for your hotel room as soon as you arrive. It will brighten your life at once.

Furs

EVER SINCE about 800 B.C., when Semiramis, Queen of Assyria, brought back Indian tiger skins to decorate the Hanging Gardens of Babylon, furs have been one of woman's favorite forms of conspicuous consumption.

Whether to take them on your trip or not depends entirely on whether you ought to make a display of them in the places you visit. In the U.S.A., which is the world's greatest fur consumer, fur stoles and coats are so commonplace that no one gives them a second glance. In many other places, however, they are still a luxury which few can afford; the fur coat you take for granted at home becomes ostentatious. So it comes down to a question of good manners. If you will be in the company of other women who are likely to wear furs, take yours. If not, leave them home. Generally you will find that many women in the large cities of Western Europe and South America own furs. In countries where the standard of living is low, there are few. Remember that being well-dressed is entirely a matter of being dressed appropriately. It's a breach of good taste to flaunt your wealth or to be more ostentatiously dressed than the women of your host country.

Besides this, consider what an irksome responsibility a delicate, expensive fur can be. In addition to the physical burden of carrying it from place to place, you may find yourself standing guard over it too much of the time. If it is lost or stolen, you will have to fuss with the local police, fill out long forms, get in touch with your insurance company, and possibly delay the rest of your trip. Recovering lost or stolen property is always a nuisance and never more so than when you are in a foreign country.

Resist the temptation to take even a fur stole, unless you are sure you will need it. First, the fashion importance of stoles is diminishing; and second, they don't look suitable in most places. American women tend to make too much use of stoles, wearing them on cruise and transatlantic ships and at warm weather resorts, where fur is not smart, no matter how cool the ocean breezes or the air conditioning. Stoles are all wrong on planes. A traveler should never attract attention by wearing something obviously valuable—or superfluous. If you are heading for big cities and planning to go to the theater, the opera or nightclubs, take a stole along to wear over your cocktail and late-day clothes. But don't put it on, as so many women do, for a simple dinner in a modest *bistro* or in a small hotel in a country village.

Buying furs abroad is a tricky business. Today, the U.S.A.—particularly New York City—is the fur capital of the world. We are the largest producers and processors of raw furs, have the greatest pool of top, skilled craftsmen and artisans (they emigrated here as a result of two wars, first from Russia and Poland, more recently from Greece), the highest styling and the lowest prices in the world. While the animal kingdom roams the globe and furs are produced everywhere, the fact that an animal is indigenous to a certain country is not enough to insure that a fur coat made locally from its pelts will be a bargain. Making a fur coat requires a tremendous amount of time, labor and skill. It is a detailed procedure, executed mostly by hand. Many countries rich in pelts are poor in skilled furriers, or ship the best of their furs to other countries. Also, styling abroad is often out of step with ours and furs look thick and old-fashioned: Shoulders are too broad, lines too boxy, silhouettes too stodgy. It is no calamity if you buy a handwoven peasant skirt on impulse, only to find that it looks more like a costume than clothing once you're home; but when a presumed bargain in fur turns out to be bearishly square-shouldered and shabbily sewn together, you have made an expensive mistake indeed.

With this warning, let me now add that there are exceptions. In some places, you will find not only good shops but fine fur buys and even bargains. Here are some that deserve to be singled out:

In Scandinavia, the icy-cold climate produces rich, thick skins— especially mink and, in Norway, fox. Denmark has the largest annual production and the best mink in Europe. In Copenhagen, there are two thoroughly reliable stores: A. C. Bang, 27 Østergade, and Birger Christensen, 38 Østergade, both of which carry a full line of furs. Christensen has the exclusive right to Christian Dior designs, and at both shops the styling is fashionable and the workmanship good. Mink coats run about 25 per cent less than in the U.S.A. If you have one shipped back to the States, there is a further discount of 10 per cent. Remember, however, that while you are allowed an exemption from duty of $100 in goods, you will have to pay duty on the difference between $100 and the cost of your coat, and you can claim the exemption only if the coat is brought back by you.

If mink is out of your reach, look into the variety of young, good-looking inexpensive furs: Danish lamb (a coat is about $200), pony, opossum, baby calf, otter, and Lakoda seal from Denmark's Greenland.

Indeed, wherever you go, look for the local specialty and buy it at the most respected and, let's face it, probably the most expensive shop in town. It will still be a considerable saving over what you can get at home—you may not even be able to find it at home—and your expenditure will be worth while. For example:

In the U.S.S.R., even children wear fur coats against the freezing winters: inexpensive sheepskin, squirrel, rabbit and others. You might bring one back to warm a little girl on your list.

In Norway, the national specialty is blue fox, which is 30 per cent cheaper than in this country. In Greece, it's stone marten.

In Argentina, Chile and Uruguay, nutria is found in rivers and lakes in the Andes. The finest skins are shipped from Argentina.

In Israel, look for inexpensive Russian broadtail; in Spain, Ireland and Austria, shearlings. Both are imported to the U.S.A.

In Bolivia and Peru, buy fur rugs of alpaca and goatskin made locally by the Indians. They cost one-third their price in the States. This is also true of the sheepskin rugs in Australia.

Should you plan, then, to buy a fur abroad, follow these rules:

1. Determine which furs are indigenous to the countries you mean to visit; then gather as much information as you can about them from a reputable furrier in your home city. Ask him about price ranges, marks of quality, and the like; and write the information down. Facts like this tend to blur when you are far from home.

2. Since fur consumers are almost completely dependent upon the integrity and knowledge of the retailer, buy from one with a long-established reputation and address. Under no circumstances let yourself be persuaded into dealing with a questionable merchant. Ask for a certificate of guarantee and a full description of the fur for insurance purposes.

3. The best buys abroad are always inexpensive local furs. Since we are in an era in which many low-priced *sportif*, even zany furs are good fashion, you can safely buy one without making a catastrophic mistake.

4. Don't buy a fur that needs special servicing.

5. Don't go haywire over raw skins, like karakul in Afghanistan or leopard in Somalia. The substantial cost of dressing, matching and sewing them into a finished coat can dissipate any money you may save at the start. Also, since the fur business is well-organized on a global basis, brokers are on the spot to pick the best pelts. The skins available to you are probably rejects.

Gardens

GARDENS have been many things to many people—palatial extensions of architecture to the Renaissance Italians and French, careless-seeming arrangements of hilly lawns and flower beds to the eighteenth-century English, austere abstractions in stone and water to the Japanese. Even if you don't know a delphinium from a daisy, visiting a country's gardens can give you a lesson in social history and art as well as many pleasant peaceful hours as you wander among good smells and fine things to look at. Looking at gardens may be a specialized way of seeing the world, but they can tell you the essence of a country as well as do its cuisine, costumes, music or museums.

There are many sorts of gardens in which flowers play only a small role, competing with fountains, streams, arbors, avenues, pavilions, waterfalls, and trees clipped in the shape of urns, crowns, elephants, or dogs downing a stag. In Britain, as one would expect of a country where every tiny backyard and window box is a garden, the possibili-

ties of garden-visiting are numberless, and—Britain being what it is
—very well organized. *Historic Houses, Castles and Gardens in Great
Britain and Ireland*, a large publication with maps, photographs and
exact descriptions, can be purchased from the British Book Centre, 122
East 55th Street, New York 10022, for $1.00. It lists every private or
government-owned estate open to the public and gives locations, with
nearest railway stations, opening times, admission fees, catering facilities, bus and railroad tours—everything you need know to plot your
own itinerary. A small booklet, *Our National Heritage—Gardens* is
available from the British Travel Association. (See page 483, for address nearest you.) The same association puts out a large brochure
with color photographs, "Gardens in Britain," which supplies a good
historical background.

It is out of the question to give even a short list of the most rewarding British gardens; there are so many, to so many tastes. You will
probably not miss the most famous—the Royal Botanic Gardens, the
restored Tudor gardens, elaborately symmetrical, at Kew; Capability
Brown's landscape park at Blenheim, in which nature is discreetly
enhanced by art; the formal water gardens at Chatsworth. But look
for others: the topiary garden at Levens Hall, the subtropical garden
of Tresco Abbey in the Isles of Scilly, the splendid garden at Sissing-
hurst Castle with its Tudor moat, roses and herbs.

A variety of garden tours is available. Galleon Tours, Eccleston
Court, Gillingham Street, Victoria, London S.W.1, offers a comprehensive 7-day tour for about $100, which includes everything and
leaves on specified dates. In late August, during the Edinburgh Festival, you can take 1-day bus tours of great Scottish gardens. They
range in cost from $1.50 to $4, including meals. For more information, write to The Gardens Scheme Desk, Festival Information Bureau, George Street, Edinburgh 2, Scotland.

Besides tours, flower shows and demonstrations (rose pruning,
manuring, composting) go on all summer long. The high point is the
great Chelsea Flower Show late in May. Two calendars of these
events are available, either from the British Travel Association or
from the Royal Horticultural Society, Vincent Square, London S.W.1
—of which anyone interested in growing flowers may become a
fellow.

The *jardin à la française* reached its apotheosis in the lucid green
vistas of Versailles, which seem to lead dreamily into infinity. If you
think of a garden as flowers, it is certainly not that, but it is one of
the most famous gardens in the world, and no visitor will want to
miss it. While you are in Paris you will also be likely to spend several

pleasant half hours in its charming parks and gardens: Parc Monceau, the Jardins du Luxembourg, the Bois de Vincennes, the Jardin des Tuileries, the Bois de Boulogne, and, nearby, the supreme rose garden of all, Bagatelle. While you are in Paris, you can arrange 3 days of garden tours, by bus or hired car, in the Ile de France. You will want to see the great, distinguished gardens of Malmaison with its roses, Saint-Germain-en-Laye, and of course Versailles. Or a 3-day tour might be taken out of Paris into the Loire Valley to see Chenonceaux, Chambord, Blois, and Villandry, the only château whose gardens are in their original state. Recently recreated in perfect sixteenth-century detail, they present intricate wonders of clipped parterres, an elaborately laid-out vegetable garden, and, in the evening, *Son et Lumière* performances. A third tour of 6 days might be taken along the Riviera and the Côte d'Azur to see the palms of Hyères, the immense flowery fields of Grasse (where French perfume comes from), horticultural establishments of every sort, and the exotic gardens of Monaco. Any garden club or individual interested in such itineraries should get in touch with the nearest French Government Tourist Office (see National Tourist Offices, page 482, for address).

Holland almost spells flowers. Besides its famous flower market at Aalsmeer (see page 233), it has superb gardens, some old, some new. One example is the Keukenhof Gardens, where 60 acres of lovely flowers bloom from late March to mid-May. Tulips, crocuses, hyacinths, narcissi, and flowering shrubs are the chief attraction; but its lake with black and white swans, two greenhouses, windmills, café and restaurant make it a delightful day's expedition. The Linnaeushof Gardens at Bennebroek near Haarlem, are open from April till October. Besides these two immense, fascinating gardens, you may visit many great gardens on private estates. For instance, there is Kasteel Twickel, which is a delightful fourteenth-century castle surrounded by lily-starred moats, elaborate parterres, sculptured box, a deer park, and an orangery. A list of estates open to the public as well as full details about garden tours is available from the Netherlands National Tourist Office.

The Italian boot, where gardens, like a number of other pleasant things in Western civilization, were invented, is rich with gardens from top to toe. In the north, the lake region is best seen in the full bloom of May. Trips by lake steamer will give you ravishing views of villas surrounded by terraced gardens. The most famous of all Italian gardens, Isola Bella, lies on Lake Maggiore, with its forest of cypress trees and obelisks, terraces mounting a hundred feet over the lake, fountains, lily pools, intricate parterres, statues, urns, green lawns planted with oranges, lemons, camellias—and white peacocks trailing like guardians through this paradise. In Florence you will certainly see the Boboli Gardens of the Pitti Palace, with an artificial lake and an island garden, planted with lemon trees and statues. At Collodi, in Tuscany, search out the Villa Garzoni, whose garden, commanding a spectacular view, has fountains and parterres, an old green theater, pebble mosaics, and troops of terra cotta monkeys playing the old version of football. In Rome, you will want to seek out the great garden of the Villa Medici, little changed after three hundred years, with its sculptures, ilex woods, cypress-crowned mount; and the villa of Pope Julius III (now housing the Etruscan Museum), which has, besides superb classical gardens, a delicious little secret garden. There are the huge gardens and park of the Villa Borghese; the garden of the Villa d'Este at Tivoli, glittering and murmuring with hundreds of fountains. If you are headed toward Viterbo, visit the fantastic ruined garden of the Villa Orsini at Bomarzo, which contains a series of huge, fabulous monsters, urns, grottoes, all carved out of natural rock outcroppings. The garden is a wilderness, but so unique and mysterious that if it lies on your path you will want to visit it.

It would take more than a summer to discover all the great gardens of Italy, but they have been beautifully photographed, described, and mapped by Georgina Masson in *Italian Gardens*, published by Abrams.

If you are in Spain, you will want to look for the Jardines de Sabatini around the Royal Palace in Madrid; and 35 miles south, the grandiose royal gardens of Aranjuez, where fountains play in a lovely island of verdure set in the tawny countryside; and the Moorish gardens of the Alhambra at Granada and the Alcazar in Seville with their patterned tiles and fruit trees and murmuring fountains. Portugal has a charming garden style of its own, which you can see in the garden of Fronteira, full of clipped box, baroque parterres, and unique walls and pavilions of blue tile.

Greece is not a great place for formal gardens, but the whole country becomes a wild garden in spring, and is well worth a special trip if you like the idea of scrambling about goat-haunted hillsides and sniffing wild basil. Orchids and wild anemones abound. Persian buttercups flourish on Crete, fiery little tulips at Delphi, mountain iris in the foothills of Olympus.

Switzerland has edelweiss, of course, and much more besides. There are fine landscaped gardens, alpine gardens up among the clouds, castle, island and botanical gardens, to mention a few of hundreds of examples.

Scandinavia, perhaps because it cherishes its summer, is rewarding to the garden lover. In Norway you might take a 7-day tour which takes in fjord scenery, hunting for alpine flora among the glaciers and visits to famous gardens (Oslo alone has over 33,000). Sweden's château country is famous for charming baroque estates. A drive through the country might take in the remarkable varied Norrviken Gardens in Båstad, a resort in southern Sweden, the garden of the Royal Summer Palace with handsome flowery parterres and parks; and a flock of turreted old castles each attended by a lovely garden. In Denmark, go to the Isle of Fyn, where old manor houses, castles and farms all cherish gardens. Copenhagen has the botanical gardens of its university, the garden of the Royal Agricultural High School, and the garden of the Royal Danish Society in Frederiksberg Garden.

Austria is famous for everything baroque—music, churches, castles, gardens too. Vienna alone has a dozen worth seeing. Innsbruck has the garden at Amras Castle; Graz the Rosegger Gardens and the Castle Gardens; Salzburg the gardens of the Mirabell Palace, the gardens of Hellbrunn, with ponds, grottoes, statuary and fountains; Linz botanical gardens and the garden of the ancient Wilhering Monastery 5 miles out of town. Germany too has rich baroque gardens: the Nymphenburg Palace at Munich with its luscious pavilions and fountains; Schloss Mainau on an island in Lake Constance; Schwetzingen near Mannheim, with obelisk, belvedere and even an enchanting mosque; and Weitschöchheim, at Würzburg, lovely with hornbeam hedges, willows, statues, swans and cherubs. The Herrenhausen at Hanover is another unspoiled baroque garden, which offers a display of fountains, ballet, music, theater, and illuminations all summer long.

The rest of the world is rich in gardens in many styles; the Moghul Gardens in the Rashtrapati Bhawan of Delhi; the Botanical Gardens in Bangalore, called Lal Bagh, laid out in the eighteenth century with terraces, trees, lakes, lotus pools, deer park, and greenhouse; the superbly colorful gardens of Bermuda and the Caribbean; the gardens of Zanzibar of a peculiar oriental splendor, sometimes surrounding ruined palaces of the old sultans; and strangest of all to Western eyes, the Zen gardens of Japan, which symbolize nature instead of manipulating it. Ripples in a pond are often represented by sand raked in wavy patterns, mountains by slabs of rock, waterfalls and clumps of shrubbery. The Ryōanji garden of Kyoto is most famous. Kyoto has many other gardens in traditional Japanese styles: the Golden Pavilion on the edge of a pretty pond containing a fine landscape garden; the Katsura Palace Garden; the Saihoji Temple and its mossy garden; the Heian Shrine and its garden with cherry trees and iris; and the gardens of the Old Imperial Palace and Nijo Castle.

The National Tourist Offices of the countries in which you plan to travel can provide you with information about itineraries and tours, and your travel agent can book you on any of the number available. (See page 479 for a list of these offices.)

Devoted horticulturists who would like an intensive garden tour of Europe, South America or the Orient should get in touch with the Jean Berke Travel Service, 518 Fifth Avenue, New York 10036. This agency offers a series of conducted tours which include enough general sightseeing to keep a non-gardening husband or wife happy, but make it their main business to enchant the garden-loving traveler with sweet sights and smells.

Gifts to Take Abroad

IF YOU KNOW that your path as a traveler will be red-carpeted with generous hospitality while abroad (or your husband will want small gifts for business associates and their wives), you will need a cache of "bread-and-butter" presents. With few exceptions most of the world's major stores are stocked with products similar to ours, from the local version of Brillo soap pads to white mink coats, and local handicrafts won't fill the bill. While you might cheerfully stock up for home consumption on sheepskin rugs, Rhodian beer mugs and worry beads in Greece, your friends in Athens will undoubtedly consider them terribly square. So it's a good idea to pack a few items that are instantly recognizable as typically American.

Two gifts are bound to be sure-fire hits with anyone on your list. The first is LP records of jazz, folk or classical music, or the scores of hit Broadway shows. The latter are especially good, for while foreigners quickly hear of our hit shows, it often takes months, even years, for the music to be recorded locally. The score of the latest American musical is prime equipment for one-upmanship all over the world. Also, records are usually far more expensive abroad than in the U.S.A., and they are easy to pack.

The second category is gadgets—the marvelous, inventive bits of hardware for which this country is famous. Don't, however, take a gadget that's a gag, unless you are certain your host will understand and like it. With our abundant supply, it seems wasteful not to give one that's really useful. Europeans, however, are slowly catching up with us, and you may see our ingenious American inventions displayed at the local equivalent of Hammacher Schlemmer.

Here are other apt presents for members of a family:

For children: clothing, especially sportswear such as T-shirts, clam diggers, blue jeans, or toys that whir or move. For little girls: a costumed doll or one that talks; a bathrobe in a fleecy synthetic; an American costume, like a squaw's dress. For little boys: a cowboy or Indian outfit or anything else related to the Wild West.

For women: nylon stockings (although these now are manufactured widely abroad, many of our yarns are a finer gauge); thick bath towels and fancy bed linens; costume jewelry (admired around the world); lingerie such as Dacron-and-cotton nightgowns; subscriptions to our women's and fashion magazines; and in the Middle and Far East, such beauty products as lipsticks and nail enamel (keep shades pale to medium), cologne, toilet water, sachet and fine soaps.

For men: sports shirts; cuff links; ties (remember the differences, however, in national temperaments: Dutchmen, for example, like theirs sober; Japanese not too conservative; and don't bring your local haberdasher's version of the Italian look to your husband's Roman business associate); after-shave lotion; cigarette lighters; a gadgety piece of office equipment; transistor radios (but not to Japan!); color film (although it can be processed abroad, the film itself is expensive); golf balls; and "name" brand fountain pens such as Parker and Sheaffer plus the special ink to go with them.

As for electrical appliances, whiskey, and cigarettes, bear in mind the following:

If you know that a country's electricity works on the same current as it does in the U.S.A., you can take anything. If it doesn't, the electrical appliance will require a transformer, or the mechanism will have to be replaced or adapted. Your gift may become far more of a problem and expense than a pleasure. As a rule, electrical appliances that are not cycle-sensitive or that have few moving parts, such as electric razors, will work reasonably well with an adapter cord. Those that have several moving parts such as clocks, phonographs and tape recorders, even toasters and coffee makers, will need major adjustments. To be safe, check the current, cycles and restrictions of the country and city for which the gift is destined, and buy only those American-made appliances that are especially manufactured for export.

General Electric sells the products it makes for use abroad through its IGE Export Division General Electric Company, and there is also the Westinghouse Electric International Company. Some manufacturers have special distributors for the sale of these export appliances, so check the pages of your local telephone directory for their names. Also, never buy an appliance to be used in a foreign country that does not carry an "International Warranty." These are honored locally and will enable the recipient of your gift to call upon services in his own country that understand the nature of the product, should something go wrong. One company whose sole business is selling and sending American electrical appliances abroad is the Arista Trading Company, 50 Broad Street, New York, New York 10004 (WHitehall 4-0085). If you write them, they will help you with sound, sensible advice about the whole subject.

Some nationals, like the wine-accustomed French, welcome gifts of Scotch and bourbon—they are expensive there and have a lower alcoholic content; others are not terribly keen about whiskey. You'd better be sure what drinking fashions are. If there's the slightest doubt, don't bother with whiskey, as it's a great nuisance to carry. The same is true of cigarettes. Once extremely welcome as gifts, they are now so universally available that unless you are sure of your host's preferences or of the fact that American brands are either not available or terribly expensive, don't haul the cartons from continent to continent. You can probably pick them up at duty-free shops as you go along.

While those who expect a tip generally prefer it in hard cash, there are occasions when a small gift is more suitable for expressing your appreciation. You might give one to the maid or housekeeper of a private house where you have stayed, a hotel manager, or an official who has been particularly helpful.

It's always wiser to anticipate the gifts you will need and take them with you than to send them after your return. There are two reasons for this. First, sending a gift means coping with a variety of international forms and practices. (To send a gift to Britain, for example, you must fill out a U.S. Customs Declaration and follow International Parcel Post Instructions.) Second, the recipient usually has to pay customs duty and purchase tax at his end if your gift is valued at $10 or more, which takes the edge off the gift's pleasure.

These levies can mount up sizably. In Britain, again, the duty for phonograph records is 15 per cent, the purchase tax about 45 per cent; on clothing made of silk or nylon, the duty runs between 20 and 33⅓ per cent, the purchase tax is 10 per cent. (Small, inexpensive gifts sent air mail are usually not subject to duty.) Some governments set down maximum quantities of specific items that may be received as gifts without being taxed, so it's best to check the individual regulations of the countries on your itinerary. Finland, for example, will allow only 1 pair of shoes, 3 pairs of stockings, and one set of underwear as duty-free gifts.

Generally, governments allow you to take in, duty free, a reasonable number of personal gifts. In France, for example, a personal gift for a national may be brought in, duty free, by any visitor if its value is not more than $10. This does not, of course, apply to little souvenirs of minimal value, which need not even be declared. At Christmas and New Year's, the regulations are usually relaxed or modified a bit, to allow gifts of greater value to go through, duty free, at the discretion of the customs officer.

In Australia a visitor may bring in up to $70 worth of gifts without paying duty; in Sweden the amount is $55; in Israel $41; in Finland $93.75. Beyond these allowable amounts, duty is levied.

If you have arrived empty-handed and suddenly need a hostess gift, go to the nearest bookstore and buy a splashy book published in America. A few years ago, I needed a bread-and-butter gift unexpectedly in Amsterdam, and after scouting around, I ended up taking a copy of *The Family of Man* from the bookstore around the corner. It was a success, as gifts go, for it was something American.

Golf

IN THE shadows of the Pyramid of Cheops, the snowy Himalayas, the castle walls at Harlech; on great seaside courses along the Firth of Clyde, the blue Atlantic, the dunes facing the North Sea; on palmy islands from Tahiti and New Guinea to Jamaica; on fairways fringed with coconut trees, umbrella pines or delicate giant ferns; around hazards created by monkeys, kangaroos and Moghul tombs; on a course brightened throughout the night by the midnight sun—golfers are teeing off. Even if you and your husband are only occasional Sunday duffers, you should pack your golf shoes and clothes and mix some quiet hours of golf in with shopping, museum-hopping and sightseeing.

Golf clubs, private and public, are probably the world's biggest fraternity and can be a wonderful entrée to the local social life, all the more welcome if you are traveling alone.

You will find good golf courses near almost all major cities and at resorts. You can play at any of the public courses wherever you go. If you prefer to use a club, no special introduction will be necessary. All you need is the membership card of your golf club back home or a letter of introduction on club paper from its secretary. If you have forgotten either, or are not a member of a club, ask the tourist office, your hotel desk, or a local travel agency to telephone ahead to the golf club. Unless it is one of the few completely private clubs, you'll be admitted easily. Even at the famous and venerable Old Course at St. Andrews in Scotland, anyone who comes to the club may play.

While golf has been the national game of Scotland for centuries, it is a relatively new fashion in other parts of the world—and the distribution of courses reflects this. There are 22 in Spain, 80 in France, 40 in Mexico, 19 in Holland and 15 in India. The four Scandinavian countries, which have taken up the sport rather recently, share about 100 among them. Britain, however, has close to 2,000—200 in Scotland alone, and more than 300 within a 50-mile radius of London; Australia has more than 1,300 (the sport is so popular there that it is often taught in the schools and Melbourne has a stretch of 40 courses —nearly all of championship class—within a 20-mile radius). Golf is booming in Japan, which has miraculously managed to squeeze more than 300 courses on its crowded islands; except for Great Britain, Japan reportedly has more golf facilities than any other country of comparative size and these days even its geisha girls are taking up the sport. There are also excellent courses in South Africa and New Zealand.

Green fees are generally far lower abroad than in the U.S.A. Some start at 35 cents for a round or $1 for a day; others go up as high as $15 for a day, but these are rare. Most of the good courses have clubhouses with locker rooms, showers, a golf shop, a pro's office, and bar and restaurant. Many also have swimming pools, tennis courts, and other sports facilities. Caddies are usually available, and occasionally exotic. Above the Arctic circle in Lapland they are colorfully costumed. In Japan they might be girls in kimono coats and slacks. Their fees, too, are lower than they are in the U.S.A. If you don't want the bother of traveling with your own clubs, you can readily rent them, but if you are wedded to your own equipment, you can take it everywhere by air for very little money. (For the costs to various destinations, see Sports Equipment, page 337.) There are many places in the world whose temperate climate makes it possible to play golf most of the year, and nearly everywhere you can play on championship courses without having to wait to tee off. If you plan a trip abroad in late fall or early spring, remember that the weather in places like Israel, Spain, Portugal, Italy and the Canary and Balearic Islands is perfect for the game. And the world of golf is such a unified world that the rules and protocol are very nearly the same everywhere.

As for clothes, wear a shirtwaist dress or tailored golf dress, or a skirt and blouse—and, of course, regulation golf shoes. On hot sunny islands knee-length shorts are permitted, but everywhere else avoid shorts, since it is not the classic costume for golf and may well be forbidden on some courses. Slacks have become acceptable in Britain and on the Continent where the weather tends to be cool. (However, don't wear them into the clubhouse or dining room.)

Since there are 7,500,000 golfers in the U.S.A., the airlines, travel agents and hotels occasionally organize special golf tours. For a single package price, they provide transportation, hotels, most meals, green fees, occasionally self-drive cars, and an itinerary that provides plenty of golf. If you want a custom-made tour of some of the world's great courses, this too can be arranged through your travel agent. In Canada several of the larger resorts offer "learn to golf weeks" with special rates. If you travel to Britain frequently, you might want to become a member of the Golf Society of Great Britain. For a fee of $14.70 for men or $8.40 for women, you can play for three years at 15 of the country's fine courses without paying a green fee.

There are four rules of thumb to observe when you play golf abroad:

1. Call the secretary of the golf club or the pro (or ask your concierge to do this) to be certain that there are no tournaments scheduled on the day you'd like to play. At the same time ask about the green fees and the rules concerning visitors' hours, weekend and Sunday regulations and special days for women players.

2. Sometimes caddies are in short supply, so it's courteous to call the club a day ahead of time to reserve one and set a starting time. Then keep your appointment.

3. Naturally, as soon as you arrive at the club, show your hometown membership card or your letter of introduction to the secretary.

4. Curb your impulse to tip as much as you would at home. Unknowingly, most Americans overtip caddies, which is a source of embarrassment for a club's regular members. Ask the advice of the professional; he'll tell you how much you should pay.

If you don't play golf and dislike the role of "golf widow," consider its fringe benefits abroad. If your husband is an avid golfer but a reluctant traveler, this may be one way to get him to go places—and to keep him happy at the same time. While he's on the links, you can wander through the shops or soak up the sun at a nearby beach.

If golfing abroad interests you, write to the tourist offices on the list that begins on page 479. Many countries publish brochures listing their golf courses.

Pan American Airways has recently started a program to give golfers who travel overseas the latest information about courses at their destination. All they need do is present a Pan Am Golf Identity Card at the local Pan Am office and they will be given a package of information with the names of local clubs where they are eligible to play, including many where the airline has made special arrangements for its passengers. The package also contains descriptions of the courses, prices, advice on tipping, meals, best times to play, best way to reach the courses and other useful data. The golf card may be obtained free of charge by writing to Pan American Airways, Box 2212, Dept. 620, Boston, Massachusetts 02101.

The airline has also recently published a guidebook to golf courses around the world called *Golf: New Horizons,* by Gene Sarazen. It covers over 400 overseas courses giving such details as location, course size, availability to visitors, green fees, caddie fees, lessons, clubhouse facilities, etc. You can buy it for $4.95 by writing to Pan Am at P. O. Box PAA, Jamaica, New York 11430, or you can find it at a higher price in local bookstores.

Handicrafts

"HANDICRAFTS" is a difficult word to define, but we all recognize the items by instinct. We know that Patek Philippe watches, Fortuny fabrics, Schlumberger jewels, Huntsman suits and gold-inlaid Belgian shotguns, all useful objects made by hand, are not handicrafts—and that porcelain mustard pots, peasant rugs and fishermen's sweaters are. Perhaps we might describe them as decorative objects made for use by people remote enough from the industrial world—either in time or in place—to have had no access to machine-made substitutes. The handicrafts of a village, province or country depend on the natural materials nearby. Where rushes grow in river valleys, there baskets will be made; where the clay is suitable, pottery will be the art. Forests produce woodcarvers; sheep, country woolens.

A lot of what is called "handicrafts" lies somewhere near the border of art; a lot more lies plainly in the wastelands of junk. Many handicrafts of times past are the objects of art you will be nosing out in antique shops, at auctions and flea markets—dower chests, quilts, old pottery, all made to furnish the house, satisfying emotional as well as material needs. Wherever you are traveling through the countryside, a treasure hunt for examples of native crafts will give you tremendous extra pleasure, and a well-chosen purchase will have the satisfying combination of functional utility and aesthetic rightness. If you have a nose for geography, a good map, and a few clues, you can set out on exciting explorations anywhere. Here are some suggestions of what to look for—and where to look—in various countries you may visit.

In the British Isles the clues may be found in a free booklet called "Country Workshops," published by the Rural Industries Bureau, which lists, according to locality, small workshops all over the islands, telling what they make and when they are open. All of them welcome foreign visitors and have things on hand for sale—from canal boats to baskets. In Sussex, for example, there are workshops which sell black metallic earthenware, cricket bats, stone carving and lettering in stone, willow baskets and wooden toys; in Carmarthenshire in Wales, one shop after another sells tapestry quilts that are copies of old tapestries and are heavy enough to be used as rugs as well as bed covers. They cost about $20; Wiltshire's workshops offer woodcarvings, saddlery, falconry furniture, fishing tackle, traditional pottery, scale models of antique furniture, fire irons and door knockers. The pleasantest thing about looking up the craftsman in his own shop is that you can have something made to your own order—a book binding, a brass doorplate, an old glass engraved with your cipher, a basket made to a special size and shape.

In London you will find refined examples of the best British crafts at the Crafts Centre of Great Britain, 16–17 Hay Hill, Berkeley Square. London is also a good source of tweeds and knitwear if you can't get to Scotland and Ireland where they originate. Woolland Brothers, Stonehenge Woollen Industry Ltd., and Hunt and Winterbotham all have full stocks.

If you do go to Scotland, the first place to visit in Edinburgh is the Scottish Craft Centre in Acheson House, where you will find traditional Scottish products such as tweeds and tartans, baskets, Shetland shawls, silverware, hand-engraved glassware, jewelry, and leatherwork. Highland Home Industries, on George Street, has a charming collection of much the same nature. Tartans are the specialty of many shops: William Anderson and Sons are specialists in Highland dress. Look for the Celtic jewelry made by Highland craftsmen, especially the traditional silver "Luckenbooth" brooch, shaped like a heart surmounted by a crown, which used to be given at betrothals. Hugh Macpherson Ltd. sells tartans and is a noted bagpipe maker too.

In Dublin you will find a splendid assortment of Irish handicrafts at Irish Cottage Industries: mostly bolts of handwoven tweeds and a sprinkling of scarves, traveling rugs, neckties, etc. Country Markets Ltd. is a handicrafts shop sponsored by the nonprofit Irish Cooperative Association, where tweeds and woolens sell for as little as $3 a yard. Carrickmacross and Limerick handmade laces are sold by the yard in the big department stores; Belfast linen and Irish crochet cost about a third of what they do in the U.S.A. Intricately handknit Aran Island sweaters and socks—recently so popular in the States—can be found in Dublin shops at reasonable prices.

French handicrafts range from copper cooking vessels to cowboy hats from the Camargue. The farther from Paris the province, the more abundant, in general, the variety of its handicrafts. The copper cooking pans come from Normandy, which is also a good place to look for provincial armoires and chests. Seafaring Bretons, who have a lot of time to kill in bad weather, produce hand-carved furniture, crocheted gloves, wicker baskets, starched lace coifs, sailor shirts and caps. The Pyrénées, at the other end of France, offer Basque linens, dolls, medlar wood canes; the Auvergne produces lace, glazed earthenware, and rosaries. From Provence and the Côte d'Azur come the ceramics of Vallauris (whose most celebrated potter is Picasso) and from Marseilles come small clay religious figures. In the French Alps you may find pottery, dolls, objects carved of walnut and olivewood, toys, wrought-iron work and cowbells; in Franche-Comté and Jura, brierwood pipes, wooden toys, and chess sets. In Burgundy look for silver wine-tasting cups, porcelain mustard pots, corkscrews set in vinestocks, wine baskets. Alsace-Lorraine makes handsome blue stoneware pitchers and steins. Bordeaux produces wineskins as well as leather pouches. In Languedoc-Roussillon look for leather gloves, espadrilles, and Catalan berets.

Every region sells dolls in the local dress, and wherever regional costume survives, interesting and often beautiful headdresses, aprons, or blouses may be found.

The main thing to remember when buying in provincial shops, in France or anywhere else, is to take your time. Examine the finish of the article: seams, bindings, joints and surfaces. Choose a rustic solid-looking small shop in preference to one obviously out to dazzle the tourist trade. A country market is always an excellent place to buy regional handicrafts, and much more fun than any shop.

The prices in Spain and Portugal are still rather low compared with most parts of Europe, but the quality of workmanship varies a good deal and you must examine your treasure carefully before agreeing to buy it. Spanish furniture, which has had a sudden vogue in the States, is an attractive buy. Look for the desks with hundreds of drawers, called *vargueños*, and the chests of all sizes. Wrought-ironwork is another traditional Spanish specialty. Metal lanterns, intricately pierced or with glass panels, are very fine; sixteenth-century examples are terribly expensive, but handmade reproductions cost as little as $15. In Madrid, go to the Mercado Nacional de Artesania (Floridablanca 1), which is the official handicraft exhibition center operated by the government. It has gathered together all the traditional types of Spanish regional work in a handsome display and sells them at reasonable prices.

In Portugal you will see a great deal of exquisite hand-embroidered work from Madeira at all sorts of prices. A tablecloth could set you back a few hundred dollars. Peasant clothes—handwoven black skirts and shawls and fishermen's sweaters—are very inexpensive (under $5) and could find a useful place in an American wardrobe. Other good buys in Portugal are magnificent handmade leather book bindings, some of them gold-tooled, which sell well below the U.S. luxury price. Portugal is famous for its special blue tiles known as *azulejos*. If you are serious about them, go to the Fabrica de Sant' Ana in Lisbon. You can order a plaque with a street number for your house or a set of tiles that will make a fanciful rococo table top with your initials and the date; or enough tiles to do a whole bathroom, fireplace, or fountain.

A greatly traveled country like Italy naturally has some of the worst as well as the best. You can live without cheap Neapolitan cameos, glass menageries from Venice, and Florentine straw skirts. But when you get out of the tourist orbit you will find valuable handicrafts. South of Naples, traditional life still goes on—for the time being. Look for coral work in Torre del Greco, inlaid woodwork (music boxes are a lovely example) in Sorrento. The famous, enchanting Christmas crèches of southern Italy include handcarved shepherds, which you may find in the shops of San Gregorio Armeno in Naples. There are ceramics in Amalfi and all over the island of Capri. In Buccino, Penta and Fisciano you can buy copper household utensils with engraved and embossed decorations; in Camerota, terracotta vases and kitchen ware shaped like ancient Greek amphorae with long narrow necks and two handles.

A few words of warning about shopping south of Rome: First, you must bargain; it is expected. Second, you must take all claims that a given object is an antique with a large grain of salt. The Italians have been faking antiques for 2,000 years. Third, Italian work is usually pretty but sometimes flimsy. Examine carefully anything that is to receive heavy wear.

Greece has joined the modern world so lately that her handicrafts are still rich and various. You can see a display of examples from all over the peninsula and the islands at the headquarters of the National Organization for Greek Handicraft in Athens. The things here are not for sale, but this is a splendid way to get your bearings. You will see the distinctive ceramics of Rhodes, Salonika, Lavrion; lace and shell ornaments from the Cyclades; brilliantly colorful woven fabrics —bedspreads, linens, shirts, sweaters, coats—from Crete and Mykonos; multicolored strings of beads, embroidered linen bags, felt slippers, silver rings and bracelets.

Carved wooden household objects—containers for butter and wine, spoons, distaffs, candlesticks, lamp stands, bread molds, which are still in daily use in the villages—can be bought wherever you go. And at the other end of the scale—too near art to count quite accurately as handicraft—are the 24-carat gold reproductions of ancient Greek jewelry made by Elias Lalaounis of Zolotas in Athens.

The Handicraft Department of Their Majesties Fund has lately sponsored a carpet-making program among the peasants. The skill is, in part, handed down from their parents and grandparents who came to Greece from Asia Minor; the designs are inspired, in part, by Greek folk motifs. The results, whatever their inspiration, are deliciously informal, freshly colored, and thoroughly pretty. Some of them vaguely resemble French needlepoint rugs of the eighteenth century, but with an airy playfulness that is very endearing.

Germany is so well-known for machine tools, Mercedes automobiles, microscopes and other products of industrialization that you might overlook the few genuine handicraft industries left in remote villages. In the Bavarian mountain village of Mittenwald, violins have been made for hundreds of years and are still being made in small numbers for people who care for fine instruments. Since it takes 150 hours to make one $500 violin, this traditional village industry is unhappily, but understandably, dying out. Tourists come to Oberammergau to see the Passion Play, but the village has been famous far longer for its woodcarving shops, which nowadays turn out almost nothing but splendid Nativity figures. In the Black Forest cuckoo clocks and regional costumes, and in Munich beautiful handmade candles, loden coats and suits, *lederhosen*, and hand-printed cloth are well worth looking for. The best buys in Austria are the engaging peasant costumes—dirndls, loden coats, felt jackets, and *lederhosen*. These you will find in Salzburg, as well as candles and tiny crèche figures made of beeswax. In all large cities, look for the Heimatswerke which sell native goods.

In Switzerland a good selection of authentic regional handiwork can be found at the Zurich and St. Gall shops of Schweizer Heimatwerk. The handmade music boxes are particularly fine; there is also a wide selection of hand-painted clay pottery, carved wood toys, and wrought-iron and copper vases.

Scandinavian handicrafts have been so highly developed that the folksy element is no longer conspicuous. The glass and crystal, ceramics, silver, stainless steel, and wooden furniture and brightly colored textiles are all highly sophisticated in their simplicity. In Denmark head straight for Den Permanente—The Permanent Exhibition of Danish Arts and Crafts. Its displays—which range from products of the Royal Porcelain Factory to folded paper lanterns and carved wooden toys—have all been approved by a hard-to-please committee and all are for sale. The simpler folk art—handwoven fabrics, lace which used to be woven for the national costume, pottery of red and gray clay, cross-stitch embroideries in peasant patterns, knitted mittens, dolls in ancient costume—may be found in the sales rooms of Haandarbejdets Fremme in Copenhagen or its branches in several other Danish towns.

The Swedish Handicraft Industries Association encourages traditional folk art—pottery, basketwork, wrought iron, wood, wall hangings, fabrics. A blue, yellow and white sticker labels any genuine handicraft item for sale in Swedish shops. Good places to find them in Stockholm are Svensk Hemslöjd and Foreningen Hantverket.

Oslo's Arts and Crafts Museum is a logical starting point for the buyer of Norwegian handicrafts. You can't buy the six hundred-year-old tapestries, but shops throughout the country sell handicrafts similar to those in the museum: wood carvings, dolls in native dress, trays and boxes decorated with painted roses, silver brooches in Viking tradition, knitted sweaters, caps and mittens. Forum in Oslo is the permanent official sales exhibition of arts and crafts. The Husfliden store in Oslo has the country's largest collection of handmade goods.

Finnish handicrafts display a peculiar elegance and flair, somehow distinctive from other Scandinavian countries. At the Finnish Design Center a permanent exhibition of textiles, ceramics, glassware and cutlery is on display and can be bought. Friends of Finnish Handicraft sell just what you'd expect, including needlework and *ryijy*, the brilliantly colored abstractly patterned, deep-piled rugs which the Finns themselves think too good to walk on (they hang them on the wall). The Tourist Office in Helsinki can give you the addresses of some of the famous makers; going directly to the source or to their home-town shops can save you a third of the Helsinki price. It is worth the trouble because they cost from $100 to $300, and you would have to pay about twice as much for them in the States.

Outside Europe handicrafts also flourish, especially where ancient ways of life are relatively undisturbed. Mexico is a wonderful example. Gimcrack objects "Made in Japan" have already made their appearance among the honest native work in Mexican markets, but the great pottery, silver, onyx ware, jewelry, dolls, mosaics, sculptures, rugs, toys, baskets, birdcages, textiles, glass, and who knows what else, are all being produced in villages up and down the country, often in a tradition unchanged from before the Spaniards found America. The simplest objects of clay, sugar, or paper are alive with a vigorous beauty that fairly explodes with exuberance. You must explore the country by bus or car to find all these delightful objects in their native places; keep your eye out for the innumerable festivals for which special objects are produced. Every major city has excellent fixed-price shops where you can't bargain; in the markets you are expected to do so. Examples of the best handicrafts from all over Mexico are on exhibition and for sale at the government-sponsored Museo Nacional de Artes Populares on Avenida Juárez in Mexico City. Go also to the Bazaar Sabado, which is filled with enchanting things.

India has a fantastic variety of handicrafts—textiles, sculpture of ivory, teak and sandalwood, intricate, boldly beautiful jewelry, enameled vessels, mosaics, pottery of every description. Like everything else about India, the handicrafts are bewilderingly rich and full of strange significance. Fortunately the state governments operate about 30 shops located in major cities, which sell crafts from their regions at fixed prices. Nothing that falls short of government-set standards is offered. Another well-regulated shop where handicrafts are offered for sale is the famous Central Cottages Industries Emporium in New Delhi. This is operated by a cooperative rather than by the government. In one large, well-ordered place goods of the highest quality, gathered from all over the country by volunteer experts, are offered for sale. These volunteers also endeavor to help craftsmen adapt their traditional techniques to current demands, since the shop exports to the U.S.A. and Europe, but quality and the intrinsic Indian character are never sacrificed. The Handloom House shops operated by the All India Handloom Board in New Delhi and Bombay have good selections of silks and cottons from all parts of India.

Colombia and Canada, Peru, Puerto Rico and the Philippines, Thailand, Japan (the list of countries with beautiful handmade goods is very long)—all have products made with infinite care and skill, that you will want to take away.

When you buy a fine handcrafted object anywhere—whether it's a Spanish lantern, a French omelet pan, or a bit of carving from an Indian temple—you have perhaps come closer to possessing a part of the spirit of that country than you can in any other material way.

Hats

IN 1884, a popular etiquette book delivered the following edict: "No lady appears at the Casino bareheaded; it is always with hat or bonnet, and she lives in her bonnet more or less even at the balls."

Bonnets are no more, and even hats are no longer *de rigueur* in or out of casinos. If you are hat-minded—if you like to collect hats and find they make you feel prettier—you can wear a hat suitable to your clothes and the occasion whenever you feel like it, just as you would at home.

On the other hand, if you go through life with nothing more on your head than hair spray and an occasional scarf, you needn't feel the slightest bit self-conscious about being hatless abroad. You may remain bareheaded on an airplane, ship, train or sightseeing bus. (Don't, as so many women do, wear an elaborate hat on a plane; if you must put on a confection only because it is too difficult to pack, leave it home.)

There is not a city where unhatted women don't look completely natural. You can in fact go around the world without once needing a hat—unless you find yourself in any of the following circumstances:

1. If you attend such an event as a garden party, a luncheon or an afternoon reception at which royalty or high officialdom are present, a hat is *comme il faut*. It need not be more than a slight pouf of veiling and a ribbon, but the dignity of the occasion demands it.

2. In northern cities where the climate can be chilly and damp, hats are seen more often and are nearly always worn at ladies' luncheons. If lunching with the local residents such as your husband's

business associates is part of your itinerary in cities like Amsterdam, Copenhagen or Stockholm, a hat might make you feel more appropriately dressed. In Helsinki, in winter, women wear handsome fur hats which they check along with their coats. Keep your hat simple, however—flowers bloom everywhere on the streets of northern countries except on women's heads. In Australia, local women wear hats and gloves to go shopping, but if you are not a hat person, you needn't bother with them even here.

3. On the other hand, wear a real milliner's dream of a hat to major sports events. While your idea of being well-dressed for a horse race at home might be a discreet shirtwaist dress, spectator pumps and the wind in your hair, elsewhere, quite on the contrary, the races bring out some of the most gala dressing you've ever seen. Should you find yourself at England's Royal Ascot, France's Grand Prix at Longchamps, Brazil's Sweepstake or Australia's Melbourne Cup meeting, you must dress to the nines. Europeans, particularly the English and the French, treat their major sports events as grand occasions (this is even true of the rowing competitions like the Henley Royal Regatta which takes place at 11 A.M.). *Not* to wear a hat, preferably quivering with organdy flowers or nodding with feathers, is to commit a fashion *gaffe*. Hats are even worn to polo matches and occasionally to bullfights, although these are usually less flouncy. Mantillas, which prettily solve the problem of covering your head when visiting churches in Spain, are never worn elsewhere except to bullfights—and then, only in white. They are definitely not right for nightclubs or sightseeing.

After dark, at the theater or restaurants, the custom of wearing hats is identical to ours. Women wear hats for flattery or elegance, never because they are socially required. And just as at home, hats are worn to christenings, weddings, funerals and church services. (See Church Dressing, page 76.)

The sunnier the climate, the fewer the hats. In cities like Istanbul, Tel Aviv, Athens, Madrid and Mexico City they practically disappear. You'll never need a hat unless you find yourself at an afternoon reception given by an embassy.

On sunny islands like the West Indies, hats are used only as sun shields, which is a straightforward, practical reason for buying the native product, usually a wide-brimmed straw hat.

The farther you go from home, the less need you'll have for a hat. Saris and kimonos are never worn with them. Even Indian and Japanese women who have adopted Western dress wear hats far less often than their American counterparts. Here what the local American community wears becomes the visitor's guide. Generally, except for the occasions given above, hats look out of place in the Orient.

However you feel about hats, keep the ones you take traveling as simple as possible (with the one elaborate exception, of course: if the Royal Ascot is on the program). Like the rest of your clothing, hats will be handled, sometimes mishandled. If you fly, the 44-pound weight limit for economy class won't give you much scope for properly packing an elaborate, fragile hat. Stick with small, neat pillboxes (they fit into corners), jersey turbans, or any of the new breed of hats especially designed for travel; they obligingly fold flat.

Health

IF YOU have any fears about staying well while you travel, banish them. It is as easy to keep well abroad as at home. Unless you intend to foray into darkest Africa, hundreds of miles from the nearest city, there will be few new or exotic dangers to your health, and you will never be far from medical help.

The world is peppered with reliable doctors (many of whom were trained in the U.S.A.) and well-stocked pharmacies; the doctor in Rome has access to the same wonder drugs as the one in Roanoke. By requiring that you be inoculated (see Inoculations, page 178), our government makes certain that you won't pick up any serious epidemic disease. Should you droop or feel ill *en voyage*, it will probably be due to one of two basic reasons: Either your body is reacting to the new physical situations inherent in the act of travel itself, or you are suffering from the same illness you might have had at home. The head cold that might just be a bother in Indianapolis becomes slightly frightening in India—not because it is more serious, but simply because you become nervous at being far from home.

Let's start with the first group of possible health hazards, their cause, and how to cope with them.

You will be in motion, on an airplane or ship. This will probably not bother you for an instant, for these days motion sickness is a thing of the past. Jets fly so high that they are above the clouds and seldom encounter sustained turbulence. Ships have stabilizers which reduce rolling and pitching. If, however, you are tense or frightened, or if you eat or drink unwisely before your departure, you may feel queasy. The best preventative is a good night's sleep before you leave and something to keep you interested—a book or a conversation— while you are en route. Ask your doctor to recommend a motion sickness remedy; Dramamine or Bonamine are usually suggested. Make it a general rule not to start any trip without feeling rested, and certainly don't start a long trip in a hot, humid climate if you're not feeling well.

You will be crossing time zones. On a ship, this doesn't affect you at all. You change your watch an hour or so each day and your body easily absorbs the slight adjustment in schedule. If you fly, however, your metabolic rhythm must make some quick adaptations, especially when you fly from east to west, or vice versa, for 5 or more hours. You may arrive, for example, at breakfast time in Lisbon, while your body is still geared to New York time, where it is midnight. Upsetting your metabolic (or Circadian) rhythm will produce temporary fatigue for the first 24 to 48 hours abroad until your body's metabolic clock is synchronized with local time. The only cure for this is rest. Try to sleep as much as you can during the flight, walk a bit to ease the cramped feeling of sitting in one place for hours, drink lots of water but little alcohol to keep from getting dehydrated. Eat less than you normally would before, during and after the flight to ease the strain on your digestion. Try to ignore the airline's forced-feeding routine. It may help to pass the time but it's hard on your system. Get lots of sleep the first two nights at your destination.

You will eat wonderful but strange new foods and drink more wine than at home. The result may be a temporarily upset stomach or an explosive diarrhea so common that it is known by several lively epithets: the trots; Cairo rumble (Egypt); Delhi Belly (India); Montezuma's Revenge, or the Aztec Two-Step (Mexico); or *turista*.

Foreign cooking has a different basis from ours; your stomach needs a little while to get used to new combinations of oils and herbs. In any civilized part of the world, your stomach upset is much more likely to come from unaccustomed food in unaccustomed quantities than to food poisoning or dysentery. (See Water, page 412; Lettuce, page 206; and Street Vendors, page 344.) Intestinal disorder seems to be triggered by changes in food, drinking water and temperature, by physical exhaustion or by several other still unknown factors. Your distress is likely to last from 24 to 48 hours; if it lingers longer or you run a fever, call a doctor. Before you leave, ask your own doctor to prescribe a remedy for diarrhea; Kaopectate and paregoric are often given.

On the other hand, you may become temporarily constipated. This frequently happens when one's personal habits are thrown off rhythm by new surroundings, or diet. Pack a mild laxative.

You may do more walking than you do at home. Take time out to rest after lunch. Either have a nap or sit in a park. Put your feet up before you change for dinner; soak and massage them—and otherwise pamper them with a cooling talcum powder.

You may be at a higher altitude than you are normally accustomed to. Where the air is rarer, you are likely to tire more easily. Take it easy for the first two days. Get lots of sleep, drink little alcohol, walk slowly—and enjoy the chance to amble along.

You may be out in strong tropical sun. Start taking the sun gradually, perhaps 10 minutes or less each day; then work up to longer exposures, never going beyond your normal limit. Stay out of the noonday sun. Walk on the shady side of the street and do wear a hat.

Since mosquitoes are often found in the tropics, it's wise to pack an insect repellent for your skin or pick one up when you get there (sand fleas, too, can be enormously irritating on the beach). Also take an insecticide such as DDT aerosol spray for your room.

The "hazards" listed above are likely to be the ones produced by your trip. You may be made uncomfortable by none, one, or all of them—but any discomfort will most likely be just temporary.

Or you might be afflicted with exactly the same aches and pains you get at home: a chest cold, for example, or an allergic reaction to shrimp, no more severe on a Greek island than in Georgetown.

To cope with the familiar contingencies, pack the drugs and medicines you use often, the ones that can give you relief from minor aches and pains. There's no need to carry a small pharmacy with you, unless you are going into the bush—and since you won't be going there alone, ask the leader of your party what to pack. I always travel with a small bottle of Alka-Seltzer (you should have one antiacid along); an analgesic (mine is aspirin); a specific against diarrhea (I carry Sulfathalidine and paregoric). You might add to these a remedy for sleeplessness; a thermometer (European ones are in centigrade) and a few Band-aids.

There are those who believe in carrying a small first-aid kit. I have never traveled with one and cannot remember ever needing it. If you have children in tow, you should of course have everything on hand to cope with their normal banged knees and scratched fingers.

If your teeth give you the slightest pain, see your dentist before you leave. A toothache in the middle of the night can be harder to relieve abroad than appendicitis.

Also, if you have a chronic disease or ailment, it's a good idea to have your doctor write down a description of it for you in Latin, should there be no English available on the spot. Have you an allergy to a specific drug or treatment, such as penicillin or tetanus toxoid, or a physical condition that may need emergency treatment? Carry some identification—a tag, bracelet or card—with you at all times with the facts clearly written out. It's useful, too, to have the card written in two foreign languages. If you are being treated for a disease or require special medication, take an extra supply of your medicine and its prescription or ask your doctor to give you its generic rather than trade name. If you depend on certain drugs regularly such as digitalis, take double the quantity you will need and put half the amount into each of two suitcases in case one gets lost. If you have had a serious illness just before your trip, it is advisable to carry a brief medical history with you. Always tell the new doctor who treats you about any drugs you are taking, since the combination of certain drugs can often be dangerous.

Should you need a doctor abroad, there are several ways of finding one. You can call the nearest U.S. embassy or consulate. Each maintains a list of competent doctors and is prepared to advise visiting Americans. If you are staying at a large hotel, or near one, ask the concierge or manager to recommend a doctor. Nearly all have "house physicians" who are on call. In Paris, there is the well-established American Hospital; in Madrid, the British-American hospital. In nearly all large cities, particularly those that the British have settled in or visited over a period of time, there is likely to be a hospital or two with a large number of English-speaking doctors on its staff. The best place to become ill is Britain where free medical and dental service is available even to visitors under the National Health Service Act, if you fall ill while touring the country. In the U.S.S.R., first aid treatment and doctors' visits are also free; you pay for medicine. If you become very ill and are far from everything but an American or British army base, get in touch with it. Naturally, if your own doctor knows any colleagues overseas, take their names with you.

About five years ago, a nonprofit organization of some 3,000 English-speaking doctors was formed in about 50 countries. Its goal was to give travelers medical care similar to what they were used to at home. Called the International Association for Medical Assistance to Travelers, it has uniform fees wherever it exists: $8 for office visits, $10 for hotel calls, and $15 for night calls, Sundays and local holidays. Most of the doctors have served internships in the U.S.A., Canada or England. Main headquarters are in Rome at 11 Via Parigi; there are also branch offices in New York at 745 Fifth Avenue and in Toronto at 18 Temperance Street. Write to any of these addresses for a roster of IAMAT Centers and a free IAMAT membership card. Should you need a doctor abroad the local center will give you a choice of two or three doctors. As the organization is relatively new—and I have had no personal experience with it—I can only report its existence, without being able to vouch for its quality. I *can* say that the American Medical Association considers it a very reputable organization.

If you have been in good health and are going to be away only a short time, I see no reason to get a physical checkup, but ask your doctor about this when he gives you his prescription for an anti-diarrhea remedy or motion-sickness pill. Also ask him whether you should take a "wide spectrum" antibiotic, "just in case" (or salt pellets or an anti-malaria preparation if you are going into the tropics). And finally, write down his telephone number. Since intercontinental telephone calls are easy to make, it will often save you a lot of worry to call him for advice if you become seriously ill.

Hotels

THERE ARE countless thousands of hotels, *ryokan*, lodges, bungalows, pavilions, *paradores*, *pousadas*, *posadas* and *Gasthöfe* around the world that can give you a roof to sleep under. They range from 35-cents-a-night youth hostels to $500-a-week resorts with private butlers and maids, and caviar at breakfast.

At the top of the scale are luxury hotels of Edwardian splendor with services to match their decor. Their hushed, well-carpeted lobbies are furnished with antiques, gilt furniture, tapestries and down-cushioned armchairs; the beds are made up with monogrammed linen; breakfast comes on gold-rimmed china; the bathrooms are as big as sitting rooms.

In the same price bracket are the jet-age tourist-boom glass-and-concrete skyscrapers. These are short on Old World charm, but comfortable and clean, with soundproof walls, push-button gadgets, air conditioning, swimming pools and television. Whether managed by American or local interests, they all seem to have come out of the same mold.

Below these two blue-chip categories the other types of hotels descend, gradually, in comfort and price. They may be smaller, not as mechanized, and more sparing of baths. But unless you pick third- and fourth-class hotels or are inordinately demanding, you should find them thoroughly comfortable, their service personal and good. Many governments grade their hotels according to fixed criteria which evaluate accommodations, facilities and location: In France, the classifications are *luxe*, 4 star, 3 star, 2 star and 1 star, with the 3 star–1 star hotels further subdivided into A, B and C groups; in Belgium, hotels are identified as de luxe, first class and second class. Within each group there is a range of prices but the standards for each, such as the requisite number of private baths, have been fixed by the government, which publishes lists of the hotels by grade. "First class" will vary a good deal from country to country, even city to city. A first-class hotel in Paris will obviously be closer to what one hopefully expects than a first-class hotel in Lille. Presumably, by the same token, first-class hotels in England are likely to be more comfortable than the same category in Thailand. What "first class" means, in effect, is the best a place has to offer. What it does *not* mean is any absolute guarantee of a private bath, dining accommodations, even a room all to oneself! That's why it's important to get these facts from the hotel or travel agent.

First- and second-class hotels, and of course de luxe, usually suit American tastes. Third- and fourth-class are unlikely to add much pleasure to your trip, but with this qualification: In countries like Scandinavia, Holland and Germany, third- and fourth-class hotels may be simple but they will be clean and reliable. In France you can also rely on the advice of the conscientious *Guide Michelin*.

There are charming hotels built, remodeled, and supervised by the governments themselves such as the *pousadas* of Portugal and the *albergues* and *paradores* of Spain. Sometimes new, sometimes converted medieval castles or Renaissance houses, these government-run guesthouses are often charming, always inexpensive. *Pousadas* cost about $4 a night, *albergues* and *paradores* from $4.50 to $10 a night, for accommodations and full board. They are usually spotlessly clean, serve regional dishes and wines and are thoroughly delightful when you are touring the countryside. All rooms in Greece's Xenia hotels

(Xenia is the Greek word for hospitality) have a private bath or shower. While hardly luxurious, these new hotels, many supervised by the national tourist association, who call them "inns," are simple in design, clean and inexpensive.

Motels are springing up in Europe (even Russia) and the Caribbean. They offer American comforts and services, but have far less charm than old-fashioned European inns. In Japan's traditional *ryokan*, the traveler sleeps and eats Japanese-style, bedded down on plump, soft mattresses spread over tatami-matted floors. You remove your shoes and wear slippers. The maid prepares all meals in your room, which functions as both sitting room and bedroom; she puts away your clothes and makes tea whenever you want it. The garden is invariably an important part of a *ryokan* and your room will often have a view of it. Charges, which run the same expensive-to-inexpensive scale as those of Western hotels, usually include breakfast and dinner. For more information about inns, see Castle Hotels and Country Inns, page 63.

Then there are pensions and paying-guest arrangements, described on pages 292-295. Some are modest, some luxe, but generally, their atmosphere is companionable and relaxed, and there is no easier way to meet people.

Youth hostels are the least expensive and most spartan accommodations available. The average cost per night for bed, supper and breakfast is 75 cents; in Greece, a particularly inexpensive country, a bed costs 35 to 45 cents. Hostels around the world are joined in the International Youth Hostel Federation. To spend a night in one, anywhere, you need a hostel pass which costs from $4 to $7 a year, according to your age. (You don't have to be a student to go hosteling. "Youth" in this context is spiritual and physical rather than chronological. In Norway, for example, more than 100 youth hostels have rooms for families with children between two and fifteen.) One night your hostel might be a fourteenth-century castle, the next a monastery, the third a modern cement-and-glass cube, the fourth a farmhouse. If space is limited and they have to choose, hostel managers (often called house parents or wardens) tend to look more sympathetically upon travelers who arrive on foot or bicycle than those who breeze in by car, and they are allowed to refuse advance reservations from people over 30, *if* accepting them means turning younger members away. (In Bavaria and Switzerland, there is, with a few exceptions, a fixed age limit of 25 years.)

Youth hostel rules are basically the same everywhere: You show the house parents your membership card, sign the house register, and pay the fee. There are limits on how long you can stay—usually 3 nights, especially in high season—unless you get special permission and space is available. You must observe a curfew—lights go out between 10 and midnight, depending on the place—and you must be awake and out fairly early. You are expected to wash your own kitchen utensils, make your own bed and perhaps help in the general tidying up before you leave. There is no alcohol (except wine with meals in France, Italy, Spain and Portugal), the food is plain and inexpensive, and the accommodations are very simple and spare. But the atmosphere is informal and relaxed, and everyone talks to everyone else.

If you are interested in hosteling, write to American Youth Hostels Inc., 14 West 8th Street, New York, New York 10011. The International Youth Hostel Handbooks list all the accommodations in great detail and give you all the information you need to know.

There are also special student hotels everywhere with low rates and simple, clean facilities. In Sweden, a good number also offer accommodations for families, and rates average $7 for a double room with bath.

The overseas branches of clubs such as the English-Speaking Union or the Royal Overseas League in London also have inexpensive rooms.

Finally, there are resort hotels whose rates range from the $500 a week charged by Frenchman's Cove in Jamaica to the $6 a day that gives you three meals, tea and room in a seaside cottage in Spain. They are intended primarily for the vacationer, not the transient, and all of their facilities are organized to give the person on a holiday a good time. If your hotel will be your vacation base, don't make the mistake that people often do of choosing one that is run primarily for businessmen.

Decide how much you can afford for each night, then handle the amount elastically. Double it in some cities so you can live in style; halve it in others by staying at a small pension. The variety will make for a much more interesting trip. Don't exaggerate the deficiencies of one type and the charms of another. In some places the native inn, however it throbs with local color, may be so seedy that the shining bathrooms and clean sheets of the local Hilton, Sheraton or Intercontinental will make you feel dewy-eyed about plumbing; in others, the latest glass-walled cube with a terrace may seem deliberately calculated to insulate you from the country you came to see.

No one has a complete list of perfect hotels up his sleeve. You will have to collect your own: from friends whose taste you trust, guidebooks and travel articles, your travel agent, and from instinct and intuition. Try to book the best or most charming room your budget will afford each time. You may not be in Paris again for years; if, for two more dollars a day, you can have a view of a garden instead of being stuck over the kitchen, it's worth it.

An average rate for a comfortable—not de luxe—hotel acceptable to most people is about $7-$8, single, $12 double with bath. Sometimes, especially at resort and country hotels, rates will include one, two or all meals, and you can't get a room without paying for some of your food. You will have to state when you register whether you want a room and breakfast (a Continental meal of tea or coffee, rolls, jam and butter), demi-pension (room and two meals), or full pension (room and all meals). Large city hotels are accustomed to charging just the room rate. When you take a room, be sure to check on what its rate includes—taxes? service? heating charges? meals?—so that you can tip and plan your meals accordingly. The rate should be posted in your room.

When you arrive, you will be asked to fill out a registration card and hand over your passport. You can safely give up your passport on this one occasion, but be sure to reclaim it the next morning or before you go out that evening. In Europe and at many resorts everywhere, a guest is expected to ask to see her room before engaging it. Europeans do this all the time. Only Americans ever take rooms sight unseen. If you don't like the room you are shown, ask for another or move on. Also, note the check-out hour carefully. Overstaying even 30 minutes can sometimes cost you another full day's rate; or you may return from an afternoon's shopping to find that all your things have been packed up by the maid and parked in the hall.

Hotels, especially de luxe and first-class, are booked solid in high season nowadays. Americans are on the move, and so are the Germans, Scandinavians, French and other Europeans. Conventions are a particular hazard. There is absolutely no way of knowing that the week you have chosen to visit Nairobi is not also the one in which the International Association of Taxidermists has scheduled its convention there. Gregariousness has become international, and congresses meet far from home. There isn't a free bed in Cannes and Venice during a film festival. Searching for a room in London during the Motor Show will make you grateful for a room at the Y. The time to book a room in Europe for the summer months is February or March; in the West Indies for winter, August or September. Reservations should be made 4 to 6 months in advance for high season. For Swiss ski resorts in winter, Caribbean resorts at Christmas and in February, and de luxe European hotels in July and August, 6 to 8 months is none too soon.

If your travel agent is to do the booking, tell him the following facts which the hotel will want to know (if you write for the reservation yourself, send along the same information): how long you will stay and the date of your departure; how many people will be with you; and the ages of your children if they are going along. Next, describe the room you would like—with or without a private bath and toilet, with or without meals. If you're traveling with your husband, say whether you want twin beds or a double bed (the latter is usually less expensive); and what you would like to pay. Ask for "minimum rate available" rather than "minimum"; if all the minimum rooms have been taken, your reservation may be turned down even though slightly more expensive rooms may be free. It is vital to mention what time you will arrive, because most hotels will not hold a reservation after 6 P.M. unless instructed to do so. If you are arriving on an early morning flight and you can afford it, book your hotel for the day *before* you arrive. Then when you get to your hotel feeling tired and grimy, you won't have to wait for your room to be made up. In confirming your reservation the hotel may or may not ask you for a deposit. Generally city hotels don't; resorts do. A resort cannot depend on passing traffic to fill the rooms and its season is short. Notice of cancelation may be required anywhere from 48 hours to 4 weeks in advance.

Be sure to get a written confirmation of your reservation. Without it, you simply don't have a reservation. Carry it in your handbag with your tickets so that you can show it when you arrive at the hotel.

If, despite all admonitions, you should decide to take your chances on finding a room, there is usually a desk at the major airports or railroad terminals to help stranded wayfarers; or you can ask the airline itself to assist you. There is also the local tourist office. Any will give good help. In Copenhagen, for example, in the arrival hall of the Central Railway Station, the tourist association maintains a Room Service Bureau (it's at Kiosk P) to find you a room for the night. It's open most months from 9 A.M. to midnight. (Never, of course, accept the offer of a stranger or an unofficial guide to show you to a hotel.) In some cities there are organizations which act as clearing houses for hotel reservations. The London Hotels Information Service, 88 Brook Street, London W.1. (telephone MAYfair 5414; cable address, Allotels, Wesdo, London) will, without charge, tell you where hotel rooms are available in the London area. While they won't make the actual booking, they will see that your space is held for a reasonable period while either you or your travel agent confirms it.

France has an extraordinary free service called Accueil de France, or French Welcome Service, which is set up to help tourists in every possible way. It has eight centers in Paris; they are at 7 Rue Balzac and the various air and railroad terminals. There are regional bureaus in eight provincial cities, most of them linked to the central office by a Telex system. Its principal activity is finding hotel rooms in Paris and the provinces for people who arrive without a reservation. There is no charge for this service, but if you make a reservation in a provincial hotel, you must leave a small deposit, which is deducted from your bill when you depart. (You leave no deposit for a reservation in a Paris hotel.) Ask any of the blue-uniformed hostesses at the airport or terminal to help you, with this or any other questions you may have.

In order not to come into conflict with established trade sources for hotel reservations, the Welcome Service acts only on immediate hotel needs. In Paris you are expected to get to your hotel within 90 minutes. If you are headed for the provinces, you must claim it by the following evening. There is, in addition, a special youth section whose chief role is to locate very inexpensive accommodations.

If you are traveling on your honeymoon, don't be shy about revealing the fact to your travel agent, the airlines, the ship lines and hotels. Your privileged state will entitle you to such lagniappes as chilled champagne on your arrival, a room with a view, complimentary dinners and drinks, orchids, breakfast in bed, and special rates. The Dorado Beach Hotel in Puerto Rico, for instance, supplies a heated breakfast cart on your private terrace; Estate Good Hope in St. Croix provides not only champagne but a sail to Buck Island Reef National Monument. The tropical Hilton Hotels and the Kahala Hilton in Hawaii offer lavish bouquets of flowers and no charge for room service all through your visit. Monaco treats you to the opera; Japanese inns offer separate cottages; Sweden gives you a "package wedding" on the island of Gotland. Special favors may be shown you in the most unexpected places, so don't hold the facts back.

This generosity is much more practical than sentimental: It is a well-known fact that honeymooners are more than likely to revisit the scenes of their first journey together.

General tips about hotels:

1. Stay away from hotels that do a big convention business, unless there's a particular convention going on that interests you.

2. The more central a hotel's location, the more expensive it is likely to be. If you're adept at using local transportation or have a car, stay a little way out of town. The hotels are less expensive and the views are often quite pretty.

3. Glorious views are, indeed, a part of the pleasure of traveling, but occasionally, as in Rome, they carry the fierce sound of street noises. In that case, forsake the view in favor of a quiet room in the back.

4. If you are tightly budgeted, take your private bath in a small hotel where the difference in price between rooms with and without bath is not great. In larger, more expensive hotels, you can use the bath down the hall. Ask the chambermaid to unlock the room and to see that it is clean. You make an appointment for a bath at a certain hour, specifying the temperature you want. You will find a well-scrubbed tub and a clean towel laid out for you, but no soap. (See Bathrooms, page 16, and Soap, page 335.) The chambermaid will expect a small tip.

5. To summon the maid, valet, or waiter, push the button beside the bed or on the wall near the door. Often there are unmistakable stick drawings to tell you which one to press. The button lights a bulb outside your door, which summons the proper person.

6. When a European waiter knocks and comes breezing into your room, it's entirely proper for you to be in your nightgown or pajamas and a robe. You may be as conservative as Queen Victoria, but embarrassment in this situation is uncalled for.

7. In many European hotels you will find a thick eiderdown on your bed instead of a top sheet. If this is too heavy to suit you, you can sometimes have sheet and blankets brought instead.

8. On your arrival at a hotel, see the concierge. Tell him what entertainment and tours interest you so that he can get started on reservations. (See Concierge, page 83.)

9. Before you check out, leave your forwarding and home addresses with the concierge. If you need a packed lunch for the next leg of your journey, the hotel will prepare one.

10. Two money-savings tips: In modest hotels the higher your room (i.e., the more floors you have to climb), the less expensive—and the quieter—it will be. If you plan to stay at a hotel for more than a week, arrange for a weekly rather than a daily rate. It usually comes to less.

11. Keep the name and address of your hotel handy, in case you should get lost or suddenly forget it.

12. Lock your door and luggage whenever you leave your room. Don't leave anything valuable in your suitcases; check jewelry and other precious items with the desk.

13. Introduce yourself to the telephone operators and be sure they know the correct spelling of your name.

14. If you are motoring without fixed reservations, telephone ahead to your next stop and give the approximate time of your arrival.

For names of each country's hotels, write to the tourist offices listed on pages 479 to 493.

Humidity

To METEOROLOGISTS, humidity is merely the amount of water vapor in a given mass of air. To women traveling, however, it is an agent of the Devil. It can make you irritable, moody and depressed; turn smoothly combed hair into a fringe of dank strings; and bring on a state of complete exhaustion usually known only after a day of unsuccessful shopping. Some of the most beautiful places in the world, however, have humid seasons—Hong Kong in March and April, for instance—but humid or not, they should be seen. Here are a few guidelines, to help you maintain your *sang-froid* even when the air is heavy and damp. (For more on this subject see Weather, page 419.)

Pace yourself slowly in humid climates. Take fewer sightseeing trips and more naps. It's better to miss one or two Buddhist temples than to remember your time in Bangkok through the misty blur of fatigue.

Instead of synthetics, wear fabrics that absorb moisture such as lightweight cottons and wools.

Keep your hair style as simple as possible. If you wear it long, try pulling it into a chignon or twisting it back in a French knot. Curly hair will frizzle; wavy hair will hang straight and limp. This is the climate for a wig or a wiglet that can transform you, come evening, into a woman with a neatly coiffed head.

Pack a supply of pale chiffon scarves or cotton turbans for keeping the hair away from your face and your head looking neat during breezy bus and ferry rides.

Use minuscule amounts of makeup so that your face can "breathe" (heavy, humid air makes the skin feel thick) and huge helpings of toilet water and talcum powder to keep your body scented and dry.

And come apéritif time, stay away from Scotch, rye or bourbon. A long gin drink or wine-and-soda will cool you without settling heavily in your legs or head.

If you were to become a resident of a humid country, you would accept the fact that it would probably take a few months to acclimate yourself. As a tourist, however, you have only a few days. Don't rush through them imprudently. You are a creature of the atmosphere, moving in a sea of air. When it is damp and heavy, take it easy.

Inoculations

IF YOU HAD sailed into Venice in the fourteenth century, from a port where disease was epidemic, or if someone on your ship was ill, you would not have been able to leave the ship for forty, or *quaranta*, days. During that time the ship would have lain at anchor in isolation just outside the harbor. If, at the end of that siege, everyone was still in good health, the cautious Venetians would have allowed the ship to enter, reassured that no one aboard was infectious. From this practice has come the English word "quarantine" and the universal recognition, followed down to this day, that governments have the right to protect themselves and their people from epidemic diseases.

Today, you can cross borders and enter countries without even a forty-second delay, provided you have had one, or at most three, shots in the arm. To keep this country—and you—healthy, our U.S. Public Health Service requires that travelers be vaccinated against smallpox and, depending on where you're going, inoculated against yellow fever and cholera. The purpose of these regulations is to protect you from the serious contagious diseases that still exist in certain parts of the world, and to prevent you, in turn, from carrying them from one country to another. In this demand it is acting in concert with other governments around the world.

Today a smallpox vaccination is practically a universal requirement. Unless you return to the U.S.A. directly from visits to Canada, St. Pierre and Miquelon, Jamaica, the Bahamas, Bermuda, Aruba and Curaçao, British Virgin Islands, Greenland, Iceland, the Panama Canal Zone and the west coast of Lower California, you *cannot* get past the quarantine officer's desk without a certificate of vaccination against smallpox. It even goes for babes in arms. With few exceptions, regulations about this are immutable—and unless you don't mind the fuss and bother of being vaccinated in the airport and are willing to risk being kept under surveillance, even in isolation, for several days after your return, be sure to get your vaccination before you leave home.

If you head for the dank jungles of Central or South America or the large central part of Africa, be sure to be vaccinated against yellow fever whether or not you are required to do so; it is endemic in these parts of the world. If you go to Pakistan, India and Ceylon and arrive by air from areas west of them, you will also need a yellow fever vaccination, for these countries are yellow-fever-prone and *they* need protection against people who might carry the disease across their borders.

Cholera is endemic in India and Pakistan and prevalent in much of Asia and the Western Pacific. Countries in this part of the world recognize that an inoculation is necessary and will not let you in without it. The U.S.A., for one, won't admit you if you have been to a cholera area unless you were vaccinated within six months of your return.

Although smallpox, yellow fever and cholera are the only *required* shots, the U.S. Public Health Service recommends vaccinations against the following diseases: typhoid, paratyphoid, diphtheria (for unimmunized children fifteen years old and younger), diphtheria-whooping cough-tetanus (for babies and preschool children), tetanus, poliomyelitis, plague (only if the possibility of exposure appears reasonably likely), and typhus (for Eastern Europe, some parts of Latin America, Asia and Africa). In addition, vaccination against yellow fever and cholera is strongly favored for those traveling to the tropics, regardless of whether or not it will be required at ports of entry.

While the list seems long and cheerless, it really boils down to the fact that whether you are at home or abroad you should have protection against poliomyelitis, tetanus and diphtheria. This leaves only typhoid, paratyphoid and typhus as additional shots to be taken because you will be traveling. Since an ounce of prevention is, in this case, infinitely worth the amount of cure necessary, and since the shots, once taken, need never be repeated (booster shots can keep you immunized after the initial set), it seems eminently sensible to go along with the recommendations of the U.S. Public Health Service.

Having decided on which shots you will have (your doctor's choice should be the final one), here are five general points to remember:

1. Your doctor can give you all shots except the one against yellow fever. This can be given only at a designated yellow fever vaccination center, usually a U.S. Public Health Station, or a county or community health department. Ask your doctor where the station is, or look it up in your local telephone directory; then telephone ahead to check the office hours.

2. Take your shots well ahead of your departure, and space them out. While protection against smallpox and yellow-fever requires only one vaccination for each, two are needed for protection against cholera, the second 7 to 10 days after the first. Also, immunization can take from 6 days to 3 months after initial inoculation to become effective, depending on the disease or the type of vaccine used. And finally, while some people have no adverse reaction to shots, others get slightly sore arms, headaches, a fleeting fever, or a general feeling of fatigue and malaise. None of these reactions last beyond a day or two, but if your reaction is unusually severe, you might have to take to your bed for 24 hours or so until the temperature disappears. If this happens just before you leave, it's a rather dampening way to start a pleasure trip.

3. Be sure that all your vaccinations are recorded on an International Certificate of Vaccination form, a small yellow booklet that you will receive with your passport application. It is the *only* acceptable immunization document for international travel. Keep it with your passport throughout your trip, ready to show quarantine officers. (If you are traveling on a tourist card rather than a passport, pick up an International Certificate from your travel agent, carrier or the offices of the U.S. Public Health Service or buy one for 10 cents from the Superintendent of Documents, U.S. Government Printing Office, Washington, D.C. 20402.)

4. Even if it is signed by your doctor, the form won't be valid until it has been given an "approved stamp" by your local or state health

department. This must be done for smallpox and cholera. You can either take your Certificate to the health department in person or mail it to the health officer with a self-addressed return envelope. The person who must endure a maddening delay at the quarantine desk instead of sailing blithely toward waiting family and friends is invariably the one whose vaccination certificate has not been properly filled out, signed or stamped.

5. If you lose your vaccination certificate while traveling, write to your doctor and ask him to send you a new card which he has signed and had validated—or you will have to be revaccinated on your arrival in the U.S.A.

6. A smallpox vaccination is good for three years, yellow fever for ten, and cholera for six months. If you are a veteran traveler, keep track of these dates as carefully as you do your passport's expiration date, or you'll get stuck, literally, when you least expect it.

Insurance

THE WORD "insurance," especially when used in connection with traveling, is apt to make people nervous. It brings to mind so many dire, dreadful—and exaggerated—things that all the hidden, groundless fears many women have about traveling may break out of hiding for an instant.

The reason it's a good idea to take out travel insurance is not that the crime rate is higher, let's say, in Copenhagen than in Chattanooga (it isn't), or that—I'll come right out and say it—you're more likely to be in an airplane crash over the Alps than an automobile crash on U.S. Highway 30 (you're not). The facts are that more people are killed by automobile accidents on U.S.A. highways in *two* holiday weekends than in 12 months of commercial aviation throughout the world; since the Wright Brothers, or a total of *more than 60 years,* about half as many lives have been lost in civil aviation (26,000) as are lost in a *single year* of our highway accidents (about 49,000). But once you leave the familiar terrain of your own neighborhood, you'll have to make physical adaptations that will be new to you. For example, the last dimly lit hidden step of your front porch might trip up a visiting Frenchman, but it's no hazard to you because you know it's there. In the same way, the last step of a bus in Paris may escape your eye whereas Parisians swing on and off buses even when they're in motion, like trapeze artists swinging from ring to ring.

The same thing holds true for your clothes. At home they hang docilely in your closets or lie neatly in your drawers. While you travel, they will be exposed, shipped, thrown, transferred, loaded, carried, laundered, dry-cleaned and more—and in each case a perfectly human error may carry them forever out of your hands. It's *most* unlikely that this will happen, but that's what insurance is for. To "insure," the dictionary says, is to guarantee against the risk of loss or harm.

There are two major types of travel insurance, but before buying either you should check with your husband or your insurance agent, or whoever handles these intricacies of your life, to see where you're already covered. There are some blanket policies that cover you for contingencies whether they happen while you're raking the leaves in your garden or skimming the rapids of the Amazon—and extra insurance may not be needed.

There is, first, short-term travel insurance which covers you on a world tour or on a Sunday picnic. This type of policy is issued by a number of companies and protects you 24 hours a day whether you go by plane, train, bus, boat, taxi, cable car, camel or canoe. You qualify for it simply by buying it. Though it doesn't protect you if you are injured while professionally engaged in sports or games, its benefits include payment for accidental death, loss of limbs or loss of sight, plus medical expenses such as physician, surgeon, nurse and daily hospital costs for accidents as well as specified hospital room and board expenses for sickness. Premiums range from less than $1 for one day's coverage to about $150 for 180 days, depending on your choice of benefits. No medical questions are asked in the application. Sensible at all times, it's especially good for short skiing vacations.

Second, even if you don't have trip insurance, you should have some form of baggage insurance. Premiums start at about 40 cents for a $100 worth of insurance for one day—and go right straight up, depending on how much you value your clothes, furs and jewelry. Coverage usually includes baggage loss by rough handling as well as theft, fire or transportation hazards on land, sea, or in the air, or in any hotel or building you may visit during your wanderings. Be sure to include items like cameras. If something valuable is stolen, go to the police; your insurance company will need their report to verify the facts of the loss. (For automobile insurance, see Motoring Abroad, page 255.)

To buy either kind of travel insurance, call your regular insurance agent or ask your travel agent to arrange it while he's handling the other details of your trip.

If you've done any amount of flying, you've undoubtedly seen insurance sales desks at airports. Their job is mainly to sell you flight insurance for a specific trip, although some sell other kinds as well. While a short-term travel policy has the advantage of covering you 24 hours a day on land, sea or in the air, flight insurance is worthwhile because you can cover yourself for a higher amount for any one flight, the maximum being $300,000.

It's important to remember that Blue Cross and Blue Shield's policies are as effective while you're abroad as when you're home. Although there is only one member hospital overseas—the American Hospital in Paris—you can go to any hospital, pay your bill, get an itemized copy and submit it to Blue Cross on your return. The same process works for Blue Shield—you go to a doctor abroad, pay him, and send a copy of his bill to Blue Shield.

If reading this has aroused all sorts of dire misgivings, remember that insurance is worth its price just for the peace of mind it buys. You practically never need it.

Islands

EVERY ITINERARY ought to include an island, whether it's one of the tiny semitropical Scillies speckling the Gulf Stream off Cornwall or a great island like Sicily, through which cultures have sluiced for three thousand years. The reason is well stated by Lawrence Durrell: ". . . I once found a list of diseases as yet unclassified by medical science, and among these there occurred the word *Islo-mania*, which was described as a rare but by no means unknown affliction of spirit. There are people . . . who find islands somehow irresistible. The mere knowledge that they are on an island, a little world surrounded by the sea, fills them with an indescribable intoxication."

Another good reason is that even those islands as central and accessible as Sicily are usually among the last places on earth to join the comfortable bland world of international hotels and cuisine. Often, the people still speak dialects and wear a dress peculiar to that particular spot on earth and go on plowing their tiny fields and fishing the sea around them the way their remote ancestors did. Except on a few, like Capri or Majorca, that have given up their own life to make tourists happy, life goes on with a rhythm almost lost in this century. You might see women sitting on doorsteps spinning black wool, or shepherds with their dogs driving sheep over stony fields, or fishermen spreading their handwoven nets over the rocks to dry.

You must make up your mind what your kind of island is. It will depend a good deal on how much comfort you want in proportion to timelessness. Decide with absolute candor whether you would prefer sunny, worldly Nassau or one of the tiny Grenadines reached by erratic motor schooners from St. Vincent; lively Hydra, where bits of the international set turn up with every boat from Athens, or half-asleep Skyros in which the only sound is the slap of checkers which the men play in the cafés by the harbor and the only amusements are walking, peering into white churches and bathing in the blue sea off the rocks.

You will also be influenced, when you decide, by the time of year. In midsummer Sicily will be a baking oven, but the Baltic islands will be lushly blooming. In February you would hardly like to set off across a choppy sea to the Hebrides or the isles of Greece either; but that is just the time when Sicily is blanketed with spring flowers and bananas are ripening in the Canaries.

If it is the rougher, not so easily found islands where time has hardly left a footprint that appeal to you, start looking for them now. Fashion and real-estate values can perform nearly instant miracles. Until the beginning of the 1960's, Sardinia was so unspoiled and out of the way, and just plain poor, few people could have told you much about it. It has become such an attraction, since the young Aga Khan bought up a great piece of the coast not long ago, that the natives have grown prosperous and Sardinia's Costa Smeralda is now the choicest island resort in Italy. Even so, other parts of the island, which is big, remain almost medieval.

You need not go far to find yourself an island. Many, even the wildest, are a short hop from big cities and populous resorts. If you have time for only an afternoon or a day or two on an island, you can find one almost anywhere. Off the northern coast of Sicily, for instance, a day's expedition from the big hotels of Taormina, lie the fantastically beautiful Aeolian Islands (remember them in *L'Avventura?*), where the swimming and skin diving are incomparable and you feel sure mermaids and mermen lurk just out of sight. And off the Côte d'Azur, halfway between Marseilles and Cannes, lie the îles d'Hyères, which are four wild little islands—one now preserved as a national park, another devoted to nudists and the French navy—where oleanders bloom in the hills and you take long walks to the pearly sea for a swim.

If you want something more ambitious, try Corsica, two hours by air from Paris or an overnight boat trip from Marseilles. In spite of clean hotels and a certain prosperity, the island remains quiet, half wild, overgrown with aromatic shrubs and flowers. A clear blue sea, white beaches, rugged mountains, quiet fishing villages, offer richly various sightseeing, underwater fishing, skin diving, mountaineering, plus—for the experienced—cave exploring, fishing, shooting, boar hunting, and even skiing in winter. The weather will be pleasantest and the tourists fewer if you go in May or June, September or October. The volcanic Canaries off the African coast, but only 2 hours by air from Madrid, combine Spain and Africa in a strange harmony. There are hotels ranging from de luxe to modest, and winter is the season.

The British Isles have their own island retreats: the Channel Islands, for example, off the coast of Normandy. The weather is always mild; the fields are pleasant with flowers, fruits, vegetables, and pretty cows. Jersey and Guernsey are most popular with British tourists (one of the attractions of Jersey is a zoological park founded by Gerald Durrell, Lawrence's brother, another island-loving Durrell); but there are the lesser-known Herm, Alderney and Sark. Sark is tiny but imposing with tremendous cliffs; the Dame of Sark, who rules it, permits neither automobiles, airplanes, movies, nor hardtop roads. The island makes up for what it lacks of the twentieth century with timeless churches, farms, flowers, horse-drawn carriages and nice old-fashioned hotels. One can feel very far away from the world.

If you have a real taste for quiet and freedom, with a lot of mist, cleansing rain and outbursts of sunshine, wet rocks and seabirds mewing, the Aran Islands, off Ireland in the Atlantic, might be for you. Gaelic is still a living language and peat fires smoke on cottage hearths. Scotland's Hebrides have the same kind of wild Atlantic beauty, with ruined castles, roofless churches, moors and lochs, tidy fishing villages, and legends of sunken Spanish treasure.

The Baltic islands of Scandinavia are cozier. East of Denmark lies Bornholm, with fortified stone churches, old towns with tile-roofed houses washed in red and yellow, cobbled streets, walled gardens planted with mulberry, fig and grape, warm coves to swim in among the cliffs, and pale summer nights haunted by nightingales. What could be nicer? Nothing, perhaps; but the islands of Aerö and Fyn are no less charming. Sweden has Gotland, where roses grow all summer among the ruins of ancient churches. There are wild orchids, wild ponies, flocks of sheep and seabirds, sunny beaches, and excellent hotels in the one town, Visby. June to September is the time for these northern outposts.

If you have a week or two to devote to a whole world of islands, perhaps the most beautiful of all, go to Greece. The tracks have been well beaten on Rhodes, Mykonos, and Hydra, but there are many many more where you might settle for a day or a week: Samos, for example, in the Sporades, which has the nice Xenia hotel and even a convent you may stay in called Aghios Yoannis. Many travelers enjoy a cruise of many islands, and cruises to suit any taste and purse are now possible. A 7-day jaunt could cost as much as $500; or you could have 3 days for as little as $60. More expensive would be an archaeological cruise accompanied by scholars who lecture on the sites. Swan's, 260 Tottenham Court Road, London, conducts the most ambitious of these Hellenic cruises. Spring and early autumn are the best times to visit Greece.

The other side of the world—the Pacific and beyond—is blessed with some of the loveliest of all islands. Hearing about flawless beauty may be a bore, but when you finally lay eyes on it, it is as fresh and astonishing as the Garden of Eden must have looked to its first inhabitants. Hawaii, in spite of electric guitars and the hula skirts, is still physically magnificent. The islands, 8 of them and 23 atolls, are full of dazzling differences—verdant, spiky mountains, volcanic craters as strange as the moon's face, precipitous cliffs at whose feet the long waves of the Pacific break. Two of these islands are not unlike their pre-civilized selves: Maui, green and mountainous, and Kauai, with deep green canyons, pinnacles, and waterfalls, haunted by clouds of exotic birds. Both are quiet, with pleasant resort hotels, and about a quarter of an hour's flight from Honolulu.

At the farthest end of the Pacific, hundreds of tropical islands are flung all along the 1,200-mile length of Australia's Great Barrier Reef. Green Island, for example, has white coral sands, tropical vegetation and a superb underwater observatory. There is Lindeman Island, if you want a pleasant resort, which offers swimming pool, catamarans, water skiing, skin diving in 78-degree water and, at night, dancing, movies, barbecue. (Princess Alexandra slept here.) Heron Island, a coral cay, is a nature preserve for countless nesting seabirds and turtles.

Those myriad marvelous West Indian islands down at the bottom of our own front yard, though visited by more Americans than any others in the world, retain plenty of beautiful mysteries as well as well-organized charms. As big and much sought after an island as Jamaica has not only the luxurious lodges of Montego Bay, the golf, tennis, swimming and cool bars, and all the pink pleasures of rum and fruit, and shellfish, but also a quiet, rural interior that is lush, mountainous and watered by many rivers. Go to Spanish Town and look for the lovely buildings and ruins the centuries have left behind among the coconut palms.

There is Trinidad, ebullient, fantastic, all its own mixture of races, occupations, languages, prejudices, foods and music; and Mexico's Cozumel, blazing luxuriously in the sun off Yucatán, where you swim in perfect blue bays, toast on powdery beaches, gorge on lobsters caught before your eyes, and wash it all down with rum punch.

But there is a plethora of little faraway-seeming islands all through the Caribbean that have been forgotten or never really discovered. There are, for instance, Les Saintes, off Guadaloupe, where the mixture (it is always a heady mix in the Caribbean) is Breton and African, and the people—some pale as taffy with golden hair—watch flitting iguanas, fish, bake bread, and engage in furious local rivalries, uncaring about the world beyond the rim of their almost purple sea.

There is Montserrat near Antigua in the Leeward Islands, as green as Ireland, its people almost all descended from slaves. Its only great commercial venture, back in the 1880's, was lime juice marketed for teetotalers. Nowadays, the lime industry having fallen on slim days, the people feast on exotic local produce, busy themselves with local politics, and dream of tourists who have not yet come.

An island once flourishing and now forgotten is Nevis, also in the Leeward Islands, where Alexander Hamilton was born, Lord Nelson married; nowadays goats browse through deserted plantation kitchens and pigs root in ruined gardens. This sad, lovely charm can be enjoyed in friendly comfort by anyone who chooses to sign up as a guest at one of the island's few delightful, simple hotels or guesthouses.

Bequia, another island that never quite joined the real world, belongs to St. Vincent in the Grenadines. It is toylike, hushed, with a harbor full of fishing boats fanned by royal palms. There are two hotels—one of nine rooms, one of six—for the chance visitor. For a few last moments a charming innocence remains intact.

If you'd like to see the nearby islands of a country you'll be visiting, it is better not to go at the beginning or the end of your stay, but rather to tuck them into the middle. Their own strong flavors cannot be rightly appreciated until you have some sense of the country. The French flavor of Jersey would be lost on you if you didn't know your England; and until you have traveled in France you can't appreciate how Italian or even Greek and ancient-in-spirit Corsica is. Aran and the Hebrides are a bit of Britain and a great deal of the ancient Gaelic world that is dying out elsewhere.

Wherever you choose to go, especially if it is an island off the beaten track, you will want comfortable walking shoes, a good book to read in the quiet evening, and a strong appetite for the unexpected.

Itinerary Building

THE SECRET of a good itinerary is counterpoint—the play of city sightseeing against country motoring, of a museum morning with a beach afternoon, of a string of capitals with a lake resort.

If you take a package trip with a ready-made itinerary, there is little you can do to change it, nor should you want to if the agent who has designed the trip knows his business. But sometimes a package trip is flexible enough to allow you plenty of free time for private meanderings. Or you may want to fashion your own itinerary, with or without the help of an agent. Or you may even be considering several different trips and need some criteria by which to evaluate them. Therefore, it's worthwhile to know the basic rules of good itinerary building:

1. Don't stay in any capital fewer than five days. This is an arbitrary rule, but my own—and I cannot underscore it hard enough. Anything less will give you that sense of breathlessness that turns all memories into a hash. Five days is the absolute minimum for unpacking and repacking, seeing and becoming even slightly familiar with a great city, and taking one-day excursions into its environs. It

allows you to sleep late the first morning after your flight, to stay up till 2 A.M. a few nights without feeling wilted the next day. It gives you time enough to gradually get your bearings and to do some leisurely shopping as well as sightseeing. From London, you will want to see Stratford and Cambridge; from Paris, Chartres; and from Edinburgh, the Trossachs and Loch Lomond. It always saves time, energy and money to find a base from which to do some of your touring. If there is a middle-sized city on your itinerary (Lausanne or Geneva, for example), you can pare down your visit to three days, but keep three-day visits to a minimum, no more than one in a three-week trip or two in a five-week one.

2. Visit a resort popular with the natives before you visit each capital: in September, Biarritz before Paris; during the summer, San Sebastián before Madrid; or Corfu or Spetsai before Athens. Or go to one that draws an international crowd: Sveti Stefan in Yugoslavia or Taormina in Sicily or Ischia in Italy. This gives you two kinds of trip insurance: the first, a few days of rest from the frenzy of preparations and flight; the second, a chance to meet people in an atmosphere more relaxed and informal than that of a big city. When you arrive afterward in Paris, Rome or wherever, you will have acquired a small circle of friends to soften its strangeness.

3. Spend about one fifth of your tour in the countryside, playing at your favorite sport or just sitting in the sun with a good book. If you're away for three weeks, do this for about four days; if your trip lasts five weeks, make it seven days—and go into the country for, yes, a rest. Travel is work—the pleasantest sort, of course, but it makes demands on your body and mind. The impact of another culture can be so stimulating that it keeps you up all night. It's wonderful, but fatiguing. On the Continent, escape to a spa, or to the Swiss or Italian lakes. In Britain, go to a country inn or a big resort like Gleneagles. Play golf, go fishing, sleep late—but don't be galvanized by your conscience into touring. A short drive into the countryside at dusk, yes; a full day's sightseeing junket, no.

4. Don't do too much in one day, and especially don't do too much of the same thing. Instead of a day of sightseeing, take two half days, and spend the other halves shopping, strolling or sitting. If you have a bus tour in the morning, swim in the afternoon. Don't plan on going to the theater the evening of the day you've been touring the countryside. You'll be tempted to cram it all in, but don't. Keep more or less to the pace you follow at home. Be comfortable within the hours and days you have. Don't let time pinch because you try to do too much.

5. Build your itinerary imaginatively, with personal predilections uppermost in your mind. Be utterly selfish, and ignore what other people have done or told you to do. Traveling is something you undertake deliberately, and you don't *have* to go anywhere. On my first trip to Europe my traveling companion spent most of her time sitting at sidewalk cafés reading Gide while I climbed resolutely to the top of Notre Dame and visited every museum I could find. We were both happy and, as it turned out, in character: She became a distinguished French-English translator and married a French college professor who teaches at Yale; I became a travel editor and writer and haven't stopped sightseeing since.

Don't think of your mimeographed itinerary as a string of musts but as a pick of pleasures that are meant to gratify you alone. If you decide, in London, that you would like to go to the theater every night and three times on Saturday, do it, sleep late the next day, and scrap your other plans. If your husband must poke his head into the local stock exchange, send him merrily along while you look at fine French furniture. Alternate, too, between the well-known, classic places, and those that are not so well known. The stopovers offered by airlines are mostly in the large cities, and tourists therefore tend to follow predictable routes—but there are air connections between capitals and many little-known places, some of them permissible on your ticket. Megève is well known to the French yet seldom visited by Americans; you can fly from London to the Channel Islands, from Rome to Sicily, from Athens to Samos, an island overlooked by the cruise ships but much favored by the Greeks. The point is, keep your itinerary loose. It was never meant to put you into bondage. You should always feel free to strike off on your own for an afternoon, a day or a week.

However long your trip, try to choose one or two places that are empty of tourists, that seem to be waiting for you alone, that give you the pleasure of discovery. And take time out from sightseeing to pursue a hobby; focusing on some interest will increase your pleasure enormously. It could be anything—collecting drawings or old clocks, visiting gardens or kindergartens or mink farms, as long as it's your own brand of madness.

6. Plan your itinerary with a calendar in hand. How sad to arrive at the Taj Mahal a week after the full moon if you might easily have come earlier to see it, incredibly beautiful, in the fullest glory of moonlight, or to run into a national holiday on the very day you planned to do all your shopping. (See National Holidays, page 277, and Sundays, page 346.)

7. Having considered all of the above, you can discuss rough plans

with your travel agent, who will help you fit the pieces together. He will see that you keep your route reasonably straight without backtracking, with suitable connections for each leg. He will tell you whether it's best to go by bus from Florence to Rome, book the sightseeing tours that save you money, and so forth. (See Travel Agent, page 382.) Tell him any hotel preferences you may have, make a list of restaurants and places you are longing to see in each city, and presto—you have an itinerary.

Some general statements are now in order about *when* to travel. The seasons at which certain places are popular are often arbitrary and have little to do with whether they are at their best then. Often travel patterns are established for no better reason than that they suit the confines of the school year or fit into vacation periods, or simply because they have become customary. If your vacation is not inexorably tied to specific times of the year like sales seasons or the school term, forget some of your preconceptions about season and start with a fresh point of view.

Since school holidays fall in the summer months nearly everywhere above the equator, July and August have traditionally been the tourist season all over the world. Just as we in America leave our cities for cottages by the lake or weekends at the shore or our annual vacation, so do the English, French, Norwegians, Finns, Spaniards and so on across the map. August in France has for so long been the holiday month that, with few exceptions, shops, restaurants and nightclubs are boarded up tight. The Frenchman is off on *his* vacation at the Riviera, or in Italy or Spain. In Paris, the streets will be filled with hordes of compatriots rather than Parisians; some of the attractions you have read about may be unavailable. So try to schedule your stay in Paris before Bastille Day, July 14 (a wonderful last night in that city, incidentally), or in September; Rome too will be asleep in August. If you *want* to be part of the tourist avalanche, know when it is and join it purposely.

You might want to consider the social season. This is when local life is at its gayest and centered in town: Calendars are filled with balls, horse shows, debutante dances. Some events are open to the tourists; many, of course, are not. In openhearted cities such as Dublin and Melbourne you will be welcomed, if you are enterprising and have the right clothes, at a number of social functions, and it will be worth your while to go during the season; in other cities, such as Paris and Rome, the only difference will be a certain electricity in the air, which you may or may not consider worth enjoying. In London, for instance, June is the peak of the season, and the city is astir with balls, debutante parties and supper dances; men in gray toppers and tailcoats, women in print dresses and flowered hats flit in and out of the hotels, off to the races at Ascot. It is worthwhile being on hand during the London season, in order to enjoy such public events as Trooping the Color on the Queen's birthday, fine opera on the lawns of Glyndebourne, and the superlative tennis at Wimbledon.

August may be hopeless in Paris, but it is exactly when you do want to be in Dublin, for Horse Show Week, which is the climax of the Irish social season. Some 120,000 people from everywhere in the world come to watch an exhibition of the finest horses in the world; there are daily jumping contests, attractive-looking spectators in superb tweeds, and at least one hunt ball each night. Even if horse shows never seemed especially compelling to you at home, you will enjoy the fizzy atmosphere of this one—and you needn't know a hunter from a hackney to enjoy it. Rome also has an important horse show in May, which marks the end of its social season and also brings out handsome men and pretty women elegantly dressed.

Madrid, like Paris, is strictly for tourists in the height of summer. Scandinavia is at its best in September, when the Design Cavalcade sets up brilliant exhibits of fresh ideas in home furnishings, in each of the four Scandinavian countries; the artists and designers are about at this time, and accessible.

In sum, if gala atmosphere attracts you, check up first on the major social events attended by royalty, and second on the big events such as races, shows and competitions built around horses. If you plan to attend any of these functions, get your tickets well in advance and book your hotel very early (4 to 6 months ahead) since natives from the provinces, as well as tourists, are competing with you for rooms.

Also, note the dates when cinema, ballet, opera, concert and theater offerings are in full swing. Throughout the temperate zone of the Northern Hemisphere the cultural season opens late in September or early in October and extends through April or May. Reverse these months for countries below the equator—summer is November through February, winter July through September. There are definite advantages to traveling then. May–June and September–October are quite safe climatically, and certainly less touristy than July and August. The natives are back from *their* holidays (the Parisians call the early fall "la Rentrée": the tourists are gone and the locals return to take over their city again), and if friends have given you the names of people to look up, they will be around to enrich your stay. Life is both livelier and more normal. In the fall, new art shows, plays, concerts, ballets and automobile shows flood the local entertainment lists.

Parliaments open, partridge shooters take to the fields, and in Ireland's pubs the conversation sparkles again after the summer's lull. Hotel prices are lower than during the rush of summer, and unless there is some special event such as a motor show, places are not so crowded. There's no jostling with crowds for a view of the guards at Buckingham Palace. Suddenly it's easy again to get a reservation at a good restaurant. On the other hand, certain events, exhibitions and tours planned especially for foreigners are closed at the end of the tourist season, and it is less easy to alternate days of sightseeing with beach resort weekends (instead you could go beagling or visit wine festivals for relaxation).

The various foreign tourist offices try to provide incentives for travel during their slack seasons: They will help you arrange visits to factories, schools, hospitals, courtrooms, farms, or distilleries, many of which may have been closed in summer. In Ireland, November is the official start of the hunting season and the hunt clubs hold from one to four meets a week, all open to visitors without special introduction. There are the great motor shows in Paris, London and Turin in the fall; Carnival in February brings revelry in Nice, Estoril, Binche, Patras, Split, Basel, Vienna and Munich. Certainly, while spring and fall can be fine, during the dead of winter Europe is no wonderland unless you're at a ski resort; the cities are bleak, and darken at 4 o'clock in the afternoon, but you may find its glittering cultural life and stepped-up pace a compensation.

Check into special events planned not for tourist consumption but for local liveliness, such as flower shows, festivals, carnivals and traditional sports events. Those that attract a large crowd of brawny outdoor men can be fun for women traveling on their own. For example, in the last weeks of November and early December, Nassau's Speed Weeks draw an international crowd of the world's top racing drivers, and Bermuda jumps with sailing enthusiasts during the Newport-Bermuda Yacht Race which takes place in June of every even-numbered year. In Norway, the King and Crown Prince, who are both good sailors, usually participate in the sailing regatta at Hankø in June and July. Tourists are welcome to join in the gaiety. In winter, the Holmenkollen Ski Week in Oslo is a famous ski meet and filled with partying. Plan with a calendar of events in hand. Each tourist office publishes one for its country annually; Pan American Airways has a particularly attractive and comprehensive one listing events around the world called *Calendar of Overseas Events* which it brings out each year. (For more about Festivals, an especially compelling attraction to most travelers, see page 132.)

Finally, adjust some of your prejudices about climate. (See Weather, page 419.) I've said above that June and September are safe; actually, they're glorious, as well as relatively uncrowded throughout the Temperate Zone. So, too, are May and October. In tropical areas such as the West Indies, the months of May and June are ravishingly pretty: The gardens are brilliant masses of bougainvillea and frangipani and the seas are at their best for sailing. In hot places where the humidity is low and trade winds blow, even midsummer can be pleasant. Don't write off the entire Caribbean area as too hot in summer: Many of the islands, though about 10 degrees warmer than in winter, are most pleasant. In fact, more people vacation in the Caribbean in summer than winter; it only seems better in the winter because you can leave the cold behind. May, when fruit trees are in bloom, is glorious in France, and from May through June thousands of pink and white blossoms cover the slopes above Norway's fjords. The rule, then, is to take a fresh look at the climate at your destination before you decide when to visit it.

Remember, too, there's a clear distinction to be drawn between off-season and out-of-season travel. If a place is strictly seasonal, it's because the sailing and swimming are probably at their best then. If you want to avoid having lots of people about, go a few weeks before or a few weeks after the start of the season, which will put you there during the off-season, not out-of-season, period. Thus you can skirt the crowds at a beach in June or September, find it warm and pleasant, and pay less for your hotel room and transportation.

Finally, don't be beguiled by a fantasy of how charming Christmas abroad can be. Being alone in a big foreign city at Christmas can be thoroughly depressing. London is not cozy and Dickensian with plum pudding and stuffed goose—it is lonely and usually cold and gray. Christmas is a time for families who are drawn together at their own hearths, behind curtained windows, and the foreigner will feel outside it all. If you must get away at Christmas, forget about St. Nick, tinsel and plum pudding—and head for a warm island in the West Indies, for Mexico, or for a ski resort.

Since everything has its price, remember that if you are going anywhere "in season," you must reserve rooms months ahead and be prepared to pay more than at other times of the year.

Knitted Clothes

EVER SINCE the 1920's, when Chanel and Schiaparelli turned knitted clothes into *haute couture*, they have been as ubiquitous on the travel scene as bright-colored posters. Today, they are not only wonderful to wear while traveling, because of their elasticity and resilience, but they have also become a favorite item to buy abroad. In the last twenty years, yarns and styling have become enormously sophisticated and various, with such U.S.A. manufacturers as Kimberly Knitwear leading the way. A mere listing of the variety of knitted fabrics on the market can make your head spin. There are knits in silk, cotton and synthetic yarns as well as in wool. There were, for example, in one recent Kimberly collection quilty cloqué knits, gossamer mohair and wool blends, whipcord knits, deeply ribbed wool ottomans, flat knits, needlepoint knits, knits threaded with metal, and handloomed Shaker knits. There are knitted cocktail and evening dresses, in addition to daytime dresses, separates, suits, and even casual coats. There are knits for every climate—string knits for the tropics, thick woolen knits for the Arctic Circle. The range is so vast and inclusive you could easily build an entire travel wardrobe out of knits—but of course you wouldn't, and you shouldn't. Just as a steady diet of caviar and champagne would soon have you screaming for beef and beer, a steady diet of knitted clothes would make you long for anything stiff and crushable.

Pack the knits that give you pleasure, flatter you, and make you feel well dressed. One of the most comfortable outfits in which to travel is a knitted suit or a knitted dress and jacket. Since nearly all knitted materials share the sterling virtue of being unmussable (it seems almost impossible for a knit to hold a crease), you can pick and choose among them. Don't feel duty-bound to take *any* knitted item just because you know it travels well. Women who do that usually end up in clothes that have about as much flair as a nurse's uniform.

While you could easily stock up on marvelous knitted clothes right here at home, it would seem a pity to do so; these days, especially if you travel to Europe, you would be carrying coals to Newcastle. Many European countries with a long tradition of craftsmanship have turned their talents to knitting. The results, whether the clothes are made by hand or by machine, are superb, and often end up on the shelves of American shops at much higher prices than on home territory.

Scottish cashmeres, for example, in the soft colors of heather and mist, which have long been imported to the U.S.A., can be bought for less in Britain. In Edinburgh, try the shop of James Grieve, a favorite among well-dressed Scots, where a knitted dress can cost as little as $20. Italy's inventive designers have done marvelous things with knits. Look especially for the silk knits of Pucci, the famous sportswear designer, many of which are now being sold in the United States. His simple silk jersey dresses fold into the size of a dinner napkin and are feather-light to wear.

In the Scandinavian countries, you will find thick bulky patterned sweaters at half the price they sell at in the U.S.A. Skiers love them, they look wonderful with slacks, and make smashing gifts. Austria, too, has some handsome patterned sweaters. In France, look especially for the sweaters made by Korrigan. Cut with the softness of a blouse, they are light in the hand and have the matchless quality of being cool in summer, warm in winter. Israel, whose fashion expertise, like so much else in that country, is growing steadily, turns out good-looking knits. They are sold, among other places, in a string of shops called Iwanir in Tel Aviv. Bring back the silk sweaters, which are especially good. In the last few years, the rugged sweaters made by fishermen's wives have turned up in the States as chic sportswear. Since fishing boats were first launched, the men who sail them have worn sweaters made by womenfolk who patiently await their safe return. The traditional patterns differ from country to country, even port to port. You will find these handsome sweaters mostly in Ireland, Portugal, Denmark, Norway, Britain and Holland. Look especially for those made by the Aran Islanders off the west coast of Ireland, and those from the British Isle of Guernsey and the Scottish Shetlands.

There are generally five points to remember about knitted fashions:

1. Although it's hard to choose the best in a fashion category of such excellence, silk knitted clothes such as ribbon hand knits (admittedly expensive), dress-and-jacket costumes of wool knit, and jerseys (generally inexpensive) come out ahead among experienced travelers. They have bounce and resilience, pack in practically no space, never crease and are so adaptable that they are suitable for both the casualness of Honolulu and the restraint of Stockholm.

2. If your knitted clothes are handloomed or porous and lacy without being fully lined, don't hang them—fold them instead with your sweaters—and don't travel—i.e., sit—in them for hours. The first precaution will avoid sagging, the second, "bagging." Tight needle-point knits and those that have great body can be hung without qualms.

3. A knitted garment should fit loosely or it will make you seem ten pounds heavier. While you needn't assume the shapeless sweatered look of your teen-age daughter, stay away from clinging knits, unless the knitted fabric has been cut and lined with all the crisp tailoring usually given to flat fabrics.

4. While knitted clothes deserve all the praise heaped on them, there is one type of knit to avoid under certain circumstances: If you are headed for the tropics, or the Orient in summer, or any hot, humid place, don't take knitted nylon underwear or nightgowns. Take cotton or silk instead, and resign yourself to having the hotel do your laundry—unless you enjoy pressing. Nylon knits in such a climate will condemn you to all the stifling discomfort of woolies.

5. In countries with a strong tradition of hand craftsmanship such as Scandinavia, Ireland, and Scotland, a good place to buy hand knits is in the central craft shop, sometimes sponsored by the government or the craftsmen themselves. Since all the profits are turned back to them, you will have the gratification of knowing that your dollars not only bought something beautiful but went to a good cause as

well. Some of these shops are the Husfliden, Møllergata 4, Oslo; the Irish Cottage Industries Ltd., 18 Dawson Street, Dublin; and the Highland Home Industries Ltd., 94 George Street, Edinburgh, where you can find heavy, brownish-black sweaters made from the wool of black sheep. They are the height of chic.

Ladies' Rooms

To MANAGE the ladies' room situation with aplomb, you must first remember an expression which sounds rather quaint and anachronistic to American ears: "water closet." While practically never used in this country, it's actually the American College Dictionary's secondary definition of the word "toilet." Its initials "W.C." mark the door in question throughout Europe and most of the world, and will at least keep you from walking into a supply pantry by mistake.

In luxurious buildings such as first-class hotels and restaurants, you will find separate facilities for men and women, and here the language problem may enter the picture. The doors will of course be marked with the suitable word for each sex. Often, you'll find a bit of decoration that makes the gender clear even to monolingual Americans. In many of India's railway stations, for example, there is a brightly painted picture of a woman pointing in the direction of the proper water closet.

Most often, however, there's a single W.C. that serves both men and women. This may nonplus you at first, but take this difference between American and foreign customs philosophically. Since the local women (who are every bit as fastidious as you are) have survived the system for years, it's probable you will too. Besides it would be ungracious of you to complain. Chalk it up to the adventures of travel, and remember that it happens in America, too, on airplanes and buses.

By and large, plumbing facilities will be good or at least satisfactory on all paths that Americans have beaten, although in out-of-the-way places such as small railway stations, obscure country restaurants and infrequently visited museums, the toilet may not be very attractive. In such cases, be good-humored and forget about it—or remember that facilities equally unpleasant exist on home territory.

At first you may be somewhat taken aback by the comparative lack of privacy in the W.C. The booths are separated by partitions so small that legs and heads are generally visible. But you'll get used to it. You may not get used to the Japanese system of squatting over a hole quite so fast (you'll find it, for instance, in Japanese department stores). By and large you needn't be concerned about this because Western-style hotels, and many new inns and rebuilt inns, have added Western facilities.

COUNTRY	WORD ON DOOR	COUNTRY	WORD ON DOOR
England	*Ladies* or *W.C.* (If you hear it referred to as the "loo," it's slang, like our "john." Going to the ladies' room is commonly called "spending a penny."	Germany ⎱ Austria ⎰	*Damen, Frauen*
		Denmark	*Damer* or *Dame Toilet*
		Spain	*Damas* or *Señoras*
		Turkey	*Kadinlar, Bayanlar*
		Finland	*Naisille, Dames, Ladies*
		Belgium	*Toilette, Dames*
France	*Dames, Mesdames*	Portugal	*Lavabos das Senhoras*
Italy	On train: *Ritirata Signore* or *Donne.* Sometimes, anywhere: *Gabinetti, Toiletta*	Norway	*Damer*
		Mexico	*Damas* or *Señoras*
		Japan	*O-tearai*
Switzerland	*Damen, Sie, Frauen, Mesdames, Dames, Signore*		

Wherever you are, when you want the toilet, ask for just that (don't ask where you may wash your hands) because it is usually in a room of its own.

Often good restaurants and hotels will have women attendants in their W.C.'s, and you are expected to give them a small tip. This can be roughly the local equivalent of a dime. If the place is very posh, raise this amount to the quarter substitute (Tipping, page 359). Tuck packets of Kleenex and Wash 'n Dri in your handbag, and you will be equipped for any contingency.

On the facing page is a list of words you are most likely to find on ladies'-room doors in several countries. If you need directions, merely saying the word for women with a large question mark in your voice will always do the trick.

Language

If the path you are about to travel is the least bit well-trodden, you will almost never need a foreign language, for English is the nearest there is to a universal tongue. It is understood almost everywhere. At the age when our children are mastering the New Math, those of most other countries are taking required courses in English. In many places, English is the second official language; everywhere it is the lingua franca of tourism and therefore of hotel-men, shopkeepers, restaurants and guides. You will hear it in the remotest corners of a country, and often see directional signs in English as well as the native language. In the Helsinki airport, for example, all signs are in Finnish, Swedish, Russian and English.

Lack of languages, then, ought never to deter you from traveling. Even if you find yourself out of gasoline in a village in Portugal or lost in a taxi in the suburbs of Istanbul, pantomime, hand language, gestures and a good phrase book will see you through. Head for the nearest hotel, tourist office or Chamber of Commerce, or a large restaurant, for where travelers pass, English is seldom far behind. Just don't shout. Voices seem to rise in direct proportion to a failure in communication—we scream our way through long-distance telephone calls or in conversations where people can hear us perfectly, even if they can't understand a word we are saying. Remember, too, that friendships and warmth of feeling have sprung up between people even without a common tongue.

If you remember anything of the language you studied in school, trot it out: It's fun, and even if your basic Spanish has no practical value, it can help to establish rapport. Your efforts to understand its language show that you are interested in the country itself—and the local inhabitants will be glad to see this. It's your responsibility as a foreigner to make the effort, although people will probably meet you three quarters of the way, often eagerly answering you in their grade-school English. They are pleased to help you, and the reciprocal language instruction becomes a charming act of friendship. While English alone will see you through in most places, it is pleasant to speak another's language, however halting your word or two may be.

With the growth of foreign travel and business, Americans are beginning to develop a long-overdue interest in other languages. Courses, especially those that can be taken in the comfort of your own home, are booming. Happily, they are based on new methods, which *don't* involve parsing irregular verbs or translating obscure passages from Corneille or Cervantes. You are thrust right into the language itself. Berlitz, probably the best-known and farthest-flung (if not the least expensive) name in language training, employs this method. You are immersed in the language; the words are demonstrated or identified with familiar objects, and repeated over and over again, by teachers who are forbidden to use English. There is rudimentary conversation—Berlitz says repeating a word or phrase in conversation thirty-five times makes it a permanent part of your vocabulary. The result is that a certain conversational agility is achieved in a relatively short time. The theory is that almost anyone can acquire a working knowledge of everyday speech after 30 hours of instruction, and a fairly good fluency after 120 hours. American businessmen who find that fluency increases sales figures have flocked to quick language courses in recent years. You can, quite easily, brush up an old facility or learn the rudiments of a new language—enough to handle your daily needs.

Tools for home study include phonograph records, film strips, sets of vocabulary cards, textbooks, and tape recorders for listening to one's voice and pronunciation. There are also phrase books, self-teaching textbooks, extensive record courses. The two Berlitz self-teaching record courses are good; the more expensive one is $75 but there is a two-record set for $12.95 in French, Spanish, German and Italian. If you are interested in French, look into the Hachette series *En France comme si vous y etiez*. The place to investigate these is your local book, record or department store. Inquire also about the adult extension courses at your local high school, college or Y.W.C.A.

Whenever you go abroad, pack a simple, good phrase book or dictionary; there are pocket phrase books especially prepared for tourists in every language an American traveler might use, including Hebrew, Polish and Greek. Buy an up-to-date one that gives you the phonetic pronunciation of the foreign words and one whose sample phrases bear some relation to reality. "Since when has your watch stopped?" won't get you very far, even spoken in the native tongue.

For courtesy's sake, memorize a basic vocabulary for each country: *please, thank you, excuse me, you are welcome, good morning, good evening, goodbye, how much, where, yes, no;* and *Do you speak English?, Slower, please,* and *I don't understand.* If you are carrying language cards with you, underscore these expressions.

If language interests you, once abroad, look at the local newspapers, especially the terse, simple headlines and the advertisments. Pronounce street and store names aloud as you drive by them. A sympathetic Finnish guide once urged me to try just such a "crash course" in her language. Feeling foolish at first, I soon began to learn the cadence and the music of Finnish, and it has remained with me ever since. Keep the radio on in your hotel room, not only for the individual words that you may be able to pick out but for the rhythm and cadence of speech.

Don't be self-conscious about syntax. Muster the best accent you can manage, but don't worry about its shortcomings. You won't be trying to pass as a native; your only goal is to make yourself understood. Above all, don't aim for perfection, the deadly enemy of the neophyte.

The Army's Defense Language Institute, West Coast Branch, the largest single language training center in the world, urges its students to be bold, never to hold back for fear of making an error. Its goal is to teach its students to understand—and make themselves understood to a native speaker; reading and writing come second.

As long as it gives you pleasure, try to speak another language but don't impose your broken sentences on a conversation if they will slow down communication or exhaust your partner. The Frenchman who speaks fluent English and has a lot to say will be charmed by your first efforts in his language—but bored to distraction if you buttonhole him with your faltering attempts.

Also, don't be surprised at the number of American words that have crept into other languages; Parisians go away for *le weekend,* they conduct *le business* and eat *le snack* at *le self service* (the name given to a cafeteria). And take advantage of the number of mechanical aids that have cropped up to dispel language difficulties. In Athens, for example, several machines have been installed around the city, through which the traveler can learn, in English, where she is by pressing a button. The machines also give the addresses of and directions to hotels, embassies and garages.

Be prepared, too, for the differences you'll find between British, Australian and American English. Aussie slang is vigorous, descriptive, and often funny. The British give many words a meaning very different from what we do. While English-speaking people share a common language, it's not an identical one. In a sense, you have to learn the language as you go along—which can be fun.

Leather Goods

THERE IS nothing very extraordinary to be seen about the European cattle grazing the green Alpine meadows or the Camargue marshes, but it's hard to believe there isn't something remarkable about their hides. Certainly the leather goods made from them are the finest in the world. Even modest pieces are exceptionally good and cost much less than they do here, while the more ambitious creations are *objets d'art.* Of course, the traditional skill with which the leather is worked is a good part of it.

You can buy handmade saddles in France for $70, handmade gloves in Spain for $3, and handmade riding boots in Ireland for $20. A few splendid shops will occasionally charge Rolls-Royce prices for their treasures, but if you can afford to buy, you will still save 40 per cent on the cost of the same thing when imported to the U.S.A. And even in these distinguished shops you will find small things such as gloves, stamp cases, billfolds and the like that sell well below $10.

Suede, kidskin, calfskin, pigskin, alligator, lizard, cowhide. Attaché cases, jackets, skirts, coats, gloves, belts, billfolds, shoes, luggage, saddles, ski, hunting or field boots, jewel boxes, picture frames, scrapbooks—leather is infinitely adaptable, but whatever shape it takes, it reflects the care, love and expertise that go into the making of it. This isn't to say that you won't run into shoddy products from time to time, but in good shops European leathers are outstanding good buys. Their excellence is the result of skills handed down through generations of craftsmanship. Many of Europe's distinguished houses were set up as saddlery shops a century or two ago and they have had the time to achieve perfection. Though machine-made products are now the rule, these shops still turn things out by hand, scrupulously sewing every stitch. Such leather goods are meant to last for decades at the very least; indeed for centuries, the honeyed gleam of well-worn and polished leather has been a mark of gentry. Most quality leather shops will look after your purchase during its entire lifetime. If, for example, you buy a suitcase or even a pair of gloves from Gucci in Italy, you can bring them back to any Gucci shop forever for cleaning, polishing and repairs.

A list of all of Europe's leather shops would fill a fat little directory, so only the "greats" are noted here. Be sure to visit them whether you buy or not, just for the pleasure of studying perfection:

Hermès, 24 Rue du Faubourg St.-Honoré in Paris, has a breath-taking—and costly—collection of leather goods of all kinds. Don't leave without a pair of their superb gloves, probably the best of France's generally superlative gloves.

Gucci is at 8 Via Condotti in Rome. It also has branches in Florence, Milan, Montecatini, Paris, London, New York and Palm Beach. The quality of its leathers, the clasps on its handbags, the strength of its frames, and the chic, intelligent design and low prices of many of its small items, plus its extraordinarily handsome high-priced goods, make this shop unique.

Loewe, whose main store is at Avenida José Antonio 8 in Madrid, has every item that can possibly be made in leather. For over a hundred years it has been turning out exquisite work, winning awards for superb leather goods. Its atmosphere has an appropriate velvety hush.

Ferragamo at Palazzo Feroni in Florence, the Via Condotti in Rome and other cities of Italy, was the greatest shoe designer of his generation. His heirs carry on, selling custom- and ready-made shoes from $25 up.

In Holland and Israel, surprisingly, leather and suede coats and jackets are among the best buys. See Metz & Company, on the corner of Keizergracht and Leibsespraat in Amsterdam, and Maskit, the government-run shop at 38 Ben Yehuda Street, in Tel Aviv. And, as a postscript, I can't resist adding two glove shops whose merchandise has pleased me for years: Gant Nicolette on Rue du Faubourg St.-Honoré in Paris and Manco's on the Piazza di Espagna in Rome. Neither is any bigger than a large clothes closet, but both house a seemingly endless supply of well-cut gloves at half the U.S.A. price.

Lettuce

THERE ARE a handful of situations that call for more caution when you are traveling than they would at home. Facing a green salad is one of them. You may have a rugged constitution that can take such exotica as squid, blood pancakes, and sheep's eyes with equanimity, but a harmless-looking lettuce leaf—or a tomato or a bowl of strawberries—can give you a sorrowful case of dysentery or a disease even more uncomfortable and hard to get rid of. So be wary—and wise.

This injunction doesn't apply to northern countries—England, France, Scandinavia and so on. Their refrigeration, food inspection regulations and farming methods are much like ours or better, and therefore you can eat what you please in perfect safety. It is only as you move south toward the tropics that the lack of refrigeration and lower standards of food handling become a menace. In *first-rate* restaurants and hotels in southern cities, you can relax, most of the time. They are so dependent on a good reputation that they have to be careful. But anywhere else, watch out.

For safety's sake follow these rules:

The water that's used to wash vegetables and fruits should be as pure as that which you drink. If you have doubts about it and find that the locals don't drink it from the tap, never eat the raw fruits and vegetables unpeeled. (See Water, page 412.)

The farther a fruit or vegetable is grown from the ground, the safer it is. In many tropical countries, human excrement is still used as fertilizer by farmers whose produce ends up on the dining tables of the small hotels in the countryside.

Don't eat fresh fruits unless you wash or peel them yourself—and don't take one whose skin has been broken. Or stick to bananas, which score high for trustworthiness; not only do they grow high from the ground, but you have to take the skin off them yourself.

Since heat destroys germs, a dish that has been thoroughly cooked and is served hot from the kitchen is safe. Warmth, on the other hand, helps bacteria to multiply. If "soft" foods such as dairy products, sauces, mayonnaise and the like are not well refrigerated, they quickly become contaminated. If food has been lying in the sun too long, avoid it.

If you will be in the tropics over a period of time and accordingly on a "no raw vegetable and fruit" regime, ask your doctor if you should pack some vitamin pills to compensate for the lost minerals and nutrients.

Be careful—but don't fuss. Simply ignore the salads and fruits about which you have doubts. One of the most unattractive sights in the world is a person who makes a public brouhaha about food.

Light and Lipstick

IF LIPSTICK that has a pretty pink glow in Lincoln, Nebraska, turns a glaring magenta in Lincoln, England, don't be surprised. From continent to continent, even city to city, there are staggering differences in atmosphere and therefore in light. The soft radiance of Paris that enchants painters will cruelly turn your face powder from rachel to orange. The brilliant light of Greece that makes the Parthenon glow with limpid clarity can make your smooth matte finish look as heavy as cement.

Since these unkind tricks of light are seldom anticipated by women travelers or noticed until you catch sight of yourself on a bus or in the noonday glare of a sidewalk café, here are a few guidelines for keying your good looks to local conditions:

If your itinerary calls for several different kinds of climate, pack several shades of makeup base, face powder and lipstick. You can then vary their depth and intensity to suit local conditions. In London's gray light, for example, you need a beigey-pink foundation.

Since good cosmetics are sold in every large city in the world, you might defer stocking up on lipstick and such until you get to the sunny cities on your list and then buy a local, popular shade. It will invariably be lighter than your own.

Use a lighter hand with makeup when you are abroad than you do at home. If possible, go without it, except for lipstick and your usual eye makeup. You will fit more naturally into the local scene. Foreigners believe that American women wear far too much in the way of cosmetics.

If you are headed for sunny islands like Hawaii, remember that lipstick with a coral undertone looks better in their bright light than pink. And in shimmering cities like Rome, Athens or Tel Aviv, go very lightly indeed on base and face powder. It's wise to remember an old maxim that where the light is brightest, the shadows are deepest—and so are the lines in your face that hold too much makeup.

Light can also play malicious tricks on your hair color. If you tint or bleach your hair, be sure to pack a "drabbing" rinse to deaden the red glints that show up in certain lights; otherwise, when you turn up in Rome, you may look as terra cotta as the ancient buildings. Ask your hairdresser for the one that's best for your hair. For more on beauty, see Beauty *en voyage* and Hairdressers, page 22.

Luggage

HANDSOME LUGGAGE is the most reassuring of traveling companions. There is nothing like it for creating a smashing impression on surly porters and disdainful hotel staff. Not so long ago, a pigskin suitcase built for the ages or a Vuitton trunk was the hallmark of the well-bred traveler. Today, fashionable luggage comes in canvas, plastic, linen, tapestry, tweed, pony hide, Fiberglas, metal, even boar skin, as well as lightweight leather. There are pretty floral prints, brilliant colors, and stunning stripes. (Even Vuitton now makes airplane luggage, though the prices remain princely.)

In fact, there is such a profusion of good-looking luggage in the shops that you may get terribly confused while shopping for it, but don't worry. Just remember two things: First, choosing your luggage is as personal a matter as buying a pair of shoes; what works for one person may be all wrong for another. Second, worthwhile luggage must be sturdy *and* lightweight *and* handsome. No matter how strong and intimidating the salesman's pitch, hold out for this trio of virtues in each piece you buy.

To determine the kind of luggage you will need in your travels, consider three basic factors:

1. How much weight you will be allowed to carry.

IF YOU TRAVEL BY	YOU CAN TAKE
Air, international	44 pounds, economy class 66 pounds, first class, regardless of the length of your trip
Air, between West Coast and Hawaii	66 pounds, economy class 77 pounds, first class, plus one carry-on bag; or, regardless of weight, 1 bag of which the total of the length, width and height does not exceed 62 inches; one medium bag, of which such dimensions do not exceed 55 inches; plus one or more pieces of hand luggage which can fit under the seat, their total dimensions not to exceed 45 inches
Bus	150 pounds
Ship	275 pounds on a transatlantic voyage 350 pounds on a transpacific voyage
Automobile	As much as trunk, seat, and roof space allow

2. What luggage can be included in prescribed rates.

Since 44 pounds is the usual minimum, let's take that figure as our guide. If you fly to Europe on a trip that lasts anywhere from 2 weeks to 2 months, all the clothes you will need can go into a single suitcase measuring from 26 to 29 inches, a shoe bag, a lightweight cosmetic case and a small piece of hand luggage. The hand piece can be either a small bag known as a "Vendome" bag (described later), or an airline flight bag in which you carry sweater, slippers, paperback and toiletries to be used during the flight.

You can also divide the 44 pounds between one 26- to 29-inch case, a 15-inch piece, and a cosmetic bag. (Except for shoes, clothing weighs little: dresses average 1 pound, blouses ½ pound; suits about 2½ pounds. See Packing, page 281.) More luggage can be added as your weight limit rises, but even if you sail and there is virtually no limit, don't take anything you can't carry yourself. This is important because once you are on land, there are bound to be rare but desperate moments when a porter will not be available. If you can't manage by yourself, you will be stuck. For this reason two bags, each of which can be lifted, are better than one huge bag which is unbudgeable. Besides, coping with a load of luggage is a bore—and expensive to boot. Each time you move it, you tip; and the heavier and more numerous your bags, the more you'll have to dole out. If you travel about with a lot of luggage, you will come to hate every bit of it.

If you sail, all your bags are brought aboard the ship and delivered to your cabin by the staff. Since they often don't get sorted for hours after sailing time, you may want to carry toothbrush, toothpaste, hairbrush, perfume, plus whatever else will make you feel fresh and pretty for luncheon. If you fly, your luggage will be divided: the heavy pieces checked through to your destination, the small ones carried aboard by you and stored under your seat or at your feet (not in the overhead rack). Since it occupies part of your space, keep it neat and compact (it makes a good footrest) or you will be fighting it with your legs all the way. The airlines, in fact, insist that hand luggage measure no more than fits under your seat. Even though it goes aboard with you, it is weighed as part of your total luggage allowance.

Many women are devoted to hatboxes, but I find them clumsy and improvident, using more weight and space than they are worth. There is also a vociferous contingent in favor of gigantic handbags, but I find them a colossal drag. A heavy bag weighs you down, numbs your arms, and is messy to plow through. You won't need it if you carry a "Vendome" bag, described below, which encloses a normal-sized handbag. Although handbags are not weighed with your luggage, they are mentioned here because women often pack them as though they were another piece of luggage. Don't allow yourself to be pressed into carrying one of dinosaur proportions. It's a nuisance. Also omit cosmetic cases, which are known generically as "train cases." They are awkward to carry, heavy, and not chic. Keep hand luggage to a minimum. Although you are allowed to carry several small pieces aboard, stepping off a plane with a load of bags and bundles can make you look foolishly disorganized. The experienced traveler rarely carries more than one hand piece and a coat.

3. How your luggage should be designed.
Luggage is made three ways: hard-sided, or rigid on all surfaces;

soft-sided, with the covering stretched over a rigid frame, allowing it to "give"; and soft construction, with no frame at all. All your major pieces should be either hard- or soft-sided. Soft construction is satisfactory only for hand pieces and shoe cases.

Since you should buy your luggage with its weight in mind, remember that lightness is more a matter of construction than of covering. Today there are leather coverings that weigh as little as canvas. The sturdiness of luggage, however, is a question of both construction and material. Given a strong frame, a piece of luggage that is covered by any one of a variety of good materials will serve you well.

As for which is better—hard-sided or soft-sided construction— much can be said for either. The "hard-siders" maintain that since luggage takes a heavy beating, a hard-sided suitcase is less likely to be ripped or squashed. "Soft-siders" like the advantages of increased space plus the substantial strength of the case. Some experts estimate that, given cases of the identical size in hard-sided and soft-sided construction, the latter will hold nearly half again as much as the former. Packing a soft-sided suitcase until it bulges is actually good for it, because the tighter it is packed, the stronger it is. I confess to being a "soft-sider" because I like the extra room it gives me. I can also report that my luggage has come through thousands of miles unscathed.

Another choice lies between the flat case and the one that hangs. The latter, a foldover garment bag, has such names as car pack, Val-a-pak or Air Pack. I have used both happily, but today I rely most on the garment bag. It is, in effect, a traveling closet with a hanging rod and hangers that slide in and out. It takes mere minutes to pack and unpack, is light as well as strong, and marvelous for trips broken up by a string of stopovers that make a great deal of packing and unpacking necessary.

You will have to decide for yourself what suits you, but whichever way it goes, be sure you buy a case with flush locks, reinforced corners, a strong handle and no bothersome fittings, which generally add nothing but weight.

Pick out your own travel accessories—for example, plastic envelopes in various sizes for lingerie, sweaters or blouses, handkerchiefs and gloves. Slip your favorite sachet into each one. When you arrive at your hotel, you need only put the envelopes into the dresser drawers and you're unpacked. Also take plastic envelopes with zippers across the top to hold each category of drugs and cosmetics (see Packing, page 281), a soft pouchy jewel case that can be wedged into a corner; plastic bottles and jars in sizes that fit your cosmetics; and finally, an inner pack which is an arrangement of pockets suspended on a single hanger that fits into any hanging bag. It will carry underwear, stockings, blouses, laundry and the like. Avoid jewel boxes with rigid sides—they take up too much space.

All small pieces of luggage must be expected to do double duty, for often, *en voyage*, you will go off on overnight or weekend excursions and won't want to be burdened with a large suitcase. After much trial and error I have found that the following small pieces work best for me:

Shoe bag—normally it carries six pairs of shoes (in shoe socks—another useful accessory), which are held in place by a snap-fastened partition. It is made of canvas, felt-lined, and weighs only 28 ounces empty. When I need a weekend case, I just snap out the partition.

The "Vendome" bag—this has two soft-sided closed compartments and an open one in the center. The open compartment holds books, papers, my handbag; the closed compartments the necessities for the flight. While you're touring, it's useful in a dozen different ways: as a shopping bag, overnight bag, or cosmetic case. It was designed by T. Anthony, 772 Madison Avenue, New York, New York 10021, a shop which carries handsome luggage in a range of colors and materials.

The best small bag of all is one that packs flat at the bottom of my suitcase and will expand into a large, soft carryall. It is, in other words, an extra piece of luggage that can be put to work carrying books, laundry, and various other accumulations—and comes in many styles.

The airline flight bag also comes under the "small bag" classification. It is handed out free to first-class passengers; economy-class travelers must pay a nominal charge of about $2. If you don't mind the airline's name emblazoned on it, you will find it eminently useful. In most cases, it is exceptionally sturdy and lined with washable plastic. While it looks small, it can absorb an impressive amount of gear, including camera, that all-important sweater, bottles and jars. Since perfumes and other liquids may leak at high altitudes, a flight bag with a waterproof lining is a good place in which to keep them.

To avoid the catastrophe of losing your luggage (it is invariably found within a day or so, but it can be maddening to be without it when you are far from replacements), be sure to tag it with your name and home address printed on sturdy leather tags. (Be certain, too, to remove all the old routing tags.) Also paste a label with the same information inside your suitcases, camera and glasses cases and coat pocket. It's a good idea to tape your itinerary with dates and hotels inside the case; then if your luggage is lost en route it can be forwarded to you. Some travelers put a piece of colored tape or a bit of ribbon on each handle so they can quickly recognize their bags in the confusion at baggage-claim areas in terminals. Except for airline flight bags, all pieces should have sturdy locks, especially the small one that carries your most expensive, fragile and valued possessions. And, of course, always keep your luggage locked when it's out of your sight. (If you want a sturdier lock on your case than the one it already has, have a small padlock fitted to it. Be sure to get an extra set of keys.)

There is another item that is favored by women who lead formal transoceanic lives requiring "big" evening dresses and lots of clothes. It's made out of a tough feather-light plastic, is indestructible, inexpensive, and has about as much flair as a grocery carton. Called "Tex-Raw," it is sold by the Airline Luggage Shop, 139 East 57th Street, New York, New York 10022. These cases are usually shipped ahead by air. Because they are so light, you can be extravagant with space and pack them with only two or three evening dresses without running into large shipping charges. There are quite nice canvas or nylon covers which slip over the cases and hide their plain exteriors.

Four final points to note:

Children traveling by air at half fare get the same allowance as adults. (Infants get none, but a portable cradle and 20 pounds of necessities like diapers will be carried free.) You may be able to borrow some pounds from your children's allowance since the luggage of people traveling in the same party is weighed all together.

If your luggage goes astray, report the loss immediately to the passenger service agent at the airport. He will put a tracer on it and have it delivered to your hotel: 90 per cent of the luggage that is lost or misplaced is recovered within 24 hours and returned to the owner within 3 days. If you need clothing replacements immediately, the airline will give you a small amount of cash on the spot.

Have your luggage discreetly monogrammed. It discourages thieves.

Try to buy several matching pieces at once. Otherwise, choose a style which is in "open stock" so that you can add to it. A matched set is far more elegant than a mongrel assortment and easier to identify in the customs or terminal pile-ups. Buy the best you can afford —luggage is no item on which to scrimp. It has to stand up to a heap of heaving, shoving, throwing, stamping, and slamming. Function apart, handsome luggage will give you pleasure each time you say "That's mine" to a porter.

Mail

ALTHOUGH your social correspondence at home may be limited to the yearly shower of Christmas cards, you will probably find, once you are abroad, that you turn into a prolific picture postcard correspondent. Consider for a moment the fact that around four *billion* picture postcards are manufactured and presumably sent every year. Once you start traveling, you are very likely going to participate in this Niagara of correspondence. How, then, do you go about sending and receiving mail while you hop from place to place?

If you stay at reasonably good hotels, the concierge and his staff should handle your mail. Turn your letters and cards over to them to be stamped as well as posted. (You could search out a mailbox or post office, but why bother?) If you insist on buying your own stamps, you can find them only in post offices and tobacco shops once you've left the front desk of your hotel. At the end of your stay, the concierge will hand you a separate bill, which includes charges for postage along with other extras. When you pay this, be sure to leave a forwarding address—either the name of the next hotel on your route or your home.

If, on the other hand, you haven't a cast-iron itinerary, have people write to you "c/o American Express" in the cities on your list. Actually Thomas Cook as well as American Express will hold mail for you for a period of time, usually 30 days unless the envelope specifies otherwise. When you arrive in the foreign city, you need only present yourself at the mail window with some proof of your identity. Ideally, these companies would like to see their mail service used by clients only. Acting as a mail drop has imposed a monumental load on them—American Express is now the world's largest private post office. In its Paris branch at 11 Rue Scribe, for example, employees sort about a million letters a year, and handle about 50,000 forwarding addresses. The agency will hold and service all mail that comes to its offices in thirty-four countries. There's no charge for holding your mail; there is, however, a tariff of $1 for any that is forwarded. If family and friends send mail via American Express or Thomas Cook, they should address the envelope with the company's name and the city and country to which the letter is being mailed.

If you'll be out of reach of an American Express or Thomas Cook office and traveling like a gypsy without firm hotel reservations, mail can always be sent to you "Poste Restante." Like our General Delivery, this insures its going to the local post office. In Italy, for example, the sender need only add the words "Fermo in Posta" to the name of the locality, and a letter will be held at the post office. In England it's called General Delivery. To claim mail, you go to the central post office of the region with your passport for identification. Officially, it will be held 2 weeks; in practice, longer. This tends to be a rather uncertain business at best, and though it *can* work, don't rely on it when important mail is involved. In addition, tell people writing you to *print* your name and address. American script is just as hard for Europeans to read as theirs is for us—often more so, as our handwriting is less disciplined.

Letters addressed to your hotel before you're due to arrive should be marked "Hold for Arrival"; those that may come after you have left should carry the words "Please Forward."

Post offices abroad work much like ours, but there is one special service which can simplify life. It is a marvelous system which beats anything we have in this country; but, alas, it exists only in Paris and Marseilles. Either place, you can mail a short letter known as a *pneumatique*, which will be delivered locally in less than 2 hours. It is written on thin paper or on a special form which you can get from your concierge or the local post office. Be sure to write the word "pneumatique" clearly across its face. Give it to your concierge, who will rush it to the post office, where it is dropped into special boxes and whisked underground to its destination by pneumatic tubes much like those that carry your money and sales check in an old-fashioned department store at home. Much faster than ordinary mail and far less expensive than a telegram, it's a wonderful way of getting a quick message to a friend.

Another economy abroad, as in this country, is the aerogramme, an airmail letter form which is always less expensive than ordinary air mail. In Britain, for example, the aerogramme costs 7 cents, while airmail letters sent the usual way cost 18 cents.

Since you'll probably send far more postcards than letters, here are two tips. One, if you plan to send out dozens of cards, buy them early in your trip, address all of them, and carry them with you. Then during snatches of waiting time—on sightseeing buses before they start to roll, at railway stations and airports, in restaurants—you can write the messages. Two, don't send them by air if you expect to be away any length of time. Surface mail from Europe takes about 3 weeks. If you are gone for 6, that still leaves plenty of time for the card to arrive before you return. The savings accumulated in sending all your mail by boat could pay for a memorable meal at Maxim's. If you do send postcards by air, be sure to mail them from a city that has air service. Otherwise they will languish for days en route.

Some skeptics will advise you to watch the stamps being pasted on your mail to be sure that the clerk or concierge does not send an airmail letter by sea and pocket the difference. This sort of petty chicanery is unlikely in large hotels but is not unknown in small towns and small-town post offices in many parts of the world, where the ten-dollar bill you put down to send a batch of airmail letters may equal a postal clerk's weekly salary. To relieve yourself of doubt and the clerk of temptation, paste the stamps on yourself.

That leaves just one more point: how to handle the mail that comes to you at home while you're away. If you live in a large apartment house with a watchful doorman or superintendent, either one can act as custodian; or possibly a friendly neighbor will look after your mail. If you can't fall back on these, the post office will hold your mail while you're away. The standard procedure throughout the country is to write to the superintendent of your post office station, asking him to hold your mail for the dates specified and giving the reason for your absence, i.e., touring. On your return, present yourself at the post office with suitable identification such as your passport or driver's license, and the mail will be turned over to you.

Making Connections

VAPOR TRAILS across Arctic skies, train tracks shining across green fields, a white V foaming in a blue sea, roads snaking up mountainsides—all testify to the passage of some carrier whisking you to some destination. Getting you there is *its* job. But getting from the plane to the bus, or from the ship to the train, or from the train to the plane is *your* responsibility—or your travel agent's.

If you leave home with a fixed itinerary in hand, your only concern will be making each connection promptly. The instructions for moving from hotel to airport or train will be as clearly spelled out as they are in a good recipe. If, on the other hand, you prefer to improvise as you go, you will have to *plan* as well as make your connections. Here is what you should know:

When making connections within a country between two flights at a large airport (for instance, between Alitalia flights from Milan to Rome and Rome to Palermo), allow about one hour. You will need every one of the 60 minutes to collect your luggage and check in for the second flight.

If you are making connections between a national and an international flight (or vice versa), or between two international flights, or between two airports, allow about 3 hours. On international flights, you must leave time for health, passport and customs clearance, processes which can take from 10 minutes to 1 hour and 10 minutes.

If you disembark from a ship and must connect with a plane or train (unless it's the boat train that stands on the siding waiting for the passengers), you must allow half a day.

Actually all the airlines, acting in concert, have agreements about what constitutes "legal" connecting periods between all flights at any airport. When your travel agent draws up your itinerary, he is guided by these officially recognized intervals. If you calculate them on your own, however, be governed by the timing given above—and don't try to beat the clock. It's far more agreeable to have time for a leisurely cup of coffee at the terminal than to dash up breathlessly as the flight is being closed down or the train pulling out of the station.

Since the best-laid plans often go *pfft!*, should you miss a connection because your aircraft is delayed, the airline is responsible for moving you along on your way and will solicitously take charge. If it can put you on the next plane, it will promptly make the booking. If it can't, and you must stay overnight or are stranded at a rerouting point, the airline will make and pay for a hotel reservation, meals, beverages, ground transportation, telegrams and even the transit taxes. If you have to be rerouted more expensively, the airline will take care of the difference. On the other hand, if the missed connection is your fault, the airline will help with all the foregoing, but, of course, you will have to pay the bills.

Some airlines go to great lengths to help their passengers make connections. American Airlines, for one, has a special agent who meets incoming ocean liners to help passengers who will be flying home cross-country via American. Pan American has radio-equipped station wagons with hostess-driver teams at Chicago, Los Angeles and New York airports, which meet domestic flights and transfer passengers to the Pan Am terminal at no charge if they are making direct connections with departing Pan Am flights.

Two final points:

If you are going from hotel to airport, go to the airlines terminal building and take the bus from there. It will save you exhausting tension and irritation. Otherwise, when you find yourself crawling along in a taxi because the road is being torn up, all you can do is fume. Even in the business of getting to the terminal, make allowances for all the variables that can delay you: detours, crowds, traffic, weather.

If you find yourself stranded at an airport for any reason, go immediately to the reservations counter of the airline on which you are booked. It will have the schedules of other carriers plus train, bus and ship connections. Unless you run into the occasional splenetic clerk, you'll find most airline personnel courteous and helpful. They will arrange a hotel reservation, take the mystery out of making telephone calls, send cables and even take care of your children in a pinch. (See Airports, page 1.)

Manners

BEFORE THEY arrive at their posts, members of American diplomatic staffs are thoroughly briefed on the niceties of local etiquette. Our State Department realizes that one can offend one's hosts through ignorance as easily as through bad intentions.

Actually, the nationals of most countries you visit are apt to be indulgent with tourists; no traveler is expected to know all the special customs of every place in the world. If a kind heart, an even disposition, common courtesy and a generous helping of common sense are the wellsprings of your behavior, you needn't worry about *gaucheries*. Even so, it is important to learn something about foreign manners and sensitivities and govern your conduct accordingly; human nature being what it is, one is always judged first by one's observance of local proprieties. These amenities are often deeply rooted in history, culture and temperament. Local residents are impressed by the traveler who is as interested in their outlook and way of life as in their monuments.

Other nations, as a rule, are more formal than we are; their manners are based on older cultures and a slower pace of life. American breeziness—the instant first-naming, the uninhibited questions, the neglect of formalities—is often taken for rudeness. To counteract that impression, try hard to be at least twice as courteous and tactful in a foreign country as you would be at home. The jet age has brought about a fairly standard code of manners throughout Western society, while other areas have become so accustomed to seeing Westerners that the manners that stand you in good stead in Innsbruck will usually see you through in India. The basic rule of thumb is to watch the people around you, then let observation and common sense guide your own conduct.

I shall try here to cover the most important specific differences between foreign etiquette and ours, as well as some variations in general deportment which are worth keeping in mind. For more on this subject, see Flowers, page 137, Pubs and Bars, page 301, Names and

Titles, page 273, Time, page 354, Shorts and Slacks, page 327, and Gifts to Take Abroad, page 148.

SHAKING HANDS: Europeans, Latin Americans and all those who have been educated in Europe customarily shake hands when they are introduced, each time they meet, and when they part. Even children follow this custom, and its breach is considered rude. As a woman, you offer your hand first unless someone is your senior in age or rank, in which case you must wait for him to make the gesture. When an older man or woman enters a room, you always rise to shake hands. When you leave a small group, shake hands all around, starting with your hostess and host or the senior member of the party.

HAND KISSING: In Austria, Germany, France, Italy and Spain, a man may bow over the back of your hand and make a gesture of kissing it, although these days women's hands are more often shaken than kissed. Since you never know which gesture a man will prefer, hold out a gentle hand prepared for either. (If you hold out a firm hand for shaking and it is raised instead to be kissed, either the man will get a karate chop or your wrist will be twisted.) Unless your gloves are heavy, don't bother to take them off as the hand is not actually kissed but raised to within an inch or so of the man's lips.

INTRODUCTIONS: When you are introduced to a European man, you will find that as he extends his hand he mumbles what sounds like either a toast or an oath in his native tongue. Actually, it's his last name, and you are expected to answer with your full name. While an American hostess customarily introduces every guest to every other guest—even if she has to recite fifteen names—at a party abroad you will be brought over to one or two people, then left on your own.

In Japan, for evident reasons, visiting cards are a must for foreign visitors. You can have them made up with your name in English on one side and Japanese on the other in a few hours after your arrival.

GREETINGS: Europeans say "Good morning" or "Good afternoon" when they enter a shop, train compartment, or any semi-public place—and all those present return the greeting. The salutation is not followed up by conversation, except in Latin countries where the salesgirl may also exchange a few pleasantries with you before getting down to business. The Japanese bow formally to each other; the deeper and more numerous the bows, the greater the respect demonstrated. Indians lightly press their hands together as if praying and incline their heads at the same time. You are not expected to do either. A Japanese or Indian, knowing Western ways, may hold out his hand for shaking. It's best to wait for his lead before offering your hand.

"THANK YOU" AND "PLEASE": Europeans punctuate their conversations with these words far more frequently than Americans. The relatively rare use we make of them helps earn us a reputation for rudeness. The Scandinavians are particularly effusive: They give thanks each time a course is served, then thank the hostess for the entire meal on arising from the table. After finishing the coffee (which is taken after the meal), they thank the hostess for it, and, of course, thank her for the evening before they leave. Moreover, the next time they meet or talk with her on the telephone, they must say "Thanks for the last time." The visitor is expected to follow suit. The British thank a waiter for showing them to a table, and again for handing them a menu. They thank an elevator operator for taking them to their floor and a ticket inspector for returning their ticket. However often the British say "Thank you," they don't say "You're welcome." If you know the equivalent of "please" and "thank you" in the country you are visiting, use them; otherwise, say the words in English. They are probably Number 1 and 2 in every foreigner's basic English vocabulary.

People in other countries, however, never say "Thank you" in return for a compliment. See Men, page 247.

Address people frequently as "Monsieur" and "Madame." It's "Bonjour, madame" and "Au revoir, monsieur" and "Merci, mademoiselle." Always use a person's title in addressing him or her, to add grace to your conversation.

INVITATIONS: In Middle Eastern countries such as Lebanon and Jordan, a guest is a sacred trust and it is considered an insult to refuse an invitation unless you have made a previous engagement.

BREAD-AND-BUTTER NOTES: You must write a bread-and-butter note to every one who extends hospitality. As in the United States, this is imperative for an overnight or weekend visit; abroad, do it as well for dinner at someone's house. Although in this country, a post-party telephone call will do, Europeans still prefer a note.

TABLE MANNERS: The European method of using knife and fork differs from ours: We cut with the knife in our right hand, shifting the fork from left to right to spear our food; they keep the knife in the right hand, fork in the left, throughout the course, unless the food does not need cutting. Both systems are correct, and you needn't change yours.

You will find the table setting slightly different from the one you know at home, with the dessert fork and spoon lying horizontally above the plate. In restaurants you will often be asked to retain the knife and fork of the first course for the second. Oriental restaurants serve toothpicks, which are frequently and casually used at table; just shield your mouth with your hands. In Japan, try chopsticks, but if you cannot manage them, ask for a knife and fork. Moslems eat with the first three fingers of the right hand, never the left, but your host will undoubtedly provide you with Western silverware. The hot scented towels that are passed around before a meal are for cleaning your hands before you plunge into your food.

FOOD: It is impolite to leave food on your plate or to refuse a second helping at a meal in a private home. You must never show that you don't enjoy the food set before you. In the Middle East it is insulting to refuse the cups of tea or coffee which are endlessly offered in shops and offices. You will occasionally be faced with foods that may be repellent to you. Grit your teeth, swallow and smile. What you can refuse is a matter of tact: No one will be offended if you leave something because experience has taught you that it disagrees with you; but they will take a dim view of your not trying it simply because it's strange to you.

DRINKING: Wherever you go, it is not good manners to be intoxicated. Worse, in Europe and the Orient, intoxication is simply an indication of bad breeding.

Cocktails are far less customary in Europe than America. An *apéritif* like sherry or vermouth is the rule before meals; it enhances the wines at dinner rather than anaesthetizing your palate.

The Scandinavian countries enjoy a regulated ceremonial toast, customary at parties of six or more, called the *skål*. As a woman, you *never* drink first, nor do you originate the toast, nor is the hostess ever toasted. But when the signal is given, you raise your glass, gaze into the eyes of the man giving the toast, nod, say *"Skål,"* and drink, never dropping your eyes. Then you raise your glass slightly once more and nod, lower your eyes and the toast is concluded.

SMOKING: Smoking between courses is frowned upon in private houses, so don't attempt it unless you see an ashtray on the dining table. The hostess will offer cigarettes with the coffee. At public dinners in Britain, one may not smoke until the assemblage has toasted the Queen—usually at the end of the meal. Women still do not smoke on the street or in public buildings abroad. On the other hand, in many parts of Western Europe you can smoke in places that are normally off limits at home, such as subway cars, the tops of buses, movie houses and in theaters during the performance. Moslem countries consider it a mark of disrespect if a person smokes when passing a mosque.

Always wait for a man in your company to light your cigarette; in this area, self-sufficiency is considered unfeminine.

PRECEDENCE: When a man precedes you, he usually does so for your comfort. If, for example, a Dutchman walks up a flight of steps ahead of you, he is only following a centuries-old rule that a gentleman never stares at a well-turned ankle. If he goes into a restaurant first, it's because he judges that in a milling *bistro* with no headwaiter, you'd be happier not facing the crowd alone. He may also lead the way into the theater, to clear a path for you. Foreign men are accustomed to opening doors for women, and your reaching for the knob first will throw a man off his stride. The American woman's independence is rather overwhelming to foreigners. Try to clip your wings somewhat: First, it's tactful; and second, it may avoid much bumping of noses and rubbing of shoulders as a man moves to serve you while you are serving yourself.

Except in Scandinavia, a woman is at a man's right both at table and on the street. European men don't, in other words, place themselves in relation to the curb as do American men. Don't try to wedge them over.

QUEUES: In Britain and the Commonwealth countries, a crowd waiting for a bus, or anything else, forms a line. There's no milling around, and no getting ahead of those already in line. The British even queue up to get into a queue which means waiting to get on a waiting line. Russia also has queuing up, first to buy something, then to pay for it, and finally to collect it.

THEATERS, MOVIES, STADIUMS: An eminently sensible rule of foreign etiquette is the Swedish one (it sometimes works in Britain, too) of entering a row of seats facing those already seated. It's considered rude to turn your back on the people you pass.

In Europe, it is customary for a woman to check her coat in a good number of public places. Be especially prepared to do this in expensive restaurants.

Even more important than these niceties of etiquette—foreigners are likely to be most generous and understanding about lapses—is the tact and courtesy of your general deportment. You are expected to recognize that you are a guest in a country, and to consider local sensitivities and outlook. If you fail in this, your hosts will be far less forgiving. Here are some of the attitudes that are likely to cause trouble:

EMOTIONAL DISPLAYS: Even in such fundamental matters as expressing love, pain, anger and impatience, there is no single way of behaving around the world. Accept others' manners while you are among them. In the U.S.A. a man and woman or two women who are close friends will kiss each other on the street as a friendly greeting. In Latin countries men kiss each other. But in Japan your new friend, male or female, will be mortified by such a gesture, since the Japanese shun public displays of affection. In the Middle East it is considered bad manners to show your impatience—and in the Far East you are expected to be dignified and inscrutable even if the world is collapsing around you. To show emotional stress is in bad taste.

In many parts of the world American women are regarded as rather bossy. Some self-reliance is, of course, necessary when you travel—but try to avoid the executive manner and all *grande dame* behavior, especially in countries where women haven't even the same legal rights as men.

OVER-DEMOCRATIC ATTITUDES: Good manners dictate that whatever the social attitudes of the place you are visiting may be, you must follow them if only outwardly. If the local treatment of servants, caste system or color bar is more than you can stomach, by all means don't go to the country at all; but the fact that you enter a country commits you to swim with its social tide for the brief time you are there. When you visit a friend at home, you don't break the rules of her house. In places whose social distinctions are similar to our own, don't do anything you wouldn't do in East Kankakee or New York. Don't become deathless friends with your guide or insist that your driver share your luncheon table if this is not locally acceptable.

CONVERSATION: Most foreigners find strange the freedom with which an American talks about his income and family affairs, subjects they consider too private to share with a stranger. Indeed, they may know someone for years without calling him by his first name or visiting his house. Friendships bloom slowly and last long. While in this country it is perfectly acceptable to ask someone you have just met what he does for a living, this question is considered rude abroad.

Unless you are talking to a very close foreign friend—of long standing—don't criticize the person's country or compare it with the U.S.A. Do try to pay compliments to the culture, beauties and achievements of the country you are visiting. Because ours is a powerful "have" nation, however, foreigners often feel free to ask questions *they* would consider sharp or rude if positions were reversed. Since you represent 196,000,000 Americans, be prepared to answer them graciously—and intelligently.

Stay away from local political sore points and oft-told bad jokes. Don't tease the Turks about the fez or the Scots about what goes on under their kilts. At dinner in Delhi don't discuss the border dispute between Pakistan and India; in the U.S.S.R. don't make light remarks about the Hungarian Revolution or Boris Pasternak; and resist the temptation to joke about the Mafia in Palermo. Let your hosts bring up delicate subjects like Sweden's neutrality or France's relations with NATO, and even then, listen more than you talk. Do your very best to show sympathetic understanding and a real willingness to learn their point of view.

Religion, American aid, and local royalty are also subjects best avoided. Many countries do not take kindly to jokes about the family and marriage. Even if your hosts make jokes about their own national customs, you may laugh at what they say, but don't contribute *mots* of your own.

Markets

DIGGING and haggling and being fleeced in markets—
and now and then coming away with a triumphant treasure wrapped
in newspaper—is for many of us one of the greatest joys of travel. In
Europe, mainly—where nothing, no matter how old, ever seems to be
thrown away—great markets still flourish, and as long as an object has
some use it can be sold. In most European cities, many of the "left-
overs" find their way to a central area where they are displayed in
stalls. Here all the merchandise is combed for treasures by tourists,
antique dealers, householders starting out in life or making a second
start, and collectors, both mad and sane.

While markets are shorter on bargains than they once were, it's
still possible to strike a "find" among the magpie heaps of trash. (In
Paris's Flea Market at the turn of the century, two ragpickers, tired of
hauling a cart filled with canvases, sold the batch for 10 francs. The
lot turned out to include works by Corot, Delacroix and Daumier.)
Dealers seem to believe that the more chaotic the assortment of articles surrounding a piece, the more the customer is likely to feel she
has found something extraordinary. The treasure seeker had better
move shrewdly, for the number of fine antiques is getting scarcer
and, naturally, more expensive, and every flea-market stall is scoured
by owners of local antique shops. Nevertheless, it's still possible to
find something marvelous among the tangle of odds and ends, and
that is the magic of markets.

If foraging in markets interests you, here are some ground rules:

1. Since few markets are open every day, check the list at the end
of this piece, and double-check with your concierge for the days and
hours they are in operation. Most markets are open only one or two
days a week. Learn when the new merchandise arrives and plan your
campaign accordingly.

2. Go early, very early; market addicts count on giving up sleep.
Many markets open at the crack of dawn, i.e., 7 A.M., and fold their
stalls by noon; your competitors, dealers from the city's fancier shops,
rise early. You will have to beat them at their game.

3. Haggling is usually in order; most hawkers would be disappointed if they weren't challenged by customers, and you'll be considered foolishly extravagant if you don't. But don't count on a slashing of prices in the markets of Western Europe. In North Africa, the Middle East and Asia, the story is different. Here you are expected to bargain hard, for the original price quoted is merely an acknowledged starting point for negotiations between you and the merchant. Bargaining is an essential part of shopping, and you must take time to do it adroitly and with style. The better you bargain, the more respect you will get from the seller. There are so many interested Europeans these days combing every stall and shop for antiques that it is a seller's, not a buyer's, market. Most dealers know the value of their wares, so don't expect to impress with your dollars when there are lots of people with perfectly good marks, lire, and kroner to spend.

4. Watch your language. Most dealers understand a smattering of English, and your *sotto voce* remarks about what a bargain you have found may push the price up. Also, guard your "body English"; if you fall hard for a portable writing desk, keep a deadpan expression or the price will rise according to the glint in your eye.

5. Cold, rainy mornings are the best time to go; an icy winter morning in January is ideal. Since dealers invariably do their business from flimsy shops, partly covered stalls or open sidewalk displays, they are exposed to the elements; they will be apt to settle for a smaller profit so they can finish their day's business early and go home.

6. Convincing imitations of antiques, to the last detail of wormholes, are turned out by the truckload in some parts of Europe. So watch out. You can detect a phony wormhole, for instance, by sticking a pin into it. If it goes right in, the hole was made by a man, not a circuitous worm.

7. Eighteenth-century antiques (and earlier) have long been much appreciated. Now even machine-made furniture and bric-a-brac of the nineteenth century are fashionable. Prices have risen steeply in the past couple of years and will keep going up. If you can still find well-priced Victoriana, don't pass it up. It's a good investment.

8. Getting the treasure home is up to you, so be sure to reckon the cost of shipment as well as that of your purchase before cheering over your bargain. The larger the piece, naturally, the larger the shipping tariff.

9. Be clothes-conscious—in reverse. Wear your most comfortable shoes. Most markets sprawl for acres—Paris's Flea Market encompasses 48; and since there is nowhere to sit down, you will be on your

feet for hours. Put on your oldest, dowdiest clothes. Dealers are quick to surmise what the traffic will bear and elegance will cost you dear. Carry a handbag with a secure clasp, since markets are the favorite haunts of pickpockets.

10. While you may save money buying at a market, remember that unlike an established antique dealer, the man who runs the stall has no obligation to sell you a perfectly restored or authentic product. If you are unsure of your ground, buy only what pleases your eye, without thought of investment or authenticity. Check the local auction prices for similar types of merchandise to get an idea of market value.

Many cities have specialized markets that are worth seeing just for their extraordinary vigor and color. Go, for example, to Dublin's Bird Market, even if you have no intention of boarding the plane home with a parrot on your shoulder. The Irish love cage birds, and on Sunday between 10 and 2, the flow of Irish wit and speech is pure O'Casey.

In the Middle East, North Africa and Asia, substitute the word bazaars for markets. In Istanbul's Grand Bazaar there are thousands of shops, clustered under one roof, that sell carpets, silver, bronzes, jewelry, and more. The stalls are small and packed together like pigeonholes. To an American eye, there isn't the infinite variety of usable goods that there is in the markets of Western Europe, but the bazaars are ancient parts of the local scene and should be visited as much as sights as for the sake of shopping.

Here is a rundown on the outstanding markets in 26 cities frequently visited by American tourists:

AUSTRIA—SALZBURG

Gruenmarkt—At the corner of Universitätsplatz and Marktgasse. Its prime purpose is to supply the housewives of Salzburg with flowers, fruits and vegetables. Sometimes a few pots and pans may be added, but most of the merchandise is perishable. Go for the color and the noise. Open every day except Sunday, from about 7:30 or 8 in the morning until around 4 in the afternoon.

Schrannenmarkt—More fruits, flowers and vegetables are sold at this market outside the Andrakirche. Open Thursday mornings (or Friday, if Thursday happens to be a holiday).

BELGIUM—BRUSSELS

Marché des Antiquités, et Marché aux Livres Précieux —Held on Place du Sablon; there are some marvelous buys here. The *antiquités* include furniture, old velvet, glassware, china (perhaps some Meissen or Limoges), sculpture, tiles and interesting old wooden cookie molds which come from Holland, Flanders and the Rhineland, carved in the figures of kings, queens, flowers, etc. You might find a valuable item among the old books which the dealers buy up in bulk from estates. Since they are often not familiar with their own wares, there may be good bindings and first editions which have escaped unnoticed. But beware—the experts have probably been there first, so go early. Held on weekends: Saturday from 10 A.M. to 6 P.M., Sundays from 10 A.M. to 1 P.M.

Marché aux Chevaux—Horse trading takes place on La Place de la Duchesse on Fridays, from early morning till 2 P.M.

Marché aux Fleurs—Held in the Grand 'Place. This flower market operates in two shifts. From about 4:30 A.M. it sells at wholesale prices to florists, hotels and restaurants. From about 7:30 A.M. to about 2:30 P.M. retail prices prevail. Go early. Takes place seven days a week.

Marché aux Oiseaux—Racing pigeons are a speciality of the bird market (this is a great Belgian sport) but there are birds of all kinds. Best time to go: between 9 A.M. and 10 A.M. Takes over part of the Grand 'Place on Sundays from 9:00 A.M. to noon.

Marché de la Place Ste.-Catherine—This is the most famous of Brussels' many fruit and vegetable markets. It's open every day from 8 A.M. to 6 P.M. in summer, till 4 P.M. in winter.

Marché aux Puces or *Vieux Marché*—The flea market, held on La Place du Jeu de Balle, is a mixture of junk—old clothes, household goods, vases, portraits, corsets, chipped plaster statues— and wares which are sometimes quaint, funny, fantastic, or just in bad taste. There is a selection of art nouveau, and occasionally something that could, with imagination, be fixed up. Held every day from 9 A.M. to 1 P.M.

There are also many small flower markets in squares throughout Brussels, and flea markets in other parts of Belgium such as Antwerp, Liege and Ghent.

BRAZIL—MANAUS

Manaus Market—If you have an affinity for the offbeat, this market, just a block away from the Amazon Hotel, is *the* place to buy animal skin rugs, a caged young jaguar or parrot, or the deadly piranha fish dried. This market's wares, which also include fish for human consumption, fruits, vegetables and flowers, are set up in stalls. Open Monday through Friday from sunrise to sunset, Saturday until 12 noon.

ENGLAND—LONDON

Bermondsey or *Caledonian Market*—Chief wares are old clothing and furniture; many antique dealers buy here. Some stall holders who work Saturday at Portobello Road Market (see below) work here on Fridays. Bargains are best early in the day. Hours: 9 A.M. to 4 P.M. every Friday.

Billingsgate Market—On Lower Thames Street, E.C. 3. The oldest of markets belonging to the City Corporation is the clearing house for the fish of Great Britain. More than 600 tons of fish (some from Denmark, Norway, Sweden, Holland and Belgium as well) pass through each day. It's housed under a roof, but the hustle and bustle are similar to that of an open-air market. Open from 6 A.M. weekdays (when every variety of fish is sold); also from 6 A.M. Sundays (when it's strictly shellfish).

Chapel Market—In Islington, on Chapel Street. You can buy almost anything: nylon stockings, herbs, a bird in a cage, an old flock mattress. It's a good place to eat things like jellied eel, or hot apple fritters, and you might round off the afternoon by having your palm read. Open every day.

Covent Garden—Covent Garden is to flowers, fruits and vegetables what Billingsgate is to fish. Roofed with a glass dome, it sells produce from all over the world: oranges from Israel, apples from South Africa, tomatoes from Holland, carrots from France. The best days to go are Tuesday and Thursday; best time between 6 and 7 A.M. Open weekday mornings.

Petticoat Lane—On Middlesex Street, E.1. This is probably London's most famous market. Go early, around 9 A.M., if you want first crack at the merchandise; later if you want a bargain (prices tend to go down as the morning progresses). The wares, displayed (and loudly advertised) in a row of stalls against the background sounds of a gramophone or a live fiddler, are endless: clothing, jewelry, leather, musical instruments, carpets. Food—fruit and fish—are also sold. Always bargain, and watch out for pickpockets. Open Sunday morning.

Portobello Road Market—This market is almost as famous as Petticoat Lane and teems with as great a variety of people and nationalities as merchandise. Many of the stall holders have smart shops in Kensington or Chelsea; their Saturday session in Portobello Road relieves them of excess stock as well as their probable pent-up desire to cajole and bargain. They sell antiques (search long enough and you might match six Georgian spoons), paintings, silver, and, perhaps, a first edition of Byron's *Don Juan*. Open Saturdays from 9 A.M. to 6 P.M. for antiques.

FRANCE—PARIS

Foire à la Ferraile—(Junk, Scrap Iron Fair)—On the Boulevard Richard-Lenoir. Wares include gates and bedposts which are a bit heavy to cart home, but you might find something that will be worth the trouble. Held from the day before Palm Sunday, to Easter, and again on the first Saturday to the second Sunday of October, all day.

Les Halles—Everyone has onion soup here early in the morning at least once. The flower market and the cheese market are probably the most interesting. The trucks are unloaded between 2 A.M. and 5 A.M., and the market is in progress from 5 A.M. to 9 P.M. Open every day except Monday. Current plans call for Les Halles to have been moved from the center of Paris by 1967.

Marché aux Chevaux, Ânes et Mulets—At 106 Rue Brancion. No winners from Longchamps here; mostly ponies, hack and carriage horses. But they're fun to see, and so are the donkeys and mules. Open Mondays, Wednesdays and Fridays from 9 A.M. to 12 noon.

Marché aux Chiens (Dog Market)—At 106 Rue des Morillons. There is a great deal of yipping, yapping, confusion, and of course, those big, brown eyes that plead for love and a home. It could be disastrous to take the children unless you have superhuman willpower. Open from 2 P.M to 4 or 5 P.M. on Sundays.

Marché de la Friperie (Clothes Market)—At the Carreau du Temple. The clothing is secondhand and hardly worth the effort of sorting through. Go to see people in action; this is a marvelous place for sociological study. Open every day except Monday from early morning to sundown.

Marché aux Oiseaux (Bird Market)—At Place Louis-Lépine. You will find everything from live parakeets to mechanical birds, bird seed and bird whistles. Cages are especially fascinating. Some are Victorian; others are from Italy, Greece, Spain, Mexico or Scandinavia; still others are just plain fantastic. Open on Sundays from 7 A.M. to 7 P.M.

Marché aux Puces—The famous Flea Market, at the Porte de Clignancourt and St.-Ouen: 4 miles of open stalls and shops with valuable antiques as well as junk, paintings, clothes with the limp, skinny thrift-shop look so popular now with the young—just about every item man has ever invented, and some you never knew existed. Best time is early Monday morning, when it tends to be less crowded; best season is winter. The stall keepers are likely to be as unusual as their wares. Always bargain. Open all day Saturday, Sunday and Monday.

Village Suisse—This is the Flea Market plus sophistication: Its stalls are operated by French artists, writers and antique collectors. Your chances of finding a bargain are fairly good. Village Suisse is within a stone's throw of the Eiffel Tower; you can take the subway to La Motte Picquet Grenelle. Open every day except Tuesday and Wednesday.

Flower markets abound. In addition to Les Halles there is the Marché de la Cité at Place Louis-Lépine, daily except Sunday from 9 A.M. to 6 P.M.; also the Marché de la Madeleine and the Marché de la République. There are food markets all over the city, traveling flea markets on Sundays, a Ham Fair dating from 1222 which is held in the spring before Easter, a Gingerbread Fair one month after Easter, and a Poets' Fair.

GERMANY—HAMBURG

Markt am Sonntag (Sunday Market)—Be there at the crack of dawn, if you want to find anything amid the jumble of bicycles, watches, textiles, etc., which constitute this market's "antiques." Takes place in the old part of town near the harbor. Ask anyone how to get there. Open every Sunday morning from 6 A.M. to 10 A.M.

MUNICH

Three country fairs, one in April or May, one in July or August, and one in late October, take place for a week or so in the Mariahilfplatz, a square within the city limits. The fair is called Auer Dult, and sells almost everything produced in and around Munich, including secondhand goods.

GREECE—ATHENS

The small shops and stalls around Monasteraki Square and Pandrossou Street constitute the local flea market, where you can buy anything: ikons, copper pots, jewelry, clothing, books, perhaps a manuscript or a Byzantine painting. There is rarely anything magnificent or of great value, but you will find pleasant items to take home. You'll find the best bargains on weekdays, but Sundays, when everyone goes, are most picturesque. Bargaining is acceptable any day of the week. The shops are open from sunrise to sunset Monday through Saturday; usually from 9 A.M. to 2 P.M. on Sunday.

Athens also has traveling food markets which move by pushcart to a different area of the city each day. They are easy to locate; you may even wake up in the morning and find a whole market suddenly encamped beneath your window.

HOLLAND—AALSMEER

Aalsmeer Flower Auction—A half-hour bus trip from Amsterdam, and you must see it. Thirty-six million carnations, five million chrysanthemums, fifty million roses, nine million lilac sprays, fourteen million sweet peas, plus millions more flowers pass through Aalsmeer each year. They're brought by barge, then sorted into lots in the huge auction hall which is divided into five rooms: two for potted plants, two for cut flowers, one for bulbs. A sample is held up, and a huge clock whose face is painted with prices starts ticking. The minute hand starts at the most expensive price and moves backward. When a buyer wants to make a purchase (only wholesalers can bid), he presses a buzzer on his seat, and the number of that seat, by the miracles of modern electricity, lights up on the clock. It's a bit like watching the Stock Exchange in action. You will marvel at the buyers' instincts for knowing which quality rose is best. Auctions take place year round Monday through Saturday, from 8 A.M. till noon.

AMSTERDAM

Flower Market—At Singel (a canal). Open every day except Sunday.

Housewares Market—On Albertcuypstraat. In addition to housewares, you can find food—with a wide variety of cheeses—and inexpensive clothing. Open daily. Another market, at Amstelveld, sells smoked eels, fruits, vegetables, live chickens and rabbits, and secondhand goods. Open only Monday mornings.

Stamp Market—At Voorburgwal, near Wijdesteeg. You can buy stamps, or, if you're a philatelist, bring your collection and trade. Open every Wednesday and Saturday afternoon.

Vlooienmarkt or *Flea Market*—Most of the items are junk; if you find anything valuable, you may make the local front page. The Vlooienmarkt is less expensive than the Paris Flea Market, but unless you have an eye for the wacky, you probably won't want to buy much, even at these low prices. Go instead for the atmosphere. Every vendor praises his goods the way speakers on Hyde Park Corner praise socialism, and a contest can develop to see which seller yells the loudest. Go on Saturday, a big day for visitors, or on Wednesday afternoon when school is out, and the children make the confusion even more colorful. If you still fondly hope for a real "find," go during the week when the market is less crowded. Bargain if you think you have a chance against a solid Dutchman, and hold on to your wallet. The Vlooienmarkt takes place every day except Sunday at Waterlooplein in an old section of Amsterdam. Its hours are from about 8 or 9 in the morning to 6 in the evening (in winter it closes earlier, when the light goes).

HONG KONG

Open-air Markets—These are better for atmosphere than for antique "finds." One is on the Hong Kong side in the Central Reclamation Area near the waterfront; the other is in Temple Street on the Kowloon side. Watch your wallet, and don't go alone—travel in a group, or use the buddy system. The markets come to life at sunset every day of the week; the kerosene lamps in the stalls burn till 1 or 2 in the morning. There are fortunetellers.

Thieves' Market—On Cat Street (nickname) or Upper Lascar Row (proper name). It is lined with shops selling secondhand goods and antiques. It is not, strictly speaking, an open-air market, but if you know merchandise, you may find some interesting bargains. Shops are open from 10 A.M. to 10 P.M.

IRELAND—DUBLIN

Bird Market—Set up in stalls which line a small square near the King's Inn in the King Street area, the center of Dublin's law courts. Caged birds are a great Irish institution; you can buy anything from canaries to pigeons or parakeets. (During the week, the birds go "inside"—to various shops in the area.) You can bargain, and often you may have to bid against another bird enthusiast. Average price for a pair of canaries is less than a dollar. Occasionally other pets are sold. Open every Sunday from 10 A.M. to 2 P.M.

Sidewalk auctions—These are held along Arran Quay (noted for its antique shops) and Merchants' Quay (bookshops that sell seventeenth- and eighteenth-century manuscripts, as well as some newer ones). Arran Quay's auctions are announced in the papers and sometimes by town crier. Most of the better manuscripts in stores along Merchants' Quay are kept inside, but you might pick up a second or third edition of Joyce lying outside in the sun, quite inexpensively. Most stores are open Monday through Saturday, from 9 A.M. to 6 P.M. Some close Saturday at noon. Some auctions take place in the evening.

ISRAEL—JERUSALEM

Mahne Yehudah—The housewares market on the Jaffa Road is worth a visit just for the character studies. Amid the pots, pans and food, cobblers ply their trade. The market is open every day except Saturday, closes early on Friday.

Tel Aviv

Shuk Carmel—Located off Allenby and King George Streets. This market has a selection of food, produce and cheeses, as well as ceramics, straw baskets and interesting copper trays made by Libyans. Try to go before 12 noon; the shopkeepers usually spend the afternoon clearing and setting up for the next morning. Don't be shy about bargaining here. Opens at 3:30 A.M. every day but Saturday, closes at noon on Friday for the Sabbath.

Shuk Ha Pishpeshim—The market in Jaffa (the port of Tel Aviv) is known as the flea market. It is off Yaphet Street near the Archaeological Museum, and near a group of shops which sell copper, brass, and jewelry. The market itself has "antiques," a vast collection of old clothing, and housewares. Some of the items are "hot." This market, like most others in Israel, is open every day except Saturday. Opening hour: 3:30 A.M.

Italy—Florence

Le Logge del Porcellino or *Straw Market*—Its name and location are one and the same, Le Logge del Porcellino, but it adjoins the Loggia di Mercato on the Via Calima. To further add to the confusion, the statue at one end of the arcade is not a little pig (*porcellino*) but a small wild boar. Florence is the best place to buy Italian straw; it makes a handsome decoration for any kitchen. Operates all day, every day, except Sunday.

On Thursday, a flower market joins the Straw Market in the same location; linens are also sold.

Rome

Flea Market—At the Porta Portese (there's no actual gate now). You can pick your way through a collection of carpets, paintings, "antiques," etc., which is 90 per cent junk, and 10 per cent possible good buys. Some of the items are stolen; the atmosphere is noisy and fascinating. Hold on to your handbag and bargain like mad. The Flea Market is fun even if you don't buy. It's a popular gathering place after a Saturday night on the town. You might make it a late night, then take a cab over. Takes place on Sunday; it's best in the early morning, peters out toward noon.

The market at the Piazza della Fontanella Borghese (a square in the front of the Palazzo Borghese) is smaller, more dignified, more expensive, and of better quality. The wares—etchings, copper, brass, old books, small statues, paintings, and little knickknacks—come from small shops on the outskirts of Rome, and the whole purpose of the market is to whet your appetite and lure you to them. The market is open Monday through Saturday, from about 3 P.M. till normal closing hours.

MEXICO—MEXICO CITY

Art Show—In Sullivan Park, just behind the Monument to the Mothers of Mexico. Artists set up their easels on the grass, and display paintings; a balloon man wanders among the benches, and birds chirp. The paintings are often good; prices range from $5 to $200. You can bargain but with restraint, for you will be bargaining with the artist himself. Takes place on Sunday mornings.

Lagunilla or *Thieves' Market*—Two rows of stalls line either side of República de Chile. You can find anything from shrunken heads to miniature cannons. Broken sunglasses and old mirrors are common items, but you may find a genuine antique if you're patient. Bargain, even if the stall keeper tells you that he has a wife, ten children, a mother *and* a mother-in-law. He will still go down 10 pesos. Open every Sunday morning.

NORWAY—BERGEN

Fisketorget—Norway's most famous fish market. Go on Saturday at noon—the best time to soak up the atmosphere. Open every day except Sunday.

OSLO

The markets in Oslo sell food only, but they are full of wonderful smells, sounds and local color. The main fruit and vegetable market is held in the Stortorget, the main square, on Saturdays from 11 A.M. to about 4 P.M. Go around noon, when the housewives do their shopping. The daily fish market is held only in the morning in front of the City Hall on the seaside. It specializes in shrimp and lobster.

PORTUGAL—LISBON

Feira de Ladra (*Thieves' Market*)—Held in the old section of the city behind an ancient church, at Campo de Santa Clara. Peddlers bring an odd collection of old clothing, pottery, paintings, glass, old lamps and rugs, copper and brass, pots and pans. Bargains are rare, but it's worth an hour of rummaging, and if you find something, you can usually bargain down to a low price. Open every Tuesday and Saturday from about 9 A.M. to 6 P.M.

Feira de São Pedro—Held at Sintra in the environs of Lisbon. There are animals, food and antiques on display. You may have a better chance of picking up a worthwhile object here than in Lisbon. A large market, held every second and fourth Sunday.

Praça da Ribeira—A vast conglomeration of flowers, plants, and all kinds of food, including a wide variety of fish, located in the downtown area on the waterfront.

SINGAPORE—SINGAPORE

Pasar Malam or *Night Bazaar*—You can find good examples of dress fabrics, rattan work, and the latest Japanese knick-knacks. This is a nomadic market; hawkers set up their kerosene-lit stalls in Prinsep Street on Monday, Guillemard Road on Tuesday, Orchard Road and Patterson Road on Wednesday, Serangoon Garden Way on Thursday, Bukit Timah (Monks Hill) on Friday, Woodlands, 14-¾ milestone on Saturday, and Alexandra Road (main road opposite market) on Sunday. Open between 6 P.M. and 10 P.M.

Thieves' Market—Goods range from the international— British woolens, Swiss watches, Japanese textiles, German cameras, French perfumes, Burmese and Ceylonese jewels—to products of Singapore and nearby countries: batik, handwoven Kelantan silk with threads of precious metal, Malay pewter and silver, krisses from Borneo, Balinese woodcarvings, Javanese masks, and Chinese basketwork. Located by the Rochore Canale. Always open.

SPAIN—MADRID

El Rastro—Madrid's famous flea market on the Plaza de Cascorro, running to the Avenida de las Americas. At its noisiest and most hectic on Sunday between 10 A.M. and 2:30 P.M. The wares, in stalls or simply spread out on rickety tables, are not nearly as interesting as the atmosphere. Most items are secondhand overcoats, shoes, and broken-down furniture that are the last thing you'd want to buy; as with all flea markets, however, you might just find something which, with a little creativity and elbow grease, could be transformed into something worthwhile. El Rastro is a favorite Sunday haunt for Spaniards, and worth a visit. Do bargain. Open every day, but Sundays are best.

The El Rastro area is lined with respectable antique shops, and you might browse. Prices are higher, but the difference in merchandise is light years apart.

SWEDEN—STOCKHOLM

Hötorget Market—The city's largest and most colorful flower, fruit and vegetable market. It is held in Hötorget Square, which is in front of the Concert Hall, and surrounded by a new shopping center. (The same type of market also takes place in Östermalm-storg Square near the Royal Dramatic Theater.) Open 8 A.M. to 6 P.M., Monday through Saturday.

Stortorgets Julmarknad or *Christmas Market*—Held only in December in Stortorget Square in the old section of Stockholm. The affair is slightly disorganized, laced with music, wandering Santa Clauses, and wide-eyed children fascinated by the mechanical toys and beautiful ornaments.

SWITZERLAND—BERN

Onion Market—Takes place on the Bundesplatz, and in the main arteries of Bern, on the fourth Monday of November. Scads of onions piled high in baskets or plaited into braids; leeks and garlic, shallots and nuts decorate the stalls. A market where onion is king has to have an interesting history. According to legend, in the fifteenth century the city of Bern set this special day aside to express its gratitude to the neighboring canton of Fribourg, whose people aided Bern after a disastrous city fire. By way of thanks, Fribourg was granted the right to hold a yearly market in Bern's public square. Onions were particularly popular around 1405, since they were believed to possess magical powers of protection against the plague. Students usually lead the merrymaking, holding confetti battles at dusk; later, disguised as onions, they go from inn to inn singing and telling tales of the past year's most scandalous events.

A geranium market is held on the Bundesplatz each spring, usually in May.

LAUSANNE

Vegetable and flower market—Takes place on the Riponne, the Palud and the Place Central in stalls topped by gaily colored awnings. The produce is brought in by cart and car from surrounding country towns. Lausanne housewives do much of their marketing here. Open from 7 A.M. till early afternoon, every Wednesday and Saturday.

TAIWAN—TAIPEI

Chung Hwa Market—Fine bargains in porcelain, pottery, jewelry, scrolls, lanterns, bamboo and snakeskin wares. Open 7 days a week, from 8 A.M. to 11 P.M. on Chung Hwa Road.

TURKEY—ISTANBUL

Covered Bazaar (also known as the Grand Bazaar, and reputedly the biggest bazaar in the world)—The sheer quantity of merchandise here—carpets, jewelry, brocades, antiques, ad infinitum

—is dazzling, but you'll find that most of it is of uncertain quality. There's a wide variety of copper and silver trays, urns, jugs, etc., but most of them will be too cumbersome to carry home, unless you've got an enormous living room wall to cover or unadorned corner that you can't bear any longer. Go to the Bazaar for the commotion instead, and if you take a friend, hold hands so you don't lose each other. Some 4,000 shops line the narrow streets and alleyways of the arcade, and wandering through them is like feeling your way through a maze where a wrong turn could cost you hours. You won't decipher it—it's too big—but doing it with someone else helps a lot. Open every day except Sunday from 9 A.M. to 7 P.M.

Meeting People

You will meet them in cable cars going up the Alps, in ferries on the Skagerrak, in sightseeing buses headed for Epidaurus, at the concierge's desk in your Paris hotel, at the soft-drink kiosk on the beach at Scheveningen, on the mail line at American Express in London, sitting beside you on the jet plane to Barbados, across the table at dinner on the train to Madrid. Meeting people is easier when you are traveling than it is at home. In fact, unless you wrap yourself in an air of freezing unfriendliness, you won't be able to avoid it.

There are good reasons for this. People are naturally disposed to be curious about strangers and, generally, kind and helpful to them as well. Moreover, it is often actually easier to talk freely to strangers than to your familiars. The curiosity and friendliness of the people you encounter and your own sense of freedom as you journey far from the paths of your ordinary life conspire to make meetings easier. And these meetings can add life, color and charm to your travels. With the right attitude and the right preparation you will get the sweetest, most durable reward travel offers—the feeling of friendship and understanding that can ignite suddenly between two strangers who belong to different countries, different cultures, different races.

However, in order to bring about the most fruitful meetings with people who share your tastes and interests, you must make certain preparations before you leave home, early groundwork that will pay huge dividends. Of course you are going to have all sorts of delightful chance meetings, but it is wiser to arrive in Florence with a list of names in your little book than to have to count on running into someone at American Express. What should you do, then, before you start, to make sure you'll meet the most congenial people abroad?

1. Try to carry a loaded address book. Friends and colleagues will supply you with names of people to look up. Tell your relatives, college classmates, and doctor about your travel plans—and follow every lead, however unpromising it may sound.

When you are collecting names, ask your friends if you can act as a courier for them, and even if it means cutting down on your own paraphernalia, take whatever small gifts they want you to carry abroad. If you haven't a letter of introduction, you may be a bit embarrassed to call a stranger with an undisguised expectation of some gesture of hospitality. It's a different matter when you can say, "I bring you greetings and a small token from Mrs. A——."

If letters of introduction are offered, accept them gladly, but you may want to ask that they be phrased in such a way that you can mail them on your arrival instead of beforehand. Then if you find that when you are in Vienna you haven't a moment to spare after all, you need not mail the letter of introduction you've been given.

2. After you've collected names, give some cool, detached thought to your assets and how to exploit them while you travel. Think of every association and connection with any sort of group that you have. What is your job? your special interest? your education? your family? your sports? your church? Then meticulously list the whole lot.

Although few people are aware of it, the key to much hospitality all over the world lies in one's interests and professional connections. There seem to be more clubs, associations, and organizations for special interests, businesses and professions than there are Joneses in a Cardiff telephone directory, and brief letters sent off to them before you leave home can start all sorts of meetings. If you don't have a chance to write ahead, look them up on the spot. If you are a professional or an executive business woman and belong to the Soroptomist International Association, you can visit one of their local meeting places. If you are a journalist, check in at the local press club. If you're interested in growing flowers, look up the local horticultural society. If you are a nurse and belong to the American Nurses Association, you'll find colleagues everywhere. Just having gone to college makes you a university woman, eligible for membership in the American Association of University Women. This gives you a key to clubs all around the world. In London, for instance, this is the British Federation of University Women, a club for women graduates of all nationalities.

If you are interested in architecture, write to societies abroad that are dedicated to the preservation of historic buildings, such as the Georgian Group in England. If you collect nineteenth-century drawings, go to whatever local art galleries are likely to be knowledgeable, and get suggestions of where to scout abroad. If you're a secretary on a magazine, perhaps there's a magazine like it whose offices you could tour. If you're a bridge player, look up lists of local bridge clubs. Any place where you can be received as a fellow enthusiast is pretty sure to give you a warm welcome.

Write ahead and say when you will be in the city and that you will call on your arrival. If your professional organization is holding a meeting or convention while you are traveling, they'll tell you where and when it is to be held and make you welcome. You'll have a flood of lunch and dinner invitations. But a good point to remember here is that you need not always expect to be the one who is entertained. Instead of half apologetically allowing everyone you call on to offer you hospitality, try inviting *them* to lunch or tea, or to have an apéritif with you.

In short, don't run away from your job, hobbies, or associations when you travel. Think of what they add to your life, in what ways they may make you interesting to other people, and look for your counterparts wherever you go.

3. After putting these assets to work, think about something you can do in terms of a special project for the trip. Collect something, anything: wooden doors, or carved angels, or photographs of French poodles. There's bound to be someone at the other end of a leash in Paris or Brussels who shares your enthusiasm. If you can't think of a special, pinpointed interest offhand, put your mind on developing one before you start traveling. It will be a sturdy bridge to people all over the world.

4. Explore the tourist offices' organized means of meeting people. Many governments sponsor "Meet-the-People" programs. The idea started in Denmark in 1945 as a means of entertaining young American and British soldiers stationed in the country. A few years later it had become such a success that it was placed under the jurisdiction of the National Travel Office. Since that time, many other countries have begun conducting the same sort of program, often with imperative titles—"Don't Miss the Swiss," "Know the Norwegians," "Find

the Finns," "Get in Touch with the Dutch." Sweden, Israel, Ireland, Japan, and India also offer such programs.

Basically they all work the same way. Before leaving home you write to the nearest branch tourist office of the country you will visit (see the list that begins on page 479 for their names and addresses), giving your name, age, profession, approximate date of arrival, length of stay, and interests. The tourist office will then check its file of voluntary hosts and make an effort to match you up with people somewhat like you. When you arrive, you check in at the tourist office so that final arrangements may be made. Some countries, Denmark for instance, make all arrangements after you arrive in Copenhagen—they like to meet you in person first. Others, like Norway, want you to write ahead so that they will have a better chance to find the most appropriate people should your occupation be out of the ordinary.

Entertainment depends on your hosts. Usually they invite you to their homes after dinner. There is never a fee, except in Japan, where the Japan Home Visit Association charges a dollar to defray office costs.

Naturally your hosts will speak English, and you, for your part, will be a good guest and take a modest bread-and-butter gift—candy or flowers. Don't present your hosts with a bottle of wine. It is a welcome, festive gift at home, but in Europe, where wine is as much a staple as beer or Coke is to us, it would be taken somewhat amiss.

A few points to remember about Meet-the-People programs:

A. They don't include lodging or meals, so don't expect them. If by any chance they should be offered, it is because you are a charmer.

B. The programs operate at different times, depending on the country. In Ireland, for example, it runs from May through September; in Norway, on the other hand, July and August are better avoided, since so many people are away on their own holidays then.

C. In countries that require advance notice, you had better make an effort to plan ahead of time. Tourist office people are genuinely obliging, but when your time or the number of suitable counterparts is limited, they are handicapped and you may be out of luck.

D. Finally, there are Meet-the-People programs not only in large cities but in smallish ones too. It is possible that you will get more out of a visit with a family in Malmö, Göteborg or Kalmar than with one in Stockholm. The smaller and more out-of-the-way the place, the cozier things are likely to be. In India, you can be invited home for a visit in Bombay, Calcutta and Madras; in Japan the list includes Yokohama, Kyoto, and Kobe, as well as Tokyo.

Besides these Meet-the-People programs, some governments have pleasant little extras. In Israel, which has been particularly inventive about ice-breaking, the mayors of Jerusalem, Tel Aviv and Haifa hold small receptions every two weeks to which foreigners are invited. In Holland several cities have their own local hospitality programs called "The Hague [or Amsterdam or Rotterdam] Invites You." They are run by prominent women who are proud of their cities and want to share them with strangers.

The French offer the American tourist a special organization called *France–États-Unis*, 6 Blvd. de Grenelle, Paris. This has a small housing bureau for new arrivals and also arranges dinner and theater parties —even picnics in nice weather—with the local French. Membership costs $2 if you are under 25 and $3 if you are over that age. The goal of the organization is to promote understanding between France and the U.S.A.

Belgium has a "Europe Meeting Club," 344 Avenue Louise in Brussels, which offers everything from chess to skin diving, plus a restaurant and bar. The membership is fairly select; you must be seriously interested in meeting people, not just out for a wild time. Dues are $6 a year.

In Holland, the Netherlands Amateur Guide Association, known locally as BBTBBA, is made up of students who volunteer as guides in their spare time and during holidays at no cost to the visitor. Write ahead to the BBTBBA Public Relations Department, 51 Statenlaan, The Hague.

The Danes have a Students Club in Copenhagen, open all the year round, which welcomes foreign students. Explore these possibilities and the many others that exist. National tourist offices are a good source of information. France and Britain both publish long, impressive lists of groups that welcome Americans.

5. Another organized means of meeting people to be considered before you leave home is Pan American Airways' New Horizons Club for women travelers. For $3 you get lifetime membership, a good guidebook full of tips (*New Horizons World Guide*), and a big packet of useful information delivered to you in the cities you visit via Pan Am. In addition, if you tell them the details of your trip beforehand, they will give you names of other members traveling at the same time with somewhat the same itinerary, and you can get together en route if you like. Also they will furnish names of members abroad for you to write to before you start.

6. Consider specialized tours—either major ones originating in this country such as the Garden Tours organized by the Jean Berke

Travel Agency, 518 Fifth Avenue, New York 10036; the archaeological tours of Greece and Asia Minor with distinguished lecturers along (e.g., Swan's Hellenic Tours, 260 Tottenham Court Road, London); or the briefer tours with special objectives that can be discovered on the spot. Any sort of bus tour is sure to be an experience rich in new acquaintances. The atmosphere is intimate and talkative (see Buses, page 000, and Tours, page 000). One thing you can be absolutely sure of under such auspices is meeting a considerable number of people with interests close to your own. Boat trips on the inland waterways of Europe offer the same lively intimacy (see Waterways, page 414).

7. While you are getting from one place to another, there are any number of tricks to surround yourself with pleasant company. For instance, if you are sailing, board your ship early and go straight to the dining room (while your friends are drinking champagne in your cabin) to consult the steward about your table arrangements. Tell him frankly that your idea of a congenial table is not five other women, but a mixture of sexes and nationalities. Even though he is apt to be harassed at this moment, he will be cooperative since this is his business. Also be sure to reserve your table for the second sitting. First is for people traveling with children.

After that go to the deck steward and pick out your chair. Tell him you want sun and company. Leave the quiet nooks to people who really want to read and sleep, period. (For more on Seating, see page 318.)

Make the most of the ship's other facilities. Browse in the library, use the pool, play shuffleboard, and don't hesitate to go into the bar alone; a woman may properly do so on shipboard. Participate in whatever is going on.

If you fly, the only opportunity for talk is with your seat partner, and everything depends on who he or she is. If he's using the flight time to work out engineering details of a new dam and has "Do Not Disturb" written all over his face, read your paperback. By the same token, if you are cornered by a bore, you mustn't feel compelled to keep up your end. Tell him plainly that you have had a heavy schedule and want to get a few hours' rest.

If you are traveling with a friend, consider splitting up during a flight so that each of you will have a chance to charm or be charmed by a stranger. Since you are together most of the time anyway, it is a waste of time to spend the hours of a flight together too when you might be promoting an invitation to a cocktail party in Madrid for both of you. Try this technique on short hops, at any rate, even if you would rather be together for the long hauls.

8. A surefire stratagem that few travelers think of is to go to a resort in each country before you go to its capital. (See Itinerary Building, page 188.) It's more natural to meet people in the relaxed atmosphere of a vacation area than in an overwhelmingly impersonal city. You will actually meet more Greeks at Nauplion than in Athens, more Norwegians in mountain lodges than in Oslo, more Australians on the Great Barrier Reef than in Sydney, and a great number of foreigners "on holiday" as well. When the time comes to storm the cities, you can make your arrival like an old hand, armed with a fresh list of names to look up.

Outside the big cities, always try to stay at places where the atmosphere is congenial to making new friends. Castle hotels or small country inns (see page 63) usually have the atmosphere of a private house party. Or go to hotels that get a big repeat trade. And wherever you are staying, at the cocktail hour go to the hotel bar. As on shipboard, this is absolutely acceptable for a woman alone. Don't on any account spend those pleasant half hours at dusk in your room, dressing.

9. Sports are by their nature a marvelous common bond, and provide a good way to find yourself in the company of active men, for men go where they can do things. If you loiter around a hotel swimming pool waiting for a man, you are likely to see one for every twenty women. But if you sign up for a scuba-diving expedition you will find the ratio almost exactly reversed.

Activity is the clue. Men go skiing—to Switzerland and Austria, of course, but also as far afield as Corsica, Scotland and Norway. They go fishing, or sailing, or they play golf (see Golf, page 151). If you already do these things well, you need only find out where you can turn up to enjoy them. To track down clubs and schools of any sort, try inquiring at the tourist office, at your own club at home before you leave, or go make a purchase at the best local shop specializing in the sport you're interested in and inquire there. If you don't know how and want to learn, go to a school abroad. England and Scandinavia, for instance, have a good number that teach sailing. Another idea is to be on hand at one of the famous sports events—in Bermuda, for example, for the conclusion of the biannual June Newport-Bermuda sailing races; or one of the innumerable regattas in the British Isles, of which the most famous is Cowes Week early in August. (Get in touch with the Yachting Association in London (167 Victoria Street, S.E. 1) for dates.

In the big cities you can go bowling and be sure of company, or look for the popular swimming pools where the young people flock on warm summer days (see Beaches and Swimming Pools, page 19). Join a tennis club, if that's your game. Europe has few public courts, but private clubs abound, and you can discover them by the sort of inquiries suggested above. In France you can find out about public courts from the Fédération Française Lawn-Tennis, 3 Rue Volney, Paris 2ᵉ.

Consider angling, stalking, hunting. If you have even the least interest in one of these, however little developed, find out about clubs, tournaments, shooting holidays, whatever. If you like horses, investigate pony trekking in Ireland and Scotland and England. These are pleasant leisurely group activities that require no particular skill or stamina and are a foolproof way of getting to know people.

Or just take a morning ride wherever it is that people ride—in Stockholm's Djurgården, for instance, or Richmond Park outside London. If you have the stomach for it, join a gliding club. Go canoeing; join a mountain-climbing expedition in Wales or Corsica or Austria. If you have an interest in archaeology, sign up for a dig or an archaeological tour.

In short, look around for the action and join it.

10. Go wherever there is activity that is likely to bring together people who share tastes in common. This might be a small charity concert, a museum lecture, a fashion show, a group walk through the city, any event organized by the local American community. For such events keep your eye on the English-language papers, bulletin boards in likely places, or consult your concierge.

Going to church, wherever you are, is another way of getting in touch. In Paris the American Church and the American Cathedral of the Holy Trinity invite worshipers to stay for coffee after Sunday services. The American Church has a "pairs and spares" dinner once a month. The American Cathedral has a visitors' luncheon every Sunday. Even on islands like Jamaica and Hawaii churchgoing is a promising way of getting to meet the residents.

11. Familiarize yourself with local customs that may work in your behalf. In Stockholm you can go alone to a Sunday afternoon tea dance at the Strand Hotel and quite properly accept any invitation to dance that appeals to you. You can do the same sort of thing in other Scandinavian countries, as well as Switzerland, Germany or Austria. They are full of open-air dance pavilions and dance halls where you can go alone and spend the early evening.

Denmark has the fairyland pleasure grounds of the Tivoli Gardens, where you may sit on a terrace sipping a Cherry Heering and watch the dancers. You are pretty sure to be asked to dance yourself.

12. Resorts make things easy for you. In places like Jamaica, Bermuda, Nassau and Hawaii, the large hotels have hostesses and social directors to see that you are brought into whatever is going on. All you need do is talk to swimmers at the pool or sunbathers on the beach or ask someone to pass the salt. The effort is minimal.

13. Finally, don't shun your fellow Americans. Of course it would be madness to sit around in the hotel playing bridge with your compatriots all afternoon, but few people travel with that in mind. You will run into Americans in all sorts of strange as well as expected places, and you will find that away from home it is surprisingly easy to get to know each other. You are very likely to get pleasure and practical benefit from these encounters, and you may make a lifetime friend. After all, you have something in common to start out with.

And wherever you are, move toward other people. Take the initiative. Remember that though you are a guest in the country, there is no rule that says you may not also play the host. Invite people to drinks, to dinner, to the theater, to join you in a visit to the *Son et Lumière* performance at the nearby château (natives are often the last people to see their own local wonders and may be delighted by the opportunity). Talk to people whenever there is a chance. Help people; nothing will make you feel better. People help you continually, which you expect them to do, but there are also opportunities to do the same for them. And when there is a choice between staying in and going out, go out, look, listen, seek. You will find friends everywhere.

For a list of various organizations abroad through which you can meet the people of the country, see page 239. Also see Traveling Solo, page 388.

Men

ALTHOUGH so many of us have been traveling all over the world in the past twenty years, foreign men by and large still make the mistake of thinking of American women in stereotypes. We are all stunning, well-dressed, rich beyond the dreams of avarice, bossy. We have beautiful legs and good figures, and we own cars. On the negative side, we also wear too much makeup, speak too loudly, travel in packs and have no souls.

By the same token, American women tend to think of foreign men as super-seducers, thoroughly untrustworthy, out for our money and position. Both pictures are totally false, but while it endures it is no wonder the relationship between foreign men and American women seems more like an obstacle course than the pleasant, simple exchange it can be.

Everywhere, men admire an attractive woman, but it's only natural that foreign men should behave somewhat differently toward us than the ones at home. They have been raised with attitudes, customs and expectations of their own. With a little adjusting on your part (don't you also attune your ear to another language, your palate to other foods, and your meals to other hours?), you can learn to get along easily with foreign men, and to relish their particular—and thoroughly attractive—flattery, charm, conversation and gallantry.

Meeting Guido—or Michel or Hans or Spiros—is the first problem. In Meeting People, page 239, you will find the *modus operandi*, and places which are geared to easy and conventional social encounters. In the Appendix, under *Organizations That Arrange Meetings Between American Visitors and Nationals*, page 455, are listed the various national and professional groups through which you can meet your foreign counterpart, man or woman. But there's still another kind of meeting, the chance encounter, which is an inevitable part of traveling. Granted that you don't openly invite a pickup, still there are going to be dozens of chances for talking to strangers, in circumstances you wouldn't dream of getting into at home, that can lead to some of the most delightful moments of the trip.

The kind of chance encounter I have in mind is the one where Audrey Hepburn drops a load of books all over the Place de la Concorde and Peter O'Toole picks them up, where Julie Christie outbids Rex Harrison for an Aubusson at Sotheby's, or even when Jack Lemmon's car breaks down on the Amalfi Drive and Shirley MacLaine fixes it with a bobby pin. Often it can lead to the gayest hours of all —it can get you to parties in Paris, show you the fascinating *tascas* in Madrid with someone who knows them well, take you to Chelsea discothèques you would otherwise never have known. And if you close your mind to spontaneous meetings, you're denying yourself an essential delight of travel. Years ago, a kind Englishman helped me through my first encounter with shillings and pence on a steamer about to cross the Channel from France to England. While I was surrounded by luggage and at a loss to figure out how much to tip the porters in this strange, new currency, he leaned over my shoulder and said, "May I help?" He then dipped into my open, money-filled hand, tipped the men, and started a conversation. We have remained good friends ever since.

But how can you distinguish between a happy chance encounter and an ordinary, garden-variety pickup? The key words are where, how, and who. Rule one: Audrey never meets Peter by sitting around a bar, nightclub or café, obviously waiting for a man to come along. She's always concentrating on something *else* that interests her. Rule two: Peter, for his part, is never idling around looking for a girl to pick up. Rule three: Peter is always cast as the sort of man Audrey would go out with at home. This can be a little difficult to determine in a foreign country where you can't always size up a man by looking at him, but in general, a sensible woman can distinguish nice men from the other kind. If you don't fall into conversation with street-corner idlers back home in Chicago, don't do it in Rome either. Remember also that your opportunities for a chance encounter plummet if you are among a flock of women. Aside from the fact that a helpless woman is far more appealing and approachable than one surrounded by a flying wedge of sorority sisters, few men *want* to take three girls to dinner. If you are traveling with friends, choose uncompetitive types with about the same degree of attractiveness as your own. Then work out an arrangement beforehand, whereby if a man seems interested in any one of you, the others will tactfully disappear, with no hard feelings.

What precautions should you take with a man you've met spontaneously? A few more than are necessary with one whose credentials have been checked. Don't go for long lonely drives in the country until you've learned to trust your companion. Take a walk around town, go out to dinner, to a café, to a museum, or, if you are lucky, a party. One or two public meetings should give you a realistic idea of how the land lies. If you have an apéritif with a man you barely know in a café and you see that you have picked a dead loss, you can always cut it short and leave.

Unlike this country, there are times and places in many European countries where men and women go especially to be "picked up" and it's all perfectly proper and respectable. The occasion is the afternoon tea dance (*thé dansant*). In countries such as Austria, Switzerland, Germany, and Scandinavia, the time is from 4 to 6 in the afternoon. Even in Spain, where women are not permitted to go out alone after dinner, two girls may go together to the tea dance, which takes place, in this late-hour country, from 7 to 10 P.M.

The tea dances are held at the good big hotels, restaurants, or the *Kursaal* (social center) of a spa. Here, a man may ask a woman for a dance without having been introduced to her, and it's perfectly permissible to accept his invitation. If she doesn't like his looks, she may refuse with a simple "No, thank you." Then etiquette demands that she not accept any other man's invitation for the same dance. When the orchestra stops, the man she has danced with will take her back to the table and ask if he may dance with her again. She can say "Yes," or she can say "I am meeting a friend"—i.e., "no." At these tea dances it is not only proper but expected for strangers to meet—and often a woman even goes alone. Use your own judgment about accepting a dinner invitation from a man you meet there.

In the larger cities on the Continent it is not unusual, if both are dining alone at the same restaurant, for a man to send a discreet note to a woman. He may extend an invitation for her to join him for a drink or dinner. She can say "yes" or "no"—either is proper—depending on her mood.

Assuming that you have met Guido—or Michel or Hans or Spiros —how will his behavior vary from that of the men you know back home?

European men, and those of every country that has known European influence, are more accustomed than Americans to feeling they are the boss in every situation, and that woman's place is not so much at their side as a little to the rear. In the Orient, attitudes about masculine authority are even stiffer. Don't expect a European to treat you as an equal right off the bat. His wishes are expected to be given priority; your role is to comply. But you will be rewarded by a gallantry unknown on our side of the ocean. Cultivate it. Let him open doors for you, light your cigarettes, spread out his coat on damp benches— and protect and cherish you in a dozen other ways.

Because he is boss and because you are accustomed to expressing yourself fairly directly, he will often find you quite a handful to deal with. From time to time he will even feel that you are overriding his right to take the initiative. To a foreign man, our willing ability to enter into serious discussions suggests a rather unbecoming boldness. Learn to modulate the way in which you present your opinions. He will be delighted by an American with whom he can converse on his own level, provided she handles her end of the conversation tactfully and without shaking his self-confidence. Since, for him, keeping the initiative is essential to a good relationship, you must help him do this—if you would like to see him again. Make a special effort to flatter his ego, make him feel important. (European women have that knack—which is what sends so many American men head over heels.)

When it comes to expressing their admiration for you, Latin men are apt to show an eloquence and vividness that are startling at first. Mediterranean men are not strong believers in repressed emotion, and the chase is their favorite sport. (On the other hand, faced with a woman so beautiful she would even stop the traffic in Piccadilly cold, the British and Scandinavians keep their traditional reserve. When he thinks you look absolutely smashing, the Englishman will break down to the point of saying, "You look rather nice.") The Latin will tend toward lyrical compliments that would dizzy the brain of any young girl from Cleveland. When you come down the stairs in your most devastating dress, the American may exclaim, "Gee, you look great." He will probably not use the word "love" unless he wants you to be the legitimate mother of his children. But the Latin will tell you that you have the face of a Raphael madonna, the body of a Botticelli nude, and that you have made sleeping and eating impossible for him for three days. A historic love is in store for you both. The compliments still mean nothing more than "Gee, you look great," and when he declares his undying passion within five minutes, just pretend that he is an American saying, "You're terrific"—which has never in American history amounted to an outright commitment. If you think Continental lyricism is unfair, remember that European girls are used to it and the man expects you to receive his admiration in the right spirit. Nothing would surprise him more than your mistaking a passionate compliment for a proposal.

If a northern European pays you a compliment, forget the good manners you were taught as a little girl, and never say "thank you." What possible answer can a man give to "thank you"? You will have let his compliment fall flat; the flow of the conversation will be broken. Instead, when he admires something you're wearing try a warm smile or a reply like "How nice of you to notice" or "Do you really think so?" or "I am very glad you like it"—anything, but bounce the ball back.

You will also find that foreign men generally have different ideas about dating and dancing then those you are used to. Don't be surprised if a European man doesn't call for you at your hotel for a date. He may ask you to meet him at a mutually convenient spot, even a street corner. In some countries it's considered rude to call for you "at home." At the end of the evening, don't be shattered if an Englishman puts you into a taxi or doesn't take you home from a dinner party. He's used to this sort of behavior with English women. Your date, of any nationality, may think that an evening of talk over a not terribly expensive meal at a *bistro* or *trattoria* makes for a wonderful time; he will take it as a matter of pride that he has chosen a restaurant where the food is good. If you want to see him again, you had better agree. Also, don't be surprised if students and other impecunious types expect you to pay for your share of an evening: Going Dutch is far more customary abroad than it is here; many Europeans just don't have the money to spend on dates that American men do. The European likes to feel that you are going out with him because you like his company, and not for all those material advantages Americans are supposed to set such store by.

The first time you dance with an Italian or a Frenchman, you are likely to be stunned. You will be held in an iron grasp that will make you feel that every vertebra in your back is about to snap, and you will be sure that every eye in the room is focused on your intimate dancing. If you really can't stand it, move away—and your partner will accept your reaction as an American eccentricity. Otherwise, relax. Like pasta and the Métro, it's their way of doing things, and you may even get to like it after a while.

On a date, there are certain things you may do unwittingly that signify something entirely different to the man. For example, remember that you should not call a man by his first name as early in your acquaintanceship as you do here; unless he is very young, it would be a familiarity to do so until you get to know him. Also, the sort of dress you wear gives him a clue; if it's cut down to there, don't be surprised if he lunges. If you smoke on the street, which Europeans consider terrible manners, don't expect to be treated like a china doll. If a European man leaps at you on your first date, you might consider whether you've given him reason to do so. Don't, for example, get yourself tiddly on Dutch gin, or jump into the Trevi, or curse freely. I am not advocating prudery—just learning the local standard for women and adapting to it, which is a different story entirely.

In Italy, don't be surprised if men follow you down the street. They are harmless as long as you don't encourage them. If anyone is too persistent, duck into a shop. Italian men may show their appreciation of your attractions by touching you, even pinching you. Inasmuch as they behave the same way with the women of their country, keep your outrage under control. It will undoubtedly be startling to feel a stranger pinch your leg or bottom, but it's not likely to happen very often, unless you spend all your time in crowds. The Italian reputation for pinching, incidentally, is vastly exaggerated; if you do run into this tactile "wolf whistle," you can be assured that however annoying it may be, it is still sport.

In Latin countries, the pleasant pastime of standing on the corner—or sitting at a café—watching the girls go by is made into something of an art. Staring is far more common in Latin, Middle Eastern and North African countries than it is here and in Britain, where it is considered rude. Even the middle-aged matron sitting comfortably with her husband and children at a café, having an ice, will look you over as though she is memorizing every detail of your costume down to the side on which your shoe buckles. Men will give you a prolonged, attentive look that travels leisurely from toe to head and back down again, with a pause at the legs. This can all be unsettling to one who generally finds such concentrated study disconcerting, but take it in your stride. It's all part of a national pattern, and you are not being singled out for especially hard treatment. Just be glad they still find you interesting enough to look at.

Being a blonde, natural or man-made, in a Latin country like Portugal or Spain is marvelously soothing to the ego, but be prepared for many hard, fixed gazes. When they are on the receiving end of such stares, Portuguese women—who of European women are most sheltered, all their lives—act as if it simply weren't happening, which is the best policy for you too.

A frequent complaint American women make about European men is the rapidity of the Continental proposition. Even if no St. Louis man has ever dared to make an indecent proposal to you, stop and think before you condemn. The American woman's particular combination of freedom and decorum seems inconsistent to a European man. He sees that you move about more freely than his sisters, that you drink hard liquor and express your opinions uninhibitedly on all subjects, and so quite logically he expects that you are equally uninhibited about sex. The European young woman—in every phase of life—is often more sheltered than you are. When her male compatriot sees you enjoying the freedom to go abroad unchaperoned, he may not realize that that freedom has limitations. Your independence of spirit is charming to him, but rather mysterious. He hopes, quite naturally, that you will be more willing and able than Maria, whom he sees under the sharp eyes of familiars. Also, your very fleetingness is a strong part of your appeal. In a few days or weeks you'll be gone, unable to gossip about him to other women he knows. No wonder he will try to sell you hard on the philosophy of *carpe diem*. Many women in Latin countries are closeted until marriage and give suitors a very rough time until they are sure of their intentions. Also remember that along with this, many European countries take sex less seriously than we do. Don't act outraged; just say "no," and make that "no" firm and abundantly clear. Don't give reasons; your admirer will delight in tearing them down. He will try to persuade you that if you don't seize this moment, something beautiful will go out of your lives. Just tell him you don't want to discuss it any further.

Finally, there are "wolf whistles" to contend with. The more southerly the country, the more elaborate and unavoidable they become, though they all stick to the basic pattern of fixed stare and vocal comment. When the language in which it is delivered is strange, the "wolf whistle" may be a little bit alarming at first. But remember that it is no different from the homely comments of the truck driver back home as you cross in front of him at an intersection or of the construction workers who cheer your passage. You pretend not to notice, but secretly you feel slightly pleased all the same. The only difference is that in Mediterranean countries the admiring comments are part of a well-developed vocabulary of idle admiration, known, in Spain, as *piropos*. Sometimes they are traditional ("Long live your mother"), sometimes colloquial modern ("So many curves and me with no brakes"). Spanish women are more likely to receive *piropos* than you are, since the point is lost if you can't understand the grace or wit of the tribute. But whether or not you understand, do as European women do: *smile and keep right on walking, without looking either surprised or irritated.* This advice is as good for Copenhagen and Paris as it is for Naples and Granada.

For the American woman, the best rules wherever she goes are those dictated by common sense. Men, everywhere, like attractive women. According to their own custom, they will try to gain her attention—by stares, winks, whistles, loud remarks, noises, smiles, following her down the street, kissing her hand, or pinching her bottom. The double standard exists everywhere too: Promiscuity is frowned upon, and no man, no matter how blatant or impassioned his approach, really expects you to succumb. He only expects you to dance gracefully in the intricate minuet of courtship—and to do this, you must understand that his behavior, though its nuances are unfamiliar, is not something to be upset about. By observing a few simple rules, you can keep the situation under control and enjoy it.

Motoring Abroad

BECAUSE a car gives you the same liberating advantages abroad as it does at home, drive-yourself touring has been booming in recent years. American International Driving Permits have shot up from 15,442 in 1953 to 191,400 in 1965. Travelers have discovered how nice it is to move about independent of timetables and the tyranny of reservations, to forget about tickets, taxis and porters, and to carry along comfortably all the bargains they discover along the way, all the while saving money. Mile for mile, traveling by car can be the least expensive way to get from here to there.

Everywhere on the Continent there are new tunnels, ferries, and international motoring routes that will take you beside fjords, glaciers, waterfalls, tiny farms perched in the mountains, fields covered with gorse and heather, rivers running swiftly to the sea. You will be able to stop at country inns, *pousadas, auberges, relais de campagne,* motels, tourist pavilions, *paradores* and *Gasthöfe.* Even if you take a beach vacation in the West Indies or Hawaii, a car will free you to wander away from your hotel, picnic on another beach, and see how the islanders live. Only in the Orient, where traffic and roads are very nearly unmanageable, is renting a car, at this time, not wise.

Of course, wherever you find good roads and an explosion of cars, you'll also find the familiar bumper-to-bumper traffic come 5 o'clock and all Friday afternoon. City traffic snarls are as common in Madrid and Sydney as in Los Angeles. Sometimes you will be competing with scooters, livestock, bicycles and pedestrians. But even with these problems, following the roads by car, stopping at local inns and restaurants, exploring byways when the fancy strikes you, will give you an intimacy with the countryside unavailable to anyone but the cyclist or hiker.

To drive abroad you will need, of course, a car, a few required documents, and a cursory knowledge of the local ways and means. Here are the basic facts:

ACQUIRING A CAR: There are three ways to go about it: You can rent one, lease one or buy one. In all cases, while you could make the arrangements while you are abroad—and perhaps even save money in the process—you are far more certain of getting the make and model you want, and of having the car waiting for you at the airport, quay or railroad station if you settle the details before you leave. It's also a good idea, whichever plan you intend to use, to look at some foreign cars in local showrooms at home to see how easily the model you have in mind will accommodate you, your traveling companion and your assorted belongings.

RENTAL: You can rent a car with either of two mileage arrangements. Under the first, you pay a flat charge for each day plus a charge for mileage; under the second, you pay a higher charge but are allowed unlimited mileage. The distance you plan to travel should be the deciding factor. But it's fair to warn you that while the unlimited mileage price may seem the better deal at first, distances in Europe are short and you may never use up what you have paid for. In either case, be prepared to pay the usual $50 deposit (refunded later) plus the cost of the estimated mileage in advance, if you use the first arrangement. Among the established sources for renting cars abroad are the World-Wide Travel Department of the AAA (the U.S. representatives of European rental fleets) and international agencies like Hertz, Avis, and Auto-Europe, the largest American company, which handles all makes of European cars and provides every sort of auto travel arrangements. (Their offices are at 25 West 58th Street, New York, New York 10019; 18 South Michigan Avenue, Chicago, Illinois 60603; 268 South Beverly Drive, Beverly Hills, California 90212; 150 Powell Street, San Francisco, California 94102; White-Henry-Stuart Building, Seattle, Washington 98101.) Your travel agent, of course, can book a car for you while he's making your other travel plans, or you can do it yourself by mail or in person. Should you suddenly decide to rent a car while abroad, check the local office of the AAA (or the local automobile club), Hertz, Avis, or Auto-Europe, or one of the rental agencies that exist at every major airport and pier. Hertz, for example, has hundreds of branches around the world and there are excellent local firms like J. Davy in London.

To get the make and model you want, make your booking at least three weeks in advance. Allow more time if you will be touring in season. Most cars are new or no more than six months old, and the kinds available vary according to the rental service and the country. Consider which car to choose on the basis of how many will be riding in it, how far you plan to drive and which countries you'll be visiting. Check it for its luggage space (a sports car, for example, without a luggage rack, cannot carry more than two people) and its gearshift. Many European cars are built with automatic transmission, but unless you reserve one of these rather early in the season, only handshift cars will be left.

Rental prices abroad are surprisingly low compared to those in the U.S.A. They start at about $2.50 a day and 5½ cents a kilometer (about ⅝ of a mile) for a Fiat in Italy and go up to $11.50 a day and 13 cents a kilometer for a Mercedes in Switzerland. They are different in every country and fluctuate from low season to high season. If you are counting pennies and plan to tour several countries, rent your car in the one with the lowest rates—then route yourself accordingly.

You will find other price variables or surcharges: For example, if you take a car from one country to another, there is usually a moderate fee; if you pick up a car in one country and leave it in another, you normally have to pay a delivery and/or collection charge which ranges from $25 to $100. The freedom to do this, however, allows you to combine travel by car with the stopover privileges in your airline ticket. For example, you can buy a ticket to Rome with a first stop in London, tour Britain, drive to Paris (the Channel crossing is accomplished by car ferry), drive on to Nice, leave the car and fly to Milan, pick up another car and drive to Rome, and then fly home. There are many such combinations. There is usually no charge for cars that are picked up in one key city in a country and left in another. If contending with foreign city traffic makes you nervous but you feel perfectly capable of dealing with country roads, a pilot driver will take you to the outskirts of town for a charge of $5.

Among other ways to rent a car aside from the regular agencies are:

In Finland, Great Britain, West Germany, Holland, Italy, Spain and Switzerland, the railways will book a car to be waiting for you at specific railway stops.

Open Road Tours, 407 North Eighth Street, St. Louis, Missouri 63101, packages a completely routed trip which includes car, insurance, and registration documents, unlimited mileage, hotels, a complete set of maps, and usually two meals a day. Your travel agent can do the booking, and whether you decide to tour the castles of the Loire or the countryside of Britain, all the details will have been arranged.

Many airlines sell fly-and-drive tours and will book your car when they arrange your transportation.

LEASING: If you plan to use a car for a month or more or to pile up extensive mileage, this a more economical arrangement than a straight rental. It also has the additional advantages of requiring less notice than rentals; you are sure of getting a new car; and there's no charge for mileage. The car is registered in your name, and you pay a flat price for a given period of time. You know in advance, therefore, what the car will cost you.

The purchase-repurchase plan is much like leasing except that you pay in full for the car before leaving, the company having agreed to buy the car back at the end of the trip at a set figure based on depreciation. If you want to keep the car or sell it yourself, you are free to do so. While this arrangement will be cheaper than the straight leasing one, its disadvantage is that you must have left behind you the full purchase price of the car while you are using it. One note of caution: Be sure that your agreement calls for the automobile company to pay you back in dollars wherever possible.

PURCHASE: As a tourist who plans to use a car in Europe and then take it home within a year, you can buy the car (exempt of local and national taxes) in the U.S.A. and have it delivered abroad. You pay the full purchase price before you leave home, take possession of the car in Europe, and ship it home when your vacation is over. The AAA, the local agency of a European make, some major transatlantic airlines, and a company like Auto-Europe can make all the sales arrangements. Buying a car for overseas delivery can save you between $200 and $3,000 but an even greater advantage is your being able to use it while touring and thus saving on rental or leasing charges. (The difference between the lower European price and the U.S. one for the same car is due to several factors: The U.S. duty is lower on the car you bring in because it arrives used, not new; for the same reason the car is exempt from foreign export taxes and the U.S. Federal excise tax; and European manufacturers lower their prices to American tourists to encourage such sales.)

To get the exact model and color you want, place your order about two months ahead of time or more. Indicate the accessories you want, delivery date and place of delivery. (This can be the factory or, for an extra payment, another city in Europe. Naturally, you save a substantial amount by picking the car up at its source, so try to make the first stop of your itinerary at the nearest port or air terminal.) Your $100 duty-free exemption can be applied to the car's price wherever or whenever you buy it. Nearly all Continental cars and British models made for export have left-hand drives like American cars; you need only indicate that you want this.

Before you leave home, you will be given a written confirmation from the factory, which will list the car you have ordered and the delivery date. The sales agent will also arrange full insurance and supply all the necessary documents. Be sure that your European car is delivered with equipment that conforms to U.S. specifications for glass and headlights; and choose a car that will perform reasonably well in your home town, that can be readily serviced and that is reasonably popular locally (this with a view to reselling it eventually). Extras in Europe cost far less than at home, so you might as well make the most of them.

At Schiphol Airport in Amsterdam, you can (at this writing) buy a car and drive it away within about an hour of your arrival any day of the week—all you need is your driver's license. This is the only place in the world where such an arrangement exists. To be sure the model and color you want will be waiting, get in touch with KLM Royal Dutch Airlines or ShipSide, both at 609 Fifth Avenue, New York, New York 10017. (See Duty-Free Shopping, page 117.)

Let the AAA or your sales agency handle shipping the car home. Or you can put it aboard a cargo ship as freight (even if you are flying home) or take it along as freight or baggage on your passenger ship. At the height of the season space is at a premium, so make your arrangements early and be sure to specify that you want the car shipped underdeck. The cost of shipping will vary according to the port as well as the size of the car: an MGB sports convertible shipped from Southhampton is about $135; a Mercedes sedan from Hamburg is about $250. In any case, it costs far less to ship a car from Europe to America than the other way around. In addition to the freight charge, allow for the fee of a port agent, usually about $25. He will take care of such necessities as washing the car, inspecting it for damages, steam-cleaning the undercarriage (this is required by the U.S. Government), disinfecting it, securing the proper documents, seeing that space is reserved and the car delivered to the ship, emptying the tank, disconnecting the battery, *et al*.

SHIPPING YOUR OWN CAR TO EUROPE: Think carefully before forging ahead. If you own a large American car, forget it. European streets are narrow—you'll have a hard time squeezing through those charming old arches and fortressed walls—and gasoline prices and consumption for American cars are so high that you'll feel like an indentured servant to your automobile. If you own a small European car and plan to be abroad for several months, the economics may work out more in your favor. Again, put the shipping problem into the hands of the World-Wide Travel Department of the

AAA and let them handle the details and documentation. You'll treasure their professional assistance. The major steamship companies will take your car as accompanying baggage, but if you handle the matter yourself, it's important to make reservations for both you and your car far in advance, as space is limited. The day before the ship sails, drive the car to the pier where it will be hoisted aboard. Try not to have a full gas tank, for it will be drained before the car is put aboard. The cost of shipping a car this way will range approximately from $300 to $675 for the round trip, depending of course on the size and weight of the vehicle and your destination. If you are traveling by air and want to send your car ahead, it can be shipped as ocean freight. Most countries allow you to bring your car in free for a period of a year, if it carries a foreign license plate. In all countries, cars which cross the borders must display an oval plaque near the license plate which indicates the country of registration. The plaque which says "USA" is available through the AAA's clubs for $2. If, however, you take delivery of a new car abroad, this will be registered locally and you should carry the appropriate plaque—*i.e.*, "F" for France, "D" for Germany, etc. The plaque indicates the country of registration of the car—not the nationality of the driver.

Remember that however you acquire a car abroad, you should be sure to pick it up during the daytime. It's exhausting and confusing to drive at night in a strange place after a long trip.

DOCUMENTS: It takes three documents to move an automobile: your permission to drive it, i.e., a license; written proof that you have liability insurance; and written evidence that the car is properly yours to drive. Rental and sales agencies help you with the second and third papers; the first is up to you.

Nearly everywhere, the driving license issued in your own state is enough if you are at least 18 years of age. However, in some countries (among them in Europe, Austria, Greece, Hungary, Italy, Poland, Portugal, Spain, Turkey and West Germany), the only recognized document for residents of the U.S. is the International Driving Permit issue by the AAA clubs on the basis of your license. Even if you are not planning to tour in the countries listed above, it's worthwhile getting the IDP since it is recognized everywhere by the local police. Should you find yourself in a jam at midnight in Toulon, you won't have to worry about the policeman's recognizing a license from Tennessee.

The IDP, which is printed in eight languages, is good for a year from the day it was issued, costs $3, and is available quickly from the AAA upon the presentation of your license and two passport-size photos. (Note: In Great Britain, if you are under 21 or over 65 you will find it difficult to rent a self-drive car.)

Written proof that you have liability insurance is most easily recognized in Europe in the form of the International Insurance Card, commonly called a "Green Card." Most countries of Western Europe make third-party insurance compulsory, but even if you are planning to drive in those that don't, you should be *fully* covered for theft, fire, and collision (you should even eliminate the customary $50–$100-deductible clause for the little extra it costs to be covered all the way). If you rent, lease or buy a car for use abroad, the rental or sales agency will arrange this coverage; a short-term insurance policy costs about 75 cents a day. If you ship your own car to Europe, ask your insurance agent to include public liability and foreign territory clauses in your policy. You can also arrange foreign coverage through the AAA. Remember that some foreign insurance companies won't accept you if you are under twenty-one, so look into the matter carefully with the car agency here. No matter what the source of your insurance coverage, be sure that it gives you the International Insurance Card, which is immediate proof throughout Europe that you are covered against third-party risks.

More insurance notes: Remember that if you ship a newly purchased foreign car home, the steamship companies will not automatically insure it. You must be sure to take out your own marine insurance or see that it is included in the overall "package price" for the full U.S. replacement value of the car. If you are driving your own car in Mexico, you will need your car title or bill of sale plus *extra* insurance, for most U.S. policies do not include coverage there. The AAA's border offices can arrange this when you arrive at the crossing points, or your own agent can add the coverage to your regular policy. Whatever insurance you buy, be sure the company is a reliable one and is represented in the U.S.A. or you'll be aged and infirm before you collect on a claim. Lloyd's of London and other English, Swiss or Scandinavian companies are likely to handle matters with greater dispatch than those in Latin countries. Also, to save headaches if you get into a scrape, take along your insurance policy number and ask your agent for some accident forms.

The third document is the registration papers of the car; these prove that the car is rightfully yours. In some countries outside Europe you may also need a customs pass for the car, known as a *carnet* (this permits it to pass through two or more countries) or *triptyque* (this is for a single country). The rental or sales agent will furnish the *carnet* or *triptyque* as well as the registration papers of the car.

Since all three documents are vital to your moving about, guard them carefully. Keep them with your other valuables; *never* leave them in the car.

GASOLINE: Known as petrol, *essence, benzina,* or *Benzin,* it will generally cost more abroad than at home, but the difference in price will be made up by the fact that smaller foreign cars give far more mileage to the gallon than do our large American ones. Prices range from about 11.3 cents a gallon in Venezuela to 80 cents for a gallon of premium gasoline in France. The wide disparity is due to the taxes that each government levies. As you drive along, you will find many familiar gasoline names: Shell, Esso, Caltex. In Britain and several other countries, the measure is an imperial gallon, which is 1.2 American gallons or 1/5 larger than ours. On the Continent, gasoline is sold by the liter, which is slightly more than one of our quarts. (To convert gallons to liters, multiply the number of gallons by four and subtract 1/5 the number of gallons. Thus 8 gallons of gasoline equals about 30 liters; 10.5 gallons equals about 40 liters.)

At this writing, Italy offers special gasoline coupons to tourists; they give you a 30 per cent discount on the regular price. Pick them up at the AAA before you leave, or in Italy at the offices of ENIT (Italian State Tourist Office) or at the Automobile Club of Italy, or at the border when you drive into that country. They are *not* good for cars which are registered in Italy; you must have rented or bought your car elsewhere. (You do qualify, however, if you have bought or rented a car for *delivery* in Italy.) You will be allowed 15 liters of gasoline at a reduced price each day for 90 days; beyond that amount, you pay the regular price. Also, you will be given a record book, and if you haven't used all your coupons, you turn the balance in for refund at the end of your trip. Gasoline discounts are also available to tourists in Romania and Czechoslovakia.

Unlike the practice in the U.S.A., the renter of the car abroad is expected to pay extra for gasoline. (Some agencies, however, have begun to include gasoline in the overall price.) You'll be started out with a full tank and expected to turn the car back with a full tank as well. On the other hand, all expenses for oil and maintenance will be refunded.

In countries such as Portugal and Yugoslavia, where tourism is just beginning to grow, gasoline stations are still rather scarce. Make it a rule to check carefully where stations are before you start.

And two hints on tipping: It is common practice abroad to tip the man who fills your tank, usually the local equivalent of 15 to 20 cents (see Tipping, page 359). Also, in the parking areas near sightseeing attractions, you will often find an official attendant whose job is to keep a watchful eye on your car. When you leave the vicinity, tip him the equivalent of 5 to 10 cents.

MILEAGE: British roads are measured in miles, those of the Continent and many other parts of the world in kilometers. The Continental car you rent or lease will have a speedometer that is scaled in kilometers. To convert kilometers into miles (1 kilometer equals about 5/8 of a mile) divide the number of kilometers by 8 and multiply the result by 5. The figure won't be exact but it will be close enough for your purposes.

SERVICES TO MOTORISTS: Where motoring and car ownership are commonplace as in western European countries, you will find road patrols maintained by the police or by national motor clubs on major highways. (Many car rental or car purchase firms automatically enroll you in their national auto club for the term of your hire.) In Belgium, Germany and Holland, for example, the major highways are patrolled by the yellow breakdown vehicles (small cars or motorcycle outfits) of the local automobile and touring clubs. If you get into trouble—even run out of gas—pull off the road, raise your hood and watch for the yellow car. In Britain the Automobile Association and the Royal Automobile Club each have uniformed highway patrols (yellow or blue) and phone booths along the side of the road for summoning help. Take your AAA membership card along; it can be useful with foreign automobile clubs, some of whose services are offered free. Even if you are not an AAA member, its World-Wide Travel Department (750 Third Avenue, New York 10017) will help you rent or buy a foreign car, give you the routings on foreign highways, and help you with travel bookings. Also, it has offices in London (15 Pall Mall), Paris (9 Rue de la Paix), and Rome (Via di Porta Pinciana 36), and about 400 representatives throughout the world including affiliations with all the major motor clubs abroad. If you plan to do most of your touring in one country, it may be worthwhile to take out a membership in its automobile club; annual fees range roughly from $6 to $15 a year.

If you travel on secondary roads or strike off into the country, take along extra cans of gasoline and oil, as well as tires, tools, and spare parts—plus some knowledge of how to use them.

ROADS, ROAD SIGNS, AND RULES OF THE ROAD: While there are splendid roads and expressways in many parts of the world (Germany's *Autobahnen; the autoroutes* of France, the *autostradas* of Italy and Britain's motorways, for example), don't expect as many good roads as we have. In some places, what is called a major highway will seem unbelievably narrow. Country roads will be tight, curving and often rough. On these sorts of roads, don't aim for more than 100 to 125 miles as a day's maximum driving, about half the distance you could do at home. Heavy traffic tie-ups and bumper-to-bumper driving have become a commonplace in every large city, so when you plan your route, try to avoid coming into a large city in the late afternoon.

Speed limits vary from country to country, even from road to road as here. In most places, you drive just as you do at home—on the right side of the road. The notable exceptions are Ireland, Iceland, Great Britain, Australia, the American Virgin Islands, and Sweden; there you drive on the left and pass on the right. (Sweden will have changed to right-hand driving in the fall of 1967.) It's comparatively easy to get used to left-hand driving. Try it slowly as you start; you should feel comfortable in about an hour, but be careful for the first few minutes every morning.

What you may not get used to as quickly is the European driver's attitude toward the right-of-way convention—known as the "Rule of the Right"—which means that the driver at an intersection must yield the right of way to any vehicle approaching from the right. Without a glance to the left, no matter how poor the visibility, cars will shoot out at you from side streets, unless you are on a road having obvious priority over intersecting roads. You must even beware of self-confident bicycles and ox-carts.

It is obvious that you should always drive more carefully in a strange place than at home, where every bit of construction, every dip and bump in the road, and all your neighbors' idiosyncrasies are known to you. Abroad, the very traffic patterns will be new and your reflexes unaccustomed to dealing with them. Paris may seem to have neither speed nor pedestrian regulations. You'll find the additional hazard of thousands of bicycles and motorbikes. For these and dozens of other good reasons, take it easy.

Basically, the motoring code observed abroad is similar to that of the U.S.A., and the small differences between one place and another are no greater than those around the U.S.A. Occasionally, you'll find local variations such as Austria's practice, as reported by the AAA, of fining motorists according to their financial status, or Russia's payment to drivers who pick up hitchhikers. In Athens, the police and the Automobile and Touring Club will give you a list of special parking areas for foreign visitors; in Vatican City traffic violations will cost you, on the average, 40 cents. Driving courtesy may be another matter. In some countries you will find yourself losing your temper every five minutes at the "lunatic drivers"; in others you will be delighted at the courtesy one driver shows another. In Britain, for example, a driver signals to tell you whether the road ahead is clear.

In many countries roads are far better marked than ours. In France, for example, it seems that you can't go for a mile or two without knowing the town you have left, the town you are approaching, and the distance to each. Reading road markers requires no great command of language since nearly all European countries use the easy, pictorial and symbolic international road signs: Circular signs say "don't," triangular signs are danger warnings, rectangular signs give information. A triangular sign with a picture of children, for example, is a warning to watch out for small fry:

 One with a man walking means pedestrian crossing.

 A circular sign with a bar thrust across it means "no entry."

 A rectangular sign with a monkey wrench means there's a garage mechanic nearby.

Although these international road signs may vary slightly from country to country, shapes, colors and pictures remain basically the same.

AND FINALLY SOME BASIC TIPS FOR THE ROAD: Don't leave your car unlocked for a minute. Your very foreignness is a terrific temptation to local thieves, and having something stolen while you're on vacation is a souring experience, costly in time and money. The chief target for thieves who prey on tourists is luggage; always keep yours locked in the trunk rather than strewn, in full view, over the back seat. Always empty the car completely each night.

Plan each day's journey before you start out. Stick to a reasonable schedule without forcing too long a drive. Start looking for a place to stay overnight, if you haven't made earlier reservations, no later than 6 P.M. in the summer, about 4 P.M. in the winter.

Don't bog yourself down with a heavy lunch and wine if you are planning a long afternoon's drive. If it is a warm day, you're bound to end up feeling drowsy. The laws concerning driving under the influence of alcohol are very strict in Europe, especially in Scandinavia. You are better off taking your heavy meal after the driving is done and asking your hotel to put up a picnic lunch to be eaten by the side of the road. If you are determined to have a long lunch at a three-star restaurant, do 75 per cent of the day's driving before you get there.

Don't travel in France without the incomparable *Guide Michelin*. There are Red Michelin Guides to the Benelux countries (Belgium, Holland and Luxembourg), Italy, Germany, and Spain. Buy them in the U.S.A. before leaving, as it may be difficult to find English editions abroad. Check your local bookstore or order them by mail from French European Publications, 610 Fifth Avenue, New York 10020.

Don't count on using your lunch hours to get your car quickly serviced. In many countries, business slows to a standstill around noontime.

Especially in remote countries, drive a popular car, or you may get stuck for days in a small village waiting for parts; this is not the time for automotive one-upmanship.

Jot down the license number, make and color of your rented car— or you may lose it in a sea of similar ones parked in the square near your hotel.

Lay in these supplies for a comfortable trip: a rooftop luggage rack and waterproof tarpaulin (the rental agency can supply these if you reserve them ahead of time), map case, flashlight, and picnic basket and accouterments. (Buy the latter abroad. Europeans love *le pique-nique*—and you'll find this equipment everywhere.)

Telephone a few hours ahead if you want to lunch at a restaurant heavily starred in *Michelin*—or you may drive for 30 extra miles and find it either booked solid for the next two hours or closed for the day.

If you get tired of driving, remember that European railways in Belgium, Britain, France, Germany and Italy will take you and your car on the same trains at a moderate cost. You can, for example, pick up a car in London and tour Britain; then go by Channel ferry to Ostend, Belgium, where you land your car; board the train for Milan; get off there, tour in Italy and fly home from Rome.

In most major cities it's virtually impossible to park in the street, but there are often special parking areas set aside for tourists. Ask your concierge about them.

If you plan to take a car ferry such as one of the Channel steamers that link England and France, make your reservation well in advance. In season they are extremely popular and space is at a premium. This is also true of the air ferries between Britain and the Continent.

If you need a basic vocabulary of useful foreign automotive terms, check the list below, compiled by the European Travel Commission:

ENGLISH	FRENCH	GERMAN	ITALIAN
axle	essieu	Achse	asse
battery	batterie	Batterie	batteria
bearing	coussinet	Lager	cuscinetto a sfere
bolt	boulon	Bolzen	bullone
brake	frein	Bremse	freno
bulb	ampoule	Birne	lampadina
bumper	pare-choc	Stosstange	paraurti
carburetor	carburateur	Vergaser	carburatore
clutch	embrayage	Kupplung	innesto
cylinder	cylindre	Zylinder	cilindro
distributor	distributeur	Verteiler	distributore
engine	moteur	Motor	motore
fan belt	courroie de venti-lateur	Ventilatorriemen	cinghia de ventila-tore
gasoline (Brit. petrol)	essence	Benzin	benzina
gear	engrenage	Getriebe	ingranaggi
hood (Brit. bonnet)	capot	Motorhaube	cofano
horn	klaxon	Hupe	tromba
hub	moyeu	Nabe	mozzo
ignition	allumage	Zundung	accensione
lights	éclairage	Scheinwerfer	fari
muffler (Brit. silencer)	silencieux	Auspufftopf	silenziatore
oil	huile	Öl	olio
piston ring	segment de piston	Kolbenring	anello de tenuta

ENGLISH	FRENCH	GERMAN	ITALIAN
pump	pompe	Pumpe	pompa
flat (Brit. puncture)	crevaison	Reinfendefekt	bucatura
radiator	radiateur	Kühler	radiatore
spark plug	bougie	Zündkerze	candela
spring	ressort	Feder	molla
steering	direction	Steuerung	sterzo
switch	contact	Kontakt	contatto
tank	réservoir d'essence	Tank	serbatoio
tire (Brit. tyre)	pneu	Reifen	copertone
transmission	transmission	Wechselgetriebe	transmissione
valve	soupape	Ventil	valvola
wheel	roue	Rad	ruota
windshield (Brit. windscreen)	pare-brise	Windschutzscheibe	parabrezza

Finally, the road of the motorist is well paved with information, available without charge, from the car rental companies, the major oil companies and the tourist offices listed in the section beginning on page 479. The AAA's guide, *Motoring Abroad*, published annually, contains details about driving in 26 European countries, lists of hotels and garages, addresses of local automobile clubs, etc. It's available to those who plan European trips through the AAA. The "Continental Handbooks" published by Britain's AA and RAC contain similar useful information, and if you cross the Channel between England and France, their uniformed port officers will be there to assist you on both sides of the water.

Museums

WHEREVER civilizations have flourished, there are museums to commemorate all man's wonderfully various arts and sciences. Even Norway, small as it is, has nearly 400 museums of one sort or another. There are national museums like Paris's Louvre and London's British Museum, each of whose vast wings could be a museum in itself. There are great picture galleries such as the Prado in Madrid; exquisite personal creations like the Soane Museum in London; and small museums that revolve around the growth and development of a single industry, sport, or hobby, such as the Lucas Bols Museum in Amsterdam, which has a collection relating to gin and liqueurs, the Museum of Bullfighting in Madrid, the museum of spaghetti in the Mediterranean village of Ponte d'Assio, Italy, and the Swiss Bread and Confectionery Museum in Lucerne. There are museums which detail local history such as the New World Museum on San Salvador in the Bahamas which contains documents and relics pertaining to Christopher Columbus. Sometimes great private collections have been willed to the community. These often have the charm of a commanding personal taste. Two examples are the Wallace Collection in London and the Lázaro Galdiano in Madrid.

There are houses where a great man lived, whose atmosphere still seems to vibrate with his genius: Rembranthuis in Amsterdam, where the artist lived for twenty years; Rodin's house in Paris, where all his greatest works, originals or plaster reproductions, are shown; the Maison de Balzac in Paris, where you can see the exit from which the writer repeatedly escaped his dunning creditors; and the radiant Fra Angelico Museum in Florence, where the spirit of the artist is alive in the cells of his monastery. There are museums of archaeology nearly everywhere, for the mysteries of man's past seem to fascinate every nation; there are museums which mirror a country's major preoccupations, such as the seafaring museums in Norway; there are open-air museums which recreate farm and village life of a century or more ago; there are museums of waxworks; there are splendid provincial museums whose unexpected superb collections are a reward for the traveler who ventures away from capitals. France is particularly rich in these: The Romanesque sculpture at Toulouse, the tapestries at Rheims, the work of Ingres at Montauban are unrivaled anywhere else in the world. Finally there are countless special museums that are pure frolics to roam through: the Wallpaper Museum in Schloss Wilhelmshoehe in Kassel, Germany, which exhibits "wallpaper" (before the end of the eighteenth century it was more likely to be leather, silk, or linen), from its earliest beginnings and from the world over; the Museum of Childhood in Edinburgh, which houses a collection of toys and games ranging from Greek terra-cotta dolls to space guns; and the Wellcome Historical Medical Museum in London with exhibits on medicine and allied sciences from the earliest time.

With these myriad manifestations of the richness of human nature awaiting the delight of the curious traveler, it's a pity that many of us left school with a dread of museums. For some, the word still conjures up boredom and aching feet, wampum, plaster casts, anomalous bronze vessels, and ivory false teeth. But such impressions are out of date. Many museums are being superbly revamped, paintings cleaned, exhibits newly installed. The National Gallery in London, for instance, has done much to make its collections more enjoyable; the Capodimonte Museum in Naples presents its paintings with great style; the Borghese Gallery in Rome and the Jeu de Paume in Paris are also first-rate. (Some of the far greater collections, alas, have yet to be shown to their full advantage: the Prado and the Louvre are vastly rich but dark; the Uffizi none too bright; the Pitti Palace a hodgepodge.)

Viewed properly, then, and—what's most important—not too much at one time, museums are exhilarating. They house—often in marvelous old palaces—some of the noblest and most ingenious work that men have done in all ages. If you expect to be entertained, and let pleasure, not duty, guide you, museum-going will be one of the greatest treats of traveling. Here are some tips for enjoying yourself:

1. Don't attack a big museum as though there's no tomorrow. Study the arrangement of its wings and exhibits first; then head for the galleries that appeal to you, giving priority to those that interest you most. The British Museum, for example, has a staggering number of exhibits. At best, you will see only part of them, so pick and choose and enjoy your selection without guilt.

2. Banishing guilt is, in fact, essential to enjoying museums. Don't feel guilty if an exhibit bores you—go on to something else. Don't feel guilty if your knowledge of a work of art is sketchy. Enjoy the harmony and rhythm, color and form, for what they are. Don't feel guilty about not wanting to go to the museum that everyone else heads for. Pick one that appeals to you. Don't feel guilty if you would rather spend 30 minutes in front of one painting than one minute in front of 30.

3. Leave a museum as soon as you feel yourself getting the slightest bit tired. Don't press on, or the pleasure will give way to bewildered exhaustion. By the same token, go to a museum when your energies are high, *never* after a wearing bout of sightseeing.

4. Mornings are probably best for seeing paintings by natural light. In the spring, fall and winter, when the days are short, the old halls of many museums get dark; and electric light kills the essential qualities of the paintings.

5. If you travel with husband or friend, there's no need to stick

together in museums. Your interests may not be the same. Separate and compare notes afterward.

6. And of course wear your most comfortable shoes, your easiest clothing, and carry your lightest handbag.

Since the hours, days and entrance fees vary not only from country to country but from museum to museum, be sure to check the facts with your concierge or local entertainment guide before starting out. In Greece, for example, the museums open in summer at 7:30 A.M. In Paris don't count on "doing" a museum at luncheontime: they are invariably closed between 12 and 2. In Japan most museums are closed on Mondays, in Paris on Tuesdays, and so it goes.

Nearly all the major museums sell post cards, art books, reproductions of paintings or sculptures, handicrafts and even sometimes records. These make handsome gifts to take home, are usually inexpensive, and are far more meaningful than, say, a model of the Eiffel Tower. At Honolulu's Bishop Museum, for example, you can stock up on shell leis, contemporary pottery made of volcanic cinders, books of Hawaiian legends and poetry, replicas of native birds, handmade dolls, and old Hawaiian games such as *ulumaika* stones (ancient-style "bowling") and *konane* (a game played by King Kamehameha resembling checkers) among other things. Often museums offer concerts, films, and lectures, all of which are inexpensive and attract attentive audiences. Under the museum's roof you should be able to strike up conversations and acquaintanceships easily.

In some museums you can find extraordinary bargains. The Louvre, for example, has a little-known department overlooking the Seine—the *chalcographie*—which was founded in 1670 by Louis XIV to record the great events of his reign through the medium of engravings. Today there are some 14,000 copperplates and woodcuts which have been carved by such masters as Van Dyke, Prud'hon, Matisse and Vlaminck. The prints that are pulled sell from $2.50 to $5. (How much more lasting and beautiful they are than the tasteless oils of Sacré-Coeur sold by the dozens in Montmartre!) The Louvre's marvelous hoard, little known to the public, is a source of supply for print shops in France and abroad, whose prices then shoot up like a fever chart. The *chalcographie* publishes a complete catalog and price list which sells for about 50 cents. It can be obtained by writing to them at the Quai du Louvre, Paris 1ᵉʳ. They will, in turn, send you the prints by mail. Another bargain in Paris is to be found at the Musée de Sèvres, where porcelain figures made from original eighteenth-century molds can be bought. The museum has an extensive collection of porcelain going back to the early days of Sèvres manufacture, when this peerless factory supplied the royal family.

Many museums are also particularly pleasant, quiet, and inexpensive places to have a simple lunch, a glass of wine or beer, or a tea. Among the agreeable ones are the Museum of Modern Art in Stockholm; the Louvre, the Jeu de Paume, and the Museum of Modern Art in Paris; the Rijksmuseum in Amsterdam; the Prado in Madrid; the Victoria and Albert Museum and the Tate Gallery in London. The peaceful terrace restaurants of the Museum of Modern Art in both Rio de Janeiro and São Paulo attract a knowledgeable luncheon crowd. And in the cafeteria and patio restaurant of Mexico's National Museum of Anthropology, you can have a pleasant meal before setting out to see what is certainly, at this moment, the world's most attractive museum.

Names and Titles

THE AMERICAN frontier is no longer with us, but it has left a strong tradition of free and easy equality. The man who removes your wisdom teeth or appendix is "Doctor"; almost everyone else is plain "Mr." or "Mrs." or "Miss"—and lucky not to be "Mike" or "Sally" on first encounter. In many older and more complex societies, however, you will find that people are normally addressed by a variety of elaborate and often descriptive titles. Sometimes, if you know the language, a man's name and title will tell you what he does for a living, where he comes from, who his relatives are—or all three.

Your head may swim at first, but accept and enjoy this difference between the other parts of the world and your own, as you do the food and the weather. No one expects a temporary visitor to master these intricacies of social and professional distinction. Wherever you go in the world, if you know the local equivalent for "Sir" and "Madam" you will be a model of tact. (One fine point: When you speak to foreigners of any nationality in English, women are addressed as Mademoiselle or Madame, men as Mister. For example, Mme. Björkssen and Mr. Björkssen.) Here are a few guidelines to help you clarify most of the titles you will hear:

Basically, titles are either hereditary or professional. In the first category are those of Prince, Duke, Marquis, Earl, Count, Viscount, Baron, Nawab, Maharajah and the like and their feminine equivalents: Princess, Duchess, Countess, etc. If you expect to be meeting titled people, it would be wise to study the pertinent passages of such etiquette books as Amy Vanderbilt's *Complete Book of Etiquette* or *Vogue's Book of Etiquette*. There are so many refinements in the correct use of hereditary titles that each book carries several pages of fine print on the subject.

In the second category are professional titles. These are the ones you and your husband are likely to run into most frequently and here's how they work:

DOCTOR: A person with a Ph.D. as well as one with a medical or dental degree is called "Doctor" abroad. Sometimes, as in Portugal, a lawyer is also addressed by this title by virtue of his extensive education. If you are with someone on the Continent who is highly educated, call him "Doctor." If wrong, you will be quickly corrected, but you will have been flattering. In England, on the other hand, use the title of doctor as you would in the U.S.A. but remember one peculiarity: Surgeons are called not "Doctor" but "Mr." The same is true of dentists.

PROFESSOR: If you hear a man called by this title, it doesn't necessarily mean that he is on the staff of a university. It can also be used to address a businessman provided he is a known and distinguished expert in his field.

OTHER PROFESSIONAL TITLES: Lawyers, engineers and architects are often addressed by the name of their profession. You will meet Licenciado Gómez, Arquitecto Bonaventures, Ingeniero Cabral. Some countries tack a "Mr." onto the titles, converting them into Mr. Lawyer or Mr. Architect. As a rule of thumb, remember that while Latin professionals are called just "lawyer" or "architect" or "engineer," their German counterparts add "Mr." Titling even extends to nonprofessional V.I.P.s: The director of a company, a hotel or government bureau is "Herr Direktor." A civil servant may be addressed as specifically as "Herr Oberinspektor" and the editor of a newspaper is called "Herr Redakteur." Furthermore, while in this country a wife's title never reflects her husband's work, abroad it often does: Wives are called "Frau Doctor," "Frau Director," "Frau Editor," etc.

The French and French-speaking Belgians give the title "Maître" to distinguished trial lawyers and venerable writers, male and female. But addressing a young writer this way, no matter how brilliant and successful he or she may be, would be absurdly stuffy.

HYPHENATED AND MULTIPLE NAMES: Unknown here, but fairly common abroad, they grow out of several sources and are handled differently in different countries.

Some result from marriage. While in the U.S.A. a woman gives up her maiden name completely when she marries and takes her husband's surname, in many other countries she retains her maiden name and places it either before or after his. In Spain and Spanish-speaking countries a rearrangement of names takes place which precisely indicates a person's history. Felicia Gómez marries Jorge Cervantes. She becomes Señora Doña Felicia Gómez de Cervantes, putting his name after hers. Their children, however, put their father's name first; they are named Cervantes Gómez. The following general rule will see you through: Address a married Spanish woman by the *last* of her two names; an unmarried Spanish woman or a Spanish man by the first of the two names.

Also, in the Netherlands, a woman never gives up her maiden name in her signature. For example, when Miss Juliana Vermeer marries Onno Brinker, she becomes Mrs. Juliana Brinker-Vermeer and she uses this name as her legal signature. You would write to her as "Dear Mrs. Brinker" and address the envelope "Mrs. J. Brinker-Vermeer."

Other double names do not grow out of recent marriages but are simply family names. If in England you run into Mrs. Robertson-Jones, call her by both names, for together they are her husband's surname and he is probably of a long line of Robertson-Joneses. The same is true in France. If names have "de" between them, use both halves. Thus in "Vaux de la Bussière," the first part is a family name, the last an honorific. If the gentleman has no title, he is M. Vaux; if titled, then he is known as Count de la Bussière.

In Japan, the polite honorific "san" is appended to the family name of the man or woman being addressed. When, for instance, Mr.

Iwata, who has been a consular officer in the U.S.A., goes back home to Tokyo, he becomes Iwata-san. For teachers, doctors, lawyers and members of Parliament, however, use "sen sei" instead of "san." "Sama" is occasionally used by women in high social circles when addressing each other. A married woman is always a "san" or "sama" with the suffix attached to her last name; a young single woman, if you have known her for a while, gets the "san" attached to her first name, i.e., Yoko-san, Mary-san, etc.

In India, while most names are made up like ours, there are some exceptions in the south. Sometimes the official name is the person's first name, preceded by the initial letters signifying the name of his native village or town and his father's name. T. K. Chandran, whose full name is Tanjore Krishna Chandran, is Chandran, the son of Krishna, from the village of Tanjore.

The list of these national variations could go on and on, but relax. No one expects you to know all these fine points. There is one thing, however, at which foreigners do look askance: *don't ever* in *any* foreign country start first-naming people as soon as you meet them. Everywhere else (except in Australia and Israel, which are even more informal than we are) the use of first names is a privilege that goes with established friendship; it is never extended to mere acquaintances. You can garble titles and hyphenated names barbarically and the locals will be tolerant—but Mr. and Mrs., Sir and Madame, are an absolute necessity until you are given express permission to call someone by his first name. You will also hear "Monsieur" and "Madame" without surname frequently repeated in French conversation; to omit them is considered rude.

Also, most foreign languages have two forms for "you"; the plural form, such as *vous* in French, which is formal; and the singular, like the French *tu*, which is familiar. The familiar form is used only after years of friendship with someone of the same age or by parents to their children. It is not, under any circumstances, suitable for you to use with someone you have just met. In Europe men who have conducted business with one another for years still employ the formal "you." As friendship deepens, they may use only each other's surname as the last step before going to the familiar "you." A younger person is *never* the first to use it with an elder.

There are some parts of the world where the pattern of names and titles is similar to that in the U.S.A., notably Australia, Canada, and South Africa. Here, except for members of the British peerage, there are no special titles. While the rule against first names is not as strict as in Europe or South America, go slowly—wait for permission.

National Holidays

FEW THINGS are more infuriating—unless you have planned it that way—than to arrive for a few days in a foreign city, eager to storm its shops and museums, and find them shuttered and the streets dead. Every nation has its sprinkling of holidays, both public and religious, when stores, banks, and sometimes even the theaters are shut tight. Some are celebrated with such joy and fanfare that despite the inconveniences you will consider yourself lucky to be there at that moment. Others have no drama to mark them and are largely an occasion for the populace to escape to beach and countryside. To come into a strange city on such a day can be a terrible letdown.

If you should arrive in Rome on August 15, the city will look like a ghost town, its streets will be empty and hushed, and none of the telephone numbers on your list will answer. Should you go to Bermuda eager to stock up on cashmeres and china, avoid the public holidays at the end of July or early August—unless you are interested in cricket, for on the annual two-day Cup Match holiday the islanders' attention is entirely absorbed in the classic game played each year between the two best teams in the colony. Even the canniest Front Street merchants place cricket higher than commerce on these days, and all the shops are tightly shuttered. If you head for Colombia during the last three days of June or December, you won't be able to buy even an emerald chip. This is when the local businessmen are making up their semiannual statements. To avoid distractions, however profitable, they close down their shops completely.

To spare yourself the frustration of having your precious few days whittled away by unexpected holidays—and to be part of those marvelous festive days marked by pageantry, music, gaiety and the displays of a nation's heart that you can't see in weeks of ordinary sightseeing—never plan an itinerary without a calendar of holidays in your hand. (See Itinerary Building, page 188, and Festivals, page 132.) The national tourist offices whose addresses are listed on pages 479 to 493 will gladly send you theirs. Your travel agent also will probably have them. If, for example, you plan a trip to India in January, you'll want to be in New Delhi on the 26th. This is Republic Day, the country's greatest national festival, celebrated on such a mammoth scale and with such gaiety that it can give you better insight into India than a fortnight of temple-gazing. And if you are in Copenhagen on March 11, you can share, with the city's children, the colorful Guard's Parade before Amalienborg Castle and the greetings of the royal family from its balcony, for this is the King's birthday, a school holiday, and a wonderful time to feel the Danes' love both for children and for their royal family.

Consider, too, the differences in the observance of the Sabbath as you travel around the world. In Moslem countries like Iran, Friday is the week's day of rest. In Israel, shops, banks and even transportation begin to shut down on Friday afternoon and remain closed until Saturday night or Sunday.

If you run into a holiday unwittingly or your itinerary forces one upon you, have the foresight to cash sufficient money the day before. You can nearly always count on your hotel's being able to change your American dollars and cash travelers checks, but they may have to limit you to small amounts if they run short. In large cities such as London and Paris currency exchange offices are open *every* day nearly round the clock at the airports, air terminal buildings and main railway stations.

If it's the sort of total holiday when even restaurants are closed, you can always count on your hotel's feeding you. And if you find yourself at complete loose ends because museums and sightseeing tours are not available, there are always the movies, a ferry or boat ride (these services never stop), a leisurely stroll down the main street, or a taxi ride to the best residential part of town, where you can amble about looking at the handsome houses.

Newspapers

IF READING a newspaper with your breakfast coffee is one of the day's more blissful moments, there's no reason to deprive yourself of it while you're traveling. Veteran travelers recognize that enjoying one's habitual small pleasures *en voyage* helps make for the big pleasure of a trip.

There are four types of daily periodicals available. Either tell your concierge what you want and he'll get it for you, or run down to the local kiosk and make this simple purchase on your own.

First, there are English-language newspapers in all large cities around the world, such as the *Athens Daily Post*, the *Brazil Herald*, the *Rome Daily American*, the *Pakistan Dawn*, the *Jerusalem Post*, the *China Mail*, the *Borneo Bulletin*, the *Egyptian Gazette*, the *Teheran Journal*, the *Bangkok World* and the *Japan Times*.

Wherever English or Americans have come to visit or settle, these newspapers have invariably been started—with the exuberance of a club bulletin—to knit the local English and/or American community together. Today, regardless of how some have branched out into covering international news, they still draw you cozily into the life of Americans abroad. They carry a listing of English-language movies, theaters, lectures, and club meetings (many of them are open to you; see page xxx). There's entertaining gossip about local comings and goings, and—depending on the available talent in journalism—such exotica as interviews with in-transit celebrities, recipes for adaptations of native dishes in terms understandable to American housewives, tips on good buys at the local stores, and news of local auctions, antique sales, charity bazaars and fashion shows. They will make you feel at home and give you a fund of small talk with local residents.

In Britain, and everywhere on the Continent, you can buy English newspapers—*The Times*, the *Daily Express*, the *Telegraph*, the *Evening Standard*, the *Guardian*, *The Sunday Times* and *The Observer* —which are in a class by themselves—compact enough to read in toto, with excellent news coverage and soft-spoken, rational manners. (Certain other English papers, of course, are notable for their no-holds-barred sensationalism.)

Next come the American standbys: The *New York Herald Tribune European Edition* and *The New York Times International Edition*. The former was a going concern when Toulouse-Lautrec was painting cancan girls. They give you sober coverage of world events plus a sprinkling of columnists to put you in touch with the European scene. You'll find them in the Middle East, Asia, and parts of Africa, as well as in Europe. The International edition of *Time*, available practically everywhere, is a welcome adjunct to the daily paper. *The Wall Street Journal* flies to London daily as well as to Bermuda, Puerto Rico, Venezuela, and Hawaii.

And last, there are the newspapers (as well as the large picture magazines like *Paris Match*) published in the language of the country you're visiting, which may be Greek to you, literally or figuratively speaking. Don't feel shy about picking one up. Newspapers are an open letter to their readers, conveying a distinct personality. You'll get some sort of impression even though you may understand virtually nothing of the language. You can fall back on your pocket dictionary, or there are always the pictures—and comic strips. Peanuts and Li'l Abner have traveled a long way from home and are no less beguiling in Spanish or Swedish.

Packing

Anyone who can unpack her suitcase after a long journey and change into something that looks creaseless and uncrushed is well ahead of the game. Packing well is a matter of assembling a comfortable basis of clothes and cosmetics, and arranging it so neatly and sensibly that pressing bills and breakage are kept to a minimum. On a fast-moving trip, there is rarely time to give your clothes up to a valet for days, or even hours; in some places like small country hotels, such niceties as quick pressing may not even exist. It's safer, then, to depend on your own packing technique than on the uncertain amenities of your stopping places.

To pack well, you should follow certain basic rules of selection, use some of the helpful packing aids that are on the market, and work systematically. Here's how to go about it:

Rules of selection: To start, think ahead. List all of the clothes, accessories and underwear (don't forget the belts) you will need for the climates and activities your trip will take in. Imagine the sightseeing, shopping, sports, motoring, theater, quiet dinners, etc.—and the clothes to wear on such occasions. Visualize and list every outfit in its entirety from brassiere to handbag. Make another list of all the cosmetics and drugs that keep you feeling soignée from head to toe (see, for example, Beauty *en voyage* and Hairdressers, page 22; Big City Dressing, page 37; Weather, page 419; Resort Clothes, page 313). Then cut the lists down ruthlessly. From the clothes list, eliminate anything you can't wear at least three times. Pare accessories to the bone—they weigh the most. Carry cosmetics that can do double duty. Take what is necessary to your sense of well-being and not one item besides. Eliminate all the "just in case" items. Too much baggage can be a millstone; generally, the more experienced the traveler the less she is likely to pack.

When there's a choice between two similar garments, pack the one of better quality—it will stay fresher, longer. Pack only your prettiest clothes, the ones you really enjoy wearing. Take nothing which you haven't worn pleasurably and comfortably at home. *Never* take anything brand new—like a knit dress, shoes or girdle. If you are bound for several different climates, airfreight ahead some of the clothes you will need instead of burdening yourself with cottons in a London May or wools in a Madrid July. By the same token, when you finally leave one climate for another, ship home the clothes you won't need again; overweight charges for excess luggage can mount astronomically on a long trip. Never take more luggage than you can carry yourself. Remember too that if you plan to motor abroad, small foreign cars can carry far less luggage than our large American ones.

After making up your final essential list, check off items as they go into your suitcase; then tuck the list into your handbag and use it when you have to repack *en voyage*. You'll probably find that ideas flash into your head days before you leave, so keep a pad and pencil handy for jotting them down.

Think also of the small things that will keep you comfortable during a long flight and pack them in a separate case (soft, light slippers, a cardigan sweater, toothbrush and toothpaste) along with anything particularly precious like jewelry that you will want to keep at your side.

You might use these clothes weights as a rough guide to how much can go into your suitcase within the weight limits set down by the airlines: 44 pounds for economy-class passengers and 66 for first on international flights.

Wool suit	2½–3 pounds
Silk suit	1½ pounds
Dress	1–1½ pounds
Slip-over sweater	½ pound
Cardigan sweater	1 pound
Blouse	½ pound
Skirt	¾ pound
Shoes	1–1½ pounds
Bathing suit	½ pound
One set of underwear:	
bra, slip, girdle and panties	¾ pound
Nightgown	½ pound
Stockings (6 pairs)	¼ pound
Robe	¾-1 pound

Wear your heaviest clothes and accessories for the flight and take as few shoes, pieces of jewelry and cosmetics as possible since they weigh the most. Remember that when you board a flight you need not weigh in the handbag, camera, coats, umbrella, binoculars and reading matter that you carry on your arm.

PACKING AIDS: One of the keys to packing well is the ancient maxim: "Divide and conquer." If you follow it literally, the entire operation will be neat and tidy. Supply yourself with plastic bags in a variety of sizes, some with, others without, zippers. They hold fluffy bits of underwear, stockings, gloves, scarves and so forth and keep them from snagging and getting separated. There are also plastic blouse "books," plastic shoe bags, laundry bags, bags for carrying a wet bathing suit or damp, freshly washed underwear. You can use small plastic bags for wet washcloths and cosmetics (more on this below). Save the thin plastic bags that your cleaner uses for wrapping your clothes; the moisture these bags hold keeps clothes fresh. You can pack dresses inside the bags or wrap the bags around the clothes. Finally, lay in a supply of tissue paper.

You are now ready to pack.

TECHNIQUES: There are several schools of packing and each has its loyal adherents. There are the roll-up supporters, the fold-it-flat loyalists, and the tissue-paper advocates. Regardless of the one to which you give your allegiance, all require that you do the following:

1. Pack in solitude. You will need to concentrate, so it's best to do the job without distractions.

2. Remove all old routing tags from your suitcases.

3. Separate hard or bulky things from soft, foldable ones; the clothes for one climate from those for another; the clothes you will need immediately from those you won't wear for a while.

4. Add up the approximate weight of your personal effects, trying to stay at least 5 pounds under the maximum weight so you will have room for what you buy along the way.

5. Divide all the small items into categories: handkerchiefs, hosiery, scarves, gloves, jewelry, nightgowns, underwear, etc. Then slip each group into its own plastic envelope, which is waterproof and practically weightless. Tuck the envelopes around the edges of your suitcase so that when you arrive you can transfer the envelopes to the drawers. Little packets of sachet in each plastic envelope are a nice extra fillip.

6. Pack tightly, without crushing your clothes. There should never be so much room in your suitcase that clothes can roll or shift about. If you use a soft-sided bag, it should be so tightly packed that its sides bulge slightly.

7. Put ordinary wire hangers into the shoulders of your dresses before stowing them in the suitcase, so that when you unpack you can transfer them straight to the closet. Also, take some foam-covered hangers (for dresses with the wide necks that otherwise end up on the closet floor) plus one or two skirt hangers, which are practically never supplied by hotels.

8. Tuck little things like film and cigarettes into the side pockets of your suitcase or into handbags, and when you repack put them back in the same places so that you can always find them easily.

9. Keep your shoes, if possible, in a separate shoe bag. (See Luggage, page 208.)

Now for the two leading systems of filling the suitcase itself.

If you use a hanging case, fill the bottom with handbags. Hang your clothes on the bar, folding sleeves and extra width toward the center. If you have more clothes than the bar can accommodate, pack them flat in the case, without putting them on hangers. Buy a separate luggage accessory which has been especially designed for hanging cases. It is divided into sections marked underwear, blouses, laundry and the like. Slip these clothes into their proper places in this bag.

If you use a flat case (and are not using a separate shoe bag), put your shoes at the bottom near the hinges, each pair in a plastic case or shoe sock. Keeping the weight at the bottom balances the case and makes it easier to carry. Also put handbags and any heavy, oddly shaped item such as a jewelry roll at the bottom of the suitcase. Now fill the valleys with things like bathing suits and the small plastic cases containing your accessories and lingerie. Pack everything in tightly to prevent sliding. When this is done, you will have a level surface for the first layer of clothes: the heavier, firmer garments such as jackets and sweaters. These should be followed by dresses and on top of these your softest blouses. Save the most crushable clothes for the topmost layer and keep tucking the filled plastic cases into the gaps that occur as the packing continues.

Many women, following the divide-and-conquer rule, put heavy cardboard, corrugated paper or muslin between dresses so that any particular one can be lifted out as on a tray. This makes it unnecessary to unpack for an overnight stay. If you decide to use this technique, cut the sheet to the size of the suitcase, and on one end pare out a semicircle, threading a cord through it. This serves as a handle for lifting out the layer.

Stand next to the case while you pack so that you can fit and fold the clothes to the right dimensions. If you use a soft-sided case, pack on bed. Its resilience helps you to fill the case to the proper bulging point.

To pack a suit, place the jacket crosswise, button it, and with the jacket front facing you, cross the sleeves and flip the lower part of the jacket over into the suitcase, so it is folded at the waist. Fold skirts in half, lengthwise, and if you have to make them shorter, make another fold as near the waist as possible. All skirts and dresses should be folded at the waistline whenever possible, rather than the hem. Always button all buttons and zip all zippers of jackets and dresses.

Dresses should be placed face down on a hard flat surface or over the case, and folded in at each side to fit into the case. Fold back the sleeves across each other and the dress itself at the waistline. Be sure the collar and shoulders are smooth. Pack one dress with the hem at the right, the following dress with the hem at the left, so that the neckline of one goes over the hemline of the one beneath. This keeps things reasonably level. Always cover as large an area of the suitcase as possible with the dress so as to make the fewest folds.

The pleats of skirts can be held in place with pins or paper clips at the hem, or with a light basting stitch. Finely pleated skirts should be rolled and drawn into a footless stocking. Roll sweaters on a long sheet of tissue paper. Button and fold blouses as though they had just come back from the laundry, slip each one into a plastic bag, and put one blouse at one end of the case and the second at the other. Arrange your belts around the inside edges of the case rather than coiling them up. Put your robe and slippers on top of the case since they are probably the first things you'll change into when you get to the hotel.

People who favor tissue paper believe that every crease is a potential wrinkle, and they pad out each fold with crumpled paper. They also use tissue to fill out the sleeves and bosoms of jackets, dresses and blouses. They say that clothes not only come out looking better but you can actually get more clothes into your suitcase. A strong believer will use as much as three packages of tissue paper for one good-sized suitcase. Other women use bits and pieces of lingerie as fillers, i.e., a slip between the folds of a dress, or the thin plastic bags that come from the cleaners.

Cosmetics and drugs are usually the most difficult items to pack. Whether or not to take a separate cosmetic case depends largely on where you are going. If you plan to spend your entire vacation in a single place, such as a resort, you can pack jars and bottles in your big bag. But if you are touring, a separate beauty case is enormously useful: You just open it up and it becomes your dressing table with no need to unpack bottles every time you stop off. (If you do decide on a separate beauty case, always tuck a nightgown and slippers into it, just in case your other luggage should go to one city while you arrive at another.)

My favorite way of packing drugs and cosmetics is an extension of the divide-and-conquer system. First, I separate them into categories; then I put each category into a separate zippered plastic bag. Into one, for example, goes all the manicuring equipment; into another, hair setting essentials; into a third, various soaps, and so on. The plastic cases are then either fitted into the corners of my suitcase or laid on top of one another in my cosmetic bag. Then, if a bottle leaks, its contents go no farther than the inside of its own plastic case. When I arrive at my hotel, I slip the plastic cases into a drawer, and when I need a nail file, I simply reach for the manicure bag without fumbling through a litter of bottles, tubes and jars.

Before putting the jars into the plastic cases, be sure to seal the caps with adhesive or plastic tape (when you remove the tape, stick it around the bottom of the bottles so you won't lose it; also it will keep moist). Don't fill the bottles more than two-thirds full since many liquids expand in a plane and trickle out of their containers. And, of course, use nothing but plastic bottles and jars with tight screw lids. Never pack liquids like perfume or nail polish remover loose in your suitcase. If they leak, it can mean disaster to your clothes.

Having packed clothes and cosmetics, what else will you need? Here is a check list of extras which, though you can buy them abroad, take little room and are useful. (Other items under the headings of Beauty *en voyage* and Hairdressers, Clothes Care, and Health are found on pages 22, 80 and 164.) Whether or not you should take them depends entirely on how exacting your sense of comfort is.

Extra hangers—in addition to those mentioned earlier, there are lightweight folding and inflatable ones.

Binoculars

Dental Floss

Corn Plasters

Scotch tape—useful for quick repairs on falling hems or slipping shoulder straps.

Personal stationery

Calling cards with your name and address

Small flashlight

Transistor radio

Travel alarm clock

Earplugs for noisy hotel rooms

Notebook and ballpoint pen

Extra set of luggage keys

Small sewing kit

Foam rubber sponge—better than a brush for removing dust and lint

Scissors

Sunglasses

Cigarette lighter and extra flints— *no* lighter fluid. It's against CAB regulations.

Games in miniature for traveling, e.g., Scrabble, backgammon, playing cards.

Extra shoelaces.

Before you lock your suitcase, make this final check:

Are your name and address attached to all your suitcases, and is the same information, plus your next destination, pasted on a card or piece of paper on the inside of your suitcase?

Are your valuables, such as jewelry, in your handbag or in the hand luggage that will remain at your side throughout the trip?

Are your documents in your handbag, not in your suitcase?

During your trip, when you have to repack, add the following rules:

1. If you do your packing on an unmade bed, go through the folds to be sure you haven't forgotten white lingerie.

2. Be sure to look under the pillows, where European maids usually put nightgowns and pajamas. These head the list of left-behinds.

3. Look under the bed for shoes or evening slippers, and on the top of dark shelves for small packages, cameras and the like.

4. Check the medicine chest for drug items you may have used at the last minute and behind the bathroom door for shower caps or razor cords.

5. Don't forget the things you sent to the laundry.

Passport

THE NEAT, sturdy little· blue book which is your United States passport has a long history. Its antecedents go back to about 3000 B.C., when Nehemiah II said, "Let letters be given me to the Governors beyond the river, that they may let me pass through till I come unto Judah." The right of an orderly citizen to travel freely in peacetime was set down in the Magna Carta. Even back in Shakespeare's time, passports were part of the travel scene. In *King Henry V* he wrote, "Let him depart; his passport shall be made."

In those distant days, as now, the passport was an official document granting its bearer permission to travel and authenticating his right to protection. Hackworth's International Law, a leading treatise on the subject, defines the modern American version this way:

The American passport is a document of identity and nationality issued to persons owing allegiance to the United States and intending to travel or sojourn in foreign countries. It indicates that it is the right of the bearer to receive the protection and good offices of American diplomatic and consular officers abroad and requests on the part of the Government of the United States that the officials of foreign governments permit the bearer to travel or sojourn in their territories and in case of need to give him all lawful aid and protection. It has no other purpose.

Applying for a passport is a simple procedure; it only *seems* complicated because the requirements are laid down in such detail. Two phrases from the Hackworth definition will help you understand the basic desiderata:

First, the passport is a "document of identity." You must, therefore, apply for it *in person*, bringing proof that you are *really* you. If you live in a small town, the Clerk of Court, acting as Passport Agent, has probably watched your comings and goings for years, and his acquaintance with you can be enough. Otherwise, you must carry written proof, i.e., a document which bears your signature and photograph or description. This can be a driver's license, a company identification card or, of course, an old passport. If you have *none* of these, you can take along a friend who has known you for at least two years to serve as an identifying witness.

Your identification must be clear to foreign officials as well as to our own consular offices. Therefore, the passport must carry your likeness. When you apply, bring two copies of a recent photograph. These can be either in color or in black and white; and they should be no larger than 3 by 3 inches or smaller than 2½ by 2½ inches. They must show you in full face with your distinguishing marks unretouched and be printed on thin, unglazed paper.

The passport is also, according to Hackworth, a "document of nationality"—which means you will have to present proof of your United States citizenship. If you are native born, this can be your birth certificate. Should you have none, bring a letter to that effect from the appropriate authorities such as the Department of Health of your birthplace, indicating no birth record exists, plus a reliable substitute such as a baptismal certificate or an affidavit signed by a parent, close relative, or someone else who has personal knowledge of the date and place of your birth. If you're a naturalized citizen, bring your naturalization certificate. If you claim citizenship through a parent, you will need proof of your father's or mother's citizenship.

With identification and proof of citizenship in hand, present yourself at one of the U.S. Department of State Passport Agencies listed below:

Boston 02116	Salada Building, 330 Stuart Street
New York 10020	630 Fifth Avenue
Washington, D. C. 20524	22nd and E Streets, N.W.
Miami 33130	Federal Office Building, 51 S.W. First Avenue, Room 812
New Orleans 70130	U.S. Customs House, 423 Canal Street, Room 228
Chicago 60604	Federal Office Building, 219 South Dearborn Street, Room 244A
San Francisco 94102	Federal Office Building, 450 Golden Gate Avenue, Room 1405
Los Angeles 90012	Federal Office Building, 300 North Los Angeles Street, Room 1004
Seattle 98101	1410 Fifth Avenue
Honolulu 96813	Room 304, Federal Building

If you don't live near any of these cities, go to the nearest Federal, state or county court which has naturalization jurisdiction. Your travel agent will know where it is located.

A new passport costs $11 if the application is made before a clerk of a state court; $10 at a Federal court or Passport Agency. You should allow about two weeks, including mailing time, to receive it. It is good for three years from the date it was issued and can be renewed for two more years. (To renew your passport, ask any of the Passport Agencies listed above or the Clerks of the Court to send you a renewal application. Fill it out and return it with your passport and $5 to a passport agency. In a few days, your passport will be mailed to you, having been stamped to indicate that it is valid for five years from the original date of issue. If abroad, you can also pick up a renewal application at a consular office; its officials will handle the processing.)

When your passport arrives in the mail, sign it at once on page 2. Fill in all the necessary information on the inside cover. (This calls for the name and address of your next of kin; ominous as the request may sound, and even though the information probably won't be needed, it's an important precaution.) Then tuck your passport away in a safe place.

Having learned the essential procedure for obtaining a first-time passport, you might also note these tips to make the process even smoother:

1. Consider your passport application as step number one in planning a trip. You may get so involved in buying drip-dries that this basic requirement is overlooked.

2. Write for your birth certificate as early as possible. While it usually takes no more than a few days to get a passport, it can often take as much as three weeks to receive your birth certificate. Most states charge a fee for furnishing a copy of one.

3. Have your photographs taken by a professional passport photographer. One is usually located close to the Passport Agency; he will know exactly what size, paper and pose are required.

4. Apropos of pose, when he tells you to smile, do it warmly. There's no rule that says a passport photograph must make you look like Ma Barker, the lady bank robber. Most travelers have the misconception that smiling is prohibited. Actually, the Passport Office, which issued and renewed about 1,500,000 passports last year, would prefer us looking cheerful. Remember, this is the most literal interpretation of that popular phrase, "our image abroad."

5. Order several prints of your passport photograph; you can also use them for an international driving license, some visas, etc.

6. Make a careful note of your passport's expiration date in your calendar and renew it even if you haven't a specific trip planned.

The occasional traveler who turns back in tears from the airport for lack of a valid passport is more often a veteran who has let the matter slide than a novice off on her first trip.

7. Although your husband can include you and your children on his passport, apply for one of your own—and one for each child, too. It's worth every dollar it costs. Should your husband be called home on business—or should the family have to, or want to, separate—you'll be absolutely stuck if you have a single passport for the family.

8. When you're traveling, your passport is worth more than gold. Don't let it out of your sight. Don't lend it, use it as security, or pack it in your luggage, which can so easily go astray. Occasionally, foreign hotels may want to borrow your passport overnight when they're signing you in; try to get it right back, but don't make a nuisance of yourself. This is the one situation where you *can* give out a passport for a few hours, providing the hotel isn't an obscure caravansary in one of the world's trouble spots. But don't leave the passport in your room when you go off for the day.

9. If the passport should get lost or stolen, *run* to the nearest American consulate, but be forewarned: Losing a passport is a serious business. At the least, it can play havoc with your itinerary, pinning you to one spot for days. (Should you lose your passport while still in the U.S.A., notify the Passport Office, Department of State, Washington, D.C. 20524.)

10. Don't change any information on the passport yourself. If you elope with a handsome Greek, don't write in your married name. Any changes must be made by an agent of the U.S. Government—either in the Passport Office or in the consulate. And though I hardly need say this, your passport is not a toy. Don't doodle, scribble, or write down the name of a "marvelous little restaurant" on its pages—or tear any of them out. If you apply for a new passport to replace one that has been lost, destroyed or mutilated, the Passport Office will require a detailed explanation and make a thorough inquiry into the circumstances. If they are not satisfied with your explantion, the issuance of a new passport may be delayed.

11. Not every foreign country requires that you, an American, present a passport. You don't, for example, need one for Mexico, Bermuda, the Bahamas, Canada, the West Indies, and a number of countries in Central and South America. In many places a simple tourist card issued by the local government will do. (See Visas and Tourist Cards, page 409.)

12. And finally, memorize the number of your passport, its date and place of issuance. You will be asked for these facts so many times

as you travel that it will be a nuisance to keep fumbling and groping for the passport itself. Learn these details or Scotch-tape the figures on the inside of your handbag, or write them on a handy piece of paper.

Pensions and "P.G.'s"

IF YOUR travel budget is Lilliputian or if you just like the warmth of a small, family-run hotel, you will enjoy a pension. This word, originally French and retaining its French pronunciation, means "boardinghouse." Equivalents in other languages are *pensjonater*, *pensional*, *pensione*, and *privaat hotelle*.

Pensions vary greatly in degree of luxury, atmosphere, and quality of service. At one end of the scale are villas in Florence, where college girls will be carefully chaperoned; at the other are seedy, slovenly houses near railroad stations that take transients. Pensions are less expensive than commercial hotels and almost all require that you take three meals a day under their roofs. (There are some places that insist only on breakfast, others on two meals a day, but most established pensions expect you to enjoy—or at least pay for—full board as well as bed.)

In pensions you live according to the rules and personalities of the owners. Meals are served at precisely specified hours, and, as in someone's home, the menu is table d'hôte, i.e., "a meal of prearranged courses served at a fixed time." (The expression "table d'hôte" means, literally, "the host's table.") Few pensions have liquor licenses and nearly all good ones require that you stay a prescribed length of time such as 3 days or a week.

The big advantage of pensions is their often staggeringly low rates. You can pay as little as $2 a day for a room and three meals in Portugal. The going rate throughout Europe is about $4.50 a day; the top price is in the neighborhood of $10. In Italy and France, countries rich in pensions, this will command a first-class room, probably with a private bath. In fact, a first-class pension in Italy is often pleasanter than a second-class hotel.

The other advantages of these lodgings are the quiet atmosphere, the ease with which a woman traveling alone can meet people, the cozy feeling of being *en famille* (Monsieur and Madame les Patrons are often helpful in a dozen different ways), and the solution to the problem of dining alone.

Their drawbacks on the other hand are directly connected to their blessings. Pensions traditionally attract students (Paris's Latin Quarter is filled with these hotels) and older people who are watching their sous. You may be thrown into the company of people with whom you have little in common. The fixed meals, while comforting, tend to be confining: If you are already paying for two or three meals a day, you may be reluctant to seek out a variety of restaurants and cuisines. If you are attracted by the throb of big-city life or want the freedom to come and go at all hours, pensions won't do. While they provide basic needs of food and shelter, they offer no social or sports programs, and finally, they have only the most modest physical facilities. There is often just one telephone to a floor, if that, and few bathrooms. In Copenhagen, for example, one pension of 45 beds has only 5 bathrooms.

In cities, distinctions between commercial hotels and pensions are easy to draw. In the country, the differences are more subtle. Both small country hotels and pensions offer regional atmosphere and cooking. But while a hotel may serve luncheon between 12:30 and 2 P.M., a pension might fix the hour precisely at 1 P.M., as a family would, since all the guests sit down together. A hotel's menu may offer a choice of dishes; a pension's would not. A hotel's atmosphere may be lively with coming and going. A pension is quieter—its guests stay for longer periods.

You can also find inexpensive accommodations with a foreign family as a "P.G.," the current euphemism for "Paying Guest." For prices that range from $18 to $55 a week, you receive food, lodging and a variable assortment of "extras," depending on your hosts. You live with the family, share its table, meet its friends. Your visit can last from a few days to a few months, any time of the year. The summer months and Easter, however, being holidays, are the most popular times. If you plan to be a P.G. then, you should make your reservations well in advance.

In France a paying guest may bask in an atmosphere of patented nobility. You can stay in any one of some 70 medieval and Renaissance châteaux and dine with the Marquis or Count who owns it. The owners of these châteaux have joined together in a group called the *Organisation de Séjours en Châteaux* or O.R.S.E.C., 40 Rue Fabert, Paris 7ᵉ, in an effort to meet tightening taxes on mansions. You can choose from three classes, and charges go from $4 to $32 per person, per day, for room, all meals, and *service*, with most prices falling between $8 and $12 a day.

In England, Take-A-Guide Ltd. (11 Old Bond Street, London, W. 1) will arrange for you to stay in one of a number of handsome and historic country homes and castles. You might choose an Elizabethan house or a medieval Scottish castle. Prices range from $33 to $54 a day for two and cover practically everything (including a certain amount to drink) except lunch.

In Turkey, an organization called Emirgan Guest Houses in the suburbs of Istanbul arranges for you to stay in select Turkish homes (each has a view of the sea and is clean and attractive) for about $4 a night, which includes bed and breakfast. Write to Emirgan Guest Houses, Değirmentepe No. 1, Emirgan, Istanbul.

Some countries have compiled lists of families that take P.G.'s, and these are usually available through national tourist offices.

Other good sources of P.G. host families are:

1. The hotel booking or tourist information services in foreign cities, such as Paris's Welcome Information Office (Accueil de France). The disadvantage of using them is that you must already be abroad when you make the arrangements.

2. Local tourist offices.

3. Religious organizations.

4. Student groups. These are so numerous that most universities can provide their students with a long list. See or write to the dean in charge of student lodgings.

5. The large number of good P.G. agencies in London. The British, who have always been intrepid travelers, have been P.G.'s in their own country and on the Continent for years. They have established several reliable agencies that set up all arrangements; these include the following:

Educational Touring Service, 10 Exhibition Road, London S.W.7

En Famille Agency, 1 New Burlington Street, London W.1

Family Friendships Service, 46 Muswell Hill Road, London N.10

Elsie M. Jackson, 110 Gloucester Place, London W.1

Lion and Unicorn Service, Ltd., 9 Western Avenue, Bournemouth, Hampshire

Gordon McGregor Ltd., 26 Brunswick Square, Hove, Sussex

The Mostyn Bureau, 52 Beauchamp Place, London S.W.3, and 19 Beaumont Street, Oxford, Oxfordshire

Scanbrit Ltd., 34 Gloucester Gardens, London W.2 (to age 25 only)

Universal Aunts Ltd., 61 Wilton Place, London W.1

There is also the official Non-commercial Accommodation Service, 64 St. James's Street, London S.W.1. (This lists London homes that take paying guests from overseas.)

6. Greece has a particularly inviting Village Guest House Program which makes it possible to stay in a simple room in a private house in a remote village—in the mountains or by the sea—for about 60 cents a day, excluding food. You can stay as long as you like. Further information can be had from the Greek Youth Hostel Association, 4 Dragatsaniou Street, Athens.

If pensions or paying-guest arrangements interest you, write to the tourist offices listed in the section beginning on page 479. Some countries have good lists, others do not; Italy's, for one, is excellent and classifies its pensions in two grades. Consider only well-recommended places; if a tourist office does not know of any, it will tell you how to find one.

Personal Products

EVEN WOMEN who are normally level-headed about snakes, how much to tip a mahout or what to do for impetigo, find themselves at a loss about how much to pack in the way of personal products, the beauty industry's euphemism for sanitary napkins et al. I still remember a traveling companion on a trip to Europe who filled one of her two suitcases with boxes of Kotex because she was sure she'd never find any abroad.

Her apprehension belonged to the era of steamer trunks, motoring veils, and 10-day ocean crossings. Today, American products such as Kotex and Tampax are found in nearly every major country of the world. You have only to walk into a large, centrally located drugstore to find them.

Tampax is distributed in the familiar blue box in more than 100 countries. The only ones in which you will not find it are Afghanistan, countries behind the Iron Curtain, South America (this is because of import duty), Borneo, Formosa, Egypt, Guinea, India, Indonesia, Laos, Turkey, Vietnam, the U.S.S.R., and Yemen. Kotex is so widely dispersed that the only places you can't buy it are New Zealand, Turkey, Brazil, India, Russia, Pakistan and Germany, as of this writing. In these countries, a comparable local product is available.

Both Kotex and Tampax will cost you a few cents more abroad than they do here, except in countries where they're manufactured, such as England.

These two well-known brands are mentioned because in matters like this the easy, familiar solution seems to be the smartest one. Since both these products have wide distribution throughout the world, as well as clearly recognizable brand names (you have to spell them out with pencil and paper in a pinch—to foreign ears, Kotex can sound much like Cutex), you can be sure of what you're getting.

There are some local variations you may want to know about: In England, sanitary napkins are called sanitary towels, and have loops at either end. As these are exported to several countries in the world, you may run into them from time to time. In French, they're called *garnitures périodiques;* in Spanish, they're *toallas sanitarias* or *higiénicas;* in German, *damenbinden;* in Italian, *assorbenti igienici;* in Swedish, *sanitets bindan;* in Japanese *seiritai.* With these languages at your command, you can manage anywhere should an "English-speaking" pharmacy be unavailable, or should the chambermaid in your hotel not speak English. (If a sudden need arises, she's the one to ring for.)

Japan is a case unto itself. Its women are extremely reticent about menstruation and wear a menstrual pantie that is quite unfamiliar to Westerners. Kotex has just been introduced into the country, however, so you need only go to a large pharmacy in, say, Tokyo, to find it.

If you'd like to start out armed with some sort of protection, Kotex puts out a box of individually wrapped napkins—eight for 39 cents—that's fine for traveling. Or break up a larger box, wrap each napkin in Kleenex and stuff it into corners of your suitcase or among the layers of your underwear. (In planes, of course, there's an ample supply of these items always available in the washrooms.)

Don't be embarrassed or have nightmares about going through customs (which does happen to young women going abroad for the first time) with Kotex or Tampax in your luggage. You can be sure that the officials are thoroughly familiar with these products and won't even give them a passing glance.

Photography

ABOUT TWO thirds of the 3,000,000 Americans who traveled out of the country last year took their cameras with them. Who knows how many millions more saw slides of their particular views of the Parthenon, the Little Mermaid, and the tombs on the Appian Way? Since it is the rare traveler who would return with *no* photographic souvenirs, some words on equipment and picture-taking are in order here.

First, of course, *don't* weigh yourself down with pounds of equipment that will have you dragging after fifteen minutes in the warm Italian sun, and *don't* carry complicated gadgets that will start your friends, other tourists and the locals drumming their fingers while you twirl dials, test the light, and peer through telephoto lenses. Your memories will be far rosier if you *see* the world, rather than busy yourself with shots of it.

If you are in the market for a new camera, look for one of the recently developed automatic ones such as Kodak's Instamatic, Agfa's Isoflash-Rapid, Yashica's EZ-Matic, or Ansco's Anscomatic that are particularly good for non-camera-minded women. They're so extraordinarily easy to use that there's no fumbling with equipment, no worry about results. Kodak's Instamatic, for example, is only 4 inches long, can be loaded simply by slipping a film cartridge in the back. Furthermore, it uses the new flashcube which permits four flash exposures, and advances film after every shot so that double exposures are impossible. Some models adjust automatically to all light conditions, so that they work as well on a misty side street as in a blazing plaza at midday. As the quality of light varies enormously from place to place, the semi-automatic adjustment of the camera is a particular boon. In sum, it's simpler than the old box Brownie but a good deal more versatile. There are also a number of easy-to-use movie cameras which load instantly and automatically. Various models range in price from about $50 to over $250. An experienced photographer might find these new cameras too amateurish, but they have the enormous advantage of being inconspicuous, handy, and absolutely fuss-free.

The Polaroid camera too is easy to operate—and often, because of its unusual character, a quick means of making friends. Your pictures are developed on the spot, and while its film is more expensive than other kinds, you are saved the bother of having it developed. (If you paste your Polaroid results on postcard backs, you can mail home your personal picture postcards.)

If you are using a more complicated camera, what other equipment will you need? Perhaps a yellow filter (to bring out clouds), flash-bulbs (you can buy them abroad, but like film they are cheaper at home and easy to pack), a close-up attachment if your camera doesn't have one built in. You should certainly take a lens hood to keep on your camera all the time you're using it to guard against glare and a skylight filter which warms the color on a gray day. Leave your tripod home. It is more trouble than it's worth: In some places you'll need special permission to use one, and it is a nuisance to carry. If you need a slow exposure, you can often find a parapet or post to rest the camera on, or press the camera firmly against your cheek or body, and hold your breath. Be sure to carry enough color film to last you through the trip; though you can buy film almost anywhere, it's definitely more expensive abroad. Rolls of film tuck nicely into odd corners when you pack. Kodak Verichrome Pan Film is the best black-and-white film for a simple camera, Kodak's Plus-X or Tri-X film for the high-speed type. The new color films are considerably more sensitive than they were in the past. You don't need sunny days to get results, and you can take excellent color pictures without an expensive complicated camera. Try such films as Kodak's Ekta-chrome-X, Kodachrome-X, or Kodachrome II with adjustable cameras. When the light becomes very dim or the action extremely fast, 35-mm. camera users can call on such fast film as Kodak High Speed Ektachrome or Ansco's Anscochrome 200. If you prefer prints to slides, the film to use is Kodacolor-X.

Whatever film you buy, treat it right. This means first of all keeping it cool. When driving keep your camera on the seat beside you, not in the oven of the glove compartment. Don't travel around with exposed film. While you can have it developed abroad, the time it takes, the quality of the work and the prices vary greatly. It is a better idea to airmail it to the U.S.A. as soon as possible, though up to a 25-day wait is safe. Any film made in America will be admitted duty free if you mail it to yourself at your home address, to a processing firm for developing, to the original manufacturer or to a dealer. You should mail it in the prepaid processing mailer; if not, mark the package something like this: EXPOSED FILM (OF U.S. MANUFACTURE)

FOR PROCESSING, NOT FOR ANY COMMERCIAL PURPOSES WHATSOEVER. In any case, it is nice to come home and find your pictures waiting for you.

Before you start on your trip, shoot *at least* one roll of film if you haven't used your camera before, under as wide a variety of conditions as possible. Then you will be at home with the camera and can avoid simple mistakes. One more precaution before departing: If your camera is foreign-made, either carry with you a bill of sale or insurance policy, or register it before you leave with the U.S. Customs inspector, who will give you a certificate. This constitutes proof that you didn't buy the camera abroad and will save your paying duty needlessly when you return. You won't have trouble with your camera in foreign customs. Some countries limit you to one still and one movie camera, without duty, but they seldom object to two still cameras of different sizes. If you plan to take more than these, you had better check how many cameras the countries on your list will allow you to bring in.

No matter what equipment you take along, it is the photographer that makes the difference between a routine and a good picture. If all you want is a record of monuments and views, you will be much better off buying the superb postcards and color slides available at every hotel newsstand. What they leave out is the personal element, the photographer's good fortune in catching the moment when a passing stranger brings a dead street to life. Henri Cartier-Bresson calls it "The Decisive Moment," which is the title of a fine book of his photographs of Europe and Asia taken over the past 30 years. You will, of course, want to include pictures of people you meet, and of yourself; these are often the most fun to look at when you're home.

Here are some general rules for posing and composing photographs:

1. You will get the best results with black-and-white during midmorning or midafternoon, when shadows offer contrast but are not overpowering. Work with the shadows in terms of design and composition. For color, a lightly overcast day will prove more successful than a bright one: The lack of shadows gives you softer, more luminous color. Don't take pictures at high noon; and in bright sunshine, try to have the light behind you or at an angle. While overhead light is unflattering to the subject, we all squint when directly facing the light. A flash is often useful out of doors. Where brilliant sunshine may cast heavy shadows into a face, the flash softens and lightens them.

2. When you're posing yourself or photographing a friend, shun

the police lineup position—a flat-footed stance with face staring directly into the camera. A three-quarter view is more professional and flattering.

3. Don't just stand there—do something. Be photographed buying violets from a pushcart vendor, feeding the ducks in the pond, or trying on straw hats in the public market.

4. In a full-face photograph, you can avoid a staring look by focusing your eyes on a spot over the photographer's shoulder.

5. Stand and sit gracefully. When seated, keep both legs together and slant them across the front of the chair; standing, place the tip of one foot slightly in front of the other.

6. If you take a picture of something moving, it should be coming toward you rather than crossing your field of vision. Crowds passing a building should be walking into the picture, not out of it.

7. If you are taking a picture of some gorgeous view or architectural masterpiece, make it you own—while at the same time giving it scale and life—by placing a person in the foreground.

8. Before you take a picture, stop to look around and sense the special atmosphere of the place. Enjoy the scene—then shoot. Let your photographs communicate your own pleasure.

9. While it may seem obvious—don't forget to remove the lens cap of your camera. Many people shoot entire rolls of film without remembering to take it off.

Finally a word about camera manners: Probably nothing has done more to damage the image of the American traveler—who actually is one of the best-mannered in the world today, despite reputation—than the disgraceful bad manners of that minority who hold up tours by stopping for camera shots, take pictures of passersby without a by-your-leave or, when they do ask permission, do it abruptly. At the height of the season the residents are continually solicited to pose and it is little wonder they get tired of it. If you must ask for a pose, do it with great courtesy, and unless the person is your social equal, offer compensation. (This does *not* apply in Japan, where a tip would give offense and thanks are all that are wanted.) If your subject asks for a copy of the picture, take his name and address and remember to send it to him.

While courtesy is essential everywhere, some countries have special taboos. In many southern countries, especially in the rural districts, older people regard the camera as the evil eye. In Morocco when you take a person's picture, you are stealing part of his spirit and have him in your power, which explains why no Moroccan mother will let you photograph her child. In Greece they don't like you to take pictures of unrepaired bomb or earthquake damage, and it is considered bad taste to photograph scenes of poverty, distress or grief. In rural Holland, pictures must not be taken on Sundays. Asking to take pictures of anyone not a personal friend is deemed rude in Denmark. Consult your concierge for further taboos.

Beside local attitudes and customs, there are official regulations that vary from country to country. In Britain you will need special permission to photograph a variety of things, ranging from footways to the Changing of the Guard, if you use a tripod. At Covent Garden permission is needed to take pictures even with a hand-held camera. You may not take pictures in Vienna's Spanish Riding School. In France pictures may not be taken in museums with a flash attachment—but since this is work for skilled professionals, and the reproductions available for a few cents are of superb quality, you'd be silly to try. In Italy flash attachments cannot be used in museums or private galleries; more surprisingly, it's a penal offense to photograph anyone without his consent (except public personalities). Italian policemen on duty are off limits to photographers. In Spain, you can't take pictures at national monuments or in a museum without permission, and no close-ups of what goes on in Spanish bullrings are allowed without consent of the management. Military installations may not be photographed in many parts of the world. No photographs may be taken inside mosques, and in Russia you must get permission to take pictures in art galleries, museums, airports, and railroad stations.

A camera can do a great deal to add purpose and pleasure to your sightseeing, but use it thoughtfully and sparingly. Photographs reinforce memory, but they must not be allowed to take over its function.

Pubs and Bars

NOTHING IS SO unnerving to even a thoroughly self-possessed woman as the prospect of going into a bar alone. And in the course of her travels, shyness will be compounded by confusion. For, depending on the country, she will be allowed in a bar with a man (of course), with a woman (sometimes), or by herself (sometimes, but not in all bars and not at all hours).

Pubs, bars, bar lounges, beer gardens, *cafés, cafetines, estaminets, tavernas, pulquerías, heurigen, sakabas, café bars, eafé terrasses, bares, mesones, tabernas* are some of the havens where men gather to drink. Until a generation ago, they were strictly male preserves. Now women are welcome, and whether you come for a sherry, a Scotch, or half a bitter, or largely for a draught of local color, you can be quite at ease if you follow a few ground rules:

Two women can go nearly everywhere; and, given the correct combination of place, time, drink and atmosphere, a woman can also go alone. Just remember that north of the Alps, customs are much like those in the U.S.A., in Scandinavia probably even more relaxed; and that south of them—in countries that are strongly Catholic—a much stricter view is taken of women's comings and goings. With a man, of course, practically no bar is off limits, although some places are so ominous that even a man wouldn't feel comfortable. (Never stand at a bar or sit on a bar stool unless you are with a man.)

But a woman is *not* welcome, alone or otherwise, in places where paid hostesses provide feminine company. In Japan, for example, a country rich in bars as well as the traditions of making a man comfortable outside his home, you would not be welcome at *sakabas* with hostesses even if you had a man at each elbow. *Sakabas* without professional female companionship, however, are fine.

The specifics that govern the where, when, what and how of your drinking abroad are:

THE SIZE AND SOPHISTICATION OF A CITY. The smaller the city, the less welcome are women at bars. In small towns, stay away from public bars altogether. While in England, for example, you may have a gin-and-tonic at London's Connaught Hotel or stop for a lager at a pub like the King's Head and Eight Bells. If you were to walk into the public bar of a country tavern in Lincolnshire, you would stop the dart game cold. (They won't ask you to leave; you will just be made to feel extremely uncomfortable.)

THE ATMOSPHERE OF A BAR. The more *al fresco* the bar, the better. Some, like the outdoor pubs of London, have such a healthy, innocent air that whole families go there. Other open areas such as rooftop bars in hotels and sidewalk cafés are certainly within bounds. And nothing could be more peaceful than watching the lights go on over Mexico City from the roof of the Bamer Hotel or seeing the sunset deepen over London from the bar of the London Hilton while sipping a drink. Even young Spanish girls—usually guarded like jewels—gather in flocks on Sundays, at noon and dusk, on the terraces along Serrano Street in Madrid; they are gay, dressed in Sunday best, filled with chatter, and seemingly impervious to the hot glances of prospective suitors. If a bar is indoors but big and well-lighted, you can include it on your list. Women alone—or with other women—should avoid any place that is small, dark and hidden.

THE NEIGHBORHOOD. Keep away from places that are obviously for the rough trade and don't explore waterfront bars in such cities as Amsterdam, Rotterdam or Genoa. Even if you are in a group six women strong, you will be asking for trouble. If you stay in a neighborhood for a while, you can treat the district pub or *bistro* as your own. London, for example, is a patchwork of villages and each neighborhood has its favorite pub. If one is near your hotel, you can use it as the locals do—and drop in whenever it's open.

THE HOUR YOU VISIT A BAR. Behavior that is perfectly acceptable at 6 o'clock may be all wrong after dark. Europeans make even more of pre-luncheon or dinner socializing than Americans. They love to escape out of doors, to sit at a café in the sun or under the cool greenness of trees on their way home from their offices. A sidewalk café at 7 in summer will be crowded with nice people exchanging gossip, but if you sit there at 10, your presence may be misunderstood.

YOUR DRINK. In southern European countries, since even the men don't drink much hard liquor, you might cause raised eyebrows if you do. Order sherry, wine, beer or vermouth. (In France and Italy, a "martini" may turn out to be merely vermouth with lemon peel.)
Outside the U.S.A., you will find fewer strictly alcoholic bars. Abroad, many serve coffee, soft drinks, ice cream, or light food. Any place which does serve food is fine for women alone. At the cafés along Rome's Via Veneto, you will see more coffee than cocktails. In most British pubs, you can have a light, inexpensive lunch.

YOUR HOTEL. At a resort hotel (or on a ship) you can use the bar as freely as the swimming pool. On palmy islands, stay away from the natives' haunts unless you are with a man. It is easier to sit alone in the cocktail lounge of a small hotel, where you will feel comfortable and relaxed, than of a big cosmopolitan hotel like the Excelsior in Rome or the George V in Paris. Even in such hotels it is not difficult if you get settled before the crowd arrives. Of course, if you are with another woman, the picture changes and you can drink and gossip to your heart's content.

Britain's 60,000 pubs are such a special case that they call for separate discussion. There are some in London today whose associations go back to Elizabethan days, and many are charmingly atmospheric with Tudor beams, oak paneling, polished brass, cut and engraved glass windows and mirrors, soft leather. Some have gardens or sit beside the Thames. While outdoor cafés have been enchanting visitors to the Continent for years, pubs have only recently begun to move into the fresh air. In London, there are charming garden pubs where you can talk, laze, sip your drink and eat a light meal. The Scarsdale, the Swan Inn, the City Barge, the London Apprentice, the Black Lion, and the familiar and still popular Prospect of Whitby are among the most fashionable at the moment. But the list could go on and on, for London is peppered with pubs, and, as with glove shops in Paris, every traveler has her favorites.

Pubs are usually open between 11 A.M. and 3 P.M. and then from 5:30 in the afternoon to 11 at night. They are most comfortable for two women or a woman alone at noontime or at dusk. The standard pub drink is "half a bitter," which is ten ounces of bitter beer or about a shilling's worth; you can also have ale; half-and-half (a mixture of mild ale and bitter beer); or lager, the closest thing to American beer. Of course, if you prefer sherry, Scotch or gin, you can have them, too. There are two parts to a pub: the public bar where workingmen gather, and the private "saloon" bar for the tweedy crowd. Women go only to the saloon bar. Since Englishmen use pubs as escape hatches, they have embellished them with classic games such as darts, dominoes, cribbage, billiards or shove-ha'penny, a game in which a small coin is shoved with one finger and score is kept more or less as in shuffleboard. In Ireland, there are singing pubs in which people in the crowd perform.

Two final points: Licensing laws have as many variations as snowflakes. In some countries bars stay open all day; in others only part of the day. Sunday hours are tricky. As at home, the whole day may be completely "dry."

In countries that don't allow their women much freedom, don't flaunt yours. The world has, however, developed a double standard of behavior—one for tourists, the other for locals. Two Portuguese women, for example, would go to a coffeeshop rather than a bar, but no Portuguese will lift an eyebrow if you and your traveling companion have an alcoholic drink in the cocktail lounge of your hotel. "When in Rome," you needn't do as the Romans do. You can usually do what pleases you, if you do it decorously—but when it comes to pubs and bars, you must do it strictly by the rules.

See also Sidewalk Cafés, page 330.

Renting a House Abroad

UNTIL RECENT years, if you wanted to rent a house abroad, you needed the shrewdness of a Philadelphia lawyer, the linguistic skill of a U.N. interpreter—or lots of money. The notion of a villa on the Riviera was pure romance, out there with dreams of Mainbocher clothes and Bentleys. These days, four secretaries rent a villa at Cap d'Antibes for $270 for two weeks (split four ways, it comes to $33.75 per girl, per week); a high-school teacher, her husband and three sons take a break in their European itinerary at a small house in Spain (a week's stay: $75 for the family); and an insurance broker and his wife spend a winter week in a cottage in Ocho Rios, Jamaica, for $150.

The idea of renting a house for your vacation is comparatively new, but it has an assured future. You can rent a log cabin in Norway, a ski chalet in Austria, a *palazzo* in Venice, an apartment in Rome, a private beach in Barbados, a castle on the sea in Tangier, a hunting lodge in Scotland, a windswept cottage in Brittany, a farmhouse in Bavaria, a mansion on Lake Maggiore, or a whitewashed village house in Corfu—where, if you are feeling lazy, you can dine on your own little terrace, watching the lights around the curve of the harbor. Majorca, Ibiza, Costa del Sol, Costa de Oro, Brittany, the French Riviera, Malta, Athens, Corfu, Hydra, the Costa Brava, Biarritz, Tuscany, Salzburg, the Italian Riviera, the Adriatic Coast, the Austrian Tyrol, Cuernavaca, Acapulco, Montego Bay, St. Croix—these are among the heady places where you can rent a house with a flowered patio, a strip of beach, a mountain view, a sense of freedom.

The term "villa," which has such a grand ring to American ears, is defined by the rental agencies as "an independent property usually detached and standing in its own ground, built primarily for holiday purposes." It's used generically in correspondence especially among the British to cover any vacation house; castles, cabins, cottages, chalets and the like are often described as "villas." A villa, in sum, is any home-away-from-home rented for a short period.

The advantages of villa vacations are fairly obvious:

FREEDOM, PRIVACY AND SPACE. Also the comfort of coming and going on your own, of having grounds for your children to play in, of a life unregulated by the demands of a hotel. There's no "But I am sorry, Madame, the dining room is closed now."

SAVINGS IN MONEY. The least expensive way to see a country is from the home base of a rented house. You can count roughly on a villa's costing you less than half the price of hotel living. The more people who are in the group, the more money is saved. If you are traveling with children, the savings are considerable. While hotels charge so much for each person, the price of a villa is fixed, and includes everyone in your party. Food costs comparatively little. In Spain, admittedly an inexpensive country, you can eat and drink well for $6 a week, per person. If you try the local restaurant, there are no pangs of conscience because you are missing a meal at the hotel for which you have paid. If you want to entertain, there are no heavy bar bills.

STABILITY. This is important when you are traveling with children. You unpack just once and sleep in the same bed several nights in a row, no matter how far afield you may wander during the days. It is easier to cope with day-to-day problems, like finding pasteurized milk or a good pediatrician, when the family has one base.

A CLOSE LOOK AT LOCAL LIFE. The local inhabitants are your neighbors, not fleeting faces on a street. The market is the place where you shop for food, not just a bit of "local color" you record with your camera.

Prices for villas range from $25 a week (some are even lower in the off season) up to $6,000 a month. An elaborate house in Jamaica in the winter season may cost $2,000 for a month; in Majorca in the summer, $1,000 for a week. For such prices you get your own swimming pool, mooring for boats, and six servants. Most of the properties for rent, however, are reasonable by our standards. You can have a villa that sleeps five on Corfu for $60 a week, which comes to $12 a person, or less than $2 a night for each. (In general the lowest price you should count on is about $10 per person, per week; a fair average is $18.50 per person, per week.) For $156 for two weeks ($310 in peak season), you can rent a villa that sleeps eight on the Costa Brava or in Torremolinos, Spain. A country villa in Biarritz for six is $150 ($230 a week in peak season). A cottage in Brittany sleeping seven costs $170 a week ($225 in peak season); one in a pretty village in Cornwall is $250 ($380 in peak season).

Rents depend on the area and the type of house, but most of all on the season. Generally, the shorter the high season, the steeper the rents—they may go up 50 to 60 per cent. Also, the more southern and sunny the area, the higher the price. For example, Adriatic Italy is distinctly cheaper than Mediterranean Italy. Villas around the Mediterranean are more expensive than those in northern Europe.

In Europe the year is divided neatly into three seasons: low, October through May; midseason, June and September; and high, July and August. If you plan to stay more than 4 weeks, the price is usually reduced anywhere from 5 to 10 per cent. In many cases, if you book your property and pay in full before March 1, you get a discount of 10 per cent.

August is the most popular vacation time in Europe, as it is in the States. In Switzerland and Austria, chalets are generally more expensive during the winter for mountain resorts, and during the summer for lake resorts, with fall and spring lower in both. If you want a villa in Europe for the high season or a house in the West Indies during the winter season, you must book it 6 months in advance. Since Europeans on their own continent face the same summer house-rental problems that you do, the earlier you begin your investigations, the better your choices. It's not unusual for good properties to be booked even farther ahead. For example, chalets in Switzerland will be rented a year in advance for July, August, the Christmas and New Year's holidays, February and March.

The total fee includes all the necessities: furniture, bedding, linens, glassware, china, cutlery, and cooking utensils. Most times the charges for electricity, gas and water are also included; sometimes they are separate. (Watch the charge for utilities; they run high in Europe, often as much as $50 a month.) Also, many rentals in Europe include the services of a part-time maid who comes in 2 to 4 hours a day to clean, make beds, wash dishes and do laundry. If you like, and are willing to pay a little extra for it, she will cook one main meal a day, do the marketing (she's apt to know her way around the market better than you) and even baby-sit. If her wages are not part of the rent, count on paying anywhere from 16 to 70 cents an hour. The rental agency can usually line up household help for you. Some rentals also include the use of a car or boat.

A reputable agency will arrange to have you met and taken to your villa, which of course will have been cleaned before your arrival. You'll be given maps of the area, in some cases a bilingual marketing list and the name of a local representative to call upon if problems arise. If you arrange for it in advance, the agency will see that your larder is stocked with food and drink on your arrival. If you want a full-time nanny, she will cost you about $35 a week extra in Europe, less in other places.

You can rent a villa from one week to several months; the most common rental period in Europe is two weeks or multiples of two weeks. The sleeping capacities of European villas range from 2 to 50 people—but you may bring only as many persons as there are beds. If you rent a villa with six beds, and show up with a party of ten, you may all end up sleeping in the street.

An established, reputable agency assures you that the villas it offers have been searched for, visited and inspected by one of its staff, that each house is well furnished and comfortable, centrally heated where the climate demands it, has hot and cold water, sufficient kitchen equipment and utensils, electricity or gas for cooking, at least one bathroom with bath or shower, a flush toilet, electric lights and outlets. The extras for which you pay are telephone calls, tourist taxes, final cleaning and sometimes utilities.

If you want to arrange for a villa through an established rental agency, write for its brochure, which is often a large, handsome volume describing available properties. If you see something you are absolutely sure you want, you can fill out the booking form then and there, and return it with a deposit. If you don't, send the agency your requirements; actually this is the safer method. Tell them where you want to go and when, how much you want to spend, how many beds you need, the ages of your children, how close you must be to the beach, and other relevant facts. The agency will analyze your needs and make specific recommendations, sending along photographs and fact sheets on the places they believe will best suit you. If you find one you like, return the booking form with a deposit and send a down payment of half the house's rental, when its availability has been confirmed; you pay the other half, as a rule, shortly before leaving this country or taking possession of the house. Normally, you can order a house as easily as you would order stationery.

The above outlines in general the way the agencies work; there may be some minor operational differences among them.

It's enormously useful to cover your agency arrangements with "cancelation insurance." Should one of your children develop measles just before you're due to leave, forcing you to cancel your reservation, the insurance company will pay your full commitment to the agency and your deposit will be refunded. Otherwise, your money cannot be recovered.

Also, you will be asked to make a small "damage deposit" or inventory charge. This is to cover any breakage of china, furniture and the like. If there is none, or if you replace the breakages, the deposit is returned to you in full; if there is some damage, the amount is deducted by the landlord from the deposit.

Should you decide to rent a villa, remember that there will probably be some minor difficulties; but while facing them, remember too that a European would have to make just as great an adjustment to your house as you will to his. Here are the things to watch out for:

1. Europeans seem to be satisfied with 40-watt bulbs, as a rule, which shed a rather gloomy light to American eyes. So lay in a supply of brighter bulbs when you arrive.

2. Americans and Europeans have different ideas about bath towels. Those provided are not likely to be as numerous or large as what you may be used to, so be prepared either to put up with this or bring several from home. Also, Europeans supply muslin sheets, which are scratchier than our percale. If this matters to you, take some of your own.

3. Hot water tanks are often inadequate, even in the best houses. Although there is enough hot water to supply ordinary needs, don't count on your family's being able to take a quick succession of hot baths.

4. Your landlord may have stripped the house bare of *objets d'art* (you'd probably do the same) so fill the emptiness with fresh flowers from the local market as soon as you arrive.

5. European landlords take an inventory of everything they leave for their tenants, including the Woolworth glasses. No need to be offended: you'll find it's as much protection to you as them.

6. Don't expect the local European shopkeeper to be overjoyed at your presenting him with a personal check drawn on your home bank, no matter how many feet of credit cards you carry in your wallet. Pay for everything, including the rent, with travelers checks or cash.

7. If you have young children, ask the rental agency about such details as the flow of traffic outside the house; banisters on the stairs; how far the house is from the water; whether there is a guardrail around the terrace, etc. A good rental agency will have definite answers to these questions.

8. If you deal with a foreign rental agency, remember that their idea of "luxe" and "modest" may be different from yours. What is considered comfortable by many Europeans would be termed "roughing it" by Americans. Our housing standards are the highest in the world, so don't expect too much from "a villa on the Riviera." Villas are usually summer pieds-à-terre; they are built and furnished for light summer housekeeping.

9. Don't go after something "picturesque" at all costs. It may have a marvelous view—and be lacking in electricity, hot water, stove, refrigerator, shower and bath, all of which can cancel the pleasure of any view in two days.

10. If you deal with a foreign rental agency, be sure to send all correspondence *air mail*.

Since, in renting a villa, all affairs are handled by mail or telephone, a great deal must be taken on trust. It's especially important, therefore, to deal with a reputable source. Most people rent houses abroad without ever seeing the agency, let alone the property itself.

Here are the leading American sources for renting a house abroad:

1. International Villas and Yachts, Inc., 28 Church Street, Cambridge, Massachusetts 02138; telephone UN 8-0500.

2. At Home Abroad, Inc., 136 East 57th Street, New York, New York 10022; telephone HA 1-9165.

3. Wakefield Fortune Ltd., 15 East 58th Street, New York, New York 10022; telephone MU 8-2671.

Villa renting is so popular in Britain that there are now many specialized agencies in London. Some have formed an organization known as the National Villa Association. Members of this group must conform to certain standards and practices. Since its membership changes from time to time, write to association headquarters for general information: 18 Sackville Street, London W.1. There are also a number of good agencies who do not belong to NVA.

As of this writing, National Villa Association members are:

1. Eurovillas Ltd., 18 Sackville Street, London W.1
2. International Villas Bureau, 16 Devonshire Road, London W.4
3. Mediterranean Villas Ltd., 139 Park Lane, London W.1
4. Renta Residence Ltd., Winterton Hall, Winterton-on-Sea, Norfolk
5. Spanish Villas, 48 Drayton Green Road, Ealing, London W.13
6. Tourist Services Centre, 50 Hillfield Park, London N.10
7. Villamar Vacations, 35 Albemarle Street, London W.1
8. Villas Abroad Ltd., 22 Upper Maudlin Street, Bristol 2

As agencies come and go, be sure to write ahead to verify their addresses and the properties they are handling.

Other agencies are:

The American Automobile Association which lists about 70 chalets in Switzerland.

Your travel agent: He will work with an agency or local realtors to ferret out the property you need.

Should you be hardy enough to undertake making all the arrangements on your own, or should you be going to a place not normally handled by villa renting agencies, write to the government tourist offices. (See page 479.) They will direct you to real estate agents or rental services that deal with foreigners in their country. They may even be able to send you a list of properties available for rental, or they will turn you over to local tourist offices who have this information.

You might also consider arranging a swap with some local resident. You could run an advertisement in the newspaper of the area in which you are interested, giving the details of your property and describing what you want. There are also agencies that serve as go-betweens, among them the Vacation Exchange Club, Inc., 550 Fifth Avenue, New York, New York 10036, directed by Mrs. David Ostroff.

For a modest fee, members of the club can place a small ad in the club's directory. They describe their homes and list what they would like in exchange. Interested subscribers answer the ad directly and work out the details of the arrangements through an exchange of letters. The Holiday Home Exchange Bureau, P.O. Box 555, Grants,

New Mexico 87020, run by Mrs. Gordon McMillan, and the Vacation Home Exchange, Inc., Box 46, Old Greenwich, Connecticut, are two other go-between agencies.

If you should be interested in sharing a flat in London with someone of similar age and background, Share-A-Flat Ltd., 175 Piccadilly, London W.1, will undertake to find what you want.

Above all, remember that what contributes most to your pleasure is your attitude. Other people live differently from Americans, which is why you're going abroad in the first place. Accept the differences instead of fighting them, and you'll find that living away from home like a native can be tremendously enriching for you and your family.

Resort Clothes

FROM YOUR current vantage point, all ski resorts blanketed in brilliant snow may seem identical, and all balmy islands bathed in sunshine may seem as alike as beads on a string. Don't be deceived.

While their terrains may be similar, their atmospheres can be wildly different. And so too the clothes you should wear. The tailored shirt that's dashing in Bermuda looks dowdy in St. Tropez; diamond earrings are bad taste in Jamaica and good form in Biarritz; the shirtwaist dress that's the backbone of a wardrobe for the Bahamas has as much appeal as a Mother Hubbard on the Greek islands.

Buying the best-looking resort clothes calls for a special kind of savvy and appreciation of subtle local differences. What's right for one island, town or even resort may be slightly wrong a few miles away. A case in point is the Dorado Beach Hotel in Dorado, Puerto Rico. This is a resort that calls for understated clothes: good simple sports clothes by day, and pale, well-bred linens and silks at night. Yet 45 minutes away by car, in the Gold Coast hotels of San Juan, the tempo is faster, the lights brighter, the music louder and the clothes more opulent: A simple sheath, however well cut, worn without a small blaze of jewelry will make you look and feel like a poor relation.

Each resort has its own "look": the fashion lapped up by the locals. In Capri and St. Thomas, it's silk pants and a bright, soft silk shirt after five; on Mykonos, it's cotton pants all day (women just don't wear dresses on this island, Hydra and the smaller islands, even if they do dress more formally on Rhodes and Corfu). But if you wore pants in the evening in the large hotels on Antigua, you would be off key. St. Tropez makes its own strong, uninhibited fashion rules—and you will enjoy your stay more if you go along with them.

Wherever you go, resort clothes are relaxed clothes. Sometimes they are even zany, with sudden fads sweeping over the scene like tropical storms.

Here, then, are some ground rules that will help you fit comfortably into any local resort scene:

1. Whatever your clothes budget for a trip to a resort, save some of it for when you get there.

2. Spend your money at home on clothes whose "engineering" counts, such as bathing suits and shoes. Many of the shops in the West Indies that make wonderful hand-printed fabrics and manufacture their own dresses, shirts and pants, import their bathing suits from the U.S.A.—and raise their prices accordingly. Limit any further home-town buying to clothes that can't fail anywhere—such as classic ski pants for a winter vacation or marvelous prints for a summer one.

3. If there's a duty-free area on your itinerary, save even more of your budget for that. It's a crime to bring a trunkload of clothes to Nassau, for example, where a splendid shop such as Ambrosine on George Street carries Pucci sportswear, Dynasty silks, and other marvelous clothes at prices well below those at home. Also, why bring ski clothes and sweaters to St. Moritz or Cortina d'Ampezzo when we import their local designs to the states? A well-established resort area is likely to abound in shops with good-looking clothes.

4. If you are eager to do most of your shopping at home because you'll be island-hopping or just traveling too fast to do local shopping, then buy the simplest, surest clothes you can find. (There never was an itinerary, however, that didn't allow a woman a gratifying hour or two to find something spectacular.)

5. Remember that formality usually diminishes with the size of your hotel. The smaller and quieter it is, the simpler your clothes can be. On the other hand, the nearer you come to the height of the season, the dressier your clothes should be. Caribbean resorts in winter, for example, call for much more serious dressing than they do in the summer.

6. Expect your resort clothes, especially those for the sun, to mirror the landscape. Where flowers are brilliant and foliage lush, splashy flower prints look wonderful, especially after 5. And they are good travelers, since they don't show creases to the extent that solid-colored fabrics do. Also adjust your color sense to the local lighting. Under a hot sun, wear hot colors—or blazing white. In the Caribbean colors that seem totally incompatible under gray city lights look marvelous together. On these islands nature mixes brilliant colors wildly; the denim and cotton-cord clothes that looked so right in Maine last summer seem totally insipid. A mango-gold hood worn over a shift in bougainvillaea pink looks absolutely right on streets where flowers blaze in every tree and hedge. Let your color sense run a bit wild; it cannot outdo nature. On the moors of Scotland, on the other hand, sweaters and tweed skirts in lavender, green and brown are as natural as scones at teatime; and on the pastel-and-white island of Bermuda, neatly styled silks and linens in soft sherbet colors look harmoniously well-mannered.

Wherever you go, however, the clothes for active sports remain absolutely fixed: for tennis, white shorts and shirt, or a white tennis dress, white wool socks, and white sneakers. For safaris, shooting or fishing, the crispest, neatest regulation clothes you can find. Sailing clothes are determined by the size of the craft. On small boats where you are expected to lend a hand, dungarees, a shirt and sneakers or any other hardy clothes will do; on bigger yachts, wear the country sports clothes you would wear ashore. The one unbreakable rule for all boats: rubber-soled shoes to prevent scratching the deck as well as to avoid slipping.

7. Leave at home: Diamonds, gold and other expensive jewelry, unless you are headed for the seaside and gambling or ski resorts of Europe, in season. In the Caribbean, Hawaii and the Mediterranean islands, one wears jewelry for decoration and color but never for glitter. In these places, too, you can omit furs, gloves, stockings, hats and raincoat.

8. Since dry cleaning is not to be counted on in most resorts, either sunny or snowy, and laundry is sometimes leisurely, travel with sturdy non-mussable fabrics.

9. For snow or sun, take two pairs of sunglasses, so you won't have to do without, should you break or misplace one pair.

10. Wherever local women are wearing a certain "look," you can be sure there's a masterful local craftsman or boutique behind it. On Mykonos, a tailor called Josef runs up the most popular pants; in St. Moritz, Davos and Klosters, skiers besiege Kaltenbrunner, the fa-

mous tailor in Davos Platz as soon as they arrive. Cast a quick eye over the local scene and ask your concierge or hotel manager for the "genius" who is dressing the locals. Then head straight for his atelier. Accustomed to sewing for travelers, these tailors or seamstresses can often turn out custom clothes in a day or two.

Now for some specifics about resort areas you are likely to visit:

SUNNY RESORTS such as those in the West Indies and along the Mediterranean:

Wherever you go, take mostly light cotton and silk dresses, and those that you plan to use for sightseeing should be neat and conservative; sleeveless dresses are acceptable, but that's as far as the bareness should go in the city. For the Riviera in winter, take a few pale, lightweight wools; this part of the world has what we consider early spring weather from November to March, with chilly evenings and days too cool for swimming. No matter where you are, the daytime resort uniform is a pair of well-cut pants and a silk shirt.

Don't take too many pairs of shorts to the Caribbean. Local women live in those simple little shifts that are as good for cocktails as for morning shopping. Their great point is that they are waistless, which is far more comfortable in that weather than anything tucked into a waistband.

At resorts with gambling casinos (such as Cannes and Monte Carlo) or floor-show nightclubs (San Juan and Acapulco), make your appearance at dinner in short summer cocktail clothes that are bare, gala and sophisticated.

Wherever you're going, take one more bathing suit than you think you'll need; one pale cardigan sweater, preferably white; and a slew of soft silk scarves for your head. Leave spike heels at home; and for comfort in a hot climate, forswear clothes made solely of nylon (Dacron-and-cotton blends are fine). Watch weaves and weights: A flat cotton beach coat is better than terry cloth, which can be terribly warm. You will need a carryall for the beach, but you can pick up a jolly basket on the spot (and help local industry along). There are three shoe "musts": one pair of low-heeled shoes for traveling, sightseeing and shopping; one pair of beach sandals, and a pair of white or pale shoes for evening. If there's enough room left, you can pack another pair of daytime shoes. Carry a pale-colored or white coat and take one or two jacketed dresses for the ups and downs of the day's temperatures: coolness morning and evening; warmth, even heat, at midday.

MOUNTAIN RESORTS IN SUMMER: Pack classics—light-weight flannel pants, light-colored woolen sweaters and skirts, silk and linen dresses.

MOUNTAIN RESORTS IN WINTER: Ski and after-ski clothes to get you through the first two or three days—then shop for fill-ins and "extras" on the spot, if you're at a large resort. But if you'll be tucked away in a mountain village with only a single boutique like Portillo, pack everything in the way of equipment, underwear, after-ski boots, pants, sweaters, jackets, a short sports coat, after-ski pants, skirts, and the like. Key the color and fashion of your ski clothes to the degree of skill with which you ski. If you're great, be as dashing as you can. On the other hand, if you're a novice, you can be sure nobody will stare at your clumsy bad moments if you wear well-cut dark clothes.

THE COUNTRYSIDE: Such terrain as you'll find in Nova Scotia, Scotland, Ireland and the Scandinavian countries calls for rugged tweeds, a suit or skirt to go with sweaters and blouses, knitted clothes. In Scotland and England, "dressing" for dinner often means a floor-length woolen skirt and a sweater.

THE SEASIDE RESORTS OF EUROPE: These are in a class by themselves. The high seasons are brief and showy. Daytime clothes are simple, marvelously tailored, discreet, but evening in season is as dressy as you can get. In August at Biarritz and Deauville, Ostend and Knokke-Le-Zoute women at the grand hotels dress to the hilt: elaborate coiffures, brilliant jewelry, even ball gowns. The clothes are as gala as the ambiance.

Seating

SOME WOMEN have a built-in Geiger counter that seems to draw them unerringly to the most desirable seat on a plane or train. They are never the ones to sit next to crying babies; on ships they are always at the gayest table in the dining salon; and on planes they have finished their dinners before others have even been served. This isn't achieved accidentally by any means. You can do the same— here's how:

When you check in for an overseas flight, you will, as a general rule, be shown a diagram of the plane's interior and asked to select a seat. In first class, the choice is simple: anywhere. First-class seats are spaced two abreast; usually there are only six rows from front to back, and everyone has an equal amount of leg room. If, on the other hand, you fly in economy class, you will find about twenty rows with three seats on each side of the aisle, which can look as bewildering as an empty theater. There are decided advantages and disadvantages to almost any location.

The rules that follow apply to seating on a pure jet, i.e., a Boeing 707 or a Douglas DC-8, since these are the planes you are most likely to use on long overseas flights. Should you find yourself on a charter flight, for example, in a propjet or a piston-engine plane, remember to reverse the rule for smoothness: In a 707 or DC-8, or even the smaller 727, the best place to sit is forward; in a propjet or piston-engine plane, it is in the rear.

If you don't smoke and are irritated by other people's cigarettes, sit in the forward part of the cabin. Smoke and the smell of a smoldering cigarette have a tendency to drift to the rear.

If you are long-legged or feel caged-in if you can't move about, pick an aisle seat. As in a theater, you will probably have row mates climbing over you, but you will be able to stretch your legs out in the aisle, even if you have to pull them in whenever someone walks by. Also, try for the first row just behind the bulkhead which divides economy from first class; it has the most leg room (see paragraph below on traveling with infants).

If you are sensitive to noise, choose a seat next to or in front of the wings. Jet noise travels back from the engines and is louder in the aft section.

If you are limp with hunger when you board your flight, sit near the galley. It is forward in first class and aft in economy. Generally passengers seated closest to the galley are served first; stewardesses go from the rear of the aircraft forward in economy class, and forward to rear in first. This is not a hard-and-fast rule, however. If meal service is important to you, check the specific procedure with the airline's personnel at the counter where you make your seat selection. Remember, though, that the worst seats on a jet are those against the rear bulkhead, because they barely tilt back. You'll have to sit up straight all the way to Europe or the Orient.

If you want nothing more from your flight than a few hours of sleep, choose a seat that's far forward or one that's near the wing. Because the wings act as stabilizers as the aircraft moves up and down with air currents, the steadiest seats are those beside them. Also, if you can fit snugly into a corner, take a window seat so that no one has to climb over you to reach the aisle; this also gives you a wall to lean against.

If you have a tendency to motion sickness (jets fly so high that this malady has nearly disappeared), avoid the rear of the aircraft, which sways more than other parts. Also, stay away from window seats. In this case, too, the stable seats near the wing are best.

If you like to look at the landscape, you can, obviously, do so better without the wing blocking your view. Therefore, avoid the mid-section of the plane; if possible, sit behind the wing. Remember, though, that while it may be fascinating to see mountains, fields, and rivers during a daytime flight, you're likely, unless the sky is particularly clear and starry, to face nothing but boring blackness on a night flight over the ocean.

When you travel in economy class with an infant, you are given the best seat on the plane: that coveted spot in the first row behind the bulkhead. The airline will board you first and provide a bassinet which attaches to the bulkhead. (If you are traveling with a child under two, he will not be assigned a seat and must sit in your lap. Often, however, if the flight isn't full, the stewardess will let him take an empty seat once the plane is airborne.)

After the mothers with infants have been seated, the remaining first-row places are available on a first-come-first-served basis. Before choosing this seat, however, remember that an infant can be a very difficult neighbor.

If for any reason an airline fails to show you a seating plan, ask for one when you check in.

If you travel by ship, you will be faced with making two seat selections: in the dining room and on deck. Since the companionship you will enjoy for several days depends on these, don't be offhand or dilatory about them.

As soon as you are aboard, go directly to the head dining-room steward or his assistant to make your table reservations. On cruise ships there is usually one sitting; transoceanic passages generally have one in first class and two each in cabin and tourist. The first, as a rule about 6:30, is for mothers with small children and for such octogenarians and sick people who must go to bed early. It offers about as much social life as a hospital. The early dinner sitting, besides cutting short your cocktail hour as well as after-dinner conversation, also ties you to an early breakfast sitting. The second sitting starts about 8; you can linger over coffee fairly late if table conversation has you riveted; and you breakfast at a civilized hour.

If you are traveling alone or with another woman, don't for a single second be shy about asking for a large table with other single people. Dining stewards are wise about human nature—and have a certain selfish interest in seeing that you have a lively time on their ship. If you are traveling with your husband, you can request a table for two or one with other couples.

While friends and family are drinking bon-voyage champagne in your cabin, slip out and see the deck steward about a deck chair. In this case, choose it in relation to wind and sun. Ideally, you should be sheltered from the wind in winter and the heat in summer, and exposed to the right amount of sun. Even in summer, choose a spot that's wind-free. Some sea "breezes" are so strong that it's impossible to keep the pages of your book from flapping and your hair from being whipped into a tangled mane. There's a small charge for deck chairs, usually in the neighborhood of $3.

On some steamship lines, you can make both dining-room and deck-chair reservations when you book your ticket. This is wise, if experience has taught you exactly which locations suit you best. If, on the other hand, such matters are new to you, wait until you are aboard. As the dining steward fills in the places on his large chart, he tries to arrange compatible groups, on the basis of his judgment of people's ages, appearances and preferences. He can do better for you when he has had a chance to size up the other passengers as they pass in front of his desk.

Passengers who sail with a line frequently, distinguished people and government officials, may be asked to sit at the Captain's table for the duration of the trip or for specific meals. It's gracious to accept the Captain's invitation unless you have a good excuse to decline, such as being in bed with raging flu.

A ship's officers also act as hosts at other tables throughout the dining room. If you are seated with an officer, it's courteous to wait for his appearance before ordering your meal.

If in spite of the good intentions of the dining-room steward you find yourself at a table with uncongenial people, you can ask him to change your place. If you do it the first day or two, it hardly causes a ripple in the arrangements, so you needn't feel the least bit self-conscious about making this request.

There are three practical points to remember about seats on trains and buses:

1. Before starting, always find out (on a bus, ask the driver or guide) which side offers the best scenery and which gets the sun. During the summer, the unremitting heat and glare of the sun streaming through the window of even an air-conditioned bus can make you acutely uncomfortable. (While the windows of jet planes, and trains have their own shades, bus windows are not usually so equipped.)

2. The middle seats are the most stable in trains and buses, as well as in aircraft.

3. In a sleeping car, remember the rule that the person who occupies the lower berth is also entitled to the forward seat; the occupant of the upper berth takes the seat that rides backward.

Finally, remember this obvious basic rule: To be sure of the widest choice of seats anywhere, queue up *early*. The early bird invariably gets the best perch.

Shipboard Dressing

THE LATIN WORD for *baggage* is *impedimenta*, a term which will seem increasingly apropos as you travel, except on ships, where baggage enters a world of weightlessness and welcome. On cruise ships no regulation is set down, and ships' personnel say cavalierly, "The sky's the limit." On transatlantic ships the sky is a little closer to earth and the limit is 275 pounds, which could roughly include all your clothes plus enough mountain-climbing gear to take a small party up the Matterhorn. Pacific crossings allow even more—350 pounds go free.

Ships—transatlantic, transpacific or cruise—are splendid floating resorts; your clothes should be casual and *sportif* by day, pretty and romantic by night. The best rule is to wear what you would find suitable for a country club. In addition to the atmosphere of the ships themselves, you must also consider the vagaries of the weather you will be sailing through plus the nature of your destination plus, of course, the class in which you are traveling.

There are also subtle though minor differences between one ship line and another. (If you sail to London in June, the appropriate thing to wear after-five, on the Cunard Line, is a pretty print; on the French Line, a sophisticated little black dress.) There are other noticeable differences between cruise and transpacific ships on the one hand and transatlantic ships on the other.

Starting with cruise and transpacific ships, remember that if you leave during the cool months you will need warm daytime and evening clothes for the first 24 to 36 hours. As soon as you enter summery waters, you can emerge like a butterfly from a cocoon. Nothing looks prettier on a sunny sea than pastels, brilliant prints and white. The "little black dress" that looks marvelous *en voyage* to Paris will make you feel drab steaming toward Hawaii or the Virgin Islands and will certainly be all wrong on shore.

While ships offer a vast range of amusements—from gambling to deck tennis—social life begins at the swimming pool. Pack two or three of your handsomest bathing suits (if you are the type, one can be a bikini) and a beach coat. As if by some perverse law, pools are invariably situated at the opposite end of the ship from your state-room. Since you will have to trudge through a labyrinth of corridors, you need to be well covered. If you hate changing several times a day, you may order your lunch at the swimming pool. (Obviously, a bathing suit, even the eighteen-nineties variety, is not allowed in the dining salon.)

For deck games like shuffleboard or tennis or for sunning in a deck chair, bring shorts, slacks, summery sport skirts and the tops to go with them. If you're wearing shorts or slacks, the dining room is again off limits. Even on deck, let your shorts be a conservative length; the brief ones you'd wear at St. Tropez are all wrong on a cruise ship.

Dressy or evening clothes are worn to dinner except in certain instances: *never* on the first and last nights, on Sundays, or when your ship lies in port or has weighed anchor late in the afternoon—in all these cases simply because dressing for dinner will only add to the confusion. Instead, wear a pretty, simple afternoon dress. On the nights when you do dress, suit yourself: you can wear a floor-length brocade or a low-cut linen sheath with equal propriety.

In matters of formality, fabric or skirt length, your own style and taste should be the guide. There is no *single* way to dress, no rigid rule about any of these matters. If you feel beautiful in a white floor-length crepe, wear it; on the other hand, if your style is a pale, cock-tail-length chiffon, you can still float into the dining room with assurance. There are only two circumstances under which formality is heightened: first, if the cruise is a particularly long one, say 95 days, in which case evening clothes are generally more formal throughout; and second, for the captain's gala, which is a party usually held the evening of the next to the last full day before the ship docks.

As for other necessities: No matter how tropical the sun or moon in the travel posters, you'll need some sort of wrap. This can be a lightweight, pale-colored coat, a bright silk stole or a white cashmere cardigan. A fur jacket is acceptable though certainly not chic—it looks out of place against the pure, trim lines of a ship. Take head scarves in every color to tie around your hair for wearing on deck, and for launch rides and shore excursions. Take lots of pale cardigan sweaters: A cardigan will serve as a bed jacket, a wrap in air-conditioned restaurants, or a lightweight cover in the cool morning air; since temperatures are bound to vary with the swiftness of a cloud racing across the sun, you should never be without a cardigan sweater at hand.

Choose most of your clothes in cotton, silk, wool or Dacron-and-cotton blends, with a fairly sturdy weave; gossamer materials have a way of going limp in the damp sea air. Pack small flat evening bags. Since any ship worth traveling on has slickly polished decks, be sure to bring rubber or rope-soled walking shoes. Add a good pair or two of sunglasses and binoculars for watching sea gulls or the excitement of a port as you steam in.

For shore excursions and sightseeing, you will need truly comfortable clothes. Landlubbers can run back to their hotels to change, but once the launch has left you in port for the day, you are on your own. In Bermuda, the Bahamas or West Indies, wear pale sport dresses preferably with sleeves (the sun can be powerful) or a pair of long tailored shorts and a shirt where suitable (see Shorts and Slacks, page 327), and low-heeled walking shoes; the shoes should have an easy fit if you will be in hot, humid climates.

If your cruise involves an excursion to a city, abandon the thought of sightseeing in shorts, slacks or any sort of décolletage. Most cities call for big-city dressing. You would look askance at anyone sightseeing in Chicago or San Francisco in shorts and halter top; if you dress this way in Rio de Janeiro or Sydney, you will get the same response. Also remember that seasons in South America and Australia are the reverse of ours, so plan colors and fabrics accordingly.

For a winter cruise in the Mediterranean, a North Cape cruise in the summer, or a cruise on an inland waterway like the St. Lawrence in early spring or late summer, pack woolens that are light in weight, pale in color. The Mediterranean in winter is not tropical as some people think, but springlike, and Scandinavia can be cool in the summer. Inland cruises are the most informal of all; you are even allowed to wear slacks and shorts to meals.

If you go on a round-the-world cruise, remember that nylon and other nonporous materials become clammy in hot climates, so pack plenty of cotton.

Transatlantic crossings are slightly more formal than cruises. Although you dress casually by day, your clothes should be better suited to a country hotel then a beach house. No matter what the time of year, if you imagine what you would wear for a walk along a country lane and pack such clothes into your suitcase, you will feel comfortable and well-dressed in mid-Atlantic.

In the evenings, the class in which you sail determines the degree of your formality. While cruise ships have only one class, transatlantic ships may have two or three: first, cabin and tourist. Naturally, first class calls for the splashiest, most sophisticated clothes. Except for the first and last nights, evening clothes, short or long, are worn to dinner. If you are a passenger in cabin or tourist class, you can scale down the glint and glitter; the sort of dress you would put on for a cocktail party back home will do nicely.

Pack the same complement of necessities as you would for a cruise: scarves, sweaters, walking shoes et al. Add a lightweight raincoat for prudence and overall usefulness for deck-strolling.

All ships, whether cruise, transpacific or transatlantic, have crackerjack laundry facilities (some cruise ships even have launderettes), and you can have clothes pressed easily.

Since there are, roughly speaking, no restrictions on the amount of luggage you can take, the pieces that you don't want to stumble over in your stateroom can be stored in the baggage room. However cabin closets do have their limits—usually about twelve to fifteen dresses— and unless you want to grope through endless layers of clothes shrouding every door and chair, don't overpack. While one of the blissful advantages of a sea voyage is not having to pack and unpack all the time, you should remember that you will be back on land again in a few days and baggage will once more be *impedimenta*.

Shoes

THESE DAYS, with the possible exception of such remotenesses as Turkey's Hakâri Mountains or the upper reaches of the Amazon, you can take off in nearly any direction carrying little more than a bottle of perfume—*and* an assortment of comfortable shoes. In a provincial town in Iran, on a Caribbean island without electricity, in a mountain village of Japan, you can buy night creams, nail polish and nylons. What you cannot find is shoes to fit your long, slender American feet.

A dress, even lingerie, can be altered to your size in an emergency; shoes cannot be re-lasted. Since American shoe lasts differ markedly from European, and certainly Oriental (the proportions of our feet tend to be narrow and elongated while those of other nationalities, even their men's, are shorter and squarer), unless you travel with the shoes that make you feel bouncy, your memory of the glories of Florence or the views of Hong Kong will be clouded by the gray haze of irritation and pain you felt when you saw them.

For a three- to six-week trip to Europe, or even around the world, if you're traveling within the 44-pound limit, five pairs of shoes are sensible: two pairs of walking shoes, one with rubber soles for cushioning the charming Old World cobblestone streets that can be murderous to walk on, and a little bit wider than you usually wear, since tired feet have a way of swelling; a pair of simple pumps with medium heels; a pair of dressy, after-dark pumps; and a pair of folding slippers to ease into whenever you're on a long transportation lap.

Dark colors are generally safest, but in the right season you can usefully break this rule so far as shoes are concerned. Bright or light colors here are not only pretty but have a way of going with almost anything: a pair of beige daytime pumps or pink evening ones can be infinitely useful.

Generally, when people are immobilized for several hours in a sitting position, their feet and ankles puff up. So don't be surprised if on the flight between New York and London you find your shoes getting tighter and tighter as the six and a half hours wear on. You should make this a cardinal rule: Never wear new shoes on a long flight or trip. Otherwise you may find yourself, as I once did, walking down the ramp in your stocking feet because it's impossible to get your shoes on. Veteran travelers slip their shoes off even before take-off and put on the pair of folding slippers mentioned above. But they don't sit altogether unshod because without something to contain them, their feet swell even more.

If you manage somehow to lose all your shoes, there are a handful of shops in Europe where you can make replacements. In London, try Abbots in Regent Street and its 18 branches, Elliott's in New Bond Street or Brompton Road, and Russell & Bromley in New Bond Street, all of which carry long, narrow lasts. In Paris, American models—they have the longest, slenderest feet of all—go to Charles Jourdan. His shoes can also be bought at his shop in London, and at the Löw shops in Geneva, Zurich and Lausanne. They cost around $20. In Switzerland you can also buy Christian Dior shoes, which have a comfortable last for American feet, at Grieder Seiden in Zurich; they cost between $16 and $20. Ferragamo in Italy can also be helpful; it has shops in Rome, Florence, Milan and Venice.

There is one last word to be said about shoes, and that concerns taking them off. In Japan courtesy demands that you leave them at the door whenever you go into an inn, private home, restaurant, teahouse, temple, or shrine. If the floor is wood, you will put on heelless slippers; if it's covered with tatami matting, go in stocking feet. In India, Pakistan and Singapore, you must take off shoes before entering a temple or mosque (in Thailand before entering a Buddhist temple). In Morocco you will also take them off when you enter a private home. The obvious moral here is that if you are traveling in these parts of the world, you should carry a pair of slipper socks in your handbag and wear shoes you can easily slip in and out of. Laces and buckles are a terrible nuisance.

William Butler Yeats once wrote, "He made the world to be a grassy road before her wandering feet." This is only true, of course, if her feet don't hurt.

Shorts and Slacks

THE ONLY person who needs never think about the propriety of wearing shorts is an English schoolboy. He can wear them at all times, in all places, and in all weathers. An adult woman is a different case.

You will have to think carefully about where you're going before packing shorts—and slacks. You won't need them on any trip that does not include a stay at a resort or a voyage by ship. Even here you won't require them, but if you like to wear pants—short or long—at home, here are the rules for wearing them abroad:

Shorts differ in their length, which falls into three categories:

Bermuda shorts—to 2 inches above the knee;

Jamaica shorts—to mid-thigh, or about 4 inches higher than Bermudas;

Short shorts—to the top of the thigh.

A length that's suitable in one place may be all wrong in another. The discreet knee-length shorts appropriate in Bermuda will look as dowdy as a mid-calf skirt in St. Tropez, where shorts are cut as high as the anatomy will allow.

Shorts that look wonderful on La Croisette in Cannes could get you run in for indecent exposure in the Bahamas. Variations in the shortness of shorts are, in fact, one of the major reasons for buying some of your resort clothes on the spot. (See Resort Clothes, page 313.)

Confine your appearances in shorts to your hotel grounds or to the resort areas where you are sure they are acceptable on the streets. In Bermuda and the Bahamas they are the uniform even in the main towns like Hamilton and Nassau, provided they come to 2 inches above the knee and are conservative in color. You can wear them literally anywhere during the day—even to lunch in restaurants and hotels. (Slacks, however, are worn less often.) On other islands, you can wear them everywhere comfortably except in the streets of the capital city. Such shorts are proper too on deck on transatlantic, transpacific and cruise ships. (See Shipboard Dressing, page 322.) And you will see plenty of women parading in short shorts along the Riviera, which is a fashion world unto itself.

Don't make the common mistake of thinking that a city which is foreign or tropical is less formal than your own. Rio, Hong Kong and Athens may be far away, sunny and relaxed, but wearing shorts on their streets, or on those of *any* city not totally committed to resort life, is unthinkable. No matter how hot and humid the country, don't wear shorts on a motoring trip. Throughout the world, the smaller the town the more conservative the people are about dress. Also, the stricter a country's Catholicism, the stronger its prohibitions against shorts and slacks. In the Province of Quebec in Canada, for example, shorts are not permitted at any time, and slacks can be worn only for active sports. In Mexico shorts are frowned upon everywhere except at "Americanized" beach resorts such as Acapulco. In Puerto Rico they are acceptable in the hotel areas but disapproved of for shopping in San Juan. Finally, shorts are not suitable on golf courses except those at resorts or on some resort islands. While you could wear shorts to play golf on Jamaica's North Shore, for example, you shouldn't wear them at St. Andrews in Scotland. Neither shorts nor slacks are traditional golf clothes for women; on some courses, especially those in cooler climates, shorts are not permitted.

Slacks—or "pants," as they are called in current fashion parlance— are much more versatile than shorts, and the places and situations in which they look natural increase constantly. If yours is the sort of figure that looks marvelous in pants, here's where you could wear them *en voyage:*

On sightseeing trips that require climbing, e.g., pyramids (even in conservative countries like Mexico and Peru).

On long motor trips into the countryside or on boat trips within a country, up the Nile, the Amazon, or the fjords, where pants are not only acceptable but natural.

On a long plane trip. A few designers, including our great Norman Norell, make pants suits for airplane travel. They have three pieces: The skirt and jacket are worn to board the plane. When the wearer is aloft, she changes skirt to pants. Mr. Norell's admirable credo about pants, which one might well heed, is: "Only for travel, only for the country, only up to size 12."

At resorts, even in countries as conservative as India, where they are always acceptable. In some resorts—St. Thomas, Ischia, Hydra, for example—they are worn into the evening, for dining and dancing at a small informal *boîte.*

On any stretch where one is "roughing it," such as hiking along wooded trails, fishing in the Chilean lakes.

On transatlantic, transpacific, and cruise ships.

On the other hand, never wear pants if you are traveling from country to country in a bus or a train. You may not shock the Americans, but the natives won't like it.

Again, never wear them in a city that is not a resort. Here a small word of explanation is in order. During your travels you may see a number of local women in pants. I remember a trip to Oslo in the month of September when the streets seemed filled with pretty young girls in pants and bulky sweaters. A housewife in London's Chelsea may run out to a neighborhood store, or a mother may play with her children in Paris' Luxembourg Gardens, and both may be dressed in pants. A local woman, however, knows the lay of the land. She knows the boundaries beyond which it would be inappropriate for her to be dressed this way. You don't—you could unknowingly commit a *faux pas.* While pants suits are currently strong on the fashion scene, they should be worn only where you are absolutely sure they are suitable.

Never wear pants to the races. In other countries these are social occasions that call for the most flowery hat and the prettiest silk dress you own. Pants at the races would be as shattering to local sensibilities as pants at church.

And of course, never wear pants to churches or to religious shrines. In addition to the above, consider these rules:

1. Look before you "leg" it. The rules for shorts and pants have local variations. Survey the scene first and make your own on-the-spot judgment before dressing in shorts or pants. If you have *any* doubts about wearing either, don't. In matters of this kind, discretion is always the better part of valor. On many of the Greek islands, for example, you can wear slacks comfortably all day. On Waikiki Beach it would be wrong to appear in them after dark if you stay at a big hotel; you should change into a dress for dinner.

2. Where the local crowd lives in pants, you can be sure that there's a local genius who is running them up for a sou. Search him out—he can probably do the job in 24 to 48 hours.

3. "Culottes," a divided skirt, actually are pants masquerading as a skirt. They are thoroughly useful, especially for women who want the comfort of pants but don't have the figure for them. And they can pass with aplomb where pants are out of the question.

4. Finally, remember that one is always judged by local standards. If you don't want to be stared at abroad, don't wear things for which a local woman would be criticized, no matter how indulgent natives are to visitors. If, for example, women do not wear pants in conservative countries like Spain or Portugal, you shouldn't either.

Sidewalk Cafés

A SIDEWALK CAFÉ is a small oasis of quiet in a thronged city where you can sit down and draw breath, visit with a friend, feel less lonely, write a letter, read the newspaper, daydream, brood, or watch the passersby. Its spindly iron chairs and tables make havens for everyone—writers finishing books, philosophers confirming theories, lovers patching up quarrels. Most Europeans use cafés as an annex to their homes or as Englishmen do their clubs. They demand so little of their patrons—a small cup of coffee can give you an hour's peaceful anchorage—that most Americans, accustomed to restaurants with a brisk turnover, find them slightly unbelievable. How a café manages to stay in business under the circumstances is an abiding mystery.

The history of the café goes back about four hundred years. London's eighteenth-century coffeehouses performed much the same kind of function that the Parisian café does now, which is to give writers a place to read the papers and discuss the news, to meet friends, and a good deal of the time to sit undisturbed and cover pages and pages of the work in progress—all for the price of a cup of coffee. The French literary world could hardly be imagined without its assortment of favored cafés, for that is where its real life goes on. Many writers prefer to use a pencil at the little table on the street than to work on a typewriter in a quiet room. Though the café has crept back into London's Chelsea recently, it has flourished best on the Continent and in a few South American countries whose social patterns were established by Europeans. A café may be just a handful of chairs spread on a narrow sidewalk, known only in its *quartier;* or it may sprawl over half a block and have such international fame that tourists head for it immediately after dropping their suitcases at the hotel. In Paris (which has the largest number of cafés in Europe—about 10,000—followed by Rome and Brussels) the Café de la Paix on Place de l'Opéra, the Café de Flore and Café aux Deux Magots on Boulevard St.-Germain, and Fouquet's on the Champs-Élysées are filled with recognizable faces from the world of art, letters and the theater. In Brussels the Café Métropole is usually swarming with "Eurocrats," i.e., men involved with the Common Market. In Rome, Rosati's on the Piazza del Popolo draws Italy's leading actors, writers and painters. The cafés along the Via Veneto are popular with those who come to pick up the scuttlebutt or to see who's new in town; Doney's is still a great favorite.

You might settle for one café because you like its atmosphere, or because it's sunny, or because you strike up a friendship with the waiter—or you could try a string of them. In none will the proprietor ever press you to leave, even if all you order in exchange for an afternoon of lingering is a lemonade. In fact, you'll probably have a hard time finding even a waiter when you want to pay your bill.

You can go to a sidewalk café for a light drink or a meal. Most of them serve sandwiches, pastries, ice cream, spirits, wine, beer, fruit juices, coffee and tea. Some offer full meals, and prices are invariably lower than in enclosed restaurants. In Paris, where prices are about the same as those in any big American city, a large sandwich at a café will cost from 30 to 50 cents; a full meal will start at $1.50; and a glass of *vin ordinaire* will cost about 20 cents. As a rule, sidewalk cafés are more popular for light lunch and after-theater supper than for dinner.

Although large cafés are open all day—and most of the night— things really start humming during midmorning coffee time; in the apéritif hours around noon and 6; at 4 for tea; and for postprandial drinking at 10 or 11 in the evening. Tables remain on the sidewalks from early spring to late autumn, then move indoors provided the establishment does not close for the winter. Some cafés have beaten the winter with heated terraces, or systems installed in their canopies which send down a soft blanket of heat.

Women alone or together can go to a sidewalk café with complete comfort any time during the day, and two women are welcome in the evening. If you are on your own, however, stay away from a café late at night. You are bound to be conspicuous and will cause an uncomfortable amount of staring. Let 8 or 9 be your curfew.

In South America and the Middle East one seldom sees a woman alone at a café even at high noon and never, of course, at night. Since South American and Middle Eastern women simply do not go out alone, it looks strange for a foreigner to do so.

While sidewalk cafés are largely an outgrowth of Latin leisureliness, they crop up elsewhere. In Britain an increasing number of espresso coffee bars and pubs serve refreshments outside their doors, come summer.

In Hawaii, Bermuda, the Bahamas and the Philippines or wherever American habits prevail, the sidewalk café, with all its opportunities for undirected leisure, is unknown. On Caribbean islands, patio restaurants take the place of sidewalk cafés.

Japan's and Turkey's coffee shops are something like sidewalk cafés, at least in atmosphere. Tokyo alone has about 4,000 of them, ranging from big brassy jazz places to quiet, dim retreats where the talk is of poetry and pop art. In any, you can order a cup of coffee (Tokyo, surprisingly, serves some of the world's best), a sandwich or pastry, and sit contentedly for hours. In Turkey's small villages the coffee shop is the major cultural center of the community; in the remote places they are meant for "men only."

In Vienna the tradition of a cup of coffee—espresso, or with mounds of whipped cream—continues. Many Viennese have two or three favorite coffeehouses where they go to have a light meal, or to conduct business, or to play cards, billiards or chess, or to read unhurriedly through the large selection of newspapers and magazines. It's a haven where they can sit all day, even if they order nothing more than a pot of coffee.

Sizes

IT WILL HAPPEN. Early in your shopping days in Europe, a salesgirl will measure your waistline, sing out "72"—and your head will spin. *Could* all those chocolate soufflés have done that much so fast? Calm yourself. The explanation is simple: In America sizes are measured in inches; in Europe and Latin American they are reckoned in centimeters—and there are two and a half of *them* to every inch. Until you get used to it, every time you go shopping for ready-to-wear, you'll feel you've become an Amazon. Size 12 in dresses, suits and coats becomes size 40; our size 6 in shoes stretches to 36; size 15 in a men's shirt is upped to 38. Only in hosiery does the process reverse; our size 10 shrinks to a European 4. Indeed, of all clothing sizes, the only one that is consistent around the world is gloves!

There's no point cluttering your mind with a catalog of foreign sizes; simply arm yourself with a good converter that gives you at a glance the American equivalents. Macy's, that Titan among American department stores, with branches throughout the country, gives away an excellent size translator. (Write Macy's, Public Relations, Herald Square, New York, New York 10001.) It carries men's, women's and children's sizes in English, French, German, Italian and Spanish. You can also get a species of translator from nearly every transatlantic airline. Actually any good shop in Europe will be able to decode your size on the spot. (In addition to a size translator, you will also want to have the sizes and measurements of anyone for whom you'll be shopping abroad, plus a tape measure. A reversible one with inches on one side and centimeters on the other is invaluable.)

Shopping differences are not, however, just a numbers game. To the dissimilarities in sizing, you must add discrepancies in cut—and this is where the gap really widens. You will probably find that you need one size smaller in European ready-to-wear than you do in American, which is important to remember when you shop for other people.

The reasons for considering yourself one size smaller are caused by some interesting diversities between Europeans and Americans. First, European clothing manufacturers create for a woman who is built differently from her American counterparts. American women, while taller, tend to be smaller-boned than European women and to run to less girth and muscle. You will frequently find waistlines and hemlines too short, bustlines and hiplines too generous. As a rule, sizes in England and Scandinavia are similar to ours; but in Holland, Belgium and Germany clothes are cut for a sturdier, more muscular figure; and in Italy they are made for women who tend to be shorter and heavier than we are. The above are generalizations about ready-to-wear, and there are bound to be innumerable exceptions. Whenever you are tempted by something pretty, be sure to try it on and appraise the fit before you buy it.

Then Europe's weather and interior temperatures influence cut strongly. Since winters in Britain and on the Continent can be bitter and houses are not centrally heated, European women wear heavy sweaters under their suits, and heavy suits under their coats. As a result, suit and coat shoulders are cut far wider than ours, and armholes are deep and roomy to the point—by our standards—of being baggy.

Finally, European women like their clothes looser than we do— although in things like ski sweaters we're quickly adapting their "look." A sweater that is marked "small" can nearly always be worn by a "medium" American.

Although nowhere do shops carry the amazing variety of ready-to-wear sizes of ours—American clothes are fractioned into juniors, half sizes, petites, diminutives and the like—many boutiques make up for this by giving you a dress or suit to measure for the same price as the sample.

And in Hong Kong, where there's a custom tailor behind every other door, it doesn't matter whether you claim you're a size 14 or a 44. They simply take your measurements and proceed accordingly.

The following chart gives the approximate foreign equivalents of American sizes, but there is so little standardization of sizes throughout Europe that you should buy nothing (except gloves) where fit is an important factor without first trying it on.

MISSES' DRESSES, SUITS, COATS, SKIRTS

U.S.A.	10	12	14	16	18	20
English	10	12	14	16	18	20
Continental	38	40	42	44	46	48

WOMEN'S DRESSES, SUITS, COATS, SKIRTS

U.S.A.	34	36	38	40	42	44
English	34	36	38	40	42	44
Continental	42	44	46	48	50	52

JUNIOR DRESSES, SUITS, COATS, SKIRTS

U.S.A.	7	9	11	13	15	17
English	7	9	11	13	15	17
Continental	34	36	38	40	42	44

BLOUSES, SWEATERS, SLIPS

U.S.A.	30	32	34	36	38	40	42
English	30	32	34	36	38	40	42
Continental	38	40	42	44	46	48	50

STOCKINGS

U.S.A.	8	8½	9	9½	10	10½	11
English	8	8½	9	9½	10	10½	11
Continental*	0	1	2	3	4	5	6

SHOES

U.S.A.	5	5½	6	6½	7	7½	8	8½	9
English	3½	4	4½	5	5½	6	6½	7	7½
Continental	35	35	36	37	38	38	38½	39	40

Glove sizes are generally identical.

* *In many European countries, hosiery sizes are the same as those in the U.S.A.*

Soap

_____ · _____

PICTURE YOURSELF in this situation: You arrive dusty and footsore at your hotel in a strange city wanting nothing so much as a hot, sudsy bath. You cross a rococo lobby, ascend to your room in a gilded cage, and open the door of your bathroom. It is glorious: the size of a miniature ballroom, with a telephone next to the enormous tub, enough marble to repair the Parthenon—and not a sliver of soap.

The presence—or absence—of soap is a classic example of the fact that what "goes" in Memphis may not in Mauritius. Once you cross the great divide of the Atlantic Ocean, you'll find that a hotel will cosset you with all sorts of marvelous service—no shoe is left unshined, maids, valets and waiters appear like genies—but only in the most exceptional cases, in de luxe American-style hotels, Caribbean cottage colonies, or high-level Japanese *ryokan*, will soap be provided.

You should start your travels armed with enough soap to last the first 10 days. There's no point in stocking up for the entire trip (even if you're staying in medium- and lower-priced hotels) because first, there's no practical reason for carrying the extra weight; second, you can buy soap everywhere you go (if you're partial to an imported brand, you may even find that it's less expensive abroad) and third, going into local apothecary shops with their sharp smells and professional hush can be fascinating. (You'll also find all sorts of familiar products staring you in the face. Pond's Cold Cream, Revlon lipstick and Cutex nail polish are just about as ubiquitous as Coca-Cola.)

Start off with a cake of face soap for soft water. If you're a perfectionist, add a cake for hard water, for often, as in London, you'll find water hard as bricks, and raising a lather a tantalizing business. Take a detergent if you plan on doing nightly laundry; it's best for all-around use. And a water softener will make bathing far more agreeable.

One experienced traveler I know spoons individual doses of detergent into each of several plastic sandwich bags, seals the bags with a warm iron and tucks them into the corners of her suitcase. If you have the temperament for this sort of thing, it's a good way to save space and weight. Cel-suds and Trav, marketed in individual packages, offer an easier alternative.

There are other reasonably useful, well-known products to remember. The soft, pre-moistened papers known as Wash 'n Dri, Wet-Nap or Tote Towel are good for freshening up during the day. Tuck a few into your handbag. They're good on long afternoons of sightseeing, during long train rides, on treks through museums (trains *never* have soap and most museums have miserable facilities), or when you have to face any sort of public bathroom that is unpleasant. The alternative is to keep a packet of cleansing tissues and a tiny cube of soap in a plastic, waterproof container in your handbag. Woolite, a cold-water detergent that also comes in easy-to-pack units, is a blessing for doing laundry when the temperature of your hotel's water runs only high enough to keep a penguin happy.

And finally, while soap is used the same way everywhere, there is one curious Japanese custom, which you will want to observe if you are using a Japanese-style bathroom in a *ryokan* or a private home. You lather yourself and rinse off the soap before getting into the big tub for a long, hot soak. In other words you get clean first and use the bath entirely for relaxation. (See Bathrooms, page 16.)

Sports Equipment

IF YOU will play better golf in Japan or ski more smoothly in Gstaad using your own equipment, you can take it with you at very little extra expense. The airlines have explicit rules and prices covering almost any situation, even taking your own surfboard to Waikiki. On ships, the allowance of 275 or 350 pounds is so generous that big game rifles, ammunition, a collapsible cook stove, and canned goods to feed a small safari could plausibly be included without extra charge.

On airlines, such light equipment as tennis rackets, fishing rods, rifles and shotguns can go as part of your regular baggage allowance. But if their weight added to that of your luggage puts you over the limit, you will have to pay the customary overweight charges. You may carry some sporting gear aboard the aircraft as hand luggage. Naturally, rackets should be in presses, fishing rods in their aluminum tubes. By law, guns, with the exception of skeet guns and shotguns, which can be carried aboard in their cases as hand luggage, must be emptied, disassembled and packed in a suitable case. Ammunition for small arms is accepted in certain quantities. Its packing is subject to special instructions which should be obtained from the airlines.

Three types of equipment are subject to special tariffs: skis, golf clubs and surfboards. The rules are as follows:

SKIS: Skis, bindings, poles and boots can be taken from your point of origin to your destination for a flat fee which is figured from point to point. This amount can never be more than the excess baggage charge for 2 kilos or about 4 pounds and is based on the rate of 1 per cent of the first-class fare. So, if you fly from New York to Zurich and the weight of your ski equipment puts you over your total baggage allowance, you will have to pay a maximum charge of about $8 one way. Carry your skis when you check in; they will be tagged with the rest of your luggage and shipped on the same plane. They need not be specially wrapped—just firmly strapped together. The charge for taking water skis from the Continental U.S.A. to Hawaii is $4.

GOLF CLUBS: A special rate for 33 pounds or less of golf equipment exists throughout the year. The fee is calculated in the same way as that for skis, though in the case of golf equipment it cannot be more than the excess baggage charge for 4 kilos or about 8 pounds. You may carry one golf bag, 14 clubs, 12 balls and one pair of golf shoes one way for these typical rates:

From New York to Nassau—about $5
From New York to London—about $15
From New York to Bermuda—about $3.25
From New York to Barbados—about $9
From the West Coast to Hawaii—there is a fixed charge of $4
From the West Coast to London—about $21
From the West Coast to Tokyo—about $28

The clubs are checked with your luggage and accompany your flight. There is no extra charge if the weight of the golf equipment does not raise the total baggage weight above your allowance.

SURFBOARDS: If you really can't face the Big Ones without your own board, you can take it with you from the West Coast to Honolulu for a charge of $20. Between domestic points and California, the surfboard travels as part of your free baggage allowance, but since a surfboard weighs about 35 pounds, you are bound to have to pay for the extra weight. It might be cheaper to send it as reserved air freight, which means it would be shipped on your flight.

There are three general points to remember in taking sports equipment by air:

1. Two people traveling together can pool their baggage allowance. Your husband's shooting gear may be heavy and your suitcase underweight; all will be added together, and overweight charges figured on the basis of your combined total.

2. If you want to ship sports equipment ahead, it must go as air freight at normal cargo rates. Airlines do not accept baggage without a passenger.

3. With the exception of skis, any equipment that does not have a special carrying case should be wrapped well to prevent damage to its surface and to allow airline personnel to handle it in their normal way. Occasionally, airlines provide special cardboard containers for shipping guns and fishing rods. Any equipment that is checked along with your luggage should be packed in a rigid container. A good one for golfers is the vinyl plastic cover made for United Air Lines by the Wilson Sporting Goods Company, available through United only for $7.50. Lark Luggage's lightweight Tennis-Pac, starting at $25 in most large department stores, has compartments for racket, tennis balls, and shoes and socks; shorts, sweaters, etc., are packed in the main part. It comes in two waterproof coverings—nylon and madras.

If you travel by ship, golf clubs, tennis rackets, guns, fishing rods, ski boots, and the like can be kept in your stateroom, as part of your personal luggage. Bulky items such as skis can be stored in the hold of the ship, where you are allowed 25 cubic feet of space without charge. If you travel with something massive that calls for more than 25 cubic feet, you will be charged $1 for every cubic foot in excess of the limit.

Shotguns must be lodged in care of the ship's Chief Purser.

You may send your sporting equipment ahead to the pier where the baggagemen will put it aboard. Just be sure to mark on it clearly the name of the vessel, the sailing date, and your stateroom number, so that it goes on the same ship as you, or it will end up in the Customs Warehouse. Getting it out again will be a time-consuming nuisance.

If, on the other hand, you would rather not bother taking your own sports equipment, you can easily rent it at resort areas and hotels. One airline, Panagra, eager to take you skiing in the Andes, will even make all the necessary equipment available at its offices in Santiago for $3.50 per day for complete gear, including clothes, skis, poles and boots; it's $2.50 for just the equipment.

Stockings

UNLESS YOU are on an anthropological expedition to the remotest villages of the Andes, you will never be out of reach of nylon stockings. Our export wizards plus foreign factories abroad that are licensed to produce the yarn have seen to that. But, except for such fashion-conscious cities as London, Rome, Paris and Munich, you may find the foreign products slightly heavier in texture, looser and squarer in shape, more orange in color, and slightly higher-priced than your favorite brand at home. So take as many pairs of stockings as you are likely to run through in the time you'll be away, but don't worry unduly about the prospect of finding yourself barelegged in Barcelona. Should that happen, you can certainly make do with the local product.

It goes without saying that you wear stockings in all cities with the possible exception of resort centers such as Nice or such capitals as Rome, Athens, and Tel Aviv, where life spills outdoors in the hot summer months. In the latter cities, you can be rather informal; if your feet are beautifully pedicured, you may want to wear sandals. The same would go for a resort city like Honolulu. In conservative places such as Madrid and Lisbon, no well-dressed woman would be seen without them no matter what the temperature.

But, except in conservative Catholic countries, it is perfectly permissible to go barelegged where muggy temperatures and humidity make nylon stockings feel like ski underwear in July. In the Orient and along the Mediterranean at the height of summer, or on a tropical island any time, invest your hosiery allowance in leg care and cosmetics. In such places, Peds, if you like them, plus plenty of talcum powder will be the very most you will need. The only exception would be if you were being entertained in Tokyo, where it is considered not quite decorous to go without stockings even in hot weather or at formal or official parties.

White anklets are also a blessing in Eastern countries where you are expected to remove your shoes before entering a house of worship. Slip them on over your stockings or bare feet; they may prove a sensible sanitary precaution.

If, on the other hand, you are going into cold climates, take some textured wool stockings and even a pair of bed socks since European buildings are kept far cooler than ours.

If you are a college girl on your junior year abroad or on a grand tour, remember that socks may look marvelous on campus but silly in foreign cities. They are a dead giveaway of your nationality, age and status.

Stopovers

As THE crow flies is not necessarily the way *you* should if you want to get the most mileage out of an airline ticket.

When you buy an international airline ticket, you are paying not to go straight from one place to another but for the right to travel a certain number of miles. This "allowable mileage" figure made up by the airlines is always higher than the straight-line distance between point A and point B. Therefore, without spending an extra sou, you can zigzag your way to a destination instead of making a beeline for it—and visit a string of cities en route.

The airlines have calculated these "allowable mileage" figures from point to point on the basis of a mathematical formula and recorded them in a tome called the Air Passenger Tariff book. When you book a ticket with a travel agent or an airline, the clerk consults this book to find out the distance between your starting point and the farthest city on your route. He is then able to tell you how many miles you are allowed and how they can be used. For example: As the crow flies, New York and Rome are 4,271 miles apart. The airlines have decided that you are entitled to use 5,125 miles flying from one to the other. You can, therefore, make your way from New York to Rome via Tunis, Sicily, or Czechoslovakia; or you could even plan an itinerary between New York and Rome that would include Scandinavia and Bermuda! None of these stops will cost a dollar more than the direct flight between the two original cities.

In short, there is far more stretch in an airline ticket than meets the eye—and you should be aware of the hundreds of possibilities for stopovers whenever you book air travel. Here are a few examples:

You can go to Tel Aviv via Warsaw; to the French Riviera via Edinburgh; and if you plan to go skiing in Lebanon, you can also try the trails in Switzerland on the same ticket.

You can enjoy the privileges of stopovers even if you sail to Europe and fly back, simply by using those granted on your one-way flight home. Even if you sail to and from Europe, you can still make the stopovers granted on a local air ticket. If, for example, you take a Mediterranean cruise which stops at Lisbon and you decide to tour some of the Continent before rejoining the ship at Naples, your air ticket between Lisbon and Naples will include stopovers in Madrid, Tunis, and Sicily.

Sometimes a small surcharge will buy hundreds of miles of extra transportation. For $6.40 more than the direct air fare from New York to Mexico City, you can also go to the Bahamas. If you sail into the British port of Southampton, and decide to fly from London to Madrid, you can go via Paris and Barcelona for a modest supplementary charge on the tourist-class round-trip ticket. If you fly from New York to Rio de Janeiro, you can go on to Buenos Aires, which is 1,232 miles farther, for only $3 more; similarly you can fly to Johannesburg for the same fare as to Nairobi even though it is 1,809 miles farther south.

Stopover privileges are so varied and numerous that each time you go into the subject, you pull out a few plums. These are the benefits the traveler derives from the competition among airlines. IATA, the International Air Transport Association, is an organization made up of the world's airline companies which regulates fares, routes, and other matters. It recognizes that its members, in order to survive, must place as few restrictions as possible upon their right to carry passengers from one point to another. Therefore, it allows you, in traveling from Point A to Point B, to zigzag on 10 different flights with 10 different airlines (including those behind the Iron Curtain). You need only follow established air routes, via IATA members or cooperating airlines (this category includes most of the world's major companies).

Your airline ticket allows stops whether you fly economy or first class, regular or excursion fare. A regular airline ticket is good for the entire year from the day you depart; an excursion ticket, naturally, is valid only for the length of the excursion period. You pay only the fare to a single destination—the farthest point on your trip —and you may either fly directly to that point or stop at any or every city along a specified route. If, for example, you fly from New York to Athens, you may stop at Paris and Vienna without extra charge.

Indeed, if you want to visit Lisbon, Madrid, Valencia, Palma, Barcelona, Nice, Milan and Rome on your way to Athens, and Belgrade, Vienna, Munich, Stuttgart, Frankfurt, Düsseldorf, Paris, Brussels, Amsterdam, London, Dublin, and Shannon on your way back to New York, you are entitled to every one of these stops as part of your round-trip air fare between New York and Athens! There is no time limit to your stay at any stopover point, but once you have completed your trip, you can't ask for stopovers retroactively. If, for example, you fly on a one-way ticket nonstop from New York to Paris, your ticket has been fully used up for that leg of the trip as soon as you land in Paris. You can't suddenly decide to backtrack to Brussels.

To make sure that you get the maximum number of stopovers on a particular flight, here is what you should do:

1. Discuss your plans with the itinerary expert at the airline, a knowledgeable clerk or your travel agent. Either tell him your final destination and ask what stopovers are available in your mileage allowance, or specify the cities you would like to visit, and let him suggest the appropriate air ticket. Stopovers are a highly technical matter, however, and you may on occasion run across an ignorant clerk who will try to sell you only his own airline's stopover plans, when actually you are entitled to use your mileage allotment on any IATA airline as long as it stays within the allowable mileage. If you have any doubts about the way you are being routed, check the matter with other airlines.

2. If you change your itinerary while in transit, remember that additional stopovers can be added to your round trip even after you have started. *Never* buy new tickets without showing the clerk your old one. David Gollan, executive editor of *Travel Agent* magazine, who writes on tariffs, estimates that about 80 per cent of those who travel overseas make at least one change in their itineraries. In seven cases out of ten, there's no need to spend additional money for the new routing since the original ticket—reissued—may well cover the additional transportation. If, for example, you are in Frankfurt and suddenly decide to visit Copenhagen, your original round-trip ticket can probably be reissued to include a free stopover in Copenhagen, whereas a direct economy round-trip ticket, Frankfurt–Copenhagen, could cost you as much as $106.30.

3. Remember that charter flights generally do not give you stopover privileges. Should you decide to visit a number of other cities than your destination, you could well end up spending nearly as much for total transportation as you would on a regular economy-class ticket, but without the attendant freedom to travel at will from

place to place. For example, suppose you take a charter flight from New York to Paris, but want to see Venice, Rome, Madrid, and London as well. Your charter fare might cost $250 round trip, but your flight from Paris to Venice and Rome, economy class, costs about $72.00; Rome to Madrid, $65.00; Madrid to London, $83.00 and London to Paris, $26.00 (to rejoin your charter flight again). All these fares add up to $496.00 including the charter fare. If, however, you buy a basic round-trip New York–Rome economy-class ticket, it will be $544.40 (a 21-day economy-class ticket is only $409.00). Besides the cities listed above, you can also stop at Lisbon and Barcelona. While charter flights have their advantages (see Charters and Group Fares, page 68), it's important to do some careful arithmetic before joining one, or you may find that you get less than you bargained for.

In short, the longest route between two cities is often the best one for the traveler. The shortest is for the crows.

Street Vendors

WHILE IT certainly would have been too bad if Henry Higgins had turned a deaf ear to the hawking of Eliza Doolittle, that is what you should do when confronted by most street vendors. Certainly, there are times when a spontaneous purchase from a street peddler is fun. But for the most part, doing business with these rootless merchants is tricky and unrewarding. Abroad, as at home, they run the gamut from being perfectly reliable (think of the Good Humor man) to utterly unscrupulous. A street vendor is, after all, a shopkeeper without a shop. If something is wrong with his merchandise, try finding him the next morning to ask for a refund.

In sunny countries like those around the Mediterranean and in the islands of the West Indies, street vendors are common sights; they are seldom if ever seen in northern countries like Norway, Sweden, or Switzerland. In Denmark, on the other hand, the sausage carts or *pølsevogne* and the flower sellers are a tradition. The careful Danish government even goes as far as to see that the quality of their merchandise and prices are controlled.

Fish, coconuts, sweepstakes tickets, hot chestnuts, lighter flints, souvenirs, flowers, newspapers, clothes, fresh fruit, ices, shoelaces, *frites* (french fried potatoes), snails, hot bread, *lechón* (roast suckling pig), pastries, herring, pencils, beads, curios, bangles, baskets, bric-a-brac, flower leis, shell jewelry, "gold" rings, "precious stones," watches, straw hats, hot dogs, woolen ponchos and sausages are some of the items hawked by street vendors around the world. Some are safe to buy; others you will regret exceedingly. If you buy a "gold" ring made of brass, you only lose money. If you eat contaminated food, you can become quite ill. To sort out the safe and the unsafe, here are a few rules of thumb covering the three general categories of goods hawked by street vendors:

1. The standbys: newspapers, lottery and sweepstakes tickets, and flowers. You can buy any of these freely. Indeed, the flower sellers in London, Paris and Rome are part of the charm of the local scene and the flowers they sell are usually cheaper than in the shops.

2. Merchandise. The injunction here is firm: Stay away from it unless you have good reason to trust it. Clothes and bric-a-brac are almost invariably shoddy; they may be eye-catching but they are junky or overpriced or both. *Never* be tempted to buy any jewelry peddled as "real," no matter how persuasive the salesman's pitch. And stay away from watches. The only place to buy this sort of merchandise is in well-established stores that give guarantees. Prices may well be lower, but so, invariably, is the quality of the merchandise. (In France, if you buy from a street vendor, you'll have to forgo the 15 or 20 per cent discount the shops offer for being paid in travelers checks.)

3. Edibles. Here the lines are somewhat harder to draw. Taking the most conservative position, you could make it a rule never to buy food from a street vendor, or, modifying this a bit, buy only in the company of a local resident who can vouch for its safety. This would keep you out of trouble, but it would also keep you from enjoying some of the specialties for which individual countries are known, such as roasted chestnuts, oysters, ham rolls and ice cream in Paris; fish and chips in London; almonds, peanuts, shrimps, sausages, oranges and sweet biscuits in Spain; *pommes frites*, snails, and oysters in Belgium; herring and lemon in Amsterdam; sausages with mustard or horseradish on a crisp roll in Vienna; and ice cream, sausages, and taffy in Italy. All these are sold from barrows or carts or stands by street vendors, and all somehow taste more delicious eaten in the hand as you walk along.

It is more reasonable to stick to these resolutions:

In hot climates, resist *all* foods sold on open stalls. In northern climates, let common sense be your guide. As you would at home, judge for yourself the cleanliness and popularity of the vendor.

Never buy—or eat—fresh fruit whose skin has been cracked or broken. Always wash and peel fruit before you eat it.

Don't buy anything if you see any flies buzzing around.

Avoid pastries, creamy foods, fresh fish and seafood that is sold in the open. Without adequate refrigeration, these foods spoil quickly.

Anything that comes in a shell, such as eggs, passes muster only if the shells are whole or if they are piping hot.

Be extremely wary of products made with ice; also ices, sherbets and ice cream. All are potentially dangerous.

Without being neurotic about it, be cautious: One delicious tidbit, bought and eaten on an impulse, can cause a long and difficult siege of dysentery.

If you do buy something from a street vendor, there's no need to add a tip. The price of the product is all that changes hands.

Sundays

FOR MOST of us, Sundays at home are lovely liberating days when we allow ourselves to do just as we like—even if it means lolling in bed till lunchtime. They should be just as free in spirit when we travel. Unfortunately, most people tend to homogenize the days when they are traveling, seeing them merely as a series of typewritten numerals on the side of an itinerary. But as every city has its own Sunday mood and offers special opportunities, quite different from those of the weekdays, it is really very important when you are planning your itinerary to pay close attention to where the Sundays fall. (If you are traveling in Moslem countries it is the Fridays—and in Israel the Saturdays, beginning Friday at sundown—which you should watch.) Do your best to make plans that are in keeping with the Sunday spirit of that particular place, and at the same time meet *your* idea of relaxation and fun. If you don't make a point of this, you may find yourself stuck at your hotel, faced with a city almost as deserted as Wall Street at midnight.

Here are some ways for making Sundays abroad pleasant and special.

Slow down the pace of your trip. Recognize that on this day one puts aside the week's business (formal sightseeing happens to be *your* business). Take time out to pamper yourself. If your idea of bliss in Cincinnati is breakfast in bed and hours with the Sunday paper, sink back into the pillow and do the same in Copenhagen. (See Newspapers, page 278.) No matter how much money you've put into your trip, *don't* feel compulsive about spending every minute "doing something" when you really want and need a few hours of quiet laziness.

Don't take any city sightseeing tours. You will see only dead streets and empty buildings. If you really feel like sightseeing, go into the surrounding countryside. If no such trips have been included in your itinerary, ask your concierge to arrange one. Green fields, rolling hills, deserts and mountains are a refreshing break in the city traveler's routine.

Since Sunday is the day you're most apt to miss your family, get involved with people. This is a good time for participating in Meet the People programs (see Meeting People, page 239, and Organizations that Arrange Meetings Between American Visitors and Nationals, page 455). Or follow the natives. They may take a picnic to the beach, or go to the country for a long, ample Sunday luncheon. The most enchanted moments on a trip are often those spent in a sunlit garden over a leisurely meal and a good bottle of wine. Ask your concierge to make a reservation at a pretty country restaurant, such as the Coq Hardi at Bougival 10 miles east of Paris or the Olde Bell at Hurley, 60 miles from London Bridge. Every big city has leafy suburbs with lovely country inns, and naturally those easiest to reach are most likely to be crowded on Sundays; so plan to get an early start. Either hire a car and driver for the day (divided among two or more people the cost isn't budget-breaking) or use public transportation.

Some things happen *only* on Sunday, so investigate special local events. In Vienna, for example, the famous Spanish Riding School performs on Sundays at 10:30 A.M. from the beginning of September through mid-December and from early March through late June. In Copenhagen there are matinees at the Royal Theater from September 1 to May 31. In Tokyo the whole family turns out to shop in the big department stores which always stay open on Sunday. It's a tremendous treat to go to the store's coffee shop for an ice-cream soda and watch the wide-eyed children and their parents.

Sunday seems to be married to music and movies all over the world. Even in Britain, where cities are like tombs on a Sunday afternoon, there are concert and movie queues come evening. Check your concierge for local events wherever you find yourself.

If you would rather bargain-hunt and go antiquing than sleep, you can spend Sunday mornings at the local markets where everything from parakeets to porcelains is sold. (See Markets, page 226.)

Just as at home, there are always the museums (in Paris, they are free on Sundays only), spectator sports events (abroad, these could be soccer games and bullfights) and active sports such as golf and riding.

And abroad, as at home, many restaurants are closed Sundays. Unless you want to eat in your hotel, make a firm reservation ahead of time in a restaurant you know is open.

Finally, you *could* scrap all these suggestions and simply spend the day at a sidewalk café doing little more than sipping a cup of coffee or a glass of wine and watching the passersby—a pleasure that *doesn't* exist at home. In cities like Madrid, Paris and Copenhagen, that, according to the natives, would be quite enough to make a happy Sunday.

Taxis

EVEN IF you often settle for a bus when you want to get somewhere at home, once abroad you will find that the shortest distance between two points is usually via taxi. You will probably chalk up more metered mileage during a three-week trip to Europe than you would in six months in your own city—but sit back, relax and banish all guilt feelings. Most foreign taxis are not expensive. Unless you are really counting pennies or genuinely enjoy being part of the crowd on a bus or tram, they will save you enormous amounts of time and confusion. Of course, you'll want to try London's great red buses, Paris's Métro and Rome's horse-drawn carriages, but if you are not a genius at grasping the local bus and trolley system, taxis are your best bet for whizzing about.

Taxis and their habits are different in every city. London's lofty, spacious cabs are a joy—probably the last in the world designed to permit you to step in with dignity and sit in comfort. They cruise for

349

passengers and also queue down the center of major streets. When empty they carry a lighted sign that says discreetly FOR HIRE. You can also summon them by telephone.

In Amsterdam and all over Holland, on the other hand, regulations prohibit taxis from cruising or stopping for passengers in the street, no matter how frantically you wave. You can get one only from a taxi stand. Either walk to one or telephone for a taxi to pick you up. In Paris, during the noon hours, if you fell in a dead faint in the middle of the street, a taxi driver would not take you as a passenger unless you were going in his direction, which is home to lunch! The cab will carry a sign indicating which way he is heading.

Rates vary enormously from country to country, but, by and large, they are considerably lower than ours. In some countries such as Ireland, Portugal and Spain, taxis are so inexpensive that everyone, resident and tourist alike, jumps into them at the slightest excuse.

In many places, when the sun goes down, the prices go up. For example, rates are doubled in France after 11 P.M., and in Lima, Peru after midnight; in Holland they increase 50 per cent between 1 and 6 A.M.; in Finland they go up after 11; and in Rome there's a surcharge of 150 lire after 9 P.M.

There are other differences, too: In Italy there's a charge for extra luggage, for taxis ordered by phone, and an additional 25 lire each for more than two people per taxi. In Portugal a driver can charge an extra 50 per cent for heavy luggage. In Spain you are sometimes charged the round-trip fare for your one-way ride to the airport. In Brussels the smaller the taxi, the lower the fare.

So don't assume you are being cheated if you are asked to pay charges that differ from the ones back home. On the other hand, never take unmetered taxis, no matter how the drivers try to entice you. They often prey on unsuspecting foreigners—and will demand that you pay excessively high tariffs.

If you are taking a long trip by taxi, be sure to arrange the price in advance. You can often bargain a little. If you wait until you arrive at your destination, you may well find the price an unwelcome surprise you can do nothing about.

Legal taxis are metered in nearly every major country. As in the United States, the tip will be 15 to 20 per cent. In Japan, where tipping is almost nonexistent in comparison to Western countries, there's no need to tip your taxi driver at all. (See Tipping, page 359).

In the face of such a hodgepodge of customs, take the easy way out. Have your concierge brief you on how to recognize a taxi, and how and where to find one once you know what it looks like.

To cover most contingencies, here are seven general rules:

1. If you don't speak the language, write the name of your hotel on a slip of paper and keep it with you at all times. This may sound elementary but it can save you untold waste and worry. It's perfectly possible that a taxi driver filled with good intentions but little English may not understand your garbled pronunciation and take you to a hotel he *thinks* you named.

2. Keep a small pad and pencil handy for writing down the address to which you're going, and the charges on the meter in case you and the driver can't understand the numbers each of you tosses about. If you get into a hassle, let the doorman or the concierge settle the tab with the driver.

3. Check into local extensions of taxi service, often less expensive than regular taxis. One example is the *publicos* in Puerto Rico. These cars take several passengers going in the same direction. In Mexico City there are taxis called *peseros* which cross the city both ways and charge you only a peso. Their drivers hold up fingers to show how many passengers they can take. In Switzerland, taxis marked KLEIN TAXI or PETIT TAXI are cheaper than regular taxis. (In Lausanne, the *tarif reduit* taxis are even cheaper than *klein* or *petit*.) Portugal has a secondary species of luxury taxi which is *more* expensive than the regular service. It can be identified by a sign saying 3$00 in the window (meaning 3 escudos, the extra cost).

4. Let the doorman of the restaurant or your hotel or your concierge summon taxis for you. His service, as here, is rewarded with a tip: the local equivalent of our American quarter. (See Tipping, page 359).

5. Don't get into a taxi without small bills and change, or you may have to chase through miles of a strange city trying to accumulate the exact amount due the driver.

6. Be prepared for the fact that most taxi drivers seem to be training for the Monte Carlo rally, only the competition is more unruly. In Tokyo, taxi drivers are called *kamikazes*, after the Japanese pilots who committed suicide by dive-bombing during the war. So before you get into a Japanese taxi, have your concierge write on a card "Slower, please." You will certainly have occasion to use it.

7. In many countries, taxis don't cruise at night. Arrange to have a taxi come back for you at a prearranged time, or you will have to telephone for one. If you are dining in a restaurant, have your waiter call a taxi while you finish your coffee. In many of Europe's out-of-the-way hamlets and villages, there is neither public nor private transportation, so get out your walking shoes.

Telephones

AT HOME, the telephone makes life cozier. Abroad, it turns into an alien, unnerving instrument whose beeps, buzzes, coin slots, levers, and buttons seem designed to create confusion. On first using a foreign public telephone, you may feel as though you are fighting the classic battle of man versus machine. Be calm. With a little practice and patience you will learn to control the seemingly demented mechanism. Start with plenty of small coins, tokens and time. Remember that a visitor to the U.S.A. will feel just as dismayed after her first encounter with the telephone in the booth of the corner drugstore as you will after your first experience with *jetons* in Lyon.

Of course, you can bypass the problem altogether by telephoning only from your hotel, where the telephone operators and the concierge can always be counted on. The English-speaking operator—and all good hotels have at least one—will not only understand what you want but will see you through a complete call if the person at the other end "has" no English. If your name is a difficult one for foreigners, be sure to introduce yourself to the operators as soon as you check in, spelling, pronouncing and writing it down with your room number. (Often, for example, given the name "Koltun," an operator has looked at her board under the letter "C" and firmly announced to callers that I was not registered at the hotel.) Also, if you have a long list of calls to make, organize them neatly on a piece of paper, give them to the operator, and ask her to put them through, one by one. If the operators work hard in your service, tip them when you leave, from $2 to $5, depending on the number of calls they have handled.

That pearl beyond price, the concierge, will gladly guide you through the maze of the telephone directory and place any particularly tricky call. If foreign telephoning seems to go at a snail's pace, it may strengthen your spirits to realize that it is simply another reflection of the same leisurely attitude toward time that results in hours of pleasant relaxation at a café. Bear it philosophically.

Whenever you confront a telephone, remember to be patient, and in addition—to make matters easier for everyone—speak in English unless you are fluent in the language of the country. If you must use the language, know how to pronounce the digits one at a time and be able to spell out words by pronouncing the letters of the alphabet accurately. If you do get confused, don't start shouting. It will only alarm the person who is trying to understand you.

Most Continental systems work in more or less the same way. If you have to use a public telephone, here is what you will face:

To make a call in many countries you must first buy a token. In France it is called a *jeton*, in Italy a *gettone*. It is sold by cashiers in cafés, at terminals, airports, kiosks, post offices, tobacconists, et al. (If you plan to make many calls, lay in a supply.) You will find pay-telephones everywhere in public places. In the telephone booth, remove the receiver, insert the token, wait for the dial tone and dial the number. When your party answers, you will be able to hear him clearly, but he won't be able to hear you *until* you push a lever or small button which releases your slug. Pushing the button deposits the slug in the cashbox and completes the connection, enabling the conversation to become two-sided. If you neglect to press the button, the call doesn't go through. If your number doesn't answer, don't press the button. Hang up the receiver and with an enormous clatter your slug will be returned to you.

If you cannot remember all these instructions, don't fret. Directions in several languages are posted next to the telephone; they will explain the various sounds, how to dial, which button to push when. In Britain and places with British ties such as Jamaica, the system is roughly the same except that instead of a slug you insert four pennies and press buttons "A" to hear the other party and "B" to get your pennies back. Once you have accomplished this series of maneuvers, remember that "hello" is not the same in every language, and the cheerful voice at the other end will answer with some foreign phrase: The Italians say *"Pronto"*; the Swiss only give their names; the French say *"Allô"*; the Greeks say *"Malista"*; the Japanese have a special, sweet rush of sound for answering the telephone. The actual words are *"Moshi moshi."*

In spite of the seeming complexities of making a single phone call, foreign telephone systems are in some respects more highly developed than ours. We have only recently installed area-code long-distance dialing; many other countries have had it for years. Also, many have such useful, even elaborate telephone information services that there is hardly a contingency that a telephone call cannot handle. Besides time and weather, they provide news, wake-up calls, prayers, recipes, lullabies, first aid instruction, spelling information and the answer to a crossword puzzle. In London, you can have a rundown of the main events of the day by dialing ASK 9211. In Switzerland, where enlightenment by telephone is particularly advanced, you can, by dialing 11, get the name of Switzerland's President, the train schedules, addresses of doctors, or of pharmacies open on Sunday, the nearest taxi stand, programs and schedules of theaters, the dates of major historic events and even arrange for emergency repairs if your car breaks down on a remote mountain pass. The same number serves as a clearing house for messages and appointments; it will answer your calls with a standard simple message and relay them to another number. In Montevideo, Uruguay, the number 213 will give you information about travel schedules, movie programs and weather reports. In Oslo you can dial for the temperature at the beaches and the departure time of buses and steamers to the beaches. In West Berlin, dialing the right number can get you an ambulance, the name of a dentist, reports on road conditions, the program at the opera, what's at the movies, and who is performing in the cabarets, among other things. In Vienna, you can dial for a fairy tale, an etiquette tip, the pitch for tuning a violin, or a suggestion for a particular walk in the Vienna woods.

The supremely practical French give you advice on money, housing, work, family problems, and, of course, *l'amour* when you dial VAL 70-50 in Paris; a Balzac exchange will furnish recorded jokes, complete with canned laughter. For more practical services, you can hire a baby-sitter, a typist, or almost any other sort of helpful person by dialing SVP; if you need an English-speaking operator in France, dial 12.

In many countries the service gives travel information and the results of sports events. In India and Australia, for example, the minute-to-minute developments in a major cricket match are available. All the ski countries offer nearly hourly ski reports. And in Portugal, if you dial 1 51 11, you can find out if your number won the lottery.

Time

WHILE every part of the globe has the same number of hours in a day, their use varies from country to country. Often, these traditional differences—and the entire local philosophy of time—stem from the climate. In equatorial countries, for example, the working day may start in the early morning coolness at 7 A.M. and end with the heat of midafternoon at 2 P.M.; in other, slightly less tropical places, where people go home for lunch and a long siesta absorbs the afternoon's working hours, offices may close as late as 8 o'clock.

Learning to fit yourself into the local schedule will help you to make the most of your stay—and give you a better insight into the life of the country.

Take meals, for example. Even if you've dined at 6:30 every evening at home for the last thirty years, break this habit when you travel. While some parts of the world (among them Canada, Australia, New Zealand, South Africa and Scandinavia) dine as early as Americans do, the hour for taking meals grows progressively later as you move south on the Continent. The Spanish dine as late as 10 or 11, and this tradition prevails in all the Latin-American countries as well. In Mexico, for example, dinner rarely starts before 9. Take these differences in your stride. Stave off hunger with an ample tea, a chicken sandwich or an apéritif. (If hunger pangs are your problem, as they are mine, fall back on the foods mentioned in Dieting, page 109.) Use the early evening hours for sightseeing while local residents finish their day's work. Then join, say, the Madrileños at a café at 9, and dine an hour or so later in a restaurant humming with non-tourist activity. In Norway, on the other hand, you may want to dine at 5 or 5:30, for this is an early-to-dinner part of the world. Restaurants start serving the evening meal at 4. Wherever you go, get a firm fix on mealtimes early in your stay, and follow the local rhythm.

Also, use these rules to guide you in coping with time:

1. Pace your day to 1 o'clock lunch, a safe time anywhere in the world except for the Middle East, Portugal, Italy, Spain and Spanish-speaking countries, where 2 or 2:30 is closer to the mark.

2. Remember that the provinces of a country tend to dine earlier than its cities, and hotel dining rooms close earlier than restaurants. If you are motoring through the countryside or depending on a hotel for sustenance, stop for dinner early in the evening. (Resort hotels, however, have fixed meal hours; in the West Indies, dinner usually starts about 8 or 8:30.)

3. Countries which pride themselves on their cuisine tend to dine late, and the evening is usually spent at the table. In France, for example, if you were to go to a fashionable restaurant at 7, you might have to while away an hour or so standing on the sidewalk, waiting for the place to fill up.

The British, who also dine at 8, are rather rigid about meal hours. If you come to a restaurant at 2 o'clock, you will probably be told that you are too late for lunch and too early for tea. Countries that dine early, such as Japan and Sweden, tend to go to bed early as well. (In Tokyo, coffeehouses are thronged with after-dinner visitors by 8 o'clock.)

Shopping hours also vary enormously around the world. In Canada, northern Europe, the Pacific, the Orient and the Caribbean, stores are open, like ours, from 9 or 9:30 until 5 or 6. But in France and countries with a Latin tradition they close at lunchtime, usually from 12 to 2 or 1 to 3:30 or 4. Therefore, it's important to check the local shopping hours carefully with your concierge before you set out. In some cities, however—Paris is one example—only small shops close at lunchtime; department stores stay open. (For more information on department stores, see page 104.)

Everywhere offices are generally open by 9 at the latest. Countries that break into their days with a long lunch hour usually keep later office hours than we do. In southern Europe, the business day ends between 6 and 8 o'clock. In northern Europe, on the other hand, offices shut down at 3 or 4 in the afternoon, come summertime, to give people a chance to enjoy these few months of sunlit weather. In Norway, for example, the Oslofjord is filled with sailboats by 4.

In Latin countries, you may be dazzled by the pace the inhabitants keep up. Restaurants are still humming at midnight, although the working day lasts from 9 A.M. to 8 P.M. Your hosts are still exuberant and fresh when you are dropping with fatigue. Their not-so-secret weapon is that civilized Latin custom, the siesta—a one- to three-hour nap following lunch. Maybe you haven't taken a midday nap since you were five, but get into the habit again, even if it means just lying or reading quietly with the shades drawn against the sun. In countries where siestas are an entrenched part of the day, there's little else for you to do between 1 and 4. The shops are shuttered, the museums closed, the streets wrapped in a stupor until the magic hour of 4. Then the city wakes again, almost as fresh as at dawn, ready to start the second half of the day.

Besides these practical differences in how the day's hours are used, there is a telling difference in the basic attitude toward time. To almost all Americans, "time is money," as Ben Franklin observed, and we tend to program our business and social affairs with precision. Other countries, particularly Latin ones, take a much more relaxed, even cavalier attitude toward the clock. They fix the hour of a social appointment as a rough approximation of when two people will meet,

not a rigid commitment to an hour. Being punctual for social engage-
ments is not only not expected; it may even be rude. When a man in
Spain (or Mexico, Brazil, Colombia, the Philippines, other Mediterranean or South American countries) says he will call for you at 8
o'clock, don't be upset if he doesn't appear until 9 or even slightly
later. And if you are invited to someone's house at 8 o'clock, it would
be inappropriate for you to show up at that hour (you may catch
your hostess in her bath, as I once did in Mexico City). Arriving at
8:30 would be nearer right, and coming as late as 9 o'clock would probably still be permissible. If you are an exceedingly punctual person,
these differences may be hard on your nerves, but don't let them upset you. Lateness is as much a Latin custom as is exquisite courtesy to
women. Accept them both, and use a paperback or postcards to help
you bear the one while you are waiting to enjoy the other.

If, on the other hand, you are engaged in business matters with a
Latin, the picture changes, for a man who will be an hour late to a
dinner party will be scrupulously prompt for a business appointment
—and he expects you to be, too. Indeed, casual unpunctuality on the
part of an American visitor is considered bad manners, largely because we are generally accepted as punctual people.

You might, then, follow these ground rules about punctuality
abroad:

Be punctual *everywhere* except Spain, Mexico, Brazil, Colombia,
the Philippines or any other country whose social habits are so firmly,
outrageously *un*punctual that you are absolutely sure of your ground.
Thus, if you are invited to cocktails at 7:30, the usual hour in Spanish-
speaking countries, you may be late. If, however, the host says "*hora
inglesa*" (English time), you must be punctual.

Even in these countries, be punctual for all but social occasions; and
for them allow yourself only half an hour to an hour's grace. If you go
to plays, concerts or an official reception, be on time. They start
promptly, as a rule. The one invariable exception to the rule of tardi-
ness is the bullfight: *Corridas* always begin on the stroke of the hour
announced.

In countries *other* than these, *always* be punctual if you are invited
to dine at someone's home. It is the height of rudeness to threaten a
dinner's finely timed cooking by your lateness. If in Scandinavia or a
German-speaking country you are asked to come at "half seven,"
don't make the dreadful mistake of arriving at 7:30—it means 6:30.

Two final notes:

While clock faces are the only public signs written in the same way
all over the world, you must learn to read them differently in Europe.

As in our armed services, the hours are called in sequence from 1 to 24: The morning hours are 1 to 11 and 12 is noon, but 1 P.M. becomes 13 hours, 2 P.M. is 14 hours and so on until 24 for midnight. If a notice reads "Dinner at 21:00" it means dinner at 9 P.M. An easy way to remember how to express European P.M. time is to add the number 12 to the hour you would name if you were in the States.

There is no shortcut to figuring the time differences between one continent and another. If you need this information, the best sources are your concierge or the overseas telephone operator at your hotel. Eventually you'll memorize it. Some parts of Europe, like London and Lisbon are five hours later than New York; others, such as Rome and Stockholm are six. Daylight saving time goes into effect at different times in different parts of the world. See the chart below for the differences in clock time between major cities of the world and the time zones of the U.S.A.

TIME CHART

IF YOU ARE IN	STANDARD TIME IN THESE ZONES OF THE U.S.A. IS:			
	EASTERN	CENTRAL	MOUNTAIN	PACIFIC
Amsterdam	6 hours earlier	7 hours earlier	8 hours earlier	9 hours earlier
Ankara	7 hours earlier	8 hours earlier	9 hours earlier	10 hours earlier
Athens	7 hours earlier	8 hours earlier	9 hours earlier	10 hours earlier
Auckland	17 hours earlier	18 hours earlier	19 hours earlier	20 hours earlier
Azores	3 hours earlier	4 hours earlier	5 hours earlier	6 hours earlier
Baghdad	8 hours earlier	9 hours earlier	10 hours earlier	11 hours earlier
Bangkok	12 hours earlier	13 hours earlier	14 hours earlier	15 hours earlier
Beirut	7 hours earlier	8 hours earlier	9 hours earlier	10 hours earlier
Belgrade	6 hours earlier	7 hours earlier	8 hours earlier	9 hours earlier
Bogotá	same	1 hour earlier	2 hours earlier	3 hours earlier
Bridgetown	1 hour earlier	2 hours earlier	3 hours earlier	4 hours earlier
Brussels	6 hours earlier	7 hours earlier	8 hours earlier	9 hours earlier
Buenos Aires	2 hours earlier	3 hours earlier	4 hours earlier	5 hours earlier
Cairo	7 hours earlier	8 hours earlier	9 hours earlier	10 hours earlier
Caracas	same	1 hour earlier	2 hours earlier	3 hours earlier
Casablanca	5 hours earlier	6 hours earlier	7 hours earlier	8 hours earlier
Charlotte Amalie	1 hour earlier	2 hours earlier	3 hours earlier	4 hours earlier
Colombo	10½ hrs. earlier	11½ hrs. earlier	12½ hrs. earlier	13½ hrs. earlier
Dakar	4 hours earlier	5 hours earlier	6 hours earlier	7 hours earlier
Damascus	7 hours earlier	8 hours earlier	9 hours earlier	10 hours earlier
Djakarta	12 hours earlier	13 hours earlier	14 hours earlier	15 hours earlier
Dublin	5 hours earlier	6 hours earlier	7 hours earlier	8 hours earlier
Edinburgh	5 hours earlier	6 hours earlier	7 hours earlier	8 hours earlier
Frankfort	6 hours earlier	7 hours earlier	8 hours earlier	9 hours earlier
Guatemala City	1 hour later	same	1 hour earlier	2 hours earlier
Hamilton	1 hour earlier	2 hours earlier	3 hours earlier	4 hours earlier
Helsinki	7 hours earlier	8 hours earlier	9 hours earlier	10 hours earlier
Honolulu	5 hours later	4 hours later	3 hours later	2 hours later

TIME CHART

IF YOU ARE IN	STANDARD TIME IN THESE ZONES OF THE U.S.A. IS:			
	EASTERN	CENTRAL	MOUNTAIN	PACIFIC
Istanbul	7 hours earlier	8 hours earlier	9 hours earlier	10 hours earlier
Johannesburg	7 hours earlier	8 hours earlier	9 hours earlier	10 hours earlier
Kabul	9½ hrs. earlier	10½ hrs. earlier	11½ hrs. earlier	12½ hrs. earlier
Kingston	same	1 hour earlier	2 hours earlier	3 hours earlier
La Paz	1 hour earlier	2 hours earlier	3 hours earlier	4 hours earlier
Lima	same	1 hour earlier	2 hours earlier	3 hours earlier
Lisbon	5 hours earlier	6 hours earlier	7 hours earlier	8 hours earlier
London	5 hours earlier	6 hours earlier	7 hours earlier	8 hours earlier
Madrid	6 hours earlier	7 hours earlier	8 hours earlier	9 hours earlier
Mexico City	1 hour later	same	1 hour earlier	2 hours earlier
Montevideo	2 hours earlier	3 hours earlier	4 hours earlier	5 hours earlier
Nairobi	8 hours earlier	9 hours earlier	10 hours earlier	11 hours earlier
Nassau	same	1 hour earlier	2 hours earlier	3 hours earlier
New Delhi	10½ hrs. earlier	11½ hrs. earlier	12½ hrs. earlier	13½ hrs. earlier
Oslo	6 hours earlier	7 hours earlier	8 hours earlier	9 hours earlier
Panama City	same	1 hour earlier	2 hours earlier	3 hours earlier
Paris	6 hours earlier	7 hours earlier	8 hours earlier	9 hours earlier
Port-au-Prince	same	1 hour earlier	2 hours earlier	3 hours earlier
Quito	same	1 hour earlier	2 hours earlier	3 hours earlier
Rangoon	11½ hrs. earlier	12½ hrs. earlier	13½ hrs. earlier	14½ hrs. earlier
Reykjavik	4 hours earlier	5 hours earlier	6 hours earlier	7 hours earlier
Rio de Janeiro	2 hours earlier	3 hours earlier	4 hours earlier	5 hours earlier
Rome	6 hours earlier	7 hours earlier	8 hours earlier	9 hours earlier
San Juan	1 hour earlier	2 hours earlier	3 hours earlier	4 hours earlier
Santiago	1 hour earlier	2 hours earlier	3 hours earlier	4 hours earlier
Stockholm	6 hours earlier	7 hours earlier	8 hours earlier	9 hours earlier
Suva	17 hours earlier	18 hours earlier	19 hours earlier	20 hours earlier
Sydney	15 hours earlier	16 hours earlier	17 hours earlier	18 hours earlier
Teheran	8½ hrs. earlier	9½ hrs. earlier	10½ hrs. earlier	11½ hrs. earlier
Tel Aviv	7 hours earlier	8 hours earlier	9 hours earlier	10 hours earlier
Tokyo	14 hours earlier	15 hours earlier	16 hours earlier	17 hours earlier
Vienna	6 hours earlier	7 hours earlier	8 hours earlier	9 hours earlier
Zurich	6 hours earlier	7 hours earlier	8 hours earlier	9 hours earlier

Tipping

EVER SINCE your first beau nonchalantly threw an extra dime to the soda clerk, you have probably assigned the intricacies of tipping—like those of car engines and Dow-Jones averages—to the gentlemen. When you travel, these mysteries will often be yours alone to fathom.

Many women are unnecessarily, if understandably, anxious about tipping. Let me say right away that if you follow established formulas and learn a few good habits, figuring the right amount should be as easy as adding up a grocery bill. First, realize that a tip is simply a light reward for services someone performs for you. Legend has it that the word "tip" had its origins in the eighteenth century when an innkeeper kept a box inscribed with the words "*To Insure Promptness*." Patrons were requested to feed a coin or two into the box if they wanted their thirst slaked quickly. In some languages today, the word for "tip" is still connected with drinking: in German, for example, it is *trinkgeld*, in French, *pourboire*, literally "for a drink."

In general, tipping is more widespread abroad than in the U.S.A.; for persons in certain occupations, it is the sole source of income. Although its purpose is the same everywhere—simply to say "thank you"—the rules for whom and how much to tip vary from country to country.

1. The common tipping percentage for all services is between 15 and 20 per cent. I tip about 20 per cent in European countries when I am using foreign currency, and 15 per cent when I use American currency, as in the West Indies. When in doubt, it's always better to overtip ever so slightly; you are paying only a few extra pennies for peace of mind. Let local custom be your guide; follow the traditional pattern except where service has been so bad or so good that you want your tip to be a direct expression of your feelings about it.

2. Learn which coin is worth about a quarter in terms of each country's standard of living—and lay in a supply. Keep them in a separate purse. The coin in question—for example, a shilling in Britain—is usually about the size of our quarter. Although its value is perhaps half, it is used in situations where we would normally tip a quarter in this country. It's also enormously useful to know the local equivalents of 10 cents, 25 cents, 50 cents and a dollar. If you don't have a pocket currency converter, write these figures on a slip of paper and tuck it into your handbag.

3. Start each day with a pocketful of local change (see Currency, page 92). This tiny reserve of small money will save you endless trouble and scurrying about for the proper coins to give porters, waiters and washroom attendants.

4. Always tip in local currency, for two reasons. First, if you use American money you are bound to greatly overtip; and second, while

hotels and shops will take American bills and travelers checks, waiters, chambermaids and porters find it hard to exchange our silver coins for local currency. Your American tip creates a problem for them. Also, use *money* for their tips; candy, cigarettes, and other such tidbits had value just after the war but are meaningless now.

5. Never try to tip immigration or customs men or other government officials.

6. Watch the escalation of multiple tips. You needn't tip a hotel porter the same fee for each bag. In Italy you might give him 100 lire for one bag, but only 150 lire for two.

7. Many tours include a large part, but not all, of your tipping in the overall cost. Be sure to check with your travel agent or tour conductor as to which tips are covered.

8. When someone is extraordinarily helpful, increase his tip accordingly. If, for example, a porter takes your suitcase from your hotel room to a waiting taxi below, the standard tip is enough. If, on the other hand, your luggage is exceptionally heavy and he must carry it a long distance, give him something extra. Remember though that in many parts of the world elaborate service is held in higher regard than in the U.S.A.—and what may seem like the red-carpet special is just local standard operating procedure. The maid in a Japanese *ryokan,* who prepares your daily bath and serves meals in your room, need not be showered with gold; she is simply doing her duty as she sees it.

9. Tipping is nearly, but not quite, universal, and the pattern varies around the world. Europeans tip more often than we do but tip less each time. Countries behind the Iron Curtain take a dim view of the custom. They have, in fact, declared tipping illegal, since they consider it a decadent capitalist habit and an insult to labor. (It still goes on, however, surreptitiously. If you decide to tip—and many Americans do—leave about 10 per cent.) Fiji says "no tipping," and Tahiti says "positively no tipping." In the Orient, tipping is lighter than in the West; hotel service charges run 10 per cent, compared to as much as 26 per cent in Argentina, and in many places in Japan, tips are not expected. In some cities like Tokyo, La Paz and Georgetown, taxi drivers are never tipped.

The following chart gives specific tipping rules. I use the expression "for special service" to apply, for example, to the ship's chef who bakes you a three-layer birthday cake, the head steward who makes crepes suzette at your table five nights in a row, the orchestra leader who plays all your Cole Porter favorites on request.

SITUATION	ALWAYS AND HOW MUCH	SOMETIMES AND HOW MUCH	NEVER
Planes	Porters at terminals; either fixed fee per bag (ask what it is) or local quarter-equivalent.		Airline personnel, such as stewardesses, pilots, counter people: tipping forbidden. If someone is especially helpful, write to airline instead.
Ships	Tip at end of trip if voyage lasts 10 days or less. For longer trips, tip at halfway mark; for cruises of 8 weeks or more, tip weekly. If ship docks at dawn, disburse tips night before. Place amounts in small envelopes and hand them personally, expressing your thanks to each recipient. Tip 15 per cent of total fare as follows: 40 per cent to room steward, 40 per cent to dining steward, 20 per cent divided among others, or $1 a day each for room and dining steward in tourist class, $2 or $3 each in first class. Suggested minimum amounts for trans-oceanic voyages: *Cabin Steward:* $5 per person or $10 per couple in tourist; $7–$10 per person, $15 per couple in cabin; $10 per person, $15–$20 per couple in first class.	*Boots:* $1 to $2 depending on how much shoe-shining done, or $2–$3 in first class. *Bath Steward:* $2 for trip, if special service given. *Night Steward:* $2 for trip, if special service given, or preferably, small tip each time he serves you. *Head Steward:* $3 in cabin or tourist, $5 in first class, for special service. *Nursery Stewardess:* if she's cared for your children (extra tip for room steward if children have had special needs) $3–$5. *Hairdressers:* 15 to 20 per cent, as on shore, to each person who served you. *Library Steward, Chef, Orchestra Leader:* for special service. $2–$10, depending on service, class.	Purser, captain, ship's officers, and anyone whose job requires him to be licensed.

SITUATION	ALWAYS AND HOW MUCH	SOMETIMES AND HOW MUCH	NEVER
	Dining Steward: $5 per person in tourist, $7.50 per person in cabin; $10 per person in first class on usual crossing of 6 days or less; double amounts on long Mediterranean trips. If there are several stewards, tip one, who will share with others. *Deck Steward:* (In addition to chair rental fee) $1 per person in tourist, $2 per person in cabin, $3 per person in first class. *Bar Steward:* 15 per cent of total bill as you are served. *Wine Steward:* If used, $1 per person in tourist, $3 per person in cabin, $5 per person in first class, or 15 per cent of wine bill. *Cruise ships* (only one class): $1 a day each for cabin and dining stewards; $3 a trip for deck stewards; 50 cents a day on long cruises. *Pier Porters:* same as air terminal porters: local quarter-equivalent or fixed fee per bag.		
Freighters	Same scale as cabin class on transatlantic voyage. Tip at least 5 per cent of your fare or give 50 cents to $1 a day each to dining and room stewards.		
Trains	*Station porters:* local equivalent of 20–25 cents a bag or fixed fee (in France, this amount is indicated on their uniforms). *Sleeping Car attendants:* local equivalent of 50 cents to $1 per person, per night, more for extra services.	If meal served at your seat, add about 5 per cent to service charge already on your check.	

SITUATION	ALWAYS AND HOW MUCH	SOMETIMES AND HOW MUCH	NEVER
Chartered Buses	*Driver and guide:* Passengers and tour director decide among themselves how much to tip at end of trip; all contribute a share to total.		
Car Hire	If you rent a car with driver, give him 10 per cent of the total bill at end of trip. If driver delivers car to your hotel, tip local equivalent of 50 cents.		
Hotel	Most foreign hotels add 10 to 25 per cent service charge (15 per cent customary in Europe). To this add a total of 5 to 7 per cent to be divided among maid, room waiter, concierge, porters, bellboys. Give most tips as you leave, but tip porters and bellboys when service is performed.	*Room waiter and valet:* same as chambermaid, if they have served you, on checkout, or tip for each service: quarter equivalent to valet, 5% added to service charge to waiter.	
	Bellboys and porters: local equivalent of 20 cents a bag or less in Europe; 10 to 15 cents a bag or less in Middle East, Pacific, or Orient; 10 cents or less in India.	*Doorman:* local equivalent 15–20 cents for each time he calls a taxi. In Middle East and Orient, 10 cents.	
	Concierge (in Britain, the hall porter): $2 to $5 for a week's stay, depending on hotel and service. See page 84. $2 to $3 is usual.	*Boots:* If you leave your shoes to be shined, tip 10 to 15 cents a night. Tuck money into shoes on last night.	
	Chambermaid: local quarter equivalent for each day, when you check out. In Middle East and Orient, 10 cents a day. If there's a night chambermaid, leave a small tip for her.	*Telephone Operator:* If you will need more than the usual amount of help, explain this to her at the beginning of your stay, tip her at the end, $2 to $5.	

SITUATION	ALWAYS AND HOW MUCH	SOMETIMES AND HOW MUCH	NEVER
	Resort Hotels have slightly higher tipping scale. Room maids get about 50 cents a day per person or $3–$5 a week. For room, bar, and poolside service tip 15 per cent of bill. Bellboys are tipped 25 cents for each service. Waiters get 15 per cent of estimated meal charges: If you are on Modified American Plan, calculate tips on basis of $2.50 or $3 for breakfast bill, $6 or $7 for dinner (per person, of course). In *Bermuda, Bahamas* and *Caribbean* tipping pattern generally same as U.S.: about 15 per cent across the board.		
Restaurants	Service charge customary abroad, especially in Europe. Check bill to see if it's there. If so, leave another 5 per cent in small change on plate. If not, leave 15 per cent (10 to 12 per cent in Middle East and Orient). *Wine waiter* or *sommelier* is not covered in service charge; leave about 10 per cent of the cost of the drink or wine.	You need only tip the headwaiter or the captain if either does something special for you: $1–$2 depending on service and size of party.	
Taxi Drivers	15 to 20 per cent of the fare. There may be extra charges for luggage which are legally permitted. In some countries drivers are not tipped.		
Ushers	In Scandinavia and on the Continent, except for Switzerland, the person who shows you to your seat, even at a bullfight, is tipped.		

SITUATION	ALWAYS AND HOW MUCH	SOMETIMES AND HOW MUCH	NEVER
	(In Britain, it's necessary only if the usher serves you tea during intermission.) Give the local equivalent of 20 cents, more if you are shown to the best seats in the house. As ushers receive no other salary, tipping them is obligatory.		
Gasoline Station Attendants		If the attendant wipes your windshield, checks radiator, etc., give about 15 to 20 cents in the local currency.	
Hairdressers	About 15 per cent as at home. *But* this figure is the total tip, to be divided among manicurist, shampooer, coiffeur, etc.		
Barbers	10 per cent everywhere.		
Guides	About 15 per cent of sightseeing tour price; if there is no fixed fee, tip local equivalent of 25 to 50 cents.		
	If a priest or nun shows you around a religious institution, leave some money for charity, anywhere from 50 cents up.		
Tour Conductors and Drivers	A joint group tip; amount depends on price and duration of tour, helpfulness of conductor. On 2- to 3-week tour each person gives $3–$7, and contributes also to group's tip to driver.		
House Servants	In Holland, Belgium and Switzerland, tip, discreetly, servant of house where you are entertained at luncheon or dinner: 25 to 50 cents.		

Tours

THE WORD "tour" carries a certain old-fashioned oppro-
brium which goes back to the massive tours at the turn of the century.
(Thomas Cook's first organized tour in 1841 carried 570 people to a
temperance meeting for a round trip of 22 miles.) In those days, travelers were shepherded along an inflexible and often unimaginative
itinerary made necessary by the sheer physical difficulties of transportation and communication. Today the word "tour" has broadened to
include any prearranged means of traveling; it can be as esoteric as a
21-day architects' view of Palladio's houses in Italy, princely as a
tiger hunt in India, or modest as a 7-day fling around Puerto Rico.
You can book a tour in twenty minutes on your lunch hour or have
several consultations with your travel agent that result in an intricate,
custom-made itinerary; like any custom-made product, it will fit you
and no one else. Some tours are still run with the regimentation of an
army platoon, but many more allow flexibility and have a number of
decided advantages.

Tours are proliferating so quickly, and are so varied, that unless
you are dead-set on vagabonding or booking yourself from start to
finish, there's probably one to suit you. The important thing is to be
honest with yourself in assessing its strong and weak points.

There are four different kinds of trips: the packaged tour, Foreign
Independent Travel (FIT), the all-expense escorted tour and the
trip whose arrangements are made directly by the traveler. The first
three categories are considered "tours" by the travel industry and
share the characteristic of having been mapped out beforehand by a
travel agent or a tour operator. You know, before you start, the
sequence of your trip, where you will stay and for how long. The reservations are made in advance and each day's sightseeing and transportation are incorporated into your itinerary.

Faced with thousands of tours, how do you choose? Do it on the
basis of price, duration, itinerary, departure date, whether or not you
want to travel with a group or an escort, and in terms of any special
interest you may have. You should also consider the amount of ad-

vance planning you want done and the degree of supervision you want during the trip. You will find packaged trips to Europe for as little as $369 for 15 days or as much as $2,500 for 55 days. There are 23-day round-the-world tours for only $1,815; others go up to $10,000 for 90 days. All four of the above prices include round-trip fare, hotel rooms, sightseeing and most meals, but the lower the price the fewer the "extras," the more limited the sightseeing, and the simpler the accommodations.

Here, then, are the different types of tours and the strengths and weaknesses of each. Make your choice on the basis of your particular circumstances and personality.

THE PACKAGED INDEPENDENT TOUR. These are planned by airlines and tour operators, then sold over their own counters or through a travel agent. You leave whenever you please and travel on your own. The itinerary of the trip is laid down and a price tag put on it. In one transaction you buy your hotel space, transportation, sightseeing by private car or bus, transfers to and from the ports, and some of your meals. The price of the package may include an occasional "extra" such as bullfight tickets. Such personal expenses as laundry, valet, liquor and wine are of course not included.

This type of trip is good for those who like a major part of the planning done for them in advance, who want to know how much most of the trip will cost—and wish to pay for it—before they leave, but who hate moving in flocks. Nearly all major airlines have expert tour departments that are constantly devising new packages. Pan American Airways, for example, puts out booklets describing dozens of tours, and you shop from them as you would from a mail order catalog. In evaluating any package trip, beware of itineraries that skim too many countries in too little time. Nine countries in three weeks can be fascinating to read about but grueling to live through.

You can also take a package tour providing a car which you drive. Ask your travel agent about the offerings of Open Road Tours (see Castle Hotels and Country Inns, page 63 and Motoring Abroad, page 255), a firm which has devised a series of itineraries to be covered in rented cars. The route is planned in advance and you are assured of reservations at charming country inns all along the way.

THE CUSTOM-MADE TOUR, known as Foreign Independent Travel or FIT. This is a trip designed to your specifications. It grows out of consultations with your travel agent, and like all custom-made articles will cost as much as you are willing to pay, certainly more than a ready-made package. You will end up with an independent but planned trip that gives you freedom and protection. You leave when you want and travel on your own—with reservations, tickets, vouchers, times, dates and transfers firmly in hand. You know each plane and train you are to take en route, the departure time of your sightseeing bus on the third Tuesday in July, and whether you'll be met at the airport in Dubrovnik. If you like, you can have couriers standing by at every terminal to take you to the hotel, and as much or little luxury as you are willing to pay for along the way (e.g., sightseeing by chauffeur-driven private car). Such a trip is good for the woman with definite tastes and a preference for advance planning. While you start out committed to a specific itinerary, you can change your mind en route with the help of your travel agent's overseas representative, or by cabling your next hotel. If you are traveling at the height of the season, however, when hotel space is at a premium, don't count on making many changes. You will feel lucky to have any reservations already booked.

THE ESCORTED GROUP TOUR, ALSO KNOWN AS THE CONDUCTED TOUR. Intelligently chosen, it can be a pleasant solution to the anxiety of traveling alone, if you are especially shy or lonely, or, on the other hand, devoutly gregarious. You travel as one of a group with an escort, sometimes called a courier, who takes care of all bothersome details from tipping to deciphering foreign menus. Even the evenings are planned. You escape all decisions. The tour escort will check you into your hotel, buy your theater tickets, see that your luggage is put aboard the train, and even make sure that you are awakened early enough to make the sightseeing bus. You won't have to talk to a desk clerk or tip a valet. Your tour escort is a buffer against language difficulties, harassing customs officials and tight timetables.

Group tours always leave on a given date. Some are limited to fifteen people; others accept as many as thirty; the average is around twenty-five. The itinerary is carefully planned and there are local sightseeing guides along the way. The price of the tour is all-inclusive and covers hotels, meals, sightseeing and transportation, all of which are paid for before your departure.

When most people use the word "tour," they usually mean an escorted group tour. It's wise to evaluate the pluses and minuses carefully (see Your Travel Personality, page 445). On the debit side: You will be thrown into a heterogeneous group of people whom you see constantly throughout the trip; some of them may be sympathetic, others not. You may find yourself sitting with an extrovert who "wouldn't be caught dead in a museum" while for you the greatest excitement in Amsterdam is seeing Rembrandt's *Night Watch*. Or you may find yourself with gadabouts who care more about night spots than local color. You may feel that a lot of the foreignness of a place is diminished because you are always in the company of Americans. Inexpensive group tours can be grim. You can be stuck at large, cheerless hotels; the charming inexpensive inn you might have found by yourself isn't large enough to accommodate a group. You may feel that your individual preferences are too often submerged, that you are getting a predigested view of a place, isolated from real contact with a country. The escort, bless him, while he takes the problems off your hands, also takes away the excuse to get "involved"—and your opportunities to experience serendipity (often called the soul of travel) diminish. There can be no digressions like a few extra days in that charming hill town you saw en route; you go only to the tried and true places. If you want to see three performances at Stratford instead of one, you can't, for the tour must stick to its schedule.

As for the credit side of the ledger: You can always be sure of companionship and conversation, and another's point of view may bring something fresh and worthwhile to you. During the height of the season or in a busy festival town you are never stranded without a hotel room, for a group booking naturally carries greater weight with a hotel manager than a single one. You never have to cope with the fatiguing vexations that travel sometimes brings. If you are plagued by fears of becoming ill while you travel, the presence of an escort is reassuring. If you are sick in bed, *he'll* miss you when he starts counting noses and see that you are looked after. For this reason alone, group tours are appealing to many people of retirement age who like to travel on tours paced to their energies.

Even if the ordinary group tour has no interest for you, look into those organized around a special interest or purpose; these days there seems to be one for every hobby. For example, in recent years there have been tours for those interested in dwarfed bonsai trees, opera, theater, mountain climbing, bird-watching, cattle raising, great houses, great churches, and great art. Archeology buffs have joined tours of Biblical sites; photography fanatics have banded together to put the world's great sights on film; and gourmets have gourmandized as a group in the noblest restaurants of Europe. There have even been specialized tours of celebrated European dog shows. Among the most popular special tours are religious trips with pilgrimages to Lourdes, Fatima, and Rome; garden tours (see Gardens, page 143), and sports tours, especially for those interested in golf, skiing and fishing.

Specialized tours are usually escorted by someone who knows the field. Their great advantages are the companionship of people with similar tastes and interests and the opportunity to see and do things that ordinary travelers cannot. (If creating or joining this type of tour interests you, get in touch with an airline or travel agent. It takes only a dozen or so people to get one going.)

Look also into study tours which are led by authorities in their fields: educators, scientists, writers and artists. Among them are ornithological safaris to Africa or archeological study trips to Mexico and the Middle East. Some are tax-deductible when they are organized for the express purpose of studying business operations abroad. A group of interior designers could, for example, arrange a trip to meet foreign counterparts, tour historic houses, see manufacturers, make business contacts. Sometimes study tours will include seminars and lectures.

A number of highly original tours start in London and can be booked there. Check, for example, into Swans Hellenic Cruises, run by W. F. and R. K. Swan (Hellenic) Ltd., 260–261 Tottenham Court Road, London W.1. Watch the London newspapers for advertisements of others. Wherever you go, look into local tours that highlight an aspect of that country's life or history. In England, for example, you can take a week's coach tour of its lovely old inns for about $100—or a self-drive or chauffeur-driven car for a higher price. This covers bed, meals, transportation and tips, plus early morning and afternoon tea. In Australia there are mail flights in small aircraft to outback cattle and sheep stations. The tour from Sydney includes a barbecue with a ranch family, sheep muster and shearing and a bit of gold panning. In Israel, there are 3-day desert tours from Beersheba which take you deep into the Negev, to the settlement of Neot Hakikar. Bookings may be made through Neot Hakikar Desert Tours in Beersheba or through travel agents in Israel.

Toys

THE PLAYTHINGS that a nation makes for its children are, in their happy way, a mirror of its society. In highly mechanized countries, toys will revolve, fly, whir, whiz about and carry on in generally noisy fashion. In others where there is great pride in creating things by hand, the love of beautiful work wedded to the love of children produces toys detailed with great delicacy. If you enjoy shopping for toys at home, you will find it even more delightful abroad. Even if there are no children in your immediate life, think ahead to Christmas.

In Scandinavia, for example, where woodcarving is a strong tradition (the forests are thick, and this pastime helps while away the long, snowy, quiet winter) handmade wooden toys are a specialty. In Copenhagen, the late designer Kay Bojesen elevated these simple playthings to the level of art—whimsical and sophisticated. Look especially for the cheerful monkeys with jointed arms and legs, and the friendly bears, and elephants. There are also brightly painted king's guardsmen in all sizes, simple wooden rattles, building blocks and wooden trains. Charming dolls' beds and perambulators made of varnished cane would thrill a girl whose grandmother wanted to pay the fairly steep price. All are available at Den Permanente, or Kay Bojesen, Bredgade 47, or at the famous four-story toyshop, Thorngreen, on Vimmelskaftet. In Norway, where the genius for wood carving created the fantastic old stave churches, the results of a winter's work are brought to craft shops like the Husfliden in Oslo and Bergen. The figures carved by one particular family in Stalheim, a small town about three hours from Bergen, are outstanding. You can create miniature pageants of village life (a wedding on horseback for instance) from the wonderful variety of characters.

Dolls are a universal enchantment, and every country makes them in all its many regional costumes, often rich with gilt, laces and embroideries. You can buy them practically anywhere—invariably at railroad stations, airports, souvenir stalls, toyshops and department stores. But when it's convenient, try to buy them at handicraft shops (see Handicrafts, page 155). Here the costumes are authentic, the standards of workmanship high, and there's added pleasure in knowing that your money goes directly to the craftsmen. In Belgium, look for dolls dressed as lacemakers; in France, coiffed Breton women; in Jamaica, rag dolls dressed as market women. The list is endless; each country, and each region within a country, has its native costumes. If you travel in Europe, note particularly the Lenci beauties of Italy, 97 styles in all, which are sold in Rome at the Lenci shop, Via Bissolati 33, from $5 to $50. At Creazioni Benny, Via Monte Maloia 30, you will find felt dolls representing historic personalities and gay twisting couples as well, from $4 to $25. You will also find hand-carved figures of Pinocchio throughout Italy. In Finland look for the

Mumin dolls, a droll family of plush trolls which represent the characters in a series of children's books written by Tove Jansson. They cost about $1.50 at Stockmann's, the major department store in Helsinki. The Japanese have always taken their beautiful dolls and puppets seriously. Even the simplest ones you buy now for a trifle, with their silk kimonos, glossy hair and guileless faces, have a real and rare charm.

Then look for each country's specialty. In London, where guardsmen in red uniforms still parade with precision outside Buckingham Palace, lead soldiers in regimental dress are the treasure to gladden any little boy's heart. You will find them in a number of shops, notably Harrod's, the great department store; the shops in the Burlington Arcade off Piccadilly and at Hamley's, 200–202 Regent Street, which has sold toys for two hundred years. While you're in Hamley's look also for a hand puppet representing Punch; a Beatle wig and guitar; knight's armor; a set of dolls dressed as the Queens of England; or doll furniture right down to an electric fire. At Benjamin Pollock's delightful Toy Shop and Museum, 44 Monmouth Street W.C.2, there are Victorian toys and toy theaters, with appropriate scripts, backdrops, characters, and other stage props. This shop also sells charming little old-fashioned wooden dolls for less than a dollar.

In Holland, the *valk* (or falcon) kites of cloth are wonderfully inexpensive. Airborne they resemble graceful swooping birds. Germany makes the world-famous Steiff toys—stuffed animals of every kind and in every size. An orangutan might cost $7, a ridable horse for a little child $35. The wistful lifelike dolls of Käthe Kruse are among the most attractive to be found in Europe.

From France, bring back "cowboy" hats and pants from the Camargue region of Provence; or marionettes from the Guignol Theater in Lyon; or wooden toys from the Jura region; or a *diablo*, the kind of yo-yo which is a disk played along a strong between two sticks; or a doll-sized Limoges tea set; or a stuffed Babar elephant; or a superb electric train with all the fittings from the shop of Allard et Cie. in Paris. From Australia, carry or send home a cuddly toy koala bear— covered with rabbit skin, not koala fur, needless to say! Indeed any of the Australian native animals—kangaroos, platypuses, wombats— will intrigue a young American naturalist. They range in size from a few inches to several feet.

In India, look for the clay toys of W. Bengal and Gujerat; the highly decorative ones from Kondapalli (Andhra State); wooden ones from Channapatna (Mysore State); teakwoods from Tirupati (Andhra State), available at the largest handicraft centers in Bombay,

Delhi, Calcutta, Madras and Bangalore. In South Africa, the Bantus make clay and wooden toys in the shapes of animals and dolls. You can buy them at the game reserves or from the Bantu vendors on the roadside.

Every large city has an impressive topshop or two. One of the most satisfactory to be found anywhere is the chain of Franz Carl Weber stores in Switzerland with branches in all the major Swiss cities. The branch in Zurich is six stories high and sells everything imaginable— ninepins, Caran d'Ache crayons, hand-carved puppets, telescopes, zoos, walkie-talkies, dolls, roulette wheels, Dinky toys, music boxes, and a marvelous selection of model trains. Also stop off at the Heimat-werk, Rudolf-Brun Bruecke in Zurich, for beautiful wooden toys. In Paris, good toy shops are Au Nain Bleu, 408 Rue St.-Honoré, and Au Train Bleu, 2 Avenue Mozart.

In Mexico, where gay flimsy toys are produced in every region and for every festive occasion, a good place to find the best traditional examples together is the government-sponsored Museo Nacional de los Artes Populares on Avenida Juárez in Mexico City. The prices are low and profits go to maintain native crafts. Go also to the markets (see Markets, page 226). Look for decorative paper work, an ancient craft in Mexico, painted animals and an especially rich assortment of dolls.

Finally, there are many foreign games or souvenirs of national sports that would enchant a youngster. What red-blooded boy wouldn't be thrilled with a pair of mounted bull's horns from Mexico; or a boomerang or "bullrearer" (a piece of wood attached to a string which makes a moaning sound when whirled around) from Australia, or a hockey stick from Canada; or a yo-yo from the Philippines or Jamaica? These days, yo-yos in one form or another are the odds-on international favorite for mesmerizing the young.

Trains

ON SWEDEN's railroads there are fashion shows, "Mothers' Compartments" (especially set up for baby care—the railroad supplies free diapers), showers, and libraries. On commuter trains with runs of 45 minutes or more, there are seminars for passengers in English, other foreign languages, modern theater and the arts.

On sleeper trains between England and Scotland the attendant traditionally wakes you bearing tea and biscuits.

Germany's new Rheingold express has a dome car, bar, individually controlled air conditioning, stewardesses, secretarial compartments, domestic and international telephone service.

In Japan there's a train between Tokyo and Osaka that zooms along at a top speed of 125 miles an hour.

Throughout Europe, Canada and Japan, the loving care that the U.S.A. pours into automobiles and throughways goes into railroads. While you may not have been on a train in years except as a commuter, your European or Japanese counterpart is apt to use trains as casually as you use the family car.

This difference in way of life is all because of something called "car density." The U.S.A. has so many automobiles—about one for every three persons—that 90 per cent of our inter-city travel is by highway. Other countries having fewer cars must depend on their railroads to get around—a necessity which has mothered the invention of some extraordinarily good train systems.

Not only are cars relatively few, but air travel is expensive. As a result the European Continent, which is just slightly larger than the United States, has about three times as many trains. (In the U.S.A., airlines transport more passengers than railroads and motor-coach lines combined.) They are streamlined, electrified, air-conditioned, and extremely fast. There are meals at your seat and soft berths. There are gleaming railroad stations with masses of flower boxes (in Sweden, the railroad is the country's biggest gardener); and while there are still rickety, dirty trains around, when they are good they are very, very good.

Since train travel, like every other mode of transportation, has its own special tricks, here are some things to know about European trains, the ones you are most likely to be using on your next trip.

SYSTEMS: Use your shopping instincts when you book train transportation. While every country has its crack or "name" trains, not all systems are uniformly good. Generally, the French, Scandinavian, Dutch, German and Swiss railroads are excellent. In other countries, trains are marvelous on the major runs but terrible off the main lines. Sometimes even the service between two major cities varies. If you are off on a long trip, be sure to check the dining facilities—and on which leg of the run they operate—or you may wilt with hunger before the ride is over.

On the Continent, the TEE or Trans Europ Express is an excellent railroad network. Launched in 1957, the group now links about 100 major cities in eight countries: Austria, Belgium, France, Holland, Italy, Luxembourg, Switzerland, and West Germany. The trains, which make swift daylight runs from city to city, have only a few cars, are painted buff and red, and hung with paintings; their first-class service includes diners, air conditioning and uniformed hostesses or stewards. Unlike other European trains, the TEE does not sell standing room and therefore requires that you reserve a seat in advance. Since all customs and border formalities take place on the train, there is no delay in entering a country. Unless you hold a Eurailpass (described later in this section) you must pay a small extra charge to ride these trains.

CLASS: Most railroads have only two classes on long runs. The difference between them is largely that a first-class compartment has slightly plushier upholstery than second class. Both usually seat six people, though occasionally you will find eight in second class. While some cars have aisles like ours, most first- and second-class cars are generally made up of several compartments which open on a long corridor, with huge windows, stretching along one side of the train. First-class tickets cost about 35 to 50 per cent more than second-class. Unless your budget has no limits, ride second class in countries with good railroad systems or on notable trains such as Spain's Talgo. The cars are clean, the journeys usually fast. There are a few third-class cars in Spain and Portugal, but these are usually on local runs. Unless you are a youth hosteler—young, strong, and poor—avoid them. In countries such as Spain and Greece, whose trains tend to be of uneven quality, go first class on all but "name" trains.

RESERVATIONS: Be sure to buy a ticket before you board the train. In some countries, you may pay a penalty of only 10 per cent for failing to do so; in others, you may be hit for double the fare. A ticket alone, however, is no guarantee of a seat, which will cost about 75 cents more. If you are traveling during the crowded months, it is worth its weight in gold. If you don't get a seat reservation, board the train early and hope that you will be lucky enough to find a seat that is not marked as having been reserved. If you leave your seat for a time, especially for a station stop, ask someone to keep an eye on it —or put a package down—so it won't be taken by a newly boarding passenger. The people who stand in the aisles for the entire journey gazing out the windows are those who boarded without a seat reservation. In the summer months, TEE trains are sold out well in advance, so ask your travel agent to make your reservations early.

Don't throw away your train ticket even after the conductor has punched it. You may have to produce it at the gate, at the end of your trip.

MEALS: All main-line trains have diners—and a unique system for running them. Shortly after your train leaves the station, a white-jacketed steward ringing a light bell will walk through the cars taking reservations for the different sittings. Reservations can also be made on the platform before the train leaves. Trains, like ships, have two, often three sittings, at fixed hours. Choose a time (don't depend on getting a place by chance) and give the steward your name and seat number. He will give you a reservation slip. When the hour of your meal is announced, go at once to the dining car with slip in hand. Once the tables have been filled, the meal is served. Although the food is generally good, there's little choice on the menus. When you have finished eating, you are presented with the check. You pay and leave. But everybody must be finished by the time the next sitting is due.

If you don't want to bother with the dining car, there are several other ways of getting a meal or snack aboard a train. 1) On some trains, there are club cars which serve light food as well as drinks. 2) On nearly all trains, there is a vendor who wheels along a cart which carries sandwiches, fruit, candy, beer, soft drinks, coffee, ice cream, biscuits. 3) If you are fleet-footed, you can sometimes catch a vendor on the station platform during a stop, or sometimes he will sell you sandwiches through the open window of your compartment. 4) Ask your hotel to put up a picnic lunch. 5) On some TEE and name trains, you can order a meal at your seat; a special table will be set up in front of you. Some trains serve meals on trays, to be eaten at your seat as on a plane. 6) If you have a long wait between trains, use the station restaurants called "buffets," which are often so good that residents with a cityful of choices go there for lunch or dinner. 7) Many trains have buffet or snack cars in addition to diners.

Many of the older, more rickety trains have no drinking water in second class. If you are also caught without a diner, you may feel as uncomfortable as though you were stranded in the middle of the Sahara. If you are traveling in the hinterlands, board the train well-prepared with your own sustenance.

SLEEPING FACILITIES: There are two types. First are the venerable Wagons-Lits sleepers which are attached to practically every night train on the Continent. These are private bedrooms for one or two persons in first class, and three persons in second class. Then, on the principal routes, there are also special coaches known as *couchettes*. These sleep four people in a first-class compartment, six in a second-class one. They cost much less than the Wagons-Lits, and offer less comfort. While the railroad gives you a blanket and a pillow in a *couchette*, the berths do not offer much in the way of springs or feathers, and you have no privacy. It is not even customary to undress—you just loosen your clothing. It is, however, a cut above sitting up all night. The charges for Wagons-Lits sleepers and *couchettes* are naturally added on to your rail ticket. Tip the sleeping car attendant the equivalent of 50 cents to one dollar for each person, each night, slightly more if he gives you extra service.

In all countries but the U.S.S.R., if you share your compartment with someone you don't know, the stranger will be of your sex. In Russia, the international trains have separate compartments for women, but on the domestic runs, women and children share their quarters with men. Soviet trains generally have two major classes for visitors: first or "soft" class; second or "hard" class. The feel of the berth fits the name of the class.

If you are on a tight budget, you can occasionally save money by traveling at night and sleeping in a berth rather than a hotel room. A *couchette*, for example, will cost about $4, regardless of distance.

SPECIAL FARES: Every railroad has so many special fares that it's hard to imagine who would ever pay a simple round-trip fare. There are discounts for families and groups. In Denmark, as few as four people rate a 15 per cent reduction. In Britain, a party of eight saves 20 per cent. There are savings if you use your railroad ticket for a day, week, month or year; for an excursion, a circular tour, or midweek travel. There are money-saving holiday tickets, extensions on round-trip tickets, regional season tickets, kilometric tickets, and student tickets. Before you buy a railroad ticket in any country, find out what fare reductions are rightfully yours.

The biggest saving of all might well be a Eurailpass, *if* you are planning to do a lot of train travel on the Continent. This is, in effect, a pass which allows you to ride, first class, without restriction on any European train including TEE and "extra fare" trains that run in 13 countries: Austria, Belgium, Denmark, France, Germany, Holland, Italy, Luxembourg, Norway, Portugal, Spain, Sweden, and Switzerland. You can backtrack, sidetrack, stop over, or stay over as much as you like. You can change your plans a dozen times en route, and board the train wherever you please. With a Eurailpass there's no lining up at the ticket window since the pass is your ticket; you simply board a train at any point—and sit down. You don't have to pay for reserving seats (although you must make the reservation); the only additional fees are those for sleeping berths and Pullman seats. (One rugged young Eurailpass traveler I know saved money by using her compartment for sleeping.)

Unlimited use of a Eurailpass for 21 days is $99 (round-trip first-class fare, Paris to Rome alone, is $77.65); for one month it's $130; for two months it's $175; for three months it's $205. In addition to being valid for trains, a Eurailpass entitles you to travel free of charge on the bus from Paris to Nice, on both the Romantic Road bus and the Castle Road bus in Germany, the Danube and the Rhine steamers, the ferries operated by the Scandinavian Railways, and the steamers operated by the Swiss Railways on the lakes of Brienz, Geneva, Lucerne, Neuchatel, Thun, Morat, Constance and Zurich. You also receive reductions on some Europabus lines in other countries besides France and Germany.

A major thing to remember about the Eurailpass is that it is sold only to permanent residents of North and South America. You can buy it *only at home;* it is never sold abroad. Ask your travel agent to arrange one or go to one of the Eurailpass issuing offices: French National Railroads, 610 Fifth Avenue, New York, New York 10020; 323 Geary Street, San Francisco, California 94102; 1500 Stanley Street, Montreal 25, Quebec; 9465 Wilshire Boulevard, Beverly Hills, California 90212; 11 East Adams Street, Chicago, Illinois 60603; the German Federal Railroad, 11 West 42nd Street, New York, New York 10036; Italian State Railways, 11 West 42nd Street, New York, New York 10036; 333 North Michigan Avenue, Chicago, Illinois 60601; 649 South Olive Street, Los Angeles, California 90014; 323 Geary Street, San Francisco, California 94102; Scandinavian Railways, 630 Fifth Avenue, New York, New York 10020; Swiss Federal Railways, 608 Fifth Avenue, New York, New York 10020; 661 Market Street, San Francisco, California 94105.

British Rail does not participate in Eurailpass but it does have a special reduced-fare plan of its own: ThriftRail Coupons which give you 1,000 miles of first-class or 1,500 miles of second-class rail travel for $45; or 675 miles of first-class or 1,000 miles of second-class rail travel for $30, which may be shared by all your family, relatives or friends. These are good for an unlimited number of years and they can be used to purchase tickets for rail travel anywhere in England, Scotland, Wales and on ships to Ireland. They may also be turned in to pay for sleeping berths, Pullman seats and seat reservations. In either denomination, they save approximately 12 per cent on all fares. The coupons must be exchanged at the station for the service you buy. This arrangement is good for those visiting these countries for the first time, or planning limited tours of Britain. It will take you to all the classic stops such as Stratford, Windermere, Glasgow and Edinburgh for a considerable saving compared to regular rail tickets. Like a Eurailpass, ThriftRail Coupons must be purchased *before* you leave North America, through your travel agent or from British Rail—International,—630 Fifth Avenue, New York, New York 10020, or 510 West Sixth Street, Los Angeles, California 90014. They cannot be bought in Britain.

PORTERS AND BAGGAGE: In all the major terminals you'll find porters outside the station when you leave and on the platform as you arrive. Although baggage limits exist, I have never known of their being enforced on a train. For practical purposes, however, impose one on yourself. The smaller terminals have so few porters that you may be stranded in the middle of a platform surrounded by your *impedimenta* for an hour before anyone notices you. In a compartment, you can put the smaller pieces in the rack over your head; the bigger pieces must be put out of the way, which means checking them through to the baggage car and the nuisance of claiming them at your destination. Often luggage is passed through the train windows to the porters. If it is not light enough for you to lift, you may be in trouble. In Switzerland, for example, a standard two-hour ride may call for four changes of train—and at each one you will have to hoist your luggage. Also, station stops may be very brief, giving you only an instant to disembark. It becomes very important then to keep your luggage manageable. When you give your pieces to a porter, be sure to note his number, usually on his cap, and the exit for which he is heading. If he is helping you to board, give him the train's name, your space, departure time and destination—and entrust him with your luggage. He will put it into the compartment. It's easy to lose a porter in a big, foreign railroad station. So follow him out, if you can. In many places porters charge a standard fee per bag. Ask your man about this, and if a fixed charge doesn't apply, tip the local equivalent of 20 to 25 cents a bag.

TRAINS AUTOS-COUCHETTES: These are literally "car trains" or car-sleeper expresses on which your automobile travels behind you on a flatcar while you are in a compartment or a sleeper.

If, for example, you are motoring through Britain and want to drive in part of France, there is a *trains autos-couchettes* which will pick you up at Boulogne, the French harbor on the English Channel, and carry you in one short night to Lyon. From there you can drive down to Provence and the Riviera. There are a number of *trains autos-couchettes* in Europe. If moving your car around this way interests you, ask your concierge to check the local railroads.

MANNERS AND TIPS:

1. When you enter a train compartment, it's polite to say "Good morning" or "Good afternoon" to your fellow passengers. You needn't get involved in any further conversation, if you don't want to.

2. European men are often gallant to a woman encumbered by luggage. I have known them to pick up my bags, carry them off the train and down a quarter of mile of platform, then tip their hats and disappear, without even exchanging a word. Don't be surprised, then, if a man offers to help you; he is exhibiting good manners, not making a pass.

3. Don't put your feet on the banquette opposite you, even if you have shed your shoes. Europeans consider this ghastly manners.

4. Unless you bought your ticket in the United States, resign yourself to the fact that there's an interminable wait to get a refund. It's simply the slow grinding of government machinery. Also a ticket purchased in the U.S. can be returned for a refund at home only if it has been endorsed in Europe as unused and its time limit has not expired.

5. The motor coach system of the European railways is the Europabuses. For more about bus travel, see Buses, page 59.

And two final miscellaneous items:

A good way to see Jamaica is by taking a rail tour from Montego Bay into the spectacular countryside. The little train was built originally to take the Governor of the island to visit the hill villages. It is a luxurious 6-hour trip with music provided by a combo, stops for strolling in village streets, visiting a cave, and eating lunch beside a river. The total cost: $11 all year round.

One really luxurious and restful way to see the glories of the North American Continent is on the Canadian National or Canadian Pacific Railways. They are considerably less expensive and far more comfortable and efficient than trains in the U.S.—with the exception of some of our Western lines. The trains are spotlessly clean, modern and well-tended; there are observation cars with sceneramic lounges, superb scenery, and excellent food. If you live in the northern U.S.A. and want to travel by train from coast to coast, you can save money by taking a Canadian railroad. One-way coach fare, New York to Seattle, is $66.82 via Canadian National Railways but $107.32 via U.S.A. railroads; the less expensive way takes about a day longer.

Travel Agent

WHAT'S THE fastest air route from Mexico City to Nassau? Can you drive from Rome to Dubrovnik? What's the best hotel in Bangkok? How can you get tickets to the Dublin Horse Show? The only way to get answers to these and other miscellaneous questions all at once is to telephone or see your travel agent.

There are 7,700 hotels in Switzerland alone; tens of thousands of scheduled flights take off every day; and hundreds of package tours are available to travelers. The travel agent earns his living by knowing about them—or knowing where to find out about them in a few moments. Among the tools the travel agent uses are the Official Airline Guide (the worldwide edition has 1,100 pages); the Official Steamship Guide, which lists schedules for about 230 different lines; and the Hotel and Travel Index, which has some 600 pages. Moreover, he or she can supply concrete, knowledgeable and disinterested answers to dozens of personal questions that pop into your mind when planning a trip. A good agent will not only book a trip that suits your needs, but will also take many of the tensions, time wasters and harassments out of arranging it, put you onto shortcuts and money savers, and generally minimize the petty details of travel.

If you do it yourself, you will have to muddle through the technicalities of timetables (all subject to last-minute changes), buy a stack of airmail stamps and stationery, write to foreign hotels well ahead of time, wait for them to answer you, and if their answer is "no," start the whole process again. In high season these hotels, incidentally, will be less inclined to honor your request for a room than that of a travel agent; you are, after all, a one-time customer, but an agent gives them business all year long. You will need to make endless phone calls to arrange sightseeing and transfers, to check on arrival times and connections—not to mention your original calls and trips to tourist offices to get the general lay of the land. In the end, since you are inexperienced, you may well have forgotten something or underestimated your expenditures. Many people, of course, do undertake to plan their own trips—but they have usually traveled before or can afford a flexible itinerary with a minimum number of reservations, or else they are planning simple trips with only one or two stops. If you are traveling during the crowded season, it is nearly always better to use an agent. Available hotel space and transportation may vary widely depending on the city, country, time of year, not to mention temporary shortages created by special events—festivals, trade shows, and so on. It is the agent's business to keep up-to-date on these matters, and because of his continuing connections with airlines, steamships and hotels, space often opens up to him which may be closed to you.

The important qualities to look for in an agent—as in any professional—are empathy and knowledge. You should be on the same intellectual beam and have similar tastes—or at least be able to talk the same language. If the agent tries to browbeat you into going to Nice because *he* thinks it's the thing, when *you* would prefer a small hill town like St.-Paul-de-Vence, find another man or insist that the one you've got make the bookings you want.

Since a travel agent is a businessman, someone, of course, must pay him. You do sometimes; the rest comes from the companies whose services he sells. When he is entitled to receive their regular salesman's commission, you are charged nothing. Here are the jobs an agent does, and what, if anything, they will cost you:

1. He books passage on airplanes, ships, buses, and railroads, and arranges car rentals and purchases abroad.

Charges to you: None for airline and steamship reservations. Because he gets his commission from the transportation company, the price of a ticket is identical whether you buy it from an agent or the carrier. Since, on the other hand, he generally gets no commission from certain domestic railroads, particularly on point-to-point travel, you may have to pay a small fee for his help in getting you a ticket.

2. He sells all sorts of trips abroad: an independent trip completely custom-made for you; a cruise; a personally escorted domestic or foreign tour; a group tour; a prepackaged tour; a special-interest tour; a convention trip (see Tours, page 367). In connection with all these, he will book your hotel or resort accommodations, arrange for meals, sightseeing, the transfer of luggage and your transfer from hotel to terminal, and get you tickets to theaters and music festivals.

Charges to you: If you are booked into a resort hotel, none. There will probably be none, too, if you need a hotel for one night in connection with an airline ticket. (His commission in these cases covers handling costs.)

If, on the other hand, the travel agent plans an entire itinerary especially for you, the tailoring of it—the string of hotel accommodations and the host of other arrangements—requires a big investment of the agent's time and that of his staff, not to mention mailing and telephone costs. He is, moreover, putting his years of experience to work for you. (Just think how much of your own time you would have to spend to accomplish the same thing.) Like a doctor or lawyer, he earns a fee for his services, some of it payable as a deposit. Any cable charges that accrue are extra. If you book an FIT tour (Foreign Independent Travel), don't be surprised if the overall price is a figure slightly higher than that of its component parts; the extra charge will legitimately defray the normal costs of his being in business. On the other hand, if you travel on some group tours, the price may turn out to be *less* expensive for you. Here the travel agent frequently has the advantage of "bulk" buying or booking, which may cost him less for travel services than it would a traveler making the reservations on her own. On an escorted tour the price must be higher than the individual components because, as with an FIT, there are extra expenses plus the cost of the courier's services.

If you take a package tour which has been devised by a wholesaler, you pay nothing additional to the retail agent; he receives his commission from the wholesaler.

3. He will advise you about and handle insurance (trip, life, health, accident, baggage and rain); travelers checks; foreign currency; duties; customs; documents (he can obtain any that don't require your presence, such as visas). He will also help you to board or ship your pet anywhere in the world, or assist you in renting a boat, trailer, or house.

Charges to you: variable. If you are taking a fair-size trip and the agent will make a moderate commission, he won't charge you for such services. However, if he has to do a lot of telephoning and cabling, the cost of these extras will mount up, and unless your arrangements are elaborate enough to guarantee him a reasonable commission, he will quite properly expect you to be responsible for these costs.

To work smoothly with a travel agent, you must shoulder the following responsibilities:

Be absolutely straightforward and specific about your budget, your requirements, your idiosyncrasies, hopes and expectations. If you prefer convenience to charm in a hotel (or vice versa), tell him. If you must be where the action is, or hate crowds, let him know. If you get sick on long bus rides, say so. He will put the facts together and plot a realistic trip. As a professional, he is obliged to hold the information you give him in confidence, so speak up.

Be sure to get a statement of the terms of the contract in writing. Know what your obligations will be, should you cancel your trip or change your itinerary. A responsible agent will explain all these facts to you when you make your initial booking so that you are not faced with unexpected fees. Should you cancel, expect to pay for the agent's out-of-pocket expenses such as cables and telephone calls, plus a reasonable amount for the time he has spent on your reservations.

After an itinerary has been drawn up and you have been presented with tickets, coupons, reservations and a detailed itinerary, ask the agent to explain exactly what you are getting: Are the sightseeing tours half-day or full-day? Does the hotel room have a private bath and toilet? Does the room rate include breakfast? He will undoubtedly tell you all this, but it's your responsibility to know what you are buying. Also, see that the vouchers for which you have paid and the tickets match your itinerary. Then stay with your plans, as even a single change can necessitate two dozen other adjustments along the line. If your agent has to start all over again, rebooking you, he will, quite rightly, charge you for the extra work.

Choose a travel agent in about the same way you would go about finding a doctor or lawyer. Take the recommendation of a friend whose judgment you value and whose tastes are sympathetic to yours. If that doesn't work, check the yellow pages of your telephone directory and call a few. Once you know your agent well, a lot of work can be done over the telephone.

As in all business, there are good firms, bad firms, and dozens in between. While big agents such as Thomas Cook and American Express, with offices around the world, can generally be relied on, they are not necessarily the best in all areas (their banking services are first-rate everywhere, however). A one-man agency whose owner has been in business for twenty years will often have better knowledge and give more personal service than a rookie clerk who has just joined a big company.

Ask if the agency is a member of the American Society of Travel Agents (ASTA), a trade organization established in 1931 to which most of the top agents in the U.S.A. and many abroad belong. Its membership includes 2,000 agencies in the U.S.A. and Canada, several hundred more in other parts of the world. An agent who is entitled to show the oval ASTA emblem must qualify for membership on several counts:

1. He must have been appointed for at least two years to two or more traffic conferences, i.e., trade organizations of carriers who can authorize him to sell transportation directly to you: Air Traffic Conference; International Air Transport Association; Rail Travel Promotion Agency; Transatlantic Passenger Steamship Conference; Transpacific Passenger Conference.

2. He must have a properly staffed and equipped office.

3. He must adhere to the Society's ethical standards.

4. He must have credentials vouching for his financial stability and reputation.

5. He must have been in business at least three years.

While there are good agents who do not belong to ASTA, there's no way of knowing that non-ASTA agents won't fold their tents and steal away into the night; the fringe operators and total newcomers are always uncertified. Unless you have personal knowledge of the agent's solidity, stick with an ASTA member. When in doubt, call your local Better Business Bureau to find out if the firm is established, spanking-new or questionable.

Travelers Checks

SINCE THE END of the nineteenth century, when people took *journeys* instead of trips, the wise traveler has carried money in the form of travelers checks.

American Express is the largest, most far-flung organization in the travelers check business, although checks are also issued by Thomas Cook, Bank of America, Perera Co., and the First National City Bank of New York, among others. You can buy them at any office, your local bank, or in many cases from your travel agent. If you are terribly busy, you can fill out an application for checks and send a messenger or your secretary to collect them at the bank. All work in substantially the same way and their cost varies from 75 cents to $1 per hundred dollars of checks.

A day or two before your departure, exchange most of your cash for travelers checks (for more on the subject of money, see Currency, page 92). Thomas Cook issues them in denominations of $10, $20, $50, $100 and $250; American Express checks come in all but the $250 denomination plus a $500 check, which is popular for groups traveling together or individuals expecting to make large purchases abroad. When you buy the checks, you will be asked to sign each one. As you spend it, you must countersign it, an act that protects both you and the recipient. American Express checks, in particular, have become so familiar throughout the world that whether you use them in a hill town in the Pyrenees, a houseboat in Kashmir or a sukiyaki restaurant in Kyoto, they will be accepted as readily as native currency.

In some countries such as France and Yugoslavia, travelers checks are even *better* than cash, for many shops will give you an official discount if you pay with them. In France this deduction even applies to the purchase of an automobile, provided you take the car out of the country. The amount you save can be substantial since, in France, the discount for travelers checks can run up to 20 per cent.

If you run out of checks while you are traveling, you can buy them locally at banks or American Express or Thomas Cook offices. You can also write or wire your bank back home, instructing it to put through an order for delivery of checks at a specified point on your itinerary.

Since safety is the primary lure for buying travelers checks, make two copies of the serial numbers on your checks. Leave one at home, take the other with you and put it in a safe place, *separate* from your checkbook. Write down the number of each check you cash and keep this record separate too. If your pocket is picked or your handbag gets lost, such a list will help trace your checks. Report any such calamity to the company at once. These days, the companies are quick to issue refunds. If, for example, you lose your checks while you are traveling by plane or ship and cable ahead to American Express, their representative will meet you at the terminal; or you may go directly to any of their offices for a refund, which is yours even if the checks turn up later, forged with your signature.

This is all very comforting, but be sure to guard your checks as carefully as you would crisp cash. Having to cope with the problem of lost or stolen travelers checks on a trip is an irritating waste of time.

Traveling Solo

IF YOU have the time and the money (and you need little of either), set out on your own. Don't wait for your closest friend or for next year. From where you sit, the notion of a place 5,000 miles away may well seem a bit alarming. But *being* there is something else again. The sight of people reading newspapers in the sun on a park bench, children shouting and laughing at their games, women testing fruits and vegetables in the local market, and all other such homely human sights put an end to feelings of strangeness. The hazards and discomforts of traveling alone have been enormously exaggerated, and the fears that give you pause are mostly imaginary. If you think of the lone woman traveler as a woebegone creature, wandering aimlessly through the forbidding streets of a foreign city or sitting in a dismal hotel dining room, lonely, uncared for and conspicuous, you must take a fresh look at the subject.

First, you are foolishly blinkering your horizons and cheating yourself of pleasure. Never before has it been possible to go anywhere in the world in less than a day and a night. A round-the-world plane ticket costs $1,263; New York to London need cost you no more than $300.

Traveling alone should not mean loneliness for you. You may start out alone but you needn't stay that way for long. See Meeting People, page 239, and the list of organizations beginning on page 455, for dozens of ways to become involved with the local citizens or with American residents abroad. In fact, there are many women, this writer among them, who would *rather* travel alone than with another woman because you can actually have a better time that way. While two companionable women can seem intimidatingly self-sufficient to those around them, a single woman traveler is cosseted and fussed over. She is invited to dine by single men or by couples who want *her* company because it brightens their meals. One of the most enduring friendships of my life started on a solitary trip to Majorca. At the small hotel, an English couple, their curiosity roused by the sight of a single American woman, invited me to dine with them. They have been my close friends since that day, thirteen years ago.

Strangers are quick to help the single woman with her luggage, with directions, with information. Nearly everyone reacts in a cheery and paternal way. Moreover, the woman traveler on her own can have as much or as little company as she chooses; and there is no omnipresent roommate for whom one must be sunny twenty-four hours a day. There are few prohibitions for women traveling alone except those imposed by good manners everywhere.

To be sure, she may miss having someone to gossip with at odd moments. It's pleasant to be able to show a friend the bargain you found in Calle Serrano, to have someone to exclaim with you about the beauty of the Taj Mahal or laugh over the day's adventures. Pleasure is often increased by sharing, true, but few relationships live up to this ideal of traveling companionship. For every one that works, there's one that doesn't. The tensions and temptations of travel frequently strain friendships to the breaking point. Other people's personalities can often be abrasive. Many are the twosomes that have spent two out of their precious four weeks in frosty, monosyllabic conversation. Far from being the ideal mate, your traveling companion may turn out to be a millstone. You may find yourself sidetracked by a friend with aching feet or one who would rather sit at a café when you are longing to look at every picture in the Prado while the daylight holds. Making compromises may turn into a constant whittling away of your pleasures. This is why true travelers travel alone; single people move singly, and couples resist the temptation to make it a foursome. Only then can they give their wholehearted attention to the things that matter most to them.

Here are some other advantages to traveling alone:

You can set your own pace, make your own plans, and then change them all around if you want to.

You are apt to be more outgoing to strangers—you have to be.

Whenever you want companionship, you need only join a local sightseeing tour for a half or full day, but you choose company when you want it, not when it's programmed for you. If you haven't joined an organized group tour or charter at the start, plan to spend part of your trip with a group, perhaps a five-day trip through the Greek islands or a châteaux tour of the Loire Valley. Unless you are one of those rare creatures who truly cherish solitude, an alternation of independent with group touring will give you the advantages of both —and you can join a different group in each country you visit.

Being free, you can also be ready to take things as they come.

Traveling alone, you will see more sights, meet more people, and enjoy yourself more thoroughly than those who go forth burdened by the cautions and prohibitions of others.

For most women, the big problem of traveling alone is an unconscious fear that they will fall prey to unscrupulous men. They picture themselves far from home, ignorant of the language, helpless—natural victims. But this is nonsense. Tourist paths are well trodden—and peopled—and if you know the rules, the same common sense that watches over you in Cleveland will protect you in Cologne. (For more on the subject see Men, page 247.)

If you go by air, the flights are comparatively short, so loneliness can't set in. You can always strike up a conversation with your seatmate. On ships, no one travels alone. Activities are so organized that you have to meet your fellow passengers. It is completely proper for you to visit the bar on your own. Ask the dining steward to seat you at a large mixed table (in this way you are bound to meet, right from the start, both men and other women traveling by themselves), join in all the deck sports and "mixer" dances, take part in a photography clinic, swim in the pool, and much, much more.

Also, since ships make it so easy to entertain—your room steward will set up a party and clean up afterward, and the chef will send up free *hors d'oeuvre* (of course, you tip the steward for his help)—you can easily encourage the friendships you make aboard by entertaining informally.

To insure that all of the advantages of solo traveling *will* be yours, start by building an itinerary that is suitable for a lone woman. Add a few wise moves to the basic plan—and you have all the guidelines for insuring a marvelous time. Throughout this book, there are dozens of hints and tips that can help the solo woman traveler, but here are a few that pertain especially to her:

When you can, stay in guesthouses and pensions. In small, well-run places, the atmosphere is much like that of a successful house party, where all gather for drinks before meals, then dine together. Try the old plantation houses and sugar mills in the West Indies, the abbeys, châteaux and manor houses in Europe (see Castle Hotels and Country Inns, page 63, and Pensions and "P.G.'s," page 292).

In large cities, if pensions don't interest you, stay in hotels that get a large repeat trade from the natives. Remember, too, that guests in first-class hotels seldom speak to strangers; those in third- and fourth-class ones invariably do.

At resorts, being alone is less chancy than touring. Large hotels in places like Bermuda, Hawaii or the Caribbean have a social hostess or a watchful manager to see that you don't sit alone too long. Often, new guests are invited to a cocktail party given by the manager to see that they meet each other.

Join a specialized group tour or a charter (see Tours, page 367, and Charters and Group Fares, page 68). On a well-run group tour all details are taken care of; you need not lift your luggage or worry about tipping. On a special-interest tour, you will be with people who are as passionately devoted as you are to gardens, dog shows, or archeology.

Go to a resort before you go to a big city. Put St.-Paul-de-Vence ahead of Paris on your itinerary, or Lake Maggiore before Milan. You will be sure to meet Parisians and Milanese on vacation who will provide you with names and places to look up when you arrive in the city.

Participate in sports, active or spectator. Tennis courts, swimming pools, golf clubs, even the grandstand of an arena, are great places to start conversations.

Expect to have some lonely, even depressing, moments. They'll come just as they would at home—and spend them the same way: washing your hair, writing letters, or reading a good murder mystery. Or go to the movies: Even if you don't understand a word of the language, it's still fun to watch the screen and listen to the voices—and it will tide you over the bad moments.

Rely on the concierge of your hotel. He is a professional at helping tourists; he knows practically everything—or seems to—about tours, sightseeing, theater tickets and the like (see Concierge, page 83).

Enjoy yourself and be approachable. Don't be glum in a crowd, or no one will come near you. Try to think more about the other person's shyness than yours.

If you enjoy a drink before meals, go to the bar of your hotel. As long as it isn't dark and sinister, you can feel thoroughly at ease, even if the locals do gaze at you with unguarded curiosity.

Use buses. A dilapidated local bus is far more conducive to conversation than a first-class railroad compartment.

If you feel your trip will not be complete without poking your head into nightclubs, join a nightclub tour. It may be an uncharacteristic thing to do, but the group is likely to include other single people as well as couples and you'll have a chance to see all those colored lights and dancing girls.

From time to time, search out another single woman and join forces with her, sightseeing or taking meals for a day or two. I still correspond with the Italian journalist-photographer I met in a rickety sightseeing bus on my way to Epidaurus seven years ago.

Don't be shy. Start conversations. Speak to strangers. Ask for a light for your cigarette, offer your cigarettes or Life Savers, ask questions about the scenery. On the theory that the person who doesn't start the conversation is shyer than you are, lead the way. Start the talk going on your overseas flight; on a ship, with the person whose whose deck chair is next to yours; in the sightseeing bus, with the person beside you. Don't worry about the proprieties—put aside your childhood admonition not to talk to strangers. In these circumstances it is perfectly correct to take the initiative.

Don't worry about not speaking the language. On the tourist paths, nearly everyone speaks English. Where they don't a warm smile, a pocket dictionary and some lively gestures will span the gap. (See Language, page 201.)

Do just the right amount of planning ahead—enough to keep you from the blank, uncomfortable "what to do next" feeling, but not so much that you can't chuck it all at a moment's notice. If you plan your time to some extent, even including the day's dinner and evening plans, you are not left feeling at loose ends. Don't commit yourself, however, to a strict schedule (except in season when good hotel space is impossible to find). Going where and when fancy strikes you is part of the reward of being on your own.

Always deal with reputable car-hire firms and guides.

Carry a map with you so that you always have your bearings in a strange city.

In the Far East, consider hiring a full-time guide, a young boy or girl who will take you sightseeing, shopping, to restaurants or the theater at night, for a few dollars a day. They are pleasant companions and will be helpful in a dozen different ways.

Don't avoid your compatriots en route. But use the same standards that serve you at home. If a man with a loud printed sports shirt and a voice to match would send you running for cover in Indianapolis, you won't find him any more attractive in India.

Look into special, personal services that will help you in many ways at inexpensive rates. In London, for example, there is Exclusive Service All Needs Limited, 17 Bolton Street, (tel. Hyde Park 1314); ask for Mrs. Alan Palmer. This is a custom service which arranges special tours of stately homes, gets theater tickets, even furnishes a female companion to take you shopping, and delights in fulfilling all sorts of bizarre requests.

For more hints and help on traveling solo, see Beaches and Swimming Pools, page 19; Castle Hotels and Country Inns, page 63; Dining Solo, page 112; Evenings, page 125; Festivals, page 132; Itinerary Building, page 188; Men, page 247; Meeting People, page 239; Organizations that Arrange Meetings between American Visitors and Nationals, page 455; Pubs and Bars, page 301; Pensions and "P.G.'s," page 292; Seating, page 318; Sidewalk Cafes, page 330; Waterways, page 414.

Traveling with Children

UNTIL RECENTLY a woman with small children resigned herself to the idea that travel was something that must be put off to the day when her children—and she, too—were a good deal older. Today, the care lavished on mothers and small fry by airlines and steamships, the reliable foreign health standards, the abundance of baby-sitting services when you need them, and the host of children's amusements nearly everywhere you go have changed all that. Now many mothers are packing up children, disposable diapers and all, and going off to bask in the Caribbean sunshine or to motor through Europe.

Whether or not *you* and your young ones can have a successful trip depends, of course, on your own temperament and that of your children. Some rugged parents can go camping in the Alps with a fifteen-month-old baby and take in their stride sleeping on air mattresses, purifying the mountain water, and making two-mile hikes to the nearest village for supplies. Other parents' nerves are shattered worrying about whether Junior should drink the water at Tour d'Argent. Children differ just as much. What is impossible to do with Johnny may be great fun with Susie, even though they are the same age.

Only you can measure the pros and cons of traveling with your children. Women who have had happy trips with theirs point to these advantages: One, it is often far easier and less expensive to take children with you than to hire a housekeeper, pay for a summer at camp, or find an obliging relative. Two, having your children with you brings peace of mind—no frantic long-distance calls back home, no worry about their falling off the swings, biting the dog or forgetting to wear their sweaters. It's calming, for you, to have them at hand under your watchful eye or a nanny's—and still to be able to go off for some shopping or sightseeing. Three, children add to the fun of a trip. They may slow down your pace, but they are geniuses at breaking the international ice and—after a certain age—at making friends and at bringing a freshness and enthusiasm to all they see. Even the sights you would normally seek out on your own will seem brighter and more joyous when they are reflected in the eyes of a child. Four, travel is a wonderful way to prepare a child for the world he will inherit. History and literature seem to have more immediacy for school-age children when they have walked on ancient cobblestones. Five, children are generally good travelers and not given to airsickness or seasickness. (Although you may feel slightly apprehensive or queasy, a bouncy eighteen-month-old will sing "Whee" when the plane hits turbulent air.) Finally, it is far simpler to travel with young children than is generally imagined. The days when a woman had to fill trunks, portmanteaus, and hampers with equipment, food, clothes, toiletries and drugs are happily gone; now a few drip-dries, some vitamin pills, disposable bottles and diapers and a game or two will carry a youngster a long way.

On the other hand, women who have come back glassy-eyed from trips with children and state flatly "Never again" paint another picture. They see it as an ordeal, not a pleasure, and point to these disadvantages: First, traveling with children limits your itinerary and the flexibility of your trip. There's no stopping at small, undiscovered villages whose ancient charm also means ancient plumbing and, probably, ancient sanitation; no exotic lunches of enchiladas, sushi or curry unless the restaurant also serves a bland local equivalent of the hamburger. Second, having to cope with children's needs while traveling cuts down on precious, expensive travel time. If your child is out of sorts for a week, it may "waste" one third of your vacation. Third, taking children abroad adds to the cost, and they may enjoy the summer with Grandma more than being subjected to a procession of strange sitters. Fourth, it certainly adds to the complexities of getting along in a foreign country. Fifth, it deprives you of the self-indulgence and privacy you and your husband deserve on vacation. Instead of getting a tranquil golden suntan, you may find yourself chasing your two-year-old up and down the water's edge or shooing the flies off his tender skin.

I have gone into the pros and cons of traveling with children because this is not a decision about which you can be doctrinaire; too much depends on the individuals concerned, and you must honestly judge your and your children's temperaments. But if these negative arguments don't faze you and you decide to take your children along, then to insure the trip's success you must plan it with these basic considerations clearly in mind:

First, while you as an adult can control your sense of discomfort, a child cannot. He is more than likely to become bored and noisy after a few hours on the plane. You must, therefore, carefully evaluate your child's ability to sail good-naturedly through such physical trials as a long flight. A two-year-old may find a three-hour flight endurable, but six hours unbearable—unless you have carefully provided for his amusement.

Two, be realistic about the fact that traveling with children is restrictive and be prepared to give up some of your freedom in order to amuse or sit with them. You must cheerfully accept the fact that you will have less time to yourself. If staying home from the theater in London to comfort a cranky child will put your nerves on edge, then don't take him along in the first place.

Third, you must create an itinerary which hews to the beaten path. Until your child is about ten, comfort is going to have to count more than charm. Also, try to maintain a daily routine close to the one he has at home. If a new one must be established, at least let it be fairly consistent for the duration of the trip. At home, your three-year-old knows he'll be getting his lunch at 12:30 and he sees no reason to wait for it just because he's abroad. A young child is not as flexible as an adult, and some familiarity of routine, surroundings and faces will help him to cope with and enjoy the many strange experiences of a trip.

Unless you are making a family visit or renting a house abroad, where you will be planted for the entire vacation, it will require uncommon patience and courage to take a baby under one year old any farther than the nearest domestic resort. A one- or two-year-old, however, will go happily to the Caribbean or Hawaii (lazy resort life with all the American conveniences); for three- to six-year-olds, this amount of exoticness will be absolutely thrilling. Only the most rugged of parents would go to Europe with a child under six except for the aforementioned family visit, but school-age children will certainly benefit from a well-managed trip abroad if the number of places is kept within reason. In sum, in this day and age, you can take a child anywhere securely, but he will travel happily only if the itinerary does not exceed his capacity to adjust.

All the rules are naturally modified as your child gets older and more flexible. His ability to control himself grows and his need for routine, care and familiarity decreases. By the time he is teen-aged, he will probably wear you out. When a trip is planned carefully to fit the child's capacities, all the benefits of travel *en famille* begin to operate, and the trip is a thrilling experience for everyone. If you can put up with the few necessary limitations, taking children to foreign places is a game definitely worth the candle.

If you do decide to travel for pleasure with children, or find that family reasons compel you to, here are the facts you should know:

Children of all ages require the same travel documents as you do. Those under sixteen may be included on either parent's passport at no extra charge; for this, you will need a group photograph of all who are included in the single passport. It is better, however, to get a separate passport for each child, so if you suddenly decide to leave Junior in a Danish camp while you tour the Continent, you can cheerfully go your separate ways.

Smallpox vaccination is the only active immunization required for re-entry into the U.S.A. from abroad, and it is necessary for even an infant. Before you travel with a child, always see your doctor for instructions; infants, for example, should be vaccinated about one month before you leave. If the doctor recommends other shots— against polio, for example—they should be taken care of well in advance of your departure since immunization may take several weeks.

When your children are old enough to understand the plans that are afoot, let them in on things from the beginning and give them a chance to voice their preferences and opinions; you'll find it easier to get their cooperation later. Have them send for the tourist office brochures. Encourage them to keep a "log" of the trip, or a scrapbook. Buy your child a book about the country he'll visit. Like you, he should do some background reading and there are many books about other lands for children from five up. Check with his school and see if there's a special project he might work on. Give each child at least one overall responsibility. Older children can note expenses, read road maps, take care of younger children. They should feel that they are helping to plan the trip.

Most hotels, especially those in Europe, are quite accustomed to receiving children. Many will put a cot in your room or arrange separate accommodations at reduced rates. If your children are old enough, give them a room of their own and be sure to specify this when you make your reservations. Let them giggle, gossip or read without intruding on your rest—and vice versa. You will all have a more enjoyable trip.

If you expect to be in a city for a while or are traveling on a budget, a family hotel or one which runs on the demi-pension plan is a good idea. The atmosphere is usually warmer than that of big-city hotels and the home cooking may be easier on young digestive systems than a constant change of restaurants. Also, stay, when possible, at castle hotels (see Castle Hotels and Country Inns, page 63); they will enchant the young with their turrets, parapets and moats.

If you are planning to tour Europe, take a supply of warm clothing such as slacks and sweaters even if you leave in a heat wave in July; also pack plenty of bathing suits and shoes. As with adults, shoes are the most troublesome items to buy in foreign countries, unless your child has wide, square feet. If your child is an in-between size such as a pre-teen, it will be hard to find clothes to fit abroad. Like their mothers, too many little American girls look silly in Bermuda shorts; leave them home unless you are going to Bermuda or Nassau. Keep each child's clothes in a small separate suitcase that he can manage by himself. Pack plenty of drip-dries like Dacron-and-cotton blends in patterns or prints that don't show the dirt, and carry the equipment listed in Clothes Care, page 80, and Soap, page 335, to make upkeep easy. Don't count on your child's wearing dungarees and sneakers on the streets of big cities. Like your active sports clothes, these are only suitable at resorts.

In addition to the drugs and medicines suggested in Health, page 164, you should also pack a small, easily reached first-aid kit containing children's aspirin, Band-Aids, antiseptic ointment, a thermometer, bandages, plenty of Wash 'n Dries, a plastic bag which can hold a damp cloth and soap, and a collapsible cup. Ask your doctor about vitamin pills. If your children wear braces, go armed with the names of some reliable orthodontists, to be called on should a sudden crisis develop.

TRAVELING ON AIRPLANES. The advantages of going by air with children are obvious: The trip is fast, clean and exciting. Raised on stories of outer space and rockets, they are natural flyers and are practically never apprehensive. You needn't wrestle with luggage or porters, and even though cabin personnel have more than your youngsters to care about and feed, they can lend a hand. The stewardess will sterilize and warm bottles, help prepare special food, bring you boiled water and fruit drinks and keep an eye on your older child while you are busy with an infant. Remember to tell the stewardess soon after takeoff what you will need, so she can help you before she gets tied up in serving a meal to more than a hundred adults. While she has been trained to take care of infants and children during a flight, don't ask her to leave her post for an unreasonable amount of time to sit with your children.

The fare for a baby up to two is 10 per cent of the adult fare except within the continental United States or between the U.S.A. and the Bahamas, Mexico, Puerto Rico, the Virgin Islands, Jamaica, certain other Caribbean islands, Canada and Alaska, where they travel free. Children between two and twelve pay half fare. Only one child under two years of age will be carried at 10 per cent or free with each adult; additional children are charged half fare.

Tell the airline in advance that you will be traveling with small children. It will arrange such special services as priority seating, early boarding and bassinets. Mothers with children are always boarded before other passengers and given the best available seats, usually those roomy ones immediately behind the bulkhead in tourist class where a bassinet can be clamped on. The ramp agents will also give you a stroller for wheeling the baby to the plane since you will have had to check yours. While it can handle last-minute provisions for infants and children, the airline can give you better service and equipment when you check in at the ticket counter if it is prepared for your arrival.

Unless you pay half fare, your under-two child does not get seat or baggage allowance. All airlines, however, will permit you to use an empty seat if it's available. On some stretches, be prepared to hold the child in your lap. You are allowed to bring aboard a bassinet filled with 20 pounds of such in-flight necessities as diapers, food, blankets and the like, free. Anything else you carry along for the baby will be charged to your baggage allowance. The young child, on the other hand, who pays half fare is entitled to the same free baggage allowance as an adult—44 pounds in economy class, 66 in first on flights to Europe.

The airline will provide necessities: bottles, disposable diapers and strained foods if it knows far enough in advance that they will be needed. If, however, your child has ardent likes and dislikes, it's best to tuck a couple of jars of his favorite food in your hand luggage.

At airports, ground hostesses will help you to and from the aircraft and see that you are made comfortable while you wait for your flight. While nursery facilities are skimpy on this side of the Atlantic, they are quite good abroad.

It's best to bring formula ready-made for younger babies. Bottles can be easily heated and sterilized on the plane. There are also disposable bottles and nipples which come sterilized. Most doctors recommend packing a small bag of cookies or crackers for the older child in case his meals are delayed or he feels slightly queasy from the motion of traveling. Remember that if your baby is still on formula, you must pack enough bottles to carry him through the flights plus transit time from home to airport, airport to hotel.

In one small bag, pack everything the baby will need during the flight: diapers, sweater, an appropriate change of clothes if you are heading for a much warmer or colder climate, and a toy. There are two prepared kits for peripatetic babies made by Johnson and Johnson. One, Johnson's Baby Travel Kit, is a neat fold-over vinyl case which can be hung open; it is packed with oil, soap, lotion, powder, etc., and costs about $3. The other, Johnson's Baby Needs Traveler, contains in addition a washable diaper tray and an insulated pocket for nursing bottles. This is about $8. You might also use the Playtex Baby Nurser, a plastic cylinder which holds a pre-sterilized disposable bottle. Only the nipple need be boiled. And, of course, disposable diapers are a great boon. Don't forget the baby's own hairbrush and spoon.

While the adult knows enough to clear her ears by swallowing or sucking a candy and so counteract changes in pressure when the plane takes off, the baby of course does not and may react quite naturally by starting to cry. When you take the hard candy that the stewardess passes around, give the baby a small bottle of water or milk—the act of swallowing will have the same equalizing effect. When the plane takes off or lands, you must hold the baby on your lap. Fasten the safety belt around your waist, but never around the baby on your lap. The stewardess will come around to check the seat belts and see that all is well.

For older children, airlines provide entertainment—but only to a point. Each airline carries a supply of balloons, toys, picture books, coloring books, children's magazines, juvenile fiction and crayons. If, however, the number of children aboard any given flight is large or the games uninspiring as far as your six-year-old is concerned, you are better off taking a few surefire games of your own to keep him from becoming bored or restless. Older children are presented with junior pilot pins, miniature wings, junior hostess pins, and certificates that commemorate their flight.

When you are served a cocktail, your child will be offered a soft drink or milk and cookies, and usually his dinner comes before yours. Normally the food given to adults is fine for children, but many airlines have a special children's menu with hamburgers, peanut-butter-and-jelly sandwiches, hot dogs, ice cream and all the other foods that fit their idea of *haute cuisine*.

Dress both infants and older children on the layer principle so that you can add and discard clothes. Also keep their clothes, like your own, simply and loosely fitted. While the plane is aloft, the temperature is kept constant, and, since airplanes are air-conditioned, they are often cool. Then there are changes in temperature during refueling stops. Speak to your travel agent or the airline about the climate of the cities along your route. If it's going to be chilly, bring woolen clothes and a blanket for the baby. If you will be landing in the tropics, be sure his clothes are easily peelable. If your baby is likely to have an upset stomach, it's a good idea for you to take a spare blouse along, just in case you get messed up.

Since travel involves adjustment to new situations and children are happiest with familiar objects that have pleasant associations, take along one or two especially beloved, familiar toys for a small child such as the cuddly teddy bear or doll that is tucked in with him at night. Also pack a folding toilet seat; a child is better equipped to cope with strangeness when he is thoroughly comfortable. Dr. Spock recommends too that "in addition to his favorite toys, it is wise to bring a few new playthings of the kind that take a lot of doing—miniature cars or trains, a small doll with several articles of clothing or other equipment, a coloring or cut-out book, a new picture book, cardboard houses or other objects to fold and assemble, a pad of paper, pencil and crayons. A child of three likes to pack his favorite toys in his own small suitcase." (From *Baby and Child Care* by Dr. Benjamin Spock.)

Pan American Airways has developed a "Take-Along-the-Baby" Island Vacation Plan in which a large number of good Bermuda and Caribbean hotels are included. All the hotels in the plan promise to supply cribs, linen, baby food, high chairs, and hot plates in the room for heating the formula. These conveniences are free except for the baby's food. The hotels carry American-brand baby foods, formula, and canned milk. In most cases the baby is accommodated with the parents at no extra cost. Baby-sitters can be arranged through the hotels; experienced ones come as low as $12 a week (which includes 7 days from morning until midnight).

As for charter flights, the general facts already outlined apply, but the fare for your child will vary according to the number of people on the flight and the rules of the chartering organization.

TRAVELING ON SHIPS: Oceangoing liners are very
small cities at sea and simply wonderful playgrounds for chi
While you are luxuriating in a deck chair, there's a whole chil
world of amusements to liberate you without a pang of consci
There are full-time registered nurses, and nurseries for children under the watchful supervision of trained attendants. The organized
playrooms, open from early morning until evening, are gay and filled
with marvelous, inventive games, books and toys. There are indoor
and outdoor play decks and children's parties. There are movies,
Punch-and-Judy shows, parties with fancy hats and balloons, separate dining rooms or sittings where children can eat alone, with their
parents or with a nurse. There are special children's menus, foods,
formulas, and all the emergency supplies a child may need. On the
S.S. *France* there are special cribs with bells that automatically signal
a wet diaper!

Children may also share many of the adult facilities such as game
rooms, lounges, library, and shuffleboard (sometimes special hours
are set aside for their use). Many of the new ships have special children's swimming pools. For teen-agers, there are soda fountains, juke-
box cafés, "coketail" parties, programs of deck sports, dances, movies.

Your room stewardess and steward will also be of tremendous help.
The stewardess will prepare formulas and special foods for the baby.
If you are laid low by seasickness, she'll keep a watchful eye on your
children and bring their food to the stateroom. Registered nurses will
keep an eye on your infant while you are at meals. Children's mealtimes are usually separate from those of their parents, but if you want
to be with them, or if there isn't a special children's dining room, you
must take them in to the first sitting. The purser will answer all your
questions and take any problems firmly in hand.

Fares for children on ships generally follow a pattern similar to
that of air fares: Children under one travel to Europe, for example,
in first class for $40 and in tourist for $20. No separate berth is provided for them in either class. The fare for children from one to
twelve is half the adult fare; those twelve and over pay full fare.
These fares vary slightly on trans-Pacific ships where children from
one to three are charged a quarter fare.

Ships are also equipped with baby bottles, nipples, sterilizing
equipment, disposable diapers, bassinets, cribs, linens and the like, all
of which are free and available, if you ask for them when you book
your passage. Ships' laundries are excellent; many also have small
launderettes for light washing. Most laundries, however, draw the

line at washing soiled diapers, so go prepared with the disposable kind. For children over a year old, the heavy training pants called "soakers" are less bulky and easier to wash than cloth diapers. They are just as effective and could be supplemented throughout the trip by a supply of paper diapers.

On all passenger ships there is a doctor who, as a rule, charges no fee to treat minor problems such as scratched knees that have been incurred aboard the ship.

As for baby-sitters, they are fairly easy to find. If, for example, you are sailing in the Far East on board an American President Lines ship, the purser will engage an amah to come aboard while you are taking a shore excursion; or you can make arrangements to have a competent stewardess baby-sit.

On ships as on airplanes, you will get better service and equipment if you tell the line in advance that you will be traveling with children.

AT YOUR DESTINATION: Once you've arrived, who will help watch over your child and amuse him if you want to go off for an afternoon of shopping, an evening on the town, or a quick tour of the country? Many people. There are baby-sitting services for temporary care, and a number of nurseries, camps, and infants' and children's homes that take children for longer periods.

Large cities in Europe and established resort areas, particularly those in the Caribbean, abound in well-trained baby-sitters and "proxy parents," many of whom customarily do a lot more than just "sit." In Europe, a baby-sitter may wash, iron and mend the baby's clothes while he naps. Also, since European sitters are unused to the blandishments of TV or a taxi home, you needn't be concerned about providing them. (It may reassure you to know that Europeans are quite used to engaging people to care for and watch over their children; only in the U.S.A. do women, even those with the means to employ someone, take complete charge of their offspring.) Also, while baby-sitting at home remains a somewhat costly necessity, abroad sitters are not only incredibly cheap—from 12 to 90 cents an hour— but are often so capably professional that occasional sallies in the care of a local sitter can be a great treat for the children. In Ireland, for example, almost any hotel will supply a sitter who can talk authoritatively about leprechauns for an hour, a day or a night at about 70 cents an hour; in Antwerp, Belgium, the Royal Dutch Theater provides baby-sitters (most are unemployed actors) free of charge to parents who want to see a Sunday performance.

The source for information about baby-sitters is the concierge or hall porter (see Concierge, page 83) at your hotel. He usually has a list of reliable ones right at his desk. In many large cities, there are specialized agencies which furnish professional sitters; you should inquire particularly about these. In London, for example, Universal Aunts, 36 Walpole Street, Kings Road, Chelsea, S.W.3, will supply baby-sitters and daily nannies who will even take youngsters off for an afternoon of sightseeing. In Paris, you can find a baby sitter by dialing SVP (see Telephones, page 352). In Rome, the American Children's Center, Via Appennini 39, keeps an eye on tourists' children and those of foreign service officers and businessmen living there. In Florence, there is a baby-sitting service called Baby's Club. In Zurich, the Kady-Kady service supplies baby-sitters to hotels. Its employees have to pass an infant-care course to qualify.

You could also call a local university. There are always students eager to earn pocket money; the faculty member in charge of student affairs can usually put you on to a trustworthy person who also speaks English. (These days with so many young Americans attending foreign universities, you might even run across a sitter from your home state.) In Copenhagen there are two excellent baby-sitting services run by students of Copenhagen University called Studinernes Babysitters, Rosenstands vej 8, Charlottenlund, and Studenternes Babysitters, Andebakkestien 4, Copenhagen. Fees range from 25 to 50 cents an hour; arrangements should be made before 5 P.M. In the unlikely event that these sources fail, you can fall back on a student nurses' home or a domestic help agency.

You might even find "baby-sitters" listed as such in the local telephone directory. In Puerto Rico, for example, the Department of Labor (San Juan 722-2010) will give you the names of trained sitters. Sitting services are also listed in the telephone directory under *Enfermeras;* two San Juan nursing services, the Borinquen Nursing Service and the Metropolitan Nursing Service, will also supply sitters.

Children's hotels are a popular institution in several European countries. The care they give, according to trustworthy authorities, is excellent. Whether or not your child will like them, however, depends on his own flexibility and gregariousness. If you plan to leave him anywhere, do your private traveling in the immediate area so you can collect him instantly without chaos in case the plan fails. Also, don't subject your child to a series of sojourns with different strange faces in different strange countries. Either drop him off, if you will, once, for a short time, and be prepared to carry him along for the rest of the journey, or hire a baby-sitter at the beginning of your trip and have her travel with you. Since familiarity spells stability to a child, having the same person look after him throughout the trip will greatly add to his security and therefore maintain his good temper. If you want the names of children's hotels or nurseries, write to the national tourist office on the list that begins on page 479.

Resort areas and hotels have long since realized that keeping children and parents happy—and therefore, when necessary, separate—is good business. For example, Vichy, the famous spa in France, charges you only about 20 cents a day extra to put your children in the care of its Children's Country Club. Some hotels, like the El San Juan in San Juan, Puerto Rico, have a special playground for children; many others like the Dorado Beach Hotel, also in Puerto Rico, have counselors to take the children off your hands during the day. In many places there are special children's tours; your concierge will be able to tell you about them, too.

As for local children's entertainment, traveling parents often forget that any large city has its own child population and that there are as many diversions for Jean and Suzanne in Brussels as for Johnny and Susy in Boston. The national tourist offices of the countries you plan to visit generally publish lists of events which appeal to children. The British Travel Association puts out a helpful booklet called "Children Visiting Britain," which lists children's entertainments and restaurants in London and tells you about everything from good family hotels to the fact that diapers are called "nappies" in Britain. Holland puts out a colorful brochure called "Holidays with Children" that lists dozens of things to do. Also look into the excellent books by Leila Hadley mentioned on page 407; check the local weekly entertainment guide or newspaper, and have a talk with your concierge. You will find that there are sights, sounds and spectacles to enchant youngsters in all cities. There are penguins to be fed, sailing ships to be run through, toy shops to explore. Everywhere there are donkey rides, puppet shows, waxworks, circuses, street corner fairs, towers, climbs, parks, lakes, ponds, swings, sandpiles, carrousels, gardens, miniature trains, dog, cat and bird markets, factory tours, ferryboats, animal rides, open-air roller skating, ice skating, movies, ballets, children's theaters, restaurants, beaches, picnics, aquariums, zoos, marionette shows, excursion boats. There are pomp and pageantry unlike anything to be seen at home. There are fairy-tale scenes and towns (the miniature city of Madurodam in Holland will enchant you as much as your children), wonderful riverboats on the Rhine, the Seine, the Thames and dozens more (see Waterways, page 414). There are Son et Lumière spectacles which bring to life many of the world's great monuments in a dramatic play of light and sound (see Evenings, page 125). There are special museums which house mementos of great adventurers such as the Viking ships and Kon-Tiki raft in Oslo. There are pageants, parades, and festivals (see Festivals, page 132). On islands and at resorts, there are bird sanctuaries, snorkeling, glass-bottom-boat trips, catamaran rides, trips to sugar and pineapple plantations, and marine life parks.

With all that's available, how do you make a happy pattern for yourself and your children?

One, be honest with yourself about your child's interests and limitations. Know clearly what your child is capable of doing, how far his energy and interest will hold out. Don't push either too far. It's best to be a little cautious at the start until you learn how your child adapts to all the new sights and sounds.

Two, establish some sort of program each day so that your child doesn't end up with a kaleidoscopic jumble of impressions. Most parents who have traveled with children believe strongly that you must alternate several days of sightseeing with either picnics in the country or easy days in the outdoors, or, best of all, outings at the beach, which is the best place to let off extra steam or wash away the crankiness of too much moving about. An unvaried diet of cathedrals and museums can demoralize and bore even the best-tempered child. You must throw in frequent afternoons at a skating rink, a zoo or an amusement park—or any place where you can wander, stroll or sit without having to be *purposefully* absorbed in anything.

Three, program at least one thing a day that's meant specifically for children. Arrange to see it leisurely, with enough preparation on your part and the children's so that all of you have an understanding of what you are seeing and why it's worth the effort.

Four, if your children are old enough to be left on their own, separate occasionally for a meal or an afternoon. On the theory that all traveling companions need time to themselves, send your children off on a tour independently when it's possible—or leave them alone to discover things for themselves.

If you'd like your children to learn a language while you're traveling, you might consider sending them to one of Switzerland's private summer schools where students come from all over the world. This small country has tended the young solicitously for generations. You can send your child to a school which combines morning study with afternoons of sports and sightseeing. Most of the emphasis is on French although other courses are available. Sports, hiking and excursions to other parts of the country are included in the curriculum. The Swiss National Tourist Office has a special education department in its New York office at 608 Fifth Avenue, New York, New York 10020, whose job it is to advise parents about schools, camps, holiday courses and children's homes.

Europe also has a growing list of American-style summer camps which are a fairly new phenomenon. While there are about a dozen such camps in Europe, three are particularly well-established. They will take children for one, two or three 3-week periods. Among the best known and run are two which are under the aegis of Mrs. Sigrid B. Ott of the International Ranger Camps: Camp Viking, for boys and girls eight to fifteen years, is situated at Asserbo, Frederiksvaerk, 35 miles north of Copenhagen and operates for two 3-week periods; Camp Lake Geneva at Leysin, Switzerland, has three 3-week periods. The third is the International Summer Camp at Montana in Switzerland.

At all three, fees are so low that it's almost cheaper to take a family of three camp-aged children to Europe, leave them at one of the camps, if you feel they will make good campers, and then go off for a while on the Continent yourself, than to pay the usual fees at home.

The staffs are half European and half American but the organization is American; the aim is to provide a replica of American camp life in Europe. When I visited Camp Lake Geneva and the International Summer Camp Montana recently, I came away impressed with the good time they offered campers and the enthusiasm of the children for their camp life.

While little French and Swiss boys and girls also go off to camp, and their camps are well supervised, your younger children will probably feel more at home in a camp which is run along American lines where language is not a problem and the practice of serving milk, fresh orange juice and ice cream, and playing taps will make him feel he has never left home. If you have fairly self-reliant teen-agers, they might enjoy many of the special camps, particularly those in northern Europe, where they can learn to sail or ride. The national tourist offices, whose addresses start on page 479, will be able to give you their names.

If you plan to motor abroad, you will face the same problem of bored and restless children that you do on tours at home. Their restlessness may be mitigated somewhat by new scenery, but it's best to go prepared for their natural wriggling and squirming and that listless, unhappy question, "Mommy, when do we get there?" Since anything that is bulky or that will add to your flying weight is out of the question, keep a list of jolly word games that you can draw on when the need arises.

There are also such diversions as spotting and counting cars, animals or license plates from different countries; alphabet games; coloring books; a few small, soft favorite toys; a "surprise" package or two made up of dime-store collections of new, quiet, lightweight items like beads for stringing or Tinkertoys, to be opened at intervals or brought out when the need arises; jigsaw puzzles; group singing (pack a songbook); changing seat arrangements at designated intervals; letting the children follow the route on road maps or taking along a supply of pipe cleaners, preferably brightly colored, fluffy ones, to be twisted into all sorts of shapes.

Stopping to picnic gives everyone a breather, a chance to run around and let off steam. Go to a *boulangerie* to pick up fresh bread, then a local *charcutier* for ham or other cold meats, an *épicerie* for cheese and fruit. Since scenery is one of the reasons to travel, picnicking is a fine way to pause and admire it.

And finally, some general tips:

1. One of the best guides for traveling with children ever published is a four-volume work called *How to Travel with Children in Europe* by Leila Hadley. It covers the subject in exhaustive detail, is written with common sense and filled with useful information ranging from how to make museums fun for children to where to find 24-hour drugstores. Start your traveling with children with Mrs. Hadley's series. Another fine book, which is both useful and funny, is *You Can Take Them with You* by Violet Weingarten.

2. So far as it's possible, take clothes for children that need little ironing. Synthetic fibers in knitted clothes are very nearly the ideal solution. And don't pack too much. Laundries are good and fast. The hotel maid will usually pitch in to do hand pieces. Avoid like the plague anything that needs starch or special care. Take two or three dress-up outfits, however, and conservative city clothes for the big cities on your itinerary. Most children abroad are dressed with more restraint than ours are.

Remember, too, that when you visit churches, even little girls are expected to observe the rules of dress (see Church Dressing, page 76) with covered arms and a scarf on the head.

3. Like you, youngsters should be dressed in loose comfortable clothes when they travel. Take along a soft pair of slippers for the flight, so that shoes may be taken off.

4. Don't take gooey candies aboard a plane or into an automobile. Don't pack bulky, messy or noisy toys; barring these, let your child decide which toy he would like best to take along.

5. Be prepared to tip more heavily at hotels and on ships because

you depend a good deal on extra service when you travel with children.

6. One trick for giving your children a sense of moving from place to place is to make a "passport" for each child, using heavy colored paper as the cover and stapling some blank pages to it. You can attach their photographs, if you like. Then, as they go from hotel to hotel, they can get their "passports" stamped.

7. If your children yearn for hamburgers and milk shakes, search out the local soda fountain or snack bar; these now seem to be an entrenched part of big-city living wherever you go.

8. Encourage your children to collect things en route—maps, stamps, hotel brochures, anything that will bring back happy memories.

9. On land, don't travel in any way that will keep your child cooped up for hours without the possibility of stopping. Don't, for instance, plan an itinerary filled with long bus rides.

10. If you have to shop for children's clothes, remember that sizes abroad are different from ours. Usually clothes are measured in inches, so be sure to pack a tape measure.

Visas and Tourist Cards

SOME COUNTRIES will admit you with only a passport in hand. Others ask you to show your passport *and* a visa. Still others will forgo both documents in favor of a simple tourist card. The day may come when the formalities at borders will disappear (much of it has already—look at the easy uncomplicated flow between the U.S.A. and Canada), but until then, you cannot travel over a wide sweep of this earth without some sort of official papers.

If you travel in Western Europe, Israel, and Turkey, your passport is all that's necessary, unless your visit extends beyond two or three months in any one country. (In Scandinavia, the three-month period begins when the visitor enters any of the countries that compose it— namely Finland, Sweden, Norway or Denmark.) For a longer stay, you will need a visa, just as you will for any visit to the Soviet Union, the Middle East, Asia, Africa, and the Pacific.

The word *visa* is a surviving fragment of the Latin term *carta visa* which means "the paper has been seen." It is, in effect, a stamp of approval put into your passport which declares that this document has been examined and found in order for passage to the country granting the visa. It is your permission to enter that country and is the reason a passport carries several blank pages marked "visa."

You must take responsibility for getting a visa, although your travel agent will steer you through the knotty red tape. Since visa regulations change so fast that what is binding today may be outdated next year, consult him as soon as your entire itinerary is firm. In many cases, your travel agent or airline will handle the whole problem; if not, you'll have to cope yourself. To show you how the situation varies from country to country, look at these examples: Australia grants one gratis, for 48 months; India, on the other hand, charges $2 and the visa is good for only three months. Some countries will issue a visa as you wait in the consular office; others will take two or three days. Burma, because home country permission is required, takes about six weeks and the visa is good only for 24 hours.

You apply for a visa at the Consulate or Embassy of the country in question. It can be done in person or by mail. Most countries have Consulate Generals in New York City, Chicago, San Francisco, Los Angeles, New Orleans, Kansas City and Houston. If you do not live in any of these cities, check your travel agent for the address of the consular office nearest you, or go to the public library and look up this information in the *Congressional Directory*. Then write to the Consulate (some countries are quite strict about your writing to the *nearest* office) for information about the forms and documents required. If you plan to go in person to the consular office, *telephone ahead* to be sure it will be open since foreign offices observe their home countries' holidays as well as those of the U.S.A. (our government does the same abroad).

There are many places which require neither passport nor visa from American citizens. They include Canada, Bermuda, the Bahamas, the West Indies, Mexico and most of Central and South America. In many areas a tourist card is all that's necessary. It can be obtained from the national tourist office, the consular office, the airline or steamship company which carries you, or upon entering the country itself (although to save your being held up, it is always best to have it with you). Sometimes it is free; other times there is a small charge.

Never leave this country without evidence of your United States citizenship and your identity. There are two reasons for this. First, many countries which *don't* require a passport or visa *will* ask for this minimal documentation; and second, if you can't prove that you are a United States citizen, you may have an awkward time getting back into the country. A passport is of course the best possible evidence of your nationality, but if you don't have one, a birth or naturalization certificate or a voter's registration card will serve the purpose.

Since the facts relating to the use of travel documents abroad change more rapidly than the prices on the Stock Exchange, be sure to bone up on the latest information about visas and tourist cards long before you set out on your travels.

Water

IF A French friend touring the U.S.A. complains that our tap water makes her feel queasy, don't be surprised. Certainly our municipal filtering systems are excellent—as are those of France —but the chemicals used to purify drinking water differ from place to place, and frequent changes while you travel can give you minor stomach discomfort or even diarrhea. Although tap water is free of contamination in capitals and large cities everywhere in Europe, Australia, Israel, South Africa, Canada (it's less safe in South and Central America, the Middle East, Asia, and Africa), try to avoid drinking it by the glassful. Stick instead to bottled water, because keeping water a relatively stable, unchanging element as you travel will keep your stomach stable, too. Obviously you will never drink from street fountains, the tap in small country hotels, or from streams, lakes, and rivers into which towns may empty their sewage. To do so is to invite serious trouble.

Make it a *rule* as soon as you arrive in a hotel to order a bottle of mineral water, plain or sparkling, for your room, and do the same at meals. Each place has its own brands, which you should learn as soon after your arrival as you learn the local value of a dollar.

A quart bottle will range in price from 20 to 50 cents. Perrier or Vichy in France, Fiuggi or San Pellegrino in Italy, Spa Reine or Spa Gazeux in Belgium, Fachinger in Germany are popular brands in this price range. (Europeans drink a great deal of mineral water too, believing it to be good for their favorite internal organ, the liver.) South America, too, has a variety of carbonated and non-carbonated bottled waters.

But don't carry things too far. If you can drink the tap water, you can certainly use it for brushing your teeth. In places where it isn't safe, you will often see a sign reading: EAU NON POTABLE (water not drinkable)—and here, use bottled water for your teeth. In remote places—many of the world's great monuments and treasures are in hot, dusty corners of the globe—hunt down the nearest supply of Coca-Cola or Pepsi-Cola. You will find them miraculously materializing everywhere: in the courtyard of the Ali Qapu in Isfahan, Iran; or in a corner of the Grand Palace in Bangkok. At home you may not drink Colas from one year to the next; abroad they are good, safe friends. Local bottled beer is always dependable and in many places— Japan, Greece and Mexico as well as the expected Denmark—superlative. Even the Pacific is full of excellent beers, such as San Miguel; but try to stick to the local brew: imports are heavily taxed. Look also for local bottled fruit drinks, which are the equivalent of our orange crush or Seven-Up. Don't, however, try the milk or you may acquire all the unpleasant symptoms that pasteurization was invented to remedy.

If you motor into the countryside or go off on a sightseeing expedition that will take you away from a big city (for example, the classic drive from New Delhi to Agra), lay in a supply of Colas or bottled water. If you get thirsty in the middle of these dusty roads and mud-roofed villages, you will be in a dreadfully uncomfortable situation without your own resources. Many travelers who would rather brush their teeth in Coca-Cola than suspect water forget all about the ice— which, as the dictionary says, is no more than "the solid form of water, produced by freezing." It stands to reason that wherever tap water is unsafe, so is ice unless it has been made from purified or distilled water. Don't make the common mistake of believing that freezing or alcohol kills bacteria; neither does. In large hotels and good restaurants, you can be reasonably sure the ice will be carefully made. If you have the slightest doubt—if, for example, a soft-drink concession is not under the management's watchful eye—skip it. Ice can be a menace.

Actually, no country except the U.S.A. makes a practice of serving water with ice, or water with meals, for that matter. So if you want ice water, you must order it specially along with your food and wine.

And finally, if you are ever in doubt about water, boil it. This is the only sure way to rid it of impurities. If you plunge an immersion heater (a blessed device described on page 124) into a cup of water and bring it to a boil for roughly five minutes, the water becomes potable.

There are also chemicals that filter water, but if you travel reasonably well-trodden paths you won't need them. However, if you go off on an anthropological expedition to the inner reaches of Mexico, for example, they will be part of the expedition's equipment. Apropos of chemicals, you should remember not to swim in pools that are not chlorinated.

Waterways

IT IS ONLY recently that anybody has given much thought to seeing a country from the vantage point of its canals, rivers and lakes. In past years, you flashed over them on railway bridges or your road ran along beside them for a little while, giving you a brief glimpse of shining water and boats at work. The centuries-old life remaining on these waterways was quiet, half hidden, and still breathed the spirit of an age where speed didn't matter. To a considerable degree this is still true.

In many places this tranquil way of looking in through a country's back door has become a delightful and easily arranged possibility, with accommodations ranging from something as grand as a big chartered fishing vessel in which to explore a country at your own pace, to the elementary simplicity of a camping punt on the Thames which shelters you from the elements with a canvas awning. You can even rent a folding canoe to portage about on trains. Wherever you go, short of the Sahara, you are likely to find some odd, delightful, unexpected ways of seeing the world from the water. A better way of seeing life unself-consciously lived—and meeting people—can hardly be imagined.

England has 2,000 miles of inland waterways, passing through some of the most beautiful, unspoiled scenery in the island, which can be explored by barge, cruiser, yacht, punt, converted "narrow boat," or canoe. There is hardly a river or canal where you can't hire a boat or join a cruise.

For example, one of the pleasantest stretches of inland waterway is the southern section of the Oxford Canal from the Thames at Oxford to its junction with the Coventry Canal in Warwickshire. In the easy course of its 77 miles you get a bit of everything—locks, idyllic scenery, the company of narrow boats at work, decked out in their traditional paintwork of roses and castles, and a winding coil of water between two villages 5 miles apart by land but 11 miles by boat. Or there is the dramatic Shropshire Union Canal which goes through a lake district, then travels through deep valleys and eventually crosses two great eighteenth-century aqueducts arching magnificently over the River Dee. Trips along such waters are experiences out of another world.

If you are alone or traveling with a friend or your husband, it would be easiest to arrange to join a cruise in a reconstructed narrow boat, which provides cabins, hot and cold water, a dining room and a bar and a seat for every passenger beside a window. Rates run from about $30 to $60 a week and the trips last 1 or 2 weeks. A comprehensive booklet describing the kinds of boats and giving a selective list of waterways can be had from the British Travel Association (see page 483). Full information about the many firms handling cruises and boats for hire is available from the British Waterways at Birmingham, Leeds and Watford; the Inland Waterways (4 Emerald Street, London W.C.1), and the Association of Pleasure Cruise Operators (Braunston, Rugby, Warwickshire).

Even if you have only a short time in London, you can explore the charming little Regent's Park Canal in the barge *Jason* to be found in Blomfield Road, Paddington W.2. Or go up the Thames to Greenwich and back on a river bus for about $1 and get an intimate view of the teeming riverside with a running commentary by a knowledgeable conductor. Cruise boats leave every hour or so from 10:30 A.M. to 7 P.M. from the Charing Cross Pier.

In Ireland the River Shannon, which is the biggest river in the country, may be followed through some of the greenest landscape on earth in any number of ways. There are camping tours by canoe, motor launch cruises, hotels for anglers, and luxury cruises organized by the Irish River Floatels Ltd. Shorter trips of an hour or a day, with picnic lunch, can be arranged through C·I·E (Coras Iompair Eireann), 59 Upper O'Connell Street, Dublin.

Scandinavia is such a sparkling network of waterways that it can hardly be appreciated unless you do some of your exploring by boat. Sweden's famous 347-mile Göta Canal threads through central Sweden from the old city of Göteborg to Stockholm, joining rivers and lakes. A cruise the length of this pastoral waterway—through locks, wheat fields, and forests whose boughs brush the boat as it slides by, past Renaissance castles, churches, villages, and an abbey where ancient kings are buried—takes 3 days on a trim little canal cruiser. The Göta Steamship Company Ltd. in Göteborg and Stockholm can provide full information.

Finland is bespangled with thousands of lakes on which you can arrange trips by motor launch (through the Finnish Silver Line), completely equipped with restaurants and bars. A 6-hour ride from Hämeenlinna to Tampere, with return by train to Helsinki in the evening, would cost you all of $9. With more time, you might take a trip on a wood-burning steamer through the eastern lakes, which includes a visit to an ancient castle. Complete schedules, fares, and itineraries appear in *Suomen Kulkuneuvet*, which you can buy in railroad stations and bookstores. Even getting to Finland can be fun. You could go by boat from Stockholm (a short trip), Copenhagen or Travemunde, Germany (long); or you could cross from central Sweden on a cosy little steamer in 5 hours.

Norwegian waterways are spectacular with fjords, islands, waterfalls, mountains, glaciers, and can be enjoyed from mid-spring to mid-autumn, because the coast is warmed by the Gulf Stream and the landscape is bright with flowers and berries. Voyages on regular coastal steamers, carrying passengers and mail, have first-class accommodations even though touring is not their chief purpose. A round trip from Bergen to the North Cape, touching into the fjords, takes 12 days, covers 1,250 miles, and costs $220. Or if you want the works, try Bergen Line's luxury ship *Meteor*. It will take you to the top of the world beyond the North Cape where the nights gleam with pale sun.

Shorter trips into the fjords, 3 or 6 days, take you from Bergen to Oslo with daily excursions to visit ancient stave churches, explore glaciers and precipitous mountain passes. The cost is $83 or $133. This cruise can be arranged through Norwegian Fjord Lines.

There is a particularly interesting 4-hour trip to be taken on Lake

Mjøsa, about 2 hours north of Oslo. A century-old paddle-wheel steamer plies the lake every day, making stops all along the way to pick up mail, deliver produce, take on and let off local farmers. At one stop you may well want to get off the boat for more than the scheduled 10-minute stop. This is Maihaugen, a meticulously reconstructed medieval village. If you decide to explore it, you can return to Oslo by train.

If you are ambitious, you can hire your own boat with a party of friends, through Norwegian Summer Ship Rental in Oslo. For example, a 6-day tour of the fjords on a 54-foot ketch sleeping four passengers with a crew of three would set you back $35 a day per head.

Holland has miles and miles of winding inland waterways, flashing back the blue of the sky and the meadows. In Amsterdam you could start with the 1-hour trip round the stately canals and harbors; but with more time you could set out from Amsterdam on a 2-week trip through Holland, Germany, France and Switzerland by "botel." These cruises offer solid Dutch comfort, with private cabins, abundant meals, shore excursions, and a bar. A 15-day cruise costs around $250. The Netherlands National Tourist Office has full information.

If you are one of a family or a group of couples, you might even rent a private yacht for around $200 a week, complete with skipper and his wife to do the cooking, and make your way at leisure through the peaceful countryside, stopping to buy cheese, smoked eel and beer, climb up and down in the locks and wave to blue-eyed children on barges.

Europabus operates a 3-day package tour via bus and Rhine steamer from Amsterdam to Lucerne, or vice versa. This trip gives you liberal helpings of the tidy Dutch countryside, with its marvelous changeable skies, medieval German towns, and the Black Forest. Or try a Rhine cruise from Rotterdam to Basel and back on a steamer operated by the Rhine Passenger Service, which takes about 4 days downstream (north) and 5 days upstream (south), past steep vine-terraced slopes and hills crowned with castles. The stops are different each way, so a round trip makes sense if you have time. You can even arrange, as many Germans do, to hire a canoe for "water wandering" on the Rhine, the Main or the Danube.

In Austria you might go out on the Danube for a day from Vienna to Linz, past flowery cottage gardens, terraced vineyards, romantic castles, and the great baroque monastery of Melk. Here the river runs blue, as the Strauss waltz would have it. Stop off and explore the beautiful old city of Linz, and if you want to continue, pick up another steamer and go on to Passau. But make the trip on a weekday;

everyone in Vienna seems to have the same idea about weekends on the river.

In France the *bateaux mouches* of Paris are famous for the days and evenings they offer on the Seine. A 90-minute tour, leaving from in front of the Eiffel Tower every 20 minutes, costs $1; a 2½-hour trip with wine, a good dinner and entertainment will set you back about $10. And a late-night trip, leaving about midnight, with a buffet and a bar, is one of the "in" things Parisians themselves do.

Lately a number of more extensive river trips by luxury yacht have been available. You can, for example, go down the Loire from Nantes to Blois, with stops at the great châteaux (Chenonceaux, Amboise, Tours, Chambord), mirrored by the water, on a 5-day cruise that costs $86. Or take a so-called "Van Gogh" cruise, a day's trip past the Île St.-Germain, St. Cloud, and the Bois de Boulogne, through the dappled green countryside the impressionists painted along the Seine and Oise. You will pass bosky islands and charming villages, and the spire of the church on the next one along the way will beckon to you over the trees. Or go south to the Rhone River. You can cruise down from Lyon to Arles and the Camargue in a couple of days, with many interesting stops en route—and finish up, if you like, by continuing to the Riviera by train. Schedules and further information about these trips and several others can be had from Entente Fluviale, Ponton Quai d'Orsay, Port de Gros Caillou, Paris 7ᵉ.

In Italy, you can take in the austerely rich Palladian villas outside Venice from the deck of the boat *Burchiello* which takes you from Venice to Padua on the Brenta River. A stop for lunch is included; the full day's trip costs about $10. From Venice you might go to Trieste and Rijeka in Yugoslavia and take an incomparable cruise down the Dalmatian Coast to Dubrovnik (with a stop at the ancient city of Split recommended), past a fairytale coast studded with walled golden cities, castled islands and rugged cliffs. These excursions are comfortable and remarkably cheap.

In Greece a multitude of cruise ships are at hand to take you anywhere you can think of, but many are touristy. You would probably have much more fun if you used the regular domestic steamships and worked your way among the Aegean islands at your own pace.

Egypt is worth visiting if only to take a Nile trip. The most luxurious possibilities now are the brand-new "botels" with swimming pools, sundecks and shopping arcades, that go from Luxor to Aswan, with stops on the way. This trip takes 4 days. These cruises are available during the winter, from November to mid-May. In Cairo you hire a felucca (sailboat) for short trips just as you would hail a taxi in front of your hotel.

In Turkey you can take an excursion along the Black Sea coast on regular commercial ships carrying mail and freight, which have excellent tourist accommodations. Or simply get on a ferry in Istanbul and sail up the Bosporus with a crowd of Turks, disembark wherever you like and take a bus back to town.

If you want to travel Russian you can cruise down the Danube to Yalta on the Black Sea; or take a delightful 2-week trip all around the semitropical Black Sea coast from Odessa back to Odessa. In Switzerland get on a steamer any time of day or evening and make a round of one of the innumerable lovely lakes. If you go as far east as Hong Kong, take a harbor or island tour, eat in a floating restaurant, or charter a sailing junk for the weekend, complete with English-speaking guide. In India, go from Bombay to the Elephanta Caves, 6 miles away by motor launch, $2 for the round trip. Or take a boat at the pier in Calcutta or Benares and cruise the Ganges for an hour or so to see the temples along the banks. If you get to the southwest state of Kerala, by all means take the enchanting 10-hour trip from Alleppey to Quilon along palmy backwaters, past villages that haven't been awakened from their thousands of years of slumber. In Bangkok take an early morning boat ride among the Klongs to see the teeming, vigorous life of the people living in slight wooden houses along the edge of the river. Green palmettos and coconut palms, laced with orchids and wisteria, shade the water.

In most countries waterways are close to the heart of the preindustrial world. They are a tranquilizing escape from the way we live now.

Weather

No ONE but a masochist likes to get sodden and damp while sightseeing, and even the most fascinating sights lose their enchantment when it's 110° in the shade. It's also rather miserable to be without a coat where the nights get cool or to be blanketed in woolens where daytime temperatures soar. So knowing the weather you'll find at your destination is an important part of your preliminary planning and preparation, and a vital factor in working out your itinerary.

Looking at a map and noting latitudes won't give you much information, for weather depends upon many other factors, including altitude, ocean currents, winds, geographical location, humidity, etc. While temperature is the single most important element in determining how comfortable you will be (68° is ideal for most of us, 60° if we are engaged in heavy physical exercise), all of these factors will influence the weather, and even your mood. Edinburgh, for example, is as near the North Pole as Moscow, yet the two cities have different climates. Mexico City, which is on the same latitude as Honolulu, has sharper daytime and evening temperature variations because of its altitude and distance from the sea. Similarly, while Quito, Ecuador, is almost on the equator, it is so high in the Andes that its nights are cool. In hot, humid weather, you are more likely to be slow-moving, irritable and cross; where the air is clear, cool and invigorating, you, as well as the natives, will be cheerful and buoyant.

Let's take a look at the major factors that shape the weather where most tourists go.

There is first the ocean and its currents. Since water covers about three quarters of the earth's surface, the oceans mother most of the planet's weather. Cities that are near the ocean or any other large body of water tend to have warmer weather than inland cities on the same latitude, for water works to moderate and equalize temperatures. Thus an inland state like North Dakota can experience searing summer heat and terrible winter frosts; but a city like London, which is on the same latitude as Greenland, has a relatively warm climate, for London's and indeed all of Western Europe's weather is strongly influenced by the Gulf Stream, the best-known and most important of the currents which, like great rivers, run through the earth's oceans. The Gulf Stream spreads out like a fan from Florida and becomes the broad North Atlantic drift as it runs toward northern Europe. Not only does the ocean current bring warmth and more equable temperatures, it also produces rainfall in nearby countries. Britain, for one, is swept by a breeze from a comparatively warm ocean which brings with it humidity, cloudiness, drizzle and frequent rain throughout the year. (About two thirds of the world's cities are on or near the sea, but remember that the farther you go inland, the less hospitable the weather will be.)

Then there are the winds, of which the two most important systems in the world are the westerlies and the trade winds. They are global in scope rather than regional. In the westerlies' main currents are the jet streams, high-altitude winds which girdle the earth from west to east like a funnel of air. Pilots ride them to increase the speed of their aircraft. (More on this below.) The westerlies, which keep the weather moving in a pattern from west to east in our Northern Hemisphere, sweep across the continental U.S.A. in winter, bringing with them the freezing blasts of our mountains and carrying them across our inland plains, thus giving Eastern cities spells of frost and cold that Western Europe seldom knows. Similarly, these winds in summer bring scorching heat from the plains to our Midwestern and Eastern cities. Westerly winds, however, when they get out over the Atlantic, are alternately warmed and cooled by the ocean's waters. So tempered and softened, they bring to Western Europe a *far* less extreme climate than ours. London is much farther north than New York, but its winter temperatures, like those all over most of northern Europe, are much milder and its summer ones much cooler. In general, the weather in Western Europe is similar to that of our Northwest. The southern part of Europe is another story, for the Alps bar the flow of the Continent's cold inland air. Consequently, Italy, Spain and Greece can be terribly hot in the summer. (Don't, however, assume that the Mediterranean's summer heat carries into the winter months. The Rivieras may be green, lushly flowered and sunny, but they are too cool for swimming from December through March.) Our country's weather is filled with enormous contrast and is subject to mercurial change. No other place on earth except Asia knows such extremes. In the winter nearly every one of our states has at some time or other recorded below-freezing temperatures; in summer, each has known 100° days or hotter. In fact, unbelievable though it seems, in summer much of the U.S.A. lives in a blazing heat much higher than that of most equatorial regions.

The trade winds were given their name because they follow a definite track. (The word "trade" comes from the old German word *trede*, meaning track.) They blow predictably and persistently, and always in the same direction. Columbus rode them to the New World each time he came. Mild and gentle, they are the steadiest winds on the planet and act as nature's air conditioners. They blow in from over the open sea, making the trade-wind belts the most delightful parts of the oceans. Islands that lie in their path—such as the West Indies, the Bahamas, and the Canaries—have a climate that is pleasantly warm in winter and not too hot in summer.

There are also local winds whose characteristics are so clearly defined and whose effects are often so startling that locals call them names as if they were enemies. (Most of northern Europe is free of these special winds.) Changes in pressure, along with those of humidity and altitude, can affect our moods tremendously, and many of these local winds that blow steadily for weeks at a time are credited with causing deep emotional reactions: extreme irritability, depression, even suicide and murder. They color local lore, literature and law. Persons who commit violent criminal acts while they blow have been known to be let off with light sentences. Since these winds affect the natives so strongly, it is not surprising that they also enervate and depress the visitor. A little knowledge about them will keep you from a sudden explosion of temper.

There is, in the regions bordering the Middle East, the harmattan, a dry parching wind charged with dust, which originates over the Sahara, and coats your eyes, lungs and skin. Along the Sudan, the haboob, a dust storm, will whirl dust as high as a mile. The excessively dry warmth of the foehn that blows off the Alps can be terribly trying. It sweeps down the mountainside, losing its moisture, and arrives in the valleys as a hot, stinging, parching wind, accompanied by extraordinarily clear air. In Tangier, the local wind, the levanter, which is an east wind that blows in from the Mediterranean, is credited with causing headaches and feelings of depression. The sirocco, which blows along the southern and eastern Mediterranean, is a dry, dust-laden, hot wind. It blows off the Sahara from North Africa and can be felt in Italy, Malta and Sicily. In Egypt, the khamsin is a hot southerly wind that blows regularly for about 50 days beginning the middle of March. The famous mistral common in southern France, especially in winter, is a cold, dry, bleak wind drawn from the French Alps down the Rhone Valley. It is extraordinarily strong and has been known to pull people from the saddle or to blow over a load of hay. The bora of the Adriatic Sea is a similar wind—violent, dry and cold. Both the mistral and the bora will roar violently through clear and sunny days. The Greek meltemi is a strong, dry flow of air from the Sahara which lasts about half the month of August.

The most dramatic of the regional winds is the monsoon, which brings torrential rains in Asia, from India to Korea. For 6 months, dry winds parch the soil, then suddenly in June the wind changes drastically and sweeps in from the Indian Ocean and the Bay of Bengal. The winds are cool and filled with moisture, and when they hit the dry earth, the result is a burst of flooding rain which is eagerly awaited and always welcome. The monsoon is keyed to the cycle of summer and winter. A breeze of sea and land, it draws hot, wet air from the Pacific into Asia in summer; in winter, it reverses and blows out from Asia back over the Indian Ocean.

Weather is also influenced by a city's altitude and geographical situation: its proximity to mountains or hills, forests and wide-open plains. Cities with exceptionally high altitudes, no matter how close to the equator, will be cool in the morning and evening, and show a wide variation in temperature during the day. For such places, you must have clothes that you can peel in layers, for the range can be as much as 40 degrees in a single day, from blazing heat at noon to nippiness at night. A high altitude also has thinner air, i.e., less oxygen. In such cities you must move slowly the first few days until your system becomes adjusted to the atmosphere.

Don't associate the comforts or discomforts of weather only with the outdoors. There are also the man-made regulators such as air conditioning or central heating which will affect you. While Europe's capitals don't get as cold as ours in January, they can often be far less comfortable because their old, thick-walled buildings seem never to warm up or dry out. Without the advantages of our ubiquitous central heating, corridors and rooms hold the chill; and with the frequent cold rains, a thin-blooded American often finds it hard to get comfortably warm. On the other hand, the West Indies are, often, far more comfortable in July and August than St. Louis or Kansas City, for most hotel rooms are air-conditioned, the trade winds blow in gently from the sea, and there is always the soft water of the Caribbean at hand to cool one's skin.

If you plan to travel during a country's rainy season, find out beforehand when and how often the rains occur and how long they last. Are they the sporadic downfalls that come, then quickly dry, as in the West Indies, or are they the drenching rains of the monsoons? The first will hardly interfere with your daily plans; the second will make sightseeing virtually impossible, fascinating as it might be to visit Asia then. If you are traveling to a hurricane belt such as the West Indies in September, you will find that it is not so much the incidence of hurricane damage that you have to fear (although it can sometimes be heavy) as the intense humidity and pressure that build up frequently during that time of year, whether or not the hurricanes occur, making a visit to the islands far less pleasant than at another time of the year.

Also, remember when you make your plans that below the equator seasons are the reverse of ours, so that in January and February in Australia, you come into a blaze of summer.

There are some weather phenomena which will add to the pleasure of your travels: the huge rainbows over Hawaii; the northern lights, or aurora borealis, the sky spectacle of Europe's northern countries; the mirages on deserts; the waterspouts one occasionally sees at sea, those extraordinary cloud formations which seem to reach down and churn up the sea beneath them; or St. Elmo's fire, which is a bright light sometimes seen on the mastheads of ships or the tops of trees and is due to atmospheric electricity.

You will occasionally run into places where the weather is so equable that hotels are willing to insure it for visitors. In the Virgin Islands, for example, all the major hotels subscribe to "weather insurance." If the mean temperature goes below 70° or above 88°, your hotel room is free for the day.

As for the weather while you are in transit, if you go by air, you will cruise above it. Jets fly at altitudes of between 30,000 and 40,000 feet. Few clouds rise higher than 7 or 8 miles above the earth; generally there is little weather 8 miles above it. From your vantage point in a jet, you will look down on white puffs of cloud—and go cruising smoothly above them in a clear, intensely blue sky.

Since winds and weather in our hemisphere move predominantly from west to east, the planes that fly from the U.S.A. to Europe are helped along by the winds going in the same direction. Between altitudes of 20,000 and 40,000 feet, depending on the time of year, there is one known as the jet stream with velocities that can exceed 250 miles an hour. An aircraft which is boosted along by it may arrive in Europe a little earlier than scheduled. Returning from Europe, the west-east winds slow down the plane's speed. Thus the flight time from New York to London is 6½ hours, whereas the same flight from London to New York against the winds takes 7½.

No pilot ever takes off without knowing every phase of the weather that lies ahead. He is fully briefed about the winds and possibilities of turbulence before he leaves the ground. As he flies, he gets half-hourly weather reports and is guided along routes that are free of storms.

Science is constantly working on ways to improve weather forecasting and the handling of planes during all kinds of weather. In use now at many airports are instruments that help airplanes fly in thicker weather than would have been possible a few years ago, and there's a constant search for instruments and methods that reduce the delays and hazards caused by weather.

As for ship voyages, storms are comparatively infrequent on most of the ordinary ocean routes. In winter you may have some rough weather, but the stabilizers with which the majority of ocean liners are equipped these days so reduce the roll of the ship that you can dance even during bad weather. Because of the tempering effect of water in cooling and heating air, the air at sea is always cooler in summer and warmer in winter than on shore. Even in July and August it may be decidedly cool on the North Atlantic as you approach Europe; you'll need sweaters and light woolens for shipboard. Cruise ships to Bermuda and Nassau seldom encounter any weather rougher than strong gales at the height of winter.

Finally, in Europe and many other parts of the world, temperatures are read in centigrade rather than Fahrenheit. To convert centigrade into the familiar Fahrenheit numbers, take 9/5 of the centigrade temperature and add 32. Thus 20° on a centigrade thermometer would be 68°F. See the diagram in the margin.

Here is a rundown of the weather you will find in the major tourist countries and cities of the world (temperature readings are in Fahrenheit; figure given for days w/rain includes precipitation of rain or snow of 0.01 inches or more):

EUROPE

AUSTRIA

Austria's climate is generally like that of New England, ideally cold and crisp (but not bitter) during the main skiing months of December through March. Spring in the mountains—when New England is usually deep in slush—is still good skiing weather, with flowers blooming in the valleys and the Danube region. Summer days are warm and sunny; at night a blanket is in order. September and October are also sunny, perfect for touring and mountain climbing. November is apt to be rainy. Vienna is pleasant most of the year.

Most hotels have central heating. There is little air conditioning—it's simply not needed.

VIENNA

	Jan.	Feb.	Mar.	Apr.	May	June	July	Aug.	Sept.	Oct.	Nov.	Dec.
Av. Daily Temp.	32	34	42	49	58	63	66	65	58	49	39	35
Av. Daily Low	28	29	35	41	50	55	58	57	51	43	35	31
Av. Daily High	36	38	48	56	65	70	73	72	65	55	42	38
Av. Humidity	78	75	68	65	68	67	68	69	71	77	80	81
Av. No. Days w/rain	14	12	13	14	14	14	15	14	12	13	15	16
Av. No. Days w/snow	8	6	6	1	x	0	0	0	0	1	3	8

(x = less than one)

BELGIUM

There are no extremes of temperature; the climate is more or less similar to the northwestern United States, as, for example, Portland, but without our sometimes strong summer heat or winter cold. There is a fair amount of rain—one reason for the beautiful Belgian countryside. May through September are probably the ideal months for touring.

BRUSSELS

	Jan.	Feb.	Mar.	Apr.	May	June	July	Aug.	Sept.	Oct.	Nov.	Dec.
Av. Daily Temp.	35	38	42	49	55	61	64	64	60	50	43	38
Av. Daily Low	30	33	35	40	46	52	55	55	52	44	38	33
Av. Daily High	39	43	49	57	64	70	73	72	67	56	48	42
Av. Humidity	89	87	82	77	77	78	78	79	83	87	89	91
Av. No. Days w/rain	15	15	15	16	16	17	16	16	16	17	18	16
Av. No. Days w/snow	6	6	6	2	0	0	0	0	0	1	2	5

DENMARK

For sightseeing, touring and sports, late spring, summer and early fall are best. The rest of the year is mild, but drizzly, with short days. Summer days are long, but it does rain a good bit of the time in Copenhagen. Summer evenings are decidedly cool, so bring a wrap.

COPENHAGEN

	Jan.	Feb.	Mar.	Apr.	May	June	July	Aug.	Sept.	Oct.	Nov.	Dec.
Av. Daily Temp.	32	32	35	42	51	59	62	61	56	48	40	36
Av. Daily Low	29	29	31	37	45	53	56	56	51	44	37	34
Av. Daily High	35	35	39	47	57	65	68	66	60	51	43	38
Av. Humidity	88	89	82	73	67	67	70	75	79	84	86	88
Av. No. Days w/rain	15	14	15	12	13	12	15	16	14	17	16	17
Av. No. Days w/snow	9	10	9	3	1	0	0	0	0	1	3	7

FINLAND

Despite its northern location, Finland has a temperate climate, warmed by the Gulf Stream. The coldest month is February. The weather is fairly dry from January to the end of April, when the Finns make good their reputation as "a nation on skis." The best skiing in Lapland is during March and April. Between the middle of May and the end of July is the time to see the midnight sun (at the 70th degree of latitude). July is the warmest month, which, along with August, is the best time for touring Finland, starting in Lapland and working south to Helsinki.

Central heating is widespread, and although air conditioning is hardly ever needed, it is available in some of the newer hotels. Even the Polar Hotel, in Lapland, has it. Dress with an eye for rain.

HELSINKI

	Jan.	Feb.	Mar.	Apr.	May	June	July	Aug.	Sept.	Oct.	Nov.	Dec.
Av. Daily Temp.	22	21	27	37	48	56	64	61	52	41	34	27
Av. Daily Low	17	15	22	31	41	49	57	55	46	37	30	22
Av. Daily High	27	26	32	43	55	63	71	66	57	45	37	31
Av. Humidity	87	84	80	77	69	68	70	78	80	84	87	88
Av. No. Days w/rain	18	16	14	12	12	13	12	16	16	17	19	19
Av. No. Days w/snow	17	16	13	7	2	x	0	0	x	4	10	15

(x = less than one)

FRANCE

Because France is a country only slightly smaller than Texas, its climate is impossible to sum up in one neat sentence, except to say that the temperatures are never extreme. Seasons are the same as in New England, yet there are great differences between northern, southern, and coastal France, to say nothing of the French Alps, whose weather is similar to that of neighboring Switzerland. For practical purposes, one can almost draw a line through the middle of France. November through March in Paris and northern France is gray, but not too cold and with very little snow. April in Paris is more a relief from winter than the ideal time. May would be better; June and September are also good. If you must visit Paris in summer, choose July rather than August, when everyone goes on vacation. For the northern and western resort areas, however, summer is delightful as well as smart.

Save your Riviera vacation until June or September; May or October could also be good. In short, May, June, September and October are the best months for visiting the length and breadth of France.

PARIS

	Jan.	Feb.	Mar.	Apr.	May	June	July	Aug.	Sept.	Oct.	Nov.	Dec.
Av. Daily Temp.	37	40	44	50	57	62	66	65	60	52	43	40
Av. Daily Low	32	33	36	40	46	52	55	54	50	44	37	35
Av. Daily High	42	46	52	60	67	72	76	75	69	60	49	44
Av. Humidity	86	81	76	69	71	73	73	74	79	85	87	88
Av. No. Days w/rain	14	14	14	13	14	12	12	12	11	15	15	15
Av. No. Days w/snow	4	3	3	1	0	0	0	0	0	0	1	2

GERMANY

German weather might be compared with that of Boston, with January the coldest month. Otherwise the winters are mild, the rest of the year extremely pleasant, and rain is pretty evenly distributed throughout the year. For touring all of Germany, choose late spring or early fall. In the southern part, add early spring and late fall. For winter sports, plan on January, February, and sometimes March—depending on what conditions have been up to that point. Indian summer lasts until late October, and spring is usually longer than in New England.

BERLIN

	Jan.	Feb.	Mar.	Apr.	May	June	July	Aug.	Sept.	Oct.	Nov.	Dec.
Av. Daily Temp.	31	33	38	46	56	62	65	63	58	48	39	33
Av. Daily Low	26	28	31	37	46	52	55	54	49	41	34	29
Av. Daily High	35	38	45	54	65	72	74	72	66	55	44	37
Av. Humidity	86	83	78	69	65	65	68	70	75	82	85	87
Av. No. Days w/rain	15	15	15	13	13	13	15	14	13	14	14	15
Av. No. Days w/snow	8	8	7	2	x	0	0	0	0	x	3	7

(x = less than one)

GREAT BRITAIN

British weather has become a worldwide joke, and a rather tiresome one. Talking about the weather is a national pastime, but it's best left to those who know the rules of the game. "You have to be British to know if it's going to rain," according to a friend. The visitor will enjoy herself far more if she forgets the subject—and concentrates on the country.

A few points are worth mentioning, however. The British Isles have a maritime climate (fog, mist, damp winds and rain), but the eastern half is noticeably drier than the western half, and there is more sun on the coasts than inland. Actual winter temperatures do not go to any great low, yet it seems colder because of the dampness, which can really get into your bones. Winter days are short, but summer days are long—in mid-summer London is light until about 10:00 at night. Don't count on constant summer sunlight, but if the day looks promising, pack a picnic and get out and enjoy the English countryside, which is nature's reward for having suffered through the dismal winter. Generally speaking, April, May, June and September are the best months to visit England; for Scotland add July and August. March is best in the Scilly Isles, where the flowers are in full bloom then. September is apt to be the least rainy, but spring is the most beautiful for flowers and those green English fields. Even if you're traveling during the warmer months (especially in Scotland), take along a few light woolens, or better still, buy them there—also a handsome English raincoat.

Central heating is still something of a novelty in Britain. When it does exist, it's kept at lower temperatures than in the U.S. You'll probably experience no discomfort in the better hotels, but if you visit a private home in winter, take along your woolen underwear and bed socks.

LONDON

	Jan.	Feb.	Mar.	Apr.	May	June	July	Aug.	Sept.	Oct.	Nov.	Dec.
Av. Daily Temp.	39	40	43	48	54	60	63	62	57	50	44	41
Av. Daily Low	35	35	36	40	45	51	54	54	49	44	39	36
Av. Daily High	43	45	49	55	62	68	71	70	65	56	49	45
Av. Humidity	85	82	79	75	73	73	73	76	80	85	86	86
Av. No. Days w/rain	15	15	14	13	12	12	13	13	12	16	16	16
Av. No. Days w/snow	3	3	3	1	0	0	0	0	0	0	1	2

GREECE

A clue to Greece's weather may be found in her many well-preserved ancient buildings, which would have crumbled to dust long ago had they been exposed to the climates of New York or London. The Greek climate is Mediterranean, but milder than the Mediterranean coasts of France or northern Italy. 320 days of sunshine a year is the official figure; unofficially, May, June and September are the pleasantest months to visit Greece. It may rain a few days during this time, but only for a couple of hours. There is practically no rain during July and August, but it's too hot for comfort in Athens then. Many Greeks choose these months to vacation on the Aegean islands, but the sun may be a bit too intense for Americans. Better stick to spring and fall.

ATHENS

	Jan.	Feb.	Mar.	Apr.	May	June	July	Aug.	Sept.	Oct.	Nov.	Dec.
Av. Daily Temp.	48	49	53	60	69	76	81	81	75	67	58	52
Av. Daily Low	42	42	46	51	60	67	72	72	66	60	52	46
Av. Daily High	53	56	60	68	77	85	90	90	83	74	64	57
Av. Humidity	72	71	68	63	58	54	46	46	54	65	72	74
Av. No. Days w/rain	12	11	11	9	7	4	3	3	4	9	12	13
Av. No. Days w/snow	0	0	0	0	0	0	0	0	0	0	0	0

IRELAND

As in England, Scotland and Wales, Ireland's celebrated greenness is due to a fair amount of rain. Winters are mild and summers comparatively cool; even in July and August the temperatures seldom rise above the mid-60's. May is usually the sunniest month in the north, west and midland, June the sunniest elsewhere. Spring comes early, in February, and summer begins in May, autumn in August, winter in November. Late spring, summer and early autumn are your best bets. Bring a raincoat and light woolens, and if you must travel in winter, stay at a modern hotel where you're more likely to find central heating.

DUBLIN

	Jan.	Feb.	Mar.	Apr.	May	June	July	Aug.	Sept.	Oct.	Nov.	Dec.
Av. Daily Temp.	41	41	42	45	50	56	59	58	54	48	44	41
Av. Daily Low	35	34	35	37	42	47	51	50	46	41	38	35
Av. Daily High	46	47	49	53	58	64	66	65	62	55	50	47
Av. Humidity	88	86	83	78	76	75	78	81	84	86	88	88
Av. No. Days w/rain	21	18	19	17	16	15	18	19	16	19	19	21
Av. No. Days w/snow	4	4	5	1	0	0	0	0	0	0	1	2

ITALY

From the top of her boot to the tip of her toe, Italy's climate ranges from freezing to subtropical. In January average temperatures are 29° in Cortina (skiing center in the Dolomites), 45° in Rome and 56° in Taormina (Sicily). It all depends on where you want to go—and for what purpose. Skiers would obviously pick winter, but could couple this with a side trip to the Italian Riviera, where the average February temperature in San Remo is 52°—too cold for swimming, yet a number of Italians do visit there in winter. The Italian Riviera is mainly a late spring, summer and early autumn watering place. Rome is mild in winter, but can become very hot in summer, like most of southern Italy. The Adriatic coast is cooler than the Mediterranean; Rimini in June averages 74°.

All of this would seem to make planning a trip to Italy rather difficult, but in general, spring and fall are the best times. Fall is better in the Italian lakes; the Dolomites (other than for skiing) are best in summer. Rome is fine in both spring and fall, as is Venice. Florence is probably at its best in spring. It can rain anywhere, and probably when you least expect it, so bring a raincoat.

ROME

	Jan.	Feb.	Mar.	Apr.	May	June	July	Aug.	Sept.	Oct.	Nov.	Dec.
Av. Daily Temp.	45	48	52	58	64	71	77	76	71	62	53	47
Av. Daily Low	38	40	44	49	54	61	66	65	61	54	46	40
Av. Daily High	52	55	59	66	73	81	87	86	80	70	60	53
Av. Humidity	72	69	66	65	61	58	53	55	62	70	73	74
Av. No. Days w/rain	10	10	9	9	8	5	2	3	6	11	12	12
Av. No. Days w/snow	0	0	0	0	0	0	0	0	0	0	0	0

NETHERLANDS

The most pleasant weather is from April to September, but there is some rainfall during these months, with lots to be expected in fall and winter. The summers are generally cool, with the average July temperature struggling up to 70°. The tulip "season" is from about mid-April to mid-May, but there are plenty of flowers during the summer as well.

AMSTERDAM

	Jan.	Feb.	Mar.	Apr.	May	June	July	Aug.	Sept.	Oct.	Nov.	Dec.
Av. Daily Temp.	36	37	41	47	54	60	62	62	57	50	42	38
Av. Daily Low	31	31	35	39	45	51	54	54	49	43	37	33
Av. Daily High	41	42	47	54	62	68	70	70	65	57	47	42
Av. Humidity	89	87	84	78	75	75	77	80	83	87	89	91
Av. No. Days w/rain	10	8	11	8	9	9	11	11	10	13	11	13
Av. No. Days w/snow	4	3	3	1	0	0	0	0	0	0	1	3

NORWAY

In spite of its location (the North Cape is Europe's northernmost point), Norway's climate is warmer than might be expected, thanks to the Gulf Stream. Winters in Oslo are about as cold as in Boston; summers more or less like those in northern Maine. The skiing is best from January through April; otherwise, Norway is more comfortable from May through September. Coastal areas are warmer, though a little wetter, during summer. It is cooler inland, and drier. The midnight sun is seen at the North Cape from about mid-May to late July, and can be seen for a shorter time in other parts of northern Norway. Nights are short throughout the country from April to September.

OSLO

	Jan.	Feb.	Mar.	Apr.	May	June	July	Aug.	Sept.	Oct.	Nov.	Dec.
Av. Daily Temp.	25	26	32	41	51	58	64	60	53	42	33	27
Av. Daily Low	21	21	26	34	43	50	56	53	46	37	30	24
Av. Daily High	28	30	38	48	59	65	71	66	59	46	36	29
Av. Humidity	82	79	74	67	64	64	69	75	80	82	83	84
Av. No. Days w/rain	12	12	13	10	11	10	12	15	11	12	12	15
Av. No. Days w/snow	10	10	10	4	x	0	0	0	0	2	5	10

(x = less than one)

PORTUGAL

Cooled by the Atlantic breezes, Portugal is not so hot as neighboring Spain, but it can be decidedly warm in summer. The humidity is low, however, and there is very little rain. In winter the weather is mild, but apt to be rainy along the coast, and there is some snow in the mountains.

LISBON

	Jan.	Feb.	Mar.	Apr.	May	June	July	Aug.	Sept.	Oct.	Nov.	Dec.
Av. Daily Temp.	50	52	55	59	62	70	70	72	69	63	57	53
Av. Daily Low	46	47	51	54	58	63	65	67	64	58	53	47
Av. Daily High	54	56	59	63	66	77	75	76	73	68	61	58
Av. Humidity	78	75	71	69	67	64	62	61	66	71	77	79
Av. No. Days w/rain	13	12	14	12	9	5	2	2	6	11	13	14
Av. No. Days w/snow	0	0	0	0	0	0	0	0	0	0	0	0

U.S.S.R.

The range and variety of climates and temperatures are as huge as the country itself, but in general, summer is the best time to visit Moscow, Leningrad, and almost any other part of Russia. The cold starts in October and continues through April in European Russia; the summers here are slightly cooler than in the Middle West. You can swim at the Black Sea resorts from May until November.

Moscow

	Jan.	Feb.	Mar.	Apr.	May	June	July	Aug.	Sept.	Oct.	Nov.	Dec.
Av. Daily Temp.	15	17	25	39	55	62	66	62	52	40	27	18
Av. Daily Low	9	10	17	31	44	51	55	52	43	34	23	13
Av. Daily High	21	23	32	47	65	73	76	72	61	46	31	23
Av. Humidity	85	82	78	76	68	73	74	79	81	84	88	87
Av. No. Days w/rain	14	13	12	12	12	13	12	15	12	13	16	15
Av. No. Days w/snow	14	13	10	6	1	0	0	0	1	5	13	14

SPAIN

Spring and fall are the best times to visit Spain, another country with a climate as varied as its scenery. Madrid has an elevation of 2,000 feet, making it comparatively cold in winter. In summer the temperatures hover in the 70's and 80's, even 90's during the day, but the air is dry and the nights are cool. July through September is the "season" at San Sebastián, on the northern coast. The Costa Brava, north of Barcelona, is popular from May to October. Barcelona itself tends to be humid, but is generally mild year round. Summer heat begins along the Costa del Sol about the end of June and lasts through September; spring is the best time here and in Andalusia. Winter is warm, but not hot, in the Canary Islands, while in the Balearic Islands spring and fall are good seasons. You'll have to plan your wardrobe according to where you're going. In summer light clothing is all you'll need, plus a raincoat. The rain in Spain falls mainly in the north, but showers do occur elsewhere.

MADRID

	Jan.	Feb.	Mar.	Apr.	May	June	July	Aug.	Sept.	Oct.	Nov.	Dec.
Av. Daily Temp.	41	44	48	53	61	68	74	75	66	56	47	42
Av. Daily Low	33	35	38	42	50	56	61	62	55	47	40	35
Av. Daily High	48	52	57	63	72	79	86	87	76	65	54	48
Av. Humidity	80	72	65	61	60	50	40	42	56	69	78	81
Av. No. Days w/rain	9	10	10	10	10	6	3	3	7	9	10	10
Av. No. Days w/snow	1	x	x	x	0	0	0	0	0	0	0	1

(x = less than one)

SWEDEN

The weather in Sweden is pleasantly tempered by the Gulf Stream. Summers are warm, without being hot, winters are brisk, generally with plenty of snow. It rains a fair amount throughout most of the year. Except for the northern part of Sweden, the climate is very much the same as in New England. The tourist season is from mid-April to the end of September, and from December to March for winter sports.

The Midnight Sun is a phenomenon that cannot be seen in the U.S.A. In the one-seventh of Sweden that lies beyond the Arctic Circle, as in northern Norway and Finland, the sun never sets from the middle of May until the latter part of July. During a similar period in winter, on the other hand, the sun never appears above the horizon. Even in southern Sweden the effect of this unbalance is felt. In the middle of the winter, dusk begins long before the afternoon is over. Conversely, at mid-summer, the sun sets for only 5 or 6 hours, and a luminous twilight lingers through the night.

STOCKHOLM

	Jan.	Feb.	Mar.	Apr.	May	June	July	Aug.	Sept.	Oct.	Nov.	Dec.
Av. Daily Temp.	27	27	30	39	49	58	63	60	53	43	35	29
Av. Daily Low	22	21	24	31	40	49	54	52	46	38	31	24
Av. Daily High	31	32	36	46	57	67	71	67	59	48	39	33
Av. Humidity	85	83	78	71	63	62	67	73	78	82	85	87
Av. No. Days w/rain	15	13	14	11	12	12	15	16	14	16	15	17
Av. No. Days w/snow	12	12	11	5	2	0	0	0	0	2	6	11

SWITZERLAND

Most of the country is much like the northern United States, and the skiing weather couldn't be better. The air is sparklingly clear and crisp, the sky a deep blue, and there's plenty of central heating (plus roaring fires) when you come in from the slopes. Socially, skiing is at its peak during the second half of February and all of March, but the whole season, January through mid-April, is good. Mountain climbing is best in September, as the snow level has receded to its farthest point. Summer in the Alps is glorious from June to September; June is the month for mountainside meadows of Alpine flowers.

In the lake region, north of the Alps, the weather is good from May through mid-October, and in Ticino the winters are mild, summers warm. Spring and fall are ideal.

GENEVA

	Jan.	Feb.	Mar.	Apr.	May	June	July	Aug.	Sept.	Oct.	Nov.	Dec.
Av. Daily Temp.	29	33	38	47	56	62	65	64	57	48	39	32
Av. Daily Low	28	28	31	41	50	57	60	59	51	42	35	29
Av. Daily High	30	37	44	52	61	66	70	69	63	53	42	35
Av. Humidity	84	80	73	67	68	66	66	69	76	79	83	83
Av. No. Days w/rain	10	9	10	11	12	11	9	10	10	11	11	10
Av. No. Days w/snow	4	3	3	1	x	0	0	0	0	x	2	3

(x = less than one)

YUGOSLAVIA

Belgrade is cold in winter, coolish in summer, with rain evenly distributed throughout the year. Winter sports are in full swing from December to April. The Adriatic coast is at its loveliest from April to October, with July and August the warmest months.

BELGRADE

	Jan.	Feb.	Mar.	Apr.	May	June	July	Aug.	Sept.	Oct.	Nov.	Dec.
Av. Daily Temp.	33	35	46	54	63	68	72	72	66	54	43	35
Av. Daily Low	27	28	37	44	52	57	60	59	54	45	35	30
Av. Daily High	39	42	55	63	74	78	84	84	78	63	50	40
Av. Humidity	80	74	69	65	66	69	62	58	60	78	75	81
Av. No. Days w/rain	12	13	15	14	15	16	12	10	12	12	12	13
Av. No. Days w/snow	8	6	3	x	0	0	0	0	0	0	3	6

(x = less than one)

MIDDLE EAST

IRAN

This country has a very dry climate that could be compared with the southwestern United States. Midsummer heat can be terrific, winters rather cold. The most comfortable times are from April to mid-June and mid-September to mid-November.

TEHERAN

	Jan.	Feb.	Mar.	Apr.	May	June	July	Aug.	Sept.	Oct.	Nov.	Dec.
Av. Daily Temp.	33	37	49	60	70	80	85	84	77	64	53	39
Av. Daily Low	20	24	39	49	58	66	72	71	64	53	43	27
Av. Daily High	45	50	59	71	82	93	99	97	90	76	63	51
Av. Humidity	76	66	50	47	51	50	46	47	49	54	65	76
Av. No. Days w/rain*	11	8	7	4	1	x	1	1	x	x	4	7
(x = less than one)												
Av. No. Days w/snow	8	4	1	0	0	0	0	0	0	0	0	4
(* approximate)												

ISRAEL

A mild Mediterranean climate exists in Israel, which can get quite hot in mid-summer, with no rain at all from June to October. Jerusalem is one of the cooler spots in the country, but can still be oppressive in July and August. Winter lasts from November to March, which is a fine month (summer is from April to October), and is mild and usually sunny. What rain there is falls during this period. In general, Israel's climate is much like that of southern California.

JERUSALEM

	Jan.	Feb.	Mar.	Apr.	May	June	July	Aug.	Sept.	Oct.	Nov.	Dec.
Av. Daily Temp.	45	48	54	61	67	73	76	76	74	70	58	50
Av. Daily Low	38	41	45	51	56	62	65	64	62	59	50	43
Av. Daily High	51	55	62	70	78	84	87	88	85	80	66	56
Av. Humidity	75	71	56	49	43	46	49	52	58	60	67	76
Av. No. Days w/rain	12	12	8	4	2	0	0	0	0	2	6	9
Av. No. Days w/snow	0	0	0	0	0	0	0	0	0	0	0	0

JORDAN

Winters are mild in Jerusalem and Amman, warm in Aqaba and the lowlands near Jericho. There are showers only from December to March. Spring is the finest season for touring.

TURKEY

April through November is the best time to visit Turkey. It is dry then, and not too humid in Istanbul, and even less humid in Ankara, where summer nights are cool. Southern Turkey is much like Florida. There is a long and pleasant Indian summer, from September to November.

ISTANBUL

	Jan.	Feb.	Mar.	Apr.	May	June	July	Aug.	Sept.	Oct.	Nov.	Dec.
Av. Daily Temp.	42	41	46	53	63	70	75	75	69	63	54	47
Av. Daily Low	38	36	40	46	55	62	67	68	62	57	49	43
Av. Daily High	46	45	52	60	71	78	82	82	75	68	58	51
Av. Humidity	79	77	71	66	64	60	60	61	65	71	76	75
Av. No. Days w/rain	10	8	9	7	7	5	2	4	6	7	11	12
Av. No. Days w/snow	4	5	3	0	0	0	0	0	0	0	0	1

THE PACIFIC AND ASIA

AUSTRALIA

Although it is an entire continent in itself, Australia does not have the extremes of temperature common in the United States. The most important thing to remember is that everything here is in reverse—it's warmer, and more tropical, in the north; cooler and more temperate in the south. Winter in Australia is June–August, spring is September–November, summer is December–February, and autumn is March–May. The best time to visit northern Australia is from April through October, when there is little rainfall. The rest of the year can be hot, humid and rainy. In southern Australia, September through November and March through May would be nearest ideal. In Tasmania summers are a bit cooler and winters sometimes snowy. Central Australia is much like America's Southwest—arid and warm. For practical purposes, one can compare southeastern Australia with the Gulf and southeastern states of the U.S.A., forgetting hurricanes and remembering to reverse the seasons.

SYDNEY

	Jan.	Feb.	Mar.	Apr.	May	June	July	Aug.	Sept.	Oct.	Nov.	Dec.
Av. Daily Temp.	72	72	70	64	60	55	54	55	60	64	67	70
Av. Daily Low	65	65	63	57	52	48	46	47	51	56	60	63
Av. Daily High	78	78	76	71	67	61	61	63	68	71	74	77
Av. Humidity	71	74	72	72	72	70	69	60	64	64	68	70
Av. No. Days w/rain	13	12	13	14	12	11	12	10	11	11	11	13
Av. No. Days w/snow	0	0	0	0	0	0	0	0	0	0	0	0

BURMA

There are three seasons: hot, rainy and cool. March through May is very hot; June to mid-October is very rainy, which leaves mid-October to March as the cool season. Best times to visit are from November to February.

RANGOON

	Jan.	Feb.	Mar.	Apr.	May	June	July	Aug.	Sept.	Oct.	Nov.	Dec.
Av. Daily Temp.	77	80	84	87	85	81	81	81	81	82	80	77
Av. Daily Low	65	67	71	76	77	76	76	76	76	76	73	67
Av. Daily High	89	92	96	98	92	86	85	85	86	88	87	87
Av. Humidity	62	62	64	68	78	86	89	89	87	80	76	68
Av. No. Days w/rain	1	1	1	2	13	23	25	24	20	11	4	1
Av. No. Days w/snow	0	0	0	0	0	0	0	0	0	0	0	0

CEYLON

The months of December to April are generally the best, but the mountains are usually cool and comfortable. Colombo is hot and humid, however; the coastal areas can also be hot from March to November.

COLOMBO

	Jan.	Feb.	Mar.	Apr.	May	June	July	Aug.	Sept.	Oct.	Nov.	Dec.
Av. Daily Temp.	79	79	81	82	82	81	81	80	81	80	79	79
Av. Daily Low	71	71	73	76	77	77	77	77	76	75	73	72
Av. Daily High	87	88	89	89	88	86	86	85	86	86	86	86
Av. Humidity	74	72	73	76	79	80	80	78	78	80	79	75
Av. No. Days w/rain	10	4	11	16	21	20	18	14	17	22	19	12
Av. No. Days w/snow	0	0	0	0	0	0	0	0	0	0	0	0

FIJI ISLANDS

Suva, the capital, is on the wetter side of Viti Levu, the largest island, so don't let the chart below discourage you. There is a dry season (from June through August) in the Nandi-Lautoka area; it's cooler then too. In general, the climate is tropical with gentle breezes.

SUVA

	Jan.	Feb.	Mar.	Apr.	May	June	July	Aug.	Sept.	Oct.	Nov.	Dec.
Av. Daily Temp.	80	80	80	79	77	75	74	74	75	76	77	79
Av. Daily Low	74	74	74	73	71	69	68	68	69	70	71	73
Av. Daily High	86	86	86	84	82	80	79	79	80	81	83	85
Av. Humidity	78	80	81	81	82	81	80	80	78	76	76	77
Av. No. Days w/rain	21	19	24	20	17	14	10	12	14	14	16	17
Av. No. Days w/snow	0	0	0	0	0	0	0	0	0	0	0	0

HAWAII

Hawaii's year-round average temperature is an ideal 75°. Temperatures vary according to elevation, and rainfall according to location. The coastal areas are warmer and sunnier, the mountains cooler and wetter. August through September is the warmest season; the coolest time is from December through February. Summer showers are scattered and light, while in the winter the rain is heavier, although brief, and the weather in general more humid. Central heating is rare; fireplaces do the job, when needed, in the mountain areas. Air conditioning is usually available in the newer buildings and hotels.

HONOLULU

	Jan.	Feb.	Mar.	Apr.	May	June	July	Aug.	Sept.	Oct.	Nov.	Dec.
Av. Daily Temp.	71	71	72	73	75	77	78	79	78	77	75	73
Av. Daily Low	66	66	66	68	69	72	73	73	73	72	70	68
Av. Daily High	76	76	77	78	80	82	83	84	83	82	80	78
Av. Humidity	70	70	68	67	67	66	65	65	65	67	69	70
Av. No. Days w/rain	14	10	13	12	11	11	13	13	13	13	14	15
Av. No. Days w/snow	0	0	0	0	0	0	0	0	0	0	0	0

Hong Kong

The British crown colony is subtropical, with summer being the hottest and wettest season, winter the driest and most comfortable for shopping and sightseeing, but too cool for swimming, which is best during summer and early fall. The best time to visit Hong Kong is from September 15 through February, although March through May shouldn't be ruled out completely. In midwinter, the days are cool enough for a light suit; tropical cottons the rest of the year.

Hong Kong

	Jan.	Feb.	Mar.	Apr.	May	June	July	Aug.	Sept.	Oct.	Nov.	Dec.
Av. Daily Temp.	60	59	64	71	77	82	83	83	81	77	70	63
Av. Daily Low	56	55	60	67	73	78	78	78	77	73	65	58
Av. Daily High	64	63	67	75	81	85	87	87	85	81	74	67
Av. Humidity	72	78	79	82	83	82	82	82	78	69	67	69
Av. No. Days w/rain	6	8	11	12	16	21	19	17	14	8	6	5
Av. No. Days w/snow	0	0	0	0	0	0	0	0	0	0	0	0

India

The climate is varied, and the temperatures sometimes extreme (summer in Delhi can boost the mercury to 110°), but in general, the pleasantest time to visit most of India is from November to March. Early summer or autumn is best for the Kashmir Valley; Bombay is also good in September, October and November; Calcutta in November. The monsoon season, when heavy rains can be expected, is usually from June to September, but it varies according to location.

Calcutta

	Jan.	Feb.	Mar.	Apr.	May	June	July	Aug.	Sept.	Oct.	Nov.	Dec.
Av. Daily Temp.	67	71	80	86	87	85	84	84	83	81	74	67
Av. Daily Low	56	60	69	76	78	79	79	79	78	75	65	56
Av. Daily High	77	82	91	95	95	91	89	88	88	87	82	77
Av. Humidity	69	64	63	66	70	79	83	85	84	79	71	68
Av. No. Days w/rain	1	2	2	3	7	13	18	18	13	6	1	0
Av. No. Days w/snow	0	0	0	0	0	0	0	0	0	0	0	0

Japan

Japan's climate is more like that of North America than other Pacific areas (except Korea, whose climate compares to Japan's). Tokyo's weather is generally similar to ours in the Middle West or that of central Europe. Japan's autumn (October and November) is very much like that in the eastern U.S.A., and these months, along with April and May, are considered the best ones for a visit. From mid-June to July the weather is drizzly and humid; during winter there is good skiing in the northern half of the country.

TOKYO

	Jan.	Feb.	Mar.	Apr.	May	June	July	Aug.	Sept.	Oct.	Nov.	Dec.
Av. Daily Temp.	39	39	45	55	62	70	76	79	73	62	52	42
Av. Daily Low	30	31	36	47	54	63	69	72	66	54	43	33
Av. Daily High	47	47	53	63	70	76	83	85	79	69	60	51
Av. Humidity	64	62	67	73	76	82	83	82	83	80	74	66
Av. No. Days w/rain	7	8	13	14	14	16	15	13	17	14	10	7
Av. No. Days w/snow	4	5	3	x	0	0	0	0	0	0	x	2

(x = less than one)

NEW ZEALAND

New Zealand's two major islands (appropriately named North Island and South Island) are rather like California turned upside down; that is to say, the seasons are reversed. Auckland is more like Los Angeles, Christchurch more like San Francisco. North Island is semitropical; South Island cooler. Summer in New Zealand, from late December to March, is the most pleasant time, with January and February the warmest months. Their autumn and spring are also good. July through September are the best months for winter sports.

AUCKLAND

	Jan.	Feb.	Mar.	Apr.	May	June	July	Aug.	Sept.	Oct.	Nov.	Dec.
Av. Daily Temp.	66	67	65	62	57	54	52	53	55	57	61	64
Av. Daily Low	59	60	58	55	51	48	46	47	49	51	54	57
Av. Daily High	73	74	72	68	62	59	57	58	61	63	67	70
Av. Humidity	72	72	74	76	78	79	79	77	76	75	74	73
Av. No. Days w/rain	10	10	11	13	19	20	21	19	17	17	15	10
Av. No. Days w/snow	0	0	0	0	0	0	0	0	0	0	0	0

PHILIPPINES

These are tropical islands, with late November to early March the best season. January is the coolest month, May the warmest. It rains a good deal from June through November in Manila, but around Mindanao the rain is fairly even throughout the year.

MANILA

	Jan.	Feb.	Mar.	Apr.	May	June	July	Aug.	Sept.	Oct.	Nov.	Dec.
Av. Daily Temp.	75	76	80	81	82	82	80	80	80	80	77	76
Av. Daily Low	70	71	75	75	76	76	74	75	76	75	72	71
Av. Daily High	80	81	84	87	88	87	85	85	83	84	82	81
Av. Humidity	79	74	71	69	75	80	85	85	86	85	83	82
Av. No. Days w/rain	5	3	3	4	10	16	21	22	21	17	12	9
Av. No. Days w/snow	0	0	0	0	0	0	0	0	0	0	0	0

SINGAPORE

The island has a nice even climate with little distinction between the seasons. The days are generally tropical and rainy, the nights cool. October and November might be considered the wettest on the west coast, however, and February to September is probably the best time for the east coast. Just bring light cottons—and a raincoat.

SINGAPORE

	Jan.	Feb.	Mar.	Apr.	May	June	July	Aug.	Sept.	Oct.	Nov.	Dec.
Av. Daily Temp.	80	81	81	82	82	82	82	82	82	81	81	80
Av. Daily Low	73	74	75	75	75	75	75	75	75	74	74	73
Av. Daily High	86	88	89	89	89	88	88	88	88	88	87	86
Av. Humidity	82	79	78	80	79	79	78	78	78	79	81	83
Av. No. Days w/rain	16	11	14	15	14	14	13	14	13	16	18	19
Av. No. Days w/snow	0	0	0	0	0	0	0	0	0	0	0	0

TAHITI

The cool and dry season is from March through November; the rainy season from December to early March. Climate tropical though cooled by sea breezes.

PAPEETE

	Jan.	Feb.	Mar.	Apr.	May	June	July	Aug.	Sept.	Oct.	Nov.	Dec.
Av. Daily Temp.	81	82	81	81	79	77	76	76	79	79	79	80
Av. Daily Low	74	75	75	74	72	70	68	68	71	71	71	72
Av. Daily High	88	88	87	87	85	84	84	84	86	87	87	87
Av. Humidity	77	78	81	80	80	81	78	78	75	73	78	79
Av. No. Days w/rain	16	16	17	10	10	8	5	6	6	9	13	14
Av. No. Days w/snow	0	0	0	0	0	0	0	0	0	0	0	0

THAILAND

November to February is the coolest and least humid season; the rest of the year is hot and damp, with May to September bringing monsoon showers.

BANGKOK

	Jan.	Feb.	Mar.	Apr.	May	June	July	Aug.	Sept.	Oct.	Nov.	Dec.
Av. Daily Temp.	80	82	84	87	86	85	84	84	83	83	80	78
Av. Daily Low	67	70	73	76	76	76	76	76	75	75	71	67
Av. Daily High	92	93	95	97	95	93	92	92	91	91	89	89
Av. Humidity	74	77	77	77	86	81	82	83	85	85	82	76
Av. No. Days w/rain	1	3	4	6	17	18	19	19	21	17	7	3
Av. No. Days w/snow	0	0	0	0	0	0	0	0	0	0	0	0

AFRICA

EGYPT

Egyptian climate is mainly dry and mild. Humidity is low, except perhaps in Cairo, where summer can be hot and sometimes humid. Evenings are cooler, and in winter the weather in most Egyptian cities is much like that of the southwestern United States—comfortable during the day, cool after sunset. Cairo has relatively the same temperatures as Alexandria and Port Said; it gets warmer as you go south. Winter is the best time almost everywhere in Egypt.

CAIRO

	Jan.	Feb.	Mar.	Apr.	May	June	July	Aug.	Sept.	Oct.	Nov.	Dec.
Av. Daily Temp.	56	59	64	70	76	81	83	83	78	75	68	60
Av. Daily Low	45	47	51	56	62	67	70	71	67	63	56	49
Av. Daily High	67	70	76	83	89	94	96	94	89	86	79	70
Av. Humidity	60	55	50	45	40	44	51	55	58	58	61	62
Av. No. Days w/rain	3	2	2	1	0	0	0	0	0	0	1	2
Av. No. Days w/snow	0	0	0	0	0	0	0	0	0	0	0	0

MOROCCO

The coastal areas are much like those of southern California. Inland, summer temperatures can rise to the extreme, but there is little humidity and in the mountains the nights are cool.

CASABLANCA

	Jan.	Feb.	Mar.	Apr.	May	June	July	Aug.	Sept.	Oct.	Nov.	Dec.
Av. Daily Temp.	54	55	58	61	64	69	72	74	71	67	61	56
Av. Daily Low	45	46	49	52	56	61	65	66	63	58	52	47
Av. Daily High	63	64	67	69	72	76	79	81	79	76	69	65
Av. Humidity	80	79	79	78	78	76	77	82	82	78	78	78
Av. No. Days w/rain	8	8	8	7	5	1	0	0	1	6	8	9
Av. No. Days w/snow	0	0	0	0	0	0	0	0	0	0	0	0

EAST AFRICA

There are usually two wet and two dry seasons a year, the wet ones from March to May and around December. In the Lake Victoria region, there is no "dry" season, but more rain falls from March to May. Other rain occurs in Uganda and the Kenya highlands from March or April. Around Nairobi, June to September is cool and cloudy, whereas January to March is usually sunny and warm.

SOUTH AFRICA

Seasons are the reverse of ours, with June a mid-winter month. The climate is temperate and gentle with no extremes of heat or cold. Spring, summer and fall (September to May) offer the best weather generally.

CAPETOWN

	Jan.	Feb.	Mar.	Apr.	May	June	July	Aug.	Sept.	Oct.	Nov.	Dec.
Av. Daily Temp.	70	70	69	63	59	56	55	56	58	62	65	68
Av. Daily Low	60	61	59	54	51	48	47	48	50	53	55	58
Av. Daily High	80	80	78	72	67	63	62	63	66	70	74	77
Av. Humidity	66	68	69	74	76	79	80	79	76	71	67	64
Av. No. Days w/rain	4	4	4	7	10	12	11	11	9	7	6	5
Av. No. Days w/snow	0	0	0	0	0	0	0	0	0	0	0	0

NORTH AMERICA

CANADA

In general, Canadian climate is like that of the corresponding longitudes in the northern United States, only usually a bit colder. There are great seasonal differences in temperature. Winters are long, spring is very brief; July and August are the warmest months. The rich colors of autumn are best in the east from mid-September through October. Winters are cold, but central heating is everywhere, and the days are usually clear. Best time for winter sports is from mid-December to April. On the west coast, winters are milder and wetter. May through mid-October is the most pleasant period for travel.

OTTAWA

	Jan.	Feb.	Mar.	Apr.	May	June	July	Aug.	Sept.	Oct.	Nov.	Dec.
Av. Daily Temp.	12	13	26	41	54	64	69	67	59	46	33	18
Av. Daily Low	3	3	17	31	43	53	58	55	48	37	26	10
Av. Daily High	21	22	34	50	65	75	80	78	69	55	40	25
Av. Humidity	80	81	75	67	66	68	67	67	75	75	76	79
Av. No. Days w/rain	13	12	12	11	11	10	11	10	11	12	12	14
Av. No. Days w/snow	11	12	9	3	x	o	o	o	x	x	5	11

(x = less than one)

BERMUDA, THE BAHAMAS, THE CARIBBEAN

BERMUDA

The most important point to remember is that Bermuda is in the Atlantic, not the Caribbean. Whereas the "season" in the latter area is the winter, Bermuda's best months are those of spring, summer, and early fall. Even August, the hottest month, is bearable. July is supposedly the sunniest, but it can rain any time. Air conditioning exists in the large hotels and many of the smaller. Winters can be dismal—cool and rainy— though they are most times mild and sunny. No Bermudian goes swimming in winter. Lightweight woolens are advisable then.

HAMILTON

	Jan.	Feb.	Mar.	Apr.	May	June	July	Aug.	Sept.	Oct.	Nov.	Dec.
Av. Daily Temp.	63	63	63	65	70	75	79	80	78	74	69	65
Av. Daily Low	58	57	57	59	64	69	73	74	72	69	63	60
Av. Daily High	68	68	68	71	76	81	85	86	84	79	74	70
Av. Humidity	78	78	77	77	80	80	77	77	76	77	75	78
Av. No. Days w/rain	16	15	15	11	11	11	12	14	13	14	15	15
Av. No. Days w/snow	o	o	o	o	o	o	o	o	o	o	o	o

THE BAHAMAS

The weather is generally good year round, although from Christmas to Easter is the so-called "season." Winter evenings are sometimes cool, the rest of the year warm. It is hotter, and rainier, from June through October.

NASSAU

	Jan.	Feb.	Mar.	Apr.	May	June	July	Aug.	Sept.	Oct.	Nov.	Dec.
Av. Daily Temp.	72	72	73	75	78	81	82	82	82	80	76	74
Av. Daily Low	67	67	68	69	72	75	76	76	76	75	71	69
Av. Daily High	76	77	78	80	83	86	88	88	87	85	80	78
Av. Humidity	76	74	71	71	73	73	72	72	73	74	74	75
Av. No. Days w/rain	3	4	2	4	9	10	15	12	13	15	7	6
Av. No. Days w/snow	0	0	0	0	0	0	0	0	0	0	0	0

THE CARIBBEAN

Average summer and winter temperatures in the West Indies vary just a few degrees, always staying in the 70's and 80's. The islands are cooled year round by the trade winds, which can sometimes be quite strong. Winter (from mid-December to mid-April) is the social, and more expensive, season. The air is drier, the sun bright, and the days generally comfortable. This period—and you can usually extend it through May—is ideal for sunbathing, golf, tennis and extensive sightseeing. From May through July it is more humid, sometimes very wet, and midday in the island capitals can often be sweltering. It is cooler in the mountains, however, and less humid. Yet prices are lower during this time, the water is calmer for cruising as well as clearer for skin diving and snorkeling, and the islands are bright with flowers. The hot nights are no problem if you stay at an air-conditioned hotel, and most hotels are. The hurricane season starts chiefly toward the end of August and continues through October, but some islands haven't known hurricanes for 25 years. Remember, too, that most islands (Jamaica and the Netherlands Antilles are major exceptions) have both an Atlantic and a Caribbean coast, with the former generally being cooler and more rugged. The Netherlands Antilles islands of Curaçao, Bonaire and Aruba are climatically in a class by themselves: They are flat, rocky and arid, with very little rain and few high winds.

KINGSTON, JAMAICA

	Jan.	Feb.	Mar.	Apr.	May	June	July	Aug.	Sept.	Oct.	Nov.	Dec.
Av. Daily Temp.	77	77	77	79	80	82	82	82	81	81	79	78
Av. Daily Low	67	67	68	70	72	74	73	73	73	73	71	69
Av. Daily High	86	86	86	87	87	89	90	90	89	88	87	87
Av. Humidity	78	78	77	78	79	78	76	79	82	84	82	80
Av. No. Days w/rain	5	4	4	5	7	6	5	9	10	12	7	5
Av. No. Days w/snow	0	0	0	0	0	0	0	0	0	0	0	0

San Juan, Puerto Rico

	Jan.	Feb.	Mar.	Apr.	May	June	July	Aug.	Sept.	Oct.	Nov.	Dec.
Av. Daily Temp.	75	75	75	77	79	80	80	80	81	80	79	76
Av. Daily Low	70	69	70	71	73	74	75	75	75	75	73	71
Av. Daily High	80	80	81	82	84	85	85	85	86	86	84	81
Av. Humidity	78	77	75	76	77	78	79	78	79	79	79	79
Av. No. Days w/rain	21	15	16	14	16	17	19	20	18	17	20	22
Av. No. Days w/snow	0	0	0	0	0	0	0	0	0	0	0	0

Bridgetown, Barbados

	Jan.	Feb.	Mar.	Apr.	May	June	July	Aug.	Sept.	Oct.	Nov.	Dec.
Av. Daily Temp.	77	76	77	78	80	81	80	80	80	80	79	78
Av. Daily Low	70	69	70	71	73	74	74	74	73	73	73	71
Av. Daily High	83	83	84	85	87	87	86	86	86	86	85	84
Av. Humidity	72	71	73	75	71	78	80	79	79	81	81	72
Av. No. Days w/rain	14	12	11	9	11	17	19	18	16	17	16	16
Av. No. Days w/snow	0	0	0	0	0	0	0	0	0	0	0	0

Mexico

Mexico City has a high altitude (7,349 ft.), which eliminates the great extremes of temperature often found in cities at the same latitude and results in a delightful mild climate year round. The country's climate may be divided into three parts: the hot lowlands such as Yucatán, with a dry winter and spring, wet summer and fall, and late spring temperatures in the 90's; the Pacific Coast (Mazatlán), with high temperature and humidity in summer, occasionally below 50° in winter, but with a pleasant mean temperature of 70° in winter, 80° in summer; the high plateau (Mexico City) with low humidity, warm days and cool nights, a dry winter and a measure of rain in summer. Mexico's "rainy season" is from June to November, but this usually means brief afternoon rains rather than continuous downpours. Light woolens are the best clothing for Mexico City at all times. On the coasts the weather is warmer and summer cottons are in order most of the year.

Mexico City

	Jan.	Feb.	Mar.	Apr.	May	June	July	Aug.	Sept.	Oct.	Nov.	Dec.
Av. Daily Temp.	54	57	62	65	67	66	64	64	63	60	58	53
Av. Daily Low	42	44	48	52	54	55	54	54	54	50	48	41
Av. Daily High	66	70	75	78	79	76	74	74	72	70	68	65
Av. Humidity	53	48	45	45	51	62	67	68	70	65	61	58
Av. No. Days w/rain	3	4	6	11	15	19	25	24	20	12	6	4
Av. No. Days w/snow	0	0	0	0	0	0	0	0	0	0	0	0

SOUTH AMERICA

ARGENTINA

The seasons are more marked in this southernmost of South American countries, with winter beginning in June, summer in December. Although it snows in Chile's mountains, to the west, Argentina is snow-free, but chilly in winter. October to March is the best time.

BUENOS AIRES

	Jan.	Feb.	Mar.	Apr.	May	June	July	Aug.	Sept.	Oct.	Nov.	Dec.
Av. Daily Temp.	74	73	69	63	55	50	50	51	55	60	65	71
Av. Daily Low	63	62	59	53	46	41	42	43	46	50	55	60
Av. Daily High	85	84	78	72	64	58	57	59	63	69	75	82
Av. Humidity	72	74	79	82	82	86	86	82	79	77	73	72
Av. No. Days w/rain	7	6	7	8	7	7	8	9	8	9	9	8
Av. No. Days w/snow	0	0	0	0	0	0	0	0	0	0	0	0

BRAZIL

The seasons are reversed in Brazil, with the tropical Amazon region in the north, the semitropical area in the central section, and the temperate zone to the south. Brasilia is mild and dry; Rio is hot in summer (December to March), but the sea breeze is always present and most hotels are air-conditioned. Winter in Rio is pleasantly cool and sunny (from April to October).

RIO DE JANEIRO

	Jan.	Feb.	Mar.	Apr.	May	June	July	Aug.	Sept.	Oct.	Nov.	Dec.
Av. Daily Temp.	78	80	78	77	72	71	69	70	70	72	75	77
Av. Daily Low	74	76	75	73	69	67	65	66	66	69	71	73
Av. Daily High	82	83	81	81	75	74	73	73	74	75	78	81
Av. Humidity	78	78	79	79	79	78	78	76	79	79	78	78
Av. No. Days w/rain	13	11	12	10	10	7	6	7	11	12	12	14
Av. No. Days w/snow	0	0	0	0	0	0	0	0	0	0	0	0

Your Travel Personality

WHO ARE YOU really? This is a question to ask before you even begin planning a trip. Take a long hard look at yourself, not as you hope to be but as you are. If you are a person who likes a beach with a clubhouse where you can meet your friends, who enjoys being seen in new clothes, who would rather go to a new discothèque after dinner than sit around in the corner of some quiet bar talking to a friend, then you certainly ought to plan an itinerary quite different from that of the woman who likes to go for long walks by the sea, looks forward to wearing levis day and night, and prefers good talk to chemin-de-fer or The Monkey. One of you will be happy at Cannes, Portofino, or on Hydra; the other will prefer a Tyrolean village, the Galician coast, or driving through Anatolia, where natives outnumber the international set.

In sizing yourself up, there are three useful particulars to consider:

1. Age group. If you are over twenty-eight, say, you won't be

particularly happy at St. Tropez, where nobody looks more than twenty-three. It is unrealistic to imagine that you will feel at ease with a crowd of people who are members of a well-defined age group that you don't happen to belong to. If you aren't the right age for St. Tropez, it probably won't suit your temperament either; and there are innumerable other lively places to go. Big cities, on the other hand, are for everybody.

2. Money. You will not be happy for a moment with people whose scale of spending is totally different from yours, in whichever direction. It is hopeless to try to enjoy yourself with people who have put themselves on a tight budget and must forgo certain extras which you can afford and will feel cheated without. You wouldn't like to sit in the top gallery at the Vienna opera if you could possibly afford the best seat, or to ride on public transport when you can manage a hired car for the day. By the same token—and this may be even worse— many a bright day will be darkened if you are straining to keep up with people to whom a picnic catered by the best restaurant in town is an amusing trifle, when sausage, cheese, bread, fruit and a bottle of *vin ordinaire* are your speed. It's nice to meet a man who will spoil you, and let's hope you do. But your daily happiness is much likelier to be unclouded if you go to places you can afford and do things with people who share your ideas about spending.

3. That vague term, taste, must serve for the third essential to be considered. This may have something to do with background, education, the way you grew up and what you've been doing since. But it really isn't so confined a matter as that. Taste easily transcends national differences, education and sometimes class. It covers, for instance, how introverted or extroverted you are, how intellectual, and how much you like your comfort. The testing grounds for it are inescapable and they crop up continually. Some people would rather read books and visit archeological sites, go to concerts and museums, visit a local fair or see a *Son et Lumière* performance; others prefer casinos, nightclubs, a day at the races or on a golf course, having lunch in Cap Ferrat and flying to Paris for dinner. One woman with only a day in Paris might make the rounds of the boutiques; another would head for the Louvre. Some people are happy to take cold showers in a shared bathroom in a private house on some obscure Greek island; others are miserable when they can't call room service. You might like to dance all night, sleep all morning, or you may be up with the roosters and off sightseeing or swimming. Nobody is a consistent type, and these tastes exist in all combinations: You might be a gregarious intellectual comfort-seeker, or an introverted, non-

intellectual comfort-seeker. Nor is it a question really of how much money you can spend, although introverted tastes, being more private, often cost less than extroverted, public tastes, which call for a handsome stage to play on. In any case, do what suits your taste and go to places where this is easy—an elementary consideration, but one that is often overlooked.

It is terribly important to be absolutely honest with yourself about who you really are, and to forget fantasies of what a trip *should* be like. If you like crowds—which does not necessarily mean the subway at rush hour, but cocktail parties, first nights at the theater, the best beach at the height of the season—then stick to cities, resorts *in* season, large hotels. Plan to surround yourself with the atmosphere that makes *you* feel happy and at ease, not with one that may have suited Freya Stark or your mother-in-law. They may make solitude sound like pure poetry, but what would *you* do after the first delicious half hour? Could you stand all that unmarred peace, however beautiful, for twenty-four hours? What would you do all evening? What would you do when you got up in the morning? If considerations like that give you pause, forget about undiscovered, unspoiled places. This is not intended to dampen your readiness for adventure, but simply to suggest that you look for your adventures where you, being who you are, are most likely to find them.

More things to consider in being honest with yourself:

1. The fatigue factor: How "dead tired" are you? How long do you really need to lie alone in the sun recuperating the energies lost during the year? Do you really want 3 weeks all to yourself, or will 3 days be enough? Chances are, if you're medium young and normally healthy, 3 days will be quite sufficient, and, if you've signed up for 3 weeks, you'll go crazy with boredom and frustration during the remaining 18. Only someone convalescing after an operation or illness is likely to want a steady diet of long dreamless nights and lazy days curled up with a good book. The answer—if you are tired and want a rest, but know that it won't take you all that long to bounce back—is to go somewhere that offers both a quiet life by day and just enough gaiety at night, if that appeals to you.

2. Not so different from the fatigue factor is the business of being keyed up. Even if the lives we live didn't keep us in a state of high tension—which they generally do—then the preparations for a trip would be apt to contribute something. It takes a person who is in a state of nervous tension a long time to unwind—weeks, perhaps. In planning a trip with your own personality in mind, you must consider the possible need for a decompression period. There are various

solutions, though all require that you plan a longer vacation than you may originally have had in mind. It isn't that you are going to want to flop on a beach to unwind—that would probably only key you up more—but that you will need steady though quiet activity. A short ocean crossing provides a pretty good decompression chamber— though of course it will add a week to your trip. Another good idea would be to go to a resort before attacking the big cities.

As important as taking enough time to unwind is knowing when you've had enough. Even if your firm has awarded you, after ten years of faithful service, a glorious 6-week vacation, you needn't stay away all that time if you find yourself chafing at the bit after 4 weeks, eager to get back to your desk or at least to your home town. Maybe Grandmother *is* willing to take the children all summer—but will you find yourself, come early August, sitting in the Istanbul Hilton longing to pick up just one toy? Once you feel ready to go home, all the kick will go out of seeing new places and you might as well face up to it. It's helpful, too, to try to estimate when that will be when you're planning the trip.

3. How adaptable are you? If you're traveling with somebody else, you had better make a big effort to be as flexible as possible; otherwise, travel alone. Don't privately fume at the cables your husband thinks he has to send his office or fuss because your girl friend takes an hour to get ready for bed. Tell yourself clearly that you can't change in 3 weeks of travel the habits of a lifetime. It's a question of looking at things as they really are, not as you think they ought to be— and not trying to bend a situation that would sooner break.

Another kind of adaptability is how you react to mishaps. One traveler might find it a hilarious adventure to be lost on the road in a countryside where no one speaks English, or to find that the weekly boat that leaves a resort island is actually a biweekly boat, and temperamental at that; another traveler would get hysterical. If the unexpected brings you to tears, stick to the tried and true—cities that are used to American tourists, first-class hotels, or, perhaps, a group tour.

4. Throw out romantic illusions. Unless you are on a honeymoon, remote cottages on the moors and lonely islands, no matter how flawless the beaches and blue the water, come under that heading. Another supreme illusion is the long ocean voyage by freighter. Freighters carry from one to two dozen passengers; the odds are that they will not be the most fascinating people you ever met. You can take just so much of the poetry of sea and sky. The dining room will be tiny, the public rooms small. It is important to face reality here, be-

cause a mistake is irreversible: You are stuck until you get to your destination. Only if you are really gregarious and can cheerfully accept the vicissitudes will you be happy on a freighter.

5. You will never get 100 per cent perfection. Accept that as a fact of life if you haven't done so already. The best you can do is to take time to sit back quietly and think: What is it that I like and want? And be prepared *not* to get it—or all of it. But you can follow your own tastes and instincts, and be sure that you will come much closer to satisfaction than you will if you think about a Perfect Trip in the abstract, instead of the right trip for you.

7. Having decided who you are and what you want, don't be embarrassed by it. Don't be ashamed if you are afraid to be alone; you aren't the only one by any means. Take a package trip; you will be a great deal happier. Package trips and group tours have their drawbacks, of course, but they have many compensations in warmth and friendliness which for a great number of people will more than make up for the herding and scheduling. Don't feel like a square for choosing what is right for you. You will be miles ahead of the person who has bought somebody else's trip and is going to be bored and lonely in some exquisite out-of-the-way fishing village she read about.

On the other hand, don't exaggerate the perils and miseries of traveling alone. You can have company so much of the time that if you arrange your itinerary well, the hazards are few and far between (see Traveling Solo, page 388).

A quotation from Erich Fromm's *Escape from Freedom* will do very well in conclusion: "Whether or not we are aware of it, there is nothing of which we are more ashamed than of not being ourselves, and there is nothing that gives us greater pride and happiness than to think, to feel, and to say what is ours."

Your Traveling Companion

SHE MAY BE the girl you have lunch with 4 days out of 5 and your closest confidante, or the wife of your husband's longtime business partner and a whiz of a bridge player, but do you know if she appropriates seven eighths of the closet space for her immense wardrobe, whether her idea of fun is getting up at 6 to go bird-watching, or if she is a compulsive spoilsport? In short, regardless of her other sterling virtues, how does she qualify as a traveling companion?

The bonds of many a bosom friendship have been broken by the tensions of traveling—a pursuit that demands a healthy respect for the other person's privacy plus the tact, discipline and good humor that go with being a congenial companion. Finding a good traveling companion is almost as hard as finding a compatible mate. Furthermore, it's perfectly possible to discover—in the wilds of Yucatán—that your otherwise compatible mate is a terrible traveling companion. The strain of being with someone 24 hours a day 3 to 6 weeks at a time can be fierce. At home you leave your office buddy at 5 and your husband can work off his tensions on the tennis courts. On a trip, it's you two against the world—married by an itinerary if not by a clergyman. Traveling with another woman, you will undoubtedly be sharing a double room, since this arrangement is cheaper—and all that togetherness may get you down after a while, if you are used to living alone. If two married couples join forces, making a decision about a restaurant or a day's sightseeing can be as complicated as labor-management negotiations.

Here are a few general rules for selecting a good traveling companion or for making life smoother with the one you already have.

1. Expect blowups—and try to keep the battle about the practical issue, not each other's personality flaws. Since you'll be quarreling over concrete things, it will be easier to make compromises and concessions. Make them like mad. A trip doesn't last a lifetime. A good friendship or marriage can. And if the friend you are with satisfies you in every way except as a traveling companion, then you needn't travel with her again.

2. Air your grievances while they are new and relatively harmless—don't save them up. Few people are really the monsters they seem for the 60 seconds you are in a hot rage. Putting the issues on the table helps to ease most situations.

3. Avoid certain personality types as traveling companions:

The Competitive Girl—she'll make your life miserable every time a man smiles at you, not at her.

The Hypochondriac—she will be seasick, carsick, have a string of stomach ailments, worry over her food and otherwise take the joy out of life.

The Compulsively Neat Person—she will fly into a rage if you leave your sweater on the back of a chair.

The Emotionally Infantile—she will need constant love and reassurance, and is likely to be selfish. She will probably, unconsciously, use you as a parental substitute and give you a hard time by playing the clinging vine or by venting rebellious anger on you.

The Rigid Person—she will be so insistent about doing things by the book, usually "her" book, that she will wipe out any chance of spontaneous fun. She's also likely to harbor grudges, and complain a lot. The beds will be too soft or too hard, the food too rich or too plain, the rooms too hot or too drafty.

Look for someone who is permissive and easygoing; someone who tends to be indulgent, and if possible, who has a sense of humor. Be sure your faults and tastes are compatible, and that her idea of adequate accommodations isn't bed and breakfast in a tiny pension while yours is a suite at the Hilton, that her only passion isn't hitting every good restaurant in Europe and yours every art gallery.

4. Go separate ways now and then. The separation can last as short a time as an afternoon or as long as 10 days. If she's dying for a day on the beach but you want to see Botticellis, take different courses. Split up some days and meet only for lunch or dinner. It will help both your dispositions.

5. Expect to be bored occasionally, but don't take it out on each other. Before you go, let's say, to Mexico, you may picture it as exotic and cosmopolitan, swarming with suave Latins who will fall at your feet. When you arrive in Mexico City, you find it a fascinating but impersonal metropolis—and your constant dining companion is Jane from the office. Don't take your temporary letdown out on her. Enjoy the city for the abundant enchantments it does offer, without bemoaning the ones you mistakenly imagined it to have.

6. Be unfailingly courteous and considerate to your companion. Good manners go far in creating good feelings.

7. Discuss your attitudes toward money and expenditures fully beforehand, and try to travel on similar budgets. Living with someone who has lots more—or lots less—to spend than you can create many conflicts.

8. Make an agreement about men. If one comes along who prefers Jane to you, be willing to "fade out" for the evening without feeling ignored or hurt—and expect her to do the same when the situation is reversed. It will be far easier to go with someone whose attitude toward men and dating, and whose general attractiveness, is similar to

yours. The girl friend who is much wilder—or much mousier—than you will make your life miserable.

9. Before you go off on a long trip which may cost hundreds or thousands of dollars, take a short weekend trip with your traveling companion. It can be a sort of "trial marriage"—and serve to show you where the booby traps may lie.

Since husbands also fall into the category of "Traveling Companions," here are some hints for handling them in that role.

1. Make a special effort to be prompt at all times. Traveling requires synchronizing schedules and timetables. If he hates being late —and you make him so several times a day—both of your tempers are sure to flare.

2. Wear easy clothes, so you needn't fuss over your comfort. He will become justifiably annoyed if you complain about aching feet because you wore the wrong shoes on the afternoon you went sightseeing in the Old Town.

3. Divide responsibilities. If he has the usual male flair for mathematics, he should wrestle with all those conversion tables. (He should handle the money, in any case.) If your high-school French is more easily recognized by the natives, you take charge of the pocket dictionaries.

4. Give in to him wherever it's possible, because, curiously, men's egos are more challenged by foreign places than are women's. He hates to feel unknowing and therefore, unconsciously, "inferior" to the natives. By this time you know the nature of the beast; do what you can to make him feel safe and secure in your estimation of him.

5. Don't complain about the plumbing, the service or minor aches and pains. At home, he escapes to his business world; on a trip, when you are thrown together 24 hours a day for weeks at a time, your reiterated complaints can become hugely irritating.

6. Be prepared for your husband's sizing up Italian brunettes and Swedish blondes—and keep your composure even when you feel that devil jealousy start to prick. If he didn't stare he'd be dead or senile, and these beauties who enter your lives for barely a moment are a part of the local scenery which deserves your admiration too.

7. If he's of a "certain age," be prepared also to hear him relive the war in appropriate parts of the world. The experiences he had there were momentous and sometimes terrible. Just be glad he's there to tell them to you.

8. If you are married to a driven, hardworking man (usually the ones who can afford expensive trips), don't nag because he stays in touch with the office. If he will really sleep better knowing that

everything is all right back home, let him make the phone calls or send the cables without resenting the time they cost.

Above all, remember there isn't just one way to "see" a country. Someone else's ideas about how to spend time and money may give you experiences you would otherwise have missed. Your extroverted friend who talks to everyone at a café may embarrass you at first, but end up bringing you in contact with people you might not have met. Your sensitivity to art may open her eyes to line and color. If she walks slowly and you walk fast, slow down—you may notice things you would have missed at your own rate of speed. Be as tolerant and adaptable with your companion as you are prepared to be with the natives.

Appendix

Organizations that Arrange Meetings
Between American Visitors
and Nationals

THERE ARE many organizations through which Americans can meet their counterparts abroad. A selection of names and addresses appears below; this section can serve as a starting point for your investigations. Much of the information can be helpful to husbands and sons, for a number of these organizations have a large, or predominant, male membership.

For additional information on meeting nationals of another country, get in touch with the tourist office closest to your home (see address list, page 479). Since you must frequently handle the mechanics of meeting the locals after you've arrived, ask each foreign tourist office in the U.S.A. for a list of its branches in the mother country.

AUSTRIA

The Official Provincial Tourist Organizations will arrange meetings with Austrians. Addresses:

BURGENLAND:	*Amt der Burgenlaendischen Landesregierung Abteilung XII/6 Eisenstadt-Schloss*
CARINTHIA:	*Landesfremdenverkehrsamt in Kaernten Alter Platz 15 Klagenfurt*
LOWER AUSTRIA:	*Landesfremdenverkehrsamt fuer Nieder Oesterreich Herrengasse 13 Vienna I*

SALZBURG:	*Landesverkehrsamt in Salzburg*
	Mozartplatz 10
	Salzburg
STYRIA:	*Landesfremdenverkehrsamt fuer Steirmark*
	Landhaus
	Graz
TYROL:	*Landesverkehrsamt fuer Tirol*
	Landhaus
	Innsbruck
UPPER AUSTRIA:	*Landesfremdenverkehrsverband Ober*
	Oesterreich
	Hauptplatz 9
	Linz a/ Donau
VIENNA:	*Fremdenverkehrstelle der Stadt Wien*
	Stadiongasse 6
	Vienna I
	Oesterreich Haus (Austria House)
	Palais Palffy
	Josefplatz
	Vienna I
VORARLBERG:	*Landesverband fuer Fremdenverkehr*
	Montfortstrasse 4
	Bregenz

Special-interest organizations such as those listed below will also arrange meetings:

AMATEUR PHOTOGRAPHY GROUPS:

Gesellschaft von Amateurphotographen
Hamburgerstrasse 10
Vienna V

Wiener Amateur-Photographen-Klub
Koellnerhofgasse 6
Vienna I

ARCHEOLOGICAL INSTITUTIONS:

Archaeologisch-Epigraphisches Institut der Universitaet
Wien
Dr. Karl Lueger Ring 1
Vienna I

Archaeologisches Institut der Universitaet Graz
Universitaetsplatz 3
Graz, Styria

Oesterreichisches Archaeologisches Institut
Dr. Karl Lueger Ring 1
Vienna I

GEOLOGICAL INSTITUTIONS:

> *Forschungs-und-Versuchstelle in der Technischen Abteilung*
> *Der Generaldirektion der Oesterreichischen Salinen*
> *Wirerstrasse 12*
> *Bad Ischl, Upper Austria*

> *Geologische Bundesanstalt*
> *Rasumofskygasse 23*
> *Vienna III*

> *Geologisches Institut der Universitaet Wien*
> *Dr. Karl Lueger Ring 1*
> *Vienna I*

PHILATELIC SOCIETIES:

> *Freie Philatelie*
> *Vereinigung der Briefmarkensammler Wien*
> *Weidmanngasse 37*
> *Vienna XVII*

> *Internationaler Philatelistendienst*
> *Schindlergasse 22*
> *Vienna XVII*

> *Tauschvereinigung fuer Postwertzeichen*
> *Gumpendorferstrasse 9*
> *Vienna VI*

> *Verband Oesterreichischer Philatelistenvereine*
> *Universitaetstrasse 8*
> *Vienna IX*

> *Briefmarken-Sammler-Verein Donau*
> *Hackengasse 30*
> *Vienna XV*

AUSTRALIA

There are two officially constituted "home-host" schemes in operation in Australia at present. One is in Perth, Western Australia, the other in Mackay, Queensland. Consult:

> *The Mackay Development Bureau*
> *67A Sydney Street*
> *Mackay, Queensland*

> *Western Australian Government Tourist Bureau*
> *772 Hay Street*
> *Perth, Western Australia*

There is also a vigorous Australian-American Association with branches in Sydney and Melbourne, and various cities throughout the United States. The address of the New York branch is 2 Wall Street, New York, New York 10005. Visitors may get introductions through these organizations.

Members of such service organizations as Rotary and the Lions are welcomed by their opposite numbers in Australia. Professional bodies such as the College of Surgeons, the Institute of Chartered Accountants, etc., have also provided valuable meeting grounds for visitors.

U.S. visitors in special categories—students, members of affinity groups, delegates to international conferences, etc.—are usually given opportunities to meet Australians during their stay.

BARBADOS

The Rotary Club and Lions Club have branches in Barbados. Other organizations which can serve as a meeting ground include the Barbados Council of Women, Barbados Teachers Association, Barbados Soroptimist Branch, the American Women's Club—and special interest clubs such as the Jazz Club, Arts Council, Mayfair Bridge Club, plus a large number of sports clubs. You can get further information from the tourist office in Bridgetown.

BELGIUM

The following offices in Brussels arrange meetings between Belgian and American individuals:

> *Europe Meeting Club*
> *344 Avenue Louise*
> *(A private club; temporary membership about $6. Has a branch in Keerbergen.)*
>
> *Institut Belge d'Information et de Documentation*
> *3 Rue Montoyer*

Professional organizations in Brussels can help you meet your Belgian counterparts. Among them:

ARCHITECTS:
> *Fédération Royale des Sociétés d'Architects de Belgique*
> *(F.A.B.)*
> *(Royal Federation of Architects' Organizations)*
> *21 Rue Ernest Allard*

ARCHITECTS, PAINTERS, SCULPTORS:
> *Association des Artistes Professionnels de Belgique*
> *(Association of Professional Artists)*
> *461 Avenue Louise*
> *1 Rue Paul Lauters*

AUTHORS, COMPOSERS, PUBLISHERS:

> Société Belge des Auteurs, Compositeurs, et Editeurs
> (SABAM)
> (Organization of Belgian Authors, Composers and
> Publishers)
> 61 Rue de la Loi

CONTRACTORS OF PAINTING AND DECORATION:

> Fédération Nationale des Entrepreneurs de Peinture et
> Décor de Belgique
> (Nat'l Federation of Painting and Decoration Contractors)
> 20 Rue d'Italie

DENTISTS:

> Association Générale des Dentistes de Belgique
> (Association of Belgian Dentists)
> 166 Chaussée d'Etterbeek

> Union des Dentistes et Stomatologistes
> (Organization of Dentists and Stomatologists)
> 218 Rue Belliard

DOCTORS:

> Académie Royale de Médecine
> (Royal Academy of Medicine)
> Palais des Académies
> Rue Ducale

> Fédération Médicale Belge
> (Belgian Medical Federation)
> 9 Rue Tenbosch

> Maison des Médecins
> (Doctors' Building)
> 54 Boulevard de Waterloo

FILM PUBLICATION:

> Association Professionelle de la Presse Cinématographique
> Belge
> (Association of Professional Writers on Motion Pictures)
> Maison de la Presse
> 4 Petite Rue au Beurre

JOURNALISTS, NEWSPAPER STAFF:

> Union Professionnelle de la Presse Belge
> (Professional Organization of the Belgian Press)
> Maison de la Presse
> 4 Petite Rue au Beurre

LAWYERS:

> *Fédération des Avocats Belges*
> *(Federation of Belgian Lawyers)*
> *Palais de Justice*

> *Fédération des Avoués de Belgique*
> *38 Rue Lambert-le-Begue*
> *(Liège)*

MAGAZINE PUBLICATION:

> *Union de la Presse Périodique Belge (U.P.P.B.)*
> *(Organization of the Periodical Press)*
> *20 Rue Belliard*

MEDICAL PUBLICATION:

> *Association de la Presse Médicale Belge*
> *(Association of the Belgian Medical Press)*
> *244 Avenue Louise*

MUSICAL PUBLICATION:

> *Union de la Presse Musicale Belge*
> *(Union of the Belgian Musical Press)*
> *Maison de la Presse*
> *4 Petite Rue au Beurre*

NOTARIES:

> *Fédération des Notaires de Belgique*
> *(Federation of Belgian Notaries)*
> *23 Rue du Nord*

PHARMACISTS:

> *Association Pharmaceutique Belge*
> *(Belgian Pharmaceutical Association)*
> *11 Rue Archimède*

> *Union Pharmaceutique Belge (UNIPRBE)*
> *(Belgian Pharmacists' Organization)*
> *30/38 Rue aux Fleurs*

PRESS:

> *Association Générale de la Presse Belge*
> *(Association of the Belgian Press)*
> *Maison de la Presse*
> *4 Petite Rue au Beurre*

TEACHERS:

> *Fédération Générale des Instituteurs Belges*
> *(Federation of Belgian Teachers)*
> *32 Rue de Louvain*

THEATER PUBLICATION:

> *Union de la Presse Théâtrale Belge*
> *(Organization of Writers on the Theater)*
> *Maison de la Presse*
> *4 Petite Rue au Beurre*

TRANSLATORS, INTERPRETERS:

> *Chambre Belge des Traducteurs, Interprètes, Philologues*
> *(Belgian Chamber of Translators, Interpreters, Philologists)*
> *11 Avenue du Barbeau*

UNIVERSITY WOMEN:

> *Fédération Belge des Femmes Diplômées des Universités*
> *(Federation of Belgian University Women)*
> *74 Rue du Namur*

VETERINARIES:

> *Union Vétérinaire Belge*
> *(Belgian Veterinaries' Organization)*
> *10 Avenue C, Vaneuken*

BERMUDA

The Bermuda Press recently instituted the Readers' Information Service. By simply calling the service at 2-5881 (Monday through Saturday 9 to 5, Thursday 9 to noon) you can get information about various organizations which introduce people and find out how to reach them, such as: the Astronomical Society; the Audubon Society; the Bermuda Boat & Canoe Club; the Bermuda Sailboat Club; the Bowmen of Bermuda (archery); the Badminton Club; the Bridge Club, which is an affiliate of the American Contract Bridge League; the Darts Club; the Garden Club; the Harrington Sound Sailing & Gliding Club; the Kennel Club and the Royal Bermuda Yacht Club.

The Altrusa Club, Eastern Star, English Speaking Union, Lions Club, Masons, Pilot Club and Rotary Club all have chapters in Bermuda, and visitors are welcome at meetings.

CANADA

No organized "Meet the Canadians" program exists as of this writing, but one is projected for the future. Before you leave, check with the nearest Canadian Government Travel Bureau (see listings under National Tourist Offices, page 481).

DENMARK

The "Meet the Danes" program, run by the National Travel Association of Denmark, arranges meetings between Danes and Americans. Visit the Personal Information Department, Main Office, National Travel Association of Denmark, 5–7 Banegaardspladsen, as soon as possible after you arrive in Copenhagen.

For students: Visit the Students' Club, 6 Hans Christian Andersen Boulevard. The club is open all year; free temporary membership during July and August is available to foreign students.

FINLAND

The "Find the Finns" program will arrange person-to-person meetings in Finland. For an application form, write:

> *Finnish National Travel Office*
> *505 Fifth Avenue*
> *New York, New York 10017*

Or inquire at the following office after arrival:

> *Finnish Tourist Association—Foreign Department*
> *Mikonkatu 15*
> *Helsinki, Finland*

FRANCE

A long string of organizations in Paris will arrange meetings between Americans and French nationals. If you share any of the special interests listed below, write directly to the corresponding organizations.

AMERICAN TRAVELERS:
> *France-États-Unis*
> *6 Rue de Grenelle*

> *Paris Welcome Information Office*
> *7 Rue Balzac*

PROFESSIONAL WOMEN'S GROUPS:
> *Association des Femmes Juristes*
> *121 Boulevard Haussmann*

> *Association des Françaises Diplomées des Univérsités*
> *4 Rue de Chevreuse*

> *Association Française des Femmes Médecins*
> *123 Rue de Lille*

> *F.C.E. Femmes Chefs d'Enterprise*
> *25 Rue Mouzaia*

> *Fédération Française des Clubs de Femmes de Carrières*
>   *Libérales et Commerciales*
> *19 Boulevard de la Somme*

STUDENTS AND TEACHERS:

American Students' and Artists' Center
261 Boulevard Raspail

Association Jeunes France-Canada
24 Rue Babylone

Centre Quaker International
110 Avenue Mozart

Centre Universitaire International (University Professors'
Center)
173 Bouleard St.-Germain

Cercle Concordia
27 Rue du Pont-Neuf
(restaurant, rooms for women students)

Office du Tourisme Universitaire
137 Boulevard St.-Michel
(or 972 Fifth Avenue, New York, New York 10021)

CATHOLIC:
Centre Richelieu
8 Place de la Sorbonne

Federation Française des Etudiants Catholiques
61 Rue Madame

Maison Diocésaine des Etudiants
61 Rue Madame

Parish Church for Students, St.-Séverin
3 Rue Prêtres-St.-Séverin

PROTESTANT:

Association des Etudiants Protestants
46 Rue de Vaugirard

STUDENT CLUBS:

Cité Abraham
4 Rue des Prêtres-St.-Séverin

Cité-Club Universitaire
2 Place Henri-Bergson

Club des Quatre Vents
1 Rue Gozlin and
Place St.-Germain-des-Prés

Sporting Club Universitaire de France
24 Rue de Chazelles

WOMEN:

Action Catholique Générale Féminine
98 Rue de l'Université

Association des Femmes de L'Union Française
184 Boulevard St.-Germain

Conseil National des Femmes Françaises
5 Rue Las-Cases

Elle Club
127 Avenue Champs-Elysées

Ligue Française pour le Droit des Femmes
3 Rue Victor-Massé

Union Féminine Civique et Sociale
37 Rue de Valois

Union Nationale des Femmes
180 Rue de Grenelle

WOMEN'S CLUBS:

Club Féminin de Paris-Lyceum
50 Avenue Marceau

*Comité d'Accueil du Comité de Liaison des Associations
    Féminines Françaises*
14 Avenue Georges-Mandel

Soroptimist Club de Paris
8 Rue de Bassano

Various organizations in Paris provide special services for doctors, architects, authors, artists, photographers, journalists, broadcasters and other professional and business people in France on business. For example:

ARCHITECTS:

Ministère Construction et Logement
Avenue du Parc-de-Passy

AUTHORS, ARTISTS, PHOTOGRAPHERS:

Syndicat de la Proprieté Artistique
12 Rue Henner

BUSINESSMEN:

Comité Franc-Dollar
31 Avenue Pierre-Ier-de-Serbie
(arranges introductions with French businessmen, can help with import problems)

DOCTORS:

Centre International du Film Médical et Chirurgical
36 Rue de Ponthieu
(Will arrange film showings of leading French surgeons
and doctors at work.)

Lions, Rotary, and other international clubs have chapters in Paris.
Consult your U.S. chapter for addresses.

SPORTS:
AIR RALLIES, FLYING LESSONS:

Groupement Bayard
64 Rue Caumartin

Touring Club de France
65 Avenue Grande-Armée

BICYCLING:

Fédération Française de Cyclotourisme
66 Rue René-Boulanger

CAMPING:

Auto-Camping and Caravaning Club de France
15 Rue du Faubourg-Montmartre

Camping Club de France, Union Camping et Tourisme
218 Boulevard St.-Germain

CANOEING:

Canoe Club
62 Avenue Parmentier

Kayak Club de France
34 Rue de Chabrol

GOLF:

Golfers Club
53 Avenue Hoche

YACHTING:

Yacht Club de France
82 Boulevard Haussmann

MISCELLANEOUS:
LITERARY CLUB:

Cercle Central des Lettres et des Arts
5 Boulevard Montmartre

GERMANY

1. America Houses (German-American Clubs) are meant chiefly to introduce Germans to American culture through films, lectures, etc., but they are good places for Americans to meet Germans. They are sponsored cooperatively by the U.S. and German governments. There are America Houses in:

Berlin W., *Hardenbergstrasse 22*
Bremen, *Domsheide, Haus Glocke*
Cologne, *Mittelstrasse*
Darmstadt, *Schustergasse 18*
Duesseldorf, *"Die Bruecke," Heinrich-Heine-Allee 49/51*
Frankfurt, *Stauffenstrasse 1*
Freiburg, *Bertoldstrasse 8*
Hamburg, *Rotherbaum, Tesdorpfstrasse 1*
Hannover, *Staendehausstrasse 5-6*
Heidelberg, *Sophienstrasse 9*
Kassel, *Wilhelmshoeher Platz*
Koblenz, *Schloss-Strasse 51*
Marburg, *Ketzerbach 1*
Munich, *Arcisstrasse 12*
Nuremberg, *Gleissbuehlstrasse 13*
Regensburg, *Am Watmarkt 1*
Stuttgart, *Olgastrasse 13* and *Charlottenstrasse 9*
Tuebingen, *Karlstrasse 3*

2. America Society, Tesdorpfstrasse 1, Hamburg, organizes meetings between groups and advises American travelers.

3. Atlantik Bruecke (Atlantic Bridge), Harvestehuderweg 9, Hamburg 13, is an organization which aims to introduce people of the same interests or profession.

4. Private automobile clubs:

ADAC (Allgemeiner Deutscher Automobil-Klub)
9–11 Koeniginstrasse
Munich 22

Automobilklub von Deutschland AVD
2 Wiesenhuettenstrasse
Frankfurt am Main

5. Rotary Club and other such international organizations meet regularly in many German cities; they are always pleased to have American guests. Check your U.S. club.

6. There are German-American clubs in various towns as well as branches of the International Women's Club.

7. The "Meet the Germans" program is established in a number of towns in South Germany, such as Ansbach, Darmstadt, Kassel, Munich, Nuremberg, Schwabach, Stuttgart, and Würzburg.

GREAT BRITAIN

Various professional organizations (e.g., Bureau of Overseas Medical Visitors; Law Society; British Engineers Association; National Union of Journalists) and hobby clubs (e.g., British Ornithologists' Club; Burns' Club; Dickens Fellowship; English Folk Song and Dance Society) offer a meeting ground for Americans and Britons in London.

A number of American associations such as the Harvard Club have branches in London, as do international organizations such as Rotary International, the International Association of Lions Clubs and Freemasonry. Other international organizations and clubs that offer hospitality or assistance to overseas travelers include:

All Nations Social Club Ltd., *83 Chiltern Street (Baker St.), W.1*
American Women's Club, *1 Cadogan Gardens, S.W.3*
British American Associates, *37 Charles Street, W.1*
British Federation of University Women Ltd., *Crosby Hall, Cheyne Walk, S.W.3*
English Speaking Union, *37 Charles Street, Berkeley Square, W.1*
Friends of Atlantic Union, *20 Wilton Place, S.W.1*
Friends International Centre, *Courtauld House, Byng Place, W.C.1*
International Friendship League, *3 Creswick Road, W.3*
International Language Club, *12 Park Hill Road, East Croydon, Surrey*
The Newman International Centre, *31 Portman Square, W.1*
Federation of Soroptimist Clubs of Great Britain and Ireland, *63 Bayswater Road, W.2*
Vita et Pax International Club, *Bramley Road, Barnet, N.14*

STUDENTS: The British Travel Association in New York City has a booklet called "Students Visiting Britain" which lists YWCAs and YMCAs, student tours and holiday centers, and suggestions for economical travel.

Organizations in London that offer assistance to students include:
Academy House, 24 Kensington Park Gardens, W.11—provides hostel accommodations, social and cultural activities for British and overseas students.

Student Movement House, 103 Gower Street, W.C.1—an international club for students and university teachers. Arranges discussion groups and social events.

GREECE

There are various organizations, mostly for students and young people, where Americans can apply for classes and/or accommodations.

FOR STUDENTS:

American School of Classical Studies—*54 Souidias Street, Athens.* classes in archeology.

Ethnikon Metsoveion Polytechnion—*42 Patission Street, Athens.* Information concerning extremely low-priced accommodations (e.g., $10 for 5 days), including use of studios, for Fine Arts students and artists in houses on Hydra, Mykonos and Rhodes.

The University Club—*Acadimias and Ippocratous Streets, Athens.* Free Greek classes for foreign students.

Many societies, cultural clubs, etc., are always happy to assist visitors with special interests, such as professional persons, artists or sportsmen. For names and addresses, write to:

> *Greek National Tourist Organization*
> *601 Fifth Avenue*
> *New York, New York 10017*

ICELAND

You can arrange meetings with Icelanders in Iceland by writing to the following organization before you leave, or calling in person after you arrive:

> *Iceland Tourist Bureau*
> *Laekjargata*
> *Reykjavik, Iceland*

INDIA

The Tourist Department of the Government of India has in recent years introduced an official program in the major cities of Bombay, Delhi, Calcutta and Madras, for introducing tourists to Indians who share their interests. Consult the New York office in advance, or one of the Indian branches after you arrive. Indicate your interests and the dates that you are likely to visit. Arrangements can be made for introductions, visiting with families or institutions.

There are, in addition, organizations such as the Indo-American Friendship Association, women's clubs, or other cultural institutions which offer similar facilities. Organizations like the Rotary, Lions Club, etc., also assist members of the overseas branches of their organizations.

IRELAND

Ireland's "Meet the Irish" program arranges individual meetings. Write for advance application forms to:

Irish Tourist Board
33 East 50th Street
New York, New York 10022

The program operates only from May through October.

ISRAEL

Israel has an official "Meet-the-Israeli" program. Meetings can be arranged through any Government Information Office of the Ministry of Tourism for Americans who want to meet Israelis in their homes, or professional people who would like to talk with their Israeli counterparts.

> *Addresses:*
> Eilat: *New Commercial Building*
> Haifa: *2 Balfour Street*
> Haifa Port: *Shed 3*
> Jerusalem: *60 King George Ave.*
> Lod (Lydda): *Lod Airport*
> Nazareth: *Casanova Street*
> Tel Aviv: *7 Mendele Street*
> Tiberias: *8 Nazareth Street*

These offices can also arrange for you to spend an evening at a kibbutz, and to visit military training camps.

The Israel Government Tourist Corporation, in cooperation with several professional groups and institutions, has also prepared special itineraries to help various visiting professional groups obtain a more comprehensive picture of corresponding local activities and efforts.

Tours (lasting up to 15 days) which include visits to varied institutions in all parts of the country as well as meetings and discussions with Israeli counterparts have already been organized for the following:

1. Archeology and archeological sites
2. The architectural profession and architecture in Israel
3. The educational profession and educational institutions
4. Industrial personnel and executives
5. The medical profession and medical institutions
6. Religion

The following tours are in preparation:

1. Farming and agriculture

2. The legal profession and judicial institutions
3. Municipal and local council activities and affairs
4. Science and scientific institutions
5. Social services and social affairs
6. Youth programs

(These tours do not preclude general sightseeing and holidaying in Israel.)

Certain groups (e.g., medical) will arrange for special events to give visiting members of the profession the opportunity to meet Israelis similarly employed. In Tel Aviv the ZOA House (Zionist Organization of America) on Frischman Street provides a good meeting place for Americans and Israelis. The mayors of Jerusalem, Tel Aviv and Haifa occasionally hold small receptions for visitors.

Other agencies to consult:

Hadassah, *Hadassah Headquarters, Jerusalem*
Pioneer Women, *Histadrut Building, Tel Aviv*
WIZO, *WIZO Visitors Bureau, Hayarkon Street, Tel Aviv*

ITALY

Americans can arrange meetings with Italians by writing to individual local tourist offices whose names and addresses can be obtained from:

Italian Government Travel Office
626 Fifth Avenue
New York, New York 10020

International organizations such as the Rotary Club, Masons, etc., can arrange meetings. Other good contacts:

Comitato della Società Dante Alighieri
Via C. Correnti 17
Milan

JAMAICA

There is no official government "Meet-the-People" program. There are, however, a large number of organizations that welcome people with common interests: Rotary Clubs in Kingston and Montego Bay; International Club, Alliance Française, Ivory Club, in Kingston; Green Room Club in Montego Bay. Various Christian Youth organizations, YMCA and YWCA, Jamaica Social Welfare Commission and farm organizations are happy to arrange meetings between members and visitors. Also, the Jamaica Tourist Board publishes a booklet called "Interesting People," which lists over 150 resident Jamaicans who have volunteered to meet visitors. The booklet gives their names, addresses and special interests, which range from bird watching to astronomy. Complimentary copies are available at Jamaica Tourist Board offices in the U.S.A. and Canada. See pages 485 and 486.

JAPAN

The official Home Visit Programs are operated by the municipalities of Kobe and Kyoto as well as by the Kanagawa Prefectural Government which covers the area in and around Yokohama. In addition, there is a privately organized Home Visit Program in Tokyo known as the Japan Home Visit Association.

In Kobe, apply at the Tourist Section offices: Kobe City Hall, Tourist Section; Japan Travel Bureau, Sannomiya Office; Everett Travel Service; Oriental Hotel; Kobe International Hotel; passenger department of your steamship company or their agent.

In Kyoto, make application two days in advance to the Tourist Industry Department of Kyoto Municipal Government, Japan Travel Bureau, other travel agents or hotels.

In the Yokohama area, get in touch with the Tourist Division of the Kanagawa Prefectural Government, 1 Nihon-odori, Nakaku, Yokohama.

In Tokyo, consult the Japan Home Visit Association, 21-chome, Ginza Higashi, Chuo-ku, or the centrally located Japan National Tourist Organization Tourist Information Center at 1 Yurakucho, Chiyoda-ku.

Another good source of contacts, with both Japanese and Americans residing in Tokyo is the America-Japan Society (Nichibei Kyokai) located on the third floor of the Marunouchi Building near Tokyo Station. This organization is comparable to the Japan Society in New York City. Further information can be secured from Mr. Douglas Overton, Executive Director of the Japan Society, 250 Park Avenue, New York, New York 10017.

Other ways to meet the Japanese are through international cultural, hobby and business organizations, professional clubs, and college alumni associations. The same organizations are likely to prove helpful when it comes to meeting Americans living in Japan. The large, handsome International House (Kokusai Bunka Kaikan) located at 2 Toriizaka-machi, Azabu, Minato-ku, Tokyo, for example, is a home-away-from-home for many resident American students, professors, artists, etc. A number of Christian churches and a Jewish Community Center in Tokyo also offer opportunities for meeting Americans.

LUXEMBOURG

American Luxembourg Society
9 Avenue de la Porte-Neuve

American Women in Luxembourg
9 Avenue de la Porte-Neuve

(The organizations above do not have full-time offices; therefore you should write ahead.)

Youth Hostels Organization, 18-A Place d'Armes, offers not only inexpensive food and board, but is an excellent ground for meeting people from all over Europe.

Additional general contacts as well as meetings with specific cultural and occupational groups can be arranged by:

Luxembourg National Tourist Office
51 Avenue de la Gare
Luxembourg, Grand Duchy of Luxembourg

MEXICO

There is a counterpart in Mexico for almost every American fraternal organization, professional association and hobby group. Get in touch with your local chapter for a list of appropriate addresses in Mexico. American churches and church-affiliated clubs are also good starting points.

MONACO

Meetings between Americans and Monegasques can be arranged by calling on the following organization after arrival:

Commissariat Général au Tourisme et a l'Information
Monte Carlo

The facilities of the Monte-Carlo Country Club, the Monte-Carlo Golf Club and the Monaco Yacht Club are available for a fee.

NASSAU

There is no official "Meet-the-People" program in Nassau, although from time to time His Excellency the Governor has an invitational cocktail party for residents and occasional foreign guests. Call on the local chapters of Rotary and Kiwanis and the local American Men's Club and its female counterpart. Hostesses at the hotels also cooperate in arranging meetings.

NETHERLANDS

The official "Meet-the-People" program is called "Get in Touch with the Dutch." You can make arrangements through the local tourist offices, called VVV's (Vereniging Voor Vreendelingenzerkeer), which are located in cities and towns throughout the country. For a complete list of tourist offices, write:

Netherlands National Tourist Office
605 Fifth Avenue
New York, New York 10017

In The Hague, Rotterdam, Amsterdam and other major cities, there are programs called "The Hague Invites You," "Rotterdam Invites You," etc., organized by prominent women in these communities who like to show their cities to visitors. The VVV offices can help the traveler get in touch with women participating in this activity. These women are volunteers, not paid hostesses; it is important that appointments be set up in advance.

There is also a student guide service called BBTBBA (Netherlands Amateur Guards Association), Statenlaan 51, The Hague. These students accept no pay, are multi-lingual, and will show visitors around Holland. They are especially good companions for young travelers. If the student guide is with you for a full day, food expenses are usually paid by the visitor.

NEW ZEALAND

The best contacts are Community Public Relations Officers. Some cities are more active in this area than others, but it's fairly certain that if you approach any of these officers with a request to meet local New Zealanders, you will be accommodated.

NORWAY

The "Know the Norwegians" program arranges meetings between Norwegians and Americans. Write in advance to one of three travel association offices:

Bergen Travel Association
Slottsgaten 1
Bergen

Oslo Travel Association
Raadhusgaten 19
Oslo

Stavanger Travel Association
Östre Strandgate 5
Stavanger

PERU

Visitors can meet other North Americans as well as Peruvians through the following organizations in Lima:

American Society
Union Church Building
Avenida Angamos 1155
Miraflores

Artesanía Peruana
1757 Prolongación de Huanuco

Casa de la Cultura
116 Azangaro

Comite Norteamericano pro Peru
615 Camana

Fulbright Art Center
Máximo Abril 599
Lince

Instituto Cultural Peruano-Norte-
americano
446 Cuzco

Museo de Arte
125 Paseo Colón

Pan American Union
Huancavelica 279

Peruvian Tourist Corporation
Casa Oquendo
Jirón Lima 298

These country clubs also welcome visitors: the Lima Golf Club, the Club Nacional on the Plaza San Martin, the Phoenix Club, and the Lawn Tennis Club. Guest cards are required, but you can arrange them through Panagra.

PORTUGAL

As of this writing there are no special facilities in Portugal for arranging meetings, but a plan is projected for the future. (There are, however, branches of the Lions Club and Rotary Club in Lisbon.) Before you leave, consult:

Portuguese Information and Tourist Office
570 Fifth Avenue
New York, New York 10036

PUERTO RICO

The Lions Club and Rotary Club have branch offices in San Juan. Other organizations that facilitate meetings in and around San Juan include:

Exchange Club
Sheraton Hotel
San Juan

Exchange Club
Top of the First
Santurce

National Secretaries Association
San Juan Chapter: Box 1647
San Juan

Puerto Rico Federation of Business
and Professional Women's Club
Box 428
Rio Piedras

SOUTH AFRICA

"Meet-the-People" programs are just getting under way in the Republic. Several dozen individuals in the major cities have instituted "Meet the South African" Committees; the largest group is in Cape Town. For details, write to:

> *South African Tourist Corporation*
> *610 Fifth Avenue*
> *New York, New York 10020*

Consult international cultural, professional and business organizations, alumni associations and hobby groups for names of the usual contacts in South Africa. There are, for example, a Business & Professional Women's Club, as well as Housewives League, Women's Agricultural Union, Maria van Riebeeck Club, various bridge and social clubs.

If you want to meet fellow Americans, get in touch with the U.S. Embassy in the Van der Stel Building on Pretorius Street in Pretoria, or the various U.S. consulates in principal cities throughout the country.

SPAIN

In Madrid, get in touch with:
> *The American Club, Villanueva 7*
> *The British-American Club, 6 Calle José Antonio*

Consult the Spanish National Tourist Department, Avenida del Generalisimo 39, for additional information.

The Spanish National Tourist Department has offices in many other Spanish cities. For names and addresses, write to:
> *Spanish National Tourist Office*
> *589 Fifth Avenue*
> *New York, New York 10017*

SWEDEN

The "Sweden-at-Home" program is the best way for foreign tourists to meet Swedes. Fourteen cities—Stockholm, Göteborg, Malmö, Eskilstuna, Halmstad, Hälsingborg, Linköping, Norrköping, Uppsala, Örebro, Västerås, Trollhättän, Falkenberg and Varberg—participate in the program. You can make arrangements in advance by writing to the Swedish National Travel Office, 505 Fifth Avenue, New York, New York 10020, or after you arrive by getting in touch with one of the following:

In Göteborg:
Tourist Office
Central Station

In Malmö:
Tourist Office
Skeppsbron

In Kalmar:
Tourist Office
Olandshamnen

In Stockholm:
The Tourist Center (Information Pavilion)
Kungstradgärden Park or "af Chapman" (youth hostel office)
(summer address)

Stockholm Tourist Traffic Society
Gustav Adolfstorg 20
(winter address)

SWITZERLAND

The official "Meet-the-People" program is called "Don't Miss the Swiss." Write:

> *Swiss National Tourist Office*
> *608 Fifth Avenue*
> *New York, New York 10020*
> or
> *Don't Miss the Swiss*
> *c/o Zurich Tourist Office*
> *Muensterhof 20*
> *Zurich 1*

Other organizations that arrange meetings:
> Geneva: YWCA, 37 *Quai Wilson*
> Lausanne: British-American Club, 27 *Avenue de Rumine*
> Zurich: American Women's Club, *Hotel Baur-au-Lac, Tal-strasse 1*

TURKEY

Get in touch with the Turkish-American Association, Mithatpasa Caddesi, Ankara, Turkey. In addition, both the Rotary and Soroptimist Clubs have Turkish chapters, the addresses of which can be obtained from their American headquarters.

Students can meet their Turkish counterparts through several students' organizations. Addresses:

Ankara:
MTTB Turizm Bürosu
Tuna Cad. No. 13
Yenişehir

TMTF Turizm Mürdürlügü
Çiftçi Ap. Bakanliklar

Istanbul:
MTTB Turizm Bürosu
Cağaloğlu

TMGT Turizm Bürosu
Istiklal Cad. 471/2
Tunel

TMTF Turizm Müdürlügü
Cağaloğlu No. 40

Izmir:
MTTB Turizm Bürosu
Fuar, Lozan Kepisi

THAILAND

Consult the Tourist Organization of Thailand, Mansion 2, Rajdamnern Avenue, Bangkok, Thailand, which may be able to arrange individual meetings between Americans and nationals.

UNION OF SOVIET SOCIALIST REPUBLICS

In Moscow, call:

Ministry of Culture
10 Kuycyshev Street

Soviet State Committee for Cultural Relations with Foreign Countries
9 Kalinin Street

Soviet Women's Committee
Pushkin Street

Soviet Youth Committee
10 Kropotkin Street

Union of Friendship Societies with Foreign Countries
14 Kalinin Street

VENEZUELA

Centro Venezolano-Americano
Edificio Easo, Mezzanina
Avenida Francisco de Miranda, Chacaito, Caracas

This organization is dedicated to advancing relationships between Venezuelans and Americans; it also offers classes in Spanish and English.

Both the Lions Club and Rotary have branches in Caracas.

Young people can meet Venezuelans and other Americans through the YMCA (Centro San Cristóbal No. 9, Las Pastoras).

If you are interested in the theater, get in touch with the Caracas Theater Club, Seccion San Román, Las Mercedes. By participating in their theater activities, you have the privilege of using all their facilities (i.e., tennis, swimming, dancing, etc.).

YUGOSLAVIA

Special contacts can be arranged through the Yugoslavia Information Center, 816 Fifth Avenue, New York, 10021, or through the local tourist associations in Yugoslavia. For their addresses, write:

Yugoslav State Tourist Office
509 Madison Avenue
New York, New York 10022

Students should call: Department of Yugoslav Youth and Students, Mose Pijade 12, P.O.B. 374, Belgrade, Yugoslavia. Cable address: NAROMTRAVEL.

All information listed above is accurate and up-to-date as of this writing, but it is naturally subject to change. To save time and avoid errors, before you leave write ahead to the organization in which you are interested, or check with the tourist office in the United States closest to your home.

National Tourist Offices:
A Comprehensive List of
Addresses At Home and Abroad

ANTIGUA
Antigua Tourist Information Office
Box 363
St. John's, Antigua, B.W.I.

ARGENTINA
Dirección Nacional de Turismo
Uruguay No. 291
Buenos Aires, Argentina

Argentine Embassy
1600 New Hampshire Avenue N.W.
Washington, D.C. 20009

ARUBA
Aruba Information Center
609 Fifth Avenue
New York, New York 10017

Aruba Tourist Bureau
L.G. Smith Boulevard 1764
Oranjestad, Aruba, N.A.

AUSTRALIA
Australian National Travel
    Association
636 Fifth Avenue
New York, New York 10020

Australian National Travel
    Association
350 Post Street
San Francisco, California 94108

Australian National Travel
    Association
Coates Building
18 Collins Street
Melbourne, Australia

AUSTRIA
Austrian State Tourist Department
444 Madison Avenue
New York, New York 10022

Austrian State Tourist Department
195 South Beverly Drive
Beverly Hills, California 90212

Austrian State Tourist Department
332 South Michigan Avenue
Chicago, Illinois 60604

Austrian State Tourist Department
2433 N.W. Lovejoy Street
Portland, Oregon 97205

Office National Autrichien du
    Tourisme
630 Ouest, Boulevard Dorchester
Montreal, Quebec, Canada

Austrian State Tourist Department
62 Richmond Street West,
    Suite 616
Toronto, Ontario, Canada

Österreichische Fremden-
    verkehrswerbung
Höhenstaufengasse 3–5
Vienna I, Austria

BAHAMA ISLANDS
Bahamas Ministry of Tourism
620 Fifth Avenue, Room 307
New York, New York 10020

Bahamas Ministry of Tourism
1230 Palmolive Building
Chicago, Illinois 60611

Bahamas Ministry of Tourism
1406 Adolphus Hotel Arcade
Dallas, Texas 75202

Bahamas Ministry of Tourism
510 West Sixth Street, Room 516
Los Angeles, California 90014

479

Bahamas Ministry of Tourism
1701 First National Bank Building
Miami, Florida 33131

Bahamas Ministry of Tourism
1015 Locust Building
St. Louis, Missouri 63101

Bahamas Ministry of Tourism
Victory Building, Room 707
80 Richmond Street West
Toronto 1, Ontario, Canada

Bahamas Ministry of Tourism
P.O. Box 818
Nassau, Bahamas

BARBADOS
Barbados Tourist Board
355 Lexington Avenue
New York, New York 10017

Barbados Tourist Board
150 Eglinton Avenue East
Toronto, Ontario, Canada

Barbados Tourist Board
P.O. Box 242
Bridgetown, Barbados, B.W.I.

BELGIUM
Official Belgian Tourist Bureau
589 Fifth Avenue
New York, New York 10017

Official Belgian Tourist Bureau
1176 Sherbrooke Street West
Montreal, Quebec, Canada

Commissariat Général au Tourisme
Gare Centrale
Boulevard de l'Impératrice
Brussels, Belgium

BERMUDA
Bermuda Trade Development
 Board
610 Fifth Avenue
New York, New York 10020

Bermuda Trade Development
 Board

6 North Michigan Avenue
Chicago, Illinois 60602

Bermuda Trade Development
 Board
111 Richmond Street West
Toronto, Ontario, Canada

Bermuda Trade Development
 Board
50 Front Street
Hamilton, Bermuda

BOLIVIA
Embassy of Bolivia
3636 16th Street N.W.
Washington, D.C. 20010

Dirección Nacional de Turismo
P.O. Box 1614
La Paz, Bolivia

BONAIRE
Bonaire Information Center
1 Rockefeller Plaza, Suite 1520
New York, New York 10020

Bureau of Economic Development
 and Tourism
Bonaire, N.A.

BRAZIL
Brazilian Government Trade
 Bureau
551 Fifth Avenue
New York, New York 10016

Secretaria de Turismo
Rua Real Grandeza 293
Rio de Janeiro, Brazil

CANADA
Canadian Government Travel
 Bureau
680 Fifth Avenue
New York, New York 10019

Canadian Government Travel
 Bureau
102 West Monroe Street
Chicago, Illinois 60603

Canadian Government Travel
Bureau
1 Second Street
San Francisco, California 94105

Canadian Government Travel
Bureau
124 South 7th Street
Northstar Center
Minneapolis, Minnesota 55402

Canadian Government Travel
Bureau
510 West 6th Street
Los Angeles, California 90014

Canadian Government Travel
Bureau
263 Plaza
Boston, Massachusetts 02199

Canadian Government Travel
Bureau
617 Vine Street
Cincinnati, Ohio 45202

Canadian Government Travel
Bureau
1250 Euclid Avenue
Cleveland, Ohio 44115

Canadian Government Travel
Bureau
1257-1259 Washington Boulevard
Detroit, Michigan 48226

Canadian Government Travel
Bureau
11 S. Meridian Street
Indianapolis, Indiana 46204

Canadian Government Travel
Bureau
3 Penn Center
Philadelphia, Pennsylvania 19102

Canadian Government Travel
Bureau
247 Midtown Plaza
Rochester, New York 14604

Canadian Government Travel
Bureau
1725 K Street, N.W.
Washington, D.C. 20006

Canadian Government Travel
Bureau
1300 Tower Building
7th Avenue at Oliveway
Seattle, Washington 98101

Canadian Government Travel
Bureau
Department of Trade and
Commerce
150 Kent Street
Ottawa, Ontario, Canada

CEYLON
Ceylon Embassy
2148 Wyoming Avenue N.W.
Washington, D.C. 20008

Ceylon Government Tourist Bureau
Queen Elizabeth Quay
Marine Drive
Colombo 1, Ceylon

CHILE
Embassy of Chile
1736 Massachusetts Avenue N.W.
Washington, D.C. 20036

Government Tourist Bureau
Catedral 1165
Santiago, Chile

COLOMBIA
Colombia National Tourist Board
140 East 57th Street
New York, New York 10022

Empresa Colombiana de Turismo
Calle 19 #6-68, Piso 7
Bogotá, D.E., Colombia

COSTA RICA
Embassy of Costa Rica
2112 South Street N.W.
Washington, D.C. 20007

Instituto Costarricense de Turismo
P.O. Box 777
San José, Costa Rica

CURAÇAO
Curaçao Information Center
604 Fifth Avenue
New York, New York 10020

Curaçao Government Tourist
Bureau
Plaza Piar
Willemstad, Curaçao, N.A.

CYPRUS
Cyprus Mission to the United
Nations (Tourist Section)
165 East 72nd Street
New York, New York 10021

Ministry of Commerce and
Industry (Tourist Section)
Passiades Street 52
Nicosia, Cyprus

CZECHOSLOVAKIA
Cedok Travel Bureau
10 East 40th Street
New York, New York 10016

Cedok
Na Prikope 18
Prague, Czechoslovakia

DENMARK
Danish National Travel Office
Scandinavia House
505 Fifth Avenue
New York, New York 10017

Scandinavian National Travel
Offices
612 South Flower Street
Los Angeles, California 90017

Turistforeningen For Danmark
Banegårdspladsen 7
Copenhagen V, Denmark

DOMINICA
Caribbean Tourist Association
20 East 46th Street
New York, New York 10017

Dominica Tourist Association
Roseau, Dominica, B.W.I.

DOMINICAN REPUBLIC
Dominican Republic Tourist Office
630 Fifth Avenue
New York, New York 10020

Dirección General de Turismo
P.O. Box 497
Santo Domingo, República
Dominica

ECUADOR
Ecuadorean Consulate General
1270 Avenue of the Americas
New York, New York 10017

Ecuadorean Government Tourist
Office
1028 Chile Street, Room 204
Quito, Ecuador

ETHIOPIA
Ethiopian Embassy (Tourist
Information Office)
2134 Kalorama Road N.W.
Washington, D.C. 20008

FINLAND
Finnish National Travel Office
Scandinavia House
505 Fifth Avenue
New York, New York 10017

Scandinavian National Travel
Offices
612 South Flower Street
Los Angeles, California 90017

Finnish Tourist Association
Mikonkatu 15 A
Helsinki, Finland

FRANCE
French Government Tourist Office
610 Fifth Avenue
New York, New York 10020

French Government Tourist Office
18 South Michigan Avenue
Chicago, Illinois, 60603

French Government Tourist Office
323 Geary Street
San Francisco, California 94102

French Government Tourist Office
9418 Wilshire Boulevard
Beverly Hills, California 90212

Commissariat Général au Tourisme
8 Avenue de l'Opéra
Paris, France

GERMANY
German Tourist Information Office
500 Fifth Avenue
New York, New York 10036

German Tourist Information Office
11 South La Salle Street
Chicago, Illinois 60603

German Tourist Information Office
323 Geary Street
San Francisco, California 94102

German Tourist Information Office
1176 Sherbrooke Street West
Montreal, Quebec, Canada

Deutsche Zentrale für
Fremdenverkehr
Beethovenstrasse 69
Frankfurt, Germany

GIBRALTAR
Government Tourist Office
P.O. Box 303
Gibraltar, Spain

GREAT BRITAIN:
British Travel Association
680 Fifth Avenue
New York, New York 10019

British Travel Association
39 South La Salle Street
Chicago, Illinois 60603

British Travel Association
612 South Flower Street
Los Angeles, California 90017

British Travel Association
151 Bloor Street West
Toronto, Ontario, Canada

British Travel Association
661 Howe Street
Vancouver, British Columbia,
Canada

British Travel Association
64/65 St. James's Street
London, S.W.1, England

GREECE
Greek National Tourist
Organization
601 Fifth Avenue
New York, New York 10017

National Tourist Organization of
Greece
4 Stadiou Street
Athens, Greece

GRENADA
Caribbean Tourist Association
20 East 46th Street
New York, New York 10017

Grenada Tourist Board
St. George's, Grenada, W.I.

GUADELOUPE
French Government Tourist Office
610 Fifth Avenue
New York, New York 10020

Guadeloupe Department of Tourism
Pointe-a-Pitre
Guadeloupe, F.W.I.

GUATEMALA
Guatemala Consulate General
1270 Avenue of the Americas
New York, New York 10020

HAITI
Haiti Government Tourist Bureau
30 Rockefeller Plaza
New York, New York 10020

Department du Tourisme
Port au Prince, Haiti

HAWAII
Hawaii Visitors Bureau
309 Fifth Avenue
New York, New York 10017

Hawaii Visitors Bureau
400 North Michigan Avenue
Chicago, Illinois 60611

Hawaii Visitors Bureau
3440 Wilshire Boulevard
Los Angeles, California 90005

Hawaii Visitors Bureau
209 Post Street
San Francisco, California

Hawaii Visitors Bureau
2270 Kalakaua Avenue
Honolulu, Hawaii 96815

HONDURAS
Embassy of Honduras
4715 16th Street N.W.
Washington, D.C. 20009

HONG KONG
Hong Kong Tourist Association
501 Madison Avenue
New York, New York 10022

Hong Kong Tourist Association
755 Boylston Street
Boston, Massachusetts 02116

Hong Kong Tourist Association
55 East Washington Street
Chicago, Illinois 60602

Hong Kong Tourist Association
211 North Ervay Street
Dallas, Texas 75201

Hong Kong Tourist Association
617 South Olive Street
Los Angeles, California 90014

Hong Kong Tourist Association
291 Geary Street, Suite 402
San Francisco, California 94102

Hong Kong Tourist Association
G.P.O. Box 2597
Hong Kong

ICELAND
Embassy of Iceland
1906 23rd Street N.W.
Washington, D.C. 20008

INDIA
Government of India Tourist Office
19 East 49th Street
New York, New York 10017

Government of India Tourist Office
Palmer House
Suite 684–5
Chicago, Illinois 60690

Government of India Tourist Office
685 Market Street
San Francisco, California 94105

Government of India Tourist Office
177–179 King Street at University
Toronto, Ontario, Canada

Government of India Tourist Office
88 Janpath
New Delhi, India

INDONESIA
Consulate General of Indonesia
Information Service
5 East 68th Street
New York, New York 10021

NITOUR, Inc.
Department of Tourism
Government of Indonesia
Djalan Modjopahit 2
Djakarta, Indonesia

IRAN
Embassy of Iran
Press and Information
3005 Massachusetts Avenue N.W.
Washington, D.C. 20008

IRAQ
Arab Information Center
757 Third Avenue
New York, New York 10017

Ministry of Social Affairs
Summer Resorts and Tourism
  Service
Baghdad, Iraq

IRELAND
Irish Tourist Board
33 East 50th Street
New York, New York 10022

Irish Tourist Board
135 South La Salle Street
Chicago, Illinois 60603

Irish Tourist Board
681 Market Street
San Francisco, California 94105

Irish Tourist Board
2100 Drummond Street
Montreal, Quebec, Canada

Irish Tourist Board
7 King Street East
Toronto, Ontario, Canada

Irish Tourist Board
Baggot Street Bridge
Dublin, Ireland

ISRAEL
Israel Government Tourist Office
574 Fifth Avenue
New York, New York 10036

Israel Government Tourist Office
5 South Wabash Avenue
Chicago, Illinois 60603

Israel Government Tourist Office
615 South Flower Street
Los Angeles, California 90017

Israel Government Tourist Office
805 Peachtree Street, N.E.
Atlanta, Georgia 30308

Israel Government Tourist Office
1117 St. Catherine St. W.
Montreal, Quebec, Canada

Ministry of Tourism
Building 3

Hakirya
Jerusalem, Israel

ITALY
Italian Government Travel Office
  (E.N.I.T.)
626 Fifth Avenue
New York, New York 10020

Italian Government Travel Office
  (E.N.I.T.)
3 North Michigan Avenue
Chicago, Illinois 60601

Italian Government Travel Office
  (E.N.I.T.)
St. Francis Hotel
San Francisco, California 94119

Italian Government Travel Office
  (E.N.I.T.)
3 Place Ville Marie
Montreal, Quebec, Canada

Ente Nazionale Italiano per il
  Turismo
Via Marghera 2
Rome, Italy

JAMAICA
Jamaica Tourist Board
Pan Am Building, 200 Park Avenue
New York, New York 10017

Jamaica Tourist Board
37 South Wabash, Room 712
Chicago, Illinois 60603

Jamaica Tourist Board
3440 Wilshire Boulevard
Los Angeles, California 90005

Jamaica Tourist Board
First National Bank of Miami
S.E. 2nd Street and Biscayne
  Boulevard
Miami, Florida 33131

Jamaica Tourist Board
278 Post Street
San Francisco, California 94108

Jamaica Tourist Board
Joseph Vance Building
Seattle, Washington 98101

Jamaica Tourist Board
Board of Trade Building
11 Adelaide Street West
Toronto, Ontario, Canada

Jamaica Tourist Board
78–80 Harbour Street
P.O. Box 284
Kingston, Jamaica

JAPAN
Japan National Tourist
    Organization
45 Rockefeller Plaza
New York, New York 10020

Japan National Tourist
    Organization
333 North Michigan Avenue
Chicago, Illinois 60601

Japan National Tourist
    Organization
1420 Commerce Street
Dallas, Texas 75201

Japan National Tourist
    Organization
109 Kaiulani Avenue
Honolulu, Hawaii 96815

Japan National Tourist
    Organization
651 Market Street
San Francisco, California 94105

Japan National Tourist
    Organization
165 University Avenue
Toronto 1, Ontario, Canada

Japan National Tourist
    Organization
2-13 Yurakucho
Chiyoda-ku
Tokyo, Japan

JORDAN
Jordan Tourist Information Center
530 Fifth Avenue
New York, New York 10036

Jordan Tourism Authority
P.O. Box 224
Amman, Jordan

KENYA
Kenya Tourist Office
750 Third Avenue
New York, New York 10017

Ministry of Wildlife and Tourism
P.O. Box 30027
Nairobi, Kenya

KOREA
Korea Tourist Association
11 West 42nd Street
New York, New York 10036

Korea Tourist Association
C.P.O. Box 328
Seoul, Korea

LEBANON
Lebanon Tourist Information
9 East 76th Street
New York, New York 10021

Commissariat General au Tourisme
Rue Justinien
Beirut, Lebanon

LUXEMBOURG
Luxembourg Economic and Tourist
    Department
Luxembourg Consulate General
200 East 42nd Street
New York, New York 10017

Office Nationale de Tourisme
51 Avenue de la Gare
Luxembourg

MALAYSIA
The Embassy of Malaysia
Information Section
2401 Massachusetts Avenue N.W.
Washington, D.C. 20008

Tourist Promotion Section
Ministry of Commerce & Industry
P.O. Box 328
Kuala Lumpur, Malaysia

MALTA
Malta Government Tourist Board
Valletta, Malta

MARTINIQUE
French Government Tourist Office
610 Fifth Avenue
New York, New York 10020

Office du Tourisme
Rue de la Liberté
Fort-de-France, Martinique, F.W.I.

MEXICO
Mexican National Tourist Council
2 East 55th Street
New York, New York 10022

Mexican Government Tourism
Department
13 West 50th Street
New York, New York 10020

Mexican National Tourist Council
9484 Wilshire Boulevard
Beverly Hills, California 90212

Mexican Government Tourism
Department
210 North Michigan Avenue
Chicago, Illinois 60604

Mexican Government Tourism
Department
809 Walker Avenue
Houston, Texas 77002

Mexican Government Tourism
Department
3106 Wilshire Boulevard
Los Angeles, California 90005

Mexican Government Tourism
Department
125 S.E. 3rd Avenue
Miami, Florida 33131

Mexican Government Tourism
Department
203 St. Charles Street
New Orleans, Louisiana 70130

Mexican Government Tourism
Department
209 East Travis Street
San Antonio, Texas 78205

Mexican Government Tourism
Department
219 Sutter Street
San Francisco, California 94108

Mexican Government Tourism
Department
707 Broadway
San Diego 1, California

Mexican Government Tourism
Department
80 North Stone Avenue
Tucson, Arizona 85701

Mexican Government Tourism
Department
1302 Connecticut Avenue N.W.
Washington, D.C. 20036

Mexican Government Tourism
Department
International Aviation Building
Annex
700 Dorchester Boulevard West
Montreal, Quebec, Canada

Mexican Government Tourism
Department
13 Bloor Street West
Toronto, Ontario, Canada

Consejo Nacional de Turismo
Insurgentes Sur 421
Mexico, D.F., Mexico

Departmento de Turismo
Paseo de la Reforma
Mexico, D.F., Mexico

MONACO
Monaco Information Center
610 Fifth Avenue, Room 612
New York, New York 10020

Commissariat General au Tourisme
et Information
2A Boulevarde des Moulins
Monte Carlo, Monaco

MOROCCO
Moroccan National Tourist Office
341 Madison Avenue
New York, New York 10017

Office National Marocain du
Tourisme
Boîte Postale 19
Rabat, Morocco

NEPAL
Embassy of Nepal
2131 Leroy Place N.W.
Washington, D.C. 20008

Office of the Directorate
Department of Tourism
Ministry of P.W., T. &
Communications
776 Sugata Chen Basantpur
Katmandu, Nepal

NETHERLANDS
Netherlands National Tourist Office
605 Fifth Avenue
New York, New York 10017

Netherlands National Tourist Office
Monadock Building
681 Market Street
San Francisco, California 94105

Netherlands National Tourist Office
38 Parkstraat
The Hague, Netherlands

NEW ZEALAND
New Zealand Government Travel
Commissioner
630 Fifth Avenue
New York, New York 10020

New Zealand Government Travel
Commissioner
153 Kearney Street
San Francisco, California 94108

New Zealand Government Travel
Commissioner
510 West 6th Street
Los Angeles, California 90014

Tourist and Publicity Department
P.O. Box 95
Wellington, New Zealand

NICARAGUA
Consulate General of Nicaragua
1270 Avenue of the Americas
New York, New York 10020

NORWAY
Norwegian National Travel Office
Scandinavia House
505 Fifth Avenue
New York, New York 10017

Scandinavian National Travel
Offices
612 South Flower Street
Los Angeles, California 90017

Norway Travel Association
Hier Heyerdahlsgate 1
Oslo, Norway

NOVA SCOTIA
Nova Scotia Information Office
30 West 54th Street
New York, New York 10019

Nova Scotia Information Office
607 Boylston Street
Boston, Massachusetts 02116

Nova Scotia Information Office
Central Station Concourse,
Montreal, Quebec, Canada

Nova Scotia Information Office
43 Eglinton Avenue E.
Toronto, Ontario, Canada

Nova Scotia Travel Bureau
Provincial Building
Halifax, Nova Scotia, Canada

PAKISTAN
Consular Division
Embassy of Pakistan
2315 Massachusetts Avenue N.W.
Washington, D.C. 20008

Ministry of Commerce
Central Hotel, Club Road
Karachi 4, Pakistan

PANAMA
Panama Government Tourist
    Bureau
630 Fifth Avenue
New York, New York 10020

Instituto Panameño de Turismo
Apartado 4421
Panama, Republic of Panama

PARAGUAY
Paraguay Embassy
1825 Connecticut Avenue N.W.
Washington, D.C. 20009

PERU
Peruvian Embassy
1320 16th Street N.W.
Washington, D.C. 20036

Peruvian Tourist Corporation
Jirón Lima 298
Lima, Peru

PHILIPPINES
Philippine Tourist & Travel
    Association
15 East 66th Street
New York, New York 10021

Philippine Tourist & Travel
    Association
212 Stockton Street
San Francisco, California 94108

Philippine Tourist & Travel
    Association
Plywood Industries Building

T.M. Kalau Street
Manila, Philippines

POLAND
ORBIS
500 Fifth Avenue
New York, New York 10036

ORBIS
16 Bracka
Warsaw, Poland

PORTUGAL
Portuguese Information and
    Tourist Office (Casa de Portugal)
570 Fifth Avenue
New York, New York 10036

National Tourist Department
Secretariado Nacional da
    Informação
Palacio Foz-Restauradores
Lisbon, Portugal

PUERTO RICO
Commonwealth of Puerto Rico,
    Department of Tourism
666 Fifth Avenue
New York, New York 10019

Commonwealth of Puerto Rico,
    Department of Tourism
11 East Adams Street
Chicago, Illinois 60603

Commonwealth of Puerto Rico,
    Department of Tourism
5455 Wilshire Boulevard
Los Angeles, California 90036

Commonwealth of Puerto Rico,
    Department of Tourism
Dupont Plaza Center, Suite 709–10
Miami, Florida 33131

Commonwealth of Puerto Rico,
    Department of Tourism
34 King Street East
Toronto, Ontario, Canada

Commonwealth of Puerto Rico,
    Department of Tourism

Economic Development
  Administration
Box 2672
San Juan, Puerto Rico

QUEBEC
Province of Quebec—Department of
  Tourism, Fish and Game
17 West 50th Street
New York, New York 10020

Province of Quebec, Department of
  Tourism, Fish and Game
12 Rue Ste.-Anne
Quebec, Quebec, Canada

Province of Quebec, Department of
  Tourism, Fish and Game
2 Place Ville-Marie
Montreal, Quebec, Canada

RHODESIA
Rhodesia National Tourist Board
535 Fifth Avenue, Room 2007
New York, New York 10017

Rhodesia National Tourist
  Department
P.O. Box 8052, Causeway
Salisbury, Rhodesia

ROMANIA
Embassy of Romania
1601 23rd Street N.W.
Washington, D.C. 20008

Office National de Tourisme Carpati
Boulevard Republicii No. 10
Bucharest, Romania

SABA—ST. EUSTATIUS—ST. MAARTEN
Netherlands Windward Islands
  Information Center
1 Rockefeller Plaza, Room 1520
New York, New York 10020

Saba Tourist Commission
The Administrator
Saba, N.A.

St. Eustatius Tourist Commission
The Administrator
Oranjestad, St. Eustatius, N.A.

St. Maarten Tourist Commission
Philipsburg, St. Maarten, N.A.

ST. KITTS—NEVIS—ANGUILLA—ST.
  LUCIA—ST. VINCENT
Caribbean Tourist Association
20 East 46th Street
New York, New York 10017

St. Kitts—Nevis—Anguilla Tourist
  Board
Basseterre, St. Kitts, W.I.

St. Lucia Tourist Board
Castries, St. Lucia, W.I.

St. Vincent Tourist Board
Kingstown, St. Vincent, W.I.

SAUDI ARABIA
Saudi Arabian Information Service
633 Third Avenue
New York, New York 10017

SENEGAL
Embassy of Senegal
2112 Wyoming Avenue N.W.
Washington, D.C. 20008

Office National Senegalais du
  Tourisme
28 Avenue Roume
Dakar, Senegal

SINGAPORE
Singapore Government Tourist
  Information Office
500 Fifth Avenue
New York, New York 10036

Singapore Government Tourist
  Information Office
510 West 6th Street
Los Angeles, California 90036

Singapore Tourist Promotion Board
John Little's Building
P.O. Box 1720
Singapore 1, Singapore

SOUTH AFRICA
South African Tourist Corporation
610 Fifth Avenue
New York, New York 10020

South African Tourist Corporation
9465 Wilshire Boulevard
Beverly Hills, California 90012

South African Tourist Corporation
2 St. Clair Avenue West
Toronto 7, Ontario, Canada

South African Tourist Corporation
President Centre
265/9 Pretorius Street
Private Bag # 164
Pretoria, South Africa

SPAIN
Spanish National Tourist Office
589 Fifth Avenue
New York, New York 10017

Spanish National Tourist Office
453 Post Street
San Francisco, California 94102

Spanish National Tourist Office
23 West Jackson Boulevard
Chicago, Illinois 60604

Spanish National Tourist Office
1418 Commerce Street
Dallas, Texas 75201

Spanish National Tourist Office
13 Queen Street East
Toronto, Ontario, Canada

Spanish National Tourist Office
Plaza Espagne
Torre Madrid
Madrid, Spain

SUDAN
Embassy of the Republic of the
*   Sudan*
3241 Massachusetts Avenue, N.W.
Washington, D.C. 20008

Tourist Section
Ministry of Information & Labor
Khartoum, Sudan

SURINAM
Surinam Tourist Bureau
10 Rockefeller Plaza
New York, New York 10020

Surinam Tourist Development
*   Board*
Box 656, Kerkplein 10
Paramaribo, Surinam

SWEDEN
Swedish National Travel Office
Scandinavia House
505 Fifth Avenue
New York, New York 10017

Scandinavian National Travel
*   Offices*
612 South Flower Street
Los Angeles, California 90017

Swedish Tourist Traffic Association
Klara Västra Kyrkogata 6
Stockholm, Sweden

SWITZERLAND
Swiss National Tourist Office
608 Fifth Avenue
New York, New York 10020

Swiss National Tourist Office
661 Market Street
San Francisco, California 94105

Schweizerische Verkehrszentrale
Talacker 42
Zurich, Switzerland

TAIWAN
Taiwan Tourism Council
126–4 Chung Shan North Road,
*   Section 2*
Taipei, Taiwan

THAILAND
Tourist Organization of Thailand
20 East 82nd Street
New York, New York 10028

Tourist Organization of Thailand
Mansion II, Rajadamnoen Avenue
Bangkok, Thailand

TRINIDAD AND TOBAGO
Trinidad and Tobago Tourist Board
48 East 43rd Street
New York, New York 10017

Trinidad and Tobago Tourist Board
2 Carlton Street
Toronto, Ontario, Canada

Trinidad and Tobago Tourist Board
56 Frederick Street
Port of Spain, Trinidad

TUNISIA
Tunisian Trade & Tourist Office
65 East 56th Street
New York, New York 10022

Commissariat General au Tourisme
et au Thermalisme
Avenue Mohamed V
Tunis, Tunisia

TURKEY
Turkish Tourism & Information
Office
500 Fifth Avenue
New York, New York 10036

Ministry of Tourism & Information
Mithatpasa Caddisi
Ankara, Turkey

UNION OF SOVIET SOCIALIST
REPUBLICS
Intourist
355 Lexington Avenue
New York, New York 10017

Intourist
16 Karl Marx Prospekt
Moscow, U.S.S.R.

UNITED ARAB REPUBLIC
U.A.R. Tourist and Information
Center
630 Fifth Avenue
New York, New York 10020

U.A.R. Tourist and Information
Center
2300 Decatur Place N.W.
Washington, D.C. 20008

United Arab Republic Tourist
Administration
5 Adly Street
Cairo, Egypt

URUGUAY
Embassy of Uruguay
2362 Massachusetts Avenue N.W.
Washington, D.C. 20008

Comisión Nacional de Turismo
Avenida Agraciada 1409
Montevideo, Uruguay

VENEZUELA
Venezuelan Government Tourist
Bureau
485 Madison Avenue
New York, New York 10022

Dirección Nacional de Turismo
Ministerio de Fomento
Torre Sur, Piso 7
Centro Simón Bolívar
Caracas, Venezuela

VIRGIN ISLANDS (BRITAIN)
Caribbean Tourist Association
20 East 46th Street
New York, New York 10017

British Virgin Islands Tourist Board
Administration Building
Roadtown, Tortola, B.V.I.

VIRGIN ISLANDS (U.S.A.)—
ST. CROIX, ST. JOHN, ST. THOMAS
Virgin Islands Government
Information Center
16 West 49th Street
New York, New York 10020

Virgin Islands Department of
Commerce
1074 National Press Building
Washington, D.C. 20004

Virgin Islands Visitors Bureau
Department of Commerce
P.O. Box 1692
Charlotte Amalie, St. Thomas, V.I.

YUGOSLAVIA
Yugoslav State Tourist Office

509 Madison Avenue
New York, New York 10022

Tourist Association of Yugoslavia
Mose Pijade 8
P.O. Box 595
Belgrade, Yugoslavia

Index

About the Author

FRANCES LANG KOLTUN is America's foremost authority on the woman traveler. She is the travel editor of one of the country's leading women's magazines and also writes a travel column, beamed at women, for the *World Journal Tribune* and other newspapers that are served by the Publishers Newspaper Syndicate, as well as *The Christian Science Monitor*. Miss Koltun, a born and bred New Yorker, has a B.A. from Brooklyn College, from which she was graduated *magna cum laude*, and an M.A. from Columbia University. When she is not traveling—she is known to have logged as much as 95,000 miles in one year—Miss Koltun lives in a mid-Manhattan apartment surrounded by drawings, sculpture and other *objets d'art* collected in the course of her world travels.